"A truly global history, a work of great richness and jaw-dropping erudition that ranges effortlessly across the continents, laying out a complex, multifaceted picture of modernity ... the book's rich and profuse detail cannot hide its author's determination to set a standard for a certain sort of new history ... A brilliantly told global story."

John Brewer, The Sunday Times

"'Globalization' may be a new term, but celebrating or lamenting its effects is clearly an old occupation. It is unfortunate, therefore, that no key figure in debates on globalization is a historian. Luckily, that will soon change – if C. A. Bayly's ambitious, masterfully executed new book gets the attention it deserves ... Though Bayly rarely directly underscores the contemporary relevance of his arguments, his book resonates deeply today."

Jeffrey N. Wasserstrom, Newsweek

"Bayly rises above the regional or national approach to present a history that 'reveals the interconnectedness and interdependence of political and social changes across the world well before the supposed onset of the contemporary phase of "globalisation" after 1945'. It is not the first time that such an approach has been attempted but his work is awe-inspiring in its breadth and authority ... Readers will enjoy an invigorating and enriching experience."

Philip Ziegler, The Telegraph

"Bayly's erudite and engrossing account of the global birthpangs of modernity is not only a landmark contribution to historical literature but, indirectly ... a pertinent addition to contemporary debates about globalization and the world order. This is a book that historians, foreign policy elites, and protagonists on both sides of the debate need to read ... Bayly has produced the most compelling and significant historical synthesis to appear for many years."

Colin Kidd, London Review of Books

"[A] bold and often brilliant book ... Empire and genocide, nationalism and modernity – these are grand themes enough for many a work of history, but they do not exhaust the range of Bayly's ambition and erudition. *The Birth of the Modern World* is as much about the writing of history as about that history itself ... It is a tribute to Bayly's skill that his discussion can be read with as much profit by those who are familiar with the historical debates he engages with as by those previously innocent of them ... [A] remarkable achievement."

David Arnold, Times Literary Supplement

This book is dedicated to
Elfreda M. Bayly,
who has lived through the consequences
of these historical events.

THE BIRTH OF THE
MODERN WORLD
1780–1914

THE BLACKWELL HISTORY OF THE WORLD

General Editor: **R. I. Moore**

Elements of World History
R. I. Moore

*The Origins of Human Societies
Peter Bogucki

The Beginnings of Civilization
Robert Wenke

A History of Africa
Paul Lovejoy

The Islamic World
David Morgan

A History of the Ancient Mediterranean
Ian Morris

A History of the Mediterranean World
David Abulafia

A History of Western Europe
Robin Briggs

*A History of Russia and Central Asia and Mongolia: Volume I
David Christian

A History of Russia and Central Asia and Mongolia: Volume II
David Christian

*A History of India
Burton Stein

A History of South-East Asia
Anthony Reid

A History of China
Morris Rossabi

*A History of Japan
Conrad Totman

*A History of Australia, New Zealand and the Pacific
Donald Denoon, Philippa Mein-Smith and Marivic Wyndham

*A History of Latin America
Second Edition
Peter Bakewell

The Early Modern World
Sanjay Subrahmanyam

*The Birth of the Modern World
C. A. Bayly

*Denotes title published

The Birth of the
MODERN WORLD
1780–1914
Global Connections and Comparisons

C. A. Bayly

BLACKWELL PUBLISHING
350 Main Street, Malden, MA 02148-5020, USA
9600 Garsington Road, Oxford OX4 2DQ, UK
550 Swanston Street, Carlton, Victoria 3053, Australia

First published 2004 by Blackwell Publishing Ltd

18   2012

Library of Congress Cataloging-in-Publication Data

Bayly, C. A. (Christopher Alan)
The birth of the modern world, 1780–1914: global connections and
    comparisons / C.A. Bayly.
        p. cm. – (Blackwell history of the world)
Includes bibliographical references and index.
    ISBN 978-0-631-18799-8 (alk. paper) – ISBN 978-0-631-23616-0 (pbk. alk. paper)
1. Revolutions–History–18th century. 2. History, Modern–19th century. 3. History, Modern–20th century. 4. Globalization. I. Title. II. Series.

D295.B28 2003
909.8–dc21

                                                                            2003001453

A catalogue record for this title is available from the British Library.

Set in 10/12.5pt Plantin
by Kolam Information Services Pvt. Ltd, Pondicherry, India
Printed and bound in Singapore
by Fabulous Printers Pte Ltd
Picture Research Jane Taylor

The publisher's policy is to use permanent paper from mills that operate a sustainable forestry policy, and which has been manufactured from pulp processed using acid-free and elementary chlorine-free practices. Furthermore, the publisher ensures that the text paper and cover board used have met acceptable environmental accreditation standards.

For further information on
Blackwell Publishing, visit our website:
www.blackwellpublishing.com

CONTENTS

List of Illustrations   xii

List of Maps and Tables   xviii

Series Editor's Preface   xix

Acknowledgments   xxii

Notes and Conventions   xxiii

Introduction   1

  The Organization of the Book   3
  Problem One: "Prime Movers" and the Economic Factor   5
  Problem Two: Global History and Postmodernism   8
  Problem Three: The Continuing "Riddle of the Modern"   9
  Conforming to Standards: Bodily Practice   12
  Building Outward from the Body: Communications and
    Complexity   19

PART I THE END OF THE OLD REGIME   23

1 Old Regimes and "Archaic Globalization"   27
  Peasants and Lords   27
  The Politics of Difference   29
  Powers on the Fringes of States   36
  Harbingers of New Political Formations   40
  The Prehistory of "Globalization"   41
  Archaic and Early Modern Globalization   44
  Prospect   47

2 Passages from the Old Regimes to Modernity   49
  The Last "Great Domestication" and "Industrious
    Revolutions"   49

New Patterns of Afro-Asian Material Culture, Production,
and Trade   55
The Internal and External Limits of Afro-Asian "Industrious
Revolutions"   58
Trade, Finance, and Innovation: European Competitive
Advantages   59
The Activist, Patriotic State Evolves   64
Critical Publics   71
The Development of Asian and African Publics   76
Conclusion: "Backwardness," Lags, and Conjunctures   80
Prospect   82

3 **Converging Revolutions, 1780–1820**   **86**
Contemporaries Ponder the World Crisis   86
A Summary Anatomy of the World Crisis, 1720–1820   88
Sapping the Legitimacy of the State: From France to China   100
The Ideological Origins of the Modern Left and the Modern State   106
Nationalities versus States and Empires   112
The Third Revolution: Polite and Commercial Peoples
Worldwide   114
Prospect   120

PART II THE MODERN WORLD IN GENESIS   **121**

4 **Between World Revolutions, c.1815–1865**   **125**
Assessing the "Wreck of Nations"   125
British Maritime Supremacy, World Trade, and
the Revival of Agriculture   128
Emigration: A Safety Valve?   132
The Losers in the "New World Order," 1815–1865   134
Problems of Hybrid Legitimacy: Whose State Was It?   139
The State Gains Strength, but not Enough   143
Wars of Legitimacy in Asia: A Summary Account   148
Economic and Ideological Roots of the Asian Revolutions   151
The Years of Hunger and Rebellion in Europe, 1848–1851   155
The American Civil War as a Global Event   161
Convergence or Difference?   165
Reviewing the Argument   168

5 **Industrialization and the New City**   **170**
Historians, Industrialization, and Cities   170
The Progress of Industrialization   172
Poverty and the Absence of Industry   177
Cities as Centers of Production, Consumption, and Politics   183
The Urban Impact of the Global Crisis, 1780–1820   186
Race and Class in the New Cities   188
Working-Class Politics   191
Worldwide Urban Cultures and their Critics   194
Conclusion   198

6 Nation, Empire, and Ethnicity, c.1860–1900 **199**
Theories of Nationalism 199
When was Nationalism? 205
Whose Nation? 206
Perpetuating Nationalisms: Memories, National Associations,
 and Print 208
From Community to Nation: The Eurasian Empires 212
Where We Stand with Nationalism 218
Peoples without States: Persecution or Assimilation? 219
Imperialism and its History: The Late Nineteenth Century 227
Dimensions of the "New Imperialism" 228
A World of Nation-States? 234
The Persistence of Archaic Globalization 234
From Globalization to Internationalism 236
Internationalism in Practice 239
Conclusion 242

**PART III STATE AND SOCIETY IN THE AGE OF
IMPERIALISM** **245**

7 Myths and Technologies of the Modern State **247**
Dimensions of the Modern State 247
The State and the Historians 249
Problems of Defining the State 252
The Modern State Takes Root: Geographical Dimensions 254
Claims to Justice and Symbols of Power 261
The State's Resources 265
The State's Obligations to Society 271
Tools of the State 274
State, Economy, and Nation 277
A Balance Sheet: What had the State Achieved? 281

**8 The Theory and Practice of Liberalism, Rationalism,
Socialism, and Science** **284**
Contextualizing Intellectual History 284
The Corruption of the Righteous Republic: A Classic Theme 285
Righteous Republics Worldwide 288
The Advent of Liberalism and the Market:
 Western Exceptionalism? 290
Liberalism and Land Reform: Radical Theory and
 Conservative Practice 295
Free Trade or National Political Economy? 300
Representing the Peoples 302
Secularism and Positivism: Transnational Affinities 307
The Reception of Socialism and its Local Resonances 308
Science in Global Context 312
Professionalization at World Level 320
Conclusion 322

9 Empires of Religion   **325**
Religion in the Eyes of Contemporaries   325
The View of Recent Historians   329
The Rise of New-Style Religion   330
Modes of Religious Dominion, their Agents and their
   Limitations   333
Formalizing Religious Authority, Creating "Imperial Religions"   336
Formalizing Doctrines and Rites   340
The Expansion of "Imperial Religions" on their Inner and
   Outer Frontiers   343
Pilgrimage and Globalization   351
Printing and the Propagation of Religion   357
Religious Building   359
Religion and the Nation   361
Conclusion: The Spirits of the Age   363

10 The World of the Arts and the Imagination   **366**
Arts and Politics   366
Hybridity and Uniformity in Art across the Globe   367
Leveling Forces: The Market, the Everyday, and the Museum   371
The Arts of the Emerging Nation, 1760–1850   374
Arts and the People, 1850–1914   380
Outside the West: Adaptation and Dependency   381
Architecture: A Mirror of the City   384
Towards World Literature?   385
Conclusion: Arts and Societies   389
Prospect   392

PART IV CHANGE, DECAY, AND CRISIS   **393**

11 The Reconstitution of Social Hierarchies   **395**
Change and the Historians   396
Gender and Subordination in the "Liberal Age"   399
Slavery's Indian Summer   402
The Peasant and Rural Laborer as Bond Serf   410
The Peasants that Got Away   415
Why Rural Subordination Survived   417
The Transformation of "Gentries"   418
Challenges to the Gentry   419
Routes to Survival: State Service and Commerce   420
Men of Fewer "Broad Acres" in Europe   424
Surviving Supremacies   426
Continuity or Change?   430

12 The Destruction of Native Peoples and Ecological
Depredation   **432**
What is Meant by "Native Peoples"?   432
Europeans and Native Peoples before c.1820   434
Native Peoples in the "Age of Hiatus"   437

The White Deluge, 1840–1890   439
The Deluge in Practice: New Zealand, South Africa, and the USA   441
Ruling Savage Natures: Recovery and Marginalization   444

13 Conclusion: The Great Acceleration, c.1890–1914   **451**
Predicting "Things to Come"   451
The Agricultural Depression, Internationalism, and
    the New Imperialism   455
The New Nationalism   462
The Strange Death of International Liberalism   464
Summing Up: Globalization and Crisis, 1780–1914   468
Global Comparisons and Connections, 1780–1914: Conclusion   469
What Were the Motors of Change?   473
Power in Global and International Networks   475
Contested Uniformity and Universal Complexity Revisited   478
August 1914   486

Notes   488

Bibliography   514

Index   533

LIST OF ILLUSTRATIONS

INTRODUCTION

1   Dressing uniformly: Japanese woman in Western dress at a
     Singer sewing machine. Nineteenth-century Japanese print.   13
2   Formality and individualism: Tomika Te Mutu, chief of the
     Ngaiterangi tribe, Bay of Plenty, New Zealand. Painting by
     Gottfried Lindauer, c.1880. National Library of Australia,
     Canberra/Bridgeman Art Library.   14
3   Embodied standards: American Indian woman in Western
     clothes. Photographed by the Royal Engineers on 49th Parallel,
     c.1870. Private Collection/The Stapleton Collection/Bridgeman
     Art Library.   16

1   OLD REGIMES AND "ARCHAIC GLOBALIZATION"

1.1 Cherishing difference: Qian Long inspecting his troops,
     by Giuseppe Castiglione. Palace Museum, Beijing.   35
1.2 A multiethnic empire: Emperor Shah Jahan receiving
     Persian general Ali Mardan Khan, 1638. Mughal miniature.
     Ousley Add. MS 173, folio 13. The Art Archive/Bodleian
     Library, Oxford.   36
1.3 Holy, Roman, bewigged, and emperor: Holy Roman
     Emperor Charles VI, statue at Schloss Laxenburg,
     Niederösterreich, by Matthias Bernhard Braun.
     Bundesdenkmalamt, Vienna. Photo by E. Beranek.   37
1.4 Caste in the Old World: Mixed marriage. A Spaniard
     and his Mexican-Indian wife, and their child. Painting
     by Miguel Cabrera. Museo de America, Madrid/Bridgeman
     Art Library.   46

2 PASSAGES FROM THE OLD REGIMES TO MODERNITY

2.1   Industrious China: Interior of a tea shop. Painting,
      nineteenth century, Chinese. The Art Archive, Musée
      Thomas Dobrée, Nantes/Dagli Orti.   55
2.2   The first multinational corporations: *Old Customs House Quay,
      London*. Painting by Samuel Scott, c.1756. The Art
      Archive/Victoria and Albert Museum, London/Eileen Tweedy.   63
2.3   Public spheres: A committee of American patriots delivering
      an ultimatum to a King's Councillor. Illustration after
      Howard Pyle published in *Harper's Magazine*, 1908.
      Private collection/Bridgeman Art Library.   73

3 CONVERGING REVOLUTIONS, 1780–1820

3.1   Transatlantic revolution: The execution of the duc d'Orléans,
      1793. Contemporary print. Mary Evans Picture Library.   96
3.2   Napoleon in glory: *Napoleon on the Imperial Throne*. Painting
      by Jean-Auguste-Dominique Ingres, c.1806. Musée de l'Armée,
      Paris/Photo, AKG London.   98
3.3   An Iranian Napoleon: Fath Ali Shah, king of Persia. Painting
      by Mirza Baba, early nineteenth century. Private collection/
      Bridgeman Art Library.   109
3.4   Polite, godly, and industrious: Norwegian followers of
      Hans Nielson Hauge at prayer meeting. Illustration by
      Adolf Tidemand, 1852. Mary Evans Picture Library.   117

4 BETWEEN WORLD REVOLUTIONS, c.1815–1865

4.1   World trade expands: Buenos Aires. Engraving, 1840.
      Photo AKG London.   131
4.2   Between repression and reform: *The Massacre of Peterloo!
      Or a Specimen of English Liberty, August 16th 1819*.
      Etching by J. L. Marks. British Museum, London/
      Bridgeman Art Library.   144
4.3   Imperial authority resists: Nanjing arsenal. Photo by
      John Thomson, c.1868. © Royal Geographical Society.   150
4.4   Imperial authority resists: British defence of Arrah House,
      Bihar, against the sepoy mutineers. Lithograph after William
      Taylor. British Library, London/Bridgeman Art Library.   153
4.5   Righteous terrorist: *John Brown (1800–59), Abolitionist*.
      Daguerreotype by Augustus Washington, c.1846–7.
      National Portrait Gallery, Smithsonian Institution,
      Washington/photo SCALA.   164

5 INDUSTRIALIZATION AND THE NEW CITY

5.1 Age of industry: Women working in Lancashire cotton mill, 1897. Mary Evans Picture Library. 173

5.2 Extracting cash crops, Sourabaya, Dutch East Indies, in the 1880s. Royal Commonwealth Society Collection, Cambridge University Library, Y30333/A9. 180

5.3 Chinese and Indian laborers mingle in one of Singapore's newly built streets of shop-houses, 1890s. Royal Commonwealth Society Collection, Cambridge University Library, YO311G/9. 184

5.4 The new architecture: The Reliance Building, Chicago, 1895. Photo Edifice. 195

6 NATION, EMPIRE, AND ETHNICITY, c.1860–1900

6.1 Nationalism at the charge: Equestrian monument to Vittorio Emmanuele II. Statue on Riva degli Schiavoni, Venice. Bridgeman Art Library. 209

6.2 Assimilation, separatism, or exclusion? Jewish scholars debating. Painting by Josef Suss, c.1900. Austria, private collection. Credit Phillips Auctioneers/Bridgeman Art Library. 225

6.3 Queen Victoria as seen by a Nigerian carver. Late nineteenth-century effigy in polished wood, Yoruba, Nigeria. Pitt Rivers Museum, University of Oxford (1965.10.1). 231

6.4 Red Cross in action: Japanese nurses attending to Russian wounded in hospital of Japanese Red Cross at Chemulpo, in the Russo-Japanese War. Popular print. The Art Archive. 241

7 MYTHS AND TECHNOLOGIES OF THE MODERN STATE

7.1 The state's lower rungs: A Chinese district headman, Wei Hai Wei, c.1909. Photo by A. H. Fisher. Royal Commonwealth Society Collection, Cambridge University Library, Fisher 14/4089. 259

7.2 The "colonial state" in undress: The British governor of New Guinea on tour, 1876. Photo by J. W. Lindt. Museum of Archaeology and Anthropology, Cambridge University, P12840. 263

7.3 The state's resources of power: The site of the construction of the Aswan Dam, Egypt, 1902–6. Royal Commonwealth Society Collection, Cambridge University Library, Y3041B/28. 269

7.4 Internal exile: Russian prisoners on their way to Siberia.
A lantern slide for teaching the horrors of despotism,
late nineteenth century. Museum of Archaeology and
Anthropology, Cambridge University, LS17785.   281

8 THE THEORY AND PRACTICE OF LIBERALISM, RATIONALISM, SOCIALISM, AND SCIENCE

8.1 Liberalism globalizes: The Indian reformer Raja Ram
Mohun Roy, c.1832. Book plate, 1870s, Calcutta.   294
8.2 Darwinism in dispute: Charles Darwin and an ape. Cartoon
by unnamed artist, in *The London Sketch Book*, 1872.
Mary Evans Picture Library.   316

9 EMPIRES OF RELIGION

9.1 Lourdes: Pilgrims at the Grotto. Lithograph by unnamed artist,
c.1885. Mary Evans Picture Library.   326
9.2 God's Word: London Missionary Society School, Torres
Strait, SW Pacific. Photo by A. C. Haddon, 1888.
Museum of Archaeology and Anthropology, Cambridge
University, N22826.   331
9.3 Pilgrimage of grace: Block-printed pilgrim's map of the
Hindu holy city of Benares, showing temples and the river
Ganges, 1903. Centre of South Asian Studies, Cambridge
University.   340
9.4 A Maulvi preaching at the end of the feast of Ramadan,
Algeria, 1905. Photo by C. J. P. Cave. Museum of Archaeology
and Anthropology, Cambridge University, P13735.   347
9.5 The Muslim Boys' School at Famagusta, Cyprus, 1909.
Photo by A. H. Fisher. Royal Commonwealth Society
Collection, Cambridge University Library, Fisher 8/1137.   358
9.6 The "Muhammadan temple," or Nagore Dargah,
Singapore, c.1880. Author's collection.   360

10 THE WORLD OF THE ARTS AND THE IMAGINATION

10.1 Revolutionary heroism: *The Death of Joseph Bara*, a nineteenth-
century version of David's vision. Painting by Jean-Joseph
Weerts, 1883. Musée d'Orsay, Paris/Roger-Viollet, Paris/
Bridgeman Art Library.   375

10.2   Art and the savage: *The Death of Jane McCrea*. Painting
        by John Vanderlyn, 1804. Ella Gallup Sumner & Mary Catlin
        Sumner Collection Fund, Wadsworth Atheneum, Hartford,
        Connecticut. Photo AKG London.   379
10.3   *The Meal*. Painting by Paul Gauguin, 1891. Musée d'Orsay,
        Paris. Photo by Erich Lessing/AKG London.   381
10.4   The character of the land: Boatmen crossing the Tamagawa
        River, Musashi Province. Print by Katsushika Hokusai.
        The Newark Museum/photo SCALA/Art Resource.   382
10.5   Exporting the classical tradition: Elementary drawing class,
        the Mayo School of Art, Lahore, India, 1909. Photo by
        A. H. Fisher. Royal Commonwealth Society Collection,
        Cambridge University Library, Fisher 8/847.   383
10.6   A Malay gamelan band, 1880s. Royal Commonwealth
        Society Collection, Cambridge University Library, BAM 1/38.   391

11 THE RECONSTITUTION OF SOCIAL HIERARCHIES

11.1   A new system of slavery? Tamil coolie labor on Malayan
        rubber estate, early twentieth century. Centre of South
        Asian Studies, Cambridge University.   408
11.2   Britain's surviving peasants: Ploughing with camels on the
        banks of the Nile, c.1902. Photo by Donald MacLeish. Royal
        Commonwealth Society Collection, Cambridge University
        Library, Y3041C/7.   413
11.3   The last mandarin: A graduate of the Chinese examination
        system, about the time of its abolition, Wei Hai Wei, 1909.
        Photo by A. H. Fisher. Royal Commonwealth Society
        Collection, Cambridge University Library, Fisher 17/4125F.   423
11.4   High noon of empire: The king-emperor and queen-empress
        in the Red Fort, Delhi, 1911. Royal Commonwealth Society
        Collection, Cambridge University Library, QM 20/170.   429
11.5   Before the deluge: Tsar Nicholas II and Tsarina
        Alexandra, 1913. Photo AKG London.   431

12 THE DESTRUCTION OF NATIVE PEOPLES AND ECOLOGICAL DEPREDATION

12.1   Shilluks repairing their boat on the White Nile, early twentieth
        century. Museum of Archaeology and Anthropology,
        Cambridge University, P6856.   442
12.2   Dance of the Eland Bull: Kalahari "bushmen" (San or Ko),
        early twentieth century. Museum of Archaeology and
        Anthropology, Cambridge University, P7289.   448

12.3   Exterminating the wild: A colonial officer with tusks, 1905.
       Photo by Ernst Haddon. Museum of Archaeology and
       Anthropology, Cambridge University, N59174.   449

13   CONCLUSION: THE GREAT ACCELERATION,
     c.1890–1914

13.1   Communicating modernity: Guglielmo Marconi sending
       a transatlantic radio message, 1902. Photo AKG London.   457
13.2   Pan-Islamism in action: Indian Muslim leaders Muhammad
       and Shaukat Ali take ship in defense of the Ottoman Khilafat
       and the holy places, c.1911. Nehru Memorial Museum
       and Library.   460
13.3   The storm gathers: A sea-plane on the Nile, 1914.
       Museum of Archaeology and Anthropology, Cambridge
       University, P13443.   486

LIST OF MAPS AND TABLES

MAPS

1.1	The world under the Old Regime, c.1750	24
2.1	Europe during the late eighteenth century	53
2.2	East Asia during the eighteenth century	54
3.1	Revolution and imperialism, c.1780–1830	84
4.1	Restored regimes, c.1830	122
4.2	Rebellion and empire in East Asia, c.1825–70	149
4.3	India and the Mutiny-Rebellion, 1857–9	152
6.1	New nations, new empires, c.1860–1900	200
6.2	The Ottoman Empire in the early nineteenth century	214
9.1	The world of Islam	346
9.2	Major religious centers in the nineteenth century	352
13.1	The industrial world, c.1900–30	452

TABLES

4.1	Regional origin of immigrants to the United States, 1820–1930	133
5.1	Estimated world population, 1800–1900	180
5.2	Population of some major countries	181
5.3	Population of some major cities	189
7.1	Government servants	278
13.1	Number of universities in different parts of the world	458
13.2	Accelerating immigration from Europe to other parts of the world, 1871–1911	458

SERIES EDITOR'S PREFACE

THERE is nothing new about the attempt to understand history as a whole. To know how humanity began and how it has come to its present condition, to grasp its relation to nature and its place in the cosmos, is one of the oldest and most universal of human needs, expressed in the religious and philosophical systems of every civilization. Only in the last few decades, however, has it begun to appear both necessary and possible to meet that need by means of a rational and systematic appraisal of attainable knowledge. History claimed its independence as an autonomous field of scholarship, with its own subject matter and its own rules and methods, and not just a branch of literature, rhetoric, law, philosophy, or religion, in the second half of the nineteenth century. World history began to do so only in the closing decades of the twentieth. Its emergence was delayed on the one hand by simple ignorance – because the history of enormous stretches of space and time has been known not at all, or so patchily and superficially as not to be worth revisiting – and on the other by the lack of an acceptable basis upon which to organize and present what knowledge there was.

Both obstacles are now being rapidly overcome. There is almost no part of the world, or period of its history, that is not the subject of vigorous and sophisticated investigation by archaeologists and historians. It is truer than ever before that knowledge is growing and perspectives changing and multiplying more quickly than it is possible to assimilate and record them in synthetic form. Nevertheless, the attempt to grasp the human past as a whole can and must be made. A world which faces a common future of headlong and potentially catastrophic transformation needs its common history. At the same time, since we have ceased to believe, as the pioneers of "scientific" history did a century ago, that a complete or definitive account is ultimately attainable by the mere accumulation of information, we are free to offer the best we can manage at the moment. And since we no longer suppose that it is our business as historians to detect or proclaim "The End of History" in the fruition of any grand design, human or divine, there is no single path to trace, or golden key to turn. There is also a growing wealth of ways in which world history can be written. The oldest and simplest view, that world history is best understood as the history of contacts between peoples previously isolated from one another, from which (some think) all change arises, is now seen to be capable of application since the earliest times. An influential alternative focuses upon the tendency of economic exchanges to create self-sufficient but ever expanding "worlds" which sustain successive systems of power and culture. Another seeks to understand the differences between societies and cultures, and therefore the particular character of each, by comparing the ways in which they have developed their values, social relationships, and structures of power.

The *Blackwell History of the World* does not seek to embody any of these approaches, but to support them all, as it will use them all, by providing a modern, comprehensive, and accessible account of the entire human past. Its plan is that of a barrel, in which the indispensable narratives of very long-term regional development are bound together by global surveys of the interaction between regions, and the great transformations which they have experienced in common, or visited upon one another. Each volume, of course, reflects the idiosyncrasies of its sources and its subjects, as well as the judgment and experience of its author. In combination, some two dozen volumes will offer a framework in which the history of every part of the world can be viewed and most aspects of human activity can be compared, at different times and in different cultures. A frame imparts perspective; comparison implies respect for difference. That is the beginning of what the past has to offer to the future.

"Every schoolchild knows" – or at any rate is taught – that the period between the later part of the eighteenth century and the outbreak of the Great War in 1914 saw the birth of the modern world. Throughout those years, four or five generations of politicians, writers, and artists proclaimed that the face of all the world was changed, separated by a great gulf from an old order which they viewed with contempt, condescension, or nostalgia. Those who have looked back upon it have agreed. Whether the transformation is taken to be the work of the American and French revolutions and the completion of the European system of nation-states, or of the "Industrial Revolution" and the subordination of most of the world's people and usable resources to the imperial and financial structures of the Atlantic powers, or of the jettisoning of the authority of religion and monarchy in favor of science and reason, it has generally been assumed at least since the 1860s that "the way we live now" is the direct result of this transformation, and that the history of the modern world is the history of its causes, course, and consequences. The resulting questions, far too important to be left to historians, inspired the foundation of the modern social sciences, and still dictate their agenda. The founding fathers, from Adam Smith to Karl Marx and Max Weber, and their successors down to the present day, differed fundamentally about every other aspect of the origins and nature of industrial society and the structures of power founded on it, but they were unanimous in seeing the argument as one about the hegemony of European, or at least Atlantic (or "neo-European"), power and culture. This they attributed, for better or worse, to developments which could be traced in European society from (in some of the most influential accounts) around the beginning of the sixteenth century, or even (in others) from the classical and Judaeo-Christian legacies of the ancient world. Dissatisfaction with this "Eurocentric" account has, of course, been widely and vigorously expressed for a long time – widely and vigorously enough, indeed, to have produced at the tail end of the twentieth century something of a reaction in a number of trenchant and well publicized accounts of various aspects of world history which unabashedly attribute the present distribution of power and wealth to the superior social and cultural traditions of its possessors. On both sides, however, the argument between those who celebrate and those who deplore the outcome has been conducted essentially as an evaluation of modernization as a European achievement: that it was a European achievement is taken for granted. One of the most consistent results of the great advances in other parts and periods of world history mentioned above has been to undermine, among specialists, the stereotypes of European exceptionalism – "the European city," "the European family", "individualism," and "enterprise" as peculiarly European characteristics, the very notions of "Islam" and "Asia" themselves – which have traditionally served as the common currency of comparative discussion, especially in the long term. The standard accounts of modernity and its genesis have been weakened in consequence, certainly, but they have not, until now, been replaced. It is the extraordinary achievement of C. A. Bayly to have described "the birth of the modern world" not as something which some people or some regions did to others less favored or deserving, but as a series of transformations in which most of the people of the world participated, and to which most of them contributed, not simply as the objects or victims of the successes of others, but actively, independently and creatively. He does so not by proclaiming any simple or simplistic formula or readily summarized "conclusion," still less by flattening the character and qualities of peoples, cultures, and generations into a grey mass of universal "trends" or "development," but by the exact and even-handed description of an extraordinary range of human actions, visions, and vicissitudes in which no group of people, and no aspect of their activities, is given more, or less, than its due. This, indeed, is modern world history at its best.

R. I. Moore

ACKNOWLEDGMENTS

ANY historical study is constructed from a partial view of the work of many other scholars. A book on this scale is deeply indebted to a whole generation of historians and to many others from earlier times. My most immediate debts, however, are to those who have been closest to this work and most indulgent of its reckless ambition, particularly the outstanding "history workshop" of St Catharine's College, Cambridge. Those who have read and commented in depth are Chris Clark (German history), John Thompson (US history), Hans van de Ven (Chinese history), and across the road at Corpus, Richard Drayton (Commonwealth history). I am very grateful to these historians, but outstanding errors of fact and interpretation are mine alone. Gareth Stedman Jones kindly commented on the chapter on political thought, while David Christian, Dominic Lieven, and Linda Colley proved to be very helpful readers. Bob Moore went well beyond a series editor's duty in providing valuable comments, especially on the introduction. Susan Bayly took time out of a holiday in Venice to suggest many improvements to the text, especially from an anthropologist's perspective. Michael Dodson drew on both his historical and philosophical training to point out many inconsistencies in argument and examples of poor phrasing. Shruti Kapila urged me to get the big picture, while Jayeeta Sharma got lots of things right that would otherwise have been wrong. Jane Samson provided a Pacific perspective and a Pacific voice. Sudeshna Guha and Rachel Rowe helped greatly with the illustrations, while Derek Beales and Kevin Greenbank provided valuable advice. Katherine Prior did the index with great efficiency. Many other people suggested reading, ideas, and insights. I thank them all most warmly. They are, of course, in no way responsible for the errors and misinterpretations that are bound to remain in a book of this range.

All maps draw to different degrees on *The Times Atlas of World History* (London, 1982). I thank the Cambridge Museum of Archaeology and Anthropology, the Cambridge University Library, and the Centre of South Asian Studies, Cambridge, for permission to reproduce illustrations.

NOTES AND CONVENTIONS

TRANSLITERATIONS of foreign words are a perennial headache. I have tried to adopt more modern and accurate versions of Indian, Turkish, and Arabic names: e.g., "Shah Abd al-Aziz" rather than the nineteenth-century "Shah Abdool Azeez." But I have abandoned the Arabic "ain," as specialists will know the word and non-specialists may be confused. With Chinese words, I have adopted the convention in Jonathan Spence, *The Search for Modern China*. That is, I have used the modern Pinyin system of romanization rather than the old Wade–Giles one ("Qing" rather than "Ch'ing") except where a name is well established in English usage: e.g., "Canton" rather than "Guangzhou." By contrast, I think that "Beijing" is now familiar enough to replace "Pekin" or "Peking."

As regards presentation and referencing, the book is erected to a great extent on the basis of a large number of outstanding regional and national histories which have been published over the last generation. These include the Oxford and Cambridge histories, the concise Cambridge histories, the Longman history series, and the recent Blackwell series, of which this is a part. Equally useful have been the great American course textbooks, particularly those dealing with east Asia, Latin America, and the United States itself. I have referenced these works quite lightly, as the reader will be easily able to consult the bibliography and refer to them. When making general points I have tried to provide examples and illustrations from different world societies which support or, in some cases, diverge from these broad trends. These have been referenced to a variety of monographs and some archival sources, especially when sources may be obscure to the reader.

Yet there is no attempt here to try to "prove" historical arguments by heaping up facts. That would be impossible from a philosophical point of view and, even if empiricism held sway, would result in a gargantuan apparatus. Rather, examples are given in order to convey some of the human texture of history and uncover some of those mental connections made by historians which constitute the substance of historical writing. The examples make it clear that historians working in different regions are often unaware that specialists in other fields are making similar arguments and, indeed, that the sets of historical processes they depict were connected. In other cases, historians are well aware of the analogies and connections with developments in other subject areas – let us say, between state building in nineteenth-century Japan and Vietnam – but have not felt the need to incorporate a broader context in their work. Above all, this book tries to start conversations between historians and historiographies in order to better understand similarities and differences between social processes.

Large numbers of individual names inevitably appear in the book. To give them all birth and death dates would have created a kind of "date soup," so I have only supplied dates sparingly for some major figures.

The work uses the word "society" a good deal. It is not only conservative politicians but many sophisticated anthropologists who have denied the existence of "societies," or at least cautioned against resort to the term. The word is not intended here to refer to essentialized, hard-edged cultural entities, so much as broad clusters of historically defined traits of human behavior which can be observed within a given geographical area. The use of the term allows a broad analysis beneath the level of the global and above the level of the local. It would be theoretically possible, of course, to break down every social entity to the village level or to individual networks within each village in the world. As the classical philosophers said, however, there are atoms "all the way down."

INTRODUCTION

THIS book is a thematic history of the world from 1780, the beginning of the revolutionary age, to 1914, the onset of the First World War, which ripped apart the contemporary system of states and empires. It shows how historical trends and sequences of events, which have been treated separately in regional or national histories, can be brought together. This reveals the interconnectedness and interdependence of political and social changes across the world well before the supposed onset of the contemporary phase of "globalization" after 1945. On the one hand, the reverberations of critical world events, such as the European revolutions of 1789 or 1848, spread outwards and merged with convulsions arising within other world societies. On the other hand, events outside the emerging European and American "core" of the industrial world economy, such as the mid-century rebellions in China and India, impacted back on that core, molding its ideologies and shaping new social and political conflicts. As world events became more interconnected and interdependent, so forms of human action adjusted to each other and came to resemble each other across the world. The book, therefore, traces the rise of global *uniformities* in the state, religion, political ideologies, and economic life as they developed through the nineteenth century. This growth of uniformity was visible not only in great institutions such as churches, royal courts, or systems of justice. It was also apparent in what the book calls "bodily practices": the ways in which people dressed, spoke, ate, and managed relations within families.

These rapidly developing connections between different human societies during the nineteenth century created many hybrid polities, mixed ideologies, and complex forms of global economic activity. Yet, at the same time, these connections could also heighten the sense of *difference*, and even antagonism, between people in different societies, and especially between their elites. Increasingly, Japanese, Indians, and Americans, for instance, found strength in their own inherited sense of national, religious, or cultural identity when confronted with the severe challenges which arose from the new global economy, and especially from European imperialism. The paradox that global

---

1

forces and local forces "cannibalized" or fed off each other, to use words of the social theorist, Arjun Appadurai, is well known to the contemporary human sciences.[1] But this ambivalent relationship between the global and the local, the general and the specific, had a long history before the present age. So, in the nineteenth century, nation-states and contending territorial empires took on sharper lineaments and became more antagonistic to each other at the very same time as the similarities, connections, and linkages between them proliferated. Broad forces of global change strengthened the appearance of difference between human communities. But those differences were increasingly expressed in similar ways.

The book argues that all local, national, or regional histories must, in important ways, therefore, be global histories. It is no longer really possible to write "European" or "American" history in a narrow sense, and it is encouraging that many historians are already taking this view. In the 1950s and 1960s the French "Annales" school of historical writing, led by Fernand Braudel, pioneered a form of global social and economic history for the early modern period.[2] The need to transcend the boundaries of states and ecological zones is even clearer for the nineteenth century. This particularly applies to the history of the imperial states of Europe, both the land-empires, such as Russia, and the seaborne empires of Britain and France. Historians such as Linda Colley[3] and Catherine Hall[4] for Britain and Geoffrey Hosking[5] and Dominic Lieven[6] for Russia have been in the forefront of efforts to show that the experience of empire in the broadest sense was central to the creation and form of these national states. Meanwhile, R. Bin Wong,[7] Kenneth Pomeranz,[8] Wang Gung Wu,[9] and Joanna Waley-Cohen[10] have begun to write Chinese history as global history, taking close account of the Chinese diasporas which predated and persisted under the surface of Western imperial hegemony.

What were the critical driving forces that account for the world's growing interconnectedness and growing uniformity in the course of the "long" nineteenth century? No world history of this period could possibly sidestep the central importance of the growing economic dominance of western Europe and North America. In 1780, the Chinese Empire and the Ottoman Empire were still powerful, world-class entities, and most of Africa and the Pacific region was ruled by indigenous people. In 1914, by contrast, China and the Ottoman states were on the point of fragmentation, and Africa had been brutally subjugated by European governments, commercial firms, and mine-owners. Between 1780 and 1914, Europeans had expropriated a vast area of land from indigenous peoples, especially in northern and southern Africa, in North America, central Asia, Siberia, and Australasia. If the gross domestic product per head in western Europe and the seaboard of North America was, at most, twice that of South Asia and only marginally more than that of coastal China in 1800, the differential had widened to ten times or more a century later. Most parts of the world which were not directly controlled by Europe or the United States were now part of what historians have called "informal empires," where disparities of power between locals and outsiders existed, but had not yet led to direct annexation.

Physical domination was accompanied by different degrees of ideological dependence. Social concepts, institutions, and procedures honed in the fierce conflicts and competition between European nations became controllers and exemplars for non-European peoples. Those peoples, however, were not passive recipients of Western bounty or, alternatively, simply the West's supine victims. Their reception and remolding of Western ideas and techniques for their own lives set limits to the nature and extent of their domination by European power-holders. At the beginning of the period considered by this book, the world was still a multi-centered one. East Asia, South Asia, and Africa retained dynamism and initiative in different areas of social and economic life, even if powerful competitive advantages had already accrued to Europeans and their overseas colonists. By the end of the period, following the rise of Japan and the beginnings of extra-European nationalisms, Europe's "lead" had been significantly challenged. A history of this period, therefore, has to demonstrate a number of different and apparently contradictory things. It has to chart the interdependence of world events, while allowing for the brute fact of Western domination. At the same time it has to show how, over large parts of the world, this European domination was only partial and temporary.

THE ORGANIZATION OF THE BOOK

The Birth of the Modern World is a reflection on, rather than a narrative of, world history. Chapters 3, 4, 6, and the final chapter attempt to construct a history of world events for chronological sections within the long period from 1780 to 1914. They contrast periods of relative stability with periods of worldwide crisis. Their aim is to select and emphasize certain connections between broad series of political and economic changes. Chapter 3, for example, reemphasizes the ideological and political links between the revolutionary age in Europe and North America in the generation after 1776 and the contemporary surge forward of European dominance over non-Europeans in the "first age of global imperialism." Recent reinterpretations of the 1848 revolutions in Europe have made it possible to view other great events, such as the convulsions in mid-century China and the great rebellion of 1857–9 in India, from related vantage points. Chapter 4 considers the American Civil War as a global event, not simply as an American crisis. In chapter 6, late-nineteenth-century nationalism, imperialism, and ethnic exclusions are considered within the same field of analysis, rather than separately, as has often been the case.

These chapters reemphasize the proposition that national histories and "area studies" need to take fuller account of changes occurring in the wider world. Ideas and political movements "jumped" across oceans and borders from country to country. For instance, by 1865 the end of the Civil War allowed American liberals to give support to the radical Mexican government of Benito Juarez, which was under assault from French-backed conservatives.

The Mexican radicals had already received enthusiastic support from Giuseppe Garibaldi and other revolutionaries who had been the heroes of the 1848 rebellions against authority in Europe.[11] Here, common experiences gave rise to a united front across the world. But, equally, exposure to global changes could encourage literati, politicians, and ordinary people to stress difference rather than similarity. By the 1880s, the impact of Christian missionaries and Western goods, for example, had made Indians, Arabs, and Chinese more aware of their distinctive religious practices, forms of physical deportment, and the excellence of their local artisans. In time, this sensibility of difference itself also created further global links. Indian artists looked to their Japanese contemporaries as inheritors of a pure aesthetic tradition and incorporated their style into their own works. The aim throughout the book is to combine what might be called "lateral history" of this sort – the history of connections – with "vertical history," the history of the development of particular institutions and ideologies.

Chapters 1, 2, 5, and the second half of the book, therefore, are more thematic in approach. These chapters consider the great social concepts which have been used by historians, as they were by nineteenth-century writers and publicists, to characterize the dominant changes of the nineteenth century. Among these concepts, the rise of the modern state, science, industrialization, liberalism, science, and "religion" appear to be the most important. The purpose of these chapters is to bring together material from a range of regional and national histories in order to demonstrate how these institutions and ideologies became rooted and empowered in different places and at different periods of time. They attempt to provide a history of connections and processes without retreating to a simple view of the diffusion outward of modernity from a dominant, "rational" European or American center. Here again, the book insists on the importance of the activity of colonized and semi-colonized non-European peoples, and of subordinated groups within European and American society in shaping the contemporary world order. So, for instance, the reconstitution of the European Roman Catholic hierarchy after 1870 was part of a much wider process of constructing "world religions" which was taking place in the Hindu, Confucian, and Buddhist worlds as much as the Christian. This is not just a matter of analogy, but of direct causation. Christian churches often began to cooperate and create new organizations at home precisely because they needed solidarity in overseas mission activity, where they found themselves under pressure from a revived Islam or other religious traditions spreading amongst their formally dependent subjects.

The book ends with a view of the period before the First World War, when diplomatic rivalries and international economic changes were facing the system of states and empires with unexampled pressures. The First World War, as Hew Strachan emphasized,[12] was decidedly a world war, even if it started as a civil war within the European core of the world system. That conflict was not "inevitable," but its explosive force, which was to echo down through the twentieth century, resulted from the flowing together of multiple local crises, many of them originating outside Europe itself.

The writing of world history raises many acute questions of interpretation and presentation. We consider three of them here, before opening the discussion by considering the growth of uniformity in one particular area, the realm of human bodily practice.

PROBLEM ONE: "PRIME MOVERS" AND THE ECONOMIC FACTOR

Most professional historians still have at the back of their minds the question of "why things changed." Historians and philosophers who lived in the nineteenth century tended to think that history was moved along by big spiritual and intellectual changes. They believed that God, or the Spirit of Reason, or the Urge for Liberation was moving in the world. Some of them believed in a European Christian "civilizing mission." Others thought that races and civilizations moved up and down according to natural laws of competition, survival, and decline. In the twentieth century, materialist explanations of change came to the fore. By 1950, many leading historians had been influenced by socialist theories and saw the logic of industrial capitalism as the dominant force explaining changes in human affairs after 1750. This perspective remains central. At one level, it must be true that the critical historical change in the nineteenth century was the shift of the most powerful states and societies towards urban industrialism. The desire of capitalists to maximize their income and to subordinate labor was an inexorable force for change, not just in the West, but across Asia and Africa.

The most powerfully written and consistent of all the English-language world histories in print, Eric Hobsbawm's great four-volume work,[13] makes this explicit, especially his *The Age of Capital*. However, as Perry Anderson remarked when Hobsbawm's autobiography was published in 2002, the great political and intellectual developments of the nineteenth century did not necessarily work on a time scale which directly reflected the underlying growth of the power of industrial capital.[14] The movements of economies, ideologies, and states were not always synchronous. They tended to be interactive. The French Revolution, the dominant political event of the period, occurred before significant industrialization had occurred even in Britain, and few historians now see the revolution as a triumph of the "bourgeoisie." Certainly, many lawyers and "middling people" took part in the revolution, but they were hangers-on of nobles and regional assemblies, rather than incipient capitalists. Even in 1870, the high age of capital, according to Hobsbawm's interpretation, landowners and aristocrats remained the power-holders in most societies. The later nineteenth century was indeed "the age of capital," but even this period cannot be "reduced" to capital. It was also the age of nobles, landowners, and priests, and, over much of the world, an age of peasants.

In view of these problems, some historians towards the end of the twentieth century cast the state and "governmentality," particularly the domineering, categorizing, Western-style state, as the "prime mover" in their historical dramas. But this does not really solve the problem either. The career of the modern state was evidently causally connected with the great economic changes of the era at some level, even if it was not rigidly determined by them. Besides, to stress the rise of the state or of governmentality in a wider sense still leaves the underlying question: why, indeed, did the modern state develop at all? The puzzle is even less tractable if we remember that the most novel political project of the era, the United States of America, had scarcely begun to industrialize before the 1830s, and its structure and constitution represented a successful revolution *against* the domineering European state.

This book is not designed centrally to address such issues of deep causation. It does, however, suggest that any world history needs to posit a more complex interaction between political organization, political ideas, and economic activity. The economy certainly retains an essential role in the argument. Patterns of local economic intensification were leading motors of change even before full-scale industrialization. Chapter 2 suggests that the economic historian Jan de Vries's concept of the "industrious revolution" can be usefully expanded to track many forms of economic intensification which had been occurring across the world since at least 1650. Over the eighteenth century, "industrious revolutions" were continuing to reorder society in a variety of different locations. Capital and labor were being made to work harder from south China to Massachusetts. Small-scale technological innovations were matched by modifications in the distribution of goods and people's material habits. Peasant families became prosperous farming families. Petty shopkeepers became urban burghers in Amsterdam, Malacca, and Fez. They wanted better-quality food and clothing, more honor and status.

Yet to stress the importance of industrious revolutions, as this book does, is not necessarily to give priority in historical causation to just another type of economic motor. For industrious revolutions were not simply brute changes in the distribution of material forces. They were also revolutions in "discourse," to use today's jargon. People's horizons of desire changed, because information about the ideals and life-styles of ruling groups was already circulating faster. "Middling people" wanted to emulate the consumption of royal courts, which were representing themselves in more pleasing and persuasive ways. It was this prior set of conceptual shifts which empowered the shopkeepers, created new demands for labor, and sent merchantmen across the oceans in search of luxuries. In turn, new, more aggressive states, particularly in western Europe, took advantage of these changes and began to link the industrious revolutions together across the world with armed shipping and monopoly companies. The slave system of the Caribbean represented the ultimate, forced, industrious revolution.

These social and economic changes were uneven and unsettling. They opened up differentials between groups and between different societies. They spawned lust for wealth, envy, and distrust of neighbors. They led to overseas wars, unequal taxation, social turmoil, and the questioning of established authority, royal and religious. The turmoil was worldwide. French philosophers and religious teachers in central Arabia felt equally the impact of the new connections and the turbulence they unleashed. It was in this context that many localized conflicts spun out of control across the world between 1720 and 1820, and especially after 1780. The aggressive French revolutionary state itself engendered many fierce enemies. The European state, its colonial offshoots, and adjacent non-European states, notably the Ottoman Empire, the Chinese Empire, and Tokugawa Japan, were forced to widen their scale of ambition. The leaders of these states had to appropriate and modify the new ideologies. They had to trench into areas of society that had formerly been autonomous.

The political and ideological changes of the revolutionary era were, therefore, "catastrophic," in the sense that they could not be predicted or accounted for simply on the basis of the contradictions and conflicts of the old regime, or even, ultimately, on the development of capitalism alone. The state, now powered by the new ideologies which crisis had generalized, developed a kind of elephantiasis. Elites battled for much of the early nineteenth century with the problems of order and legitimacy that this caused. Ideological and political conflict had, in fact, achieved a global scale, *before* economic uniformities were established across much of the world. The rise of capital was not, therefore, a force in itself. It spread in a social ecology which had already been created by wider aspirations to power, ownership, justice, and sanctity.

It was only after about 1840, in fact, that the patchy, but now relentless shift toward industrialization began to "kick in" at a global level. It did so at the time when another series of crises had shaken the world order: the 1848 revolutions in Europe, massive rebellions in Asia, and the American Civil War. Ruling groups worked to stabilize the social order by promoting industrialization, or at least providing a framework for it. Industrialization provided new resources for the state and new weapons for its armies. The age of capital had indeed arrived by the 1870s, as Hobsbawm surmised. But the men of capital could still only acquire status and respectability by sharing influence with kings, aristocrats, landowners, and bureaucrats who staffed the offices of the new, hard-edged nation-states. The age of capital was therefore also a period when hierarchy was perpetuated and religions became more forceful and demanding, as chapters 9 and 11 attempt to show.

In the broadest terms, then, historical development seems to have been determined by a complex parallelogram of forces constituted by economic changes, ideological constructions, and mechanisms of the state. Developments in the world economy do not really seem to have been "prior" to the ideological and political structure in any straightforward sense. These domains penetrated and influenced each other to different degrees and at different times. So there were periods when the state and the powerful narratives people created about it were the "driver" of historical change. There were periods of flux and fluidity, as for instance between 1815 and 1850. Again, there were indeed periods when significant economic restructuring cumulatively determined the direction of governmentality and its ideologies. And just as it differed over time, so the balance of these elements differed from society to society across the continents.

PROBLEM TWO: GLOBAL HISTORY AND POSTMODERNISM

A second problem in writing world history, however, derives from the recent rise to prominence of some historians who do not think in this way at all and tend to reject all "grand narratives" of capital, the state, and even ideological change. After about 1980, some historians were influenced by a trend of thought that has been called postmodernist[15] or postcolonial. Writers taking these positions are often hostile to broad comparative histories, or so-called meta-narratives, which, they argue, are complicit with the very processes of imperialism and capitalism which they seek to describe. The narratives of the state or of capital, described above, would constitute two of the targets of such authors. Instead, historians writing in this style try to recover the "decentered" narratives of people without power. These disempowered people are held to have been subordinated by the European and American male capitalists who wrote the political speeches and government minutes of the time. Consequently, their voices have been systematically expunged from the grand narratives of world history constructed by later historians. The postmodernist turn in some history writing has therefore created an area of tension. The academic and popular demand for world histories seems to be expanding enormously as "globalization" becomes the most fashionable concept of the day. Yet some of the basic assumptions of world history writing have been subjected to stringent criticism by postmodernists on the grounds that they homogenize human experience and "airbrush out" the history of "people without power."

There is no reason why the human sciences should all adopt the same methodology. Controversies of this sort can be quite productive. History has always flourished when different types of historical writing are available on the same bookshelf, when questions about "what happened" are challenged by the questions "Who said so?" and "What did it mean?" This was true in the 1970s and 1980s, when a still influential Marxist school was challenged by neo-conservative historians in Europe and North America. One thing is clear, however. Even when writing of the particular experiences of the poor, the subordinated woman or the "native," the postmodernist and postcolonial historians make constant reference to the state, religion, and colonialism, all broad phenomena, but ones which are sometimes taken for granted in such accounts. The postmodernist works, therefore, usually conceal their own underlying "meta-narrative," which is political and moralizing in its origins and implications. For example, many of these accounts appear to assume that a better world might have evolved if such historical engines of dominance as the unitary state, patriarchy, or Western Enlightenment rationalism had not been so powerful. All histories, then, even histories of the "fragment" are implicitly universal histories. Writing world history can therefore help to uncover a variety of hidden meta-narratives. This is particularly the case when causation is at issue. Why things change has always been a predominant concern of historians. For this reason, it remains important to consider the resources and strategies, and mutual collisions of dominant groups and their supporters, at a world-historical level, as well as to chart the experience of the people without history.[16]

This is not to argue that histories of the experience of individuals and groups isolated from the main centers of the production of history are unimportant. The marginal has always worked to construct the grand narrative as much as the converse has been true. Especially before the mid-nineteenth century, it was common for people on "the fringes" to become historically central. Nomads and tribal warriors became imperial generals. Barber-surgeons became scientists. Dancing women became queens. People easily crossed often flexible boundaries of status and nationality. Historical outcomes remained open. Certainly, to do no more than insist on the rise of capitalism, the modern state, or the concept of the nation hides and excludes much of what was really interesting about historical change. Yet it is difficult to deny, and few, even amongst postmodernist historians, do deny, the importance of the weight of change towards uniformity over the "long" nineteenth century.

Of course, in 1914, the heterodox, the transgressive, and the fluid were still everywhere in view. The triumph of modern Christianity was challenged by the efflorescence of spiritualism and esoteric healing cults even in its European heart. The rise of orthodox Islam was challenged by a pervasive ambiguity which still allowed Hindus, Buddhists, or African tribal healers to mingle at shrines with Muslim worshippers. New centers of power proliferated to deny victory to the modern state and nationalism, not least the powerful phalanx of organized labor. All the same, these unpredictable and unstandardized forms of human life and thought were increasingly marked by the imprint of common forms of governmentality. They were influenced by common ideas about the nation and the workings of international capital markets. Seers and spiritualists came to use the printing press, while the protagonists of organized labor kept bank balances and updated their minutes and memoranda like the great corporations. This book therefore rejects the view that any type of contradiction exists between the study of the social fragment or the disempowered and the study of the broad processes which constructed modernity.

PROBLEM THREE: THE CONTINUING "RIDDLE OF THE MODERN"

It is now worth directly addressing the issue of "the modern," a word which is used in the title of this book and in all the contemporary human sciences. In the 1950s and 1960s, S. N. Eisenstadt[17] and others used the word to denote a clutch of global developments, which combined to create a step-change forward in human organization and experience which they called "modernity." The changes they charted affected many different domains of human life. These included the replacement of big, extended families with small nuclear families, a change which was often associated with urbanization. They encompassed industrialization, the notion of individual political rights, and secularism, the supposed decline of the religious mentality. In many ways their model built on the seminal work of Max Weber, the German sociologist, written 50 years earlier. Weber himself always had Karl Marx in mind, even though he emphasized the independent role of ideological change in his theory. Consequently, the chronology of Eisenstadt and other liberal writers of this period had a lot in common with that of Marxist writers. All of them tended to locate the origins of the modern in the sixteenth century, but saw the nineteenth century as its critical phase. All of them tended also to privilege the West as the source of all global change, the non-West as a mere recipient which would eventually "catch up."

By the 1980s, the postwar "modernization theorists" had come under attack from a number of mutually hostile quarters. Demographers became wary of the idea of the shift from the extended to the nuclear family. Economic historians began to doubt that human evolution "needed" to have gone through a phase of industrialization. Sociologists invoked the Islamic revolution in Iran in 1979, or the onward march of evangelical Christianity in the USA, to challenge the idea of the triumph of secularism. After about 1980, scholars began to talk of "multiple modernities," implying that a Western modernity might be quite different from, say, a Senegalese or an Indonesian one. In this, of course, they were arguing along similar lines to politicians and intellectuals in Germany, Russia, and China who, even in the nineteenth century, argued for "modernity in our own way." In the first decade of the twenty-first century, the issue remains confused. The postmodernist philosopher Bruno Latour stated, "We were never modern," pointing to the resilience of sensibilities, emotions, and apprehensions of magic, which contradicted the idea that the bourgeois individual subject is yet dominant. Meanwhile, other social theorists, notably Ernest Gellner,[18] Alan Macfarlane,[19] and David Landes,[20] resolutely insisted on the reality of the "riddle of the modern," the once-and-for-all step forward of mankind.

In the first place, this book accepts the idea that an essential part of being modern is thinking you are modern. Modernity is an aspiration to be "up with the times." It was a *process* of emulation and borrowing. It seems difficult to deny that, between about 1780 and 1914, increasing numbers of people decided that they were modern, or that they were living in a modern world, whether they liked it or not. The Scottish and French philosophers of the eighteenth century believed that a good deal of all previous human thought could safely be dumped. By the end of the nineteenth century, icons of technical modernization – the car, the aeroplane, the telephone – were all around to dramatize this sensibility. By 1900, many elite Asians and Africans had similarly come to believe that this was an age when custom, tradition, patriarchy, old styles of religion, and community were eroding and should erode further. On the other side, a minority of thinkers was beginning to deplore these developments, though they believed equally strongly in the deluge of the modern.

At one level, then, the nineteenth century was the age of modernity precisely because a considerable number of the thinkers, statesmen, and scientists who dominated the ordering of society believed it to be so. It was also a modern age because poorer and subordinated people around the world thought that they could improve their status and life-chances by adopting badges of this mythical modernity, whether these were fob watches, umbrellas, or new religious texts.

This statement does not imply that people before the nineteenth century had never perceived epochal changes in human history. They had done so, but in general they explained and described these changes in two ways which did not imply the same type of step forward in secular human affairs essential to the idea of the modern. These earlier commentators generally understood changes in human society as "renovations." The scholars of Renaissance Europe, for instance, believed that the perfect learning of classical antiquity was being restored even while they were changing the way people understood history and diffusing their ideas in the novel medium of print. Equally, Chinese scholars of the eighteenth century believed that the pious and learned world of earlier reigns was being restored under the aegis of the transcendent rule of the contemporary Qing dynasty, even though the scale of that dynasty's rule was much greater than that of earlier monarchies.

A second way in which people had thought about major changes in human history was the millenarian mode. In this sensibility, people believed that in some way the supernatural or the heavenly had "leaked" into human history, bringing a new age of godliness or virtue or prophecy. This again differed from the idea of a secular shift toward modernity which obsessed many thinkers and statesmen after about 1760. These two earlier styles of thought persisted into the nineteenth century, tincturing the idea of the modern. Indeed, one of the most intriguing aspects of the period is the way in which these sensibilities all bonded together. So, for instance, scientific, modernist Marxism still had a whiff about it of the idea of the restoration of Paradise on earth. Equally, resolutely millenarian leaderships with old-style ideologies, such as those of the mid-century Taiping rebels in China, tried to get hold of gunboats and telegraph lines, as symbols of modernity as much as because they were practical tools. The aspiration to modernity was indeed something novel.

Yet, for historians, it is surely not quite enough to say that something was the case only because people in the past thought it was. How far do recoverable political, social, and economic trends "out there," beyond the overtly stated ideologies, discourses, and texts, bear out the impression that something that could be designated the modern was coming into being over this time period? This book takes the view that contemporary changes were so rapid, and interacted with each other so profoundly, that this period could reasonably be described as "the birth of the modern world." It encompassed the rise of the nation-state, demanding centralization of power or loyalty to an ethnic solidarity, alongside a massive expansion of global commercial and intellectual links. The international spread of industrialization and a new style of urban living compounded these profound developments. The merging of all these trends does point to a step-change in human social organization. The scope and scale of change broadened dramatically. Modernity, then, was not only a process, but also a *period* which began at the end of the eighteenth century and has continued up to the present day in various forms.

Where, then, was this modernity born? Nineteenth-century thinkers tended to argue that societies evolved into more complex organisms almost like living creatures. The more complex societies, the Western ones, would therefore survive, because they were the "fittest." This book accepts the argument that some Western societies retained a competitive advantage in the medium term because of the way they did business, made war, and publicly debated policies. These were not inherent advantages, however. They were contingent, inter-active, and relatively short-lived. States and societies outside Europe quickly adapted new forms of political and social action. This book therefore relativizes the "revolution of modernity" by showing that many different agencies and ideologies across the world empowered it in different ways and at different times. Thus old-style Chinese family firms were as important as the gentle-manly capitalists of Hamburg or New York in bringing about the expansion of world trade in the China seas and Southeast Asia. Islamic teachers in West Africa, looking to the days of the Prophet, were the agents who brought rule by law and the written word to the region. The shift to modernity certainly occurred somewhat earlier, and initially much more powerfully in western Europe and its North American colonies. Before 1914, people in most parts of the world were grappling in very different ways with this common modernity and were not simply imitators of the West. For a time the West was both an *exemplar* and a *controller* of modernity. By the mid-nineteenth century, there were many new controllers and exemplars around the world, among which Japan's partially self-fashioned modernity was the most important.

Over the 140 years covered by this book, then, the societies of the world became more uniform. Comparable processes of change had been proceeding for millennia, of course. The spread of the world religions had itself entailed significant shifts towards uniformity, particularly in bodily practice. After about 1750, however, the scale of social organization and aspiration became vastly wider in the course of perhaps only two generations. More rapid communications, larger political entities, and more ambitious ideologies of "civilization," Western and non-Western, powered this change. At the same time, societies became internally more complex and more stratified. Differ-ences of wealth and power between societies became more glaring. This is the phenomenon which people in many different societies have understood in many different ways as "the modern." These broad statements provide a starting point for an analytical history which attempts to bring together polit-ical, cultural, and economic change and show how they influenced each other, without giving any one of them overriding weight.

CONFORMING TO STANDARDS: BODILY PRACTICE

This chapter now takes as an example *uniform*ity in one obvious sense: dress and bodily deportment. Of course, people can think and believe totally differ-ent things, even when they dress and deport themselves in similar ways. Yet, at the very least, the creation of uniformity in this sphere speaks to a powerful

ILLUSTRATION 1   Dressing uniformly: Japanese woman in Western dress at a Singer sewing machine. Nineteenth-century Japanese print.

need for people to represent themselves publicly in a similar way. In 1780, the most powerful men in the world were dressed in a large variety of different types of garments which ranged from Chinese mandarin robes, through French embroidered frock coats, to ritualized undress in the Pacific and parts of Africa. By 1914, a growing number of the most important men operating in public arenas wore Western-style clothes wherever they lived. Chinese nationalists and the leaders of the new Japan dressed in the top hat and black morning coat which had come into favor with the early-nineteenth-century evangelical Christian revival in Britain and white North America.

This sobriety expressed responsibility and self-discipline, as opposed to the luxurious complexity of the dress of males of the old aristocracy and contemporary women. It went along with the abandonment of practices like dueling and riotous feasting. It is important that this change was registered not only in the adoption of explicitly Western dress, but also in the growth of analogous uniformities within "non-Western" or hybrid forms of dress. In China and Japan, dress reform movements attempted to provide models for the making and wearing of robes and kimonos. Here again, growing uniformity in dress went along with the discouragement of all sorts of erotic and transgressive behavior. Indian reformers, for instance, tried to stop people singing bawdy songs in public during the Holi festival.

This uniformity came in subtly modulated guises, of course, because people still wished to mark their distinctiveness for a variety of reasons. Uniformity is not the same as homogeneity. Uniformity means adjusting practice to create similarities on a larger scale. The paintings of the Maori chiefs of the later nineteenth century which gaze down from the walls of the National Gallery in Auckland, New Zealand, still display their variegated ritual tattoos, but several of the chiefs wear a black coat and white bow tie (see illustration 2). Contemporary photographs of the great American Indian war chief Geronimo (Goyathlay) show him dressed in a suit and jacket as well as specially posed, rifle in hand, as a warrior. In his later years, he made a living selling such autographed pictures.[21]

Military clothes were also moving toward a uniform, but internally modulated, style. The padded armour and metal helmets of samurai, Ottoman palace-guard janissaries, or Austrian mounted cuirassiers began to be replaced

ILLUSTRATION 2 Formality and individualism: Tomika Te Mutu, chief of the Ngaiterangi tribe, Bay of Plenty, New Zealand. Painting by Gottfried Lindauer, c.1880.

worldwide in the course of a century by drab operational garments. Typical of these was the dun-colored clothing which the British Indian army called "khaki"; this had given British soldiers some cover against sniper bullets during the South African War of 1899–1902. At the same time, the so-called traditional dress of elite men was itself becoming more uniform. Reformers in Egypt, Algeria, and Malaya wore the Ottoman fez. This was an adaptation of the Western hat. It was still appropriate for Islamic prayer, but made of a single piece to avoid the tedious process of tying the traditional turban in place.

The trend towards uniform clothing was less evident among working-class, peasant, and subaltern men. The historian Richard Cobb's study of the poor dead of Paris at the time of the revolution[22] showed that they dressed in bits and pieces of different styles and eras, cast-offs and elaborately patched garments. In 1900, most of the poor could still not afford much better. Yet factory conditions and the influence of social reform and religious movements had ensured that men in public arenas were beginning to dress more and more like each other, regardless of differences of region and culture. Leather shoes, cloth cap, shirt, and trousers had begun to replace the profusion of skirts, dhotis, pyjamas, kimonos, and smocks which had prevailed in 1780. Uniform markers of working-class status had spread to African and South American Indian workers in the mining industries. Conversely, in some parts of the world, especially the Pacific and Africa, settlers and colonial administrators had deliberately set out to mark the inferior racial and civil status of non-white populations by insisting that they retained "indigenous dress." British civil servants in Nyasaland objected to Africans wearing shoes, for instance. But such legal impositions themselves disregarded the resourcefulness of older dress customs and imposed their own type of servile uniformity.

The clothes of elite women had not yet converged to quite the same degree. Many male reformers proposed modified forms of traditional dress for their women, rather than Western styles. Modernity, both a dangerous process and a dangerous aspiration, was thought to be more appropriate for men than for women. In many societies, women were expected to inhabit a domestic space which was, if anything, more rigorously demarcated from the world of men and their affairs than it had been in 1780. The idea of the domestic was in itself a product of public uniformity. Women's clothes remained ornamental and impractical. In this, Chinese foot binding resembled the European use of stays and corsets. Even for women, though, the trend was towards uniformity. In 1780, modesty required many women throughout the world from Bengal to Fiji to keep their breasts bare. By 1914, Christian missionaries and indigenous moral reformers had made sure that bare breasts were associated with indecency. This was itself an extraordinary reversal of bodily practice. In the Muslim world, the Islamic *burkah*, the full body covering of Muslim women, was growing in popularity. Often wrongly regarded in today's West as a mark of medieval obscurantism, the burkah was actually a modern dress that allowed women to come out of the seclusion of their homes and participate to a limited degree in public and commercial affairs. Even in this insistence on tradition, therefore, one glimpses the mark of growing global convergence.

ILLUSTRATION 3 Embodied standards: American Indian woman in Western clothes. Photographed by the Royal Engineers on 49th Parallel, c. 1870.

This trend towards uniformity had been brought about partly by fashion and advertising. The spread of manufacturing and expansion of western European and American overseas trade aided the diffusion of common styles. But the action of the state and its agencies,[23] and a more general aspiration to modernity, was just as important as these economic imperatives. Uniformity registered an intellectual change in the aspirations of the self as much it did the expansion of industry and empire. In Japan in 1894, for instance, the new Meiji regime, asserting its place amongst modern imperial nations, ordered its functionaries to come to work in Western dress. Even in a lightly governed society such as the United States, the spread of the idea of respectability, as much as the regulation of the local court system, gradually made hoary local justices appear in court in regular gentlemen's coats. Uniformity of dress denoted an outward display of the uniformity of bureaucratic procedures and an inward mark of trustworthiness and respectability.

Not everyone applauded the growth of uniformity. It was the essence of the process that it was always controversial and contested. Westerners lampooned "natives" who mimicked them,[24] while cultural nationalists objected to the servile imitation of foreigners. A Muslim Ottoman conservative objected in the 1880s: "The fallacy that everything seen in Europe can be imitated here has become a political tradition. For example – by simultaneously introducing Russian uniforms, Belgian rifles, Turkish headgear, Hungarian saddles, English swords and French drill – we have created an army that is a grotesque parody of Europe."[25] He might have added that it was ironic that the most exemplary piece of Ottoman clothing which the world knew, the fez, was generally manufactured in Austria until a boycott in 1908 revived the manufacture of camel-hair hats in Syria.[26]

The body is a site on which anthropologists and social historians chart the influence of the state and methods of social discipline which became global norms in the course of the nineteenth century.[27] Alongside uniformity of clothing, another significant bodily discipline was the practice of timekeeping. Already in the late seventeenth and eighteenth centuries, the small pocket timepiece or fob watch had spread across Europe and her colonies of settlement. Slave plantations, where so many of the methodical practices of labor control had been brutally invented, were controlled by bells sounded to the time of the master's watch. By 1750, small farmers and skilled workers in the Thirteen Colonies and in the wealthier parts of Europe such as England, northern Germany, and Holland could afford watches. Across the world, the time that these watches and clocks displayed was also itself converging. Russian imperial expansion into Siberia and eventually to northern China required that schemes of local time had to be coordinated. As the nineteenth century progressed, more exact and synchronized timekeeping was also required in dependent non-European societies. The spread of the electric telegraph made possible the standardization of time systems across the world and within populous societies such as China and India, where local systems of time still prevailed as late as the eighteenth century. Here, as in Indian and Chinese coastal cities, municipal grandees began to build great clock towers to regulate the rhythm of bazaars and offices where once they would have put their money into temples or mosques.

By 1900, human languages, another aspect of bodily practice, were also coming to resemble each other. Western administrators, missionaries, and educationalists wanted languages reduced to easy transparent rules, which would, if possible, follow the pattern of western European languages. So did indigenous statesmen and educators who desired their own national languages. The sentence structure of the emerging Indian common languages – Hindi and Urdu, for instance – began to follow that of the English language. Even newly formed hybrid languages which reflected migration, slavery, and globalization – Creole, Swahili, and Pidgin – were armed with their own books of grammar and rules. As the public man staked his place in politics, religion, and science across the world, he needed a public voice. The political speech and the sermon took on common forms from Philadelphia and Rome to Kyoto and Fiji. The models were not only Christian and Western, but also Muslim sermons on the life of the Prophet and pro forma block prints telling stories of the Buddha.

Another consequence of growing global uniformity can be seen in the practice of naming. Personal names became more standardized as printed media and movements of religious and cultural change spread across societies, erasing differences in local naming patterns. The state was a powerful influence, because administrators wanted increasingly to tag and docket people for the purposes of taxation and military service. But it was not simply a matter of coercion; ordinary men and women needed to use the forms of the state to obtain parochial relief, education, or passages as emigrants. Religious belief also played its part. More and more Indians were named after the various attributes of the great god Vishnu, especially his *avatars* or reborn forms, Ram and Krishna. In Islamic societies in Asia and Africa the personal names of the Prophet and his consort, Ayesha, were increasingly adopted as a more standardized form of Islamic practice was once again propagated by teachers and governments. Their efforts were reinforced by the global contacts generated through pilgrimage to Mecca and Medina. The twin levelers of slavery and Christian evangelization spread European "Christian" names, most themselves once Jewish, of course, to millions of Africans, American Indians, and dwellers in the Pacific in the course of the nineteenth century. At the same time, the working of government and the courts demanded that everyone have a standard personal and family name for official purposes. This had some anomalous outcomes. In Scandinavian countries it meant that hundreds of thousands of people were called "Johanssen" and "Christiansen," for instance, while in Burma the practice of birthday naming meant that much of the population was called after the Burmese days of the week and a small number of astrological signs.

People's food in different parts of the world became similar. Wheat bread and beef had become the standard meal of the British and north Germans in the early modern period. This fare was exported to Britain's American colonies, and later to Australia, New Zealand, and southern Africa. Indigenous peoples who came into contact with missionaries or began to live in European towns took up the food of northwestern Europe partly because this was what was available in the market, partly because they were forced to conform to the standards of their new masters. In the later nineteenth century, as reforming governments came to power or Westernized elites became influential in Asia and Africa, new pressures to food conformity emerged. The Japanese began to eat beef, whereas previously their Buddhist faith had forbidden it – hence the appearance of beef *sukiyaki*. This, it was thought, would enhance their racial fibre and help them to confront Western imperialism. Mahatma Gandhi also briefly considered the idea of a meat diet to build up Indians whom he thought had been made "effeminate" by imperialism and bad domestic habits. He and his generation later came to reject that idea. All the same, Indians were quickly adapting to the use of tomatoes, potatoes, and chilli peppers, all of which had originated in the Americas and been spread across the world by their Spanish and Portuguese conquerors in the course of the sixteenth and seventeenth centuries.

This last example is a further reminder that it was not simply a question of the one-way adoption of European foods or bodily practices. Empires and commercial expansion had created multilateral links between different world societies which tended towards greater uniformity. So, for instance, eighteenth-century Caribbean and American slaves were fed on Asian white rice and clothed in Indian cotton goods. West African chiefs prized printed cloths from the same continent. This connection between Asian commerce and the Atlantic slave plantation system had been created by European expansion. Indian weavers and African entrepreneurs became active agents in the commerce as time went on.

By the end of the nineteenth century, uniformity had expressed itself in one further area: sport and leisure. The haphazard and ad hoc nature of many earlier games had been reduced to order and rules, now increasingly sanctioned by world bodies. Even the form of those quintessential British exports to the rest of the world – football, rugby, and cricket – seemed to bear the hallmarks of this powerful desire to discipline the body, seen equally on the battlefield and in the factory. Even games which moved from Asia to the West, such as hockey and polo, gave up their original appearance as genial melees and became orderly competitions. Meanwhile, French patterns of disciplined and orderly cooking and eating, French patterns of polite diplomacy, and German concepts of the proper ordering of scientific and humanist knowledge moved across the world in similar trajectories.

BUILDING OUTWARD FROM THE BODY: COMMUNICATIONS AND COMPLEXITY

This growing uniformity at the level of bodily practice, and in external markers of personal identity, was mirrored at the level of ideas. Systems of ideas and the discourses generated by economic and political power began to converge across the world. The nineteenth century – variously called the "age of industry and empire" – was also the age of global communication. There was a massive expansion of book printing worldwide. Societies that were not highly literate by standard measures became sensitive to printed forms of communication. It was not always Europe itself which was in the forefront. In 1800, more printed titles were produced in Calcutta than in St Petersburg and Vienna. In 1828, it was estimated that 3,168 newspaper titles were published around the world, nearly half of them in English-speaking countries. But as early as 1831, *Le Moniteur Ottoman* stood side by side with *The Times* of London. By 1900, the total of newspaper titles had reached 31,026, the print runs of many being in the hundreds of thousands. The 1900 total included 600 in India, 195 in Africa, and 150 in Japan.[28] The almost geometrical progression in the expansion of standardized information across the world can be appreciated if we remember that people begged, borrowed, and stole copies of the newspapers. In some societies men read out pages to illiterate people. In others, scribes reduced them to manuscript form in numerous copies.

The electric telegraph became an international system following the opening of the Europe–Asia cable in 1863 and the two Atlantic cables in 1866. The railway, the steamship, and, later, the telephone revolutionized the speed of communication. It would be wrong to deny the sophistication of pre-print and pre-telegraph communication in Asia and Africa. Yet the new density of messages did make possible an unparalleled diffusion of common ideas. Modern nationalism – a product of the French Revolution and subsequent wars – was itself "globalized" in the generation after 1850. Irish, Indian, Egyptian, and Chinese nationalists corresponded along the telegraph lines and met together in Paris, Tokyo, London, San Francisco, and Shanghai. Scientific and medical ideas spread round the world with equivalent speed.

The argument should not, of course, be pushed too far. Close inspection reveals that formal similarity and mutual translatability still often masked significant difference in intrinsic style. The rising trend towards uniformity was contested, partial, and uncertain in its outcome, therefore, rather than an all-powerful force for homogeneity. Even in 1880, Americans meant rather different things by "liberty" than did Europeans, though parties dedicated to the concept and articulating apparently similar philosophies held sway on both sides of the Atlantic. In Islam and Hinduism, religious uniformity meant more often a common religious rite, rather than the doctrinal uniformity that Christian churches sometimes sought. All the same, I shall suggest that Islam and Hinduism seemed more like Christianity in 1914 than they had been in 1780, if only because these "faiths" were now more easily distinguishable from each other. And in the meantime, representatives of the world's "religions" had met and conversed at the famous World Parliament of Religions held in Chicago in 1893. What they said to each other was probably less important than the fact that traditions which had once been bundles of rights, shamanistic practices, rituals, and antique verities could now be formally ranked as "religions," with their own spheres of interest and supposedly uniform characteristics.

The second major theme which will run through the book is the growth of internal complexity in the world's societies which developed within this trend towards outward uniformity. This complexity of function was quite different from the local cultural variety of the old order. By the later nineteenth century, most large societies had a wide range of specialist professions and occupations, with their own forms of training and rites of solidarity. Associations of this sort were now doing much more of society's "work" than solidarities created by kinship and marriage. Administration had been separated off from military prowess in a way which had not been the case in most of the world in 1780 outside China and, to a lesser extent, Europe. Even societies such as those of the Islamic Middle East, where soldiers still held much influence, had created cliques of civil administrators who stood somewhere between the military and the men of religion, the two poles of authority in the older society. A distinct legal profession had emerged in most colonial territories, in the Chinese treaty ports, and in Japan, where, a century earlier, legal argument had been conducted by religious functionaries or varieties of articulate middlemen employed individually by families. Medical systems had been written down and formalized. Even traditional forms of Asian, North African, and Middle Eastern medical practice had their own academies and certified practitioners. The world was increasingly governed by sets of discrete, though interrelated expertise.

In the domain of economic life, specialist bodies of managers, accountants, and insurers had come into existence in all the major urban centers. Management had widely been separated from ownership and marketing. Special classes of financial speculators, limited to London, Paris, and Amsterdam in 1780, had come into being in cities such as Shanghai, Tehran, and Nagasaki. For ordinary people, work itself had become more specialized. In particular, the millennia-old link between seasonal agricultural work and urban labor had been broken across much of the industrializing world for those living and working in major cities. In fact, a kind of international class structure was emerging. This greater specialization gave rise, paradoxically, to an impression of uniformity. The ruling groups, professions, and even working classes of different societies looked more and more similar, were subject to similar types of pressure, and began to harbor similar aspirations. Convergence, uniformity, and similarity did not mean, again, that all these people were likely to think or act in the same way. At the very least, though, they could perceive and articulate common interests which breached the boundaries of the nation-state, even if they were profoundly influenced by it.

In order to chart these broad trends, the book takes as a bench mark the world of the mid-eighteenth century. It is not intended to suggest that this world was static or parochial. On the contrary, powerful forces for change and globalization had been working on human societies for centuries. This was only a world of old regimes or archaic social organization because people later came to differentiate it from their own times so sharply. It is from this time, however, that the forces for change outlined above began to pick up speed dramatically, as contemporaries noticed as clearly as later historians. Chapter 1 considers in broad terms the organization of political and economic life in the mid-eighteenth century. Chapter 2 goes on to show how developments in material and political life across the world were beginning to unsettle these patterns before the onset of the world crisis of 1780–1820.

PART I

THE END OF THE OLD REGIME

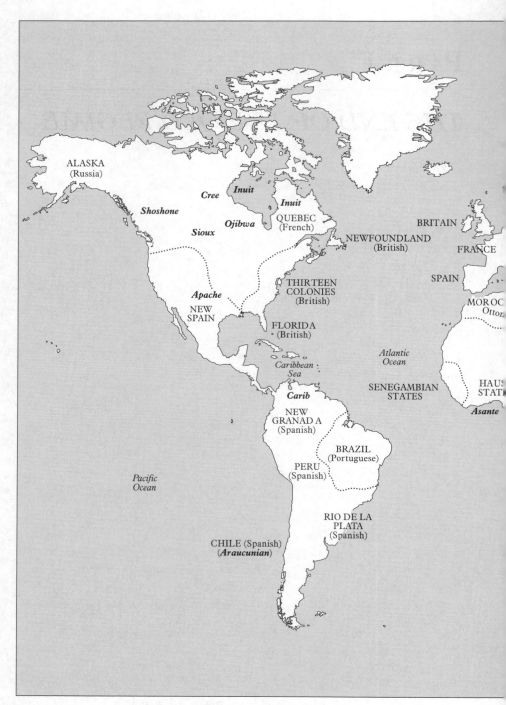

MAP 1.1 The world under the Old Regime, c.1750.

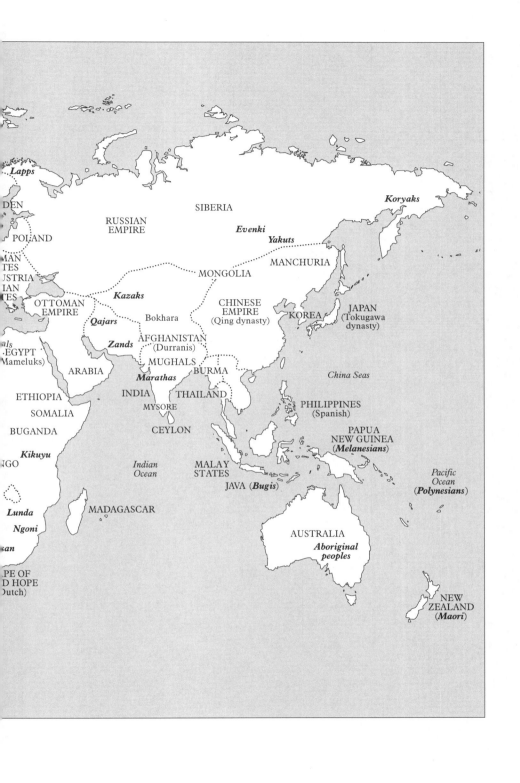

Lapps

DEN

POLAND

MAN
TES

USTRIA
IAN
TES

OTTOMAN
EMPIRE

als
EGYPT
(Mameluks)

ETHIOPIA

SOMALIA

BUGANDA

Kikuyu

NGO

Lunda

Ngoni

san

PE OF
D HOPE
Dutch)

RUSSIAN
EMPIRE

SIBERIA

Koryaks

Evenki

Yakuts

MANCHURIA

MONGOLIA

Kazaks

Bokhara

CHINESE
EMPIRE
(Qing dynasty)

KOREA

JAPAN
(Tokugawa
dynasty)

Qajars

Zands

AFGHANISTAN
(Durranis)

MUGHALS

BURMA

Marathas

INDIA

THAILAND

MYSORE

CEYLON

China Seas

PHILIPPINES
(Spanish)

PAPUA
NEW GUINEA
(Melanesians)

ARABIA

Indian
Ocean

MALAY
STATES

JAVA (Bugis)

Pacific
Ocean
(Polynesians)

MADAGASCAR

AUSTRALIA

Aboriginal
peoples

NEW
ZEALAND
(Maori)

[1] OLD REGIMES AND "ARCHAIC GLOBALIZATION"

IN THE eighteenth-century world, political power and religious and cultural authority were highly variegated and intertwined in complex ways. Economies, however, were relatively simply, dominated by agriculture and still dependent on the seasons. The next four chapters attempt to explain how and why there occurred over little more than three generations a worldwide shift to political and cultural uniformity accompanied by the emergence of more complex and recognizably modern social and economic patterns. They will give prominence to the rise of European dominance across this world, while at the same time acknowledging the multi-centered origin of the shift toward this common, yet fiercely contested, modernity. The present chapter considers aspects of the ideology and political organization of the world in the early to mid-eighteenth century.

PEASANTS AND LORDS

In 1750 the largest part of humanity still lived within the domain of what historians have called "agrarian empires." Agrarian empires were large, ethnically complex states which subsisted at their core by intercepting the surplus product of peasant producers. Strictly, peasants were farmers who cultivated small plots of land largely with their own family labor. Above peasants in social ranking were local elites, who might sometimes farm the land themselves but also took rents from other peasant-tenants. Below "peasants proper" were landless laborers who worked on the lands of peasants or the local ruling groups for wages or a portion of the crop. Culturally, though, local lords, rural tradesmen, and agricultural laborers were all intimately linked to the "peasant proper" and generally subscribed to similar values.

The agrarian empires of Qing China, Mughal India, Tokugawa Japan, Safavid Iran, Java, the Ottoman Empire, the Russian Empire, and the Habsburg monarchy together must have accounted for at least 70 percent of the world's population. Large parts of the Spanish Crown's territories in Central and South America were still farmed by peasant descendants of the original Amerindian populations. Societies which regularly grew crops were also scattered across Africa, subsisting in complex relationships with nomads and forest-dwellers. Peasants, broadly understood, must have accounted for 80 percent of that gross population, though in some areas the emergence of nodes of early capitalist commerce may have pushed the urban population to above 20 percent of the total. This appears to have been the case, for instance, in parts of northwestern Europe, maritime or riverine China, and coastal Japan.

The political and religious orders of these old polities continued to be fragmented and complex to one degree or another. Yet the societies and economies which maintained them were relatively simple by comparison with those of the later nineteenth century, which had experienced early industrialization and the growth of the state. Because most people living within them were peasants, agricultural laborers, or landholders and merchants dependent on agricultural produce, the quality of the harvests dominated everyday life as it had for thousands of years. Many western and southern European peasant-farmers were hardly wealthier than their Asian and African equivalents, and often had less ready access to plentiful food. John Komlos has argued persuasively that much of central Europe was suffering from a severe nutritional crisis during the eighteenth century.[1] Even culturally sophisticated France was plagued by constant *crises de subsistence* (subsistence crises) throughout the eighteenth century. Most Asian, African, and many European societies suffered debilitating scarcities or famines every 20 years or so. These scarcities were deepened by wars and foreign invasions, both by old-style bands of nomadic warriors sweeping in from the steppes or deserts and by new, European-style model armies.

Yet only in the broadest sense were peasants worldwide a single category. The life-styles of lords and peasants in different societies indeed bore a family resemblance to each other, but displayed many significant differences in detail. These differences depended to some extent on the different types of basic crops which they grew. For instance, rice-growing lands such as southern China, Southeast Asia, and the Indian river valleys required large efforts by local communities to maintain the irrigation systems which watered the crops. Intensive rice areas typically supported large numbers of tied laborers or very poor dependent peasants, who were needed to weed the crops and dig the ditches. North China, northern India, the Middle East, along with western Europe and the bulk of its American colonies were, by contrast, dry grain and pastoral areas where population was less dense. Here, farmers were often more independent, but often poor because they lacked irrigation or access to markets or were indebted to moneylenders and other magnates. Between these two poles were innumerable local combinations, in which the form of agriculture depended on the specific mix of crops or micro-ecology and the balance between agriculture, animal husbandry, and surrounding pastoralists. Even areas where peasants cultivated the same type of crops varied a great deal in social forms. Religious institutions and the pattern of organization of political elites intervened to dictate the complex forms of land tenure and subordination which had developed within them. Peasants, in addition, were often part-time artisans, carriers, and soldiers, by no means tied to the land as earlier social scientists sometimes thought. Until the emergence of mechanized farming and scientific crop nutrition toward the end of the nineteenth century, therefore, there were intricate differences in the ways in which peasants and lords lived their lives and related to each other.

Peasants were not "boors" as some learned people of the time thought; nor, by contrast, were they charming inhabitants of an unspoiled arcadia, as many indulgent literati had begun to assert by the end of the eighteenth century. Nor again were they engaged in perpetual wars of resistance against landowners and states, as many modern radical historians prefer to claim. There were violent and determined peasant risings, of course, and the later eighteenth century was replete with them. Yet these rebellions usually reflected near-despair at the accumulation of abuses and imposts heaped upon rural people rather than any inherent tendency on their part to resistance or violence. Peasant communities did indeed have a strong sense of morality about the doings of their own members and the chicanery of outsiders. Yet most peasant families were quite entrepreneurial. They wanted more land, more money, and more honor. They would try to maximize their opportunities. This provided a huge fund of canny talent whenever and wherever the political order and economic circumstances were propitious. In many parts of the world, and especially in southern and eastern Europe and in Japan, it was to be the unlocking of the huge development potential of peasants, or, in the new worlds, transplanted peasants, which was to provide much of the economic dynamism of the nineteenth century.

Generally, social hierarchies in the old order were also more malleable than most commentators believed. The old regimes were bound by status, but they were not rigid. This was true even in China, India, Japan, and the Middle East, which eighteenth-century Europeans thought of as unchanging realms of custom and conservatism. New men from the middling strata, and even some rich peasant families, could and did make it into high office and secure land and privileges within a generation or two in most societies. There are even examples of people of poor peasant or low status rising to power. Yet the hierarchy *per se* was relatively simple: peasants, merchants, landowners, and aristocrats. Insofar as professions were beginning to form in some societies, they were still unorganized and tended to be hereditary in nature. Even the bodies of specialist Asian and west European artisans which dominated the growing intercontinental trades were still greatly dependent on the protection of petty rulers and the out-turn of harvests.

THE POLITICS OF DIFFERENCE

In the 1960s several historians, led by Marshall Hodgson,[2] began to write of the early modern Islamic or "gunpowder empires" of the Middle East, India, and Southeast Asia. Some authors extended the category even further, suggesting that the Chinese Qing dynasty (c.1644–1911) had gone through a rather similar evolution to that of the Ottomans (c.1326–1922), Safavids (c.1501–1736), or Mughals (1526–1858). They had all transformed themselves from the status of "great khans," nomadic lords of herdsmen, horsearchers, and cossack-type soldiers, into dispassionate and enlightened emperors of broad agrarian domains.[3] It was even suggested that the Russian tsars and, from some perspectives, the Austrian Habsburgs, represented a Christian version of the same sort of development. Historians of courtly display and "representations" of rule have also traced exhilarating parallels between the court ideology and ritual of Louis XIV, the Qian Long emperor of China (1736–99), and Peter the Great of Russia.[4]

Such broad "family resemblances" between many of the political regimes of Eurasia and northern and western Africa certainly need to be borne in mind. This is because these polities contrasted so sharply with the world of bounded nation-states and demarcated colonial provinces which was to be dominant a little over 100 years later. The most recent body of scholarship, however, has tended to stress the differences between the old regimes. Within the agrarian empires, and even in the commercially buoyant regions of western Europe, there was a great variety of political and ideological forms, many of which were to be suppressed or to begin to become more uniform over the next century. Italy and Germany, for instance, two of the next century's new nations, displayed a degree of cultural and linguistic unity but were fragmented into a plethora of kingdoms, grand duchies, papal states, and, in the German case, attenuated imperial jurisdictions.

People are used to thinking of the France of the pre-revolutionary ancien régime, symbolized by the routine of the palace of Versailles, as a centralized, autocratic state where great royal officials intervened constantly in local society. In the same way, the idea of "oriental despotism," an artefact of early modern Europe, hangs over the common understanding of the Qing Chinese or Indian Mughal empires. There were indeed aspects of social and economic regulation in which these emperors and kings routinely and purposively intervened, and these examples should not be discounted. For instance, William Beik[5] has shown that the French monarchy in the eighteenth century was quite effective at bringing in taxation revenues, even in the Mediterranean south. It was much stronger around Paris and in the northeast. In Europe, before the nineteenth century, monarchs often had particular charge over roads, ports, and postal systems. Again, those parts of western Anatolia, northern Syria, and the Balkans within a thousand miles of Ottoman Istanbul were ruled quite tightly,[6] at least by comparison with Egypt and the outlying Arab provinces of the empire, let alone Safavid Iran or Mughal India.[7]

Even in Persia and South Asia, the Muslim emperors were directly responsible for the maintenance of canal systems which watered the semi-arid areas of their domains. In China, similarly, the emperors directly managed the irrigation systems of the Yellow River and maintained the Grand Canal north of Nanjing which supplied grain to the imperial heartlands.[8] With these examples in mind, some European commentators developed the idea that these political systems were examples of "hydraulic societies," in which the provision of water required the centralization of power. Large, directly managed royal estates were also a feature of these kingdoms, so that in Islamic and Arab domains a distinction was often made between the royal province, the *khalisa*, and less formally ruled areas. In China, Manchu Banner Lands and imperial hunting grounds had a similar status.[9] In Africa too, several precolonial states also exhibited some centralized functions. The West African Asante kingdom (in modern Ghana), in particular, developed a form of bureaucracy, state trading organizations, and a common legal code.[10] Its rulers carefully maintained the communications system and had a fairly clear idea of their own boundaries.

Yet these examples only serve to reinforce the general rule. This was that the old imperial centers and bureaucracies intervened in the working of society and the economy only in particular cases and in quite specific geographical areas. It was not the case that the old states were uniformly "weak," more that they husbanded their moral and physical authority for specific tasks. Throughout the world, for instance, the majority of irrigation systems and roads were probably maintained by local communities or magnates. Where complex bundles of royal privileges and powers had come into existence, there was often a tendency for them to be broken up, becoming part of the patrimony of some other prince or noble. Kings and emperors often found it lucrative and convenient to "farm out" their rights to the highest bidder in order to raise money. Even in fiscally centralized France, the state widely handed out to revenue contractors in "farms" and to big magnates in privileges what it squeezed out of the restive peasantry. Here and elsewhere in Europe, it was often grievances against the extra imposts levied by such financial entrepreneurs, rather than royal taxation itself, which lay at the root of rural revolts. In the Spanish New World, successive attempts by the crown to centralize power were stubbornly resisted by local governors and mayors who made money not so much through the free market, as by forced sales of goods and the requisitioning of labor from the Indian peasantry. Not surprisingly, "tyrannical abuse," as the Spanish officials termed it, sparked off numerous local rebellions.[11]

The picture was similar in Asia. By 1800 in China, the royal granaries, the Grand Canal, and the Yellow River dike systems were in decay.[12] Other royal institutions were foundering. Initially, the emperors had been content to cede their power in one area in order to strengthen it elsewhere. In the longer run, however, the decay of these imperial functions gravely compromised the regime's legitimacy. Recent work on the West African Asante has also shown that this aspiring centralized power was severely limited by local feudatories and lineage groups. Here, commoners developed trading contacts with the world market in spite of, not because of, the interests of the rulers.

So government in all these great states was often something of a trick of the light. State power was powerful and purposive in defined areas, though constant vigilance was needed to stop it seeping away to magnates and local communities. Elsewhere, it was patchy and contingent. Over large areas it was deliberately not exercised at all. Rulers found it difficult to mobilize military forces quickly. In the monsoon areas of Asia where great kings vaunted their magnificence, warfare and tax gathering regularly came to a halt when the roads annually became impassable. The state could only deploy a small number of officials or exercise royal justice in particular cases. In general, rulers were only just beginning to find out who and how many people lived within their diverse territories, what languages they spoke or what religious rites they performed. Because of the history of religious persecution in Europe, most regimes even here avoided "making windows on men's souls." In Muslim and Asian societies a broad recognition of the supremacy of the emperor's cult, not uniformity of belief, was what was required. Everywhere, therefore, the panoply of state and imperial power rested in the longer term on the co-option and honoring of local elites or self-governing local communities. Rulers had to accept and make the most of the political forms and religious beliefs of the localities and leave them to their own devices.

The means of co-option varied widely. The two ends of the spectrum were analyzed by nineteenth-century social theorists, notably the German sociologist Max Weber. On the one side was the pattern of military aristocracy. Here the dynasties of great soldiers and controllers of land were allowed effective lordship within their domains, provided that they paid allegiance to the supreme ruler and directly or indirectly furnished the resources and manpower for wars of conquest and defense. This was largely true, for instance, of the Hungarian nobility within the Austro-Hungarian Empire. The northwestern Indian territory of Rajasthan, controlled by local kings and nobles owing a broad allegiance to the Mughal emperor in Delhi, was not dissimilar in some respects. On the other side were the old-style bureaucracies. China had its elaborate hierarchies of civil magistrates trained in the Confucian classics through lineage and imperial schools and then sent to far provinces to create order and plenty through agrarian redistribution. They represented the ideal type of archaic bureaucracy. France, with its nobility of the sword, drawn from great families who had fought for the crown of St Louis since the Middle Ages, apparently lay at the other extreme. In practice, though, military aristocracies needed managers of paper and information, while in bureaucratic systems, officials nurtured their own power as land-controllers at the local level. So France, a society in which government needed to be literate and penny pinching, had its *noblesse de robe*: civil, bureaucratic nobility drawn from the lower-status commercial classes and lawyers. By contrast, in China, the ruling Qing dynasty had to allow the land tax to be fixed in perpetuity when it consolidated its power in the mid-seventeenth century. This meant that the scholar-gentry families from which the bureaucrats were recruited had accumulated further landholdings and the perquisites of commerce in their own localities, becoming a landowning and even a trading class in their own right. The pure scholar-gentry bent with the wind of local conditions. On the fringes of the Vietnamese state, members of its own Chinese-style mandarinate made multiple marriages with the Tay minority group in order to stabilize the dangerous border areas. In reality, then, the distinct ideal types of bureaucrat, warrior-landholder, and man of religion merged into each other in complex patterns.

Even the most powerful of agrarian emperors, therefore, continued to deal with jumbles of rights, privileges, local autonomies, and "family circles" which had been inherited from the past or created through the very act of imperial or royal political consolidation. In the words of William Doyle, even over much of Europe, "[t]he reality of the ancien régime was intense confusion of powers and perpetual overlaps of unequal jurisdiction, in which the king, so far from imposing an unchallengeable authority, was constantly bargaining with his subjects at a number of different levels."[13] In the later eighteenth century, the authority of the supposedly absolute kings of France was still limited by regional courts or *parlements* with appellate jurisdiction and by "estates" invested with powers over taxation. Russia was an extreme case in "Europe" where the tsar's theoretical autocracy was limited in practice. In 1763, the Russian government employed 16,500 officials, while Prussia, a mere 1 percent of Russia's size, employed 1,400.[14] In Russia, therefore, despite the fact that the landowners had never built up feudal privileges on the scale of western Europe, they effectively controlled this vast empire. Again, this was not simply a question of weakness. Monarchs could sometimes strategically deploy the resources of these different powers and jurisdictions to gain their political ends. The tsars could deploy formidable arbitrary powers if they wished. But it was not always in the interests of rulers to iron out these particularistic jurisdictions. The English kings and their ministers, for instance, found the separate status of Ireland and its patronage an extremely useful resource with which to oil the wheels of politics across the three kingdoms of England, Scotland, and Ireland.

One feature of the old regimes on which historians have often remarked was their tendency to go through "developmental cycles" in which periods of relative centralization were followed by decentralization, and then sometimes by attempts at recentralization. In some cases, "imperial overstretch" had already become only too apparent by the eighteenth century, and the high kings and emperors had ceded most of the powers they had seized during periods of conquest. The Ottoman rulers in Istanbul had virtually relinquished command to powerful *ayan*, or regional magnates, in Egypt, Syria, Mount Lebanon, and North Africa by 1700, though their rule remained strong in the center of the empire. In India by 1720, the Mughal emperor could count on only a diminishing volume of revenue and public obeisance from his over-mighty Hindu, Muslim, and Sikh subjects, ranged in expanding kingdoms distant from Delhi. The Habsburg empire of Austria was a "conglomerate of separate territorial units, most of which had deep rooted and powerful individual identities,"[15] and below the central level almost all authority was exercised by landowning nobles, the Church, and semi-autonomous cities, at least until the mid-eighteenth century. The German state-builders of the nineteenth century came to regard this image of decentralized, overlapping powers in the German and Austro-Hungarian empires as frustrating, verging on the ridiculous.

Ideological power within the old states was as segmented and complex as political power, and often intertwined with it. Far from being straightforwardly a "Buddhist," "Confucian," or even "Daoist" realm, the Empire of China was a cosmic spirit empire. The Qing emperors maintained close connections with the spiritual power of the Dalai and Panchen Lamas of Tibet and the shamanic holy men of Mongolia, as their steppe-raiding ancestors had done. Again, this should not necessarily be put down to the ideological "weakness" of these powers. On the contrary, a good case can be made that the great dynasties often promoted these very differences. The Chinese historian Pamela Crossley argues that the later Qing ruled by fostering separate ethnicities under leaders who were often also heads of cults.[16] Qing imperial ideology, especially under the Qian Long emperor, elevated the emperor to a transcendent and dispassionate role. His very greatness was reflected in his universal monarchy as great Khan of the Mongols and Manchus and Confucian father for the Han Chinese (see illustration 1.1).

Similar arguments have been made for the Ottoman dynasty. The Sultan was an Ottoman khan, a Caesar, an emperor for the "Romans," and later Khalifa, or successor, to the Prophet and a universal king in the style of Alexander.[17] As a Muslim ruler, he could not head other cults, but he patronized Jewish, Druze, and Christian institutions. The Muslim Mughal emperor, regent of God on earth in succession to the holy Prophet, regularly cast his blessed gaze over the hordes of naked Hindu holy men who gathered on the River Jumna below his ramparts in the Red Fort of Delhi. This was despite the fact that they were the very embodiment of Hindu "polytheism." It was in the emperor's armies that were firmed up once-shifting social categories such as "Rajputs,"[18] "Mughals," "Turks," and Persians. In some cases there is little doubt that local religious and "ethnic" communities were powerful enough to reject imperial ideology and policy. Yet these examples are a reminder that the old regimes had quite different ideals and cultural aims from those of most nineteenth-century nation-states and empires. They helped to create, even gloried in, complexity and difference.

Even in Christian Europe, where religion had already become more closely associated with the identity of states, rulers sought to reflect their power by patronage of different religious groups. After Peter the Great, Russian monarchs tried at the same time to represent themselves as enlightened embodiments of European reason, sacred kings of the Orthodox Christian Church, and great khans to their increasing numbers of Mongol and Muslim subjects. They had to deal with intransigent Old Believers among the Orthodox and, by 1800, Polish and Lithuanian Catholics and central Asian Muslims. In the Austrian and German lands, the "toleration" of diverse beliefs had been legislated for by the 1648 Peace of Westphalia. On its eastern frontier of Austria, Vienna ruled over communities of Orthodox Christians and Jews. Whether they liked it or not, the Habsburg monarchs had to keep on board Catholics, Protestants, Orthodox and Uniate Christians, Jews, and even a few Muslim stragglers.

The relationship between the Catholic kings of western and southern Europe and the papacy remained complex and watchful. The Bishop of Rome across

ILLUSTRATION 1.1 Cherishing difference: Qian Long inspecting his troops, by Giuseppe Castiglione.

the Alps could still deflect a French sovereign's power at the height of so-called enlightened despotism. Even in Britain, where Roman Catholics were debarred from holding most public offices, the monarch was the head of an Episcopalian church in England and a Presbyterian one in Scotland, though their clerics professed different and mutually antagonistic doctrines. By 1815, the English king ruled Roman Catholics in Quebec and Malta, Orthodox Christians in the Greek islands, and Hindus, Muslims, and Buddhists in South and Southeast Asia.

ILLUSTRATION 1.2   A multiethnic empire: Emperor Shah Jahan receiving Persian general Ali Mardan Khan, 1638. Mughal miniature.

All these features of the global "old order" of the seventeenth and eighteenth centuries emphasize the significance of the transformation which was to occur by the early twentieth century. The ideas of the state, the nation, the "ethnic minority," science, and the professions emerged out of, or were to be imposed, on the more shifting, ideologically complex, yet economically simple world which preceded it.

POWERS ON THE FRINGES OF STATES

Just as the inner agrarian space of most eighteenth-century dominions was populated by powerful independent land-controllers, masterful bureaucrats,

ILLUSTRATION 1.3 Holy, Roman, bewigged, and emperor: Holy Roman Emperor Charles VI, statue at Schloss Laxenburg, Niederösterreich, by Matthias Bernhard Braun.

and free-trading cities, so the outer perimeters were generally porous and undefined. Regimes survived longest if they incorporated resourceful soldiers and administrators from outside their realms. People from present-day Albania and Romania ruled in the Ottoman Empire and founded a new dynasty in Egypt as late as 1802. An Armenian dynasty ruled in what is now Iraq. The Chinese Empire was in large part a Manchurian domain which continued to incorporate Mongol, Uighur, and Tibetan tribal notables from beyond the Great Wall into its ruling group.[19] The Qian Long emperor supposedly learned the Uighur language in order to converse more easily with his peripheral commanders. Cossack horsemen and "pioneer" peasants were only just being made reliable tools of the Russian Empire. But at its heart, many noble families traced their origins to Turkic or Mongol enemies of old Muscovy, who had later been incorporated into expanding Russia.

Skilled and assertive minorities from outside the borders of states established circles of office holding. Baltic Germans ruled in Russia. Hanoverian Germans ruled in England, where they were joined in their military commands by Scots and Irish. Some of the fathers or grandfathers of these men had once been Catholic and "tribal" enemies of England. If many European and non-European societies saw a growth of patriotic display and sentiment, as we shall see, it was at least in part because they were ruled by outsiders. In India, people made a distinction between "locals" (*deshis*), "foreigners" (*bideshis*), and a category of "outsiders we know from just over the fuzzy border," called *pardeshis*. Much of the world in 1780 was ruled by such "pardeshis."

Most of the great empires also lived in symbiotic contention with varieties of commercial cities, maritime trading corporations, or seaborne states which controlled or "took a cut" from their external trade. Privateering still flourished in the Atlantic and eastern seas. In the Mediterranean, a motley group of ship-owning powers, ranging from the Knights of St John of Malta, through the Beys of Algiers, to the Republic of Venice, held sway. In eastern waters, the traders of Muscat and Oman cruised the African and Indian coasts, while the Bugis, a vast corporation of Southeast Asian port-princes and shipowners, struggled over the control of trade with the "Dutch" of Batavia and their mixed-race progeny.[20] Studies have found that even in the agrarian empires, powerful bodies of merchants and local gentry effectively controlled maritime cities which were formally dominated by imperial officials and soldiers. It was to avoid this kind of creeping autonomy and the rise of "King Silver," or commercial greed, that emperors from the sixteenth century onward attempted to close down China's maritime trades when they were not directly controlled by state trading corporations.[21] It is, however, easy to underestimate the importance of these sea-borne supremacies because they had all disappeared or been beaten into submission by the mid-nineteenth century. Their final indignity was often to be castigated as "pirates" by the commanders of Britain's Royal Navy.

Historians have traditionally viewed the world through the perspective of the great regimes and their chroniclers or the emerging nation-states of western Europe. But over recent years more attention has been paid to the large swathes of humanity who lived in neither of these contexts. Complex agrarian societies, such as the Oyo, Great Zimbabwe, or Asante empires, existed in Africa. Yet many other Africans, especially in the east and south of the continent, lived in what have been called state-less societies, and their livelihoods were made up from the exploitation of a range of agricultural, forest, and animal products.[22] Cities were common in West and North Africa, but there were few in eastern and southern Africa, except where Arabs or Europeans had settled. The wheel and the plough were unknown, or at least unused, across much of the continent, and because land was plentiful, African hierarchies were more often constructed of age-sets and not, as in Eurasia, by differences in landholding and wealth.

Over much of Africa, as in the native American and Pacific worlds, the apparatus of "the state" therefore did not exist as a separate entity. These societies were regulated internally by lineage heads who represented the interests of different "segments" of society arranged in real or assumed kinship units. Many African "high kings" were constrained by the counsel of the heads of the great lineages. Their power was largely ritual, concerning mediation with the spirit world, rather than the exercise of power over resources. In these societies conflict was widely between different age-groups among the lineage leaders, rather than between classes or ethnicities.[23] Even in such societies dependent groups did exist, of course. Sometimes they were descendants of slaves, sometimes people whose parents had pledged their property in exchange for help during bad times. But such people were more like servants of the superior lineage than serfs or plantation slaves on the Caribbean and American model.

The same was true of the indigenous populations of North America and Australasia and the Pacific, which provide many examples of nomadic, forest-dwelling, and hunting populations. These were culturally sophisticated, linguistically diverse, but even more closely tied to the cycles of the natural and animal world than the populations of the agrarian empires. Social and religious life was not regularized or predictable. Gender was a powerful force shaping social relations. In the Polynesian Pacific, for instance, communities were bound together through the exchange of women, often over quite long distances.[24] But elsewhere, as among the Maori, groups led by bodies of male warriors contended fiercely with each other, forming the pattern of social life. Religious activity centered on cults and mysteries rather than on preaching and regular ritual. The cultural shock generated amongst such people by the sudden arrival of missionaries and European military units or administrations is difficult to exaggerate.

Even the great agrarian realms of Eurasia were fringed and internally complicated by diverse societies of this sort which lived within them in a symbiosis occasionally ruptured by war and invasion. Inland Eurasia supported nomadic polities. There were the still-powerful Manchurian herdsmen, who had long before spawned the world-conquering Genghis Khan. In Arabia there were the nomadic camel-keeping tribes who had once provided the warriors of the Prophet, and even in the eighteenth century were the bedrock of Wahhabi resistance to the Ottoman Empire in the name of pure Islam. In Persia during the eighteenth century it was families from the semi-nomadic tribal groups Zands and Qajars who came to power.[25] This was, however, almost the last generation in which tough nomads and desert-dwellers were able to break in to settled states to revive their governments and purge their religion in the classic historical process described by the great medieval Muslim thinker Ibn Khaldun. On the fringes of the European states of western Eurasia, Lap reindeer herdsmen or Kazak sheep herdsmen provided resources, but also irritants, for the settled kingdoms. Cossack pioneer peasants and horse-soldiers were a powerful interest on the fringes of the Russian Empire. When, in the 1770s, some cossacks revolted against the Empress, the peasant armies of the pretender, Pugachev, who claimed to be Tsar Peter III, roamed across the empire for several years.[26]

Forest polities, dependent on the animals and wood products or selling their skills as sappers, miners, and forest-men to the kings and officials of the settled, represented another distinct type of polity. Here again, scholars have recently demonstrated that as late as the eighteenth century forest- and fastness-dwelling chieftain marauders could still deal with the agrarian states of the plains on the basis of something like equality. This was true of the "tribal" forest-dwellers of India, Burma, Thailand, and the Indonesian archipelago, or even the Siberian frontier, where such peoples not only provided scarce resources and military skills but were also regarded with some awe as white magicians and healers. In North America, the historical record has been dominated by wars between settlers and Indians. But there were at least as many examples of cooperation and interpenetration, at least before more vigorous policies of discrimination were introduced after 1812.

HARBINGERS OF NEW POLITICAL FORMATIONS

Finally, consideration must be given to those polities that were to become so critical in the following 100 years at the international level and which are considered in more detail in the next chapter. These were the emerging commercial societies which were heavily concentrated in northwestern Europe, but had also established colonial offshoots in the Caribbean and North America. In economic activity, life-style, and attitudes, much of the population of northwestern Europe was not far removed from its peasant origins. The idea that western European development was wholly exceptional in world history is no longer fashionable. Yet in scale and style, it surpassed the growth of entrepreneurial societies which had come into existence in many other parts of the world. For a start, rural as well as urban societies in these regions were much more heavily specialized than even those centers of commercialization which could be seen in the central Yangzi valley, or in rural Bengal or in the hinterland of Istanbul. Only Japan and parts of coastal China really provide a convincing parallel.

Even in the seventeenth century, central Holland, which Jan de Vries sees as the first modern economy,[27] was importing more than one-third of its food from some distance. Well-developed regional specialization was also a feature of southern England, where London was a massive market, importing fresh fruit and vegetables from southern Ireland and coal from as far north as Newcastle in the eighteenth century. Financial and credit instruments were equally well developed, and capital was increasingly becoming transnational. So, for instance, Dutch financiers invested in the stock of the English East India and Levant companies and in the British Caribbean, even though Holland remained Britain's rival. In some ways, the most advanced form of economic specialization and the long-distance deployment of capital were the slave plantations of southern North America and the Caribbean. The violence and cruelty of the slave trade and of the exploitation of slaves cannot obscure the fact that this was a flexible, financially sophisticated, consumer-oriented, technologically innovative form of human beastliness.

Where Europeans went overseas, they might have continued to operate according to older communal and religious norms, as did the Dutch farmers settled in southern Africa since the 1650s, for instance. But they rarely became a peasantry in the classic sense. Land was too plentiful in these settler continents. People had emigrated in order to acquire their own land rights, not to become a new peasantry dominated by large owners. Big pastoral and woodland landlords were, therefore, generally opposed in the New World, and later in Australasia, to sharecroppers and small owner-occupier farmers. Even on the Cape of Good Hope, the black population formed something more like a labor reserve than a peasantry cultivating its own land predominantly with family labor.

These modern-looking forms of labor, produce and capital markets in such global growth centers did not always overlap with polities in which state power was clearer and more delineated. Holland and England still had numerous subsystems of law and status, curious anachronisms which had sometimes even been strengthened by the growth of the market. Germany remained a patchwork of principalities, prince-bishoprics, free cities, and so on. In general, though, the more commercialized and specialized types of economy sooner or later became coterminous with more specialized and powerful states. The transparency of power was something that merchants and commercial landholders have always found attractive. Yet the yeast of commercial growth had still had only a patchy and limited effect, even in the core areas of western Europe and its North Atlantic colonies by 1780.

THE PREHISTORY OF "GLOBALIZATION"

One theme of this book is the growth of a more integrated international society in the course of the long nineteenth century, one which, in the medium term, was dominated by the West. For the nineteenth century we can certainly use the term "international." This, above all, was the period of the "internationalization of nationalism," when the ideas and practices of the nation-state became rooted among the elites in all major world cultures. It is important, however, to consider the nature of globalization in the seventeenth and eighteenth centuries, before the high point of the nation-state. The world crisis of 1780–1820 was a climacteric precisely because political and ideological shock waves were passed backward and forward between the centers of a world which was already linked. In addition, the networks of what I am calling here "archaic globalization" and "early modern" globalization persisted under the umbrella of the nineteenth-century international system. At times they empowered it; at times they challenged it.

This section uses the term "archaic globalization"[28] to describe the older networks and dominances created by geographical expansion of ideas and social forces from the local and regional level to the inter-regional and inter-continental level. As the previous pages have implied, archaic globalization had many centers. In its early stages, the "expansion of Europe" was simply one among several contemporary examples of globalization, rather than a world system in the making. Yet we can detect some common underlying principles in these patterns from classical antiquity through to the early modern period. Vast political and economic changes occurred during this era, of course. By the seventeenth century, the new cultural and economic network of the slave plantation system and New World silver had ushered in the era of early capitalist globalization in part of the Atlantic region. Nevertheless, the rationale underlying global networks of people, monetary transactions, and ideas for much of the population of Mediterranean Europe, Asia, and Africa in 1750 bore some similarities to that underlying those which had existed five or even ten centuries earlier.

People have always made long-distance contact with each other for reasons of profit, through the desire for power, and as a result of pure inquisitiveness. In the world of the old regimes, these drives took subtly different forms from those typical of the modern international system. Three general principles underlay archaic globalization: first, universalizing kingship; secondly, the expansive urge of cosmic religion; and thirdly, humoral or moral understandings of bodily health. These forces created some underlying patterns in the global exchange of ideas, personnel, and commodities.

First, the idea of universal kingship drove monarchs, their soldiers, and administrators over vast distances in search of individual and family honor, whether in the service of the Most Christian Spanish Empire or of Manchu Supremacy. As the previous section indicated, the courts of these world conquerors prized difference and "cherished men from afar."[29] Their kings and administrators valued representatives of different peoples for their qualities: Turks for toughness, Christians for science, Persians for refinement, and so on. The great courts and their petty imitators down to the large villages also acted as magnets for honorific commodities drawn from distant lands. Kashmiri shawls, Chinese silks, Arab horses, and precious stones of all kinds were prized across huge distances, and were critical to the workings of long-distance trade links. Even in the more isolated cosmos of the Pacific chiefs, high kings sought exotic and charismatic objects or foods to embody and represent their greatness. Prestige trades of this sort fitted into a much broader pattern whereby social relations were constituted through the long-distance exchange of prized goods between different communities.[30] As the anthropologist Marshall Sahlins pointed out, this valuation of rare products predisposed Hawaiians to trade eagerly for commodities such as European and American cloth, Chinese porcelains, and prized sandalwood once "first contact" had been made.

The intelligentsias of the archaic globe transmitted mythologies and ethical systems which complemented these political ideologies. Along with the charisma of Rome or Rum, the story of Alexander was widely remembered across Eurasia and Africa. Seventeenth-century Mughal kings modeled their meetings with Hindu renouncers on the reported deportment of Alexander before the ascetic Greek renouncers, the cynics, and self-abnegating Indian Brahmins.[31] Even in the nineteenth century, British travelers penetrating into the high passes of Afghanistan looked for Greeks, throwbacks to Alexander's army, among the tribal peoples.[32] The philosophy of Alexander's teacher, Aristotle, also retained its potency across a vast area of Christendom and Islam, even in the eighteenth century. Aristotelian ethics had passed through the hands of medieval Islamic writers into the everyday moral language of the Indo-Islamic world. Works of Muslim ethics patterned on Aristotle were read daily at the courts of many Islamic rulers. They informed the decisions of local judges.[33] Meanwhile, Aristotle and his followers remained an important element in the intellectual landscape of Europe and its colonies until the nineteenth century. As late as 1860, churchmen in Spanish- and English-speaking America were using Aristotle to justify slavery.

The idea of the "civic republican" tradition of thought has informed European and early American intellectual historiography since John Pocock's seminal work in the 1960s.[34] According to this view, most thinkers still looked back to the ancient world, stressing sturdy virtues uncorrupted by the state or the market. Perhaps, however, we can also glimpse another, wider civic republican tradition which limited the power of kings in Asia and in North Africa. As in the European republican tradition, kings were supposed to rule well in order to preserve the balance of the ideal polity, preserving pious householders and balancing the interests of different professions. These common elements in the world mythology and political ideology provided points of contact between Europeans, Asians, and Africans up to the mid-nineteenth century, even in situations otherwise characterized by ruthless exploitation and religious conflict. This theme will be explored further in chapter 7.

Secondly, even after the growth of Atlantic slavery and migration, many of the greatest global movements of people still remained pilgrimages and the wanderings of seers in search of traces of God. These reflected the imperatives of cosmic religion. Jerusalem and Rome retained their magnetic attraction for Christians in the Age of Enlightenment. For example, Napoleon and the Irish revolutionary of 1798, Wolfe Tone, both took time off from more pressing engagements to consider how to bring the Jewish people back to the Temple in Jerusalem.[35] For Muslim rulers from Sumatra to Nigeria, organizing the pilgrimage to the holy places remained the prime duty of external relations. The expansion of the Sufi mystical orders within Islam, especially the movement of the "mystical" Chishti order, provided a religious analogy to the globalizing of great kings. Even in the Atlantic world, Christian belief established patterns of long-distance godly migration. The diaspora of the Franciscans and Jesuits, the expansion of the Mormons, or the regular wanderings of English and Irish Quakers across the Atlantic in the eighteenth century are cases in point.

Thirdly, bodily practice helped to provide the force behind archaic globalization. The transmission of ideas encouraged the movement of goods, which in turn spread new ideas. The world's biomedical systems, from the Greek, Islamic, and Hindu through to Daoist and Confucian, overlapped. Specialists read each other's texts. They sought out similar spices, precious stones, and animal products which were thought to enhance reproduction, sex, and bodily health. Along with markers of royalty such as precious metals, weapons, and horses, the search for prized medicines imposed deep patterns on world trade and the movement of peoples.[36] They helped to create the archaic "ethnoscape," a global pattern of cultural mixing, to borrow a word from Arjun Appadurai again.[37] In the eighteenth century, for example, much of China's overseas trade was designed to capture life-enhancing products and tokens of kingship. It was as medicines that tea, then tobacco, and finally opium entered China. Each of these commodities became, first, tokens of leisure and then, in the nineteenth century, items of pathological mass consumption. To some degree, this was also true for western Europe and the Atlantic world.

Archaic globalization worked, then, in several different and mutually reinforcing ways. At the broadest level, there was the ideology and imagined community of the Old World constructed by universal kingship and cosmic religion. In the intermediate register lay the uneven patterns of diasporic trading, military, and specialist communities generated by these values. These were the links that scattered Armenian merchants from the kingdom of Hungary to the South China seas. Finally, in the register of bodily practice, the human being constructed global linkages through acts of bio-moral transformation of substances and goods. The logic of such consumption was strategically to consume diversity. This pattern of collecting charismatic goods and substances differed significantly from the market-driven uniformity of today's world.

ARCHAIC AND EARLY MODERN GLOBALIZATION

The inter-regional trades in tea, tobacco, and opium characterize the second level, transitional phase in the emergence of the modern international order. This was early capitalist expansion, beginning in the Atlantic in the seventeenth century and spreading to much of the rest of the world by 1830. This phase was associated with the growth of Atlantic slavery. It also saw the rise of the European chartered companies, arms of mercantilist state power, and the royal trading entities created in the Asian world to handle and control these burgeoning trades. Proto-capitalist globalization developed by filling out and becoming parasitic on, perhaps "cannibalizing," to use Appadurai's phrase again, the earlier links created by archaic globalization. For instance, the capture of slaves, once a strategy in the building of the archaic great household in Africa and the Ottoman world, became a brutal proto-capitalist industry.

These new globalizing entities tried methodically to subordinate and redistribute labor on a vaster scale. They tried, as the next chapter shows, to link together and exploit the regional reorientations of production and consumption which de Vries called "industrious revolutions." Still, the change was uneven. In the register of bodily practice and personal deportment, the transformation was particularly slow. In Europe and outside, the trading companies carefully maintained the cultural and bio-moral repute of what were originally charismatic products, substances which were thought to alter both a person's body and spirit. So, tobacco was seen, and still is seen, as a stimulant to mental capacity. Aristocratic and burgher taste preserved the rituals of sociability and the aura of rareness surrounding what were now industrial goods, as far as production was concerned.

The first age of truly global imperialism, 1760–1830, is discussed in chapter 3. It looked both backward and forward if we consider the forces promoting global interconnection. There were new elements emerging especially from the European-Atlantic economy. Here for the first time changes in the Americas directly affected Asia. For example, the American Revolution significantly altered trading patterns in Asia by forcing the English East India Company to redouble its purchases of tea in China, and eventually to introduce Indian opium into Qing territory. Yet, during this same period, the instruments of international statecraft and the ideologies which informed them retained archaic features.

At the ideological level, hybridity and mixing characterized these years. On the one hand, the French admiral Louis Antoine de Bougainville (1729–1811) and Captain James Cook (1718–79), who explored the Pacific, used rationalistic and methodical methods of survey. The learned men of the British and French royal and oriental societies sought to make a "Map of all Mankind" by which all species, peoples, and products could be categorized.[38] On the other hand, archaic ideologies still prevailed. For instance, travelers in Egypt set themselves to tap the cosmic power of the pyramids. What modern Egyptologists call "pyramidiocy" has a very ancient pedigree. In the 1790s, an Anglo-German official in India believed he had found descriptions of the ancient British Isles of the days of Joseph of Arimathaea in the Sanskrit texts.[39] At this time too, a Scotsman became an Amerindian king in Honduras, and a British Indian officer carried floats of the Hindu deities around in his retinue. An Anglo-Irish British officer, Sir William Johnson (1715–74), learned American Indian languages, married Indian women, and became father of his people. Widely, religious practice remained both ritualized and flexible. In the British and American world, neither belief nor race but simple baptism widely remained the qualifier for public office. Even in the central lands of Islam, sultans made royal gifts to Christian monasteries and to synagogues.

At the level of bodily practice, the boundaries of the ethnic nation-state were not yet in evidence. Sexual relations were not heavily policed in practice. Large Eurasian, Afro-Asian, and, later, Euro-Australasian communities developed across the world. People used a wide range of remedies to strengthen and protect their bodies. Despite the beginning of a separate medical profession in Europe, most people still opted for a portfolio of different types of medical treatment, reinforced with prayer and magic. The consumption of exotic and charismatic herbs and other products continued the exchange of bio-moral information at the global level. The smallpox variola traveled from Persia to England. From here it was disseminated by direct bodily contact back to European trading posts in India and the China coast, and on to the royal centres of the interior.

How were honor and value assigned to people in these patterns of global interconnection? Neither race nor nationality, as understood at the end of the nineteenth century, was yet a dominant concept. Rather, what characterized this period was a series of interlocking rankings of people in terms of their embodied status, their honor, or purity or lineage. This was a "caste system" in the original Portuguese use of the term. In this scheme, European aristocratic blood purity provided one pole of embodied status, and slave origins the other. As in the eighteenth-century Mexican manual of pedigree, *Las Castas Mexicanas* ("The Castes of Mexico")[40] all other human groups could be intricately distinguished in a hierarchy stretching between these poles (see illustration 1.4). This archaic notion of caste, *casta*, or race (*raza*), prevailed in

ILLUSTRATION 1.4   Caste in the Old World: Mixed marriage. A Spaniard and his Mexican-Indian wife, and their child. Painting by Miguel Cabrera.

the Caribbean, Iberian, and English American worlds. This notion of caste also proved serviceable in the Muslim and Asian worlds, because it seemed compatible with current understandings of embodied status in these societies.

In the Indian world, prevalent ideas of purity and impurity could be fitted into the grid of caste in the towns of the west coast, where the Portuguese settled from the sixteenth century onwards. Muslims could loosely identify European "caste" with their own forms of status discrimination. These were based on humoral principles and historic closeness to the family of the Prophet. In turn, Chinese merchants in port cities adapted these Eurasian and Islamic categories to their own concepts of refinement and barbarity. As Frank Dikotter has shown in his book on race in modern China, classical Chinese bio-moral rankings assigned highest value to yellow races. Whites were associated with mental dullness, and blacks with uncontrolled passions.[41] Caste as a global measure of embodied status remained the key discriminator in the interaction of peoples in the archaic and early modern diasporas. It operated at a deeper level than nationality, which remained a flexible and rather indistinct category at this period.

PROSPECT

These connections of ideas, faith, and material acquisitiveness operated to give form and structure to the old world order as it began to change more rapidly under the influence of Atlantic trade and the great world empires. Yet ideological movements, as much as sharp changes in material life, could also spread conflict and uncertainty. Sanjay Subrahmanyam, developing an idea of Jean Aubin, showed how sixteenth-century Christians and Muslims had been affected by currents of millenarian thought which could be used to justify political expansion, war, and conflict. Christians had been unsettled by the coming of the first millennium-and-a-half since Christ's birth. The expectations of Muslims had been roused by the millennium of the Prophet's message which came a few decades later. The ripples of these respective anxieties and aspirations flowed together into what Subrahmanyam calls a "millenarian conjuncture."[42] This is of relevance to the present book. For in the same way, Buddhist, Muslim, and Sikh millennial aspirations, flowing strongly after about 1720, were to act on, and interact with, the secular millenarianism which flowed from the French Revolution. This time, however, states and empires were both larger in scale and more embattled than they had been in the sixteenth century. The resulting political maelstrom surged on through the generations after 1780.

The effects of this latter "millenarian conjuncture" were very powerful, in part because the world in 1780 stood on the brink of what the Chinese historian Kenneth Pomeranz has called "the great divergence."[43] The economic and social future of the human race was beginning to point in sharply different directions. The next chapter considers in greater detail the accelerating divergences between the economic performance of different world societies, especially between western Europe and the rest of the world. It goes on to examine the much subtler differences which emerged in the organization of states and civil societies across the continents.

[2] PASSAGES FROM THE OLD REGIMES TO MODERNITY

FIFTY years ago, if professional historians or students had been asked what was the major economic change taking place at world level in the second half of the eighteenth century, they would probably have pointed to the Industrial Revolution and the beginnings of mechanical production in Britain. No one can doubt the long-term importance of industrialization for how people lived across the world. But many historians are now skeptical that the Industrial Revolution had proceeded very far by 1800 and have downplayed its significance even for most of western Europe and America before the 1830s.

THE LAST "GREAT DOMESTICATION" AND "INDUSTRIOUS REVOLUTIONS"

From a global perspective, two other major types of social and economic change besides industrialization loom much larger in world history, at least before about 1830. The first of these shifts constituted the final phase of what could be called the "great domestication." Several millennia earlier, human beings began moving from nomadism, foraging, and shifting, with small-scale agriculture, to regular, intensive agrarian exploitation. The process moved into a final and very rapid phase on the remaining nomadic frontiers after about 1650.[1] There were a number of reasons for this. Human population began to grow much faster as a result of the ending of the great pandemics of bubonic plague and other diseases. Population even began to recover in Central and South America, where European-imported illnesses had cut back numbers savagely in the preceding century. Disease now became endemic in more resilient populations. New, nutritious varieties of food from Central and South America spread across the Old World in the wake of the Spanish and Portuguese "discoveries," improving fertility and resistance to disease. As populations grew, so pioneer peasants from nodes of settled agriculture and high population spilled into less populous forested and grazing lands, bringing them under cultivation.

From the Indonesian islands to northern Scandinavia, the growth of larger states encouraged the expansion of cultivation and the settlement of nomadic peoples and slash-and-burn agriculturalists. Settled people were easier to tax, and states needed soldiers, labor, and money. With the extermination of most of the indigenous fur-bearing animals in Russian Siberia by 1700, for instance, pioneer peasants began to move into this vast European hinterland. Almost everywhere European agriculture expanded on its hill, forest, and marshland frontiers. The destruction of forest in Scotland and the division of the peat bogs in Gaelic Ireland were part of this process. At about the same period, European colonists in North America began to push cultivation beyond the Atlantic seaboard up the river valleys into areas where indigenous peoples had once lived mainly by hunting and herding. During the eighteenth century, the export of cash crops, such as grain, sugar, and tobacco, from the ports of Latin America and the Caribbean greatly expanded. The production of these commodities also spread into lands which had once been forest or pampas. In the hinterland of Buenos Aires, indigenous nomads were driven away from better pasture or settled as ranch servants as the trade in cattle hides boomed and was regularized at the end of the eighteenth century. Here the old-style "domestication" was associated with a much more modern form of commerce. African slaves were brought in as the leather was shipped out.[2]

These agricultural changes usually accompanied the expansion of pioneer human communities. Along the internal and external frontiers of the settled Islamic world, the hospices of Sufi mystics often provided the stimulus to the growth of settled agriculture in their environs, just as did the networks of Christian mission stations and monasteries in Central and South America or southern Africa. Buoyant external trade sometimes acted as an important stimulus to intensive agriculture, but population expansion and agrarian development within individual societies were generally more important. A powerful urge to settle, colonize, and build up the fertility of the land had been the major dynamic of African societies since the eleventh century. In East and South Africa especially there existed a long-term relationship between more effective forms of animal husbandry and more intensive cultivation.[3] The island of Madagascar, for example, provides a good example of the essentially internal nature of these changes. It was only distantly and indirectly influenced by outside trade and the Muslim state building on the East African coast. Yet, during the course of the fifteenth to the eighteenth centuries, intensive rice agriculture in Madagascar expanded considerably.[4] In this forced domestication, labor was provided by a dependent serf population drawn from conquered peoples. Ambitious petty chieftains, wishing to defeat their enemies and become high kings, drove these changes forward by trying to increase their own wealth. Only later were such new types of economic activity reinforced by slave trading with the outside world and by the appearance of the Maria Theresa silver dollars in Madagascar's trading marts.

An example from an even more self-contained universe is to be found in the Pacific. Here, as immigrant Maori pushed into the north island of New Zealand between 1500 and 1800, forests were cleared, indigenous species exterminated, and earlier settlers displaced, as large areas were turned over to gardens for the cultivation of sweet potato.[5] Even in enclaves of Australia, pig raising and gardening had been introduced from New Guinea at some time in the recent precolonial past, modifying Aboriginal life-styles.[6]

In many parts of the world, the last great domestication – the more rapid ploughing up of prairie, jungle, or steppe and pioneer peasant intrusion into forests – provided raw materials and labor for the emerging commercial economies of the nineteenth century. Former forest-dwellers and "sedenterized," or settled, herdsmen were to become "coolies" and indentured laborers for the dominant white populations of the nineteenth-century world. Yet the great domestication had gathered pace over many preceding generations and was not confined to areas of European dominance alone. It was also to be a formative force in the creation of modern societies from Indochina to central Africa.

A second set of broad cultural and economic changes, distinct from the great domestication, but often related to it, was taking place in the heart of the old arable societies. These were what have been called "industrious revolutions." In some places, the resulting reorganization of demand and resources provided an essential complement to a slowly emerging industrial revolution. But this was not always the case. The concept of an "industrious revolution," developed by a historian of the Netherlands, Jan de Vries, has done much to make the picture of economic exchange under the old regime more complex and intriguing.[7] Yet it has also made it more uncertain, because Europe, its American colonies, and the Atlantic slave economies were not the only regions of the world which were experiencing something we might call industrious revolutions in the seventeenth and eighteenth centuries.

De Vries argued that people in Holland, southern England, north Germany, and the Thirteen Colonies were experiencing a series of industrious revolutions. This meant using family labor more efficiently by buying in goods and services from outside the household. Families acquired new "packages" of consumer items which worked on each other to produce yet larger gains in productivity and social satisfaction.[8] For instance, the consumption of coffee and, later, tea went along with the purchase of sugar, fine breads, and easily replaceable plates off which to eat these items. The resulting package – let us call it "breakfast" – gave people a higher calorific intake, a new time discipline, and a new pattern for sociability and emulation in the household. It also gave a boost to the trade in specialist foods and, later, disposable crockery which replaced the old and heavy family possessions which had been passed down from generation to generation. In the case of England, Hans-Joachim Voth has studied one aspect of an industrious revolution in detail, demonstrating how the whole society was pervaded by a new sense of time discipline between 1750 and 1830.[9]

The demand which arose from "the invention of breakfast," along with household furniture or household privacy, might well have provided consumers for the early industrial revolution, as it did in Britain. But industrious revolutions did not necessarily lead to early industrialization. They were not always forms of "proto-industrialization," to use a less precise concept which was in vogue among economic historians in the 1960s and 1970s. On most interpretations, the Industrial Revolution was a "supply-side" revolution, resulting from the mechanization of production. Industrious revolutions, by contrast, could increase prosperity in a much stealthier way without benefit of a rapid ratcheting up of industrial production. They were indeed supply-side revolutions in a modest way. But they also reflected changes in demand and in the patterns of consumer desire which stoked up demand. This pattern of industrious revolution without early industrialization was common in the Low Countries, Germany, and coastal North America. It was visible over patches of the valley of Mexico and coastal Brazil before 1850. These areas turned to large-scale factory production only quite late.

This chapter greatly expands the concept of industrious revolution by widening its geographical scope and giving it a cultural twist. First, it can be usefully extended to regions outside Europe, for which social historians have already built up a picture of changing consumer values and local-level production and distribution. Consumer values were, of course, culturally specific. In China it was the desire for the refined luxuries of the mandarin elite which was generalized to middling people and the merchant classes. This demand helped reorient production and labor in many localities. In Japan, it was the lordly style of samurai which mandated certain dress codes and the carrying of swords as a matter of status. This gave a boost to metallurgical industries and to inter-regional specialization, as it had in Europe. The "objectification of luxury" took widely different forms across the continents. All the same, broadly similar social changes flowed from industrious revolutions. Because people tend to like the "exotic" and had heard of wonderful substances from distant lands, they inserted themselves into the patterns of "archaic globalization" and began to transform them.

Secondly, then, these micro-level changes contributed a new dynamic to the expansion of commerce. Merchant capitalists in many societies quickly became aware of potential markets and new producers and began to link them together in new patterns of world trade. This happened before significant industrialization took place in Europe. It is striking, too, that some of the key consumables in the industrious revolutions of Europe and the Americas were tropical products: tobacco, coffee, sugar, and tea. The corollary of this, however, is that Europeans and their American colonists were the greatest beneficiaries of this networking. Chinese, Arab, and African merchants certainly prospered. Yet by far the greatest "value added" was grabbed by Europeans.

There were a number of reasons for this. From a very early period, their operations in mining and exploiting the Americas had given the Europeans a competitive advantage in world trade. The expansion of the slave production

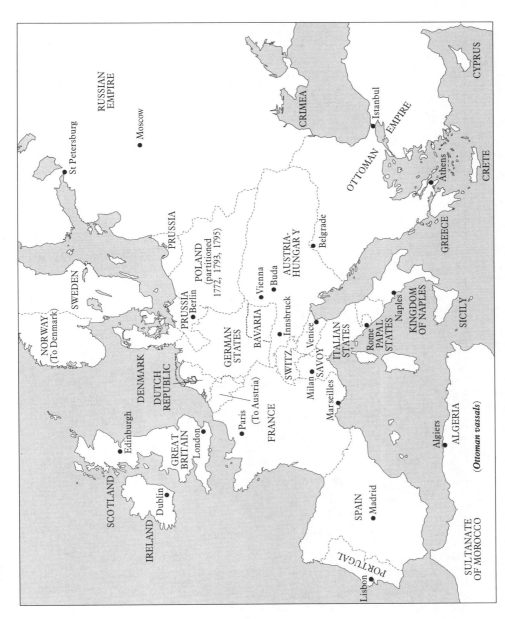

MAP 2.1   Europe during the late eighteenth century.

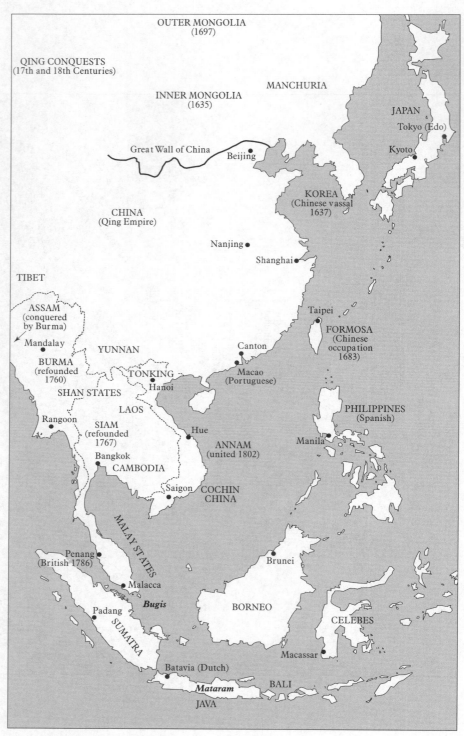

MAP 2.2 East Asia during the eighteenth century.

ILLUSTRATION 2.1   Industrious China: Interior of a tea shop. Painting, nineteenth century, Chinese.

system gave them a second great advantage. De Vries's industrious revolutions sometimes sound tame and domestic, redolent of Delft vases and the Dutch painter Cuyp's lustrous and contented cattle. But this was far from the case. In the Caribbean, the source of two of the most important items of "breakfast," brutality and subjugation were the order of the day. This forced and violent industrious revolution swelled the pool of European armed shipping and honed Spanish, Dutch, French, and British techniques for projecting their power across the world. Finally, as the later sections of this chapter will show, Europe and the North American colonies were information-rich societies in which inquisitiveness and cupidity turned information into tools for world exploration and, later, world conquest. This, however, is to leap ahead. The next section considers the strengths and limitations of industrious revolutions outside western Europe.

NEW PATTERNS OF AFRO-ASIAN MATERIAL CULTURE, PRODUCTION, AND TRADE

Historians have long wondered why China, with its great technical expertise and complex systems of internal marketing, entered the nineteenth century apparently suffering a gathering social crisis. The White Lotus Rebellion, which came to a head between 1796 and 1804, appeared to be the first of a succession of millenarian peasant revolts which weakened and impoverished China in the face of Western aggression. In the past decade the question has become even more pressing. A succession of historians of eighteenth-century China have presented a picture which modifies the view of decline. They depict buoyant trade, increasing inter-regional specialization, and a positive engagement by peasants and gentry with the emerging market.[10] These, of course, are all features which characterized the industrious revolutions of Europe, though the cultural context was rather different. Even as late as 1820, the Chinese economy displayed extensive production without large-scale urbanization,[11] it has been said. Labor became increasingly free and mobile, while credit expanded with small moneylenders and traders disbursing increasing volumes of New World silver into the interior.

In China, as in the European industrious revolutions, a critical development was the reorganization of household patterns of labor and, more importantly, consumption. Women were increasingly set to work as artisans, raising clan and family income from outside sources. From the sixteenth to the eighteenth century, the consumption of fine handicrafts spread from the upper scholar-gentry to lower gentry and even to merchant families and some rich peasants. Poorer peasant families found a market amongst them for goods such as fine printed kerchiefs and lacquered sweetmeat boxes. An eyewitness of the seventeenth century recorded a change in consumption patterns, which evidently proceeded further in the eighteenth. He observed: "now even lower officials began to use fine wooden furniture and cabinet makers opened shops where they made wedding furniture and other objects."[12] The same was true of the rather florid pink and blue porcelains which we associate with the Qian Long reign. Antique shops throughout Europe and North America still sell large numbers of these items, testimony to the flourishing export trades of the English and Dutch East India companies. Large volumes were also exported to Southeast Asia by Chinese merchants. Yet a large part of the huge volume of porcelain production in eighteenth-century central and south China was destined for the internal market, for the consumption of middling and lower state officials and merchant people. Luxury became a goal in its own right, and it was one marked by the acquisition of goods, rather than, as in the past, the control of people by righteous magistrates. Luxury, indeed, was "objectified," an essential motor of industrious revolutions within and outside Europe.

Similar patterns were appearing in Japan over the course of the late seventeenth and eighteenth centuries. Economic growth was not as fast as it had been during the seventeenth century, and it was often "country places," not the big cities, which prospered. Still, markets became more numerous in a relatively peaceful countryside. Labor became more specialized, and suburban elites accumulated goods as they did in parts of northern Europe. The knightly class, or samurai, set the patterns for consumption. Merchants and rich peasants increasingly bought silks and metal items. Ceramics flourished mightily, as the Japanese samurai and merchants reinvented and domesticated the Chinese tea ceremony after 1600. The demand for finely honed swords and ceremonial armor kept artisans busy. The population of the empire may have reached about 26 million by 1730.[13] Japan's low level of population growth, resulting from late marriage and abortion, ensured that slow gains in productivity were not "eaten up" by too many new mouths. The steady growth of demand helped to maintain incremental improvements in technology, especially in the agricultural sector and fishing. There were no major inventions such as the spinning jenny or the steam engine in England, but farmers, fishermen, and merchants, secure in their property rights, made many minor improvements to their methods of production and employment of capital. The Japanese market became more closely interconnected, even though political power was dispersed among the many domain lords.

More surprising, perhaps, in terms of the old historical literature is the impression that parts of India and the Middle East also experienced broadly favorable economic conditions at least to the middle of the eighteenth century. Traditionally, historians of eighteenth-century India, Iran, and the Ottoman Empire have seen these countries' economies as "tribute economies," in which the cities were parasitic on the countryside, and peasants produced only because they were forced to do so by the need to pay state land tax or rent. That view has recently become less tenable. Substantial parts of South and West Asia experienced a degree of relative prosperity even during the political turmoil of the early eighteenth century. In the western Indian uplands, where new regional polities were emerging after the decline of the Mughal supremacy, there is persistent evidence that rural people acted as entrepreneurs, buying and selling in local markets. Prasannan Parthasarathi has estimated that the standard of living of weavers in contemporary south India was actually higher in real terms than that of British ones in the mid-eighteenth century.[14] Other writers show how country people of low status gained wealth and renown during the century, controverting the old idea that precolonial India was a society of rigid caste divisions.

Throughout West and South Asia, political revolution created distortions in society and production, the effects of which it is easy to exaggerate. If warring magnates sometimes destroyed their own or others' patrimonies in pursuit of battles with overlords or underlings, others sought to capture artisans and peasants, starting their own local industries or areas of intensive farming. In a situation where labor, not land, was still a scarce resource, artisans and laborers could also be drawn off by promises of better treatment. Production was more often relocated than it was destroyed by war and faction. New, aspiring consumers rose to replace the "tall poppies" which had been lopped off by war and invasion. For instance, though the great Mughal and Safavid cities may have declined, new men such as the western Indian Marathas or the Zands and Qajars of Persia had become purchasers of fine silks, cottons, horses, and rice by the end of the eighteenth century.[15]

THE INTERNAL AND EXTERNAL LIMITS OF AFRO-ASIAN "INDUSTRIOUS REVOLUTIONS"

Many histories, especially those written by Asian and African nationalists, continue to ask the question, "What went wrong, then?" Why were Asians and Africans unable to nurture the sprouts of development which were clearly in evidence about 1700 or even 1750? This question was usually asked of the industrial, mechanizing revolution, rather than of industrious revolutions. That is because until recently most economic historians were concerned with questions about the supply of goods at the expense of the study of demand. The answers that historians came up with to explain relative decline indicted a range of internal factors. These included problems of communication, the tributary role of the state, which sucked out wealth from the people, especially from peasants, and the destructive effects of peasant rebellions against the lords of the old order.

These older accounts then went on to indict Western expansion and capitalism for dealing the deathblow to the already weakened victim and then subjecting Asia and Africa to a century of exploitation and misery. The slave trade, it was argued, sucked the developmental potential out of west and central Africa which, if not on the brink of an industrial revolution, was certainly experiencing growth, with the development of local trade and consumption. In India, the great textile centers were pole-axed by the East India Company, which depressed weavers' wages by the use of force and eventually ceased purchase and export of Indian goods. Much the same happened to the smaller textile and iron manufacturing sector of the Ottoman Empire and North Africa, which was already suffering corrosive French and Italian competition in the eighteenth century. This argument has recently been resurrected by André Gunder Frank. But Gunder Frank goes further, arguing that there was nothing very special about Europe.[16] What happened was that an almost fortuitous set of crises in non-Europe merely gave the appearance of the "rise of Europe."

Both sides of these arguments need to be rebalanced. First, the "decline of the rest" was only a patchy and relative process. There is indeed some evidence that benign agricultural and commercial growth, which was outlined in the previous section, was beginning to slacken by 1770 over much of the world outside northwest Europe and North America. The political systems of Asia and Africa were definitely experiencing difficulty in sustaining the momentum of expansion, and this impacted on prosperous and industrious regions. By this date, for instance, the Qing regime was showing signs of "imperial overstretch." It was devoting more and more resources to war on the frontiers, particularly in prized inner Asia. Meanwhile, there seems to have been a dwindling of interregional trade in China, as coastal areas looked towards the sea and inland zones became more self-sufficient.[17] Some parts of the country also began to experience serious ecological problems. By contrast, recent assessments by R. Bin Wong and Kenneth Pomeranz, among others, suggest that agricultural and commercial expansion held up quite well in China at least until the crisis following the opium war of 1839–42.

There is good reason not to overstress the "optimistic" view of the eighteenth century in South Asia, too. However buoyant some Indian regional economies may have been, the subcontinent still seems to have been locked into a zero-sum game in which people, capital, and resources moved from region to region, rather than sustaining cumulative growth in any one area.[18] In the Ottoman Empire, economic improvement was held back by the tussle between regional notables, cities, and "tribes" and the central authorities which sought close administrative control of provision and supply for their urban centres.[19] The periodic "breakouts," perhaps better "break-ins," of tribal groups led by monarchs aspiring to universal kingship, noted in the previous chapter, suggest that the African and Asian peripheries were not sufficiently pegged down as yet. Incipient industrious revolutions were unable to root themselves very deeply as a result of this geographical and political fluidity.

None of this, however, suggests a "decline of the rest" consonant with the huge differentials of wealth, productivity, and life expectancy which had opened up between the West and the rest by 1900. The early nineteenth century was to be a relatively successful period of adjustment to global change for large parts of the Ottoman Empire, especially Egypt. In South Asia, the Indian textile industry lived on borrowed time until at least 1820, and some parts of the subcontinent remained relatively prosperous until the agricultural depression of the 1830s, despite the "drain of wealth" to Britain.

The argument for the "decline of the rest" can, therefore, be pushed too far. We can go too far also in assailing the idea of the exceptional nature of European development. The "rise" of Europe and European America between 1750 and 1850 was more than simply a result of the relative "failure" of Asia and Africa. Nor do the reasons for northwestern Europe's and European North America's dynamism lie simply in the domain of economics. They can also be attributed to certain features of society and the state. Northwestern Europe's particular style of industrious revolutions – and, later, its industrial revolutions, too – was lodged in an economic and a social context which gave them significantly greater cumulative force for change than was the case in southern and eastern Europe and the rest of the world. At least in the short and medium term, this meant that these patches of social and economic transformation had more staying power than those of Asia and Africa. The remainder of this chapter considers aspects of European financial dynamism and then its essential ideological and social contexts.

TRADE, FINANCE, AND INNOVATION: EUROPEAN COMPETITIVE ADVANTAGES

The first chapter has already alluded to some of the features which gave this added economic dynamism to western Europe in its transition to what people began to describe as modernity. Firstly, as Kenneth Pomeranz argued,[20] Europe had a truly massive hinterland of underused resources, even in comparison to China and India, both in its own continent and in the Americas. In addition, its seizure of labor and resources through the expansion of the slave plantation system provided it with a series of massive, cheap agricultural provinces. In the course of the eighteenth century, huge quantities of timber were cut in western Europe, the Siberian north, North America, and latterly on the west coast of India, Burma, and the north coast of Australia, to support naval construction. Already in the eighteenth century, Europe exported surplus population in large numbers to the Americas, reducing the problems caused by high population density, which increasingly affected parts of Asia in the course of the nineteenth century.

The productivity of agriculture was probably significantly higher in parts of India and China than in Europe in the seventeenth century. But new crop varieties and more intensive forms of production allowed some regions of Europe to leap forward in the eighteenth century, though shortfalls between production and consumption still existed. To this was added the import of foodstuffs, such as sugar and protein-rich fish, from the Caribbean, Atlantic Ocean, and the Americas. Northwestern Europe could thus feed a growing urban population, which accelerated much more rapidly than Chinese, Indian, and Middle Eastern urban populations over the course of the century. Outside Japan and parts of coastal China, Asians and North Africans do not appear to have brought in significant quantities of food from the seas. Investments in transport in Europe rose rapidly, whereas Chinese transport and internal trade had already reached a "high level equilibrium trap."[21] They were efficient enough to satisfy demand at a low level, but not to create a real breakthrough.

As Pomeranz also pointed out, northwestern Europeans moved rapidly and efficiently to exploit the use of coal. This commodity was carried over long distances to provide fuel for industrious revolutions in household organization and, later, for industrial production. By comparison, Chinese resources of fossil fuels, isolated in its northern backwaters and Manchuria, were perhaps less efficiently exploited. Coal also helped initiate a chain of innovations in Britain. Deep mines required pumps. In turn, the development of pumping technology encouraged iron casting and further promoted an understanding of the nature of the vacuum, which was critical to the breakthrough in steam power. Even if inventions such as the spinning jenny and the steam engine took a long time to raise overall growth rates in the economy, as some economic historians now argue, by the 1820s and 1830s they were beginning to give Europeans a further edge in military technology.[22]

Northwestern Europe and its North American colonies increasingly capitalized on three other advantages which lay more in the social and political domains than in the economic but did help its populations to project their power internationally. These must be considered alongside Pomeranz's economic conditions. First, relatively stable legal institutions guaranteed that economic advances were rewarded. Intellectual property rights were slow to develop outside Britain, but English common law and mainland European Roman law did provide significant support for family and personal property in general. Inventors and innovators could become wealthy if they played their cards right. Rural and urban landed property was relatively safe from seizure by government or escheat, at least in western Europe. The geographical stability of dominant groups also meant that there was an incentive to invest in small improvements generation by generation. The inheritance of Europe's seventeenth-century ideological wars meant that governments and elites had reached an unspoken agreement not to tamper with property rights overmuch. Even during the French and European revolutions, it was generally only the Church and a small minority of nobles who saw lands and privileges permanently confiscated. These families, too, were often able to claim back their property after 1815.

In eastern European, Middle Eastern, Asian, and African societies, property does appear to have remained rather more vulnerable to state intervention. This should not be exaggerated, as did theorists of oriental despotism, such as the seventeenth-century writer François Bernier. Yet there was still a significant degree of difference between western Europe and its competitors. Ruling dynasties in Asia and Africa often frustrated the development of wealth outside their own immediate dependants. Among the Asante, for instance, slaves and commoners were largely excluded from state-controlled opportunities for advancement, and rich families were hit by punitive death duties.[23] The Ottoman sultans saddled their greatest commercial families with state contracts which impoverished them.[24] This was apparently less true in China, where political change did not generally see lineages forfeiting their rights. Yet, during times of crisis, wealthy merchants were "asked" to make donations to the state. Here, too, the system of multiple inheritance tended to split up rewards and "cut off the tall poppies" generation by generation. In South Asia and the Middle East, powerful consuming groups emerged and reinvested, despite the rapid rise and fall of dynasties. Nevertheless, the rapid geographical relocation of political and commercial centers after 1680 meant that capital investment did not produce the same long-term cumulative rewards as it did in some parts of western Europe.

Russia may well have been closer to the Ottoman than to the western European model at this time. Richard Pipes has shown how the state selected head merchants in much the same way, and this sometimes made them vulnerable to political change.[25] But from Peter the Great's time onward, several regions of Russia, particularly its newly acquired Baltic territories, seem to have become prosperous from localized preindustrial growth which the state fostered rather than snuffed out. The tendency of regimes to over-exploit emerging commercial classes was not universal outside Europe, of course. Japan, for example, possessed a form of primogeniture, and its political leadership was relatively stable and geographically rooted. The country achieved relative economic stability and benefited from a flexible and mobile work force. This ensured that, in the long run, Japanese leaders were in a better position to respond to the global changes of the nineteenth century and, ultimately, to plan their own industrialization on the back of a strong pre-existing industrious revolution.

A second, medium-term competitive advantage enjoyed by northwestern Europeans and Americans lay in the commercial sphere. They had developed financial institutions which were relatively independent, both of the fortunes of individual great merchants and of the whims of governments. The Dutch had pioneered the joint-stock company specifically as a way of avoiding risk on long mercantile voyages. The Dutch East India Company began the process of pooling risk and dividing management from ownership which has been central to modern capitalism. Indeed, from the early modern city-states of Italy onward, western Europe seems to have been able to sustain a continuous chain reaction of commercial innovation. By contrast, even the most successful and dynamic of Chinese firms continued to guard resources by keeping management within the family unit. In Britain, the Bank of England provided an independent check on the state of the economy. The idea of a national debt, funded by the mercantile and property-owning classes, gave public accounts a transparency unattainable elsewhere. In fact, the national debt became something like a national icon. People thought it revealed the perfect trust which subsisted between the elite and government. Paper money and the explosion of regional banks in Britain and North America made borrowing and lending easier. All this put European governments and financial institutions into a position to capitalize not only on their own industrious revolutions, but on those of other continents as well. Chinese tea and porcelains, Javanese spices, and Indian textiles were all gulped down their capacious maws.

Recent historians have pointed to the relative sophistication of the great merchants of Asia and the Middle East. Indian, Chinese, and Middle Eastern merchants were certainly among the richest in the world as late as the early eighteenth century. In their accounting techniques and entrepreneurship they were in no way inferior to their European contemporaries.[26] It was, however, the framework of law and corporate organization within which great commercial firms could operate which gave western Europe and, arguably, Japan, their advantage. Ironically, it was the nineteenth-century colonial state, otherwise indifferent to African and Asian economic progress, which provided indigenous merchants and financiers with legal guarantees and stability of property rights.

The final competitive advantage enjoyed by parts of Europe lay in the relationship between war and finance. Crudely, Europeans became much better at killing people. The savage European ideological wars of the seventeenth century had created links between war, finance, and commercial innovation which extended all these gains. It gave the Continent a brute advantage in the world conflicts which broke out in the eighteenth century. Western European warfare was peculiarly complicated and expensive, partly because it was amphibious. Governments needed to project their power by both land and sea. Highly sophisticated systems were required to finance and provision navies at the same time as armies. The value of Caribbean slave agricultural production was so great by 1750 that huge sums were invested in creating

ILLUSTRATION 2.2   The first multinational corporations: *Old Customs House Quay, London*. Painting by Samuel Scott, c.1756.

systems for maintaining and supplying navies that protected the islands. The British, in particular, reduced their vulnerability to invasion by placing a large fleet permanently in the waters off their western coasts.[27] This required a high level of systems of supply and control, but also created a permanent pool of ships which could be dispatched to more distant waters in the Caribbean or the East. Any European navy in military contact with the British, however distant from the British Isles, needed to catch up. Famously, Peter the Great of Russia modernized his army and navy at the beginning of the eighteenth century, just as the Japanese rulers were to do a century and a half later. The farther away, however, the less the stimulus for innovation became. Asian powers and the Ottomans could, of course, assemble large fleets, but the techniques for maintaining them at sea for long periods were less well developed. Naval technology also fell behind the westerners after 1700. One historian of the Ottomans has remarked that the sultans had superb navies in the eighteenth century, but ones for fighting seventeenth-century wars.

The mutual struggles of medium-sized states in Europe gave a great incentive to innovate in land warfare to produce new, more deadly weapons and financial systems to support growing numbers of professional soldiers. This in turn conferred a significant competitive advantage on European and European-controlled international trade. It was European ships and commercial companies, not the Asian or African producers of slaves, spices, calicos, or porcelains, which were able to capture the greatest "value added" as world trade expanded in the eighteenth century. For it was they who controlled transport and sales in the world's largest markets. Equally, the sale of protection and military services to non-European powers balanced Europe's world trade, as Niels Steensgaard has argued.[28] This was true even when, before the industrial revolutions, the Continent's products remained more expensive and less prized than those of Asia and North Africa on the world market. Europe connected, subjugated, and made tributary other peoples' industrious revolutions.

THE ACTIVIST, PATRIOTIC STATE EVOLVES

In addition to flexible and expanding economies lodged in a relatively benign institutional framework, Europe, for better or worse, was already beginning to develop forms of the modern state which were infused with a variety of local patriotisms. These were to be forged during the revolutionary crisis into the aggressive nation-states of the nineteenth-century world. This again conferred on Europe only a temporary competitive advantage, for amidst the fluidity of identities and the complex bundles of political powers that prevailed, parts of Asia and Africa also appear to have been moving in a similar direction. But 50 years is a long time in world history.

In 1790, as the first chapter suggested, the boundaries of many European states remained as fuzzy as they were in Asia and Africa. Their internal structure was complex and variegated, with overlapping forms of power and authority, rather than close centralized control. At one extreme and closer, it was often said, to the Chinese Empire was Russia, in which only 44 percent of the tsar's subjects were Russians by 1897.[29] If the tsars intervened too aggressively in their more distant lands, they ran the risk of unsettling the very lords and tribal elders who kept the empire together. Germany remained fragmented, despite the stirrings of a powerful cultural nationalism. Goethe, the foremost German Romantic poet and polymath, is widely associated with the beginning of German nationalism. Before 1793, however, Goethe was an ardent supporter of the Holy Roman Empire, an institution which perfectly embodied the old supremacies. Robespierre, later icon of the all-conquering

French centralized nation-state, began his career as a spokesmen for the local patriotism of the Artois region,[30] though he probably tried to forget this later.

Even Britain and France, which were to typify the new aggressive national and imperial states of the nineteenth century, exhibited some of these older features. The Irish Ascendancy Parliament was one such anomaly in the British case, guarding its powers at the same time as it was tied by the executive in London and constrained by royal patronage. The patchwork form of the French body politic was still apparent as late as 1793. Local *parlements* remained powerful in many regions and tried to subvert the authority of Paris. Britain and France remained culturally diverse well into the nineteenth century. Gaelic, Irish, Manx, Welsh, and even Cornish were spoken by large numbers of people in the British archipelago, while in France more than a third of the total population could not speak the language which was later to embody the perfect culture of the French nation. Despite a history of internal war, imperial expansion, and homogeneity, Spain remained a deeply provincial society in the eighteenth century.

All the same, there were long-lived developments working to create wider connections and to make people's culture, manners, and political activities more uniform in both Britain and France. These processes operated in different ways and at different speeds at the ideological, social, and economic levels. But they were important in giving substance to the new ideas of nation and state once they were more coherently and vigorously articulated in the aftermath of the French and European revolutions. Similar processes were seen working more fitfully in other European polities, and even outside Europe and its vigorous colonies of settlement.

Historians and theorists of nationalism do not find economic explanations for the rise of national sentiment as convincing as they once did. Yet the emergence of big, integrated regional markets made people aware of each other and created regional solidarities which transcended local class interests. An economy is, after all, as much a matter of culture, social links, discourses, and representations as it is a matter of brute materialism. Money is a supremely representational phenomenon: it has no value beyond the discourse of value which it embodies. E. A. Wrigley showed some years ago how London achieved dominance over much of England as early as the seventeenth century.[31] Local tradesmen and farmers – there were few real peasants any longer – saw the capital as the market and source of supply of the last resort. Similarly, networks of agricultural and proto-industrial specialization brought food and other products to the capital or diffused them outward from it. The growing export of English goods to Scotland has been credited with easing the path to the union of the two countries in 1707, creating a kind of British "patriotic economy." To a lesser extent, the Île de France had achieved a degree of economic dominance in France, though the revolutionary wars were to show how easily this might be undermined. This long, slow integration of economies underpinned a growing sense of patriotism among gentry and merchants. They were increasingly subject to similar forms of training and education, similar legal systems, and similar patterns of consumption and leisure. The rituals of the French court brought representative nobles to live for long periods in *hôtels* in Paris, cementing a sense of common identity.

Religion and war were two other forces which accelerated the pace of this piecemeal building of homelands. Identities were formed in the face of dangerous "others," people with different beliefs, languages, and values. Many historians now trace a distinct sense of English identity and an English national state, sometimes even an English national character, to as early as the High Middle Ages.[32] Later, according to this view, the fifteenth-century wars with France spurred in to life a virulent sense of English patriotism. This remains controversial, but there is probably now a consensus amongst historians that the Reformation and the long wars of the eighteenth century transformed this sentiment further and generalized it to something increasingly called "British." British Protestant Christianity was invoked on many occasions in the eighteenth century when the country still fought against Catholic and foreign foes. The after-shocks of the wars of religion were still being felt. To the same degree, a French identity was being shaped by the sense people had of being the redoubt of a specific form of Catholic statehood. Again, this had only recently fought off the challenge of regional Protestant separatism.

Adrian Hastings observed that the consolidation of "Frenchness" was as much a matter of literacy and religion as of politics. Its locus was the city of Paris, rather than the court of Versailles. One sign of this rising sense of French identity was the widespread use of the French language for prayers and sermons after the Latin mass had been said in churches during the eighteenth century.[33] The combination of fierce patriotism with the conviction that France upheld a universal spiritual mission was rapidly to take on a secular guise during the revolutionary wars. For the revolutionaries, France would remain both a special location of virtue and yet a bearer of universal human values. Such patterns of change were also working in polities which were more complex yet than France. Novelists and dramatists in the wider German area lauded ancient heroes and reinforced the sense of "Germanness" in distinction to the French "other."[34] This occurred even when the German political order remained fractured between a hundred smaller states.

A more cohesive sense of patriotic identity associated with warfare does seem to have been characteristic of at least the dominant groups of most eighteenth-century European states and also, of course, of their American colonies. Territorial politics was replacing dynastic politics. The rhetoric of the French-hating, anti-Gallican societies in Britain was equalled by the denunciation of Britain in France. The French also made vigorous attempts to use the hostility of Protestant and Catholic Irish patriots against their British enemy. French Canadian settlers were mobilized against the largely Protestant colonies to the south. While the Prussia of Frederick the Great remained a dynastic state at war, and the mass of the peasantry probably did not feel any sense of identification with their ruler, international conflict was consolidating a sense of "Prussianness" amongst the more privileged subjects. During the Seven Years War a vigorous volunteer movement emerged in

Prussia, aiming to replace the men killed in action as a matter of patriotic duty.[35] As T. C. W. Blanning showed, anti-French sentiment fitted into a long-lived Germanic discourse about the "invader" which went back to the Renaissance, when antique German exploits against the Roman imperialists had been cast in a patriotic mode. Even the brilliant, tesselated pavement of powers that made up Italy could not entirely obscure some unities. As John A. Davis writes of the nineteenth century "[n]ationalism was not new and from much earlier times there had been a clearly defined sense of the shared cultural and historical identities derived from language and custom, from ways of dressing and eating, forms of recreation and of religiosity that made Italians distinctive."[36]

There is some evidence, too, that protection of far-flung dynastic territories by rulers may have been giving way to a more rooted sense of geopolitics in Europe. Governments were increasingly fighting to protect "their" land and abandoning older alliances based on royal marriage links. Austrian ministers in 1749 argued for an alliance with the old enemy, France, against the threat of a revived Prussia, which was now seen as a more direct threat to the Austrian heartland.[37] This very example, though, warns us that the emergence of patrias was a messy process. Geopolitics and culture did not necessarily point in the same direction. Frederick the Great may well have been consolidating a Prussian patria which would one day form the core of a German nation. But he still despised the German language as a boorish, peasant tongue and habitually spoke French. Equally, the Austrian ministers may have had a stronger sense of Austria as a geopolitical heartland, but they allied with France at the very time when a sense of common German culture was beginning to develop, embracing both Protestant Prussia and Catholic Austria. By a final irony, the new alliance with the old Habsburg enemy was one of the most important of the revolutionaries' charges against the French royal government in 1793, and a spur to French patriotic mobilization.

Nevertheless, this emerging sense of elite nationality, overlapping unevenly with cultural identification, was solidified, breaking down the boundaries between the different orders of nobles, gentry, burghers, and tradesmen in some of the big regionally dominant cities: Berlin, St Petersburg, Turin, and Paris. Peasants still fought for kings, icons, and relics, but urban people exhibited a growing sense of patriotic solidarity which was independent of regimes. Kathleen Wilson has shown how a venture as mundane as fishing rights in the North Sea could become the object of national fervour when they were challenged by French or Spanish interlopers in the mid-eighteenth century.[38] Patriotic songs such as "Rule, Britannia!" or tableaux in the Palais Royale, Paris, or Vauxhall Gardens, London,[39] representing overseas conquests, signaled the onward march of a more aggressive and expansive patriotism.

War and the integrated proto-national market were no doubt important, but benign acts by rulers also helped to build identities in eighteenth-century Europe. The so-called enlightened despots began to pioneer state education, for instance. By the end of the Empress Maria Theresa's reign in Austria, "the state boasted well over 6,000 schools and 200,000 students."[40] Prussia and Russia had pioneered state education, and while the effect may have been to spread common European ideas, it also helped to build standardized languages and a sense of commonality within old dynastic realms. The Jesuits in the Habsburg territories and the Pietist Christians in the German states were spreading lower-level literacy. Originating in a religious mission, these groups nevertheless helped create a deeper sense of regional patriotic community. Once the authorities had adopted a common ideal of education, this almost inevitably meant the standardization of teaching and literate expression. The "print culture" of nationalism, described by the theorist Benedict Anderson, spread as much through the schoolroom as through the newspaper.

The arguments made here are not intended to detract from the importance of the French Revolution in sharpening notions of citizenship and territorial nationhood. After 1793, Europe was engulfed by much more general ideological changes and by armed conflicts between states which drew millions of young men into military service for self-styled nations. Ideologues and politicians promoted the more unitary and harder-edged concept of the sovereign nation, with its sharply defined boundaries and more vigorous policies of excluding or suppressing the ethnic or religious "other." Yet the interaction of earlier patriotisms did much to provide the context for the new nation-states of the nineteenth century. The latter were not conjured out of nowhere. From the later Middle Ages, Europe had witnessed a gradual, often imperceptible and always ambiguous, transformation of old symbols of dynastic and religious identity into something which had a more popular, patriotic aspect. It is not surprising that the wars of commerce and the creation of national markets in the eighteenth century should have made these processes more visible.

Yet, by stressing the piecemeal, contradictory, and shifting pattern of emerging patriotic identities in premodern Europe, historians have actually begun to diminish the distance between Europe and the rest of the world. Traditionally, of course, historians and theorists have clung to a narrative of human history which sees nationalism exported fully formed to the rest of the world in the course of the nineteenth century. The mutual collisions and conflicts of Europeans, Asians, and Africans scattered the seeds of nationalism to all parts of the world. The cultural baggage of nationalism is supposed to have made landfall in India and Egypt about 1880, China in the 1900s, and the Ottoman Empire and North Africa after the First World War. Somehow, it had already washed up on the Japanese shore at an earlier date. Sub-Saharan Africa, by contrast, acquired the cargo too late, after the Second World War, and proceeded to misuse it. This account was the staple of Victorian and later imperial ideologues, who either deplored or praised Europe and North America for bringing nationalism to the East and the South in the baggage train of colonial government and Western education. The theory has recently been given new life by Asian and African intellectuals. Detesting the world capitalism of which they are the products, they have sought to portray their own earlier histories as stories of benign, decentralized, shifting peasant identities only later ruptured by the monolithic nationalisms and ethnicities imposed on them by the West and its stooges.

It cannot be doubted, of course, that British rule created India, French rule Algeria and Vietnam, Dutch rule Indonesia, and Spanish and American rule the Philippines as tightly delineated national spaces. The Jesuits wrote about China as a "Confucian" culture, and missionaries in Africa assigned "tribes" to specific homelands and wrote down "their" languages. Borders, passports, national currencies, and national prison services all flowed from European domination. The international conflicts of the nineteenth century made political leaders everywhere aware of "their" boundaries and "their" people. In Asia and Africa, however, just as in Europe, more focused identities, patriotic homelands, owing allegiance to wider values than simple loyalty to dynasties, had also formed, dissolved, and reformed before European expansion or in its early days. These social forms and processes were active agents in the creation of the nationalisms of Asia and Africa in the nineteenth and twentieth centuries. They were not simply "invented traditions," or false consciousness unleashed by self-serving, westernized intelligentsia. Nor, like the European patriotisms of the seventeenth and eighteenth centuries, did they always merge happily into later popular nationalism. The Irish patriotism of the eighteenth century may have been anti-English, but it was also in general anti-Catholic, a far cry from the Catholic peasant nationalism of the nineteenth century. In the same way, the eighteenth-century patriotism of the western Indian Marathas was too high caste and exclusive easily to fit with the patterns of popular mobilization in the nineteenth and twentieth centuries.

The activity of states, markets, and religious teachers had given many areas outside Europe types of fluid patriotic identity before the colonial deluge of the nineteenth century. This is self-evident in Europe's colonies in the New World and southern Africa, where the locally born Creoles, Americans, and "Africans" were already exhibiting strong resistance to incoming European governors and commercial interests, well before 1776. It was also true of some of the great Asian realms, where the promotion of the idea of "nationality" or ethnicity might sometimes have resulted from the actions of the rulers themselves. The Qian Long emperor celebrated the deeds of Han Chinese soldiers led by his Manchurian dynasty, but in doing so he seems to have perpetuated a sense of Han Chinese identity.[41] This stood in contradistinction to Manchu solidarity. It had been passed down from family to family, had lain dormant in the Confucian texts, and had always been manifest in the dress codes and hairstyle which the Manchus had legislated for the Chinese.

This sense of identity was, however, often strongest in the most peripheral and smallest homelands, vulnerable to distance and foreign enemies. Sri Lankan rulers and nobles had long nurtured a sense of local pride in the face of Tamil South India and the depredations of the Portuguese.[42] The Burmese, Koreans, and Vietnamese – at least, the northern Vietnamese – also displayed a sense of identity born of specific religious practice, a common language, and long wars with aggressive neighbors well before the nineteenth century. For these cultures and polities, China was a model to be emulated, but also to be held at a distance as a stronger sense of the worth of the homeland emerged. The embracing patriotism of the Japanese had long flourished. It marked itself off from a variety of outer "barbarians" and also from inner "barbarians" such as the Ainu, who were steadily penned back into the more desolate parts of Hokkaido island in the fifteenth to eighteenth centuries by a Japanese "great domestication."[43]

In these cases a preexisting sense of identity provided the basis for an unsteady emergence of Asian national polities. Elsewhere, emerging kingdoms created spaces in which new identities could flourish. In the later eighteenth century, a range of more closely defined regional kingdoms sprang up within the ambit of the earlier empires: Gurkha Nepal, a new, unified Burma, the new Thailand of Rama I, and Qajar Iran emerged on the fringes of the Chinese, Mughal, and Safavid domains. The Egyptian rulers tried to create state monopolies of produce, while to the west of the former Ottoman domains, Sidi Mahomed brought in Western military and technical expertise in an attempt to shore up his kingdom against Spanish and Portuguese incursions on the coast.[44] This was dynastic-led state building rather than, as in the case of Japan or China, the reconfiguration of old cultural entities. It did, however, provide a space within which nineteenth-century literate people could define themselves as nations.

While lineage-based states in which centralized royal functions were very limited remained the norm over much of sub-Saharan Africa, changes had become apparent there even by the mid-eighteenth century. Some kings and ruling groups had achieved an uncertain and temporary victory over their relatives and associated lineage leaders. The Yoruba in West Africa and the Baganda peoples in East Africa certainly displayed a sense of identity married to their own flexible political system long before the colonial impact. One historian has commented:

> If there existed one nation state in nineteenth century black Africa, Buganda would have a good claim to be it. It had grown over centuries; it had a strong sense of its own history, centralised government, an effective territorial division in counties (*Saza*) and possessed in its clan organisation a horizontality of social consciousness to balance the verticality of royal and bureaucratic rule.[45]

East and central African rulers had begun to create states which collected dues and mobilized men for warfare, enhancing group identity in the process. There is some danger in seeing this as a "progressive" change, because Europeans, Asians, and other Africans had moved in this direction some thousands of years earlier. Certainly, the existence of more centralized and belligerent polities may have helped some African peoples to resist the European onslaught, at least for a time. Others, such as Benin and Kongo, collaborated with Europeans and grew temporarily stronger as a result. Yet anthropologists remind us that the conditions of life were in many ways better in the stateless, decentralized social forms, where access to goods and honor were less restricted. When these moves towards "statishness" and identity formation did come, they were sometimes the consequence of limited contacts with Arab or Creole European societies, where the claims of the state were better known, as in the Portuguese areas of East and West Africa, or the Dutch settlements on the Cape. Rulers, impelled by ambition or seeing a useful future in trading in slaves, ivory, or diamonds, capitalized on the hostility of younger men to the lineage chiefs who had privileged access to women and honor. They built praetorian guards for themselves.[46] In the classic case of Basutoland on the fringes of the European Cape during the early nineteenth century, the Mthethwa chief, Shaka (d. 1828), built up an army of young men armed with stabbing spears and created a large authoritarian polity, the state known as the Zulu Kingdom by Europeans.[47] The statements of later European observers suggest that war and the pooling of honor within these kingdoms created some degree of local pride and common identity among their inhabitants. In the Pacific, too, some historians have glimpsed the emergence of larger polities with stronger identities before the colonial deluge. The slow growth of population, trade, and knowledge within pre-contact societies belies the notion that they were static.

What was distinctive about the western European example was not always, therefore, the existence of strong, determined states or even of inherited, if still fluid, patriotic identities. What was striking was the convergence of these forms with economic dynamism, well-honed weapons of war making, and fierce rivalries between medium-sized polities. Europe's temporary and qualified "exceptionalism" was to be found not in one factor, but in an unpredictable accumulation of many characteristics seen separately in other parts of the world. For instance, it is significant that one area of Asia where precolonial identities were quite sharp was mainland Southeast Asia, where conflicts between middle-sized kingdoms had an ancient history. And, of course, Europe's exceptionalism was a wasting asset. As early as 1870, the Japanese had glimpsed their own way to a parallel modernity. One element, however, is missing if we concentrate only on economic contingencies, patriotic identities, and state power. That is the texture of society, developing fast in eighteenth-century Europe and North America, which allowed individuals to congregate, debate, and adjust their institutions and, ultimately, to make them more effective tools for accumulating money, power, and knowledge. The next section turns to what sociologists have called "civil society" or the "public sphere."

CRITICAL PUBLICS

Until the 1970s most historians of the ancien régime concentrated on trying to describe the social and political forces which brought it down: the fiscal and political crisis of European monarchies and empires or the expansion of European-led trade in the East. Slowly, after that date, the ideas of the German social scientist Jürgen Habermas[48] about the emergence of civil society as a domain between state and society began to influence scholars. The "critical public" soon came to be seen as the main solvent of the old order. As historical analysis, Habermas's theory was rather lacking in novelty.

British historians had actually been writing about this kind of development for a long time. But, because they were allergic to social science theory and keen to avoid pretentious words, no one had really noticed what they were saying.[49] After 1970, historians of France, particularly in the United States, began to turn to issues of public culture and representation, trying to discern in the popular disturbances and displays of the ancien régime and the early years of the Republic the emergence of a new style of politics. Both of these shifts merged with the "linguistic turn" in contemporary thinking. For historians in the 1980s and 1990s, the exchange of ideas, the creation of cultural connections, and the invention of ceremony became social events in their own right, as important as flows of revenue or the integration of markets had been for the earlier liberal and Marxist historians. This concern with the modernization of discourses and representations replaced earlier studies which emphasized the modernization of economies or formal ideologies. Traditionally, intellectual modernization was a process that was supposed to have started in the West and spread out from there. How far can that type of approach still be sustained in an age of global history?

On the face of it, there does indeed seem to have been something distinctive about the Western urge to create clubs, societies, and meeting places in the eighteenth century. If we take the *Autobiography* of the American founding father Benjamin Franklin (1706–90), for instance, we glimpse a world in which religious ideas, the use of the printing press, and ideas of liberty converge with an extraordinary proclivity to set up clubs and societies for argument and talk.[50] Franklin came of clever artisan and farming stock. Wherever he went in later life, he tried to urge on the authorities small practical improvements. His famous experiments with electricity were matched by papers on the improvement of street lighting and cleaning in London and the improvement of taxation and fire fighting in Philadelphia. This sort of link between scientific theory and practical application seems to have been an unspoken assumption in the Atlantic world. It is one which is more difficult to perceive in other great civilizations, where debates usually offered more overt deference to issues of tradition and religion.

This is not to say that religious belief was unimportant to the practical *philosophes* of the eighteenth-century West. Max Weber's link between Protestantism and capitalism is now often pooh-poohed by social scientists. Yet it is more difficult to dismiss the idea that the cellular organization and individualistic codes of Protestant churches – and Protestant-influenced Catholic churches – provided a congenial medium for ideas of civic republicanism. The roots of Franklin's thinking about public virtue, for instance, lay in his Protestant, dissenting background, an upbringing which insisted on personal moral improvement through sociability and brotherhood. Franklin later rebelled against strict Puritanism, becoming a Deist, or a believer in a transcendent, rational deity rather than the divinity of Christ. He also appears to have been influenced by the Quaker culture of Philadelphia. Franklin acknowledged Methodists, Baptists, and German Moravians as his brothers in virtue. He was the founder-member of a club called the Junto dedicated to

ILLUSTRATION 2.3   Public spheres: A committee of American patriots delivering an ultimatum to a King's Councillor. Illustration after Howard Pyle published in *Harper's Magazine*, 1908.

social and personal improvement. Later he helped found another society whose main aim was to found yet more clubs for discussion of good causes and new knowledge. It was inevitable that as one of the first journalist public men in history he should participate in the American Revolution. His insistence on ground-level sociability embodied a new idea of freedom, while his emphasis on frugality and personal initiative made state taxation without representation a perennial problem for him. Hardly anywhere in his narrative does Franklin even mention the word "king," though he was happy enough to accept the patronage of British governors in New York, Boston, and Philadelphia.

Throughout Europe and its colonies there was a similar stirring of societies which bound together members of the middle classes of society and upwardly mobile artisans. In England, the patronage of nobles and royalty remained important, but commoner and merchant families participated in the creation of a myriad new clubs dedicated to sociability, education, trade, and sport throughout the seventeenth and eighteenth centuries. In France and other Catholic countries, the Church (though not the Jesuit order) often looked askance, particularly when the new sociability was expressed through semi-mystical societies such as the freemasons or in clubs and societies which mocked the established order, such as those established by the French *philosophes*. Not all these societies were devoted to either freethinking or Deism, which de-emphasized doctrine and creed. In the German lands, Pietist Christians greatly extended their organization between 1770 and 1820. Nevertheless, the expansion of associations, with their subscriptions, minutes, and printed journals, played a vital part in providing the basis for the wider political class and a more critical public, which slowly consolidated itself during the years of global war.

Where social theorists and historians of the 1970s and 1980s painted an incomplete picture was in not paying sufficient attention to who was excluded from the new associations and the new vision of society. Women were sometimes the center of salons which debated the ills of state and society, but only aristocratic ladies and ladies of less than perfect repute could generally enter these male enclaves. Working people began to organize themselves in friendly and self-help associations to fight the decline of old artisan industries and the appalling conditions of the new ones. But any attempt to combine for sectional good against employers was met with hostility and, after 1789, with severe repression. Slaves remained, inevitably, outside the vision of society being propagated by most of these associations, although many Quakers, Methodists, and other humanitarians were arguing vigorously for their emancipation by the 1770s. Religious minorities – Catholics in Britain, for instance, and Jews virtually everywhere – were also excluded. Native peoples in the colonies of white settlement were equally regarded as outside the pale. The virtuous Franklin described a scene of drunken American Indians happily dancing as a vision from hell and seems to have hoped that liquor would wipe them all out and make room for honest, industrious white settlers. In British Calcutta, where racial boundaries were fluid and European men took Indian wives, Indians were generally kept at arm's length from European public spaces and arenas of discussion.

While the picture of civil society which historians began to paint was initially too rosy and homogeneous, there is no doubt that the proliferation of associations and societies of self-organization gave Western societies a considerable staying power and solidity, for both internal cohesion and external aggression. It was rooted in the rapid social mobility created by the expansion of internal production and external commerce in the eighteenth century. It reflected the expansion and development of Christian and humanist education and ideas of personal responsibility in a society which had greater access to them in an age when printing techniques were being diffused rapidly. In turn, the expansion of sociability facilitated the further expansion of capitalism through friendly societies, stock exchanges, and insurance brokers. The public sphere created a wedge of expert opinion which could criticize or lampoon the doings of the state, or kings and nobles, with deadly accuracy, contributing to the efficiency and dynamism of political institutions. In Britain and America, the common law, with its slow accumulation of judgments and different legal perspectives, was ideally suited to benefit from, and extend, this civil society.

So far this picture seems to give support to David Landes's arguments[51] that the West had some decisive advantages over the rest of the world in the early modern period. It does, but only up to a point. The link between capital formation and sociability, print culture, warfare, and organization of government finance in western Europe and the North American colonies suggests that they had a structural advantage, and not merely a relative advantage created by the short-term problems of Asia and Africa. But the issue is rather more complex. The weakness of Landes's position lies in its reversion to old ideas of Asian stagnation: "cycles of Cathay" or "eternal Ind." As we have seen, Asian and African historians have painted a much more dynamic picture of the eighteenth century. During this century, serious economic and social decline in some areas was matched by cultural change, economic stability, and adaptation to global modernity in others. It may be most satisfactory to write of different and slower adaptations to change in Asia and Africa, rather than to see their societies as "failures." Social forms which bore some similarities to those we have seen in the West – new types of sociability, more integrated patterns of commerce, and some technological innovations – were in evidence in Asia and Africa. These continents were, after all, subject to similar patterns of international trade, the diffusion of armaments, and even the spread of ideas which were affecting Europe and the Americas over the period 1600 to 1800. Indeed, it was Amerindian and African agricultural expertise with crops such as rice that had allowed Europeans to develop lucrative plantations in the Carolinas and Caribbean in the first place.

In Asia and Africa, however, the state's relationship to society was organized, not necessarily better, but at least differently, from that prevailing in the western European model. Ironically, the very success of the great Asian and North African kingdoms during the sixteenth and seventeenth centuries may have made it more difficult for them to adapt to the rapid changes of the eighteenth century. Their kings retained charismatic authority, but their regimes were widely less intrusive than the post-Reformation European ones. Even the Mughal emperor Aurangzeb (1658–1707), widely denounced in the nineteenth century as a Muslim fanatic, was not generally concerned with what people believed. He was mainly concerned to assert the sovereignty, not the exclusive practices, of Sunni Islam. Empires continued to incorporate hostile groups, rather than seek to eliminate them, as the French monarchy did with the Huguenot Protestants, for instance. The state in these African and Asian lands was more concerned with protection of the peasantry than in guaranteeing commercial wealth. It did not so single-mindedly seek to fund more and more weaponry for wars of aggression against small neighbors.

Asian and African states generally avoided the equivalent of Europe's wars of religion. Yet their own problems of overextension and resource distribution in the eighteenth century were made infinitely worse by the intervention of those same Europeans who had mastered new tools of aggression and social organization in the course of those very wars. Some aspects of those processes of adaptation were aborted or thrown into reverse during the age of European empires which was to follow. Some were followed through, in their own interests, by the Western empires. But in Japan they were allowed fully and rapidly to play out under the protection of an indigenous government.

THE DEVELOPMENT OF ASIAN AND AFRICAN PUBLICS

Important changes in social organization continued to manifest themselves within African and Asian societies even during the disturbances of the eighteenth and early nineteenth centuries. We have failed to give them sufficient weight because historians have long observed them under the rubric of "religion." Because kings, nobles, and intelligentsia expressed the need and desire for change in religious terms, whether as Muslims, Confucians, or Buddhists, they are seen as modifications within the traditional order. Yet Benjamin Franklin understood his modernity in terms of a residual Protestantism and Deism, and Isaac Newton, the British astronomer and physicist, plotted a new world while still remaining an adherent of astrology and alchemy. Neither of them is portrayed as a traditional man in the general historical literature.

During the late seventeenth and early eighteenth centuries, movements of sociability and modes of critical thought continued to develop in Asia and Africa. These provided people with spiritual and social resources with which to confront the rapid changes which they saw around them. Criticism of the prevailing political order was expressed in a religious idiom, but this is not to say that its proponents were simply looking to the past. In Islam the end of the first millennium since the Prophet's revelation led to powerful reappraisals of state and society, accompanied by movements of purification and assaults on the moral laxness of the world's rulers. Even before the turn of the nineteenth century, the Ottoman intelligentsia had become acutely aware that it was slipping in the face of the revived West, in this case Catherine the Great's Russia. Many of the intellectual and political remedies for decline which were put into practice after 1830 were already being discussed in the previous generation. Well before the nineteenth century, networks of intellectuals debating the need for reform had formed in different societies across the world and had often done so with reference to each other.

In the eighteenth century, radical monotheists in the Arabian peninsula began an assault on traditional interpretation and on Arab and wider Muslim custom which has continued into the twentieth century and has spread to Africa and central Asia. These so-called Wahhabis were distantly aware of the problems gripping the Ottoman Empire. In turn, more inclusive thinkers in Cairo and North Africa, who believed in the efficacy of Sufi mystical teaching, restated and strengthened their own traditions. The changes were received and reinterpreted as far away as in North and West Africa, where a series of literate Muslim reformers tried to build states which they hoped would guarantee a more orderly form of Muslim life. They sought to set in train not a reactionary "holy war," but a process of struggle and debate which would institute in West Africa a proper, modern Islamic society in place of the mixed, syncretic society which they saw around them. They were reacting to change and seeking to assert their own brand of modernity.[52]

In India during the eighteenth century, learned men created new systems of teaching which were intended to help Muslims to operate in a complex world of bureaucracy. One of South Asian Islam's greatest teachers, Shah Wali-Allah, acutely aware again of the relative decline of Muslim power in India, attempted a major reinterpretation of Islamic law, urging the amalgamation of its different schools and the purging of the mystical tradition.[53] He stressed the importance of education, including women's education. His program was directed at a pattern of social regeneration, not merely religious purism. In Malaya and Indonesia, for many decades before the onset of European rule, Islamic teachers had criticized the customary rights and deportment of indigenous rulers. In this sense, the Islamic public sphere, which had always revolved around the debates of pious men in the mosque square, the *madina*, was spurred to new intensity by the disasters and problems which overcame eighteenth-century Muslims. Muslims founded new associations, stressed the importance of learning and literacy, and lauded personal and social discipline. These movements, therefore, were not simply products of the "Western impact." They represented a response to global change as profound as the rise of nationalism and the centralized state in Europe, and one which may yet outlast them.

Muslims were also alert to changes in the outside world. Rulers in central Asia, post-Mughal India, and North Africa continued to perfect medical and astronomical law by observation and practice. Towards the end of the eighteenth century, European astronomical works were translated into Arabic and Persian, reversing the late-medieval flow of knowledge. The older revaluation continued, whereby the doctrines of Copernicus were gradually accepted over much of Asia and Africa. The traffic in ideas and practices was by no means one way. For instance, techniques of dyeing and glazing from Asia and herbal medical remedies developed by indigenous peoples in Africa and South America were still being borrowed and adapted by Europeans in the eighteenth century. Historians have gradually become aware of the extent to which many small technical advances in the European world associated with the Industrial Revolution were originally drawn from non-European exemplars.

The Islamic world had, of course, been in intellectual dialogue and conflict with Christianity and Judaism for many centuries. This was not the case to the same extent further to the east. Here, ironically, it was often the continuing experience of Islamic expansion which stirred other traditions into self-reevaluation and new organization. Indian society had periodically been galvanized by movements proclaiming the coming of the rule of righteousness (*dharma*). These were often centered on charismatic teachers or gurus, who preached the unimportance of worldly hierarchies, including the tight restrictions on sociability maintained by caste. Such movements had redoubled in the relative peace of Mughal rule; some had clearly been influenced by Islamic monotheism. They also created new types of congregation and association, which provided connections and contacts for South and Southeast Asian commercial communities. One notable reforming religious movement of this sort were the North Indian Sikhs, whose prescriptions were so radical that they regarded themselves as technically outside the Hindu world altogether. In the eighteenth century, the Sikh movement spread not only among commercial people, but also among the great North Indian peasant castes.[54] All these movements were otherworldly in the sense that they pointed people towards spiritual salvation. But all of them also offered solutions to political and social problems of the age. They show Asians grappling with their own forms of modernity no less vigorously than the freemasons and *philosophes* of western Eurasia.

Historians have also reinterpreted the world of eighteenth-century China. The Chinese Empire and its commerce continued to expand throughout the eighteenth century. China was on the point of neither political implosion nor intellectual stagnation. The long period of peace under the Kangxi and Qian Long emperors saw a major reinterpretation of the Confucian classics.[55] The emperors also turned their efforts to statecraft and government, founding new academies of learning, which drew on Western learning through Jesuit sources. Scholars rejected the high-flown metaphysical theories of the first years of the dynasty and turned instead to "practical evidential research," seeking out the hard facts, as it were, in fields such as astronomy, linguistics, mathematics, and geography. The new mood was typified by Gu Yanwu (1613–82) who traveled across the whole of China recording aspects of local technology, mapping the land, and collecting old inscriptions. Gu sought to develop a body of rationalistic writings that would counter what he saw as the "hollowness of the dominant schools of Confucianism with their emphases on metaphysical dualism and initiation."[56] Scholars and officials of this ilk later tried to reform the examination system for the bureaucracy, which they considered was tired and old-fashioned. These movements were by no means limited to a tiny elite. People from the non-official class, notably merchants, patronized these rational investigations and sometimes made contributions themselves. Historians have noticed a great increase in the volume of letters written by intellectuals passing from one region to another.

This suggests that the fabled "republic of letters" of eighteenth-century Europe had analogues elsewhere. In China, painting and calligraphy reached new heights, while printers and booksellers flourished in catering to this new and wider audience. Of course, this rationalist thought was often backward looking, in the sense that its highest goal was to correct editions of the classics and collect the fine artefacts of the sage-like ancestors. Yet did not classical studies remain the pinnacle of European thought in these years, and was not one of the great practical investigations of eighteenth-century Europe the discovery of the buried Roman cities of Pompeii and Herculaneum? While the past loomed large, it is difficult not to conclude that it was the growing scale of Manchu government and of internal and external commerce which provided the spur to this counting, sorting, and analysis. This effort to achieve a more concrete sense of land and people found echoes among China's satellite kingdoms, which looked to her with both reverence and fear. In

Korea, for instance, literati adherents of the "Northern Learning" were eager to keep up with China's new knowledge. Yet they wanted this knowledge in order to improve the Korean education system, and their successors increasingly turned to detailed studies of the patria of Korea itself.[57]

World history becomes more comprehensible when we abandon the picture of China and its satellites as being caught in intellectual stasis. It is as enlightening to abandon the idea of "feudal Japan" awaiting the sailor's kiss of the American admiral Matthew C. Perry, who invaded Japan's territorial waters in 1854. This was the picture painted not only by the British and Americans of the mid-nineteenth century, but also by the young Japanese reformers of the 1870s, who wanted to blacken the picture of the old regime. Two generations of modern scholars have worked to show that eighteenth-century Japan remained adaptable, despite its political decentralization stigmatized as "feudalism." Its economy remained buoyant, and "Dutch" learning – western European medical and botanical lore – penetrated Japan through samurai schools in the different domains. As in Europe, there was an interesting conjuncture between print, learning, and commerce. Great Japanese firms developed their own systems of commercial reporting and market research and sometimes had the products printed and sold. Japan's culture of aristocratic honor ensured that scholars maintained their status by being "up with" the latest developments from China or, more problematically, from the West. Samurai and populace criticized the Tokugawa government by comparing it to ideal Japanese or Chinese kingdoms of the past. Still, their criticism concentrated on the abuses, ills, and inefficiencies of the present.[58]

These examples, which have come to light in the historical writing of the last 20 years, illustrate the fact that the cultures of the non-Western world were responding to global political and economic changes throughout the eighteenth and early nineteenth centuries. Behind Confucian "revivals" of knowledge or Islamic "doctrinal controversies" we can discern rulers and intellectuals attempting to grapple with the problems of organizing society and human experience. All this helps to explain the complexity and richness of non-European thought in the nineteenth century. It was never simply derivative of Western norms, but was heavily inflected with creative versions of multiple traditions. Western ideas and techniques, especially in areas such as timekeeping and warfare, were no doubt already becoming more influential across the world. Knowledge systems had always been interactive, as, for instance, when Chinese literati came into contact with the ideas of Aristotle through the good offices of the Jesuits. But European ideas were taken up and used by indigenous rulers and intellectuals who were already attempting to forge intellectual tools with which to grapple with their own "early modernities."

This said, however, the picture of global intellectual endeavor cannot be made completely relative. There were, to repeat, competitive differences, at least in the medium term, between the West, Asia, and Africa. Even if "science" as a modern, integrated doctrine hardly came into existence before the mid-nineteenth century in the West, certain routines of intellectual endeavor had become common in western Europe and North America by the eighteenth century. These significantly contributed to the dynamism of its political and economic institutions.

The complex and contested public sphere which had developed in western Europe as a result of its culture of association and printing contributed to what has been called "scientific egotism." In Asia or Africa, scholars were constrained by Chinese Boards of Rituals and Islamic schools or their equivalents. By contrast, Europeans and Americans could make a name and a fortune in public controversy about astronomical knowledge, mechanics, and medicine. Universities in Europe were more active and innovative during the eighteenth century than is sometimes thought. In them, religious conformity was widely quite superficial. But it was the dense networks of associations of philosophers and gentlemanly enthusiasts, whether holding chairs in universities or not, which made the running. This was as true of the effort that went into the Swedish biologist Carolus Linnaeus's mapping of plant species as in the rush to chart the solar system. The state contributed, particularly in its military and naval provision. It was, however, the gentleman-scholars, in uniform or out of it, who provided the impetus. In Britain and the United States the slow emergence of a system for patenting inventions and a well-developed market economy diminished the distance between artisanal innovation and this scholarly world. Even if the thinkers of the Admiralty and the British Royal Society scorned developments in naval technology when they were first presented to them, enlightened amateurs and the Royal Navy captains eventually took them up. Practical and philosophical knowledge could not be kept apart when it was a case of making money, whether by bringing the cargo ashore fastest or by growing the best crop of corn in the locality. In India or China, by contrast, the distance between the artisan and the manufactories of the royal courts appears to have been greater. It is probably, therefore, in the intellectual buoyancy of the European idea of the advance of knowledge and its material rewards, rather than any practical application of any particular technology as such, that we must seek the most significant difference. In the emerging social sciences, too, new patterns of thought emerged from the gentleman's study as much as from the royal courts or universities. Giambattista Vico (1668–1744), whose theories of human historical evolution were as important in their way as Isaac Newton's physics, was a professor in Naples. Yet his intellectual life was nourished by networks of learned men across Italy and Europe.

CONCLUSION: "BACKWARDNESS," LAGS, AND CONJUNCTURES

What we have seen in all these cases are people both inside and outside Europe grappling with related, interconnected problems. These were problems which arose from the conflict between a just ideal and a changing social order. They arose from the uneven distribution of wealth which resulted from patchy economic growth. These people were all struggling to create their own modernity by critiquing the disposition of political power. The first revolutions which were designed to resolve these intolerable conflicts are discussed in the next and subsequent chapters. They came at different times. In the Arabian lands, they came in the 1740s. In France and across much of Europe and the Americas, 1776 and 1789 were key dates. In Britain, it was 1832; in Japan, the Meiji restoration of 1868 achieved a similar revamping of the old order. Colonial nationalisms in the 1880s in India and China, along with a great variety of movements of religious reform, sought the same ends.

Historians have come to sense that many of the great advantages which their predecessors attributed to Europeans and North Americans in order to explain their vaunted nineteenth-century global preeminence can be seen in some form in many parts of Asia and Africa even as late as the mid-eighteenth century. As K. N. Chaudhuri[59] and Janet Abu Lughod[60] emphasized, Asians had made use of flexible forms of merchant accounting and credit for centuries. The state and literati had institutions which processed and organized information. Accumulations of technical change and innovation were building up in Arab and Chinese archives. Government was made more efficient, if not more accountable, by the criticism of bodies of learned men, religious and administrative experts. Commerce and useful knowledge were not simply the preserve of Europe and the Americas.

All the same, the relatively long-lived preeminence of Europe and North America in technical, political, and social innovation cannot simply be explained by the short-term political failures of Asia and Africa in the late seventeenth and eighteenth centuries. The relative time lag in innovation had some longer-term and more general reasons. We have pointed to some of these. First, Europeans were more generally more mobilized for warfare and more ruthless in prosecuting it than Asians, Africans, and Polynesians. The terrain of Europe required a rapid adaptation between fighting at sea and on land, in the mountains and on plains, in fierce cold and in baking heat. Relatively small political units all had to innovate constantly in order to deal with these different terrains and climates, while in the great empires of the East and the South, looser, less specialist styles of army were developed for the task of controlling huge areas of land. In Europe, intense competition within a relatively small area forced states to spend more in technical developments for warfare and to make sure that their weapons matched those of their enemies. Asian, African, and, at first, Russian armies often incorporated a huge variety of subordinate troops, which supplied their own weapons and horses. These armies were massive, but difficult to control. Military finance drove the state across Eurasia, but more efficient systems of payment and taxation emerged to deal with the endemic wars of Europe. In some ways, Asia's relative peace in the seventeenth century was its undoing.

This European preeminence in warfare fed into other aspects of the economy, making it easier for rulers to raise money and provision cities, easier for its entrepreneurs to innovate in metalwork, chemistry, glassmaking, and many other premodern industries. But the emergence of codes of law which bound rulers as well as subjects, foreigners as well as locals, peasants as well as urban people, also gave Europeans and Americans a structure within which to create trust and the long-term expectation of justice. In Asia, political stability had been guaranteed by "farming out" jurisdictions to a much greater extent than in Europe. Communities made their own law. Religious law tended to encompass civil and commercial law. The emperor could often override the property rights of his court servants, if not of the local land-controllers. This had become less common in Europe after the great wars of religion of the seventeenth century. It was the overall structure guaranteeing the reproduction of capital which proved to be a European advantage, less than specific features of merchant practice, the organization of cities, or the entrepreneurial abilities of peasants.

Finally, if we stand back from the debate about civil society and associations, it seems, again, that Europe and its American colonies possessed, in general, a density of civil institutions outside the state which were not yet matched in Asia and Africa. No Asian or African ruler was really a despot, enlightened or otherwise. Even the Qian Long emperor had to adjust to the needs and interests of local gentry and merchants. But the articulation of public opinion through print and associations in the European case does seem to have been of a different order of magnitude. Information on politics, commerce, and useful discoveries was produced and reproduced at a massive rate. None of this is to say, as the Victorians did, that other societies were morally or politically backward. The Chinese Empire guaranteed the welfare of its peasantry more effectively than western Europeans protected their proto-industrial cities before the beginning of the nineteenth century at least, despite rapid population growth. Indians were spared the vicious and very general wars of religion and trade which afflicted Europe, at least until the eighteenth century, even if localized religious riots sometimes erupted. Asian and African religion generally eschewed the moral aggression which, paradoxically, lies at the heart of Christianity, a religion which had, long before, comfortably accommodated itself to the conquest ethic of the Roman Empire.[61] Still, it is difficult to deny that it was Europeans who hit upon the trick of combining this aggression with well-defined, medium-sized states, burgeoning commerce, and a culture of vigorous critique. The Chinese social Darwinist scholar Yan Fu seems to have understood this rather better than his contemporaries among late-nineteenth-century European liberals.[62]

PROSPECT

These were decisive European advantages, but they were ones which were maintained only for the medium term. Even at the height of the age of imperialism after 1850, people outside Europe were challenging its preeminence, drawing on their own forms of economic expertise, political ethics, and sociability. Between 1780 and 1820, however, Europe's lead in warfare and conquest was given a further great boost, which is discussed in the next chapter. This was not, as yet, because the industrial revolution had "kicked in." Instead, it was because the attempts of Europeans and their American colonists to solve these global problems of uneven wealth and entitlement brought new and dangerous actors onto the world stage: the revolutionary state and its bitter conservative enemies. The slowly emerging patriotic and information-rich state, discussed above, was quite suddenly inflated to a massive degree. It grew gargantuan in its ideological ambitions, its global reach, and its demands for military and civilian labor. Its appetites stretched across the continents. Before the impact of the steam engine or the electric telegraph had been registered, the European state, its soldiers and bureaucrats, became hyperactive in what was an "axial age" for world history.

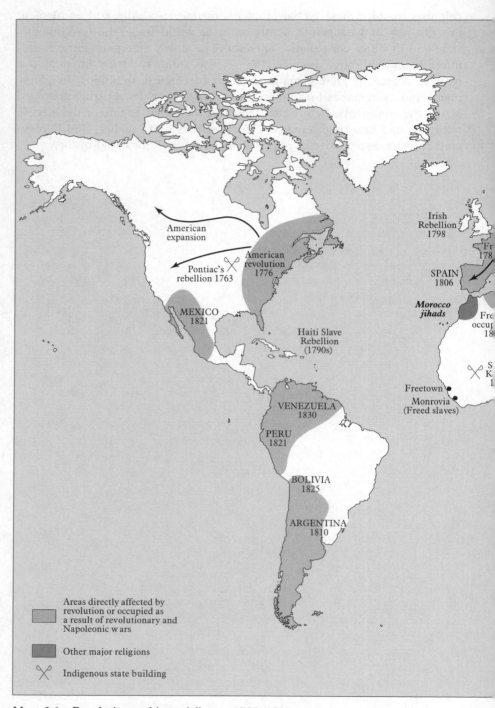

MAP 3.1   Revolution and imperialism, c.1780–1830.

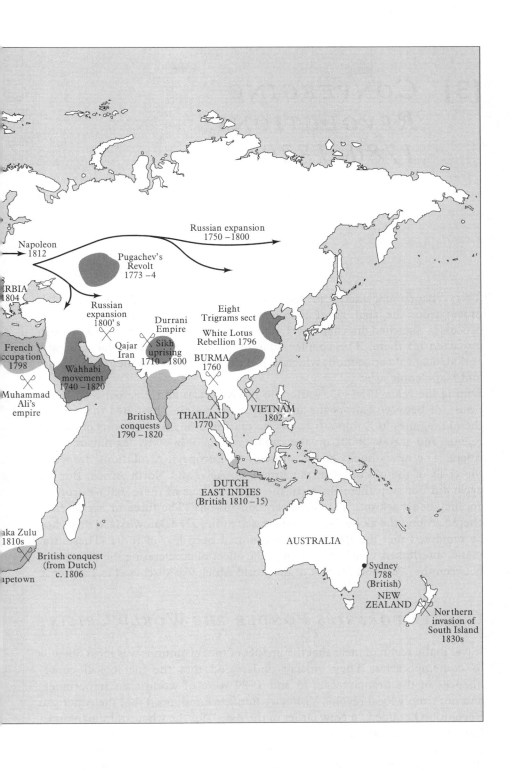

Russian expansion
1750 – 1800

Napoleon
1812

Pugachev's
Revolt
1773 –4

RBIA
804

Russian
expansion
1800's

Eight
Trigrams sect

Durrani
Empire

White Lotus
Rebellion 1796

French
ccupation
1798

Qajar
Iran

Sikh
uprising
1710 – 1800

BURMA
1760

Wahhabi
movement
1740 – 1820

Muhammad
Ali's
empire

British
conquests
1790 – 1820

THAILAND
1770

VIETNAM
1802

DUTCH
EAST INDIES
(British 1810 – 15)

aka Zulu
1810s

AUSTRALIA

British conquest
(from Dutch)
c. 1806

Sydney
1788
(British)

apetown

NEW
ZEALAND

Northern
invasion of
South Island
1830s

[3] CONVERGING REVOLUTIONS, 1780–1820

THIS chapter considers the "age of revolutions" in its global context. It moves from the analysis of long-term changes in political and economic processes sketched in chapters 1 and 2 to the "history of events" which impacted on them. The chapter analyzes the complex economic, military, and ideological connections which linked the world crises of the revolutionary and Napoleonic ages.

During the years 1756–63, warfare in the Americas and Asia between Europeans, or between Europeans and indigenous peoples, hastened the crisis of the old regimes in Europe. It helped to crack the financial systems of the old regime and throw doubt on the capacity and, ultimately, legitimacy of its rulers. The after-shocks of the subsequent European revolutions deepened the crisis of the old order in the Americas, Asia, and North Africa. But the cycle did not stop there. In turn, the repercussions of these extra-European conflicts fed back into the European convulsions. The force of events ricocheted around the globe. Napoleon himself indirectly acknowledged this when he remarked that the Battle of Waterloo had been lost in India. These dramatic, interlinked social conflicts had the effect of accelerating the divergence between the West and the rest of the world which was discussed in chapter 2.

CONTEMPORARIES PONDER THE WORLD CRISIS

It was in the realm of ideas that the impact of the revolutions was most obvious to contemporaries. They quickly understood that the ideological consequences of the dramas of 1776 and 1789 were of world-class importance, and not simply local revolts. Visionary thinkers announced that the American Revolution heralded "a New Order of the Ages" for the whole of humankind.[1] French Jacobin radicals later proclaimed the epochal importance of the French Revolution as they tried to extend it throughout Europe and beyond. Black slaves in the Caribbean seized on the idea of revolution for their own emancipation. The clear enunciation of the principle of "No taxation without representation" and of the "rights of man" had an extraordinary impact. After a century or more of philosophical discussion, the content of these "rights" may not itself appear shocking. What was remarkable was that these rights were held to be "self-evident" and freestanding: no king, no divine authority, no imperial interest, no superiority of race or creed could nullify them.

The echoes of these doctrines continued down through the nineteenth century. Intellectuals of both left and right – for this distinction began to structure politics worldwide – continued to believe that the Declaration of the Rights of Man threatened to blow apart all the old forms of moral and political authority. In order to survive, feudal rights, religious supremacies, local clan or caste loyalties, all these had to be reconstituted with reference to this novel concept of universal rights, whether for them or against them. The era's best-known English-speaking liberal philosopher, John Stuart Mill, felt as a child that "the most transcendent glory" he could achieve would be as a French revolutionary in British garb: "a Girondist in an English Convention."[2] Simon Bolivar and other liberators of Latin America from Spanish rule pondered the lessons of the French Revolution. In Calcutta in the 1840s, the first generation of young English-educated Bengalis read Tom Paine's *Rights of Man* and derided the authority and caste prejudices of their elders. Asians and Africans quickly began to argue that human rights stood prior to any "civilizing mission" that their white rulers might announce.

Many Asians, Africans, and South Americans, however, received and transformed these dangerous new doctrines in situations *already* riven by conflict between ideologies with a global reach. Well before the onset of the American and European revolutions, the great agrarian world empires and the smaller states on their margins (discussed in chapter 1) were suffering severe social tensions. In part these arose from similar problems of taxation, war finance, and legitimacy which provided the context for Europe's own epochal convulsions. In part, they arose from more particular problems of ideological cohesion and incorporation which surfaced when great states encroached on the diverse culture of their respective localities. Quite localized movements of resistance could now access and use universalistic ideas of godliness and deploy them against the world empires.

Early in the eighteenth century, for instance, the Sikhs of North India announced a revolution of *dharma*, or righteousness, which put them at odds with Mughal power. The Mughal elites' attempt to take resources from the rich and industrious Punjab provided the context. The Sikhs' growing sense of belonging to a separate and militant community, a "fourth way" after Hinduism, Christianity, and Islam, however, sowed the seeds of a wider moral conflict. Shortly afterwards, in central Arabia, Wahhabi Muslim purists hailed a new age of spiritual struggle for the pure, antique Islam which threatened the religious and political establishments of the Ottomans, Cairo, and the African emirates. As early as the 1760s, too, some Chinese sectarians began to claim that the Qing emperor no longer held the "Mandate of Heaven," since the magistracy was corrupt and the people oppressed. Asians and Africans were already announcing their own "new order of the ages." As in Europe and its colonies, it was provincials, cherishing old, godly beliefs and resisting intrusive empires who began to pull apart the big polities and recast the global links which had emerged under their aegis.

Europe and North America were, then, not alone in inaugurating the dangerous new doctrines of this revolutionary age. Nevertheless, the ideological backwash of the European revolutions and the new aggressiveness of European states engendered by them spread across the world and deepened these conflicts. The American Revolution, for instance, accelerated the pell-mell advance of white settlers in North America and, indirectly, in the central Pacific. The European invasions of Egypt and the quickening expansion of European power in India, Southeast Asia, and southern Africa were direct consequences of the French Revolution.[3] Many Muslims now feared a new age of Christian crusading, following Napoleon's appearance before the mosques of Cairo in 1798. Meanwhile, to the east, the Napoleonic struggle propelled the British and Dutch into central Java.[4] The collapse of old supremacies and the sudden appearance of aggressive foreigners ruptured indigenous histories across the world. In many places, the revolution constituted a Christian invasion. It created a spiritual void, compromising the power of high kings and destroying the ancestral spirit houses. Worse, in parts of the Pacific, the importation of Eurasian diseases by soldiers, seamen, and entrepreneurs, scattered far and wide by the world war, led to a staggering rate of mortality which wiped out half the population.

The regimes of the early nineteenth century were to confront the longer-term effects of this ideological and social turmoil. The creation of yet stronger, more intrusive states, European, colonial, and extra-European, was the most potent legacy of the age of revolutions. But there were other consequences which most people have traditionally regarded as more "progressive," or even benign. Liberalism and a sharper sense of nationality also sank shallow roots in many societies across the world, though their consequences were slower to mature. The events of the years from 1780 to 1820, therefore, greatly speeded up two of the longer-term changes examined in chapter 1: the emergence of the resolute, aggressive modern nation-state and the rise of "polite, industrious, and commercial societies" across the world.

A SUMMARY ANATOMY OF THE WORLD CRISIS, 1720–1820

Historians probably use the word "crisis" too much. Pointing to a historical crisis seems to suggest that societies and polities are normal most of the time and then suddenly become critical. In fact, conflict is a built-in feature of human societies, and it is wrong to portray them as "systems in balance." All the same, it seems legitimate to use the word "crisis" for the epochal changes of the years 1780 to 1820. The level of conflict greatly escalated, and profound ideological conflicts erupted alongside struggles over material resources. It is the global interconnectedness of the economic and political turbulences of this era which is so striking. They culminated in radical changes in the form of government and economic regulation for one large part of humanity, and the loss of local autonomy for another large part.

This chapter first examines the interlinking of financial and military crises across the world. It then goes on to consider the ideological turmoil of the revolutionary period and the new principles which animated the post-revolutionary state. Finally, it considers the "polite and commercial" revolution which was maturing beneath the surface of these dramatic events.

THE END OF THE LONG PEACE: ASIA AND NORTH AFRICA

In general, the period from 1660 to about 1720 had seen a broad upswing in economic activity across the world, with relative peace and stability following the consolidation of the great agrarian states of Asia and Africa described in chapter 1. Their populations benefited from the consolidation of the Qing, the Javanese Empire of Mataram, the Mughal, Ottoman, Safavid, and tsarist regimes. The East Indies may have suffered a trade depression in the seventeenth century, but there is little sign that this seriously affected South or East Asia. Europe, too, was past its wars of religion. Internal commerce flourished; cities grew rapidly as many killer diseases of the earlier era became endemic in populations rather than epidemic. For the better for Europe and for the worse for Africa, the Atlantic slave plantation economy moved into a higher gear, and the European colonies in the Americas expanded and became more sophisticated.

The first cracks in this picture of broad stability and expansion began to appear, not so much in Europe, as in the Middle East and South Asia at the beginning of the eighteenth century. Historians have argued long about the reasons for this. In a general sense, the Asian and Middle Eastern polities suffered from what Paul Kennedy called "imperial overstretch." They were forced to fight wars on the internal and external frontiers of their realms and had neither the financial resources nor the manpower to do this. Another suggestion is that the expansion of world trade had put money and power into the hands of local men and peasant bosses who would no longer put up with imperial control, or reacted against it when the rulers tried to raise taxation. It was the very success of these big regimes that caused their decline.

At all events, the simultaneous collapse of two Eastern regimes had profound consequences for their neighbors and also for European trading interests on their peripheries. After 1722, the century-old Safavid regime in Iran fell apart.[5] Its crash ushered in more than a century of warfare between local tribal-based polities. The beautiful cities and high arts of the Safavids suffered or disappeared. At about the same time, the Mughal dominion in South Asia also began to fragment. Provinces became semi-independent while north India was invaded by Persian and Afghan armies in 1739 and 1759.[6] Delhi was sacked and looted: "the face of the sky and earth was changed," as one

Mughal poet put it. There began a long political standoff between Muslim adventurers from the north and the western Hindu warrior kingdoms of the Marathas, all of whom had designs on the riches of Delhi. The decline of the Safavids and the Mughals let loose a great wave of turbulence which stretched from Mesopotamia in the west to Thailand in the east. The main beneficiaries were the European powers, perched hungrily on the periphery. Between 1757 and 1765, the English East India Company seized the rich weaving and rice-growing territory of Bengal. Local conditions and local conflicts made this possible. But its implications were of global importance. The British could now build an army in India. This subtly tilted the balance of world power well before the Industrial Revolution got up steam.

Regimes in East Asia survived longer than those in South Asia, West Asia, or even Europe. Yet even here there were warning signs. In Japan, the Tokugawa hegemony was under strain, but it staggered on for another 70 years. During the reign of the Qian Long emperor, China continued to expand territorially, though there were some ominous premonitions of the decay of imperial institutions as early as the 1760s. Philip Kuhn has shown how a scare about "sorcerers" nearly got out of control in this decade, because the emperor did not have enough power at the local level to clamp down on dissident monks, sectarian leaders, and bandits.[7] To the south, turbulence increased markedly. China's expansionism added to the pressures faced by her southern neighbors. The rapid development of the coastal trade of the Southeast Asian river deltas and the consequent population movements had already changed the pattern of politics there. The spread of European and Ottoman forms of warfare raised the political and economic stakes in a region which had long been the scene of mutual struggles between ethnically based kingdoms. Burma and Thailand were beset by savage warfare in the mid-eighteenth century. What was to become Vietnam also experienced peasant rebellion and prolonged conflict between regional warlords. This lasted until 1802, when the kingdom was formally reunited. In the East Indies, Dutch power reaped the benefit of a long cycle of decline and fragmentation in the Javanese state of Mataram, just as the British were handed an advantage by the political decline of the Mughal center in India.

To the west, the Ottoman Empire had fallen into a serious political and economic impasse by the later eighteenth century. In the long run, the Ottomans were to have greater staying power than the Mughals, the Safavids, and perhaps even the Qing. But military failure against the Austrians and Russians in the 1690s and 1760s had humiliated the regime and sapped its resources. A series of severe internal power struggles between the center and powerful regional magnates accompanied these external disasters. Throughout the eighteenth century, Egypt, the empire's richest province, was virtually independent. Ottoman power, if not Ottoman authority, in North Africa had vanished, while taxation and graft snuffed out the possibility of economic expansion.[8]

All these striking developments were directly, though distantly, linked through military invasions, the ambitious mutual emulation of warlords, and the disruption of trade which followed in the wake of armies. For instance, the collapse of the Iranian Safavids released the gargantuan ambitions of the Persian conqueror, Nadir Shah, who invaded India in 1739. This weakened indigenous Indian regimes facing European expansion. Further economic decline in Nadir's Persia consequently destabilized the Ottoman Empire's eastern provinces. Conflict spiraled outward, attracting the greed and ambition of the Europeans on the coasts.

This, then, was a truly global crisis. In some ways, perhaps, it was the first global crisis. But can we see any underlying pattern beneath the myriad outward forms of these convulsions? Part of the answer has already been foreshadowed in the preceding section: regimes across the world were particularly vulnerable to the financial pressures of warfare during this period. The "military revolution" in Europe, hailed by the historian Geoffrey Parker,[9] had its global dimension.[10] Changes in military technology, some originating in Europe and some outside, appear to have pressed increasingly on the finances of the Muslim empires and even China from the late seventeenth century onwards. Asia and the Ottomans lost their lead in ordnance and galley warfare to Europeans, who meanwhile developed new styles of small arms and fortification.

The costs of war had risen rapidly. This was a particular problem for Muslim empires and the Chinese Empire, which were loosely knit and absorbative on their borders, precisely in order to incorporate and accommodate local leaders. The general economic climate was unpropitious as well. The long-term influx of silver from the New World during the sixteenth and seventeenth centuries had pushed prices up. Some parts of northwestern Europe were able to offset these costs against the increasing productivity associated with industrious revolutions. The economy of Russia, too, seems to have been doing relatively well in the course of the century, despite acute problems of political control. Over much of southern Europe and West and South Asia, however, governments and ruling groups found themselves under strain. The cost of war and strategic goods was rising, but this was not offset by higher productivity there. Besides, the great Asian kingdoms were also hobbled by their internal organization. If rulers raised land taxes too high, they risked peasants deserting their fields and sparking revolt among local magnates. If they expanded on their frontiers and tried to seize new areas of trade and agriculture to tax and exploit, they risked being drawn into desultory frontier wars, and these, once again, raised the costs of warfare to the state exchequer.

This no-win situation was precisely the one that faced the Mughal Empire. After 1670 the emperor Aurangzeb became bogged down in a long war of occupation against the Maratha chieftains of western India at the same time as he faced peasant desertion and rebellion nearer his imperial capital. Aurangzeb's military costs rose at the same time as the flow of revenue to his exchequer was interrupted, in a classic case of imperial overstretch. His successors in the eighteenth century found themselves forced to extreme solutions in order to solve the "military-fiscal" conundrum. The rising costs of warfare, as new European- and Ottoman-style armaments became available, added further pain. The emperors could introduce dangerous Afghan, Abyssinian, or, worse, European mercenaries to do their fighting for them. They could hive off areas of revenue to such dangerous foreigners or "farm out" their revenues to their own over-mighty subjects in order to raise money to buy arms. Again, they could spend money and blood on constant campaigns of internal pacification against their local notables and peasantries. Any of these solutions could, and did, easily get out of hand. Much the same problem faced all the other Afro-Asian regimes during the same period. The Safavids and the Javanese succumbed first; the Ottomans struggled on into the nineteenth century, but in the meantime they had been forced to concede their richest provinces to powerful subjects. Effectively, they were caught in the same vice of rising military expenditure and stagnant or falling revenues.

WAR AND FINANCE IN EUROPE

A similar and related dilemma faced contemporary European governments. In 1700, their taxation systems and networks of internal control had generally been greater than those of the Asian and North African states. Yet, at the same time they also had wider global interests, which brought them regularly into conflict with each other and with Asians and Africans. Whereas in the seventeenth century, European wars had centered on religious belief and the power of the state to suppress dissidence and heresy, those of the eighteenth century were about dynastic resources and the control of towns, trades, and customs. European elites were beginning to supplement their incomes as landowners from the proceeds of the Atlantic slave economies and trading with the Mediterranean and Asia. So great corporations, such as the English, French, and Dutch East India companies or the branches of Spanish and Portuguese agency houses in Central and South America, gained considerably in political importance. Overseas commerce, therefore, reflected directly on European credit in a way which politicians and political economists could no longer ignore. European wars in the 1740s and 1760s became wars of the Asian and American littoral, with Britain often bargaining for advantage with the continental powers by using forts and trades it had captured in Asia or the Americas.

This sort of warfare was particularly costly: "breaking windows with guineas," as William Pitt the Elder, the British prime minister, called it. Naval forces swallowed up huge resources. Nelson's flagship, HMS *Victory*, cost five times as much as Abraham Crowley's steelworks, one of the most important investments of the Industrial Revolution.[11] The effect of new conventional military techniques and weapons, such as the flintlock gun which had been pioneered between 1680 and 1730, were now feeding through to all major conflicts. The stakes were raised by the disciplined methods of deploying firepower developed by Frederick the Great of Prussia. Smaller European and non-European powers began to employ European methods and to build new, scientifically engineered defensive fortresses by the middle of the eighteenth century. This further raised the costs of warfare.

A final escalation of costs in worldwide warfare was to result from the French Revolution itself. The idea of the mass levy of young men to defend the fatherland was adapted and extended by Napoleon. The emperor threw huge armies of men against Austria, Prussia, and Russia. This required a response from states such as Britain which did not have the same numbers of young men of military age. At the Battle of Minden in 1759, the British deployed a mere 5,000 infantrymen; at Waterloo in 1815, they had to use 21,000, itself a relatively small number by comparison with the huge German, French, and Russian armies.[12] What the British spent most of was money, not blood. They used their fiscal power to give huge subsidies to their allies in order to keep them in the war.

The problem for European states, then, was that although they were increasingly being forced into warfare worldwide, most of them did not have the resources to prosecute wars, which were so costly in terms of men and treasure. The mid- to late eighteenth century was no longer a time of rapid economic expansion. In fact, population growth seems to have outrun the capacity of farming to innovate in many parts of the continent. Governments were still dependent on cliques of large landowners, even in the relatively commercialized societies of northern Europe. The wealth-generating effects of industrialization were still minimal and would remain so for two generations. Governments fighting their wars inside and outside Europe with military and naval resources could scarcely cut into the earnings of the great landlords. This would risk revolt or undermine the positions of ministers in regard to the consultative assemblies which operated fitfully in much of Europe and to more serious effect in Britain and its Irish and North American dependencies. Equally, given the growth of large, unruly cities dependent on commerce and government jobs, the authorities could hardly tax the urban lower middle and laboring classes. Continuous riots over taxation, excise duties, and the cost of bread brought this home to all the European governments. Problems of this sort drove the attempts of the so-called enlightened despots of Germany, Russia, and Austria and their allies among the intelligentsia to try to reform some of the old European autocracies. As is well known, reforming governments are extremely vulnerable.

THE EUROPEAN MILITARY FISCAL CRISIS KICKS IN, 1756–89

It was in the 1760s that these discrete pockets of turbulence in Eurasia and the Americas flowed together more strongly, deepening conflict within and outside Europe. Events in the European-Atlantic sector were critical here. The Seven Years War (1756–63) in which Austria, Russia, Prussia, France, and Britain all took part, put a great strain on all European states. Inside Europe, war revealed the military and financial weaknesses of the great monarchies. Outside Europe, it became a costly game of grabbing colonies. In either case, the experience of war pushed governments into risky types of internal political reform and external expansion. The Spanish monarchy, for one, attempted to rebuild income and honor by revamping its American empire after defeat by the British. Spain, however, was not strong enough to reassert firm control of its rich and populous colonies, whose most important residents increasingly identified with America, not the Old World. Latin American independence was not really on the cards until after Napoleon invaded Spain 30 years later. But the lines of battle between the Creole settlers and imperialist parties in Latin America were already firmly drawn in the 1770s and 1780s. The resources of Spain were sapped by the great effort of ruling its empire and suppressing the Amerindian revolts which resulted from its policy of squeezing the peasantry for cash.[13]

Another fissure in the international system which widened after 1757 was the almost ceaseless warfare between Britain and France. They fought in the Caribbean, Canada, and India. Following a series of stunning victories against the French, Britain met its own nemesis. After 1763 it tried to recoup the vast cost of its wars against France and Spain in North America. The British ministry determined to raise taxes in the Americas, and also stationed a large royal army in the Thirteen Colonies to police the territories newly conquered from France and protect them from possible Indian attack in the west. This offended the fiercely independent local American legislatures, to whom centralized royal government, especially royal government by High Anglicans, was an anathema. American pamphleteers were particularly suspicious of the East India Company, which monopolized their trade to the east. This they saw as an engine of corruption specially protected by ministers in London.[14] The American Revolution started on a small scale as a revolt against taxation and petty tyranny. It aimed to restore the powers of local assemblies, which were being eaten away by the intrusion of the Crown. Americans were jealous of their religious freedoms and doubted the good faith of the British establishment, which had already allowed French Catholics in Canada extensive rights. The entry of France and Spain into the war on the American side in 1779, however, ensured British defeat and transformed a regional conflict into a worldwide convulsion. The French saw this as an opportunity to break Britain's growing stranglehold on international trade, which was only too evident after her victories in Canada and India.[15]

The loss of the colonies did not prove fatal to the British political system, in part because Britain retained the wealthy Caribbean islands.[16] Yet defeat in the Americas did introduce significant changes into British imperial policies, which fueled the gathering crisis of the Eastern world. British government in Asia became more grasping and more interventionist. A generation of South Asian historians have argued that the expansion of the East India Company from its Bengal base to conquer much of India between 1783 and 1818 was largely due to its voracious need to finance its military forces. The Company forced Indian rulers to pay for its troops or, alternatively, seized their revenue-bearing territories. The prize of India's trade goods was dimmed by comparison with the riches of its territorial revenues. British eyes began to fall on China, too, within ten years of the American defeat. The China trade began to bulk largely in ledgers of the embattled and cash-strapped East India Company. There was an almost infinite demand for China tea in Britain, and Indian raw cotton and opium provided valuable resources with which to purchase it. Britain sailed successfully through the choppy waters caused by its American defeat partly by exploiting its Asian and Caribbean colonies.

Ironically, therefore, it was the French monarchy and ruling classes, rather than the British, which were to be the most visible victims of the financial problems and political controversies created by the American war in which the country had ostensibly triumphed. Unsettling ideological change was in the air, too. The American cry of "No taxation without representation" was particularly meaningful in France. Volunteers in France paraded singing American songs and were mobilized by the French hero of the American war, the marquis de Lafayette. The American example brought to Europe ideas of reform and representation through popular assemblies which were rapidly to germinate on French soil. The free-trade philosopher Condorcet wrote that "the spectacle of the equality which reigns in the United States . . . will be useful to Europe."[17] More prosaically, the large financial burden taken on by the French Crown in order to help the Americans pushed royal ministers into risky, but incoherent, programs of reform. These gradually undermined the basis of the monarchy itself. In order to push through political changes, ministers needed a degree of elite and popular consent. Yet they were never bold enough really to trust the old powers and assemblies, or far-sighted enough to enlist the support of the lawyers and new professional men of Paris and the other big cities. In the end, the reforms simply stimulated more opposition. In order to resolve this crisis, many experts argued that a new, American-style constituent assembly was essential. But as no agreement could be reached, the older, more cumbersome representative body, the Estates General was summoned in 1789. Because the Estates worked on the archaic principle of the representation of orders, conflicts between nobility, church, and the middle classes become more and more bitter.

The resulting impasse in France's central government in 1789 and 1790 allowed a whole host of local revolts and social conflicts to catch fire, to become nationalized in a sense.[18] Peasant protests, anticlerical explosions, and constant outbreaks of popular disorder in Paris and other large cities buffeted a succession of ministers, who were pushed in more and more radical directions. Already, by 1792, the elements of the coming struggle were in place. The fragmentation of the old order had allowed full rein to strong feelings of regional and local autonomy which had continued to exist under the surface of royal government. The "federalists," represented in Paris by the so-called Girondins, were faced by a bloc of radical centralists, the Jacobins. The Jacobins believed that strong government could create a "republic of virtue" and sweep away church, nobility, and monarchy in a single purge. The volatile crowds of Paris and other large cities, which had been increasingly active on the cities' streets during the previous generation, fed the sense of panic. Conservative reaction, especially in the northwest of the country, where landowners, clerics, and a pious peasantry tried to thwart the aims of anticlerical republicans, enraged the radicals and drove them to institute the bloody massacres of the Terror of 1793.[19]

CLIMACTERIC: REEXPORTING THE WORLD REVOLUTION FROM FRANCE, 1789–1815

The thing that did most to radicalize the Revolution was the invasion of France by the great powers, horrified by the execution of the king and the aristocracy, but keen to gain the lands, colonies, and territories which they had eyed throughout the wars of the previous century. The presence of foreign armies on French soil released a wave of resistance which was to sweep the Revolution and, later, the armies of Napoleon Bonaparte across the borders of France, and even those of Europe itself. Radicals committed to the ideals of the Declaration of the Rights of Man came together in alliance with those richer peasants and bourgeois who were fearful of losing the aristocratic and church lands which they had occupied. Together they empowered an extraordinary

ILLUSTRATION 3.1 Transatlantic revolution: The execution of the duc d'Orléans, 1793. Contemporary print.

explosion of political and military energy. The danger to the Republic and, later, Empire posed by foreign invaders provided a powerful incentive for recruitment to the large new armies that took to the field.

Everywhere the revolutionary and imperial armies ventured, in the Rhineland, Italy, Spain, or the German states and eastern Europe, even Egypt, they found people eager for change. Merchants envious of state or guild monopolies, peasants resisting feudal dues, anticlericals eyeing with hatred the privileges of the Church – all these provided support for incoming French proconsuls and the princes of the Napoleonic family who later became rulers of Europe.[20] Before the domineering aspect of French imperialism became inescapable, young radicals everywhere thought it was "bliss to be alive" when ancient and corrupt supremacies were foundering all around them.

Cautious modern historians have tried to show that the empire created by the revolutionary and Napoleonic armies in Europe, Egypt, and even as far distant as the Dutch East Indies, had only limited social effects. Outside France and nearby parts of Belgium, Holland, and Italy, it is said, aristocracies managed cleverly to reorganize themselves in order to preserve their lands and privileges. As in the English East India Company's empire, the invaders, however revolutionary their intentions, had to deal with prominent men in society simply to stabilize their new dependencies for taxation. Napoleon's commanders sought order above all, and, whether in suppressing the Parisian crowds in 1795 or in putting down the rioters of Cairo's bazaars after Napoleon's invasion of Egypt in 1798, they looked for local notables to preserve the peace.

Yet there were changes. The new state was grasping and intrusive. At the very least, it melted down and fused together different elements of the old elite. The Napoleonic state within Europe, and briefly in Egypt, itself provides a good example of the same explosive combination of military ambition and financial need which had driven on the world crisis from its origins.[21] In intention, the short-lived but radical transformation of Europe and its frontiers by Napoleon was a consequence of the strategic and ideological needs of the French revolutionary state. But the empire, conquered by the transformation of the revolutionary mass conscription into a fighting force of two million men, soon developed its own momentum. The enormous indemnities and subsidies demanded from cowed or conquered territories and the allied armies they supported helped to offset the cost of the war to France. Control of the European economies also helped to compensate France for the loss of so many colonial and overseas territories to the British. Venice was stripped of six million francs and its most valuable territories in 1797. Other defeated states were reorganized so that their finances could provide a surplus for the French Grand Army's further advances. During the brief French occupation of Egypt, its land revenues were streamlined to provide Napoleon with a million francs per month.

Enlightened French rule was supposed to sweep away the corruption and venality of the old order. Ironically, it often created a system of stipends and revenue grants for the upkeep of the military which bore a striking resemblance to those of the Ottomans, the Russians, or the Mughals and their

British successors in India. Napoleon established a system of "donations" and "entails" in conquered territories for the support of his soldiers and administrators. For instance, the rich territory of the Veneto was assigned to the French-controlled kingdom of Italy on the understanding that 10 percent of its revenues were set aside for making grants of this sort. Similar policies were implemented in central and eastern Europe. The emperor needed to support and placate the huge numbers of officers of French and other nationalities who commanded his armies and staffed his client administrations. By 1814, 5,000 people were receiving grants of this sort, for a total in excess of 30 million francs per month.[22] This was quite apart from the large number of regular officers and administrators who were supported on the various forms

ILLUSTRATION 3.2   Napoleon in glory: *Napoleon on the Imperial Throne*. Painting by Jean-Auguste-Dominique Ingres, c.1806.

of subsidy and tribute paid by conquered territories to the French exchequer. As with the other states at war, the continental European economy was supported by what the British called "the old corruption." Military contractors and entrepreneurs made massive fortunes. For example, G. J. Ouvrard, an associate of the empress Josephine, created a ramshackle army of subcontractors and clients which stretched across the whole Empire and linked up through Madrid with another set of entrepreneurs in Mexico and Peru.[23]

The impact of the revolutionary and Napoleonic state carried well beyond the penumbra of French conquest itself. In the Caribbean, the early liberation of slaves by revolutionary decree was later reversed by Napoleon. Yet everywhere, slave revolt, which was already surging dangerously before the revolution, took on a new, ideological dimension. In Haiti, the armies of the slave revolutionary Toussaint L'Ouverture, the great "black Jacobin," even helped to preserve the revolution from its enemies in Europe by absorbing nearly 100,000 British troops, most of whom died of tropical diseases.[24] Later, in 1800, when Napoleon attempted to reintroduce slavery, his armies met their first defeat on land in Haiti, slowing the forward pace of the new empire. These were particularly good examples of how the European crisis was not simply passively received by the rest of the world, but "bounced back" to Europe, where it created further waves of change. Like the famous image of the butterfly fluttering its wings in Tokyo but ultimately creating a storm over New York's Central Park, the shock-waves carried over great distances. The fall of Spain to Napoleon's armies triggered the revolt of Spain's American colonies. In turn, the disruption of the slave trade and the interruption of the production of Mexican and Peruvian silver created ripples of change in West Africa and Asia, especially in China, which had become dependent on imported Mexican silver.[25] In southern Africa, too, more intensive conflict between European powers and ideological conflict within European settler communities had a knock-on effect among the surrounding African kingdoms, already more militarized and contentious.[26]

The British, for their part, tightened their grip on Ireland after the French-supported rebellion there in 1798. They also revamped their regime in Canada following the war of 1812 with the United States, which broke out over their blockade of Napoleon's Europe. Meanwhile, in the East, international war gave aggressive local commanders the opportunity to crush the remaining independent states of India. In acts of local "sub-imperialism," the British also invaded the Dutch East Indies, which was allied with Napoleon through its colonial master, the Dutch Batavian Republic.

Worldwide, the new military vigor and aggression of the European states, whether revolutionary or reactionary, served therefore to intensify the internal conflicts and contradictions which had troubled the old Asian polities since 1700. The Ottoman Empire, bereft of Egypt and suffering new military pressure from a reinvigorated Russia following the tsar's defeat of Napoleon in 1812, was forced to reform or die. Mughal India and central Asia were carved up by newly aggressive Russian and British mini-Napoleons. Soon China was to encounter a British offensive much bolder and more arrogant than Lord Macartney's ill-fated mission to Beijing of 1793–5, which was told that the middle kingdom needed no Western trinkets.

Even in the distant Pacific Ocean, the events of the global age of revolutions were indirectly, though equally powerfully, felt. In different ways, the military, economic, and ideological shock waves impacted on Australia, New Zealand, and the Polynesian islands. Some of the huge buildup of European and American naval power was released into the region. Commercial rivalries during the British "continental blockade" of Napoleon's empire intensified the search for whale oil in the southern oceans, releasing whalers and "beachcombers" onto its shores. Britain's establishment of penal colonies and mission stations in Australia was intimately connected with the new definitions of state and evangelical religion which flowed from the revolutionary conflicts. American missionaries spilled over into Hawaii, symbolizing their thanks to God for his creation of a righteous republic. Here, too, the overspill of European weapons and ideologies combined to bring about internal reorientations of power. Maori groups of New Zealand's North Island were the first to begin to learn to use the new European military technology. This allowed them to invade and overthrow the chieftains of the South Island.

SAPPING THE LEGITIMACY OF THE STATE: FROM FRANCE TO CHINA

As the previous section has suggested, there is a powerful case to be made that the world crisis of 1780–1820 had its origins in a growing imbalance between the perceived military needs of states and their financial capacity. This tension first afflicted the large, porous, and multiethnic states of West and South Asia. After 1760, it soon became apparent in western Europe and its American colonies, finally bringing down the whole edifice of European monarchies after 1789. Thereafter, the need for military finance motivated aggressive states within and outside Europe.

Yet this surely cannot be a complete explanation of what contemporaries called the "universal wreck of nations." Of course, financial crises and military defeats have, throughout history, been the major reasons for the collapse of regimes. Typically, as in the years 1780–1820, these shocks also released underlying economic tensions arising from slow economic growth and the unequal distribution of economic rewards and penalties. The world crisis of this period, however, was deeper and more fundamental than the largely materialistic explanation outlined so far suggests. This section examines the connection between social crisis and modes of opposition to authority in different societies across the world.

Everywhere, poverty, deprivation, and social conflict raised fundamental questions about the right of rulers to rule. There is no real distinction between "culture" and "economy," particularly in societies poised on the brink of starvation. The buoyant growth of printing and political associations in eighteenth-century Europe and America, which was mentioned in the last chapter, had made people more skeptical of, and hostile to, established authority. To account for different manifestations of this hostility, we must turn to histories of ideological conflict and popular belief. The nature of the "culture of opposition" in different contexts seems to have been critical in transforming economic conflict into wholesale social crisis. This will help us to understand why different societies took different trajectories through an age of revolution which had different origins, but broad global consequences. It will also help to begin to heal the breach between the older history of economic and political processes and the new histories of representation and discourse. While it is likely that many of the champions of these contending schools would deny that this is possible, or even desirable, the historical materials are already partly to hand to do it.

In the case of America, some of the deepest lineages of opposition had emerged around hostility to "tyranny" and Roman Catholicism. In the 1770s, these had been stirred up by British conciliation of newly conquered Catholics in Canada. They "bonded" easily with resentment about taxation. The First Continental Congress denounced

> [t]he act passed in the same session [of the British Parliament] for establishing the Roman Catholic religion, in the province of Quebec, abolishing there the equitable system of English laws and erecting a tyranny there, to the great danger (from so total a dissimilarity of religion, law and government) of the neighboring British colonies, by the assistance of whose blood and treasure the said country was conquered from France.[27]

Similarly, recent writers have shown how the representation of royal financial incompetence was turned into a moral issue in the case of France. If the court was grasping and raised taxation irresponsibly, this was because it was luxurious, degenerate, and sexually perverted. Examining what French people read in the two or three decades before the revolution, Robert Darnton uncovered a whole world of forbidden books, debates, and rumours.[28] These systematically eroded the moral bases of the monarchy, the aristocracy, and the Church through obscenity and political libel. People were so inured to regarding the court as corrupt, self-seeking, and even ludicrous that when the political crisis reached its height in 1791–2, anything and everything could be believed. Darnton and Mona Ozouf have shown how many of these representations of corruption were expressed in terms of gender. Scurrilous pamphlets and stories persistently played on allegations about the lewdness and debauchery of Queen Marie Antoinette. A foreign libertine, it was believed, could very easily corrupt her husband, the king, and encourage him in an act of treachery to the new and aggressive form of French patriotism which was growing up in Paris and the big towns, from which the royal court of Versailles was so distant.[29]

The uncompromising doctrines of popular sovereignty, fed by radical intellectuals distant from the process of government, flooded in to fill a vacuum where no authority existed. Because royal, noble, and religious rituals had been so utterly tarnished, wholly new ones drawn from classical or millenarian sources had to be invented, as Lynn Hunt showed in the 1980s.[30] It is hard to think of a deeper mental rupture than the abandonment of the Christian calendar which the revolutionary regime briefly achieved. Once the hollow symbols and discourses of the old order in France collapsed, the crisis accelerated. Fierce resistance from embittered Catholic and loyalist circles brought counter-reaction and terror in its turn, because no moderating discourse of law, religion, or polity could establish itself as legitimate for a short but devastating span of years.

Over the last 20 years Robert Darnton, Keith Baker, François Furet,[31] and Gwynne Lewis have argued that the very nature of the French autocracy and its archaic but ruthless policing served to magnify the importance of this popular culture of libel and scandal. Britain, too, had its own political caricatures and vicious lampoons. Still, Parliament and the London press served as a pressure point where political rage and contempt could be both concentrated and defused. Historians have shown that the older, more violent tradition of radical protest and rioting in Britain was actually being domesticated during the years of revolution. The London Corresponding Society of the 1790s, a reforming organization of intelligentsia and artisans, regarded as seditious by conservatives, was actually a rather well-behaved and sedate talking shop, true great-grandparent of British socialism. Once war had begun, a powerful system of communication spread fear of France, Catholicism, and Jacobinism amongst a wide range of gentry and commercial people who had a stake in the social order even when they despised the court and the capital. Few were prepared to stand outside the law. Loyalty to the Crown acquired a status quite independent of the doings of the bizarre and unpopular royal family. Even government indebtedness, which was used in France to pour scorn on the court, was taken in Britain to be a sign of national maturity. The existence of the "national debt" was taken as evidence that Britons were joined in an unbreakable social contract, not evidence of aristocratic debauchery and libertinism.

In the same way, the doubts about the Church expressed by public philosophers and the zeal of evangelical religious reformers did not signal a wholesale attack on the Church such as that which was seen in France. Many of Britain's – and Germany's – Enlightenment thinkers may have wished to "put God in the back seat," but few wanted to dispense with him completely. On the contrary, British evangelicals, Methodists, and the German Protestant reformers known as neo-Pietists aspired to a form of conservative Enlightenment. These worthies wished to improve society by the application of rational benevolence to the problems of poverty and ignorance. Untouched by the explosive anticlericalism of Catholic France or northern Italy, British Methodists and German or Scandinavian Pietists were not going to line up behind social revolution and the expropriation of property. This restraint, of course, was not apparent 20 years earlier in Britain's American colonies. There, routines of opposition and appeals to right government had been brought to bear against a Crown administration which had come to have no more legitimacy for much of the population than had royal government in France.

Far from being protector of religious and community liberties, the Crown was thought to be a tyrant.

So, popular culture, beliefs, and representations of politics give us an important middle stage in a "model" of revolution, standing between social tension and radical political breakdown. They acted as a kind of conceptual "accelerator," which brought fundamental political and social conflicts to the point of chaos. And the great strength of the new history of "representations" is that it can be applied to any human society. The work of Furet, Ozouf, and Darnton has parallels in historical writing about the world outside Europe. A similar interpretation can therefore be applied to some of the other key events of the world crisis, the decline of the great kingdoms of Asia and North Africa. Movements to purge the power-holders and submit them to ancient and universal virtues had already emerged in several parts of Asia and Africa. Thus Philip Kuhn's *Soulstealers* paints a different picture of Qian Long's China from the one that emerges from standard political and economic history. China in the eighteenth century may well have continued to grow economically and to expand on its imperial frontiers, as many social and economic historians have argued. But, as early as 1767, the Chinese regime was encountering severe problems in the handling of a variety of dissident movements which both fed on and deepened these economic strains.

Kuhn reveals a Chinese popular culture of apocalyptic rumor, always alert to the appearance of witchcraft or malign spirits. Wandering monks spread the ideologies of millenarian Buddhism: the idea that salvation might come soon, and on earth, and that earthly powers were about to vanish away.[32] This helped to erode the legitimacy of the Confucian scholar-gentry, especially in frontier areas, much in the same way as libelous books corroded the nobility, the Church, and the court in France. The Chinese Empire had itself served to stoke up the feeling between Manchu and Chinese, between establishment and popular Buddhism. Beijing insisted on the precedence of Manchu claims for jobs and offices and also fostered Tibetan and central Asian lamaistic religion at court, provoking further resentment among ethnic Chinese. The death of the Qian Long emperor in 1799 revealed the extent of corruption in government, as factions of Manchu nobles fought over the perquisites of office and control over the new monarch. A few scholars themselves began to insinuate that, though superior to the Ming dynasty, the Qing were now themselves losing their grip on the Mandate of Heaven. In the following 20 years, a series of revolts flared across North and South China. The rebels claimed legitimacy from a variety of ideologies: millenarian Buddhism, "social" banditry, popular Taoism, the Chinese spirit religion, and local Christian millenarianism. These all acted as carriers for a central idea: that corrupt officials and misgovernment had violated the moral economy of the middling and poor.

The early rebellions of the new century, however, were a premonition of turbulence rather than the beginning of the collapse of the Qing Empire. Like the "sorcery scare" of the 1760s, they revealed the strains developing in Chinese society. They showed, in addition, how these strains could be deepened by the economic and political backwash of the European and

Atlantic revolutions. Yet, until as late as 1900, some Chinese scholar-gentry continued to come to the aid of the regime. Critical discourse was at this time concentrated more on the corruption of the bureaucracy than on the court itself, unlike in France. The dynasty in China was not critically wounded as far as its legitimacy was concerned until well into the nineteenth century. Neo-Buddhist and Daoist messianic leaders certainly attacked the emperor, but the more successful movements at this time concentrated their invective on local officials and often preached a kind of schism in which godly people would go off and live on the margins. To repeat, tried and tested rituals of resistance varied from society to society, and these affected the scale of protest movements independently of the degree of actual material distress.

Though the point should not be pushed too far, one can see some analogies between the cases of Britain and Japan, just as there were between China and France. It was not that Japan was immune to the tensions of the age of revolution. Japan, too, was to face civil war, foreign attacks, and replacement of the ruling dynasty over the three generations after 1789. The country certainly experienced severe social strains. The pace of economic expansion slowed, and complaints about the competence and legitimacy of the Tokugawa regime grew more insistent. Peasant rebellions sputtered on in the countryside, and the towns were restive. A great riot took place in Edo in 1787, for instance, which scholars have compared with the contemporary ritualized bread riots in Paris, lovingly described by the historian Richard Cobb. An observer of the events in Edo wrote of the surging crowds: "Day and night, ceaselessly, they broke into the shops, tossed bags of grain into the street and ripped them open."[33]

Yet Japan's transition to the status of industrial power was to be much easier and faster than China's. It avoided foreign occupation, the bankruptcy of the regime, and the tens of millions of deaths that were suffered by China. To some degree this reflected the underlying economic differences to which I alluded in chapter 2. Japan's population grew much more slowly than China's, and its local economies remained linked and complementary, despite political decentralization. Further explanations for these divergences, however, can be found in the content of political culture and ideology. Late Tokugawa scholars and administrators were apparently able to counter dissident or heterodox movements more effectively than the Chinese elite.[34] State power in Tokugawa Japan may indeed have been quite decentralized, but government and its systems of communication were much denser at town and village level than in China. It was, after all, a smaller and less populous society. The established order of samurai and prosperous merchants was able to exercise leadership and control dissent by means of educational programs and movements of religious reform. Even at the time of the great revolt against the Tokugawa in 1868 – Japan's own "French Revolution" – the ruling groups managed to regain control quite quickly.

The issue of why the state stayed on top cannot, then, be simply reduced to the political or economic "factors." Where ancient forms of power and civility suffered a revolution, or *inquilab* (the word used to designate political cataclysm in Persia and South Asia), historians need to examine contending ideologies and discourses.[35] But they also need to consider how these discourses communicated themselves through local-level systems of sociability. In Britain, "the gentlemen were thoroughly frightened" by the echoes of the French Revolution. Social tensions were widespread across the land as riot and tumult in town and country before and after the wars demonstrated. The difference between English "stability" and French, Italian, or German "chaos" is easy to exaggerate. Nevertheless, the English gentlemen do seem to have been able to count on a widespread popular belief in the law and a concern for property and order, as I have suggested. This united gentry, merchant, and the middling sort of people. The French had been taught by two generations of scurrilous pamphleteering and public ridicule that authority, the law, and the Church were basically corrupt. Equally, in Japan the gentlemen or samurai may have seen their incomes eroded by commercial growth. Yet they could still assume their role as leaders of society and take control of the new religious, social, and educational movements which fed on the widespread sense of popular unease.

In India, by contrast, the ruling dynasty and the Indo-Muslim ruling elite were unable politically to counter the growing restiveness of emerging local powers which could deploy new claims to legitimacy. So, for instance, the Sikh movement in eighteenth-century north India was not inspired simply by peasant economic deprivation. As suggested, it was also a moral campaign to establish *dharma*, or righteous rule, across the world in accordance with the tenets of the gurus, the Sikh teachers. The Delhi rulers, who were, in general, broad-minded Muslims, were at both a military and an ideological disadvantage in opposing them. On the one hand, new Sikh or Hindu regimes were able to appropriate aspects of the old Mughal charisma. On the other hand, their more zealous supporters called for a new order of godliness which explicitly or implicitly found less room for Muslims.[36]

The Ottoman Empire stood somewhere between these extremes. The sultans lost power in their outlying provinces. However, after 1823, Istanbul's tight-knit administrative cadres, long embattled with Russia and the Western powers, were able to coordinate a movement of reform, the Tanzimat.[37] This was consonant with both the survival of the sultanate and the protection of religion. All the same, the radical challenges to the nature of the form of the Islamic community released during the age of revolutions continued to threaten rulers and the religious establishment throughout the world. As the first section of this chapter pointed out, the Wahhabi purist movement, originating in Saudi Arabia, had become a threat to Ottoman government even before the European revolutions. In some respects it was the Islamic world's "revolution," and, like the European revolutions, it was turned back but never stopped. Abd al-Wahhab, its originator, condemned the religious "innovations" and corruption of the Arabian towns which had grown wealthy on expanding trade. It was old-fashioned, in that it sought a renovation of the godly old Medina of the Prophet. Yet Abd al-Wahhab's message was also political, directed to the poor of the towns and spartan Arab nomads. An Arab chronicler wrote:

> And the chiefs and oppressors of the towns knew only how to oppress their people and tyrannise them and to fight among each other. When the Sheikh [Abd al-Wahhab] realized what constitutes the unity [of God] and what constitutes its denial, and into what misleading innovations many people had fallen, he began to deny these things.[38]

Ibn Saud, a local tribal chief, vowed to spread Wahhabi teaching and create a new "abode of Islam." Deeply conservative in doctrine, Wahhabism nevertheless became a badge of modernity for later generations. After an initial surge of conquests which took them into present-day Iraq, the Wahhabis were held in check by Ottoman Egyptian armies. But teachers influenced by their radical monotheism continued to spring up over the next two centuries in places as far distant as central India, the Chinese border, and West Africa.

In all these cases, moral discourses acted conjointly with social processes to bring about varied political outcomes. On the face of it, the linguistic and "representational turn" in history over the last 20 years has made the task of accounting for the different fates of the world's societies during the world crisis of 1780–1820 much more difficult. No grand narrative seems to hold. This is partly because historians of discourse and the representations of power through ritual, print media, or art have been less interested than their predecessors in why change occurred in the first place. Possibly, they have a sense that their approach is simply too limited to "model" change. It was easier in the 1960s and 1970s when historians would baldly contrast the depth of France's subsistence crises with the agricultural revolution in Britain, or point to differential levels of population growth between China and Japan. The task is not hopeless, though, because the distinction between the economic, the political, and the linguistic is more in the minds of historians than it was in the minds of contemporaries. The legitimacy of rulers depended on their perceived equity in managing the moral economy. Equally, the moral economy was itself subject to fluctuations brought about not only by changes in popular expectations, but also by the unintended consequences of changes in the flows of goods, services, and labor.

THE IDEOLOGICAL ORIGINS OF THE MODERN LEFT AND THE MODERN STATE

The currents of turbulence and ideological dissidence which flowed more strongly after 1789 forced ruling groups to reconstitute the ideological foundations of the state and partially to modernize it. They drew on a variety of sources, especially the vision of mankind's unity and the possibility of "improvement" which was announced by the thinkers of the European Enlightenment. But indigenous ruling groups in Asia and Africa were also able to reconfigure aspects of the rational sciences in Islam and in Chinese understandings of the proper deportment of person and state as they confronted global political turmoil and even invasion. This section considers the moral rearmament of the state during the years of world crisis.

As observed at the outset, contemporaries and commentators of the early nineteenth century drew attention to the liberating effects of the ideologies of the revolutionary years. The state seemed an unlikely beneficiary. The notion of popular sovereignty appeared to have achieved a decisive victory. Controlled and directed, the urge to equality could bring great benefits to mankind in the view of most liberals. Superstition had fallen victim to the ideas of the French philosophers. Corruption and monopoly had been assailed by the ideas of the Scottish economists and their continental European equivalents. Libertarian ideologies which sprang from, or were related to, those taught by the *philosophes* and revolutionaries were widely registered in the demands for the franchise and for labor rights which affected most commercial societies over the next generation. The idea of a mass citizenry of enlightened individuals proved irresistible in the United States. In Europe, the continuing rash of revolutions which spread from Spain (1820) to Naples and Sicily (1820), Piedmont (1821),[39] and finally to France itself (1830) were testament to the continuing appeal of liberty, equality, and fraternity. Similar ideas caught the spirit of young men as far afield as India and Spanish America who wanted to throw off the burden of aristocracy, caste, or church privilege. They flowed strongly in the antislavery movements in Britain, France, and later the United States.

Perhaps more important than any political philosophy as such was the symbol of "the people" itself. The idea that the people had rights and could also act as a creative, even revolutionary force in politics was globalized. It provided a sort of cultural template which could strengthen and sharpen ideas of just deserts and resistance to oppression everywhere. Slave rebels in the Caribbean, low-caste activists in India, rebelling artisans in Genoa could all invoke the rights of "the people" and be understood, even feared, way beyond their localities. It matters little that historians have shown that many of these popular revolts were not really led by the "wretched of the earth," and that the revolutionaries were often men who were embittered but relatively privileged. What matters is the worldwide recourse to the idea of "the people." This was a novel feature of the post-revolutionary age, even if it had been indirectly foreshadowed by the idea of God's people in earlier struggles within Christianity and Islam.

Radicalism did not have it all its own way, of course. There was a flip side to liberty, equality, and fraternity. According to the Anglo-Irish conservative thinker Edmund Burke, the revolution had led directly to the tyranny of the mob and the madness of the Terror of 1793, during which the Jacobin French government slaughtered thousands of its own citizens. Indeed, the revolution made explicit an active, conservative style of thought which was quite different from the "politics of difference" of the old order. It was not only the privileged who responded to these new currents. A profound shock had been delivered by the revolutionary wave and consequent economic changes to corporate bodies, especially artisan guilds. The status and honor of these poor but respectable people had been undermined. In some cases, women had been introduced into the work force, which had the effect of reducing overall wages.

In the longer term, the resentment of weavers, artisans, and the respectable poor gave a powerful boost to corporatist ideologies which demanded a return to protection and social justice. In Europe, communal ideologies revived in reaction to revolutionary change. These stressed the value of small communities and old ways of doing things. They sometimes nourished anti-modernist and anti-Semitic right-wing reactions.[40] Sometimes they nourished very conservative forms of early socialism. Outside Europe, the economic changes and legislative rationalizations which swept away the corporate bodies created a context for the emergence of ideas of nativistic economic protection. In India, for example, intellectuals quickly began to voice the need for protection of "our own valued products" (*swadeshi*). In Egypt and the Ottoman Empire, which suffered from both European competition and post-revolutionary attempts to discipline the urban guilds, artisans rallied to Islamic purist and anti-Western movements as their means of livelihood was destroyed. These were not simply negative responses. The pious merchants and sober artisans who, since the beginning of the previous century, had approved of movements to discipline the "excesses" of mysticism, were also making a claim to their own type of honor, civility, and modernity.[41]

Yet it was the state which learned most, and ultimately benefited most, from the ideological turmoil of the years after 1780. The sole exception to this, right at the outset of the period, was the United States itself. The American Revolution remained a "revolution against the state," partly at least because the new nation was not thrown into a long war for survival after 1783. Elsewhere, the state "got on top" again, even in the most turbulent of the seats of revolution. This was not simply because people craved protection, and reactionary conquerors reimposed the old order. To a much greater extent, it was because the revolutionary age had, ironically, furnished the domestic European and colonial state with a new set of ideological tools. Close to the notion of the universal rights of man was the ideal of universal standards of enlightenment and benevolence. Such ideas could easily be turned to the service of the new, invigorated state which emerged from the wars of revolution and imperialism. Generally speaking, the new empires of military fiscalism had less time for religious orthodoxy than the old regimes, whose monarchs had been protectors of the faith. Napoleon himself had stated that he wanted to govern peoples as they wished:

> It was by making myself a Catholic that I won the war of the Vendée [the war of counter-revolution in western France], by making myself a Muslim that I established myself in Egypt, in making myself Ultramontane [a devotee of the papacy] that I won men's hearts in Italy. If I were to govern a Jewish people, I would re-establish Solomon's Temple.[42]

Everywhere the intervention of this new and alien style of governance raised questions about the source of political legitimacy, even when the immediate social changes were limited in scope. As Stuart Woolf has shown, Napoleon at first emphasized race and ethnicity, rather than dynasty and tradition, in his reorganization of Europe.[43] This had powerful effects on the ways in which

Europeans saw themselves thereafter. Napoleon was the greatest of all post-dynastic figures. In this fashioning of a new justification for hierarchy and stability, he followed Nadir Shah, the Persian who seized the city of Delhi, or George Washington and Thomas Jefferson, the Americans. Napoleon, like these earlier post-dynastic figures, drew on aspects of the ancien régime, while at the same time claiming to embody the pure principle of revolutionary or imperial reason, without benefit of the divine rights of kings or the sanction of tradition. Napoleon's example proved powerful in turn. Whether we look to enlightened despots such as Muhammad Ali in early nineteenth-century Egypt, Bernadotte, Napoleon's general who was to rule in Sweden, or even the statesmen of revived and reorganized post-Napoleonic Germany or post-Bourbon Latin America, the appeal to "reason of state" and modernization acquired new vigor.

ILLUSTRATION 3.3   An Iranian Napoleon: Fath Ali Shah, king of Persia. Painting by Mirza Baba, early nineteenth century.

Revolutionary regimes in other parts of Europe began cautiously to liberate Jews from the ghettos and to remove the religious disabilities of the earlier era. Even the restored monarchies in France, Italy, and the German states reluctantly followed suit. While still dressed in the tatters of the Anglican establishment, the British Empire began to acknowledge religious diversity precisely in order to impose a uniform type of citizenship. Catholics were commissioned in the British army, having long fought for the East India Company's forces. The Emancipation of Catholics in Ireland took another 20 years, but a substantial part of the establishment, particularly imperialists such as Lords Cornwallis and Wellesley, former governors general of India, already believed that it was inevitable. Dissenters in India and new British colonies such as Canada, Australia, and the Cape achieved social and political influence that would have been unthinkable a generation before. It began to seem absurd that an imperial state which recruited Hindus and Muslims to the colors should still exclude other denominations of Christians.

The relatively relaxed view of the new states and empires towards religious affiliation did not mean, however, that difference was not taken into account. Novel theories of history and society were abroad. These encouraged the ruling elites to rank peoples, races, cultures, and religions according to the degree to which they had risen on, or fallen down, a ladder which represented a common standard of judgment for all mankind. Enlightenment philosophers, especially Adam Smith and William Robertson, provided some good theoretical underpinnings for these administrative ideologies. An implicit hierarchy was accepted in which tribal peoples and Africans represented the least developed of societies because they had failed to generate a commercial society or a recognizable state. In this scheme, other cultures, the Islamic, the Hindu, and the Chinese, were stuck at the level of rationality achieved by the ancient Greeks or Romans, but they could progress no further without the benevolent effect on them of other, superior races.[44]

Such racial attitudes were not yet systematically based on biological and evolutionary theories. In the learned discourse of the period, discovering the whole "map of mankind" was seen as an end in itself. Connections were discovered, as well as differences. So, for instance, the work of William Jones on the ancient Indian and Persian languages discovered connections with the classical and European languages, which German linguistic scholars of the early nineteenth century worked out in detail. Observation became an end in itself. Captain Cook's and Admiral Bougainville's voyages in the Pacific discovered a whole new arc for human and natural history. Observations were ranked in encyclopaedias and in great mapmaking ventures such as the Survey of India or of Ireland which allied the skills of the military cartographer with the precision of the new science of astronomy.[45] Governmental projects for the acquisition of knowledge became grander and more coherent. Napoleon took the learned men of the French Academy with him to Egypt, while in Britain, Sir Joseph Banks, once a private gentleman sailing with Cook, organized a network of officially sponsored surveys and scientific investigations through the Royal Society, the Admiralty, and the East India Company.[46]

The greater sway over the land and the seas wielded by those who controlled the post-Napoleonic armies made this data collection much easier than it had been under the old regimes.

Though they were officially sponsored, these early attempts to systematize data in anthropology and natural history did not always have a direct practical purpose. They often seem to have been declaratory rather than practical: that is to say, they set forth the power, knowledge, and enlightenment of a particular nation, state, or ruling group. But, as Richard Drayton has shown, the fashionable theorists of the era were keen to "improve" the peoples and areas which had been conquered since the 1780s. If the native peoples were so irremediably primitive, corrupt, or trapped at the level of the ancients, then the British, French, Americans, or Germans would have to bring them the benefits of state, commerce, and freedom of trade. Recent studies of Napoleonic armies and government in Italy have shown how strongly held was the notion that the Italians were degenerate, unable to move beyond primitive, family-based values and corruption. According to condescending French administrators, they lacked a civil society and a sense of "mine" and "yours." Their civic institutions would need to be purged of old privilege, their landed society freed of feudal accretions, and power within it invested in powerful landowners protected by strong and transparent property rights.

These ideologies were implemented in practical policies during the short-lived French government of Egypt and, after 1830, in Algeria. They were common currency in British India, where Lord Cornwallis expelled people of mixed race and Indians from high positions in the state on the grounds that centuries of tyranny had bred "corruption" in them. He also created a land system in Bengal which vested rights in would-be whig landowners, and trade was purportedly freed. Ranajit Guha argued in 1963 that Cornwallis's Permanent Settlement of revenue in Bengal in 1793 owed something to French ideas of "physiocracy" – that is, the theory that social value would spring from the benign management of landed property by men whose taxation was fixed and moderate.[47] Land revenue arrangements from the Cape to India to continental Europe began to resemble each other more and more. This aided the state by providing it with a stable group of notables to whom it could devolve local responsibility. The more adept of the old class of notables were also able to manipulate the intentions of the new state and protect their power effectively. The landowners (*zamindars*) created by Cornwallis and his successors in Bengal soon adjusted to the new levels of taxation imposed on them. But the legal and institutional framework created by the British also gave them a whip hand over the peasantry beneath them. This created a highly unequal agrarian society, subject to frequent peasant rebellions.

Related ideas were implemented by the new conquest-state in the very different conditions of the Rhineland under Napoleon. The French sheared away many old rights and dues, making the landed class the basis of their "modernized" administration. In the process, landlords accumulated new powers in relation to agricultural laborers and tenants.[48] Their dominance in the Rhenish economy and politics went virtually unchallenged before 1870. In fact, this setting of universal standards for the holding of property was one of the most important changes of the whole era, and one which was to be further confirmed during the second wave of revolutions after 1848. In important senses it preceded the emergence of a new commercial stratum in most parts of Eurasia and South America. It resulted from the ideological projects of the newly invigorated state and facilitated, rather than followed from, the "rise of the middle class."

In areas of European settlement, these new definitions of property rights could become blunt instruments to bludgeon the weak. They made it possible for white settlers, and sometimes for indigenous elites, to expropriate the common lands and labor of the original inhabitants. In American Hawaii, all land was privatized in 1841. In Australia and New Zealand, European settlers fenced off land and tried to assume freehold rights. Sooner or later this led to conflict with the original inhabitants, who continued to believe that land was a common good for everyone's use.[49] The tally of losers and gainers was not simply a racial one. In the codification and organization of society which followed the rebound of the state, some elite indigenous people played an active role in the new order. They remained administrators and informants at the lower levels of government. A number of native intellectuals took over and adapted the concepts of civilization and barbarism that the conquerors wished to force upon them.

NATIONALITIES VERSUS STATES AND EMPIRES

The very success of the new type of state and empire bred its own opponents and critics. The turmoil of the revolutionary age, which saw huge armies moving over large swathes of land, plundering and conquering, enhanced the sense of identity of those who lived through the cataclysm. It has long been recognized in European and Latin American history that the revolutionary wars and, even more, the experience of Napoleon's occupation, began to galvanize the fluid patriotisms of the eighteenth century into the harsher lineaments of the modern nation-state. In less obvious ways, the accompanying "revolutionary imperialisms" sparked into life the beginnings of a sharper sense of national identity among some indigenous intellectuals and political leaders in the overseas world.

Let us trace the eddies of these new identities in different continents. In Europe, of course, they were most intense. However buoyant had been the old patriotisms of the eighteenth century, the experience of conquest and occupation by French armies greatly heightened the sentiment of nationality. As a boy, the Italian patriot Giuseppe Mazzini learned about "Italy" and freedom from French newspapers.[50] His flirtation with the universal freedom of the revolution soon gave way to a concern for the honor of the Italian patria, one which he defined as the land of Dante's language and the inheritors of Giotto's art. Equally, it was the mass mobilization against Napoleon which helped to turn Russia into a country, rather than the realm of the tsar and the seat of the

Orthodox Church. The Russian nobility "discovered" the peasantry on the battlefields of 1812. An officer who was to become a leading radical noble told the tsar: "You should be proud of them, for every peasant is a patriot."[51] In Germany something similar happened. After 1793, Goethe no longer looked to the Holy Roman Empire, but to the German *Volk* after the experience of the defeat of the German states by the French. Even in Britain and America, an already strong sense of identity was forged anew by the popular recruitment which accompanied the Napoleonic wars. The victories of Trafalgar and Waterloo and the burning of Washington by the British powerfully reinforced these nations' sense of themselves.

The leaders of subordinated peoples within Europe also began to think of themselves as prophets of future nations. Russia's partition of Poland in 1795 gave a fillip to a sense of embattled "Polishness," which was to grow stronger throughout the nineteenth century. With the old order of nobles and assemblies gone, Poles had no choice but to imagine their future as a nation. Between 1780 and 1820, again, the Protestant Irish patriotism which had given rise to an Irish Parliament in 1780 had been supplanted by a sense of a specifically Catholic Irish identity. Originating among the middle classes, it showed signs of being taken up by the peasantry. Two critical changes encouraged this. First, at the height of the revolutionary wars, Ireland was politically united with Great Britain, creating in the longer term a wide range of grievances among Irishmen. Secondly, the activity of Protestant missionaries amongst the Catholic peasantry sparked off a religious reaction and provided another potent stimulus to a broader-based sense of nationality.

This was a worldwide phenomenon. In North Africa, India, and Ceylon, the wars of revolution and global imperialism also strengthened hitherto fluid patriotic identities, sometimes injecting them with a sense of religious revival. In Morocco and Algeria, faced with what they saw as a new Crusade by Napoleon and his successors, Muslims came to identity their faith with their homeland. *Jihad*, or holy war, became a patriotic, as much as a religious, imperative. In a weaker version of this sentiment, Muhammad Ali consciously fostered a local sense of identity in his newly reorganized satrapy of Egypt.[52] Arabic-language scholars began to write of "Egypt" and its history. Faced with British conquest, the rulers of the regional states of India also called upon an implicit sense of regional patriotism – of commitment to home, hearth, and custom – in order to galvanize their subjects against invasion. Even if there was often no direct connection between these embattled patriots and the Western-educated nationalists of later years, the heroic deeds of the forefathers provided a powerful residue of emotional symbols for later leaderships.[53] The new, united Vietnamese kingdom displayed deep distrust of French and British trading and missionary ventures, and invoked the spirits of the land, stressing its identity as both a Vietnamese and a Confucian kingdom. In China, Vietnam, Japan, and Korea, rulers and literati of the 1830s had a much sharper sense of the outside world and the dangerous foreign races which beset their kingdoms.[54]

As in Europe, the opening to the world and the expansion of communications, as much as sudden and abrupt conquest, helped to forge these new identities. By the late 1820s Bengalis in the new city of Calcutta, with Raja Ram Mohun Roy at their head, began to discover what they called the "Hindu race" and, a little later, "India" itself. They began to speculate that this race or culture had "rights" and needed representation, pointing to both the Hindu past and to the European present. Newspapers, which fed on the events of the world crisis, made them aware of the post-revolutionary struggles of the Irish and the Genoese. If there were bodies of people called Irish or Genoese who had rights as peoples, then surely there must be rights for "Indians" as well.

Even in the nineteenth century, historians asserted that the revolutionary and Napoleonic era saw the emergence of a new form of the nation and of the state in Europe and its colonies. The previous section broadly accepted that judgment. It has argued, however, that this was a worldwide development. The crisis of the old order had Asian, African, and American, as well as European, origins. Its consequences were also global. The more demanding states and the more resolute nationalities which emerged from the turmoil certainly drew on European Enlightenment philosophies. They also enlisted, in different parts of the world, elements of Muslim, Hindu, Buddhist, and other systems of thought. These evolving forms of regional and national identity appealed to some of the newly prosperous middle or administrative classes in these societies. Over the following century, the ideologies of national identity and state power, which were forged in the revolutionary and imperial wars, were themselves shackled tightly together to create a powerful, and often destructive, tool in the hands of political leaders across the world.

THE THIRD REVOLUTION: POLITE AND COMMERCIAL PEOPLES WORLDWIDE

The impact of the first age of global imperialism and of the political revolution in Europe and the Americas was accompanied in the years 1780–1830 by a third, quieter revolution. This was the emergence in northwestern Europe, North America, and in several other bridgeheads in the global economy, of the commercial middle class and its values. This development was not as yet associated with a profound revolution in industrial production. Modern-style industry before the first railways was still mainly confined to a small area of northern and central England. Industry here was already acting as an accelerator to the expansion of commerce, but elsewhere the rise of the commercial middle class owed more to a reorganization and globalization of consumption patterns and to the accumulation of changes in the artisan sectors of the economy. Insofar as this was an "industrial revolution," it revolved more around the rationalizations of master weavers and slave planta-tion owners than it did around the spinning jenny or the steam engine. It more closely represented an accelerated form of the industrious revolution, motiv-ated by the economic consequences of the events of the revolutionary age. The worldwide struggle scattered bodies of European soldiers, seamen, merchants, and settlers across Asia, Africa, and the Pacific, where they created new patterns in the exploitation of resources, labor, and trade.

The United States provides the best example of this third revolution. Even as late as 1830, the young republic was overwhelmingly agricultural, with only New York above 100,000 in population. This led some mid-twentieth-century historians to ignore the significance of the years 1780–1830, insisting that colonial society was mobile and commercial, and that real change came only with industrialization and the railroad. More recently, a different picture has been painted. Late colonial society was still aristocratic and caste-ridden in style if not in forms of production. During the next two generations a slow but fundamental change occurred, historians now argue. In 1780 there were only a half-dozen business corporations in the Thirteen Colonies. By 1830 there were hundreds of thousands: "an extraordinarily high proportion of society, at least outside the South, was engaged in buying and selling. . . . People began to realise that a society could become more prosperous not simply by selling abroad, but more importantly by selling to each other."[55] The individual states chartered scores of new banks, all of which issued the paper money which made possible this expansion of commerce. Private consumption burgeoned, so that ordinary families could now afford chinaware, fine cooking utensils, and quilted bedclothes.

This, then, was one of Jan de Vries's most powerful and continuous industrious revolutions which was satisfied not yet by industrial mass production, but in the main by smaller-scale improvements in artisanal activity. Such a "virtuous" division of labor, along the lines advocated by Adam Smith, was accompanied by a significant growth of population, concentrated in particular in small towns. Between 1790 and 1820, New York State's population quadrupled, and Kentucky's grew by eight times.[56] Though emigration from Europe only began to accelerate rapidly after 1815, "in a single generation Americans occupied more territory than they had occupied during the entire 150 years of the colonial period." To the north, the British colonies of Canada expanded equally explosively into their hinterland. This huge expansion of land acreage unlocked massive quantities of resources of virgin forest for cultivation and grazing, timber and minerals. In a small way, the growth of Cape Town and Sydney registered similar changes.

The growth of population, consumption, and exchange in the United States was accompanied by changes in social, political, and intellectual life which were yet more profound, though announced with less brio than the original Declaration of Independence. By 1830, white adult male suffrage was widespread in state elections. Literacy had reached a high level, and large numbers of newspapers were now available in all parts of the country. Despite their archaic dogmas and doctrines, the leaders of the Whig and Democratic parties were now, in effect, dealing with the first educated mass electorate. The notion of individual conscience was quietly triumphant with the widespread disestablishment of the Anglican Church and the flourishing of Baptists, Methodists, and Catholics. Americans remodeled their cities and their landscapes, and came to regard culture as a consumable for the majority rather than the preserve of a high-minded republican elite, as it had been as late as 1783. Older American ideas of revolutionary equality were increasingly reinforced by new ones coming from Europe. Economic pressure here was beginning to push out more emigrants, and, consciously or not, many of these had been touched by ideas of liberty and equality which had been so sharply focused by the experience of the continental European revolutions.

When the inhabitants of other British and Irish colonies of settlement – in Canada, Australia, and New Zealand – emerged to political self-awareness in the 1840s and 1850s, they also displayed rather similar mentalities to those of the United States of a generation earlier.[57] The depiction of early Australian colonization as a brutal penal colonialism was overdone by the leftist historians of the 1960s, as Alan Atkinson cogently argued.[58] Aspects of eighteenth-century Enlightenment thought were present here right from the beginning. In white Australia, too, the doctrine of the respectable tradesman came later to coexist and contend with the idea that the independent farmer was the fount of all virtue. Here, too, as in the United States, landlordism had been shorn of the caste status of aristocracy. Religion had been de-linked from the state, and local churches went their own way implanting notions of self-help and respectability.

This type of middle-class, consuming society developed with almost as great speed in Britain as in the United States, though here it remained sandwiched between the still-powerful landowning aristocracy above it and a class of poor agricultural laborers and a growing urban working class below. Modern British historians of all periods notoriously espy the emergence of the middle class. But there is much evidence for their emergence over these years. Patterns of consumption changed, making it possible for ordinary people to dress in the cloth produced by the new factories. Wedgwood famously mass-produced styles of classical china tableware which could only have been afforded by the aristocracy a generation before. Large numbers of modest but clean town houses for people of middling income were constructed in north and east London, the emerging industrial cities, and the old ports.

This social change was, once again, registered in the political and intellectual sphere. The rise of evangelical Christian belief, as in America and commercial north Germany, was accompanied by a new emphasis on education, sociability, and the foundation of political and moral societies. The established churches retained their grip on doctrine, but able and enterprising people directed their attention to missions to the domestic poor and the overseas heathen. Evangelicals believed that the world was in a premillenarian phase, and that the mass conversion of non-believers would indicate the imminence of Christ's second coming. The taming of the world's savage soul was to be accompanied by the taming of savage nature by industrious commodity producers and pious family patriarchs. The global missionary effort of British, American, German, Dutch, and Scandinavian societies in the first half of the nineteenth century was to have a lasting impact on the social and economic patterns of large areas of the globe, especially in southern Africa, the Pacific regions, and Asia. Subscriptions to mission and improving magazines and disseminators of "useful knowledge" achieved mass levels. Though it slackened between 1807 and 1825, the antislavery movement became the greatest voluntary movement for moral reform in history. The concerns of those same middle-class and industrious people were registered in the political arena with the Reform Bill of 1832. This did not create a mass electorate like that of the United States, but it gave a great impetus to the reorganization of local government and the poor law, to the expansion of education, and to free trade throughout the empire. It also led directly to the abolition of slavery. In Ireland, the demands of the majority, voiced through the new middle classes of Cork and Dublin and orchestrated by Daniel O'Connell, made Catholic Emancipation irresistible by the later 1820s.

Middle classes with similar interests emerged over much of northern Europe in the aftermath of the revolutionary years. Hamburg had begun to develop as a world center of commerce after 1783, when it secured the right to trade directly with the newly independent United States. It suffered badly during the later stages of the Napoleonic wars, but resumed its upward path very rapidly in 1815. In 1816 the first steamboat appeared on the river Elbe as the alarums and excursions of war faded into the distance. The stimulus given to some centers of production during the wars and the return of agricultural prosperity in the 1820s were no doubt important. But the expansion of the

ILLUSTRATION 3.4 Polite, godly, and industrious: Norwegian followers of Hans Nielson Hauge at prayer meeting. Illustration by Adolf Tidemand, 1852.

state and the abolition of the old society of orders and grades by the revolutionaries and Napoleon's lieutenants were of equal significance. Outside Hamburg and some other commercial port cities, the new German middling sort was made up largely of lawyers, teachers, and administrators. Political activity over much of continental Europe remained constrained until the 1830 revolution in France, but the hectic publishing trade which had flourished during the revolutionary years continued to prosper into the 1820s.

Some related changes were registered outside Europe, its settler colonies, and North America. Even before the great administrative reform of the Tanzimat or reorganization in the Ottoman Empire during the 1830s, new, educated state servants had emerged as a class apart from the old military orders and court officials. They established schools, libraries, and debating societies, which were ultimately as influential as anything the newly galvanized states had planned. In the commercial towns of the Greek, Jewish, and Syrian fringes of the Ottoman Empire, a quietly prosperous commercial middle class had grown wealthy from the expansion of Mediterranean trade. Beirut[59] and Alexandria[60] began to expand and buzz with new ideas, while the older inland centers stagnated. In European colonies, settler populations mingled uneasily with representatives of indigenous people who had made fortunes in alliance with the Europeans. Before 1820, a small but vigorous Indian and Southeast Asian middle class had emerged in port cities such as Calcutta, Bombay, Penang, and Batavia. They differed from the older commercial communities in these societies in that they read English and Dutch for political information, and not just for business. They organized in societies, clubs, and libraries to press for education and religious change. The literati and professional people who frequented these societies began to be aware of each other and to adapt ideas and techniques from each other. There began to emerge what theorists have called an "international civil society." This was constituted by a set of networks of information and political advocacy which, though less obvious than the rising national and imperial state, was no less important as a product of the age of Enlightenment and revolution. Here again, the Christian mission stations, which spread rapidly across the globe after 1800, provided important stimuli, both positive and negative, to these indigenous literati. Missionaries pioneered libraries, printing, polemics, and public debates. They began to investigate Asian classics and African legends. Local intellectuals adopted their methods, often for reasons of self-protection.

Western European and North American models were, then, important in this self-fashioning, but the imperative was wider changes in the organization of states and global commerce, which required public men and businessmen to behave in sober, rational ways in order to be allowed to participate. Participation was very unequal. In many respects, for instance, gender divisions were reinforced in the post-revolutionary cities. Whereas the formal rhetoric of the French Revolution had made women symbols but confined them to the domestic sphere after the model of the Roman senator Brutus's wife, Portia, the quiet revolution began to provide women with small openings through which to infiltrate civil society. Religion, education, and charity were the spheres in which they were most active, but this as yet was true only in the United States, the new British and European societies, and the European settlement colonies. Similarly, these new sober, polite societies were often more blindly racist than the old "mestizo societies" of aristocratic plantation owners and merchants, which were divided on the principles of Portuguese *casta*, Indian caste, or Chinese homeland association. In the new age, Europeans began to seclude themselves in leafy suburbs of the commercial cities. Chinese, Arabs, and Indians were excluded.

The age of revolutions had quite dramatically speeded up those two changes in human life which were discussed at the outset of this book: the growth of uniformity between societies and the growth of complexity within them. Forms of land and property rights, commercial activity, government, and even ideology looked increasingly similar over a large part of the globe. At the same time, European conquests had spread more complex, specialist knowledges to new parts of the world. By 1830, the works of the French and Scottish philosophers could be found in public libraries from Madras to Penang to Sydney, and in places where the concept of the public, the library, or even the book was entirely new.

That other feature of the long nineteenth century, the growth of European and American dominance over the world's economies and peoples, had also been significantly advanced. A large part of humanity had been converted into long-term losers in the scramble for resources and dignity. The polite, commercial societies of London, Boston, and the ports of Brittany flourished, in part because of the huge volume of cheap raw materials which slaves and dependent peasantries across the world produced to fulfill their labor or revenue dues in the wake of national independence or colonial conquest. Brazil's coffee industry greatly expanded production in the first decades after the world wars, on the backs of a growing number of slaves. Indian and Indonesian peasants grew cash crops, often at the expense of food crops, to service their new colonial masters.

The end of the war also released large numbers of white settlers into parts of the world where indigenous populations were even more vulnerable: southern Africa, the Pacific, and the American frontiers. Here they clashed with indigenous people, themselves on the move. Some of these settlers were political refugees. Some were economic migrants escaping the postwar downturn. Yet others were shipped off by complaisant governments, keen to thin out fractious working-class people and peasantries or rid themselves of petty criminals. In Australia, the European population had already risen to 30,000 by 1821. The settlers and their animals had begun to expel Aboriginal people from their lands, and massacres of those who resisted were already being reported.[61] The home societies of these settlers were also increasingly polarized. Even in the matter of industrial growth, the pendulum of judgment among economic historians has now swung back to the view that the growing industrial working class suffered a lower standard of living than earlier artisan communities.

PROSPECT

All these social and regional imbalances were to ensure that the age following the "restoration of order" in Europe and the wider world after the great wars was to be, at best, a period of political equipoise, at worst, a period of flux and hiatus. This will be discussed in the next chapter. The equation between control and revolt, prosperity and starvation, liberalism and repression, was everywhere finely balanced. The hyperactive post-revolutionary and imperial state discussed in this chapter deflated after 1815. Many of the trends established by industrious revolutions across the world were resumed. Early industrialism registered its effects. Yet no class or type of state power, whether democratic or neo-absolutist, decisively established itself within Europe or outside. Europe and North America, however, consolidated their domination of the world between 1815 and 1860.

PART II

THE MODERN WORLD IN GENESIS

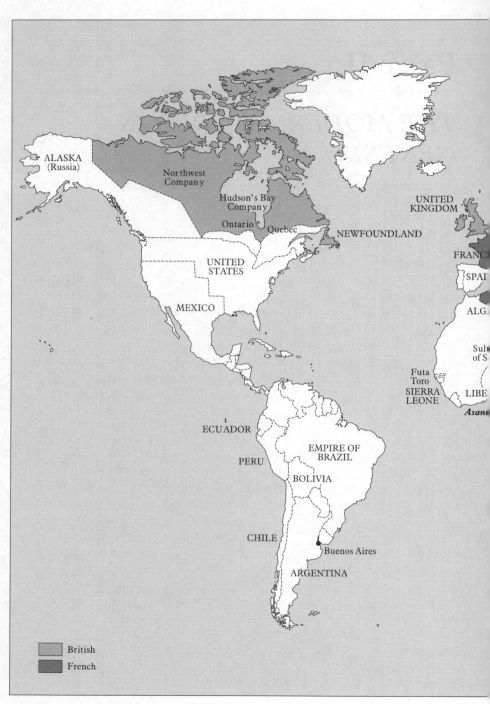

ALASKA
(Russia)

Northwest
Company

Hudson's Bay
Company

Ontario   Quebec

UNITED
KINGDOM

NEWFOUNDLAND

FRANC

UNITED
STATES

SPAI

ALG.

MEXICO

Futa
Toro
SIERRA
LEONE

Sul
of S

LIBE

Asan

ECUADOR

PERU

EMPIRE OF
BRAZIL

BOLIVIA

CHILE

Buenos Aires

ARGENTINA

British
French

MAP 4.1   Restored regimes, c.1830.

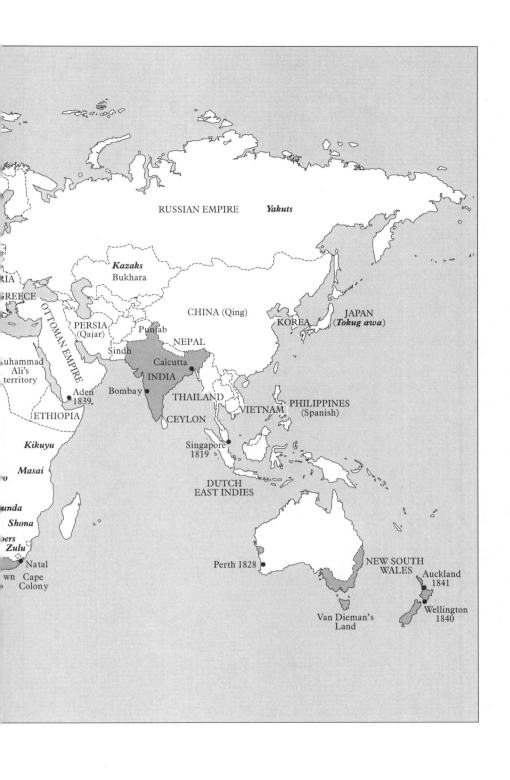

RUSSIAN EMPIRE   *Yakuts*

Kazaks
Bukhara

GREECE

IA

CHINA (Qing)   JAPAN
                                (Tokug awa)
PERSIA   KOREA
(Qajar)   Punjab
        NEPAL
    Sindh
        Calcutta
    INDIA
Bombay   PHILIPPINES
        THAILAND   (Spanish)
                VIETNAM
    CEYLON

OTTOMAN EMPIRE

uhammad
 Ali's
 territory
Aden
1839

ETHIOPIA

Kikuyu
                Singapore
Masai   1819

unda   DUTCH
Shona   EAST INDIES
ers
Zulu
Natal
wn Cape   Perth 1828
    Colony   NEW SOUTH
                                        WALES
                                            Auckland
                                            1841

                            Van Dieman's   Wellington
                                Land   1840

[4] *BETWEEN WORLD REVOLUTIONS, c.1815–1865*

THIS chapter examines the lineaments of the fragile "new world order" which was constructed as the defeated Napoleon was consigned to exile on the island of St Helena in 1815. I characterize this as a period of flux and hiatus, when new forms of state, economy, and ideology had announced themselves but had not yet been consolidated. A more modest form of the patriotic state had "got back on top" by 1820, but only just. It had barely vanquished the global ambitions of the revolutionary state and the popular explosions that accompanied its rise and demise. Old autocracies revamped themselves and drew into their ambit a small range of administrative experts and representatives of the "polite and commercial" people. Yet the problems of political representation and economic equity were unresolved. Over parts of Asia, Africa, and the Pacific region, Europeans had replaced indigenous rulers, but their rule was widely resented and still fragile. Its survival depended on the threat of force and the uneasy support of privileged fragments of restive societies. The chapter goes on to chart the new tensions in which the post-revolutionary settlement had foundered by the mid-nineteenth century. The great mid-century rebellions in China, South Asia, and Europe and the Civil War in North America were all global, as well as regional, shocks. Their consequences again intertwined across the world.

ASSESSING THE "WRECK OF NATIONS"

The wars and revolutions of 1780–1820 had exacted a high price in lives lost and economic disruption. Earlier conflicts had seen Europeans fighting on other continents. But these wars had been fought along the coasts, on the islands, and on the margins of settled agriculture. The consequences of the global crisis following the decline of the old Asian regimes and the American and French revolutions had penetrated deep inland in every continent. Cairo, Moscow, Delhi, Jogjakarta, and Paris, all great and famed political and commercial centers, had fallen to conquering armies. The British had burned Washington, the new American capital. According to the grim reckoning of Charles Tilly, deaths on the battlefield jumped tenfold between the European wars of the 1750s and those of the 1800s.[1]

The worldwide silver famine, which accompanied the struggles between Spanish forces and Creole rebels in Mexico, deepened the economic damage of war. The sudden shortage of cash after 1810 exposed growing economic tensions in foundering Eurasian and African polities, from eastern Europe to Java. China began to show signs of that long turbulence which was to mark its dismal nineteenth century of economic and political turmoil. In Europe itself, the lesions of war gave way to industrial and agrarian problems, as the slump in demand which inevitably follows peace set in. Unemployed soldiers demanding work battled with militias. Landlords who had done well from high grain prices during the wars were pitted against tenants who faced a new austerity or found old feudal disabilities reimposed on them. Industrial laborers, beginning to combine into trade unions to demand better wages and conditions of work, found themselves treated as criminal conspirators.

The economic dislocation felt across the globe in the years from 1800 to 1820 was surpassed only by the ideological and doctrinal shock which had been released by revolution and world war. Leaders of the new American Republic had deliberately broken with aristocratic decorum, one receiving foreign ambassadors in a dressing gown and carpet slippers. In a more sinister fashion, the bright dawn of the French Revolution had given way to the first systematic secular political purge carried out by a vaunted popular government. The murder of the French royal family and its aristocracy was played out across the whole continent in less bloodthirsty ways. The Pope was driven from Rome. The thousand-year-old republic of Venice disappeared, and its art treasures were looted. War had exposed the vulnerabilities of the Prussian, Austrian, and even Russian autocracies and aristocracies.

Then, revolutionary change was itself stopped dead in its tracks. Many groups and orders of people who had drawn hope from the first flush of revolution had been disappointed. Radicals viewed with horror the reimposition of dynastic police states after 1815. Irish Catholics felt betrayed that emancipation from religious disqualifications did not follow the union with Britain of 1801. The old Polish republic had been partitioned between Austria, Russia, and Prussia in 1795. Slaves who had briefly smelled freedom during the French Revolution contemplated a new age of bondage. Slave revolts erupted periodically in Barbados, Jamaica, South Carolina, and Brazil. In Spanish America, the vision of liberal constitutional government promoted by its liberator, Simon Bolivar, did not prevail. The great southern continent of liberty split into contending pseudo-nations. For two decades the developing commercial cities were at risk from fierce rural military bosses, the *caudillos*.[2] The revolution, too, had rapidly turned patriarchal, and the Napoleonic regime had discouraged the fuller entry of women into public life, an outcome which had briefly seemed possible in the aftermath of 1789.

Outside Europe and the Americas, it was not only ancient supremacies, but the self-confidence and autonomy of whole civilizations which seemed to be under threat. French infidels temporarily controlled the al-Azhar mosque in Cairo, the greatest teaching institution in the Muslim world. Within a few years, purist Muslim zealots sacked Mecca, Medina, and Karbala, Islam's holiest places. The British had seized the person of the Great Mughal and the tooth relic of the Buddha in Ceylon. The Dutch and the British had penetrated the royal enclosures of Java's palaces, the *kratons*. Early in the new century, too, peoples designated "savage tribes" by European theorists began to suffer. In the Pacific and the Americas, the culture and sacred places of indigenous peoples were soon under threat from logging, the extermination of animals by hunting, and the outward push of white settlers which built up powerfully as postwar distress in Europe flooded the outer world with new immigrants. The British and, temporarily, the French government had interdicted the slave trade. Yet slavery continued, and the trade simply transferred itself to different ports and to the shipping of Spain and Portugal. The commerce in people continued to distort African society, dissipating productive resources, occasioning inter-necine wars, and spreading slavery within the continent. In the Caribbean and the southern states of America, slavery also persisted, though widely denounced by reformers, both white and black, as a primal human evil.

Across the world, governments and ruling groups tried to respond to the consequences of this "wreck of nations" which had so profoundly upset the assumptions about deference and reason on which the old order had theoret-ically been based. Thinkers, from the French liberal conservative Alexis de Tocqueville[3] to Shah Abd al-Aziz, the leading theologian of Delhi,[4] sought to accommodate change while preserving what they could of cherished beliefs and practices. In China, He Changling attempted to summarize what was best in Qing statecraft, to repair the Grand Canal, and to rebuild the dynasty's legitimacy, aware that dangerous foreigners were drawing near.[5] During the early part of the nineteenth century power-holders and intellectuals sought to find ways – political, economic, and ideological – to constrain the forces of change which had been unleashed. To some extent they were successful. The period can best be seen as one of "unstable pluralism," when a small indus-trial economy and limited representative governments in western Europe flourished alongside a patchwork of dynastic states, shored-up imperial thrones, and dubiously legitimate European colonial provinces.

Yet the political artificers of the 1815 settlement of the European peace and their coevals in America, Africa, Asia, and the Pacific were only partly suc-cessful, and then only in the medium term, if we take into account the numerous coups and minor conflicts that followed. By the 1840s and 1850s, attempts to hold together a streamlined version of the old order of states had evidently failed. It had been ripped apart in 1848, the second great revolutionary year after 1789, across much of Europe and its colonies by a new radicalism of peasant and artisan. A series of savage wars between whites and non-whites erupted as Chinese, Indians, and native peoples in North America, Australasia, and southern Africa made their last stand against

European assaults on their religion and monarchies or fought the seizure of their lands. The regimes of the 1860s and 1870s were quite different from those of 1820. Even those, such as Bismarck's Germany, Russia, or China, which still seemed to bear the stamp of the old order, had been forced to concede more power to the bureaucrat, the bourgeois, and the idea of nationality. In Europe's colonies, political power had been grasped yet more firmly by expatriate Europeans. The illusion of shared sovereignty in which indigenous rulers cooperated with a limited European presence had been thrust aside.

BRITISH MARITIME SUPREMACY, WORLD TRADE, AND THE REVIVAL OF AGRICULTURE

When the statesmen who dominated the world at the end of the Napoleonic wars tried to secure greater international and domestic stability for their generation, they devised political systems to hold in check the political radicalism and cultural and class tensions which had increased during and in the aftermath of the global wars. The rulers badly needed a rapid expansion of trade and commerce to pull the international economy out of the postwar slump. This would restore their finances and secure complaisant supporters among businessmen and substantial farmers. Of course, prosperity did not automatically guarantee political quiescence, but hunger and deprivation certainly gave radicals justification for their cause. A number of political and technological developments helped the conservative statesmen in this, at least for a time. The first two sections of this chapter will examine the political, economic, and ideological sources of stability – and of instability – in the early-nineteenth-century world.

First of all, Britain had become the unchallenged sea power as a result of its defeat of the French, Spanish, and Dutch navies. This eliminated one of the great sources of international tension of the previous century, the conflict between armed European trading nations, which, in its turn, drew non-European peoples into warfare. Even though the land war of 1806–14 in the Iberian peninsula and across the globe had stretched British military resources to the limit, the country emerged at the peace of 1815 as the world's commercial arbiter. There were gaps in Britain's supremacy, of course. Russia emerged from the wars with a surprisingly large navy in the Baltic and the Black Sea, keeping the Ottomans and Britain in a state of suspense. In North American waters, the Monroe Doctrine, which theoretically interdicted European intervention in the Western Hemisphere, at least created a northern sphere of influence for the new United States. But the British still emerged dominant in South American and Pacific waters.[6]

After the Anglo-American war of 1812–14, relations between the two countries improved rapidly, based on a mutual interest in transatlantic trade, migration, and Protestant evangelicalism. Britain retained the whip hand in dealing with the new republics of South America. The restored French monarchy maintained some influence in the western Mediterranean and along the West African coast. Elsewhere, though, the Royal Navy and the British merchant marine, along with its East Indian surrogates and Arab or overseas Chinese clients, remained in firm control of the seas. New British strong points and staging posts in Cape Town (1806), Fernando Po on the African coast (1820s), Malta (1802), Aden (1839), Singapore (1819), through to the growing settlements of Australia and New Zealand, made it possible for Britain to project amphibious power across the world. Along these routes, naval forces suppressed independent port-kings who had taxed and controlled shipping in their maritime domains before 1815. The British now called them "pirates." The transmission of strategic and commercial information across the European world system seems to have improved in the early years of the century, even before the installation of the electric telegraph and the development of the steamship.[7] Private firms built up bodies of commercial data and posted agents in previously inaccessible port towns. Meanwhile, the spread of cheap marine insurance and attempts by the authorities to regulate shipboard conditions improved the transparency and the reliability of commerce. World trade boomed in the 1820s and again in the 1840s, though there was a significant hiatus in between.

For all their volatile swings, the recovering trades gave dynasts and imperial governors struggling with the aftermath of revolutionary change a fragile range of allies among merchants, canny landlords, and calculating peasant-farmers. Much of this burgeoning trade was directed to feeding and clothing the still-growing populations which had been so gravely exposed to the subsistence crises of the eighteenth century. European, American, and East Asian populations continued to expand rapidly during this period, even if those of the Middle East, Africa, and South Asia continued to be savaged by famine and disease. New cash-crop-exporting provinces began to form under the pattern of older commodity trades. Whereas woollens and linens had been earlier staples of local consumption and trade, "cotton was king" in the nineteenth century. Cotton farmers and slave plantations fed raw material to hundreds of thousands of older artisan weavers across the world, as well as to growing numbers of power looms.

Egypt provides a good example of how economic growth and medium-term political stability marched hand in hand. The province had long produced grain for the Ottoman Empire and the Mediterranean ports of southern Europe. After the French invasion of 1798–1800, the Ottoman sultan's deputy, Muhammad (Mehmet) Ali, an Albanian by origin, took power and eliminated the old landed ruling class.[8] He aimed to make the country a formidable military power by exporting cash crops and ploughing the proceeds into public works and a European-style army. By 1840, Egypt had become a key exporter of raw cotton to Britain and France. The Egyptian delta became a huge cotton field. Alexandria, since the fall of ancient Rome a quiet Mediterranean port, began to turn into one of the classic hybrid Eurasian port cities of the nineteenth century. Muhammad Ali's regime proved powerful enough to overawe his neighbors and suppress internal dissidence, even though his plans for expansion into Palestine were halted by Britain and France. Income from cotton had made this possible.

By 1850, again, a large trade in raw cotton was also moving out of ports of the west and southeast coasts of India.[9] Most of it was designed to supplement the shortfall in production in China, whose population was still surging forward. Some, however, was designed for the power looms of Britain and northwest Europe when demand was particularly high. Cotton and other cash crop exporters and producers in coastal India provided the new British imperial governments with a number of commercial and landlord supporters, or at least neutral parties, to set against the sullen and hostile denizens of the old Indian royal centers inland, which were now in sharp decline. Zoroastrian Parsi merchants in Bombay played an important part in cotton and opium exports from western India to China, Southeast Asia, and East Africa. They were also among the most anglicized and complaisant of the new Indian elites, demanding economic protectionism less urgently than their contemporaries in other Indian port cities.

In the New World, rapid expansion into sparsely occupied land helped the new American Republic to stabilize itself. There was continued political conflict over the form of the constitution between federalists and advocates of states' rights. But American ideological and political conflicts were not deepened by social conflicts over land and resources to the same extent as they were in the Old World. External trade helped, too. The southern states of the union did handsomely from the export of slave-produced raw cotton to the factories of Britain and northwestern Europe.[10] The southern slave plantations had formerly exported rice to the Caribbean plantations, and tobacco and indigo to Europe. But these commodities were available from other sources, and the South could not continue to expand exports. Cotton provided a much-needed new resource, which temporarily held at bay the South's economic and ideological crisis. For half a century it allowed its leaders to stand on an equal footing in federal politics with the leaders of the northern states, which were, by mid-century, beginning to industrialize. Cotton also helped to perpetuate the slave system, by providing an incentive for southern slave-owners to fund at least a minimum of social support for their work forces.

This happened on a smaller scale elsewhere on the American continent. Even in remote parts of Central and South America, cotton produced by the Amerindian peasantry for distant markets and occasionally, after 1840, for local cotton mills provided an important stabilizing resource for merchants, cities, and landowners in a period of constant political turmoil. The great success story here was Brazil, which emerged as one of the largest coffee exporters in the world. This allowed it to finance its debts more effectively than the formerly Spanish American states and to avoid some of the political turmoil which affected them well into the century.[11]

Growing commodity trades bailed out the farmers and merchants of other vulnerable producing regions. The profits of these trades also helped sickly European economies. In the early part of the century, for instance, Holland

ILLUSTRATION 4.1   World trade expands: Buenos Aires. Engraving, 1840.

was virtually saved from extinction by the wealth that it drew from taxing in kind Javanese peasants and making them produce tobacco, sugar, and rice for the world market under the so-called Cultivation System.[12] Piedmont and Tuscany, by contrast, were dependent on supplying agricultural produce to the volatile markets of France and Britain.[13] In turn, the Bushatli magnates of Albania exported raw cotton to Italy in the late eighteenth and early nineteenth century. The Cape of Good Hope, since 1806 a fragile and troubled British colony, produced wine and hides for the European market, at least until French exports soared back in the 1820s.[14] Even the new garrison and settlement colonies of Australia were transformed by the quite sudden discovery, in the late 1830s, that intensive wool production would give them a *raison d'être* in the new world of free trades, beyond that of being a large penal institution.[15] British settlements in West Africa began slowly to develop their exports of staple commodities such as palm oil. There was even a short moment when the enterprising black merchants of Lagos, or Accra, seemed to stand on an equal footing with European settlers in the racial dispensation of the British Empire.[16] This so-called legitimate trade also provided a key resource for interior kingdoms such as Asante, which found the going harder after the British officially banned the slave trade on the coast after 1807.

The technical innovations of the period helped landlords and entrepreneurs in town and country. The mechanization of harvesting and threshing was well established across western Europe and North America by the 1820s. Later, by the 1840s, the railways had begun to transform access to regional markets for those farmers and landlords who had the spare cash to take advantage of them. The prairies of North America supplied its east coast cities along the railways, and their produce was exported in volume to Europe.[17] The canal and road systems of western Europe, already improved during the Napoleonic wars for reasons of security, continued to expand for commercial reasons. On the great rivers of eastern Europe, the Middle East, and India, the coming of the steamboat after 1830 gave a great boost to the grain trade. Cotton, tobacco, and rice production famously expanded with the coming of the Mississippi steamboats.

The legal framework of agriculture was also being modified across the globe. In many areas, this brought into being for the first time true markets in land. Governments in post-revolutionary western Europe abolished many of the old feudal dues, rights, and church tithes which had been such irritants to peasants in the previous century. These legislative moves gave greater stability to farming communities. In the British colonies of Canada, southern Africa, and Australia, legal entitlements gave ordinary settler-farmers control over land, where previously big owners leasing out to "squatters" seemed likely to become the norm. Native peoples, of course, were generally excluded from these provisions, or at best were established on dwindling reserve lands, as they were in the United States. In Cape Colony and Natal, British legislation strengthened the power of landholders and allowed them to encroach on the lands of African peasants and pastoralists. In Ceylon, stronger provision for landowners helped the emergence of a new plantation system in the central highlands.

Land-based European empires achieved temporary stability, too. In Austria and some other states of the German-speaking world, the effects of the moderate land reforms of the late eighteenth century began to pacify rural society, once the economy began to pull out of the postwar slump.[18] In general, this aided landowners, who were compensated for the loss of peasant dues, rather than the peasants themselves. Still, some of the worst causes of agrarian conflict were alleviated in the short term. Even in regions such as east Prussia, where tenurial reform was slow in coming, changes in communications and the growth of larger urban markets made it worthwhile for landlords and some smaller farmers to invest in agriculture and improve productivity. To the south, Venice and the Veneto had been prized from the grip of Lombardy, which had controlled it under Napoleon. This rich wine, olive oil, and maize-growing region now reluctantly paid its dues to the masters in Vienna. Yet the Habsburgs' demands for cash and conscripts were less pressing than those of the First Empire, while some of the more effective features of French-style administration, such as the gendarmerie, had been maintained by the Austrian rulers.[19]

EMIGRATION: A SAFETY VALVE?

A corollary to the export of commodities was the export of peoples.[20] In the first half of the nineteenth century, African slavery persisted and even expanded, as chapter 11 will show. The British abolition of the slave trade in 1807 was hardly a revolution. It merely drove slave trading into other nations' ships, particularly those of the Spanish and the Portuguese. Slavery as an institution was not even abolished in the British Empire until 1834, and it lingered on in other guises until the mid-1840s. In the USA, Cuba, and Brazil, it had several more decades to run. What was new about the export of people in the first half of the century, however, was a rise to even higher levels of the numbers of "free" migrants to other parts of the world, especially from Britain, Ireland, and northwestern Europe. The trade depression of the postwar years and stories of fortunes made in the Americas, South Africa, and, later, Australia and New Zealand, attracted hundreds of thousands in a self-conscious age of improvement. European statesmen hoped this would rid them of troublemakers and radicals. They were probably right to some degree.

The European exodus to North America and other areas of "white" settlement was accompanied by an equally large, but less well-known, exodus of Asians across the seas in conditions which ranged across the whole spectrum from near-slavery to free migration.[21] This took some of the pressure off the land and kept Asian coastal areas relatively buoyant. Chinese continued to spread across Southeast Asia as laborers and merchants. Later, Chinese and Japanese migrated across the Pacific to North and South America. The Indian historian Rajat K. Ray has argued that the new burgeoning of the old bazaar economy throughout Asia[22] was a key feature of the emergence of the modern economy, as important in its own way as industrialization. Indian indentured laborers went to Ceylon, Mauritius, the Caribbean, and later to Fiji and Natal, to produce tea, coffee, and sugar. Because they owed the cost of their fares and subsistence to their employers, their export formed a virtual "new system of slavery."[23] Migration along land frontiers was also picking up speed, especially after 1840. Russian settlers pushed further into the steppe lands and Siberia, as the country's population growth speeded up in the first decades of the century. French settlers moved into North Africa after 1830, and Dutch settlers on the Cape moved inland from the irksome restrictions of the British administration of Cape Colony and its attitudes of cultural disdain for them.[24]

These accelerating movements of people helped to provide the underpinnings of the new global division of labor in which Europe supplied manufactured and semi-manufactured goods, and the rest of the world produced

Table 4.1 Regional origin of immigrants to the United States, 1820–1930

Continent of origin	Number emigrating in 1820–1930
From Europe	32,121,210
From Asia	1,058,331
From the Americas	4,241,429
Total	37,420,970

Source: Based on Chris Cook and David Waller, *Longman Handbook of Modern American History 1763–1996* (London, 1997).

primary commodities. Whole ranges of commercial towns and producing regions sprang into being, some penetrating into the interior of India and North and South America. The mass movement of peoples also relieved the pressure of population in northwestern Europe and China and, conservatives believed, the danger of popular radicalism in the Old World.

Yet the lineaments of stability were matched by the visions of conflict which emigration carried with it. The British and Spanish home authorities already knew that vigorous overseas Creole populations would throw off allegiance to the mother country and eventually compete economically with their lands of origin. British and French provincial governors and military commanders knew, too, that the hunger of settler populations in terrains as varied as Algeria (French after 1830), southern Africa, Canada, and Australia, could lead to endemic warfare with the people of "first nations" who were desperately protecting their patrimony from the invaders. The scene was set for a series of wars between settlers and indigenous peoples which exploded in the 1850s and 1860s.[25] The balance between social and economic security and the forces of conflict and economic collapse remained delicately balanced everywhere.

THE LOSERS IN THE "NEW WORLD ORDER," 1815–1865

This section moves on to discuss areas of decline and conflict which threatened the fragile stability of the postwar settlements and anticipated the wider conflicts after 1848. In the first place, some of the old producing regions which had been world centers of production in the eighteenth century went into decline. They did not benefit from the new international division of labor. The Caribbean sugar islands, for instance, began a steady collapse as slave revolts and competition from other world producers hit them in the 1820s and 1830s. Indian textile exports slumped in the 1820s, even before manufactured products from Britain flooded in with the railways and the steamship. British expatriates no longer used the textile trade as a way of remitting their dubious profits to Europe. The Southeast Asian spice trades languished. Yet the problems of these victims of early globalization did not spill over into other regions as they might have done in the eighteenth century before the British rose to maritime dominance.

In many parts of the world, too, ordinary peasant communities felt these improvements only very late and very partially, if at all. Rural economies were vulnerable to cycles of bad seasons. There had been a rash of these natural disasters across the globe in the 1780s, adding to political turmoil in both Europe and Asia. The years 1815–18 had seen widespread misery in Europe, as poor harvests coincided with the slump in demand at the end of the war. The 1830s and 1840s, again, seem to have had more than their fair share of harvest failures and famines across Eurasia. Periodic droughts and floods were compounded by disease. During the years 1847 and 1848 a disease in continental Europe, Scotland, and Ireland caused the failure of the potato crop. In Ireland, which was dependent on the potato, more than a million people died.[26] The plight of the Irish rural economy, however, was a major example of a wider problem. Revived population growth, especially in the large Asian economies, squeezed the margins for poor farmers, who had to be content with smaller and smaller plots of land. Meanwhile, the relative decline of older artisan industries throughout the world, in the face of British and later continental European industrialization, seems to have had the effect of forcing more people on to the land as dependants.

For the early nineteenth century was not the ideal world of the Scottish philosopher and economist Adam Smith, who hoped that a virtuous global division of labor would signal an inexorable increase in human virtue. Severe conflicts persisted within the international trading system. These fed into the international crises of the 1840s and 1850s which will be discussed in the second half of the chapter. In the first place, this "integration" of world trade, as the economists call it, was still in its infancy. Economic information, though certainly more reliable than 50 years earlier, remained imperfect. The electric telegraph was only beginning to stabilize prices by the early 1850s, and speedier communication would anyway lead to bouts of "irrational exuberance" and panics among investors. Most of the key export commodities were agricultural ones, still subject to the vagaries of the seasons, peasant production, and local political conditions. Huge bottlenecks could emerge and then collapse, so that no one could be quite sure of future profits, or even survival. Peasant-producers might make a killing one year and fall deeply into debt the next. Some of the largest-volume trades, such as those in the blue dye indigo and in tobacco, served to remit home the fortunes of soldiers or the ill-gotten earnings of colonial governments within the British, French, and Dutch empires. This meant that these trades were never subject to the usual laws of supply and demand. Demand of this sort could suddenly switch from one commodity to another. And since production had been stimulated artificially, peasants might suddenly find themselves without a market for their crops, or artisans for their products. Thus, even where standards of living improved, inequity between different groups of people increased.

In general, it was the European merchants, shippers, and insurers who made the real money. The only indigenous people who usually came out of this well were moneylenders or big merchants such as the Parsis of Bombay or the Greeks, the Maltese, and Syrian Christians of Alexandria, Beirut, and Istanbul, the metropolitan Spaniards, the Portuguese, and the British of Rio or Valparaiso. Trades went through hectic cycles of profitability and decline. The whole economy suffered a severe depression in the late 1820s, when overproduction of indigo and cotton in Asia and North Africa combined with a commercial slowdown in Europe. The same thing happened with more serious consequences in the mid-1840s. Cotton was an especially volatile commodity well before the stoppage of American production during the Civil War distorted world trade in this commodity. Consumption and production of raw materials across the world were balanced only imperfectly.

The conflicts surrounding these early-nineteenth-century trades were not simply about profit and loss. They also concerned politics and ideology. Eighteenth-century wars abroad had turned around the issue of "mercantilism." Theorists and politicians of the ancien régime had thought that the world's wealth was a finite amount, and mainly denominated in bullion. If someone got more of the cake, someone else would get less. Governments, therefore, fiercely supported their national companies and trades in an attempt to establish monopolies. In the new century, however, the British and Americans in the southern states, in particular, came to believe in the virtues of free trade and the evils of monopoly. This was not just an economic theory, as it had been in the works of the Scottish economist Adam Smith or his French equivalent François Quesnay. It became an article of faith to the extent that some statesmen and theorists believed that the laws of the free market were virtually the cornerstones of God's plan for mankind. Regimes which maintained monopolies in either internal or external trade were increasingly regarded as positively wicked, not simply as economically inefficient. A fierce battle was fought in 1845–6 in Britain over the archaic Corn Laws. These restrictive measures had aided British landowners who produced food grains by taxing foreign imports. The legislation derived from the days of the Napoleonic wars, when Britain feared being unable to feed its own population and wished to boost local production. To the free-traders of the 1830s and 1840s it seemed an anachronism. The abolition of the Corn Laws split Britain's governing Conservative Party and ushered in the beginnings of popular economic politics in the guise of the agitation of anti-Corn Law leagues.[27] From now on, Britain would seek to service its growing and now rapidly industrializing population with foodstuffs and basic raw materials gathered from all over the world.

The national wealth of Britain came to depend more and more on the sale of manufactured products and the acquisition of raw materials and food from abroad. Consequently, the desire to gain access to large markets in Asia, Africa, and Latin America without paying high tariffs became a key aspect of policy. British statesmen in general and Lord Palmerston, British foreign secretary and prime minister, in particular, wished devoutly to open up world trade and believed it right to do so by force of arms if necessary. As this blunt policy of forcing open markets became more insistent, so too did the risk of conflict with regimes and business interests which saw no gain for themselves in freeing trade. Tensions rose within Europe and outside. Some newly enfranchised elites in Europe and Latin America followed free trade blindly, sometimes to their own disadvantage. Elsewhere, there was resistance. In Germany, Friedrich List, realizing that the British were becoming addicted to free trade because it was in their interest as the dominant industrial power, wrote in favor of a system of "national political economy."[28] This model urged less favored producers to keep tariff barriers high, in order to allow nascent industry to get off the ground free from damaging external competition. As copies and translations of List's ideas spread, political leaders, from Hungary[29] to Ireland and India, began to see merit in his prescription as their indigenous production was battered by western European imports.

Wars arose over access to markets. Ronald Robinson and John Gallagher argued in the 1950s that the economic hegemony which Britain sought to impose by forcing other regimes to submit to free trade was a kind of "informal empire." In this type of imperialism, the British did not control territory as such, but their military clout and political influence curtailed the independence of these regimes to such an extent that it is reasonable to talk of empire.[30] During the 1820s and 1830s, for instance, British governments were in constant conflict with the authorities in some independent states of Latin America which did not sign up to free trade, about the tariffs and taxes which British merchants were forced to pay to import their goods. In 1840, Palmerston sent a fleet into the Bay of Naples to force the Bourbon Neapolitan government to bring down tariffs. The trade depression and unemployment caused by the resulting influx of British goods did much to bring about the 1848 revolution in the kingdom.[31] The Middle East provides other good examples of the "empire of free trade" in action. The powers bludgeoned the Ottomans into reducing important tariffs wherever they could. This was one reason why they supported the independence of Greece from Istanbul. Once the British and French had forced the Ottomans to reduce their tariffs in 1838, the attempts of the sultans and the rulers of Egypt to build up small industries to compete with the West were doomed to failure.[32]

The most striking example of conflict between the self-interested moralizing of the British about free trade and the concerns of non-European governments is to be found in the case of China and the Opium War of 1839–42. Since the 1820s, the Chinese government had worried about the outflow of silver from the country. The silver was going to pay for the growing consumption of opium brought to China from the subcontinent by the English East India Company. Opium was also undermining the effectiveness of the Chinese army, and its use was spreading to the peasantry. Matters came to crisis point after 1834. In that year, free-traders managed to abolish the East India Company's monopoly of the opium trade from India to China. The result was that British and American free merchants who took over the trade from the Company pumped an even greater volume of opium into the country. A fierce internal debate took place between Chinese officials who wanted to legalize the trade and conservative ones who sought to reestablish the control of the regime and ban it altogether. As contraband opium piled up in the port of Canton, the imperial court sent a magistrate to destroy the drug. This attack on British property drew an armed response from the British government.

The British went to war with the Chinese and hastened the decline of its fragile dynasty because they wanted to keep Indian opium flowing into China. The revenues of the government of India, and so of the British government itself, were at risk. Opium duty accounted for roughly 20 percent of total Indian revenues. Chinese goods sold on the international market guaranteed that Britain could buy raw materials such as American raw cotton. In danger, too, were the livelihoods of the many European and American traders who had come into the China trade when it was freed in 1834. A second clash about "opening China to trade" – that is, selling Indian opium and other commodities to a growing Chinese market – came in 1856–60. This was the so-called Arrow War, named after the British ship *Arrow*, which was the supposed cause of war.[33] On this occasion, British troops burned the summer palace of the Chinese emperor, an almost unparalleled example of imperial vandalism. Here again, the British used the cry of "free trade" and international law to justify a policy of economic penetration in the interests of an underlying monopoly.

If the conduct of international commerce in the nineteenth century avoided the great inter-European wars of the eighteenth, it nevertheless saw the widespread economic subordination of peoples outside the core of north-western European development. Often this was simply a matter of force. Europeans were now too well armed to allow themselves to be frustrated by indigenous governments, as the Mughals had frustrated the British, and the Beys of Algiers the French, a century earlier. Sometimes it was because Indian, Chinese, or Arab merchants could not gain access to the information, mercantile techniques, capital, or insurance which the great European and American merchants and shipowners could now deploy. Ironically, once the dominant British began to legislate to improve shipboard safety and conditions after 1815, this made it more difficult for ill-equipped and poorly capitalized indigenous merchants to compete. This mercantile subordination helped bring about the decline of indigenous artisan industries as surely as did the slow process of mechanization in Europe and America. European merchants now used primary cash crop exports to remit fortunes to Europe or fill their hulls for return voyages. They no longer patronized the South and East Asian or Middle Eastern artisan products which had been so popular in eighteenth-century Europe. Indigenous merchants had neither the range nor the techniques to export on their own account. They were also increasingly put at a competitive disadvantage as more and more regions began to produce the precious products of yesteryear: tea, opium, spices, coffee, tobacco, and sugar. With the gathering pace of industrialization in Europe, the "terms of trade" turned decisively against areas outside the economic core.

This, then, was the critical period, when industrial production was repatriated to Europe and North America. Already in the eighteenth century, European and North American naval power had allowed the merchants of these regions to capture a disproportionate percentage of the value added to world trade by industrious revolutions. In the early nineteenth century, these disparities in power became wider, as European military power became unassailable and industrialization began gradually to gather pace. In the longer term, these developments reinforced the great disparity in income per head at the international level between what we would now call the rich "north" and the poor "south."

PROBLEMS OF HYBRID LEGITIMACY: WHOSE STATE WAS IT?

This section turns from the economic conditions for the fragile political stability of the restoration regimes to the related issue of their legitimacy and ideology. It was not enough for rulers to find ways of banishing hunger and assuring to at least some of their subjects a degree of prosperity. In view of the violent debates about the nature of good government during the revolutionary years and the persistence of radical challenges to their authority, they needed even more to be seen to act with the authority of both God and man.

The reemerging state systems of 1815 managed to neutralize their most radical ideological opponents across the world. The balance was hard to maintain, and it was widely overturned after 1848. In the medium term, though, monarchy and aristocracy were shorn of their worst abuses and shored up with stronger cliques of lawyers and career bureaucrats. People remained godly, and kings were still widely thought to derive their powers from God. Fear of continuing anarchy and, as the last section argued, the patchy growth of prosperity also gave the forces of order a boost.

Ironically, it was Napoleon himself who had begun to address problems of post-revolutionary stability and legitimacy, both in France and across his Grand Empire. To cement his rise to power, he had vigorously repressed the riotous revolutionary crowd in Paris and other great cities. On the other hand, he accepted and consolidated the new class of landlords which had been created by the seizure of church and aristocratic land by the revolutionaries. Napoleon's Concordat with the papacy ensured that the Church also accepted the finality of the loss of its property, and this greatly simplified the problems of the returning Bourbon kings after 1815.[34] Napoleon reorganized the French judicial system through the celebrated Code Napoleon and perfected the form of centralized government through prefectures. These units remained the steel framework of metropolitan France and its empire in the nineteenth century. Even where aristocratic power-holders returned after 1815, as in central Italy, the Rhineland, eastern Europe, and Egypt, the lineaments of the state were sharper and more "rational" than they had been in the eighteenth century. At the same time, Napoleon had implicitly conceded a role both to the Church and to the dynastic principle. Between 1806 and 1809 he desperately tried to marry into the Austrian royal house, and he introduced members of his own family into conquered territories as kings, princesses, and princes. Republicanism was already severely compromised by 1815, and the Bourbons slotted back into the system with only minimal purges and social conflict.

Napoleon's most supple enemy, Great Britain, also sought to head off the radical challenge by reinventing its monarchy and purging the most egregious political abuses. Linda Colley has traced the way in which a new cult of royalty was established around the unpropitious person of the mentally disturbed

King George III. George IV, *bon viveur* and womanizer, a scarcely more likely proponent of the dignity of monarchy, tried to create a more glorious and sparkling court worthy of his continental coevals. This, too, foundered amongst rumors of immorality and the celebrated divorce of his wife, Queen Caroline. Yet, even before the 1832 reform of Parliament and extension of the franchise to the middle class of the major cities and some yeoman-farmers, reformers had done something to make the British polity more acceptable to its fractious inhabitants.[35] Arguably, the concession of parliamentary reform, the end to slavery, and Catholic emancipation between 1829 and 1835 saved Britain and its empire from more dangerous turbulence during the 1840s. British "reform" during this period, however, was lodged much more in the activities of voluntary associations and individual aristocratic activists than in the doings of the state. The latter, by contrast, were much more a feature of Germany, and, in particular, Prussia.[36]

The union with England snuffed out well-known corruption of the kingdom of Ireland, though this was a palliative for the Catholic Irish only in the short run. Humanitarian reform had pruned away some of the barbarism of the legal system, while imperial government was strengthened. Some of the worst excesses of the slave plantation system were removed by the abolition of the British slave trade in 1807, and the government pruned the East India Company's privileges in 1813. None of this silenced radical or even Whig reformers, but it did give the old regime a new lease of life and placated the rising evangelical middle classes well before the country was revivified by the large-scale new wealth of the industrial revolution.

In their vigorous attempts to establish political equipoise, the men of Vienna and the veterans of Waterloo who ran the new British and French imperial provinces had several key advantages, beside the purely economic. First, memories of revolutionary upheaval meant that conservative regimes could usually count on the support of their middle-class and urban citizens to put down anarchists, proto-socialists, and secessionists. Despite their ultra-loyalist protestations, most of the power-brokers of the post-war world displayed a canny pliability, born of fear of disorder. Where conservative regimes lost legitimacy, as did the unreformed parliament of the Duke of Wellington in Britain in the late 1820s, the Bourbon regime in Spain in 1820,[37] and ultimately France in 1830, they were replaced with slightly less conservative ones, which paid lip service to representative government. In the Austrian Empire, representative assemblies (the diets of Hungary and Transylvania) brought in some weak reforms after 1825.[38] In Piedmont, the dynasty was ultimately hurried into piecemeal reform, such as the new law code of 1837, by a series of failed coups masterminded by the hyperactive revolutionary Giuseppe Mazzini. Autocracy unwillingly acknowledged liberalism. An unsigned proclamation, which appeared in Paris in the summer of 1830, nicely illustrated the compromise. It stated that "The Duc D'Orléans is a prince devoted to the cause of the revolution... The Duc D'Orléans is a citizen King. The Duc D'Orléans has declared himself; he accepts the charter as we have always wanted it. It is from the French people that he will hold his Crown."[39]

Where nationalist movements became irresistible, as in Ireland and Greece, concessions were made. The powers recognized the independence of the latter in the course of the 1820s, while Catholic emancipation in 1830 temporarily quieted Irish demands. The revolutionary tradition was domesticated in France, where the new Orleanist monarchy partly accepted the Napoleonic tradition and recognized popular sovereignty. In Austria, Italy, and Spain, an alliance of churchmen, magnates, and bureaucrats held nationalist and republican forces at bay for another decade or so.

In Spain, the Catholic northern peasantry rebelled against the liberals in Madrid in defense of what they took to be the principle of proper royal succession. This, the so-called Carlist war, represented the largest counter-revolutionary movement in nineteenth-century Europe and resulted in the deaths of more than 3 percent of the total population. A liberal commentator wrote:

> Many things contributed to the insurrection of the Navarese. A superstitious religious spirit is a particular influence in Navarra. Its inhabitants, especially in the mountains, still preserve, together with their language, a primitive simplicity which cannot be paralleled in the rest of the peninsula. They are so blindly credulous and subject to the will of their priests that they neither see nor can see any other guide to their judgements.[40]

Elsewhere, the forces of order remained strong. During the early nineteenth century, Russia remained a huge reservoir of conservatism perched on the frontiers of Europe. Napoleon's invasion had given rise to a stronger sense of nationhood in urban Russia, even if, for the peasantry, patriotic sentiment remained centered on the tsar and the Orthodox Church. Population growth and exploitation of the eastern frontier lands had improved the empire's relative economic clout. A growing bureaucracy, European in taste, began to knit together the provinces dominated by landowners and military settlements. Yet society was still too hierarchical and rural to provide much comfort to the liberals and radicals in such cities as Moscow, St Petersburg, Riga, and Warsaw. The state was in a dilemma. Alexander I and Nicholas I might, temporarily, concede some constitutional advances to the Poles. But they could not really do the same for the Russians, since this would merely entrench the power of the serf-holding nobles. Autocracy was repaired and strengthened, but it was not strong enough to move against entrenched local interests until the 1860s. The weight of this revived conservatism could be enlisted to check liberalism and anti-Russian nationalism in Poland, where a major rising was suppressed in 1831, and in eastern Europe. It intimidated Germans and Hungarians in Austria. It was eventually brought in as a military counterweight to European revolution in 1848–51.[41]

Outside Europe, too, some of the causes of the most radical attacks on the traditional order which had boiled over during the revolutionary crises were removed or circumvented. In Latin America, the new rulers faced difficulties in legitimating their rule and suppressing the Amerindian and poor Creole revolts which had accompanied independence. In the first years, they often somewhat bizarrely claimed descent from the ancient Aztec and Inca monarchies which had preceded the Spanish Crown. Later, after the 1830s, they sought to make Bolivar and other leaders of the liberator's generation into icons of republican virtue, rather as the French gradually recovered Napoleon and his family. In the Ottoman Empire, autocracy was revamped, culminating in the reorganization (Tanzimat) decree of 1839 which gave civil bureaucracy a greater role in the management of the state and appears to have helped give the eastern parts of the Empire a functioning government for the first time.[42] Across the empire, the powerful notables who had asserted their autonomy in the eighteenth century were brought to heel. The Ottoman viceroys had moved to suppress the purist Arabian Wahhabi movement and pen back tribal Muslim millenarian rebellions into the Sudan. These had been a threat not only to the state, but to the religious hierarchy itself.

Where small numbers of Europeans ruled over large non-European populations, the problems of legitimacy were even greater. Colonial governors sometimes tried to shore up existing royal courts. This was a dangerous tactic, because they often became centers of dissidence. In India, under governor-general Wellesley and his immediate successors, the British administration temporarily paid lip service to Mughal authority. They also reconstructed some princely regimes, maintaining the old order, if only in appearance. In Mysore, for instance, the East India Company's wealthiest princely milch cow, the supposedly "ancient Hindoo constitution" was reinstated, but the political reorganization accomplished by the eighteenth-century rulers was not tampered with.[43] At the same time, colonial governors worked with magnates to put down millenarian movements and peasant risings. Another tactic was to try to draw indigenous elites into dialogue with European values and culture. Even before the great rebellion of 1857, so-called modernist thinkers arguing for accommodation between Western knowledge and Islamic faith had emerged in several Islamic societies in South and Southeast Asia and in the Middle East. Moreover, the countervailing, purist Islamic movements rarely demanded holy war against infidels. In 1804, it is true, Shah Abd al-Aziz, the leading proponent of revived Sunni Islam in the subcontinent, declared India a "land of war" and no longer an "abode of Islam." He also implicitly gave his followers leave to join British service, since none of the conditions for a successful holy war could be met in India itself. In fact, the tendency of most Muslim clergy throughout the world was pacific. When, in the 1820s, Sayyid Ahmed Barelvi preached *jihad* in South Asia, moreover, it was the Sikhs of the Punjab and not the Company's government which came under attack. The Indian clerics preached moral reform from within. They were concerned to ameliorate the social and intellectual effects of the world crisis before seeking the political kingdom.

Almost the opposite problem faced the remaining independent regimes in China, Japan, Vietnam, and the Ottoman Empire. Any deviation from political or religious orthodoxy might encourage the dangerous foreigners and their agents. Yet some acknowledgment of change was necessary. In the medium term, again, a fragile stability held. In China, conservative Confucian scholars and local gentry urged loyalty to the empire as the first flush of millenarian

Buddhist movements subsided after 1803. There are few recent historical studies of the period 1800–50. It seems wrong, however, to read back the crisis of the Taiping Rebellion of the 1850s into the early part of the century. The regime seems to have recovered quite well for a generation after the White Lotus Rebellion. It consolidated effectively both politically and culturally in central Asia and Tibet, earning the admiration of Brian Hodgson, the British Empire's man in Nepal. It continued to receive the support of the vast majority of the scholar-gentry. The economy, while not strong, was not yet in disarray. Irreversible ecological problems, with their implications for the Mandate of Heaven, began to appear only in the second half of the century. In the 1820s, the governor-general of Canton established a "Sea of Learning Hall," which was designed to centralize practical knowledge and statecraft in the interest of the dynasty. He also attempted to deal with opium smugglers in a subtle but vigorous manner.[44] The Qing monarchs were, in fact, far from paralyzed rabbits in the headlights of Western expansionism. The assault on the legitimacy of the Manchu Mandate of Heaven only really got into full swing after 1842, with the increasingly devastating defeats of the regime by the Western powers and, later, Japan.

THE STATE GAINS STRENGTH, BUT NOT ENOUGH

Revamped eighteenth-century regimes therefore retained some degree of legitimacy and room for maneuver. Yet force remained the ultimate arbiter of state power. In military terms, the restored monarchies and revived empires were generally able to exert somewhat greater control over their inner frontiers than their predecessors before the world wars. The experience of deploying millions of men under arms against foreign enemies aided them in suppressing domestic dissidents and extending imperial control. Cavalry soldiers and riflemen were in good supply after 1815. They were used to suppress British working-class activists in the infamous Peterloo massacre of 1819 (see illustration 4.2). French troops were employed to overthrow the dangerously radical Genoese and Spanish republics, which raised alarming memories of 1789 among the conservative statesmen. The forces raised to fight Napoleon in Austria, Prussia, and the Russian Empire were similarly used to suppress urban radicals who still followed revolutionary ideas. They were also used to pin down the turbulent frontiers of empire. Emperor Alexander I scattered colonies of retired soldiers on land grants throughout the Ukraine and into central Asia. As agricultural colonies, these were far from successful, but they did help to tame the turbulent agrarian frontiers.[45]

The military detritus of world war also helped to spread European empires overseas. When the French government decided to annex Algeria in 1830, as a distraction from domestic conflict, it was conquered using bored and discontented officers who remembered the glories of Napoleon's campaigns. The British Empire, from India, through the Cape to Canada, was ruled by the men who fought against Napoleon at Waterloo. Irish soldiers, many of

ILLUSTRATION 4.2   Between repression and reform: *The Massacre of Peterloo! Or a Specimen of English Liberty, August 16th 1819*. Etching by J. L. Marks.

them rebels during the rebellion of 1798, unwittingly stiffened the sinews of Britain's world power. The tactics of fast light cavalry columns used on the Cape of Good Hope against African resisters were modeled on the commandos of the Spanish peninsular war. Irregular military forces of Khoi and mixed-race people patrolled the frontiers against intrusion by Xhosa to the north. Even in North America, the alarms of the Anglo-American and Indian wars gave the military state a much sharper edge than it had commonly had over much of the English-speaking world. Western and northern Canada were conquered by the military and paramilitary mounted police, as much as by pioneer settlement. In the United States, the army emerged as a more powerful and more bureaucratic institution from the wars, which had so often taken the form of campaigns of protection against Indian raiding parties. The combination of military and logistical control with new ways of deploying force gave national and colonial governments much greater dominion over the countryside and its resources than had been the case in the previous century.

Lawyers and bureaucrats were also the longer-term beneficiaries of the era of world wars. They thrived and prospered under all forms of government because all governments needed to increase taxation. The German principalities were the paradigm here. On the face of it, the old system of states, culled of its excesses and reduced in number, was reestablished after 1815 and survived until 1848. In fact, the restored princes were now much more dependent on university-educated lawyers and pen-pushers. The greater activity of the state in taxing and regulating was matched by an increasing penchant to theorize about it and about the progress it could foster. We think of Prince Metternich and the duc de Talleyrand, the aristocratic survivors of the old regime as the typical figures of the age, but Hegel, great academic theorist of the state and its ideas of improvement, was no less representative. France was rather different. Here, one of the great causes of the revolution had been the legal jungle of the old regime with its different courts and practitioners. In the medium term the number of legal cases, separate jurisdictions, and lawyers tumbled. From 1830 onwards, though, rapid commercialization created new opportunities, and the tribe came back with a vengeance. By 1876, there were 30,341 members of the legal profession in France.[46]

Lawyers prospered mightily in the British Empire, too. In England their numbers and wealth greatly increased between 1800 and 1850, way ahead of population growth, as a vigorous land market was given greater impetus by the expansion of the canal system and railways.[47] Lawyers seized their chance in the colonies, too. By mid-century, India and most dependent territories had flourishing local legal professions made up of expatriates and a few trained local people. These lawyers enriched themselves by battening on land litigation, and especially on buoyant sales of land rights, which were being expropriated from indigenous people. As the Crown's justice began to cut into the criminal jurisdictions of local populations, this side of legal work also flourished. Much the same conditions prevailed in the United States, where, from an early period, battles about constitutional matters and social and economic disputes were settled by lawyers as often as by politicians.

One rather sinister aspect of the deployment of state power was the rise of the police and, in particular, the secret police. There had been secret government agents and forms of mounted police under the old regimes. But the idea of a paramilitary bureaucratic agent of surveillance was new in many societies before the beginning of the nineteenth century. In the late eighteenth century, the "enlightened despot" Joseph II of Austria was ahead of his time in this, as in many other respects. He instituted a network of political policemen to keep an eye on his internal enemies. Announcing the arrival of a new form of secret police, deployed by governments increasingly worried by revolutionary subversion, was Joseph Fouché (1763–1820), minister of police and government spymaster under Napoleon, who became a byword for "dirty tricks" across Europe. The political police sniffed out not just crime, but sedition and heterodox ideas.

It was, however, the periods of reaction after the 1830 and 1848 revolutions which saw the most significant upward step in power and effectiveness of both civilian and secret police. As Napoleon III imposed his empire in France in the early 1850s, *procureurs généraux*, police bureaucrats, made no fewer than 26,000 political arrests. Many of the victims were sent into exile in Algeria.[48]

Meanwhile, the French revolutionary gendarmerie provided a model for everyday policing, crowd control, and information gathering. Many German states, Italy, and Russia had such bodies before 1830, while the Irish, Sindh, and Hong Kong constabularies represented the spread of the form to the British Empire. Even in mainland Britain and America, whose people associated the idea of central police with "continental" despotism, police gradually replaced informal agents for debt and crime control, though they remained under the control of local bodies.

All this shows the governments of the early nineteenth century attempting to enforce control over justice and violence within their own territories and to map and control dissidence. To do this, they entered into alliance with the powerful remnants of restored magnate authority, but, to one degree or another, they also needed to accommodate the new professions and commercial classes. What stands out clearly, though, is that in most cases these aims were only partially realized. Quite apart from the growing rumble of dissidence and revolt which we will chart in the remainder of this chapter, large areas of social life continued to remain outside the control of the central authorities. Factions of militarists and landowners inherited the revolutionary regimes of Mexico and South America. Slave-owners in the American South and bodies of landlords and middlemen over much of Eurasia continued to exercise power and patronage, which was anathema to the theorists and administrators of the regimes. The continuing incompleteness and contingency of the power of the authorities was reflected in the upsurge of "information panics" about the wicked and murky doings of particular groups of ill-understood subjects. In the growing British cities, the elites were frightened of garroters who strangled unwary travelers, and of Irish tinkers and "boweries" of criminals who were supposed to steal from the respectable. France and other Roman Catholic countries feared the sinister power of freemasons or, if they were of the revolutionary tradition, Jesuits and other supposed reactionaries. German authorities worried about the persistence of revolutionary clubs in which men did military drill, while the Italians fretted about radical Carbonari secret societies. In the European colonial empires, an assortment of Islamic fanatics, Thugs (stranglers, again), Chinese triads, or Malays "run amok" stoked the fears of fragile colonial regimes relying on indigenous informants and rudimentary police systems. Even in the United States, the fear was rife that great corporations, predatory immigrants, or slave revolts might threaten the constitution.

One reason for these periodic panics was the continued physical inability of authorities to control enough of society's resources or its educated personnel to effect closer control. Central government and its financial clout actually retreated in Britain between 1820 and 1870, as the propertied classes fought off the high taxation which they had suffered during the period of world wars. In the United States, power remained divided, split between the states and the federal government, and deeply suspect to the inheritors of the revolution. But, as the last two chapters have suggested, in many parts of the world the continuing relative lack of competence of the state in resources was mirrored by its ideological fragility. Since 1789 in Europe, and the concurrent weakening or destruction of many centers of authority in the non-European world during the wars, there had been a pervasive vacuum of power, a widespread crisis of legitimacy. Popular sovereignty had been mooted, but the old ruling groups had reinvented themselves both in their own countries and through international agreements, of which the Holy Alliance against revolution in Europe was the most obvious example. The papacy, the Church's orders, and orthodox kingship had all been challenged, but, through interest, fear, or faith, people, especially in the rural areas, continued to give them credence.

In the new Latin American republics, wordy constitutions, echoing the language of the French republic, were issued. Yet a generation of military leaders rose to power and fell again, dependent on the unstable support of cliques of landowners. Antonio López de Santa Anna (1794–1876), eleven times president of Mexico epitomizes this political roller coaster. Many times called to the balustrade of the presidential palace and then expelled through the back door, he lost large chunks of Mexico, including Texas, to the United States during his rule. With no clear source of political authority at hand, he could offer only a piece of himself. Santa Anna, "having lost a leg in a battle against French invaders of the country in 1835, had it disinterred from its first resting place in 1842 to be ceremonially reburied, with funeral discourse in Mexico City."[49] A few years later, when Santa Anna was out of power once again, an enraged mob invaded the church and destroyed the tomb in which his leg was buried.

This age of flux and hiatus thus drew to an end in a series of gathering conflicts with their epicenters respectively in Europe, South and East Asia and North America. The degree of turbulence was impressive. Its cumulative character has been forgotten in those European histories which still tend to see the nineteenth century as an age of relative stability between the cataclysms of 1789 and 1917. The year 1848 in Europe witnessed an upsurge in revolutionary activity and rebellion which stands comparison with the events of the French and Russian revolutions, even if it was ultimately rolled back. The ideological consequences of 1848 in the early enunciation of a class-based revolutionary socialism were momentous, even if the ensuing wars were less destructive. Yet, at a global level, the loss of life and property was massive. The Taiping Rebellion in China and the Indian Rebellion, which broke out in the following decade, were among the most destructive civil wars in history. The American Civil War, one decade later again, saw the destruction of a long-lived culture and economic system and sent economic shock waves across the globe, affecting most of the cash-crop-producing regions discussed at the start of this chapter. Its ideological repercussions were yet greater, even if only subtly registered.

The final sections of the chapter will examine each of these concatenations of turbulence separately, and then try to identify some common features and specify the differences between these mid-nineteenth-century climacterics. In the longer term, they were to bring about further advances for the nation-state, Western colonialism, and international civil society.

WARS OF LEGITIMACY IN ASIA:
A SUMMARY ACCOUNT

As the previous section has suggested, in Asia, Africa, and the Middle East, the forces of dissolution and reconstruction were very evenly balanced in the early nineteenth century. In the 1820s and 1830s the Ottoman Empire was convulsed by a series of internal coups which reordered its state institutions and abolished the military and bureaucratic systems which had served it for 300 years. In 1827–31, it suffered a humiliating defeat at the hands of the European powers during the Greek wars of independence. Some Muslims glimpsed a wider crisis for their coreligionists. In 1825–30, the Muslim kingdoms of central Java fought and lost a final war of liberation against the Dutch colonial government. In Persia in 1848, the Babi millenarian sect staged an armed uprising against persecution and hailed the coming of the Islamic "messiah" (the Mahdi). Thereafter, however, the pace of revolt increased exponentially across Asia. In 1851, there began in south China the millenarian Taiping Rebellion against the Qing dynasty. Over the next 15 years this revolt cost the lives of an estimated 20 million people, destroyed the finances of the Chinese Empire, and fatally weakened it in the face of British aggression during the Second Opium War of 1856–60. All these events had profound political consequences. They also signalled collective moral crises that affected people whose beliefs and cherished icons had been uprooted by the gathering pace of global change.

The Taiping Rebellion began in late 1851,[50] when a religious mystic declared a new religion which mixed Christian themes with Buddhist millenarian aspirations to create a new order on earth. The Taipings, or followers of the "Heavenly Way," attracted support from substantial numbers of peasants, immigrants, and dissident gentry in the Canton province. In its early days they redistributed land, emancipated women, and promulgated themes of community which some later commentators interpreted as a kind of indigenous socialism. Soon the rebel armies spread over south China, capturing the city of Nanjing. The movement now seemed much more like those many revolutions in Chinese history which succeeded in establishing a new dynasty. Hong Xuiquan, its leader, even proclaimed that he was restoring the pre-Qing Ming dynasty. The rebellion failed, however, because provincial Chinese governors who had access to more advanced weapons and local gentry, fearing loss of their status, combined to field pro-Beijing armies. The Taipings were not completely crushed until about 1862, and even then local revolts and Muslim rebellions continued to sputter on in south and southwest China into the 1870s.

The Taiping Rebellion, like all great rural resistance movements, had many causes, and some of these will be discussed in greater detail in chapter 11. Population pressure and the outflow of silver to finance the opium habit had exposed peasants to inflation. Peasants had to pay their revenues in silver, but only got copper cash in return for their own produce. Some disgruntled gentry

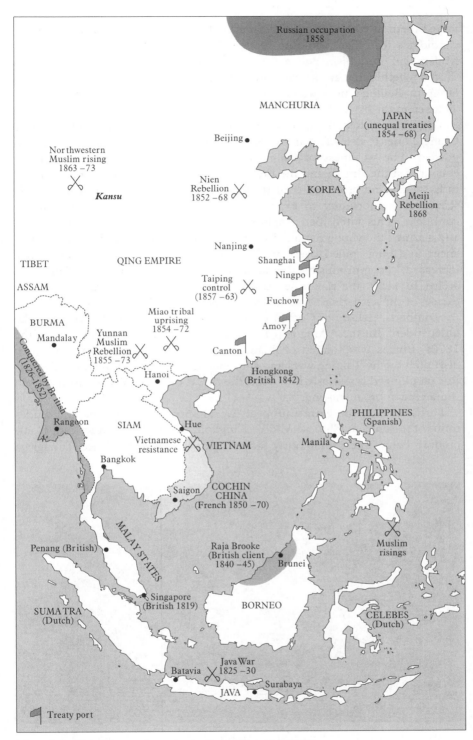

Map labels:

Russian occupation 1858

MANCHURIA

JAPAN (unequal treaties 1854–68)

Beijing

Northwestern Muslim rising 1863–73

Kansu

Nien Rebellion 1852–68

KOREA

Meiji Rebellion 1868

Nanjing

Shanghai

TIBET

QING EMPIRE

Ningpo

ASSAM

Taiping control (1857–63)

Fuchow

Miao tribal uprising 1854–72

Amoy

BURMA

Mandalay

Yunnan Muslim Rebellion 1855–73

Canton

Hongkong (British 1842)

PHILIPPINES (Spanish)

Conquered by British (1826–1852)

Hanoi

Rangoon

SIAM

Hue

Vietnamese resistance

VIETNAM

Manila

Bangkok

Saigon

COCHIN CHINA (French 1850–70)

MALAY STATES

Raja Brooke (British client 1840–45)

Brunei

Muslim risings

Penang (British)

Singapore (British 1819)

BORNEO

CELEBES (Dutch)

SUMATRA (Dutch)

Batavia

Java War 1825–30

Surabaya

JAVA

Treaty port

MAP 4.2   Rebellion and empire in East Asia, c.1825–70.

joined them in revolt, as population growth increased the number of eligible candidates for office, while no more offices were available to satisfy them. Millenarian Buddhism and a Chinese version of Christian millenarianism flowed together to make a heady brew in the southern provinces of the empire, far from Beijing's now waning authority. All these tensions exploded into violence in the early 1850s.

The Taiping Rebellion, however, was an Asian cataclysm, not merely a Chinese one. It also affected the longer-term relations between the European powers. The weakness of China at the height of the Taiping movement encouraged the British and the French to renew their struggle for supremacy in East Asia and projected their rivalries across the world. Soon after, Russia seized the opportunity to expand her territories in the northwest of the continent. This intensified Anglo-Russian competition throughout Eurasia and alarmed the young nationalists of Japan. The religious and social disturbances in China spilled over into Vietnam. Here, too, French interference increased,[51] compromising the stability of Vietnam's neo-Confucian monarchy. In 1859, the newly self-confident French Second Empire used the excuse of the gathering persecution of Vietnamese Christians to intervene in the southern territory of Cochin China. Further to the west, the rump of the independent Burmese kingdom had survived on British sufferance. By the 1870s, Burma was starved of finance, because its Chinese trade had been disrupted by the Taiping wars and subsequent revolts in southwest China. As Burma plunged hopelessly into debt, the threat of a final British assault from India grew more menacing.[52]

Turbulence in the extra-European world spread well beyond the feudatories of the ancient Chinese Middle Kingdom. In 1854, the American, Commodore Perry, unceremoniously kicked open the doors of closed Tokugawa

ILLUSTRATION 4.3   Imperial authority resists: Nanjing arsenal. Photo by John Thomson, c.1868.

Japan and persuaded its young leaders of the moral and financial bankruptcy of their regime.

The Taiping episode overlapped with that other, related Asian crisis which divided the nineteenth century. The Indian Rebellion of 1857–9 began as a mutiny of the sepoys or indigenous soldiers of the East India Company's Bengal Army in May 1857. They were protesting over pay, conditions, and loss of status. The collapse of British power allowed a whole variety of peasant movements, risings by dispossessed rulers, and revolts by urban artisans to take fire. The now powerless Mughal emperor, confined by the British to Delhi, became the main symbol and center of revolt. Other dispossessed heirs of eighteenth-century regional rulers also took to the field against the reconquering British armies. The British won, partly because the rebellion was confined to north-central India, and partly because they could throw into the struggle armies from other Indian provinces and a force which was simultaneously in transit by sea to fight the Taipings on behalf of the Chinese emperor.

ECONOMIC AND IDEOLOGICAL ROOTS OF THE ASIAN REVOLUTIONS

All these movements had quite profound, and profoundly different, internal social and ideological roots. Yet they also had common features. Three broad sets of conditions seem to have held true. First, these outbreaks were reactions to the worldwide expansion of Western colonialism, along with the new forms of government, commerce, and economic activity which it brought. Since the earlier turbulence which announced the world crisis of 1780–1820, these pressures had grown infinitely stronger as western Europe lengthened its economic and military lead. Secondly, internal problems of dealing with ethnic and religious communities in these great polities were deepened by the expansion of new ideologies, especially Christianity and its indigenous forms. Finally, population growth and local economic imbalances, only very indirectly related to the world system, played their part.

The explosive combination of these conditions was already signaled before the climacteric of the 1850s and 1860s. Russia, itself a semi-Westernizing power, had pressed harder on the Ottoman Empire and Qajar Iran since the Napoleonic world wars. A struggle ensued to redefine the internal structures of government and provide these states with new bureaucracies, more transparent taxation systems, modern armies, and military academies with which to face down the Western threat. But this internal renovation raised issues of legitimate rule. Were the sultan and the Persian padishah still Muslim kings, and if not, who would protect the faith? Once modernization was in the air, many claimants to modernity came forward. The Persian Babi revolt of 1848 and the subsequent emergence of the Bahai faith, for instance, occurred in an area heavily subject to Russian and British pressure. Some of its strongest

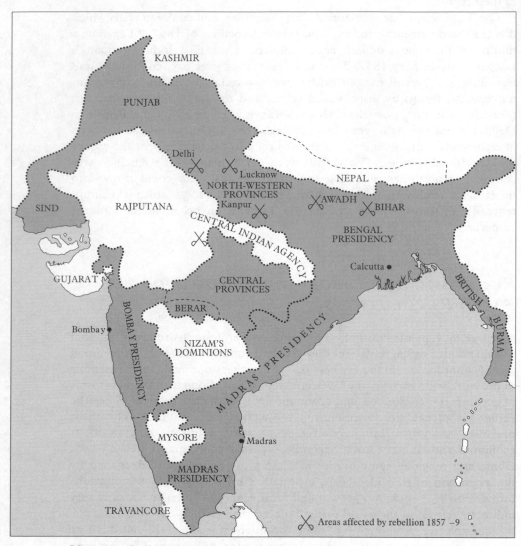

KASHMIR

PUNJAB

Delhi

Lucknow

NORTH-WESTERN
PROVINCES

Kanpur

NEPAL

AWADH

BIHAR

SIND

RAJPUTANA

CENTRAL INDIAN AGENCY

BENGAL
PRESIDENCY

Calcutta

GUJARAT

CENTRAL
PROVINCES

BERAR

BOMBAY PRESIDENCY

Bombay

NIZAM'S
DOMINIONS

MADRAS PRESIDENCY

BRITISH BURMA

MYSORE

Madras

MADRAS
PRESIDENCY

TRAVANCORE

Areas affected by rebellion 1857 –9

MAP 4.3   India and the Mutiny-Rebellion, 1857–9.

supporters were among clerks and workers for the new telegraph lines who had glimpsed an alien modernity and wished to transform it into their own. In the Ottoman Empire, the reorganization of the state raised issues about the relationship between Christians and Muslims. Revolts ravaged the Balkan provinces of the Ottoman Empire in the 1860s. The Christian population was well aware of the growing power of Austria and Russia to the north and west.

ILLUSTRATION 4.4 Imperial authority resists: British defence of Arrah House, Bihar, against the sepoy mutineers. Lithograph after William Taylor.

In the same way, the Taiping Rebellion registered many echoes of the advance of the West. Its millenarian leader, Hong Xuiquan, proclaimed himself to be the younger brother of Jesus Christ. He stirred biblical quotations which he had learned during his missionary education into the movement's millenarian ideology. According to his followers, the founder of the sect died, rose from the dead, and "exhorted everyone to worship God and cultivate virtue. Those who worship God must not worship other deities. Those who did worship other deities would be committing a crime."[53] One leader of the movement argued for a modernizing program which included the building of railways. Equally, many of the followers of the Taipings had been damaged by the advent of the West. They were soldiers abandoned by the regime following its defeat in the First Opium War of 1839–42. Others were tea porters and tradesmen thrown out of work by the depression which hit the Canton province after the fighting. The Taiping forces also included pirates and bandits, driven inland now that European navies patrolled the China seas and the coastal cities. Above all, the rulership of the Mandate of Heaven was cast into doubt when British diplomats trampled Chinese dignity and their gunboats blew apart the light Chinese junks.

India, of course, had felt yet more directly than China the pressure of European government and economic penetration. As elsewhere in the world, the radical changes of the Napoleonic age had given way to a more cautious period in which the old Indian supremacies had been partly preserved alongside the new state apparatus introduced by the East India Company.[54] It proved cheaper to rule India through Indians. Many Company officials believed that the preservation of Indian kings, landholders, and priestly supremacies would help buy the acquiescence of Indian people. After 1848, however, a new generation of British rulers became impatient with the petty politics and pertinacious financial independence of the Indian states. They scorned the "self-sufficiency" of the post-Mughal courts and became suspicious of the guild-like British Bengal Army. Distantly, these Anglo-Indian attitudes reflected the high tide of early Victorian self-confidence in industrializing Britain. A new wave of acquisition of territory and tinkering with the army, combined with palpable scorn for Indian manners and royalty, threw together a combustible pile of grievances. This was set ablaze in the army mutinies and rebellions against the British in 1857–9. These conflicts at the political level combined with a wide range of local tensions arising from the emergence of new-style landlordism, conflicts over forested and nomadic land, and inequalities in the levy of revenue. In the north Indian towns, impoverished artisan communities, suffering from the competition of British imported manufactures, played a role. Here the rebellion sometimes took on a popular Islamic form.

As in the case of Persia, the Chinese Empire, and Java,[55] religious differences and patriotic self-assertion played an important part in all the major rebellions we are considering. They may not have been proto-nationalist, as some Indian historians have asserted. But they did reflect commitment to community and homeland. The 1857 rebellion was neither "Hindu" nor "Muslim," yet it reflected a fairly universal hostility to Christians, whether Indian, Indo-Portuguese, or European, as privileged factions set outside the local ethical community and ones favored by alien authority. In the Chinese case, millenarian Buddhism and evangelical Christianity merged to give strength to the Taiping call to oust the Manchu foreigner and bring a new reign of harmony and justice on earth.

For their part, the Manchu rulers and their Han Chinese-led gentry armies proclaimed their hostility to the foreign Christian religion, so that patriotic movements in China, through to the Boxer Rebellion of 1900 and beyond, were infused with anti-Christian themes. In Vietnam, the emperors of the early nineteenth century regarded their growing Christian populations as sinks of sedition. Even in Indonesia, where the Dutch rulers had displayed little interest in missionary activity, the revolts of the 1830s in Java and later movements in the island of Sumatra spoke in an Islamic messianic language of the "return of the Just King" and restoration of a godly society. The reaction of old religious orders and of local communities to religious plurality was not simply a question of the Asian response to the challenge of Europe, however. It was part of a much broader apprehension of the consequences of the global reach of Christianity and its new mores. Most agents of Christianity were indigenous people, not European missionaries and administrators. So, while it provides some common points, the role of European influence in the origin of these Asian wars of legitimacy should not be exaggerated.

The Asian crises of the mid-century, finally, revealed the buildup of agrarian and social tensions. These conflicts reflected deeper strains on patterns of economic entitlement, not simply the effects of Western expansion. The long-term growth of the Chinese population left it at 450 million by mid-century. Much of this growth had taken place before 1700, as a result of peace and better nutrition. It put pressure on agricultural resources, especially in south China, where minor climatic setbacks or internal disturbances could create great hardship. Internal migration to the more stable agricultural areas of the south reduced living standards there and increased conflict between resident population and the immigrants. Here was an important cause of the Taiping Rebellion and the consequent decline of the Chinese central power. Population pressure was not unimportant in India either. The old dominant peasantries of north India were affected by a long-term decline in their income from land as the number of rentiers swelled. Their fragile status was challenged by internal social changes as much as by the doings of British revenue officers.

Even in the case of these deeper social and economic strains, however, inter-regional comparisons and contrasts remain useful. The rapid expansion of population and commerce from the later seventeenth century onward had been a global phenomenon, and an interlinked one. Europe's advantages in confronting this common pressure on resources, alluded to in chapter 2, had grown steadily greater by the first half of the nineteenth century. For instance, Europe's growing populations had been absorbed by emigration to the Americas or Australasia and the effect of increasingly rapid urbanization. This widely avoided a dangerous decline in living standards. Many northern European farmers had been responsive to the industrious revolutions which reoriented the consumption and labor of households. These adaptations were made only patchily in Asia, Africa, and South America, and were often aborted by European intrusion. Earlier historians have spent much labor trying to find out where to place the blame. Depending on their political predilections, they indicted colonial rule or indigenous lethargy. What can be said, though, is that the difference between Europe and Asia has been exaggerated. The rather tentative transformations in Europe reflected the coming together of a number of different conditions which raised living standards, rather than inexorable European economic progress. As the conflicts which culminated in the 1848 European rebellions showed, that continent and its colonies of settlement were certainly not immune to the strains of economic and political adaptation. Yet the fact that European powers and the United States now possessed a huge network of global commerce, widely rooted in direct colonial control, certainly helped them negotiate this adaptation.

THE YEARS OF HUNGER AND REBELLION IN EUROPE, 1848–1851

In accounting for the mid-century turbulence in Asia, we have emphasized several key dimensions: the introduction of new and alien forms of government, the reaction of local communities to the uprooting of old rights, a closing of ranks against religious change, and reactions to uneven demographic and economic development. Up to about 1980, historians saw the revolutions of 1848 in Europe as "wars of progress," not as apparently backward-looking movements of this sort. They were understood, following the classic formulations of Karl Marx himself, as class conflicts reflecting the self-assertion of the new industrial proletariat and of vanguards of radical intellectuals. These upsurges looked forward to the revolution of 1917, not backward to the religious riots and peasant jacqueries of the European past. The changes in recent historiography have here, as in so many other cases, diminished the difference between Europe, Asia, and Africa, even if they have not ultimately erased it. For one thing, historians' emphasis has now moved to the countryside. The uprisings of radical intelligentsias, artisans, and young nationalists in the towns which occurred in the spring of 1848 threatened governments and even overthrew several of them. It was of great symbolic importance that they occurred in Paris, Berlin, Munich, Vienna, Budapest, and Venice, great centers of the old order. Urban revolts, however, could be put down by predominantly conservative armed forces supported by more prosperous citizens for whom the folk memories of 1789 were still fresh. Yet these urban revolts were only part of the story.[56]

What was more dangerous for the authorities was that the revolutionary outbreaks occurred at the same time as widespread movements of rural protest. Determined agrarian unrest was more difficult to suppress, because many regimes still had only a tenuous hold in the countryside. Movements of rural protest and no-rent campaigns endangered those old-style landlords who had survived, particularly in eastern and southern Europe, and continued to levy their seigneurial dues. They also threatened new, commercially adept rural magnates who formed the basis of support for the neo-conservative regimes which had come into being since 1815. One potent source of rural unrest was dwindling access to forested lands in which communities had found fuel, pasture, and other goods. Peasants in central Europe and Italy invaded forested lands which had once been held in common but which had gradually passed into the sole ownership of large landlords. They attacked forest guards and estate employees. Newly planted commercial tree varieties which provided no food for animals were cut down, and village livestock was let to roam freely in the pastures. Elsewhere, peasants reoccupied common lands that had been divided, uprooting fences and boundary markers. There were numerous assaults on moneylenders and rich peasants who had lent money and were attempting to regain their loans through the courts. The links between these rural movements and the democratic demonstrations in the towns were rather distant. Country people often invoked the language of liberty and marched under the banner of the tricolors of the aspiring nation-states proclaimed in city squares. But the urban dwellers were inclined to denounce the peasant rebels as anarchists who had misunderstood the language of liberty. It was fear of the untamed countryside, as much as disorder in the towns, which ultimately inclined many liberals to side with the forces of law and order after 1849.

The putsches of liberals and nationalists in the major towns were accompanied by revolts among less well-off townspeople. One thing these movements do not seem to have witnessed very widely was any flexing of muscles by the new industrial working class, as the myth of socialist history once had it. Industrialization was a very limited phenomenon in 1848, outside Belgium, the Ruhr, and parts of the Rhineland, where the revolutions were not especially successful. Elsewhere, factory workers seem to have been no more, and often less, inclined to strike or indulge in acts of industrial sabotage. Instead, the center of revolt lay among the old artisan population and the employees of the putting-out system in which big manufacturers allotted contracts to smaller, family-based units. The sources of grievance here were almost all connected with the loosening control of artisan families and their organizations over the labor market. Attacks on machinery were only one part of this. Workmen joined together in hitherto illegal combinations or trade unions, attempted to intimidate owners, and attacked the police who protected them. In one south German town, thousands of weavers attacked a merchant who had been short changing them for years over the amount of cloth they were producing. As in the case of the peasant communes, the impetus seems to have come from a sense that new work practices and impersonal market forces were violating what E. P. Thompson, the English radical historian, called "the moral economy of the crowd." If, as the governor-general of India had put it a few years earlier, the "bones of Indian weavers were bleaching on the plains of Hindustan," the lifeblood was simultaneously bleeding out of the master weavers of central and eastern Europe.

These outbreaks also reflected conflicts over culture and religion within Europe. One aspect recently noted by historians was widespread anti-Semitism in both the urban and the rural movements of 1848. As the most visible debt collectors, local merchants, and wholesalers in many areas, Jews were often scapegoats for the whole petty capitalist economy which was creeping forward in town and country. Jews attracted violence just as did the *bania* moneylenders of India in 1857 and the moneylending gentry in Taiping China. These tensions, though, went beyond the purely economic.[57] New representative assemblies in the towns began to erase differences between classes of citizens. Some of them emancipated Jews and disestablished dominant religious groups. These measures opened up a large range of hidden fears of scheming "others," which had been fed by the moral and political panics of the previous 30 years.[58] In some parts of southern Europe there were scattered Protestant–Catholic brawls. Conflicts between guest communities and locals of all sorts were widespread throughout eastern Europe, and this was another point of comparison with the contemporary eruptions in Asia. The European legitimacy crisis, however, had both a secular and an ecclesiastical face. In Italy, hatred of Austrian rule turned popular mobs to anticlericalism. For it was the Church that had offered the strongest support to the Austrian rulers, because it feared indigenous liberals and radicals. After the restoration of 1815, the Church had cleverly filled the vacuum of legitimacy for a time. But Pope Gregory XVI (1831–46) had been a profound reactionary who aborted all change in his own territories and worked assiduously to export

THE MODERN WORLD IN GENESIS

conservative policies elsewhere. His successor, the "liberal Pope" Pius IX, shook the Church twice, first by his championing of Italian unity and later by his rapid retreat from liberalism.[59]

It would be wrong, of course, to insist on only the popular, communitarian, and religious aspects of the 1848 revolutions, without taking account of political and nationalist demands. These were at the forefront of the intentions of the educated participants themselves and were the main staple of historians' discussions until the last 30 years. The leaders of 1848 demanded suffrage reform and self-determination. The language of the rights of man and the invocation of the revolutionary tradition distinguished these revolts from the more inchoate sense of patriotism displayed in the near-contemporary Asian events. Bengal certainly had its young urban radicals – "Young Bengal." By the 1850s, Chinese who spoke European languages in cities such as Penang and Hong Kong were also beginning to speak the language of Western radicalism and ponder their own modernity. Yet the connections of such men to the contemporary inland rebellions in north India or Guangxi province, where the Taiping Rebellion began, remained much more distant than the connections between the urban and rural rebels in Europe.

In Europe, by contrast, urban discontent had already turned into urban, nationalist revolt. Forcible peasant occupations of land and attacks on cloth merchants aside, the revolutions in Italy were revolutions of patriotic lawyers, merchants, and liberal landowners against the domination of Austria, which had been reimposed following the defeat of Napoleon. Carlo Alberto, king of Piedmont, demanded an end to foreign rule on Italian soil, and other Italian towns and provinces followed his lead. In Germany, the new liberal ministry in Berlin supported a movement for unity and for the end of Danish rule in the border areas. In Vienna, a modestly liberal regime replaced the long-lived rule of Prince Metternich and cautiously put its weight behind a pan-German crusade to unite all German-speaking lands. In Poland and Hungary, both ruled by foreign regimes, local patriotism also sprang to life. Abetted by small but vigorous political nations, drawn together by a burgeoning press, a society of taverns and coffee houses, and an associational culture of "improving" societies and scientific bodies, liberal nationalism enjoyed a brief heyday between 1848 and 1851.

One feature of this nationalist upsurge, more pronounced than in the 1790s, even, was its international character. German, Italian, and particularly Polish radicals were found on each other's barricades, and some fled eventually to the Americas. For instance, Ludwig Mieroslawski (1814–78) began his career in the Young Poland movement and the Carbonari. In 1846–50 he was found leading radical movements in Berlin, Paris, Hungary, Sicily, Posen, Baden, and finally supporting the Paris Commune of 1871, all to little effect.[60]

The radical movements of 1848–51 were soundly defeated. Monarchical authority returned, though further modified by its compromises with the interests of coalitions of property-owners and commercial magnates. This must be laid at the door of the soldiers loyal to the Russian tsar, the Austrian Empire, and Louis-Napoleon Bonaparte. The line of military authority held in all these regimes in a way it did not in 1789 or in 1917.[61] The Hungarian revolutionaries led by Lajos Kossuth had defeated the Austrian imperial armies time and time again, but they could not contain a million Russian troops as well. In part, reaction was effective because people still remembered and feared the consequences of 1789, as mobs went out on town streets again. In part, it was because radical ideas were still held in check by awe of the revived monarchies and ideas of religious duty. The revolutionaries were themselves split by class, ideology, and ethnicity. Some of the aims of the activists of 1848 were accomplished 20 years or more later as a result of the unification of Italy and Germany and the creation of the Third Republic in France. Yet the democratic ideals and themes of social redistribution which the 1848 rebels enunciated were, by this time, much feebler.

One country that did not follow the pattern of 1848 was Britain. Though even here, one must make a partial exception of Ireland. Rural Britain had been transformed into an economy of tenant-farmers and laborers rather earlier than continental Europe. The revolt against mechanization in the 1810s had really been the last fling of the reaction by embattled local farming communities. Outside Ireland, the age of flux gave way more quickly to the age of improvement. The rapid growth of industrial employment in the towns after 1820 and foreign emigration had absorbed some of the social discontent in the countryside which built up so strongly across the European continent. Administrations of liberal landlords had moved to concede a degree of representative government in 1832, and a vigorous associational and religious culture had blunted the development of radical politics. The Chartist movement of 1846–7, when urban radicals and tradespeople demanded universal male suffrage, was Britain's first mass political movement. The ideologies which animated it, however, represented not so much an early form of class-based socialism as a harking back to eighteenth-century demands for an end to corruption and taxation. Radical Chartists promoted a vision of virtuous communities of pious freeholders. It challenged government, but not personal property and wealth when appropriately used.

Yet, as Miles Taylor argued, the wider British Empire did witness a degree of social turbulence in the 1840s. This modifies the argument for England being the exception and provokes some comparisons with conditions in continental Europe. Social and racial tension in the Caribbean mounted again throughout the 1840s and early 1850s, especially in Jamaica.[62] Emancipated slaves proved to be a labor force which was not easily cowed by the planter class. Ideas of rights to land and political participation spread rapidly amongst them. The economic position of the islands was meanwhile deteriorating. British free-traders had secured the equalization of duties on sugar across the empire. This and rising labor costs, compared with those of remaining slave systems, such as those in Cuba and Brazil, damaged competitiveness. The European economic crises of the 1840s also reduced demand.

Spurred on by poor economic conditions and resentment against archaic colonial government, local patriots were in action in Canada, Australia, and southern Africa in the same decade. The ethnic divisions between British and Dutch settlers in South Africa and between British and French settlers in Canada gave these movements a dangerous edge from the point of view of the authorities. These were all societies of striving individualists, so demands for self-determination among contemporary European radicals found attentive audiences. Ireland, which was part both of the British Empire and of domestic British society, also showed all the widespread symptoms of rural and urban unrest combined with the flowering of a religious-based nationalism in the years immediately before the European revolutions. There was even a brief upsurge of agrarian violence in 1848 itself. Only the devastating famine, which carried off a million people, preempted a widespread political movement in that year. Ireland followed the dismal Indian pattern of the 1830s famines, not the violent one of 1857, though many Irish radicals later applauded the Indian mutineers.

Before leaving the mid-century wars in Eurasia and North Africa, it is worth reiterating that these events were not only distantly comparable in terms of their social origins, they were also directly connected by chains of causation. So, for instance, after 1850, Louis Napoleon attempted to stabilize his post-revolutionary regime by appealing to France's Roman Catholic sentiment. He did this in part by promoting a more aggressive policy of missionary endeavor in the Middle East and East Asia. On the one hand, this policy embroiled the French in wars with the Vietnamese kingdom. On the other hand, French and Russian conflicts over the holy places of Palestine were an important trigger for the Crimean War of 1853 between France, Britain, and the Russian Empire. The events of the Crimean War set off a new chain of consequences. It forced the pace of Russia's modernization and shocked the British into reconstructing their armies at home and in India. Blundering attempts to reform the East India Company's Bengal Army set off the great mutiny of 1857–9 in India. Events spiraled out of control in an already globalized world.

Chains of causation worked in the other direction, too. The Asian events impacted on Europe, albeit less directly than had those of the 1750s and after. But subtle changes were registered in ideologies and organizations. British embarrassments during the Indian Mutiny gave a great fillip to Irish radicalism in Ireland and North America, for instance. For the first time, perhaps, a few of these white radicals began to see an analogy to their own political predicament in the revolt of a non-white "people." That analogy had been made by representatives of India's "people" some years before. Conversely, the mutiny also helped confirm a new form of racialism in the English-speaking world. Again, Anglo-French competition in Asia during and after the Taiping Rebellion intensified rivalry between France and Britain in Europe and the Pacific. The appearance of French influence in the latter region encouraged the consolidation of British dominion in New Zealand and forced the Australian colonies to consider a degree of cooperation, even though they refused to federate during this generation.

THE AMERICAN CIVIL WAR AS A GLOBAL EVENT

The third of the inter-regional shocks which divided the nineteenth century was the American Civil War. With a death toll of 600,000 in a population of 40 million, the loss of life in this war was proportionately less severe than that in the Taiping Rebellion. Yet its ramifications were even wider, because it occurred in a semi-industrial society, using the most modern weapons.[63] What is the justification for treating the "war between the states" in the same interpretive framework as the European and Asian events we have been discussing? Whereas historians might recently have softened the lines of distinction between what were once regarded as "backward-looking" Asian societies and the "modernity" of Europe in the 1840s and 1850s, the intrinsic similarities between the Eurasian conflicts and the contemporary American ones were limited. For one thing, most of the United States was occupied by prosperous farmers, rather than impoverished peasants dominated by landholders. The political institutions of the USA were of very recent coinage, and religious and ethnic controversies were muted, at least as far as the white population was concerned. Despite widespread sympathy for the southern Confederacy in conservative circles in Europe, this did not become a world war, because neither Britain nor France had a direct interest in intervention.[64]

Yet the American Civil War had widespread consequences across Eurasia as well as in Central and South America. This is a further testimony to the tightening connections within the world economy and diplomatic order. The distraction of the United States during the war, for instance, allowed a brief independence in foreign policymaking to Mexico. The Civil War also encouraged France to make its foray into the sacrosanct territory of the Monroe Doctrine with its ill-fated attempt to support the creation of a French-leaning Mexican Empire in 1862–3. The end of the Civil War, in turn, put pressure on the French invaders and saved the Mexican liberal republic. Blatant foreign intervention stirred peasant patriotism to a new bravado, which was still felt during the full-scale Mexican revolution of 1911. Meanwhile, the defeat of Napoleon's adventure also gave France's European competitors, notably Bismarck, a strong sense of the limitations of French power. The Civil War may also have aborted the emergence of a more aggressive American expansionist policy in the Pacific and the Far East, where Japan was afforded a short, but critical respite from Western pressure.

In addition, chains of economic causation can be followed as they spiraled outwards from this Western center of turbulence. For instance, the defeat of the South caused a commercial depression in Cuba, once American exports of raw cotton and tobacco resumed. This reinforced the demand of the Cuban Creoles for independence from irksome Spanish rule. In turn, the Cuban revolt contributed to the overthrow of the Spanish liberal regime, which had also been nurtured by Emperor Napoleon III of France. Cuban revolutionaries had meanwhile carried the flame of war and revolution to the Dominican Republic.

Britain's dominance of the Atlantic carrying trade, which appeared to be threatened before 1861, was given a new lease of life by the Civil War.[65] The country's cotton factories also boomed. After the period of temporary hardship that followed the abrupt loss of cotton supplies, the textile industry recovered, as overstocking of raw cotton was eliminated. Britain, the great consumer of American raw cotton, now turned to other sources of supply as war blockaded the ports of the southern states. Long-staple Egyptian cotton was the best replacement, but short-staple Indian cotton wool also found itself in great demand across the world. Large fortunes were made by Indian and Middle Eastern cotton exporters. The Egyptian government of Khedive Ismail borrowed yet more heavily on the European money markets to sustain an ambitious program of military modernization and public works. British entrepreneurs tried to initiate cotton cultivation in Ottoman Anatolia. The Civil War era, therefore, became the high point of the boom of the mid-Victorian British imperial economy. Growth was fueled both by this sudden rise in cotton and tobacco prices and by the contemporary discoveries of gold in south Australia and western North America. Merchants built huge, neo-gothic palaces in Melbourne, Bombay, and Alexandria. Newly rich cotton-growing peasants in India were rumored to have shod the wheels of their carts with silver.

When the crash came, following the resumption of American production, it was a very severe one and began to propel the world economy into the doldrums of the long depression of the 1870s and 1880s. The collapse of cotton prices after 1867 was a terminal wound for Egyptian finances and ushered in the constitutional crisis which racked the country throughout the 1870s. The simultaneous collapse of Indian cotton prices and concurrent famines in western India encouraged the growth of a new militancy in town and countryside. Though the links were indirect, the prevalence of rural poverty in the cotton tracts powerfully assisted the growth of anti-British nationalism in western India. Even in distant Russia, the dangerous dependence on American cotton supplies revealed by the Civil War gave militarists a justification to seize the rich black soils of central Asia which were ideal for growing the crop.

The American Civil War was, then, a global event in the same sense as the Taiping Rebellion or the 1848 revolutions, because direct connections of trade, government, and ideology spread its effects across the globe. Yet did its origins and outcomes have any generic connection with contemporary events in Europe and Asia? There do appear to be some distant comparisons. In crushing the emerging Confederate state, the Union was itself following, and contributing to, a much wider realignment in which large and unified nations and more centralized and economically sophisticated supremacies replaced the still loose and varied polities of the early nineteenth century. Across the northern states of America, a more self-conscious economic and political nation was emerging. Northerners feared the rivalry of a "slave nation" to the south and west, because it might have been amenable to foreign influence. Like the denizens of emerging Germany, they were protectionists who wished to build up their nascent industries, and they were suspicious of the free-trading proclivities of the South and its links with the British.

Before 1860, the American federal government was a weak institution, even by the standards of contemporary European polities. This was one reason why the southern states were able to secede from the Union in the first place. To fight the war, President Abraham Lincoln called on the northern states for armed support. The war itself brought into being, at least temporarily, a more powerful, armed, and centralized government with a distinct line of interventionist policy and an enlarged bureaucracy. Yet even after the power of the federal government had waned again, individual states retained some of the new forms of governance which they had developed during the war. Wider than this, something akin to American nationalism, though still fractured by loyalty to state and locality, began fitfully to emerge. In this sense again, the bloody birth of a stronger federal America was distantly related to the movements for Italian or German unification and the modernization of Japan. In the English-speaking world, the Canadian Confederation (1868) and the consolidation of British New Zealand during the same era represented parallel developments. Economic change now seemed to demand the creation of larger, unified nation-states. More educated and self-aware middle classes craved the psychological protection that such states were believed to afford. There were exceptions, of course. The scattered British colonies in Australia did not finally pool their resources until the beginning of the next century. Here, state building worked slowly from the bottom up, as colonists found they had more and more in common as they traded, legislated, and worshipped together in the vast southern continent. Their pattern of development resembled what that of the United States might have been had it not been for the explosive issues of slavery and expansion to the west.

The American Civil War also signaled the final demise of a core constituent of the Western arm of the old eighteenth-century British world economy. It was of symbolic importance that the great, and mainly British-founded, slave plantations of the southern American states disappeared within ten years of the demise of that other key institution of the British world of the eighteenth century, the East India Company. That corrupt old monopoly had finally been displayed as incompetent even in regard to its residual military and government functions. In the eyes of American liberal reformers, slavery and slave ownership had come to be regarded as inefficient and corrupting to the same degree. Slavery, that "peculiar institution" of labor control outside the market, could not be allowed to take root in the new lands which the republic was opening up in the west of the continent. Though states' rights remained enshrined in the constitution, they could no longer invoke history and culture to protect social forms which were deemed abhorrent by a dominant opinion emerging among both Republicans and Democrats in the north.

In their intertwining of moral and economic arguments, reform movements on both sides of the Atlantic were often quite directly connected. The 1848 revolutions in Europe, the Chartist movement in Britain, the Fenian upsurge in Ireland, and the abolitionist tide in the United States expressed similar ideologies. At one level, they all concerned the right of the individual as a citizen. The movement of activists and printed matter across the Atlantic linked temperance and antislavery movements, women's movements and church groups. The Salvation Army became active in the United States at the same time as it emerged in Britain and its empire.

The moral effect of the vision of mass emancipation, however flawed in practice, should not be underestimated either. John Bright, the British radical, took up the example of the American war as a worldwide struggle for "democracy, liberty and the dignity of labour."[66] Bright and, after him, Gladstone himself drew an analogy between American slave emancipation and the enfranchisement of smallholders and working people in Britain, which was to be accomplished in 1867 and 1885. A new charismatic tone entered popular politics in Protestant Europe, and this had roots in the moral discourse of abolitionism. Moral rearmament was reinforced by hard political concerns. Initially, the industrial disruption in Britain caused by the loss of cotton supplies seemed to foreshadow the reemergence of labor radicalism. But the working classes of Lancashire did not riot or revolt, and many of them actually supported the Union's cause, even though it was apparently against their own interests. The political maturity of the textile workers did much to

ILLUSTRATION 4.5 Righteous terrorist: *John Brown (1800–59), Abolitionist.* Daguerreotype by Augustus Washington, c.1846–7.

persuade both Conservative and Liberal politicians that a further extension of the electoral franchise was appropriate.[67] Across the British Empire, early colonial nationalists were also distantly but powerfully affected by the outcome of the Civil War. Following its setbacks in 1848–51, democracy, or at least representative government, now seemed to be on the march again.

Inevitably, though, the most pervasive and long-term effects of the Civil War were registered in the domain of war making itself. In many respects, this was the first heavily mechanized war in history. Heavy guns devastated troop formations, and whole cities were destroyed by bombardment. Cameras were now on hand to record suffering and to stimulate patriotism. The commanders of European armies learned quickly. A huge increase in the production of war matériel spread new forms of weapons, especially small arms, across the world. Legally traded or smuggled weapons found their way to Europe, Asia, and Africa, strengthening the forces of royal and colonial armies, but eagerly sought by revolutionaries, anarchists, and peasant rebels.

CONVERGENCE OR DIFFERENCE?

This chapter has sketched the direct and indirect connections linking the great conflicts which divided the nineteenth century. It has not tried to "homogenize" world history. Even in the contemporary age of electronic communications and instantaneous movement of capital from continent to continent, sociologists such as Arjun Appadurai argue that localism remains formative, "cannibalizing" and incorporating forces from the wider world. In the conditions of the mid-nineteenth century, the particular and the "fragment" remained infinitely more important. People caught up in the American Civil War, the Taiping Rebellion, or the Indian Mutiny would have understood these events in terms of the social and mythical geographies of their district or country. Their leaders were local gentry or pious artisans. In many of the movements discussed in this chapter, the collapse of wider political authority allowed the self-assertion of the poor, whose moral claims had little or nothing to do with the ideologies of the dominant groups in society, or even of their enemies among dissident gentry and settled peasants. In India, China, and Southeast Asia during the 1850s, "tribal" people took advantage of the turbulence to assert rights to lands and produce which had been denied them for decades. Within the European movements of the 1840s, we also glimpse the assertion of the rights of many groups from the margins: unskilled laborers, early feminists, religious sectarians, and socialist anarchists. The "war between the states" briefly opened the door to the agency of African-Americans as runaways from slave plantations and as soldiers in Union armies.

Even amongst the main protagonists of the mid-century wars, ideological positions remained much more diffuse than they would be even 50 years later in 1917, when peasants and town-dwellers distant from the war fronts knew quickly of the Bolshevik Revolution or the dishonoring of the Ottoman caliph.

In the 1850s and 1860s, the powerful urging of millennial religion remained pervasive. Men and women spoke of the return of the Maitreya Buddha or of Christ's younger brother in China. They prophesied the advent of the final age, the Kali Yuga, in India, and of the Lord's vengeance on slave-holding sinners in the United States. As history of experience, the flurry of revolts which ended the age of flux was a patchwork of disconnected moments, special histories which should not be wrenched too casually into common patterns. Here, historians of the "fragment" are right.

This chapter has argued, by contrast, that historians must also examine the moral and material connections between these, and that these emerge strongly when a global perspective is adopted. Consider some of the leaders of the 1850s ruptures. The chief prophet of the Taiping Rebellion had been educated in a Christian mission school. Nana Sahib, the Indian rebel of Kanpur in India, had been taught to read English and French novels by his British tutors. Both these men hoped that France or the United States would intervene in their conflicts. The major leaders of the European popular movements of 1848, and the contemporary proponents of home rule in the settler colonies, inherited a picture of the world in which the French Revolution and the Declaration of the Rights of Man were the fundamental events. Both sides in the American Civil War used the Declaration of Independence as a universal charter of human rights. Contrast this with the past. It had been different 60 years before, at the start of the first age of global imperialism. Then, in the 1780s, the Mughal emperor, Shah Alam, and General George Washington had, in their very different ways, confronted the global reach of British power and searched for a counterpoise in France and Spain. Yet their understandings of the world were wholly different. Then there was little enough to link the Chinese idea of the Middle Kingdom, the Mughal concept of Timurid charisma, and the ideology of old Whig republicanism as it had flourished in North America. By the 1840s and 1850s, the leaders and perhaps even some of the more important followers of the great dissidences which swept the world had a clearer understanding of the global hegemonies which confronted them.

The emerging left took particular note of slave emancipation and the coeval Asian rebellions. Karl Marx himself was perhaps the first contemporary to consider the European and Asian rebellions using the same set of concepts, even if he did, ultimately, relegate "the Orient" to a different conceptual box. This chapter and previous ones have given a rather mixed picture of the implications of popular or "subaltern" revolt for global history. Its direct importance cannot be written off, of course. Rebellion did profoundly affect structures of power and economic exploitation across the world. The Paris crowds of 1789–93 and 1848 did help sweep away old autocracies. The slave rebels of the Caribbean between 1815 and 1831 terminally weakened the plantation system. The peasant rebels in Russia in the 1770s and India in the 1850s did irreparably damage existing systems of exploitation. Yet, in general, they were effective only where these institutions had already been severely corroded by the sustained criticism and subversion of elite activists and the "middling sort" of people. There were as many urban revolts and peasant or slave uprisings which had no effect, or even strengthened the status quo, in cases where the institutions of government were not already compromised by elite attack.

It is a myth, therefore, that popular or subaltern rebellion in itself became an irresistible force for change in the course of the nineteenth century. Yet it was precisely this mythic status which made the idea of popular rebellion such a powerful political artefact at global level. Already, in the 1850s and 1860s radicals and early socialists were making connections between the rebellions of the suppressed Irish and the Indian "mutineers," or between the struggle of American blacks and the European working classes of 1848. The idea of the global struggle of "the People" of all races had already taken root. In the longer run, the history-making power of this myth was to be registered in many centers away from the temporarily dominant core of the world economy. The revolutions were to come in China and the distant Russian coalfields. The mass movements were to take place in Indian cities and African plantations. That these upsurges were seen as part of a global movement was itself of huge importance, even if the real connections between them were tenuous.

Finally, what of the connection between these events and future outbreaks of conflict? The wars of nation building which followed in Germany, Italy, Japan, and Mexico in the 1860s and 1870s in many ways represented the tidying up of issues left over from the turbulence which ended the age of flux. In the meantime, the state, gaining strength from rapid economic growth, had achieved greater definition and purpose. Bismarck, Cavour, and the reformers of Meiji Japan knew much more precisely where they were going and what they were trying to achieve than the rebel peasants and intellectuals and poets of a few years earlier. The meaning of the nation had become, by the same token, narrower and less inclusive, the state more intrusive.

One final set of issues needs to be put into context. Across the world, and with increasing ferocity after 1860, land wars began to erupt between European settlers, on the one hand, and nomadic, forest-dwelling, or semi-settled people, on the other. Chapter 12 will elaborate this point. Land was the prize, but more often the occasion for war was the clash of European notions of state, sovereignty, and land use with those of the indigenous people. From 1846 onward, the Xhosa and Zulu wars in southern Africa and the Anglo–Maori conflict in New Zealand were paralleled by new invasions of the American prairies and the Brazilian forests. The assaults on the common rights of Hawaiians and other Pacific islanders had become annihilating drives for exclusive rights over land. In Asian countries, the depredations of pioneer settlers on indigenous peoples expanded their scope, while colonial entrepreneurs ruthlessly pressed home their demands for wood for railway sleepers and mineral products to supply new industries.

The disturbances described in this chapter acted as a kind of catalyst for these colonial land wars. The great European "hunger" and the European revolutions after 1848 speeded the emigration of settlers into virgin territories. British veterans of the Indian Rebellion participated in the New Zealand and

South African wars. In French New Caledonia, the revolt of the local Kanak population did not come until 1878. But the political and agrarian tensions that caused it began to escalate in the early 1850s as post-revolutionary emigration increased. Thousands of French convicts in the colony were later joined by political prisoners from the 1871 Paris Commune.[68] In the same way, the American Civil War cleared the way for mass invasions of the remaining Indian territories. Even in China, the collapse of the regime during the mid-century rebellions let loose a wave of peasant diasporas into the hills and high plains of the empire's fringes, especially in Yunnan and Manchuria. All this serves to remind us that any attempt closely to delineate periods in global history, whether they are economic or cultural, is fraught with difficulty. The unintended consequences of earlier political and economic decisions spiraled uncontrollably outwards from world centers of power, deepening and changing as they were absorbed into continuing local conflicts over rights, honor, and resources.

REVIEWING THE ARGUMENT

In many ways, the origins of the mid-nineteenth-century world crisis formed an extension of the earlier "wreck of nations" of 1780–1820. Once again, from 1848 to 1865, uneven economic growth, and the associated questioning of the legitimacy of all forms of power, formed the crucible of conflict worldwide. Europeans and North Americans resolved these crises with great slaughter. Many old institutions were overthrown. Yet, in the West, the state emerged more strongly and was able to project its power overseas even more effectively thereafter. Asians, Africans, Latin Americans, and residents of the Pacific suffered wars, conflicts, and revolutions of comparable violence. There were distinct global connections between these upheavals. The reverberations of Asian and African conflicts sometimes "bounced back" into the Western crisis and exacerbated it, as they had done between 1780 and 1820. In general, though, the flow of events was now more firmly from Europe and North America outward.

Of course, non-Europeans continued to be active agents, appropriating, transforming, and resisting the outside forces loosed on them. Yet the differentials of power and in the use of knowledge between the West and the rest of the world had become even greater than they had been in 1780. They were to be at their greatest between 1860 and 1900. The further honing of European weapons of war and statehood was partly responsible for the widening differential. By 1850, however, some profound economic changes were also apparent. Chapter 2 argued that "industrious revolutions" and a connected growth of world trade, rather than early industrialization, was the dominant trend in global social history at the end of the eighteenth century. Europeans and North Americans had done particularly well out of these developments, and the nature of their civil societies emphasized these benefits. Theirs was not a unique transformation, however.

By the time that the great exhibition of 1851 opened at the Crystal Palace in the suburbs of London, full-scale industrialization had begun, latterly, to transform what was now an international order. This did not mean that industrial capitalists or their agents suddenly came to grasp political power, as some Marxists once argued. Industrialization widely came to the aid of kings, priests and aristocrats. Until the end of the century, even the West was to be ruled by a combination of landowners, middle-class bureaucrats, industrialists, and shopkeepers. Still, Europeans, their colonists, and their former colonists in the USA, looked around them at the electric telegraph, steam power, the new, planned cities, and the vast accumulations of knowledge in universities, government departments, museums, and art galleries. They began to believe passionately that they had made that once-and-for-all step upward to the modern age mentioned in the introduction. To understand the background of this, the next chapter turns back from the history of global political processes to underlying changes in the organization of production and urban living.

[5] *INDUSTRIALIZATION AND THE NEW CITY*

INDUSTRIALIZATION worked unevenly across the world, creating new powers, new dependencies, and new ways of living. By the mid-nineteenth century its transforming effects were clear to see. This chapter considers why the spread of modern industry was erratic, and why it came particularly to benefit parts of the Western world. It examines the changes in urban living which these new forms of production and new manifestations of political power were bringing into being. Chapter 6 then goes on to consider the apogee of nationalism which occurred within the same two generations as the fuller emergence of industrial society.

HISTORIANS, INDUSTRIALIZATION, AND CITIES

Of all the dynamic changes that the people of the later nineteenth century associated with their own era, industrialization and the rise of the huge, impersonal metropolis were the most striking to them. Very often they perceived a close connection between these two developments, whereas, in reality, much early industrialization actually took place in the countryside, with large "factory cities" developing only later. These two phenomena were linked in the broader sense, however, in that they represented radically different ways of creating, consuming, and living from those which had been common 150 years earlier. This explains why so much of the intellectual energy of the century went into trying to understand them. At the beginning of the period, the ideas of Adam Smith about economic specialization and economies of scale provided intellectual tools with which people could analyze the phenomenon of accelerating economic growth, though the critical developments in manufacturing came long after his death. By the end of the nineteenth century, economists such as Alfred Marshall had evolved a science for the study of the rhythms of industrial society.

Reflection on industrialism and the city spread to all facets of social and cultural life. Marx and Engels argued that industrialization had even created a new type of human being, the proletarian, with nothing to his name but his own labor power. The public moralists and poets of northern Europe and North America denounced the vices of the industrial city: drunkenness, disease, prostitution, irreligion, and poverty. The first generation of sociologists, notably Emile Durkheim, pondered the effect of alienating urban living on social solidarities. In France, Britain, and Germany the new science of statistics was developed with an eye to monitoring the number and health of burgeoning urban populations. Artists such as Toulouse-Lautrec painted the exotic and erotic denizens of the city. Richard Wagner supposedly modeled his dismal world of the mythical Nibelungen in his operatic "Ring" cycle on his memory of the bleak industrial skyline of London which he had observed in the 1840s. Others reacted with enthusiasm to the new world. Before the end of the century, American architects had created in the skyscraper a new form of machine for living in the modern industrial city.

Historians of the last third of the twentieth century tended to downplay the importance of industrialization in their accounts of the nineteenth century. Many economic historians argue that industrialization had little effect outside Britain and Belgium until the mid-1850s and assert that rhythms of agricultural production remained the critical determinant of economic and social life. The idea of a long proto-industrialization from the later Middle Ages onward developed by Franklin Mendel in the 1970s also tended to suggest that there the slow accumulation of the conditions for industrialization was more important than any sudden acceleration. As chapter 2 noted, Jan de Vries pioneered the concept of "industrious revolutions" to highlight savings in efficiency and reorientations of consumption patterns which were independent of the Industrial Revolution itself. Most writers seem to agree that, outside the United States, industrial fortunes merely consolidated existing social hierarchies rather than revolutionizing them. In the case of Britain, once seen as "the first industrial nation," Peter Cain and Anthony Hopkins use the phrase "gentlemanly capitalism" to argue that the dominant feature in both the country's domestic and its imperial economy was financial services, banking, and the stock exchange, rather than industrial production.[1] Martin Wiener[2] tried to show that anti-industrial values snuffed out British industrial entrepreneurship before it even got off the ground. Patrick O'Brien, among others, has constructed complex statistical analyses for the British economy which suggest that growth in gross domestic product hovered around a sedate 1.5 percent per annum for much of the period 1780–1861.[3] Whereas economic historians once spoke of the Industrial Revolution, if hard pressed, they might now agree that the trends were gently upward. They signaled what at best might be called an "industrial evolution."

In recent years scholars have become more skeptical about the political impact of industrialization and urbanization, too. Earlier chapters have noted that where socialist and even conservative historians once saw the industrial worker as in the vanguard of political change, modern historians have argued that the rebellions of 1848 and the Paris Commune were really caused by dispossessed, old-style artisans. In accounts of the Russian Revolution of

1905, peasants and soldiers, rather than industrial workers, now hold center stage. In the case of Russia, China, and India, many historians working since the 1970s have insisted that the tiny nineteenth-century industrial working classes were really made up of "peasants in disguise," rather than a true urban proletariat; their mentalities were resolutely preindustrial and agrarian.

As other chapters of this book show, many features of the old agrarian and political order survived to the beginning of the twentieth century. However, to insist that a revolution in means of production and life-styles spread only slowly, and only gradually revealed its true potential, is not the same as saying that no revolution took place at all. This chapter argues that, by the later nineteenth century, the percentage of gross national product generated by industrial production within the dominant world powers was very substantial. Politicians and urban leaders were forced to come to terms with issues of nurturing, controlling, and providing for this growing industrial work. They became dependent on products of scientifically based industries to fight wars, and on taxation derived from industry to finance them. The effects of industrialization spread well beyond the still small part of the global population actually employed in industries. Agriculture in industrializing countries had been transformed by the presence of large new urban markets and by mechanized tools. The most dynamic sectors of agricultural economies were those producing goods for export to the industrializing world. These were palm oil and cocoa from West Africa, cotton from Egypt and India, and the "protein chains" which brought meat to Europe or the eastern seaboard of the USA from Australia, New Zealand, Argentina, or the North American Midwest to feed the growing industrial working class.

In 1880 few cities of the world outside America and northwestern Europe were truly industrial. But many centers such as Naples, Alexandria, Calcutta, Shanghai, Lagos, or Buenos Aires had already become bulking points for outward-bound food and primary produce of this sort, and distribution points for the reception of industrial produce. Their elites were as much implicated in the industrial world system as those of the West. Above all, this was the period when long-term, profound differentials in industrial development significantly widened the gulf in standards of living between the richer and poorer parts of the world. In 1780–1820, before significant industrialization, international differentials in power and wealth were already growing. By 1880, they were enormous, and industrialization was one key reason why they continued to grow. Equally, the chapter will show that the modern urban life style, which was associated with industrialization, became a reference point for intellectuals and political leaders across the world, even where it only distantly affected them.

THE PROGRESS OF INDUSTRIALIZATION

British industrialization remains the starting point for a general study of industrialization, though British historians have been particularly insistent on de-emphasizing industrialization as a turning point in both British and global history. All the same, the transition to industry was striking. By 1881, 44 percent of the British labor force was employed in industry or industry-related occupations, compared with 26 percent in the United States and 36 percent in Germany.[4] More striking yet was the fact that only 13 percent of British workers were employed in agriculture in that year, compared with 52 percent in the United States and 43 percent in Germany.[5] Even if it is argued that agriculture had long been commercialized in Britain, the change since the 1780s was very great. By 1881 much of the non-industrial British working population was employed in transport, which included railways, or in commerce, which included the marketing of industrially produced foods and clothing. Moreover, Britain accounted for as much as 45 percent of the world's industrial production by 1840, and even in 1880 it still accounted for nearly 30 percent. Recent calculations suggest that Britain's industrial production was growing at the rate of about 3.5 percent per annum between 1815 and 1861.[6] This may not look very robust by the standards of today's tiger economies, but it was extraordinary at that time.

Some historians attribute Britain's early industrialization to technical advances: the iron blast furnace, the steam engine, and the spinning jenny; others to relative scarcity of skilled labor in Britain, especially during the Napoleonic wars, which encouraged mechanization.[7] The great French historian Fernand Braudel seemed, typically, to suggest in the 1970s that it was

ILLUSTRATION 5.1   Age of industry: Women working in Lancashire cotton mill, 1897.

Britain's position on the margins of Europe which turned its entrepreneurs to the outside world. Prasannan Parthasarathi has further developed the argument that British industrialization was a response to efficient artisan textile production in other parts of the world, particularly in France and India.[8] Indian weavers were producing high-quality goods at very low cost and threatening Britain's own textile industry. British manufacturers' response in the mid-eighteenth century was to try to exclude the Indian products. By 1800, they were responding to external competition by introducing machines which produced cloth even more cheaply. This is an interesting line of thought, because it makes it clear that technological change, whether of the "industrial" or "industrious" sort, was multi-centered and global right from the beginning. It was also thoroughly embedded in social relations: technical change was inevitably social change as well. This consideration is also germane to the issue of capital formation for industrial investment. Wealth generated in the outside world, through either the slave and sugar trades or the commercial and fiscal activities of the East India Company, certainly added to Britain's growing stock of capital for investment. Whether it amounted to 5 percent, 10 percent or 15 percent of the total will probably never be known.[9] It should be remembered, though, that this step-up in world trade had occurred before industrialization, reflecting the cultural and economic realignments of industrious revolutions. More important, the activities of these international corporations had created the concept of a global market where rising industrialists could now seek markets.

The best resolution of these different positions about the origins of British industrialization is to assume that pressures on labor and production during the wars between 1793 and 1815 combined to convert a number of diverse technical breakthroughs into a slow, but much broader, change in economic structure. By 1750, British agriculture and mining were already highly commercialized and drawn together into a national market. Outside northern Scotland, north Wales, and Ireland, the peasantry had disappeared, and land was freely marketable. Property and capital had been protected by a long period of internal peace and the benevolent vindictiveness of the common law. Above all, since the 1680s, Britain had possessed a flexible capital market which could provide large sums of money for investment. When labor shortages and growing demand powered by industrious revolutions in family consumption made manufacturing profitable and attractive, entrepreneurs, financiers, and inventors rushed into industrial investment in order to reap the profits. As always, military and naval technology received heavy inputs of capital. The new battleships, field guns, and armed steamboats then helped batter a way into protected markets in the Ottoman Empire, China, and South America.

American industrialization followed a similar path at a later period and, ultimately, on a vaster scale. By 1885, the USA accounted for 30 percent of world industrial production, much the same as Britain's share.[10] As in the British case, industrialization reflected the investment of capital by successful Atlantic trading merchants and landowners in mechanized production through a flexible capital market. American industrial products were designed for a rapidly growing and very prosperous consumer market. Import substitution – Britain had been a major supplier earlier – took place very fast once the railroads had opened up the huge internal economy in the west and the south of the country to the industrialists of the northeast states and, later, the Midwest.[11] Before the 1890s, however, American manufacturing production had taken on a significantly different appearance from that in Britain, Belgium, and France. In those early industrializing countries, ownership and management often remained in the same hands, especially in leading industries, such as textiles and machine tools. In the United States the management of companies was beginning to be divorced from ownership, which was dominated by large stockholders. Their distance from direct ownership allowed managers in the USA to concentrate on innovative production and marketing without the hindrance of family interests and personnel. The first stages of mass industrialization rapidly led on to innovations in labor organization. A critical breakthrough here was Henry Ford's invention of the production line for motor cars in 1896, which allowed more flexible deployment of management and workers.[12]

In the case of German, Austrian, Italian, and Russian industrialization, historians have always stressed the role of the state as investor and promoter of manufacturing, especially in heavy industries and defense industries. This can be overdone. In the Saar-Ruhr and Carinthia, private investment by merchants and landowners seems to have been as important as it was in Britain and the USA. The German states certainly helped create the conditions for a large, protected internal market, first through the customs union which began in 1834 and later through the system of preferences within the German Empire.[13] But the sharp distinction between the role of the state in these different venues has been blunted somewhat in recent studies. After all, even in Britain, the imperial state's interventions overseas helped to create favorable conditions for manufacturing enterprise. The huge slave economy of the Atlantic provided one motor of growth and market formation throughout the later eighteenth century. In the guise of the Royal Navy, the state provided the essential protection for this system, and at great cost. In the nineteenth century, imperial expansion created lucrative subsidiary markets for British textile and arms manufacturers, even if North America and Europe remained the destination for most manufactured goods. In Scotland, industrialization was quite closely associated with empire, and so with the activities of the British state.

Belgium was the first country in continental Europe to industrialize. In its case, the desperate need of a weak and dubiously legitimate state provided the spur to investment. Belgium's position and resources also proved favorable. Close to Britain's Channel ports and an early recipient of its railway technology, Belgium also possessed huge resources of coal and iron, which most specialists now believe to have been one of the major factors in promoting early industrialization in Europe as a whole. Equally important was Belgium's access to the large internal market of northwestern Europe in France,

Germany, and the Netherlands, countries which remained relatively prosperous because of their agriculture and artisanal industries, but had not thus far industrialized very fast.

The heartland of continental European industrialization was, however, the arc of land which stretched from the Ruhr through to the western provinces of the Austrian Empire. Though Germans, Austrians, Hungarians, and Czechs were relatively prosperous by world standards in the early nineteenth century, a clutch of changes which occurred in the 1850s, after the trauma of revolution had passed, combined to unlock their productive potential. Harvests were markedly better in the 1850s than in the difficult years of the 1840s. As part of the movement to political unification, the German and even Austrian governments continued to demolish internal barriers to the free market, and concern about British competition began to diminish. Worldwide changes were important, too. The influx of gold from California and Australia helped to boost world trade. The eastern crises and the American Civil War actually increased German trade, as they did British trade. Textile manufacturing, mining, and metal industries all grew exceptionally fast in the three decades after 1850. Thus, for instance, employment in the Ruhr coal mines grew from 13,000 to 51,000 between 1850 and 1870.[14] Later, in the 1880s and 1890s, the chemical, electrical, optical, and precision instrument industries, with which German economic strength has been so long associated, developed rapidly. The availability of chemical deposits such as potash was a valuable asset, but more important was the skilled and educated work force which the united Germany supported. A steady flow of science and engineering graduates attested to the modernization of German universities, which had been brought about both by the demands of war and by the very rapid growth of the pure and applied sciences.

In France, too, the decade of the 1850s seems to have been critical for industrialization, and once again the state gave it a distinct push forward. Louis Napoleon proclaimed, hypocritically beating Bonaparte's sword into a ploughshare: "The Empire means peace ... we have immense tracts of uncultivated lands to clear, roads to open, ports to create, rivers to make new, canals to finish, our railway network to complete. These are the conquests I am contemplating and all of you ... are my soldiers."[15]

In France, the Lille area took on some of the characteristics of Britain and Belgium, while Lyon capitalized on its artisan silk-weaving past to modernize its textile industries in the later nineteenth century. Silk textile production was an industry in which relatively cheap, low-level investment in mechanization could transform an older industry. Access to plentiful supplies of raw silk from the Far East and the Middle East also attested to the importance of France's international and colonial trade links in this case.

Nodes of industrial activity became established in several other parts of Europe from the 1850s onward. Northern Italy, and especially the Piedmont region, developed its own textile and metallurgical industries, becoming the industrial heart of the new Italy. Here state investment during the protracted wars of Italian unification was important, as was the existing inheritance of skilled artisan workers and a good transport system.

Russia, by contrast, industrialized only very slowly, though with increasing speed after 1890. Between 1890 and 1900, Russian production of pig iron increased by over 200 percent, and railway mileage by 70 percent. In many respects, Russia should be compared with China and with territories in the European colonial empires, rather than with western Europe. Indeed, in 1900, there were more power textile looms in India than there were in Russia. The problems Russia faced were dreadful weather, poor transport, lack of investment, and a badly educated work force. Even in 1900, the majority of industrial workers still lived in the countryside. When industrial enterprise developed, as, for instance, did coal mining in the Don region or iron production around Smolensk, foreign expertise and management were needed to start up most operations. This weakness in industrial capacity was one reason why the Russian Empire, despite its huge resources of men and material, had a very patchy record in the international conflicts of the century. It was defeated in the Crimean War with Britain and France, and its fleet was sunk by the Japanese in 1905.

POVERTY AND THE ABSENCE OF INDUSTRY

What were the factors which accelerated or retarded industrialization? Industrialization should be seen as much more than building factories. It meant establishing systems of management and control of skilled labor, sourcing raw materials, and establishing transport and outlets. A favorable governmental and tariff regime was critical. However, precisely which types of government intervention helped or hindered industrialization remains a matter of ideological controversy among historians and economists. When one moves outside Europe and North America to the roughly 15 percent of industrial output which, in 1895, was accounted for by what would now be called "developing countries,"[16] these external and political factors become even more significant. A substantial part of this balance of 15 percent was accounted for by primary produce processing in cash crop and mineral production regimes. Typical examples here include canning plants in the meat-exporting areas of Australasia and Latin America and cotton ginning in the subtropical regions. In the best of all worlds, primary producers could move on from fairly low-level industrial processing to the production of heavier industrial products. This happened to some degree in the British dominions and South America, where canning factories for meat and fruit complemented export trades in those commodities. In the later nineteenth century, primary producer status was by no means a sentence to low standards of living. By some calculations, in fact, Argentina, a meat and grain producer with relatively little industry, had one of the highest per capita incomes in the world around 1900. Several of Brazil's regions did especially well out of the international expansion of coffee consumption and the inflow of British investment for railways and ports, while others stagnated under the weight of population growth. By contrast, statesmen from British dominions visiting Britain remarked on the poor health, nutritional standards, and services available to British workers by comparison with the bounty available in their still largely agricultural countries.

What seems to have stranded much of the developing world in a state of relative poverty was a combination of circumstances. Being an agricultural producer made a territory poor, but only when this was combined with an external trade regime which prevented any significant degree of local industrial protection. Conversely, having a large, skilled artisan industry, like much of South and East Asia, was an advantage, but only where the state was able and willing to aid the process of transition. In addition, it was important who exactly owned the new enterprises and banks. Control of local shipping, banking, and financial services by expatriates meant that the value added by participation in international trade largely ended up in the pockets of foreigners. Finally, internal factors, such as rapid population growth, the relative immobility of labor, and poor educational provision, were also significant, quite independently of the external regimes of formal or informal empire.

Mexico was perhaps the only Latin American country to attempt to industrialize in the decade or so after independence from Spain, in the 1820s. A healthy textile industry had developed there by 1850, though initially it was heavily dependent on government finance. The effort was not extended to other industries, however, because the external tariff regimes were not sympathetic, and also because Mexico's economic leadership was heavily influenced by British free-market ideology and was suspicious of government intervention.[17] Healthy foreign investment in transport and infrastructure after 1880 helped the region to become a major exporter of foodstuffs and raw materials before 1900. But the relative lack of secondary industry made it difficult for Mexico to maintain its relatively high living standards into the twentieth century or to combat rural poverty. These circumstances, as well as religious and cultural conflicts, set the scene for Mexico's revolutionary decades after 1911.

The international free-trade regime championed by Britain widely had a stifling effect except for regions in northwestern Europe and North America, which were already industrializing fast. In the Ottoman Empire, Persia, and even China, for example, early attempts by indigenous entrepreneurs to set up manufacturing plants were aborted by the tariff regime forced on them by the great powers, led by Britain, which remained rigidly committed to free trade until the 1890s. The Ottoman Tariff Convention of 1838 which reduced import duties on foreign manufactured goods throughout the Empire, threw into disarray Muhammad Ali's attempts to develop secondary cotton-manufacturing plants and military industrial production in Egypt, and damaged industry elsewhere in the Ottoman Empire.[18] Foreign imports squeezed out home industries, so that what little industrial capacity existed in the region in 1895 was foreign-owned. A special problem in the Middle East was the existence of capitulations – areas of cities set aside for European expatriate residents who benefited from special legal codes and taxation regimes. Indigenous entrepreneurs found themselves at a legal as well as a financial and cultural disadvantage. The very rapid population rise in Egypt compounded these problems. Yet it also has to be admitted that the Ottoman state did not always use its influence in the market very wisely. The bureaucracy seemed much more concerned to reestablish its control over the magnates, merchants, and guilds of the provinces than to encourage the development of new financial tools and economic initiatives. Even in the mid-nineteenth century, the revived Ottoman state remained quite suspicious of wealthy merchant-industrialists and often attempted to bring them down to earth by punitive taxation or by saddling them with impossibly demanding supply contracts. Many of the most promising commercial ventures, therefore, took place far from Istanbul, in the Balkans, and were in the hands of Jews or of the increasingly restive Christian subjects of the empire.

Of all the non-Western polities, China was in many ways the most comparable with the Ottoman Empire, though Kenneth Pomeranz has contended that it was in a much stronger position at the turn of the nineteenth century.[19] Despite the Western contention that the "Confucian mind" resisted modernity, the Chinese tried to adapt to military and naval technology as soon as they encountered it in earnest, during the opium wars. Gentry and Qing officials opposed industrialization not, in general, because they were implacable conservatives, but because of the loss of judicial and moral authority over their own citizens that the importation of European technology, management, and skills often seemed to involve. Where that control could be guaranteed, modern technology was embraced with alacrity. In the 1870s and 1880s the viceroy Li Hongzhang attempted to rebuild Chinese power by modernizing the south China coast. He founded arsenals and tried to develop a modern coal industry. He founded the China Merchant Steamships Navigation Company, which pooled state and private capital.[20] The Chinese reformers of 1898 and 1911 were even keener to develop the country's industrial infrastructure, especially given the great reserves of iron and coal in the north of the country, which were beginning to attract the envious gaze of the Japanese. But China faced considerable problems in getting its infant industries to grow. Expatriate European, American, and, later, Japanese firms provided stiff competition. China's dependence on foreign loans and the maritime customs income, which was also collected by foreigners, made it difficult for the government to raise tariffs against foreign imports. The treaty port system, which installed the jurisdiction of foreign powers in cities on the coast, gave foreigners further advantages. The Chinese government did not have the same level of financial independence as the Japanese had when it came to planning direct investments in industrial enterprises. External constraints on Chinese industrial development did not, however, abort all internal change. Historians have noted the spread, especially in the later nineteenth century, of merchant-owned handicraft workshops making silk, cotton goods, paper, and so on. These shops were serviced by a large proletarianized labor force of people drawn initially from the massive internal transport sector and from displaced peasants.[21]

Japan has always been taken as the example of the "non-European society that succeeded," in the sense that by 1895 its industrial production amounted to more than 1 percent of total world production, which put it within range of

ILLUSTRATION 5.2 Extracting cash crops, Sourabaya, Dutch East Indies, in the 1880s.

Russia's per capita industrial production at about the same time.[22] Japan's relative success points up the importance of an overlapping set of favorable conditions for the growth of a modern economic sector. Internal endowments, over-stressed by the economic historians of the 1960s and 1970s, worked together with a more benign external trade regime, which was in turn over-stressed by "world systems theorists" of the 1980s and 1990s. Certainly, Japan had an old metallurgical, silk-weaving, and dyeing tradition.[23] It had a

Table 5.1 Estimated world population, 1800–1900 (millions)

	1800 (a)	1800 (b)	1850 (a)	1850 (b)	1900 (a)	1900 (b)
Africa	90	100	95	100	120	141
North America	6	6	26	26	81	81
Latin America	19	23	33	33	63	63
Asia	597	595	741	656	915	857
Europe and Russia	192	193	274	274	423	423
Oceania	2	2	2	2	6	6
Total	906	919	1,171	1,091	1,608	1,571

(a) Figures taken from A. M. Carr-Saunders, *World Population* (London, 1936), pp. 30–45.
(b) Figures taken from W. F. Wilcox, "Population of the world and its modern increase," in Wilcox (ed.), *Studies in American Demography* (Ithaca, NY, 1940), pp. 22–51, 511–40.
Source: A. J. H. Latham, *The International Economy and the Undeveloped World 1865–1914* (London, 1978), p. 104.

Table 5.2 Population of some major countries (millions)

Year	Austria[a]	Great Britain	France	Germany	United States	Ottoman Empire	China	Japan	India	Latin America
1750	—	7.4 (includes Scotland)	21.0	18.0	1.59		179.5	26	100	
1800	14.0	10.5 (excludes Ireland)	27.4	23.0	5.30		295.3			12
1850	17.82 (A); 31.10 (A-H)	20.8 (excludes Ireland)	35.8	33.4	23.26	36	429.9		206.2 (1872)	
1900	26.15	37.0 (excludes Ireland)	38.5	56.4	76.09			44	294.3 (1901)	

[a] Austria = Austria-Hungary (A-H) (1760–1860) and Austria (A) (1830–1910).
Sources: Austria and USA from Mann, *Sources of Social Power*, vol. 2, and Colin McEvedy and Richard Jones, *Atlas of World Population History* (Harmondsworth, 1978); Great Britain, France, and Germany from Cook and Waller, *Longman Handbook*; China from Ping-ti Ho, *Ladder of Success*; Japan from J. D. Durand, *Historical Estimates of World Population* (Philadelphia, 1974); India from ibid. and *Census of India*, 1872, 1901; Ottomans from Davison, *Reform in the Ottoman Empire*.

disciplined, skilled, educated, and mobile labor force. The population was growing, but not at a rate fast enough to eat up all the profits of growth. Its great merchant houses had long been adept at sampling local consumer opinion and creating marketing structures. Japan's government, even in the late Tokugawa period, had sent missions to Europe and the United States in search of new military and industrial techniques. Even if its leaders are sometimes described as "feudal," they had a keen sense of national loyalty and a deep competitive instinct as regards the West.

After the "revolution" of 1868, the new Meiji regime[24] was in the lucky position of having a "development fund" – that is, the monies taken from erstwhile samurai aristocrats in exchange for government pensions. Chinese and Ottoman state finance was draining away to local magnates or to the archaic Manchu Banner and Green Standard armies,[25] on the one hand, or the Ottoman debt managers, on the other. By contrast, the long-term presence of political authority in the Japanese countryside ensured that the new state had a much greater control over society. The Meiji statesmen were therefore able to spark investment in shipyards, munitions, and railways. Some historians argue that they would have been better employed leaving entrepreneurs to make these investments, but this perhaps underestimates the fragility of the "animal instincts" of these potential investors before 1905. A lead from authority, especially from the emperor's ministers, was essential.

All the same, some aspects of Japan's relatively rapid industrialization were contingent, determined by the play of favorable political and economic factors outside her control. For instance, she was lucky that world demand for silk remained buoyant throughout the later nineteenth century. By introducing quite small-scale technological improvements into silk weaving and process-ing, Japan could maintain her external balance of payments in reasonable shape. Again, fortuitous external diplomatic circumstances favored her. Unlike China, Japan was not subject to a full attack by the imperialist powers, at least not after Commodore Perry kicked open the door in the 1850s. Again, the huge indemnity she took from China after its imperialist war of 1895 helped to keep the government in the black for a time. Her emerging industrial strength allowed it to crush Russia ten years on. This in turn caused a surge of beneficent foreign investment in its industries. British interest in having Japan as a defense partner after its defeat of China and Russia was matched by the desire of British firms, especially Scottish ones, to export skills and tools. Japanese development appears, therefore, to have been aided by a rather fortuitous mixture of state initiative and local skills and experience. The Japanese example suggests that when thinking at a world level about industri-alization, as in the case of broad political and intellectual changes, a combin-ation of diffusionist models of change with models which stress endogenous endowments and developments seems to have the greatest explanatory power.

In the colonial world, the picture was one of very slow industrial develop-ment, because the colonial powers were unwilling to put any competition in the way of their own national industrial producers. British, Dutch, and French colonial governments levied only very low rates of tariffs on manufactured imports, insufficient to provide much protection to nascent industry. But some growth, nevertheless, did occur. Naturally, the first sustained industrial activity in India occurred as the colonial armies tried to develop local produc-tion of gun carriages and military steel making around Calcutta. The need for local supplies was always balanced by the fear that military technology would fall into the hands of dissident Indians or, in earlier days, rebellious Euro-peans. But, given India's potentially huge demand for cloth, it is not surprising that both British and Indian entrepreneurs opened textile factories even when external tariff conditions were quite hostile to them. India in 1895 had a substantial number of power looms concentrated in the cities of Bombay and Ahmedabad. Bengal supported a large, though mainly foreign-owned, jute-processing industry.[26] Indian entrepreneurs had already begun to invest in industry as early as the 1850s, and they were able to carve out a niche for themselves in low-value, volume cloth production where they were less subject to competition from Britain. Though the argument suffers from vagueness, it does seem that the particular cultures of commercial trust and cooperation common among the older merchant classes of western and southern India were a distinct advantage to India's struggling industrial entrepreneurs. British businessmen also invested in low-quality and low-wage textile production as a way of skimming off easy profits.[27] For all the colonial neglect, however, India did enter the twentieth century with some viable industry. The problem was that it made little impact on the huge inheritance of rural poverty.

One of the key claims of colonial nationalists was that European and Ameri-can manufactured imports devastated indigenous artisan industries. As late as 1800, these had continued to produce valuable commodities for the world market and dominated local markets. There is no doubt that European industrial growth concentrated production in the West and reduced non-European artisan production to a marginal status in both European and world markets. But indigenous artisan textile production should not be written off completely. As in Europe itself, artisan industry adapted to mechanization to some degree and made use of low-level technical improvements. Semi-modernized weaving and other artisan communities remained socially significant in most parts of the world, long after the onset of industrialization. Some of them have survived to flourish again in the post-industrial age of small-scale production within household units. Economic historians now quite commonly argue that it was not absolutely necessary for industrial societies to go through a period of concentration in huge factories. There were, as we have seen, examples of dispersed artisan industries, such as the Lyon and Japanese silk-weaving industries, becoming modernized without intense industrial concentration in modern factories. This was more about the perceived need to discipline labor than about productivity as such. If this is so, then here again the distinction between "backward" African, Asian, and southern European artisan production and "advanced" northern European and American factory production begins to look a bit threadbare. The vast disparities in world living standards which were apparent by the end of the nineteenth century may have been more about external regimes of money and military power than about relative technical progress. The industrial life-style was as much about the desire of the wealthy to control the poor as about economic efficiency in its own right.

Historians, therefore, have come to argue that mass factory production was not really an essential "stage" in the development of human society. Industrialization, like Western domination, has now come to be seen as a slower, more patchy process than it appeared in previous generations. Its social consequences in urbanization and the development of class-based politics are also treated with more skepticism. The balance is difficult to strike. Clearly, forces such as nationalism, urbanism, and industrialization have been seen as too monolithic and inevitable in the past. Their capacity to transform small communities has been both overstated and dated too early. In consequence, the stagnation of the old regimes has been overdone, as has the dynamism of the "age of industry and empire." This book argues that real and rapid changes did occur, especially in the last 10 to 20 years of the nineteenth century and the first decade of the twentieth. Up to this point, different systems of hierarchy and localism, many of them surviving in a modified form from the old regimes, showed a striking capacity to accommodate these changes.

CITIES AS CENTERS OF PRODUCTION, CONSUMPTION, AND POLITICS

The term "urbanization" refers to a process. It is used to mean the growth of the percentage of the population living in cities of over 10,000, but it also

ILLUSTRATION 5.3   Chinese and Indian laborers mingle in one of Singapore's newly built streets of shop-houses, 1890s.

refers to a cultural change which implies the dominance of city values over those of the countryside. In the first sense, the pace of urbanization speeded up considerably in the nineteenth century, but it did so in a rather patchy way. In North America and in sub-Saharan Africa and the Pacific region, where cities had been small or had not existed before white settlement, urbanization was rapid. In the great agrarian societies of China, India, and the Middle East, where general population was growing fast during the nineteenth century, the percentage of the population living in urban areas increased only marginally. New forms of commercial and semi-industrial city certainly came into being, but their growth was balanced by a decline of some of the older centers. In the second sense, however, the consequences of urbanization were profound and had implications well beyond the economic realm. Bigger cities made possible the emergence of new social relationships and speeded up the passage of information. The "associational culture" which was seen in embryo amongst the middle class of the cities of the late eighteenth century spread to lower social groups and to women. This section will consider the changing form of the city at the global level and then discuss the cultural and political changes which urbanization and urban industrial production brought in its wake.

    In 1780 the basic patterns of spatial organization, function, and culture of cities remained recognizably the same as they had been at the outset of the great sixteenth-century expansion of the world economy and the concurrent development of large, grandiose states. Many cities were emporium-style ports or inland bulking centers dominated by rich merchant communities and hinterland landowners. Other cities were centers of political power, mostly of ancient foundation, but now much larger by dint of the expansion of royal court life and the beginnings of bureaucracy. A few cities in northwestern Europe and East Asia, notably London and Amsterdam and perhaps Edo, had spawned recognizably new types of financial institutions – stock exchanges, national banks, insurance brokers – in the seventeenth and eighteenth centuries. Still, the pattern was recognizably the same. About 9 percent of the world's population was urbanized in 1600. By 1800 it may have been nearer 12 percent, but the pace of change still remained slow. Britain was one of the few countries in which the rate of growth of the urban population was very much faster than that of the total population, even in the first three decades of the nineteenth century.

In the eighteenth century, most of the inland centers of power took the form of complex agglomerations of fortresses, aristocratic dwelling quarters, royal courts, specialist markets, and religious buildings. Most also displayed an underlying cosmological organization which placed religion and royal power in contrast to each other. The ancient Christian pattern of placing the church-basilica opposite the royal court-fortress and the grouping of aristocratic houses and processional routes around it had been exported to Central and South America and even to places such as Goa, Malacca, and Macao in the East. Mosque, sultan's palace, and *madina*, or city square, formed a similar triad in Islamic society. In Indian and Indian-influenced cities, primacy in residential patterns was given to priestly Brahmin families, who lived in "pure" quarters around the temple area. In China, the traditional conception of the city as a "pivot of the four quarters" was maintained even in the huge land area of Beijing. Most aristocrats spent part of their time at court and part in their ancestral rural seats, a pattern which was institutionalized in the *sankin-kotai* system of Tokugawa Japan. The Japanese ruler, the shogun, like his European and Ottoman contemporaries, had an arm lock on the great nobles when part of their families and possessions were in striking distance of his court. Court life and proximity to the centers of power were attractive in their own right. In Paris, *hôtels*, in the original sense of great town houses, represented the metropolitan palaces of regional elites. In London, clubs had begun to spring up to provide for the social life of young aristocrats seeking jobs and excitement in the city. In Chinese and Chinese-influenced cities, urban associational life was structured around guilds or associations of people claiming to share a common regional background.

The urban populations of South Asia, Southeast Asia, and Africa remained quite mobile, with large bodies of soldiers, servants, and their families following the rulers around their territories in visitations or on campaigns. In India, the mobile Mughal camp sometimes had a population half the size of the capital city itself, Delhi, which was proportionately reduced in population. Many cities also exhibited distinctly rural features, especially on their fringes, where peasant families retained strong links with villages which provided them with food and marriage partners. In times of distress or warfare, large parts of the urban populations retreated to the countryside. In these cities, as in the port emporia and inland bulking centers, small-scale artisan production remained very important. Master artisans, financed by local merchants and drawing on local produce, were themselves local notables. Through guilds or professional associations, they provided charity for the poor and patronized large numbers of local religious institutions – friaries and nunneries, Sufi settlements, Buddhist monasteries, and gurus' hospices.

THE URBAN IMPACT OF THE GLOBAL CRISIS, 1780–1820

The first major rupture to these old-established patterns was delivered, not so much by industrialization, as by the wars of revolution and European imperial expansion which erupted between 1776 and 1815. Some of the great cities of the old order actually declined in size. Others continued to expand slowly but forfeited some of their political and cultural primacy. At a deeper level, the expansion of world trade and industrialization gradually made commercial towns more wealthy and created new working-class conglomerations. These "new" cities developed their own forms of social and cultural life, which were often more self-consciously modern than that of the older centers. Here economic growth led to rapid urbanization and cities which were divided by class as well as status.

Over much of western Europe, cities suffered from the revolutionary wars but continued to expand. What was more striking were the political and ideological conflicts over the use of space. In Paris, large areas of royal and aristocratic dwellings, notably the Louvre, the Palais Royal, and the Place des Vosges, were converted into public spaces, museums, and tenements during the revolution and empire. The royal tombs at the church of Saint Denys were desecrated. A similar fate overtook ducal palaces and chapels all over north Italy and in parts of Germany. In Spanish America, royal palaces were occupied by Creole political bosses who became presidents and governors of the new republics after 1820. The revolutionary period certainly opened more space in cities to a bourgeois public. By the same token, experience of war and revolution began a slow process by which elites sought to separate themselves from, and control, the spaces of the poor more effectively. In other respects, the revolutionary period opened up the use of space.

In some parts of Asia and Africa, the change was more abrupt. The great Mughal cities – Delhi, Agra, and Murshidabad in Bengal – were already in decline before the dismemberment of the empire, and the flight of nobility reduced them to shadows of their former selves.[28] This pattern was played out in Iran and Java, where imperial decline and foreign conquest felled other ancient cities. Struggles between the sultans and regional magnates damaged some of the great centers of the Middle East. The Persian cities of Isfahan, Qom, and Shiraz, fabled homes of great Quranic scholars and the poetry of Saadi, were neglected for the new capital, Tehran, which resembled a Russian provincial capital. Cairo lost influence to the typical Mediterranean metropolis of Alexandria for more than a century, even though it continued to expand slowly and function as a religious and royal center. Alexandria became the seat of a wealthy commercial oligarchy, part Egyptian and part European. Its developing urban culture reflected "European" more than "Islamic" influences.

A more subtle and powerful threat to the integrity of these old cities was the direction of general economic development. Even before substantial industrialization, the large growth of trade was beginning to give new commercial centers a great edge. The Atlantic world saw the rapid growth of Nantes, Bristol, Glasgow, Bordeaux, and Boston. Beirut and Alexandria grew substantially in the Mediterranean. On the Indian Ocean and in the China Seas, Bombay, Calcutta, Madras, Shanghai, Singapore, and later Hong Kong, Tianjin, Port Arthur, and Darien challenged the cultural preeminence of the older inland cities and became the forcing houses of new ideas and styles well before direct colonial rule was imposed. The patterns of middle-class sobriety established in Boston and New York set the social norms of the new republic. In Britain, aristocratic and landed society survived or even flourished in the nineteenth century. But here, as in other parts of northern Europe, the bourgeois city became politically and culturally significant. The antislave trade movement in Britain and France was closely correlated with the rise of new commercial centers such as Liverpool and Nantes. The demand for constitutional reform in Britain also came predominantly from this quarter.

In coastal Asia and Africa, patterns of trade already in the process of expansion before industrialization had likewise produced rich commercial classes which re-created the independent city-states of the past, even within a colonial or semi-colonial world. Manila and Batavia, respectively the Spanish and Dutch centers of Southeast Asia, emerged as new hybrid cities. Locally based European naval power forced or attracted local merchants to trade in these ports. Within a generation from 1770 to 1800, Calcutta, Madras, and Bombay all overtook in size even the largest of the centers of inland political power in South Asia. Their merchant princes constructed palaces and reinvented a new style of public Hindu worship and a form of hybrid aristocratic display. It was these *bhadralog*, or gentry, like their contemporaries in Liverpool, Cork, and Boston, who made the first circumspect demands for indigenous political representation of a modest sort. They also demanded that the colonial power and the missionaries leave their religious practices strictly alone. These powerful commercial magnates soon found their equals in all the great seaports: Singapore, Canton, Aden, Alexandria, and Beirut. Inland centers of communication, though still dominated by landowners, also threw up a commercial middle class eager for news, commercial and political, and ready to adapt to the printing press, the railway, and the electric telegraph. Manaos on the Amazon, Chongquing (Chungking) on the Yangzi, and Kanpur on the river Yamuna were all examples of what might be called "inland port cities." They also participated in the newly modern life-styles which had spread through the coastal cities.

Predominantly manufacturing cities were quite late to develop, as the previous section suggests. This was partly because industrialization itself came late, partly because much early industrialization took place in "green field sites" around coal mines and at railheads. Manchester, Birmingham, Liège, and Essen stood on their own in the 1850s. Quite rapidly during the next decade, manufacturing and mining cities sprung up in the United States and in parts of Europe. The gold and diamond rushes created cities such as Melbourne, San Francisco, and Kimberley. Cotton mills opened up in western India, and jute mills in eastern India, in the 1860s, with Indian owners demanding protection from imported British textiles. Between 1870 and 1900, the rate of urbanization speeded up appreciably worldwide, rising from about 12 percent to 20 percent over that period. The industrial working class appears to have risen from about 15 million to 50 million over the same period.

The change was particularly striking in Africa south of the Sahara and in Australia. Large traditional trading cities had existed in northern Nigeria, and big royal centers were recorded in Ghana and Zimbabwe before the nineteenth century. The Swahili and Guinea coasts both had slave-owning city-states. But in the area that became the Union of South Africa, the urban population rose from about 7 percent to 25 percent of the total population between 1865 and 1904, as mining settlements and big agricultural exchange points developed. Cape Town, Durban, and Kimberley quite suddenly overtook the cities of the East and West African coasts as the largest cities south of the Sahara. A similar urban boom had started earlier in Australia. Victoria's 36 gold-mining towns had a population of 146,000 in 1871, though many of them declined later.[29] In Australasia, some Maori settlements had town-like qualities, but to an even greater extent than in southern and eastern Africa, the town was a European import.

RACE AND CLASS IN THE NEW CITIES

These cities saw a reformulation of social and economic life not quite as profound as that glimpsed by those socialists and sociologists who saw only alienation and anomie, but profound nevertheless. Family structures changed with urbanization, though this argument was overdone in the past. In many parts of the world, the large extended families of the past broke down into smaller units, but people still retained connections with their rural kin for reasons of security and marriage. By 1900, most internal migration in Britain and Belgium was between cities rather than from country to town. Mass cheap urban housing developed, often without proper drainage or access to water. The unpleasantness of the new urban life for the poor was deepened by industrial pollution, long work hours, and the lack of medical provision.

Table 5.3 Population of some major cities (thousands)

Year	Berlin	Bombay	Calcutta	Edinburgh	London	New York	Sydney	Edo/Tokyo
1800	172	—	—	83	1,117	60.5	—	1,200
1850	419	644.4 (1872)	633 (1872)	194	2,685	515.5	54	500 (1863)
1900	1,889	776 (1901)	847.8 (1901)	394	6,586	3,437	500	1,750 (1908)

While few historians doubt that great gaps in living standards opened up between rich and poor, fierce debate has raged over the condition of the working class in Europe and North America. Recent work has tended once again to the pessimistic view, that life spans, nutrition, and health declined somewhat in the first stages of industrialization, even if people had access to a greater variety of goods. Mortality rates varied greatly between different social classes. A study of Berlin between 1855 and 1860, for instance, revealed that professional people lived on average to the age of 54, but industrial wage-earners only to 42.[30] The situation was even bleaker in the non-European world. Universal distinctions between rich and poor were complicated by rapidly growing inequality between the rich "north" and the poor "south," which have persisted to the present day. In large measure, these growing differentials reflected the adverse terms of trade between Europe and North America, which produced technologically advanced goods, and Asia and Africa, which produced mainly agricultural raw materials and minerals, whose value added in world trade was much less.

Institutional forces, however, were equally important. Outside Europe, in areas where indigenous workers had less clout with their alien or Creole employers, the position of laborers in cities deteriorated more rapidly, and their economic position became bleaker, even than that of the peasantry. The concentration of population in the new cities made them particularly vulnerable to disease. Deaths from malnutrition remained stubbornly high, year in, year out, because people in cities did not have easy access to social networks to provide them with food, as they did in the countryside in all but the most exceptional years of famine. Casual urban workers in colonial and semi-colonial societies suffered from a structural lack of entitlement to food, goods, and services. Average life expectancy for the poor of colonial urban centers, such as Shanghai, Bombay, or Batavia, may have been as low as 28 years, lower even than that of the surrounding peasantry.

The size and poverty of the urban working classes which developed after 1870 worried the middle class and the rulers of the towns. Periodic panics about seditious syndicalism, crime, vagrancy, and violence convulsed most urban societies.[31] European colonial cities imprisoned large percentages of their young male urban populations, a practice reserved mainly for important political prisoners in the early days. Fear of "crime" was widespread, but anyone from drug-takers through religious mystics to inarticulate tribal people who had wandered into the towns could find themselves imprisoned in these impressive neoclassical or neo-Gothic establishments. More rigorous urban policing methods were introduced in Britain and France in the 1840s and 1850s, and particular attention was paid to "boweries" and *bidonvilles*, slum tenement areas which were supposed to be particular nurseries of crime. The level of policing was extraordinarily high. During the Chartist riots in Britain in 1848, 20,000 police were deployed in central London alone. Those who migrated to the towns who were different in religion or language were particular targets of uneasy urban propertied people, and likewise of urban mobs. In Britain, the east coast of the United States, and the British dominions, the Catholic Irish who migrated in their millions after the famine of 1848 were particularly suspect as carriers of crime, disease, and later, with the surfacing of the Fenian nationalist movement, political sedition. In Germany and Austria migrants from the Slavic lands to the south and east were equally suspect. While much hatred was directed against commercial Jewish families in most European cities, and especially in central Europe, poor Jewish urban dwellers were the victims of riots and harassment in Russia and Austria. Here urban political anti-Semitism became particularly virulent in the 1890s. In Russia, the humiliation of the defeat by Japan in 1904–5 gave further license to the security police and conservative mobs to attack Jewish shops and houses. Jews could easily be portrayed as anti-national. There were occasional attacks on Jews in the cities of the USA.

Just as formal legal emancipation did not improve the position of poor Jews in European towns, the few city-dwelling blacks in the United States found themselves excluded from urban services, jobs, and even white churches. By the 1880s and 1890s, a brief period when interracial democracy appeared to be on the cards had given way to a system of discrimination much subtler than that of slavery.[32] Here, as in South Africa, the vociferous white lower-middle and working class acted in concert with urban elites to create informal systems of segregation by race in the expanding cities. Vagrancy laws were used to criminalize, imprison, and segregate blacks in the mining towns of South Africa, Aborigines in Australia, urban Maori in New Zealand, and American Indians throughout the New World. In fact, the 1880s and 1890s seem to have been a period when racial awareness and segregation on the grounds of race became more obtrusive in almost all societies. Clearly, elite ideologies of race war and eugenics were important here, but it was because these ideas could be applied as a set of practices in rapidly growing cities that they became so prevalent. Since they appealed not only to the middle classes, but to suspicious and embattled white workers protecting their own livelihoods, they were enacted into law and political programs.

It seems that class divisions became more politicized to a similar degree. This should not be taken to mean that class-war was in the offing, only that governments, the middle classes, and working people were now much more aware of the significance of the "problem of labor." In the societies of the old regime, the classification of people according to social order was generally an inbred matter of bodily practice. Yet the cities of the later nineteenth century saw competition for space between middle-class and working-class people. This came quite late. The public demonstrations and demands for rights which accompanied the revolutions and constitutional upheavals of the early nineteenth century appear to have been powered by a loose congeries of the discontented: artisans, small shopkeepers, urban journeymen, petty clerks, and so on. From the 1880s, however, many urban centers began to see the active involvement of manufacturing labor in local politics, in rallies and marches, and their appearance in public places such as parks or "public" drinking houses. The politics of class therefore became a measurable and observable thing, much written about in the newspapers. The lower class, like subordinate ethnicities, became increasingly suspect as criminals and carriers of disease.

WORKING-CLASS POLITICS

How far, though, was the radical industrial working class an active agent in the new industrial and urban politics, and how far was it simply a "representation" engineered by the middle classes and administrators? By the turn of the twentieth century, radical activists and socialist thinkers had elaborated a myth of social development which saw in the world's working class the harbinger of a new type of human being. Class consciousness among the industrial proletariat was growing everywhere, they thought. The spread of trade unionism and the French form of small syndicalist societies of labor was seen as evidence of this. Most social historians until the 1970s followed this line of argument. The debate was about why revolution or radical industrial activity had not come about as widely as it ought to have done. British labor historians argued that an aristocracy of labor had been "co-opted" by the middle-class life-style and liberal political values. In the United States, the "ethnic" differences between immigrants were implicated, while historians of the largely agrarian societies of India, China, and Japan believed that workers there were still gripped by "peasant mentalities."

Recent work has developed more subtle explanations of the nature of working-class politics. Labor historians now tend to argue that the degree of working-class activity in different centers across the world was determined much more by the particular form of industry and by urban living conditions, than by any general features of "consciousness," whether working-class, ethnic, or peasant. The rash of strikes which arrived with the new century was more a product of cycles in the world economy, which caused employers to try to squeeze down wages at a time of rising prices, than of any general social change, let alone a lurch toward revolution. Just as nationalism was a consequence, more than a cause, of European wars, so working-class consciousness was a consequence of turmoil and revolution, rather than its cause. Revolutions had immediate political and military origins, rather than being the consequences of inexorable and uniform changes in class relations. An approach of this sort still allows historians to give weight to the emergence of the urban working class and the new types of social relations which characterized the late-nineteenth- and early-twentieth-century urban world. But it liberates them from the assumption that nineteenth-century working-class histories inevitably saw the growth of a unified class consciousness which eventually exploded in revolution.

The most developed industrial societies – Britain, France, the United States, and Germany – saw labor conflicts which reflected the flexing of muscles by highly skilled workers, particularly in technological industries like telegraphy, shipping, and chemicals. The coal industry, especially in France, was the scene of large-scale "industrial action" over these years. Many contemporaries, as well as later historians, saw these as harbingers of revolution. But what was mainly happening was that relatively well-off workers were trying to secure for themselves some of the benefits of rapid economic expansion which occurred once the depression of the 1870s and 1880s had ended. The prevailing sense of political change brought about by the electoral rise of the Liberals, Democratic Progressives, Radicals, and Social Democrats in these countries raised the temperature of labor negotiations. Strike action had been largely decriminalized. Despite the substantial increase in the rate of industrial stoppages in the advanced industrial economies between 1905 and 1914, it is difficult to argue, therefore, that these societies were on the verge of large-scale class conflict in 1914. On the contrary, the prevalence of strikes suggests that radicalism had been domesticated and neutered. Only the experience of total war after 1914 could redraw the lines.

Since activists and working-class intellectuals across the world now read translations of Marx, Lenin, Bakunin, Proudhon, and other radical thinkers, these industrial movements were connected. Yet, in each context, they responded to different conditions. The Russian Revolution of 1905 was not primarily a workers' revolution, or even a peasant revolution. Instead, the prevailing crisis of relations between state and society in the Russian towns had encouraged workers to express their long-term grievances about working conditions and security of employment in undercapitalized and primitive industries. There had been a growing wave of industrial strikes since the 1890s. It was strikes by students and the congress of radical local government bodies (the *zemstvos*) which set the ball of revolution rolling in the winter of 1904–5. The legitimacy of the autocracy had been dealt a mortal blow by abject failure in the war with Japan. The working class became involved only when large numbers of unarmed workers were massacred in St Petersburg on 9 January 1905. These workers, far from being radical revolutionaries initially, had been organized by a priest. His message was moral reform rather than class war, and he wished to create a loyalist trade union to preempt socialist teaching.[33] Over the spring and summer of 1905, about half a million workers in various Russian industries staged strikes. These were mostly directed to improvements in working conditions and appear to have been unorganized and adventitious, an attempt to take advantage of the state's weakness and the move towards representative government in the Duma. Though workers' representatives were sent to the short-lived St Petersburg soviet of the autumn of 1905, this was basically a creation of radical urban politicians and had relatively little connection with the emerging trade unions. After 1905, the waxing and waning of strikes among Russia's industrial workers reflected the fact that trade unions had been sanctioned legally. It gives no prima facie evidence of an increase in working-class militancy directed to political ends.

The contemporary strikes in Bombay, occasioned by the imprisonment by the British of the radical Congress leader Bal Gangadhar Tilak, drew on a deep vein of resentment among the textile workers of the city. These people were not in general striking because they were peasants in disguise, moved by the religious symbolism of the Tilak party. Nor did they withdraw their labor out of a new homogeneous class ideology. For they were fragmented in status, origins, and crafts. It appears to have been the widespread attempt of the management, both British and Indian, to keep down wages and benefits at a time when the cost of housing and food was rising which explains the outbreak.[34] Broadly, as in Europe, the best-organized strikes in China, Africa, and the Middle East before 1914 occurred among privileged workers. These were generally European expatriates: men working in the docks in telegraph offices, on the railways and tramways in places such as Shanghai, Cape Town, and Port Said. In South America, labor conflicts were particularly violent. In 1906, the Chilean authorities put down labor disputes in the coastal town of Antafagosta, killing hundreds. In 1907 alone, 231 strikes took place in Buenos Aires.[35] Such people were jostling for advancement, like their European contemporaries, rather than harbingers of social revolution.

While urbanization transformed life-styles and projected class differences into the political arena, then, urban workers do not appear to have suffered mass alienation by the beginning of the twentieth century. Nor did they desire to purge the world of private property. Where cities were important was the way in which they dramatized the politics of industrial relations and allowed people to adopt new ways of thinking and acting politically. Cities became great stages on which were played the dramas of popular and radical politics. Even in the most industrialized parts of the world, a stable "working-class consciousness" had probably not come into existence. But the idea of the working class as a worldwide phenomenon had become entrenched. In part, this was because governments now feared networks of syndicalists and anarchists, who had staged some extraordinary coups in the assassination of Russian tsars and French presidents. The rhetoric of international socialism was often in front of their eyes as left-wing newspapers disseminated what had become known as Marxism. In part, however, it was because the spread of the uniformities of industrial and urban life imposed similar conditions on working people in different continents and began to give them a sense of their aggregate power. The practice and, even more, the ideology of working-class activism was to be a critical feature of the early and mid-twentieth century.

WORLDWIDE URBAN CULTURES AND THEIR CRITICS

There have always been cities of great reputation as the seat of kingdoms, republics, or holy men. During the course of the nineteenth century, however, global urban culture emerged as a more uniform and distinct pattern of living. Already at the end of the eighteenth century, American and north European cities had begun to be the scene of common patterns of leisure and sociability among the gentry, upper mercantile elites, and even working people. This became much more general in the following century. In addition to the profusion of urban societies, clubs, meeting halls, and community associations, the café provided a potent symbol for the urban public space, both as a meeting point for men and women and as a scene of political and philosophical discussion. To reinforce the importance of the revolutionary period in quickening these changes, one need only point to the "bistro," or French-style eating house. This had its origins in the "fast food" kitchens organized for the Russian troops who occupied Paris in 1815. The original coffee houses, places such as Quadri's and Florian's in Venice, the former the pro-Austrian, the latter the nationalist drinking haunt, spawned a thousand imitations across Europe, especially in the two great seats of radical politics, Paris and Vienna. Radical editors such as Karl Kraus, the Viennese socialist and social reformer, and Émile Zola, curse of the French political and military establishment, organized their campaigns and movements through the cafés. Equally important was the fact that, by the 1880s or 1890s, respectable women could be seen – indeed, very much wished to be seen – in cafés and big public restaurants. Public space remained deeply gendered in most big cities across the world. Yet the significant inroads made by women into these redoubts of male sociability in the café and the restaurant were as important as the great campaigns for female suffrage in shifting the balance of power between the sexes a little.

The great American contribution to the reordering of public space was the department store. Paris had its *supermarchées* as early as the reign of Napoleon III, but the Americans did it bigger and better. Originating in the need of dispersed agricultural communities to purchase a wide range of specialist goods in one place and at one time, the great urban shop had, by the end of the century, become the fount of a new consumerism. The stores had become places to enjoy sociability through common patterns of luxury consumption, especially for women. The pattern established by such places as Sears Roebuck in Chicago was extended to Harrods and Selfridges in London before the First World War. All these shops provided facilities specifically for women. In the extra-European world, great hotels often came to fill the roles of club, store, and restaurant for the large mobile population of European expatriates and even for Chinese, Indian, Malay, Indo-Chinese, or Egyptian aristocracy or rich mercantile magnates. Elsewhere in colonial cities, public space was not only gendered but racially divided. There were a few exceptions to this. Humanist movements such as freemasonry, theosophy, and spiritualism transcended the racial divide, as did some churches, Young Men's Christian Associations, and a handful of polo grounds and racecourses. Generally, though, the growing indigenous middle classes of these cities founded their own clubs, associations, and guest houses to cater for a population which now needed to move frequently for court cases, higher education, and marriage. These societies became the forcing houses of political discussion and debate. Calcutta University's Coffee House in College Street and the Shanghai YMCA common room were as potent symbols of the emergence of anti-colonial politics as Dublin Post Office and the killing ground in Amritsar were to become after 1914. In addition, these symbols of urban living were universal. Young radicals from the European colonies, China, and Japan could find fellow spirits in similar common rooms and coffee houses in London, Paris, Amsterdam, and Berlin. Ho Chi Minh, future leader of Indo-Chinese Communists, worked in "Polidor," the Paris restaurant, before the First World War. The global

ILLUSTRATION 5.4   The new architecture: The Reliance Building, Chicago, 1895.

uniformity of professional and academic training brought Mahatma Gandhi and Jan Smuts to London, Sun Yatsen to Honolulu, and B. R. Ambedkar, future leader of India's "untouchables," to New York.

With the expansion of industry, common patterns of urban sociability also began to emerge among the working class. Traditional forms of male sporting interest were pressed into service. Wrestling circles had been a feature of traditional aristocratic society in the Ottoman Empire, Iran, and central and south Asia. Now wrestling clubs, or *akharas*, proliferated in great numbers among the male workers of Bombay, Ahmedabad, and Tehran.[36] They provided a powerful network of organizations and interests outside the work place, which could be used for social and political mobilization. More, they became symbols of national popular culture. Similarly, in European cities, the rapid spread of sociable games – especially football, boxing, and greyhound racing – after 1870, allowed men, at least, to develop interests outside both the work place and the home. The phenomenal spread of the game of football throughout the world at the end of the nineteenth century was evidence of the power of the desire for companionship amongst ordinary people. The sports club, working man's café, or public house became a central place for social and political discussion, as also an outlet through which common patterns of consumption were encouraged by advertisement and emulation.

So cities across the world became more uniform in appearance than they had been even 50 years before. Earlier patterns of segmented residential areas and quarters, which retained the diverse character of large urban villages, broke down. Governments and ruling groups had a clear interest in disciplining urban space, providing broad highways and grid-like patterns of urban living. This helped the authorities to maintain public order in an age of great street demonstrations. It also made it easier to contain the great urban fires which had been a constant feature of the timber, mud, or wattle housing of the past. They could also quarantine populations in the face of the epidemics of cholera and plague which broke out through the century. The result was to make middle-class and working-class, white and non-white, more homogenous groupings and foster the growth of exclusive and sometimes antagonistic identities among them.

One development which was particularly important for the future of world-wide residential patterns was the development of the middle-class "suburb." In the old urban world the outskirts of great towns were a straggling mass of transport areas and wholesale marts. The houses of servants and poorer people mingled with and surrounded those of the rich. Towards the end of the nineteenth century, as people of middle income withdrew from town centers, large islands of superior housing began to appear on their outskirts. The development of transport as a result of industrialization, represented by the train, tram, and car, made this feasible. In the suburbs, the middle classes could enjoy a sanitized, secluded life distant from the din of political tumult or the sight of poverty. Sometimes the architecture of these enclaves was consciously archaic, as in the neo-Gothic of suburban Manchester, Melbourne, and Bombay, or the "neo-burgherish" of outer Amsterdam and Batavia.

Sometimes it was modernist, as in the suburbs of New York or Barcelona. The state was sometimes active in forming such enclaves, especially in colonial societies where civic improvement trusts created space for settlements of European expatriates and rich indigenes by sequestering the lands of suburban villagers. Large military settlements, inhabited by white soldiers, were built up on the fringes of many cities in the Asian and African world. Suburbs also reflected the self-modeling of the middle classes themselves: the desire to live in secluded, garden-rich settings, though ones not too distant from centers of power and wealth.

Yet governments were also making symbolic gestures when they widened streets, provided lighting, and stopped residents encroaching on newly demarcated public space. They announced their modernity and their adherence to science. St Petersburg became the neoclassical symbol of modern Russia in the nineteenth century, while Moscow remained a religious center, place of royal coronation, beloved of the "Slavophiles," who honored the traditions of old Russia.[37] The tension between old royal and religious centers, and the need for the state to proclaim its modernity in the great arena of the city, was particularly sharp in the non-European world. The khedives of Egypt and the post-Tanzimat rulers of the Ottoman Empire made a special project of establishing boulevards, opera houses, public squares adorned with statuary, and flower gardens adjoining the new railways stations in their cities. Much of this was wasteful expenditure by the standards of strict economic management. Yet it distanced them from the old oriental societies of the past and complemented the vaunted power of the state, invested in great official office blocks, chancelleries, and law courts. The great *art nouveau* buildings of the city center of Madrid symbolized a new type of power from the old Habsburg palace with its studied closeness to the cathedral. Equally, it is difficult to imagine an urban scene more different from the old low-rise Chinese city, "pivot of the four quarters," than the waterfront Bund at Shanghai, packed with neoclassical hotels and banks.

By no means all the world's intelligentsia applauded these changes. Despite the protests of a few nostalgics in the Victorian arts and crafts movement in supposedly traditional Britain, the British public appeared unconcerned about the creation of huge areas of urban jungle. The new wealth of the United States was even more determined to establish a whole new image of urban modernity for itself, initiating massive, high-rise developments in the 1890s, even before the rise of real-estate prices in cities really justified this. Instead, the strongest reaction against the alienation and anomie of the cities came from continental Europe and from some parts of Asia, from both conservatives and radicals, both sociologists and artists. The idolizing of "deep France" (*La France profonde*) and the emergence of a "back to the land" movement in Germany came well before the urban population moved above 70 percent of the total in either of these societies. In China, the Confucian tradition had always registered deep ambiguity about cities, which were regarded as the realm of the merchant and often the seat of corruption. Modernist writers reinvented these themes and turned them against capitalists and foreigners. The deep distrust felt by many urban intellectuals in Asia for the alienness of the city was also being expressed by the writers of Bengali popular farces, who excoriated the new middle classes, as well as Japanese poet idolizers of the "noble peasant." They were signaling their revulsion two decades before Gandhism and Japanese political expansionism urged a return to the village and the dignity of labor in the rice fields.

CONCLUSION

The nineteenth-century intelligentsia regarded industrialization and the expansion of urban life as the most important features of their age. They were both right and wrong. Historians have demonstrated that industrialization came relatively late in the century, was often rural, and that its effects, though powerful, were quite patchy even as late as 1914. The idea that industrialization gave rise to a large, homogeneous, self-conscious working class is also now difficult to sustain. Yet the contemporary intellectuals were right in the sense that, as political, social, and even artistic symbols, the idea of the working class and the modern city had been invested with great power by the end of the century. Politicians of the right and left alike acted with an eye to encouraging or placating what they believed to be a growing and powerful working class. Most social thinkers and artists were equally preoccupied with the life of the modern city, whether they feared the moral and aesthetic corruption which it spawned or celebrated the liberation and equality which it offered.

Even if industrial capitalists and a stock-owning middle class had not been able to grasp unchallenged political power before 1900, industrialization and the politics of cities had registered powerful effects from at least the mid-century. In the 1850s, European rulers took a more active role in sponsoring railways, telegraphs, the development of war industries, and the planning of cities. Even that modestly inclined state, the US federal government, flexed its muscles here. Japanese and Chinese authorities soon followed suit. These interventions gave the nationalism and empire building of the late nineteenth century a broader scope and a harder, more aggressive edge. But the post-1848 statesmen of "blood and iron" had another advantage on which to capitalize. These were the nationalist aspirations of their subjects, forged in war, diffused by print, and reinforced by propaganda. The next chapter considers the new nationalism, the new imperialism, and new definitions of ethnicity.

[6] NATION, EMPIRE, AND ETHNICITY, C.1860–1900

THIS chapter follows the later nineteenth-century career of nationalism and empire building, which were among the dominant features of the age. It integrates discussion of these two great incubuses of historiography, but also examines the peoples, ethnicities, and religious groups that were excluded by nations and marginalized by empires. The chapter argues that the more vigorous stirring of nationality in the late nineteenth century was a global phenomenon. It emerged contemporaneously in large parts of Asia, Africa, and the Americas, rather than first in Europe, later to be exported "overseas." In many cases, the tide of nationalism also drew on indigenous legends, histories, and sentiments about land and people, rather than being a malign imposition of the West. In future, theorists of nationalism will have to bring the extra-European world into a central position in their analyses, rather than seeing it as an "add-on extra." Finally, the chapter considers the many links between emerging national institutions which began to create an inter-*national* civil society at the end of the nineteenth century. Again, the paradox of globalization reveals itself. The hardening of boundaries between nation-states and empires after 1860 led people to find ways of linking, communicating with, and influencing each other across those boundaries.

Nationalism (along with empire) is among the few thoroughly "theorized" historical topics. It will be useful, therefore, to consider "theories" of nationalism before examining the questions "When was nationalism?" and "Who or what created it?"

THEORIES OF NATIONALISM

"Theories of nationalism" were a major talking point for historians of the later twentieth century. This was partly because nationalism refused to die, as it was supposed to in the socialist theories which had earlier influenced historians. It was partly because historians were stirred into action by the programmatic

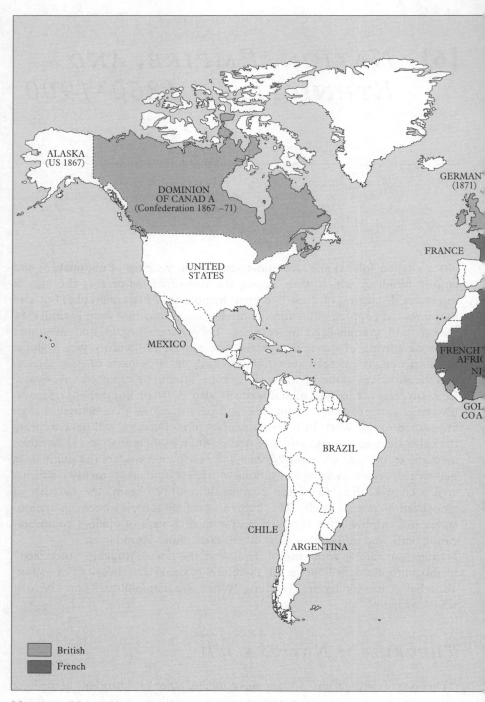

ALASKA
(US 1867)

DOMINION
OF CANAD A
(Confederation 1867 –71)

UNITED
STATES

MEXICO

GERMAN
(1871)

FRANCE

FRENCH
AFRIC
NI

GOL
COA

BRAZIL

CHILE

ARGENTINA

British

French

MAP 6.1   New nations, new empires, c.1860–1900.

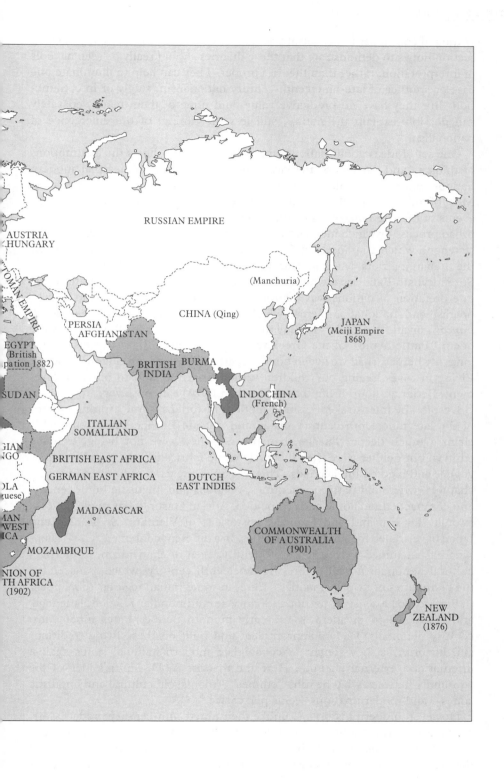

RUSSIAN EMPIRE

AUSTRIA
HUNGARY

OTTOMAN EMPIRE

(Manchuria)

CHINA (Qing)

JAPAN
(Meiji Empire
1868)

PERSIA
AFGHANISTAN

EGYPT
(British
pation 1882)

BRITISH
INDIA

BURMA

INDOCHINA
(French)

SUDAN

ITALIAN
SOMALILAND

GIAN
NGO

BRITISH EAST AFRICA

GERMAN EAST AFRICA

DUTCH
EAST INDIES

OLA
uese)

MADAGASCAR

AN
WEST
ICA

MOZAMBIQUE

COMMONWEALTH
OF AUSTRALIA
(1901)

NION OF
TH AFRICA
(1902)

NEW
ZEALAND
(1876)

writing of colleagues in the social sciences, at least on this issue. The following section hopes to demonstrate that these theories should really be seen as tools of interpretation, rather than theories proper. They can help to illuminate one case or another of late-nineteenth-century nationalism, singly or in conjunction. But they have no predictive value, and none of them taken separately can possibly explain the nature, still less the timing, of the emergence of nationalism.[1]

One set of ideas about nationalism, which directly follows the assumptions of thinkers and patriots of the late nineteenth century, argues that modern nations emerged naturally out of earlier communities of language and culture. Most of today's cultural nationalists still hold to this view. They assert that the events of the late nineteenth century were no more than the culmination of a broad process by which incipient peoples claimed nationhood and claimed the statehood which guaranteed it. This was the historical legitimation sought by the Italian patriots Mazzini and Garibaldi, and by their Indian admirer, Surendranath Bannerjea, who wrote of "nations in making." This naturalistic interpretation of nations was the message proclaimed in a thousand novels, operas, and national anthems, which lauded the German *Volk, le peuple français*, or an "Egypt for the Egyptians." Typical of these effusions was the poem "Battle hymn" of the Greek revolutionary poet, Rigas Feraios: "How long, my heroes, shall we live in bondage, alone like lions, on ridges, on peaks. Living in caves, seeing our children turned from the land to bitter enslavement. Better an hour of life that is free than forty years in slavery."[2]

Despite the intense skepticism of modern historians, some aspiring nations of the late nineteenth century inside and outside Europe could reasonably claim a much deeper lineage than others. They were not living, evolving entities, but neither were they the lately come fabrications of populist demagogues and bigoted intellectuals. This was often the case, as implied in earlier chapters, where old patriotic identities, religious and linguistic homogeneity, and compact ethnic homelands coincided. Adrian Hastings has made the case strongly for England and France.[3] Historians of Vietnam, Sri Lanka, and Japan have argued for similar continuities. In a different context, T. C. W. Blanning has examined a deep sense of identity, even of chauvinism, in German cultural nationalism well before the nineteenth century, which transcended the boundaries of its principalities.[4] Elites in some Indian regions, too, appear to have forged a sense of patriotic identity around popular religion, language, and resistance to invaders in the early modern period. Later nineteenth-century nationalist leaders appropriated and built on these living traditions and histories as they sought to consolidate modern national states against internal and external enemies. Here the theorist A. D. Smith's idea of the continuity between what he calls "ethnies" – that is, old cultural and linguistic zones – and modern nations seems persuasive.[5]

However, modern historians, unlike their nineteenth-century predecessors, are very skeptical about such claims, with the majority arguing that nations were recently "constructed" by political forces or acts of imagination, rather than growing like living organisms. And there is no doubt that in many regions

during the late nineteenth century, it was indeed these state-driven constructions of nationalist sentiment which were most in evidence. Here, the debate
has turned, therefore, on the conditions which made it possible for elites to
invent or construct nations. In the 1980s many professional historians
followed the anthropologist and philosopher Ernest Gellner,[6] in arguing that
nationalism was closely connected with urbanization and industrialization. He
observed that in nineteenth- and early twentieth-century Europe, and in Asia
and Africa after the 1930s, it was people congregated in new urban centers
who were most likely to portray themselves as unified peoples and to demand
statehood. It was, for instance, the melee of Hungarians, Serbs, and Italians in
nineteenth-century Vienna and their competition for resources and jobs which
tended to harden the distinctions between these "races" and propel their
demands for national autonomy.

Gellner's, then, was a modernization theory. It saw nationalism as the
functional equivalent in politics of capitalism, industrialization, the nuclear
family, and "possessive individualism," forces which were all believed to be on
the march to dominance across the modern world by steady stages. In this
view, nationalism moved from west to east to south, finally coming to rest in
Africa in the twentieth century, as the "last continent" was penetrated by
capitalism and urbanization. Rather predictably, Gellner's thesis works best
for the central and eastern European societies which were to the forefront of
his mind. So, the confrontation between Czechs, Germans, and Hungarians
within the Austrian Empire took place in an atmosphere of rapid urbanization.
Prague's population, for example, rose from 157,000 in 1850 to 514,000 in
1900.[7] It also speaks to the German case and to Italy, insofar as Piedmont at
least was a new industrial center. There are many other cases, however, where
vigorous national movements emerged in societies where industrialization
remained at a very low level.

Writers who were less sure about the onward march of capitalism and
individualism came to argue, somewhat later than Gellner's book, that nationalism was the product of the state itself, the working of a pure principle of
power. As Eric Hobsbawm puts it, nationalism follows the state, not vice
versa.[8] He and John Breuilly,[9] above all, have argued that the conscious policy
of new political elites, especially in the later nineteenth century, was what
created nationalism. States promoted popular education, defined citizenship
and its duties, counted and imprisoned people. Their sense of urgency was
enhanced by the needs of capitalism, the rise of socialism, working-class
activism, and the fear of crime. This was a period when governments began
to institute regular censuses and to control immigration and emigration more
closely through the use of the passport system. All this was consciously or
unconsciously directed to strengthening the sentiment of nationalism and
making people on the margins choose one or another nation-state. Even the
United States in the later nineteenth century fits this model quite well.

A corollary of this theory, rather than a separate theory in its own right, is
found in the formulation of Benedict Anderson made in the 1980s.[10] This was
a more anthropological view, which emphasized the role of the imagination

and shared feeling in the invention of nationalism, rather than changes in power and resources. Nations were "imagined communities" created by "print capitalism." The diffusion of books and newspapers across the world inscribed a sense of belonging in the minds of those elites and, later, ordinary people who read them. Anderson's position has one great advantage. It can explain why people in territories not yet subjected to capitalism, industrial urbanism, or even strong states could begin to advance claims to nationhood. This is why his work, which was generated out of a study of Dutch Indonesia, and has been particularly popular with historians of India and Africa in the nineteenth century.

A complete account of the emergence of the competitive nationalisms of the late-nineteenth-century world would incorporate all of these discrete "theories" as preconditions. Some of them would have to be given more weight in some situations than in others. So, for instance, the emergence of nationalist movements in the still-rural societies of Asia, the Middle East, and North Africa widely predated modern industrial urbanization and even the widespread diffusion of print capitalism. In these societies, urbanization rarely went higher than 10 percent before the end of the nineteenth century, and male literacy was probably a few percentage points less. Nor, in fact, was this simply a condition of the non-European world. It is important to remember that even in 1848, when something which could be called nationalism was clearly on the march, the same was true for Germany, where 75 percent of the population still lived on the land, and the urban population was made up predominantly of officials and old-style artisans.

Again, the emergence of nationalism was not a single event so much as a process. An inchoate sense of nationality, generated by memories and traditions of earlier patriotisms, could be honed and molded by the activity of a newly powerful state, if we follow the arguments of John Breuilly and Eric Hobsbawm. This is not to say that the state created a sense of nationalism out of nothing. In the United States, for instance, the Civil War forged more firmly a sense of American nationality, at least among the dominant northern population. After 1865 the word "nation" was heard more often across the North American continent.

This last example reminds us of a condition for the emergence of nationalism which has remained rather marginal in most of the major "theories": the importance of armed conflict, particularly armed conflict between states, but also conflict among their constituent populations. The intensification of nationalism during the nineteenth century was itself preeminently a consequence of war and invasion. Nationalism defined itself against "others." The experience of common military service, basic education in the ranks, and elite leadership widely transformed peasants and workers into nationalists. In turn, this militarized nationalism often gave rise to further wars and invasions. The world wars at the end of the eighteenth century speeded up the process by which the regional patriotisms of the old order were transformed into more exclusive and aggressive nationalisms. The multiple crises of the middle of the nineteenth century widely confirmed that transition, not only in Europe, but also in the Americas, the Middle East, and Asia. The new industrial machinery and communications discussed in the last chapter made a national community more visible, or at least more feasible.

WHEN WAS NATIONALISM?

For historians, then, if not generally for theorists, the timing of the emergence of the new nationalism at world level is important. This needs elaboration. As stated, nationalism has often been seen as a sentiment which was passed from supposedly advanced white people to less advanced Asians and Africans. This diffusionist theory needs to be greatly modified. It is true that many sub-Saharan Africans lived in local or regional communities without deep social hierarchies in which broader social identities had little relevance. Yet even here, the mid-nineteenth century was a period when, in response to missionary propagation of the Bible, local intellectuals writing in African vernaculars began to assert the claims of African "peoples." Moreover, vigorous independence movements existed in India and Egypt by the 1880s, and across other parts of Asia by 1900. Japan was in many respects a nation-state before the end of the Tokugawa regime in 1868. It may well have had as strong a sense of nationalism as contemporary Germany, and one more developed than Italy's. The contrast with Europe should not, therefore, be overdrawn. After all, few of the nationalist revolutionaries of 1848 in Europe had widespread support. As Jonathan Sperber notes, the leading Romanian nationalist newspaper of that year had only 250 subscribers.[11]

With this caveat, it still seems possible to set out some broad periods of change which would make sense at a world level, and not simply for Europe. The two interlinked sets of world crises, those of 1780–1815 and 1848–65, gave a great impetus to incipient national identities. It is generally accepted that Napoleon's conquests in Europe gave a fillip to national identities in Germany, Italy, and Russia. Equally, French and Russian invasion made Ottomans, Egyptians, and other North Africans aware of a heightened sense of vulnerability and of the need to reorder their societies. Two generations later, the Eurasian wars of the mid-nineteenth century convinced the elites of late Tokugawa Japan of the need for self-strengthening. In India, the 1857 rebellion and the new British invasion which it brought about forced the merchants and professional people of the seaboard regions to reconsider their status within the empire.

This heightened and broadened sense of nationality was not simply a consequence of the rolling tide of global wars, however. It also reflected new opportunities for inter-regional communications and the transfer and adaptation of ideologies. In the 1820s, the Indian reformer Raja Ram Mohun Roy was able to read about the post-Napoleonic revolutions in Europe in Calcutta's English newspapers and wrote about national self-determination. Before 1914, Nguyen Ai Quoc, alias Ho Chi Minh, was reading about the thought of Thomas Jefferson, the American founding father, in his French school books. Nor did these ideas and models simply move from the West to "the rest." Even by the 1880s, Japan's own hybrid modernity had become a powerful model for other Asian and African nationalists.

The classic general histories of Europe describe the later nineteenth century as an age of alliances and tension between newly industrialized nation-states. These nations projected their power abroad in the guise of a "new imperialism," exemplified particularly in the partition of Africa. This broad periodization still holds true, though it was a global, not merely a European, one. After 1860, political leaders within and outside Europe rapidly extended their project of making nation-states. By 1870, Italy was unified under the leadership of a rapidly industrializing and modernizing Piedmont, following the intervention of France and Prussia against her erstwhile overlord, Austria. Though landed magnates still retained great influence, especially in the south, a small industrial middle class based in Milan and Turin, which consciously adopted the Tuscan form of the Italian language, provided the country with a degree of unity. Germany was unified in 1871 following the military victories of Prussia over two former overlords of the German-speaking regions, Austria and France. While the German fatherlands still attracted the loyalty of their people, a common culture and language and a growing role in the outside world brought together the landowners of the east, the bourgeois of the Rhine valley, and the Catholic peasantry of the south.

In the same span of years, rapid social change and the reestablishment of the Union in the United States brought into being a more vigorous sense of American nationality. The British dominions, Canada, Australia, and New Zealand, became federated states between 1860 and 1901. In Japan, meanwhile, young reformers refashioned the authority of the Meiji emperor as the center of the nation. In eastern Europe, pan-Slavism, encouraged by a newly assertive Russia, began to partition the European parts of the Ottoman Empire into small, aggressive Christian principalities following the Balkan War of 1878. When the British occupied Egypt in 1882, they were confronted by a coalition of military officers, clerics, and landholders which signaled the emergence of a new sense of identity in this former southern province of the Ottoman Empire. In Asia, the foundation of the Indian National Congress in 1885 and the strident denunciation of the Manchus in the 1890s by young coastal and overseas Chinese registered the desire of new Asian elites to capture "their own" embryonic nation-states.

WHOSE NATION?

Even if warfare and social changes brought into being nationalisms over similar periods, it is important to remember that the form of the national community remained highly contested and ambiguous in almost every case. It is unwise to "read back" the form of today's nationalisms into the later nineteenth century, let alone an earlier period. Irish home rule, for instance, did not require a separate Irish nation-state for many so-called Irish nationalists of the 1880s or

1890s. Thousands of Irish people, including many Catholic Irish people, were to fight in British armies in both world wars. Leaders of Britain's white dominions also remained intensely loyal to the British connection, but social and economic integration had begun to create distinct regional nationalisms in Australasia and Canada by the time of the South African war in 1899. In a very different context, proponents of what is called Egyptian nationalism certainly began to cry "Egypt for the Egyptians!" during the years of European intervention after 1876. Yet many of them were at the same time "Ottoman patriots," for whom Istanbul remained the center of the world. Some Chinese nationalists after 1896 may well have been denouncing "Manchus," oblivious to the fact that this category was partly created by the very Qing Manchu dynasty itself. But that ethnic divide became critically significant only after the Japanese occupation of Manchuria in the 1930s. So, while many more intellectuals and statesmen were talking about "the nation" after 1860, this does not mean that there was any consensus about whose nations they were, or what the nation was.

Yet we need not completely retreat to the cover of ambiguity. It may be useful to classify types of nationalism on a spectrum. This in turn makes it easier to specify historical turning points. At one end of the spectrum were the nationalisms which emerged out of "old patriotisms" – that is, relatively homogeneous communities of language and religion. These were often fortified by relatively long-lived centralized states and traditions of virtuous government. England, France, Japan, and, less surely, Indian Maharashtra and Sri Lanka fall into this category. Ireland definitely had an old sense of patriotic identity in the seventeenth and eighteenth centuries, though this identity was rather different from the Catholic mass nationalism of the end of the nineteenth century. So, too, did at least the northern part of "Vietnam," what the French called "Annam." In these areas ruling groups were able to marshal more active forms of nationalism at the end of the nineteenth century precisely because they could be rooted in an already existing sense of common purpose, reflected in common language and culture and old regional connections. Late-nineteenth-century nationalism here was not simply a top-down phenomenon, nor simply a creature of the state or its elites.[12] People from poorer and subordinate groups sought a stake in what they thought of as their nations. Sometimes, too, emigrants outside the borders of states played a powerful part in stimulating the desire for a unified national territory. Irish emigrants to the United States or Australia and Chinese emigrants to Hawaii and Southeast Asia were very important in the emergence of Irish and Chinese nationalism respectively. This type of nationalism, then, falls firmly within the camp of A. D. Smith, Adrian Hastings, and others who are skeptical that nationalism was easily "constructed" in very recent times.

At the other end of the spectrum were nationalisms which were *created by states*, as opposed to states which were created out of old patriotisms. Britain, as opposed to England, was forged during the long wars with France, and particularly during the world crisis of 1780–1820, as Linda Colley has argued. Belgian nationalism was fostered by the government after the creation, in

1831, of the Kingdom of the Belgians from a set of polyglot northern European provinces. Latin American nationalisms, similarly, followed, rather than preceded, the creation of independent states there in the 1820s and 1830s. True, literate people and landowners had a vague sense of "Creole-ness," of being American as opposed to Spanish, as early as 1760. But there had been little sense of being a "Colombian" or "Venezuelan" – the very names were later inventions. Again, there was certainly an ideal of patriotic commitment in the United States before 1860. Yet it was the Civil War and the growing, if still marginal, US participation in world affairs after that date which bred a more robust American nationalism.

Somewhere in the middle of this spectrum were located those large states whose leaders were not really sure whether to foster or suppress the various proto-nationalist leaderships which emerged within their borders during the later nineteenth century. The rulers of Russia, Austria-Hungary, the Ottoman Empire, and China all faced the problem that, by patronizing an emerging sense of nationalism in one section of their population, especially if it was a dominant one, they might pull apart the whole façade of empire. If, conversely, they failed to give such nationalist leaders their head, the rulers themselves might become politically irrelevant. These cases will be considered in more detail later in the chapter.

PERPETUATING NATIONALISMS: MEMORIES, NATIONAL ASSOCIATIONS, AND PRINT

The origins of nationhood have been treated in greater detail than has its perpetuation. In recent years, however, historians have become more interested in how the idea of nationality was represented and "read" by ordinary people. As important in the rooting of nationalisms as the brute experience of armed conflict were memories of it. Memories and traditions, education,[13] and the emergence of national politics ensured that this heightened sense of nationality was reproduced generation by generation. Sites of memory – battlefields, graveyards, the dwelling places of national liberators, the statues of patriots and martyrs – all these created the sacred landscape of nationalism. The attempt to link and formalize these sites in public memory was particularly widespread after the wars of the mid-nineteenth century. The new French Third Republic defied monarchists, Bonapartists, and the Church to impose public celebration of Bastille Day. Streets throughout France were renamed after the heroes of the Enlightenment and the 1789 revolution. In America, Washington DC was adorned with monuments to the heroes of the Union, including one memorial to the black soldiers who died in its defense. In united Italy, a huge cult developed around Garibaldi and King Victor Emmanuel, whose equine statues can still be seen galloping or strutting through the *piazze* of hundreds of Italian towns and cities (see illustration 6.1).

The state's insistence on drilling and paramilitary volunteering, which accompanied the European wars of unification, became one means by which the

ILLUSTRATION 6.1   Nationalism at the charge: Equestrian monument to Vittorio Emanuele II. Statue on Riva degli Schiavoni, Venice.

new sense of national destiny was imprinted on the mind of the following generations. School textbooks, romances, atlases, museums, public entertainments, military and naval parades kept them always in front of the eye. Outside Europe, too, aspiring leaderships could warm their hands around the memorial fires of old patriotic resisters. The tradition of "Vietnamese" resistance against the Chinese or Japanese resistance to the Mongols were embroidered in many nationalist speeches and books of the late nineteenth century.

"Racial" struggle and the military mobilization of nations had been the dominant themes of the mid-century crisis. Nationalism was heightened by these conflicts. But how did the political theory of the liberal nation-state accord with all this? Another theme of 1848 in Europe and of the Union's war against the Confederacy had been the representation of all the people. Popular politics and the democratic urge have long been recognized as the brighter side of the tarnished force of nationalism. The paradox that the search for an equal citizenry often led to a narrow nationalist autocracy is recognized in the phrase "plebiscitary dictatorship" which was used of Napoleon III, paragon of the 1848 barricades turned emperor. How far can the expansion of popular democracy be seen as a forcing house for the new nationalisms of the years after 1860?

On the face of it, it cannot. The nationalism of the leaders of the new Germany and Italy, Bismarck and Cavour, led them to be more suspicious of an extension of representative government than had been the leaders of the "springtime of peoples" in 1848. Both aristocratic liberals and the men of blood and iron were suspicious of the hold of priests and socialists on the masses. In America, the liberation of the slaves did not lead to their mass enfranchisement, as local whites soon began to rig electorates. The British elite was turned against the idea of extending the franchise in part by their observation of Napoleon III's "tyranny" in France.[14] The representation of interests through parliament was held to be a good, but democracy was still equated in the eyes of political leaders with oppression. In the new Germany, where a wide franchise did exist, electoral support carried little purchase in the inner organs of government. Elsewhere, the franchise remained severely limited, and concessions were wrung only reluctantly out of governments, in the case of Russia in 1905 by force. Non-European subjects of the colonial powers saw at best tiny local electorates or minor concessions in the right to govern parochial affairs according to the old norms. In the 1880s, for instance, the British Liberal government established municipal and district boards in India with tiny direct electorates of Indian worthies.

Even if popular sovereignty played only a muted part in the development of nationalism after 1860, the period did see the emergence of national political parties. These tended to project local events on a wider scale and to make people aware of the politics of the nation, even when they could not themselves vote. The mobilization of people through political parties and pressure groups to capture and give meaning to the state arose in the context of the decline of royal and aristocratic legitimacy after 1789. This, as chapter 4 noted, was merely halted, but not reversed after 1815. The corollary of this was the massive expansion of social and political pressure groups, from labor unions through women's movements to religious associations, which claimed the nation as a whole as their constituency. Nationalism was cemented by the constant reiteration of claims to national legitimacy made by such sectional associations, as well as by pressure from elites "at the top." So, even in the highly decentralized USA, the national political arena became more important for both Democrats and Republicans as economic and technological changes brought different parts of the Union into contact with each other.

In Britain, the Liberal Party emerged from a congeries of Nonconformist and reforming associations under the leadership of W. E. Gladstone. When the franchise was extended to include working men after 1884, the Conservatives began for the first time to enlist the support of working-class supporters. Consequently, appeals to the national interest and national symbols became an increasingly important part of British elections, and indeed of the vigorous world of voluntary associations throughout the country. In Germany, where political parties were unable to exercise much influence on ministers, the conflicts between the conservatives, the Catholic Center Party, and later the Social Democrats similarly drew politics away from the state and lodged them at a national level. In the Russian Empire, too, where popular politics was virtually non-existent before 1905, bureaucratic factions or patrimonial political interests attempting to demonstrate support were forced to campaign and build opinion in the Russian localities, Siberia, and the Ukraine. This growing sense of Russian-ness among elites in the major cities jostled uneasily with the emerging nationalist sentiments of urban Poles, Lithuanians, and Finns. In the colonized world, electorates remained tiny, if they existed at all. Yet national parties and lobby groups existed throughout the British, Dutch, and French colonial empires by the 1880s.

One further change, which fostered stronger allegiance to national political entities, was the growth of means of communication, especially of newspapers which sought to appeal to a national interest. Here Benedict Anderson's notion of imagined communities of print again becomes highly relevant, though not so much in creating nationalism as in spreading and generalizing it. In 1840, the European press had been overwhelmingly provincial, speaking to the interests and need for information of small groups of readers. After 1860, there was an impressive growth in mass publication, and the new syndicated newspapers published in their millions, many of them being directed almost at national markets. Press "barons," such as the British radical W. T. Stead and the American William Randolph Hearst, saw newspapers as vehicles for education, drawing working people to an understanding of their duty as citizens. The communications revolution had a literally electrifying effect on the aspirations of people outside Europe, too. What made the Persian "constitutional revolution" of 1909 possible, for instance, was the linking together of different centers across desert and mountain by telegraph messages. This created a much stronger sense of shared national endeavor.

The political effects of these developments were ambiguous. They strengthened national governments as well as national civil society. As so often with the development of communications media, an initial pressure towards freedom of communication was frustrated by the implementation of powerful measures of control. Governments became the protectors of telegraph lines. News syndicates such as Reuters controlled and channeled news. These controls tended to ensure that governments and national political elites read little that they did not want to hear. The war correspondent, whose despatches detailing the belligerence and brutality of the enemy were now found on middle-class breakfast tables in every major country, was the forward standard-bearer of combative nationalism. The British populist liberal politician Winston Churchill began his career as a war correspondent during Britain's African wars, for example. For even in Britain and the USA, where a long-lived sense of nationality had to some degree stifled the birth of a sharper nationalism, the joint stirrings of political parties and a hectoring press began to create a vigorous chauvinism. Before 1898, when the United States went to war over Cuba, the press stirred a wave of anti-Spanish sentiment. The strident British campaign against the

Boers, Germans, and French, which accompanied the South African War (1899–1902), and Anglo-French tension in central Africa, prepared British public opinion for the deepening of European conflicts after 1900. On the other hand, colonized peoples eagerly plugged into these novel news media. Indian nationalists eagerly read Stead's *Review of Reviews*, while North African nationalists bombarded the British and French authorities with telegrams.

FROM COMMUNITY TO NATION: THE EURASIAN EMPIRES

This section moves on from a consideration of "theories of nationalism" and their broad development to chart in more detail the emergence of nationalist leaderships in areas where the old agrarian empires had been dominant. As a type of nationalism, these cases were located in the middle of the spectrum between old patriotisms and state-constructed nationalisms which was outlined above. The rise of nationalism in these polities was perhaps the most important development of the later nineteenth and early twentieth centuries. Of course, as chapter 11 will argue, it is important not to write off the great empires too early. One can point to parts of the world, and even parts of these same imperial polities, where nationalism was of little salience before 1914. All the same, there were large tracts of former agrarian empires where vociferous nationalist leaderships emerged quite rapidly after about 1860. This created severe strains in these complex societies and often resulted, as the next section will show, in the harassment and exclusion of "ethnic minorities," a tendency which also became sharper after 1860.

Multiethnic empires faced a severe dilemma in the late nineteenth century: whether to patronize or suppress these stirrings of nationalism. European and quasi-European empires had particular problems. The Habsburg dynasty and its German ruling groups were forced to cede more and more influence to their Hungarian partners in power, if only to fend off a growing challenge from spokesmen for the "Magyar people" reflected in newspapers, books, and growing resentment among urbanizing Hungarians hungry for jobs and status.[15] This in turn raised questions about what it meant to be a Czech, a Slovak, or a Romanian in the Habsburg lands. Most historians of the Austro-Hungarian Empire see the 1890s as an important turning point. During this decade, nationalist spokesmen appear to have gathered widespread support, especially in the big cities and amongst the more prosperous farmers. Russian rulers faced similar difficulties. Tsar Alexander III realized that he had to give a degree of latitude to Russian Orthodox nationalism within his empire. The danger was that this could easily spark into life leaderships which claimed to represent Polish, Lithuanian, and other nationalities. For these non-Russians continued to make up 60 percent of the tsar's subjects. The palace looked on in horror during the late 1870s when Russian nationalist agitation in the press and society forced Russia into a costly war with the Ottoman Empire.[16]

In Middle Eastern, North African, and Asian polities, the dilemma of how to handle national aspirations was heightened by economic backwardness and European dominance. In the European parts of the Ottoman Empire, the Orthodox Church, the Greek language, and the success of Greek entrepreneurs within the eighteenth-century Mediterranean had spurred Greek patriotism. The old Christian commonwealth of the eastern Roman Empire was already showing some fissures at this time, as Greeks and "Slavs" began to create different lineages of nationhood for themselves. It was, however, the intervention of Ottoman armies in Greece during the 1820s which forged a more cohesive sense of nationhood among Greeks and made possible the creation of an independent Greek kingdom. The contemporary European discovery of the ancient Greek past invested this nationalism with an invented historical lineage and encouraged the Western powers to accord Greece the trappings of nationhood. Successively, over the next 80 years, the other Christian parts of the Balkans – Serbia, Romania, and Bulgaria – progressed towards independence. At a deeper level than the intervention of the Christian powers, the main force aiding the intelligentsia in fragmenting the empire was the practical calculation of the peasantry that it would gain more secure property rights after national independence from the Ottomans.

Elsewhere in the Ottoman Empire, particularly in Syria, some historians have argued that there was a vague sense of "Arabness" emerging in the eighteenth century. This did not imply any hostility to the adjacent Ottoman Turkish populations or the Ottoman governors who ruled Syria. It was reflected, though, in a sense of sacred and historical geography, a kind of "soft" patriotism. It was the wars of the late nineteenth century between the Ottomans and the Russians and Austrians which began to create wider fissures outside the Balkans. Ottoman rulers facing Christian aggression sometimes tried to rouse Muslim feeling against the foreigners. But this was problematic, because it was bound to raise questions about the status of the many Christians and Jews who still owed allegiance to the sultan in the central Ottoman lands. Alongside religion, ethnic origin became a site of political debate. If Greeks were a nationality, what on earth were the Druze, the Orthodox Christians, and the Shias of Syria and Mount Lebanon? The Ottomans were by no means as ineffectual in brokering and compromising these disputes as was once thought. On Mount Lebanon, a mid-century civil war between sectarian groups gave way after 1860 to a new political system under the sultans. Decentralized government made room for a distinct sense of Lebanese identity, while bargaining between community leaders remained peaceful and effective until the Western powers again intervened during the First World War.[17]

Nevertheless, the dilemma of managing difference yet creating a strong state became more acute after the so-called Young Turk revolution of 1908. Pan-Turkish feeling was, as yet, not very widespread, though a number of literati had begun to write passionately of Turkish language and culture. The young military officers, who took power in 1908 and restored the constitution, were in a dilemma. They felt that they needed to consolidate the empire and make it more like a European state. Most of them were still Ottoman patriots at heart,

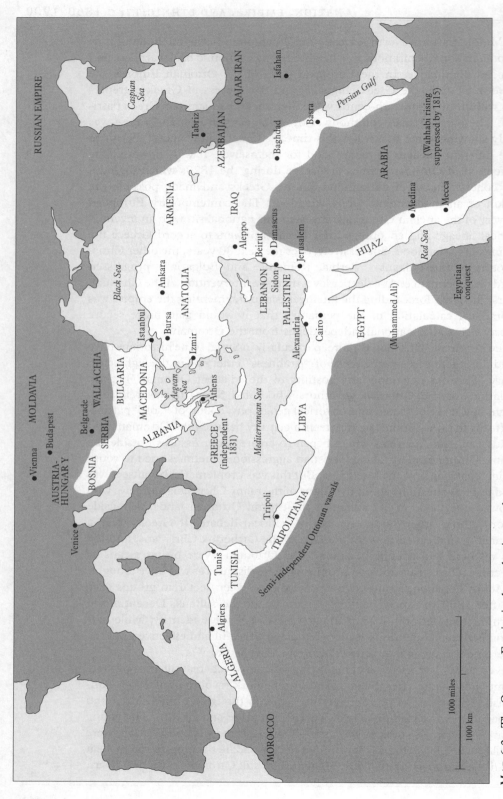

MAP 6.2 The Ottoman Empire in the early nineteenth century.
Source: William L. Cleveland, *A History of the Modern Middle East* (Boulder, Colo., 2000), p. 45.

rather than Turkish nationalists, and were to remain so until the 1920s, as Hasan Kayali has argued.[18] They included Arabs and Armenians as well as ethnic Turks. Yet they did put in train some measures for expanding Turkish language education in the Arab provinces, though these were later watered down. The world Arab Conference which met in 1913 was, in part, a reaction to these tentative moves. Locally, as in Mesopotamia, pro-Arabist societies began to query the purpose of the empire.[19] Nationality was indeed becoming an issue within the empire, though much opinion, even amongst the Greeks of Asia Minor, remained broadly Ottomanist in attitude as late as 1916.

Egypt, by contrast, had always been a unique province within the Ottoman Empire. This was partly because Egyptians spoke a distinctive form of the Arabic language and partly because modern Egypt was set amongst the remains of ancient Pharaonic civilization. With its relatively large population, intensive riverine agriculture, and strong economy, Egypt had a long history of local autonomy. Ironically, it was the Albanian and Turkish-speaking ruling family of Mehmet, or Muhammad Ali, which encouraged the Egyptian sense of separateness in the early nineteenth century through its military and fiscal reforms and tactic of promoting local people to office. Though there is some disagreement between historians about the extent of this "Creole" policy, it does seem that Egyptians displayed a well-developed sense of regional identity by the 1880s and 1890s.[20] As in the German case a decade or so before, the need for a "national political economy" to protect local industry and fend off rapacious European moneylenders and bondholders also created an economic alliance between landowners, entrepreneurs, and bazaar people, reinforcing this sense of regional identity. By the 1870s, Egypt had become a virtual colony, with upward of 200,000 European residents in its cities and its ruling house hamstrung by British and French commercial interests.[21] After 1878, the Western powers forced the Egyptian rulers to cut back their army, raise taxation, and accept foreign advisers. The result was the transformation of an Egyptian feeling of resentment into a widespread nationalist movement demanding "Egypt for the Egyptians!" That movement was by no means anti-Ottoman in ideology, but it was nonetheless testimony to a growing sense of Egyptian solidarity.[22]

Elsewhere in North Africa, the theme of "holy war" in defense of a particular homeland situated within the wider world of the Ottoman Empire and Islam was as conspicuous as it was in the plural society of Egypt. North Africans tenaciously remembered the Spanish reconquest of the Muslim lands of southern Spain three centuries before. When Napoleon invaded Egypt in 1798, the inhabitants of North Africa feared Christian invasion and began to consider their political future. In the wars after 1830, they responded to the danger with a sense of solidarity that was peculiarly North African.[23] Their fears were confirmed when France invaded Algeria, precipitating a long war of occupation and an almost constant succession of revolts through the 130 years of French rule. This was no homogeneous "Islamic reaction," nor was it a simple response to economic desolation. In its commitment to land, people, and traditions, it was as much and as little nationalist as the sentiments that Napoleon had once stirred through his Italian conquests.

Some black Africans, too, began to talk of an "African nation," even though the continent remained divided between many different polities. By the 1860s, West African Creoles, freed slaves, and mission-educated men trained in Britain and the United States were arguing that Africans deserved independence and humane treatment. They were not under "the curse of God." This sort of pan-Africanism had few supporters, but it did have a growing literature, newspapers, and congresses well before 1900.[24] The tone was set by men such as Edward W. Blyden, professor of Greek and Latin. Born of slave parents of Ibo origin, he went to the USA and later to Liberia under Presbyterian auspices. A pan-African nationalist by the 1880s, he wrote:

> During all the years that have elapsed since the commencement of modern progress, the African race has filled a very humble and subordinate part in the work of human civilisation . . . [but] there is a peculiar work for them to accomplish both in the land of their bondage and the land of their fathers. I would rather be a member of this race than a Greek in the time of Alexander, a Roman in the Augustan period, or an Anglo-Saxon in the nineteenth century.

Here, race and the idea of progress come together with the idea of Christian redemption to create the beginnings of a sense of shared nationality.[25]

Outside the west coast, Africa south of the Sahara did not really throw up anything that could be called nationalism before 1914. Yet African kingdoms embattled by European advance north from the Cape, such as the Ndebele and Shona, embodied a sense of pride in land and community. They were more than military despotisms. Adrian Hastings argued that the appropriation and use of the Bible by African elites during the later nineteenth century also created a new sense of local patriotism. Significantly, Hastings and a new generation of African-born historians are beginning to argue that, while missionaries and colonial officials helped categorize Africans into "tribes" in the years between 1860 and 1900, there already existed in many parts of Africa a sense of "peoplehood" which went beyond simple loyalty to a king.

The 20 years after 1860 were also critical in the building of an all-India nationalism, broader and more self-consciously modern than the older patriotism of the Indian regions. Already, as early as the 1830s, Indian reformers and conservatives were calling for what amounted to a national political economy in both Bengal and western India. This was a response to Britain's importation of its early industrialization to the subcontinent and to resident Europeans' pressure for free trade. The commercial and landed magnates of Bengal were as aware as any European of the wars between republicans and monarchists in the aftermath of 1815. They understood the import of the British Reform Bill of 1832 and bewailed the plight of the Irish during the 1848 famine. Perhaps again, the small elites of merchants and professional people were probably no more or less "nationalist" than Hungarians or Neapolitans during these years. Many of them were worried by the apparent anarchy loosed by the rebels of 1857 and rejected the notion that the mutiny was a patriotic movement.

Further experience of British invasion and of humiliation by the new breed of post-mutiny white expatriates created amongst the Indian elites a clearer sense of the need for political revival through the creation of a national community. Though large parts of India had seen no war since the end of the eighteenth century, their elites increasingly came to see themselves as citizens of an occupied country. The greater visible presence of white British troops after 1857 and the construction of railway lines and new military and civil stations fed this sentiment, at least among urban people. The various associations and varied elites which hesitantly came together in the first Indian National Congress at Bombay in 1885 drew on a sense of conflict and economic and racial disadvantage. These leaders inherited some of the themes of the old patriotisms of the Indian regions. They also lauded the virtues of the homely artisans and their products, the need for kings to obtain good counsel, and the need to keep the land free from the pollution of cow killing and alcohol.[26] Yet the leaders of these associations were also aware of British liberal doctrines of popular representation and control of bureaucracy.

In China, as in the Ottoman Empire, sentiments of solidarity were complicated by the emergence of a new rhetoric of ethnic division which began to pit Chinese against "Manchu." Ironically, these distinctions had been institutionalized by the regime itself during the eighteenth century, as part of imperial ideology. By the 1900s, however, it was possible to speak of an incipient Han Chinese nationalism, fortified by an idea of racial uniqueness, as well as Qing imperial patriotism. Both sentiments were redoubled in their strength by the experience of defeat and occupation. The Chinese humiliations of the opium wars were deepened by the unequal treaties forced on the empire by the Western powers after 1860. Christian missionary intrusion along the coasts brought traditional Chinese literati and ordinary people to a stronger sense of their own identity. Sometimes this feeling of rage against foreign intervention turned the Chinese against the regime. Sometimes it created a popular patriotic movement of Chinese elites and populace hostile to all foreigners who supported the regime. This was the case in 1900, when a martial and religious movement that westerners called the "Boxers," rose against foreign missionaries and businessmen, declaring its loyalty to the Chinese empress.[27] The threat to Western economic and cultural assets in China was averted only by a full-scale invasion by European, Japanese, and American troops.

Meanwhile, a more modern and sometimes explicitly anti-Qing form of Chinese nationalism was emerging among the missionary-educated middle class and business people of the coastal regions and the Chinese diaspora in Southeast Asia. Sun Yatsen, first president of the Chinese republic after the First World War, was a case in point. He had been educated in Hong Kong, Hawaii, and Japan. He also had contacts amongst the Chinese in Bangkok and Malaya. In 1895, Sun Yatsen and his supporters attempted a coup against the Manchu authorities in Canton. His aim was to create a new Chinese state, dedicated to the salvation of the Chinese people. This new regime would stand up to Western cultural and economic intrusion in a way that the Qing regime had failed to do. Following the coup's failure, Sun and other young Chinese reformers and nationalists fled to London. Here, in the imperial capital, they encountered a host of colonial nationalists and radical students, Indian, Irish, and Egyptian. They read of other movements against the colonial power, and Sun began to draw together in his mind the threads of what would be his "Three Principles of the People," one of the key documents of Asian nationalism in the twentieth century.[28]

WHERE WE STAND WITH NATIONALISM

Previous chapters and the first sections of this chapter have been developing what amounts to a three-stage proposition about the emergence of nationalism. In summary, this argues, first, that in several world regions, including non-European societies, such as northern Vietnam, Korea, Japan, and Ethiopia, leaderships steadily and over long periods transformed older sentiments of patriotic attachment to land into more aggressive and exclusive understandings of nationality. This occurred under the pressure of war, economic and cultural change, and the development of communications. Often these "old patriotisms" were connected with an early history of statehood, so that a cultural region, an economic region, and a state emerged as overlapping forms. But some old kingdoms did not overlap with well-defined cultural zones in this way, while some cultural zones did not throw up old states. Often, too, these old patriotisms had emerged on the boundaries of great multiethnic polities and in reaction against them. Yet this, again, was not always the case.

The growth of the market and social connections among ordinary people in these emergent old "motherlands" solidified connections amongst the regional elites. The process, therefore, was "bottom-up" as well as "top-down." It was accelerated by the world conflicts of 1780–1820 and 1848–65. It was deepened by global forces towards the end of the nineteenth century, but it had a longer history. In these cases, if nations had indeed been "constructed," it had been over a very long period and was in part the unintended consequence of much wider social and economic changes.

The second proposition is that in other areas, and particularly in the complex large polities of eastern Eurasia and North Africa, the change came more abruptly, in the nineteenth century and especially in the years after 1860. Here, international war and colonialism drove intellectuals and publicists to adopt the language and practices of modern nationalism. While this was true of many non-European areas which were coming under extreme pressure from European imperialism after 1860, something similar occurred in the Russian and Austrian empires. Here also, the attempts of statesmen to modernize and industrialize their societies to face war and economic conflict galvanized regional leaderships, which cherished a history of cultural difference, into a new assertion of their separatism and claims to nationality. In this sense, the development of a more assertive nationalism in Hungary and Poland after 1860 was related to the emergence of Indian and Egyptian nationalism and occurred over very much the same span of years.

Thirdly, there were areas, such as the central Ottoman lands and parts of Austria-Hungary, Russia, and even parts of southern Ireland, where nationalism had still not emerged as a coherent set of ideas and political practices even in 1914. None of these different trajectories can, however, be summed up in any easy distinction between the timing or nature of nationalism inside "Europe" and in regions outside "Europe."

As far as "theory" is concerned, continuity with old patriotisms was not a necessary condition for the emergence of nineteenth-century nationalisms. Or, as Ernest Gellner wittily put it in a debate with A. D. Smith, nations need not have "navels."[29] They did not *need* to have been born out of some earlier patriotic solidarity. That, however, does not mean that "navels" were unimportant where they did exist, as Gellner seems to imply. Some nationalisms, indeed, had more pronounced navels than others. Some were clones with false navels; some were designer-babies with no navels at all. Others again were virtual children, drawing-board imaginings, like nineteenth-century Zionism. But for historians, the existence or otherwise of such navels is important, because they helped form the political sensibilities of national leaderships and common people. The relative youth of the United States, its "constructed" nature as a nation, for instance, is one reason why it has retained its archaic eighteenth-century constitution. Change to such a recent construction was too fraught with danger. By contrast, the longevity of the common law and the sense of English nationhood has blocked the creation of a written constitution. Navels have unintended, unexpected, and sometimes deep consequences.

PEOPLES WITHOUT STATES: PERSECUTION OR ASSIMILATION?

This section turns to those groups which found it difficult to assimilate into the more homogeneous national movements that were widely in evidence by the later nineteenth century. It deals with peoples that were too small or too scattered to effectively press home their claims for autonomy or, conversely, were marginalized and oppressed by the emergence of the "big" nationalisms considered earlier. For almost everywhere there were, within these real or aspirant national territories, other groups marked off by religious affiliation, assumed racial difference, or language and life-style. Sometimes these minority groups were located on the fringes of national domains, as were the Russian Tatars and the American Indians, sometimes near their heart, like the plains-dwelling Karen of Burma and the German Jews. Sometimes they were scattered across their whole territories, like the Armenians and the Catholic Irish immigrants to the Protestant states of the English-speaking world.

"Others" of these varied types provided a perennial challenge for nationalists and state-builders. The lexicon of nationalism insisted that such groups should be assimilated for strategic as much as cultural reasons. Paradoxically, the very act of nation building and the very symbols of resurgent big nationalisms tended to increase the perception of difference, spawning obdurate subnational movements and militant ethnicities among those excluded or put under surveillance. Some colonial governments found it useful to exploit difference through policies of "divide and rule" and welcomed the existence of such fragments. The leaderships of most nations and emerging nationalist movements, however, sought to melt them down and meld them with the nation as a whole. Outside the United States, this was a tactic which had only mixed success.

The great empires of the old order before 1780, and even old national states such as England, France, and Japan, had developed ways of handling cultural, religious, and life-style differences which minimized, even if they did not eliminate, persistent tensions. In societies where statuses were complex and intertwined, it was simpler to devise schemes to separate, segregate, and avoid conflict. If the king, rather than the people, was the fountain of authority, issues of "us" and "them" were less important. All were subjects of a universal monarch. In Europe, Jews, for instance, were widely denied the rights of the wider populations, being seen as aliens and religious anomalies. Yet the kings and aristocracies of the old order offered them some degree of protection some of the time. The politics of accommodating difference was particularly successful in the Ottoman Empire. Non-Muslim minorities were grouped in semi-autonomous orders called *millets*. Each millet was governed by supposedly traditional heads: bishops in the case of Christians, rabbinic councils in the case of Jews. The Ottomans devised similar structures for dealing with their Muslim minorities and the Bedouin tribes of the internal frontier. They were allowed to practice their own ritual and customary forms, provided they paid allegiance to the sultan and served in his armies when required. The administration of revenue collection by provinces was generally kept separate from the millets and tribal organizations. The Ottomans, like the Mughals, the Safavids, and, particularly, the Qing, made a virtue of cultural difference. Though Middle Easterners and Asians had a complex hierarchy of racial types, determined by climate and supposed bodily substance, this was not a rigid ladder of superiority and inferiority. After all, it was thought, the best Muslims and the best servants of the sultans might come from the lushness of Africa or equally from the barren cold of the northern, Christian mountains. After all, the Prophet himself had been a man from the desert fringes.

The Ottoman Empire, like the other empires, was multinational or multiethnic, except that nothing like nationality existed in its modern sense and the notion of ethnicity is a little exclusive. In the late eighteenth and early nineteenth century, however, a number of changes occurred which highlighted the issue of difference and began to create a "nationality problem." First, the growth of the Atlantic economy and its tributaries within the Mediterranean and the Indian Ocean began to give economic advantages to some groups and disadvantage others, sowing the seeds of envy. Greeks within the Balkans and the eastern Mediterranean capitalized on old seafaring skills and connections with the Venetians to capture much of the carrying trade. Armenians prospered over a wide area. On the Levant coast and in Egypt and Mesopotamia, Jews, Assyrians, and Coptic Christians also flourished. As non-Muslims they were not debarred from taking interest, and they benefited from connections with the Christian ports and the Knights of St John of Malta. In Egypt, Muhammad Ali's regime, trying to fill its coffers and build up a new army, found the Copts to be good clerks and accountants and rewarded them with local office. Paradoxically, the slow strengthening of the notion of "Egyptianness," noted in the last section, tended to enhance the sense of separateness of some Copts.

Secondly, the rising Christian powers of Europe gave encouragement and support to the Ottoman minorities, out of business acumen but often simply because their members were effective middlemen in trade and diplomacy. The British and the French made Jewish merchants honorary consuls in the coastal cities. Under Napoleon III, harbinger of the new French imperialism, missions to the Christians of Mount Lebanon redoubled their efforts to cultivate a sense of allegiance to France and its culture. Meanwhile, British and American Protestant churchmen and missionaries put out feelers to the Egyptian Copts and Assyrian Christians. European consuls intervened at Istanbul to press the sultan to give relief to the Christian minorities from the disadvantages from which they were supposed to suffer. This pressure became more insistent as European and American pilgrimages to the Holy Land began to increase when communications improved.

Thirdly, as mentioned earlier, the Ottoman Empire was itself undergoing significant internal change, particularly after 1830, when successive military defeats forced modernization on the state under the Tanzimat decree. The old military corps and Sufi orders were dissolved; a form of constitution was set up. If even a hint of popular representation was conceded, then the question of who were "the people" inevitably rose to the surface. After 1870, when the Ottoman Empire was periodically involved in "Balkan wars" against the Russians and the Austrians, religion and the question of the identity of the state came to the fore, as we have seen. In a world in which Christian anti-Turkish rhetoric had become a successful rallying cry, it was not surprising that the later sultans began to see themselves increasingly as Muslims. Battle lines drawn against the West, however, raised the issue of the internal foe. Armenian and Lebanese Christians, Jews, Arabs, and Kurds, who were thought to be dallying with foreign powers, became a potential enemy within. Even before the onset of world war, local servants of the now more self-consciously Muslim state had sometimes taken the decision to stifle dissent by mass killing.

For colonial powers, the existence of religious and cultural difference among their subjects posed both difficulties and opportunities. The European empires did not always find it easy to deal with the heterogeneity of their conquests. These differences might complicate attempts to impose common forms of law and administration or impede the economic exploitation of their possessions. The British, French, and Dutch, therefore, often separated off those parts of conquered territories which seemed to be inhabited by "minority peoples," especially when they were located in hill lands, forest, or desert. This is how the Shan and Karen states of British Burma came into existence after 1886, and the different kingdoms of French Indo-China. In many parts of newly conquered Africa, a system of "indirect rule" was created under special commissioners, ostensibly to maintain "native administration" rather than to impose European government. Thus at the Cape, the San or "Bushmen" territories were always under a separate administration from the colonies of white settlement and also from the surrounding enclaves of African farmers and settled nomads such as the Xhosa. In northern Nigeria, Lord Lugard made a virtue of reconstructing "traditional" Muslim kingdoms after the British conquest of the 1890s. "Indirect rule" saved money and also stifled the growth of English-educated elites like those who were causing such trouble in India and Egypt.

Special administrative arrangements of this sort and the colonialists' tendency to treat these forest-dwelling, nomadic, or culturally different Africans, Asians, and Latin Americans as special "peoples" inevitably enhanced these very differences. It disrupted many earlier and subtler economic and cultural relations between the predominant agricultural groupings in these territories and the "tribal" people. The latter had once served as hunters, providers of forest produce, men of magic, and even mercenaries for the rulers of the settled. Under colonial rule they lost these functions and were often transformed into little more than pools of poor labor. They were often now suspect to those defined as majority populations.

More significant for the future of non-European nationalisms and nation-states was the tendency of colonial powers to privilege differences of religion and race within the majority societies of their territories. Here the advantages of policies of "divide and rule" became more prominent. In part, this arose from political calculation. An army composed of indigenous minority groups, different from, and suspect to, the majority populations was less likely to turn against the colonialists. The headmen, rajas, or chiefs of such groups might also provide a useful counterweight to aspiring nationalist leaderships. More often, these aims were unspoken and unacknowledged. The contemporary prejudice about race and nationality made it impossible for the colonizers to see colonial peoples as anything more than a congeries of mongrel groups between which it was their function to arbitrate.

For instance, very subtle differences of language and culture between different forms of North African were elaborated by the French into the idea that recent Arab invaders were set against supposedly indigenous Berbers, or Kabyles, the latter being much closer in civilization to the peoples of the European Mediterranean. This distinction did not prevent Berbers from revolting against the French, which they did as late as 1912. But it did tend to set Berber politics and society moving in a subtly different direction from those of their Arab neighbors and coreligionists.[30] Similarly, the British authorities in the Malay states often found it prudent to treat the incoming Chinese tin miners and rubber tappers rather differently from the Malay

Muslim smallholders. Yet they were too suspicious of Chinese businessmen and laborers in the tin mines to push this too far, fearing Triads, secret societies, and the seditious politics of these articulate settlers more than the sedate conservatism of the Malay Islamic courts. The Dutch, in turn, made much of the difference between the inhabitants of Java and those of the "outer islands," especially the Moluccas. Likewise, the French preferred Melanesian and even Vietnamese indentured laborers to the indigenous Kanaks of New Caledonia.

There were parallels in India. Here complex histories of difference separated Hindus, Muslims, and Sikhs. Yet the difference was very subtle, Muslims having adjusted to centuries of relationships with surrounding Hindus, while Sikhs continued to operate to some degree within norms and cosmologies derived from a common Indian religious past.[31] As in other colonial territories, British rulers found it easier to rule a continent divided into religious and racial blocks. The legal system, the census, and the emerging "science" of anthropology recognized and to some degree enhanced these differences. In the late nineteenth century, however, leaders within these communities also insisted on difference on their own account. Some Sikhs argued forcefully in the 1870s that "We are not Hindus." Some Muslims argued that Muslims were an incoming, conquering race, wholly different from and superior to the mass of Indians, and that they deserved the support of the colonial rulers.

These attitudes reflected the spread of the idea among the indigenous intelligentsia that religions and races were real, substantial entities, and that they needed men to speak up for them. The colonial power tended to think, govern, and write with these rigid categories in mind. Indigenous intelligentsia also attempted to enhance their status by describing their histories as communities or peoples. At the same time, some adherents of these often still-fluid religious traditions began to think of themselves as "minorities," threatened both by the steamroller of the modern state and by the timid beginnings of the politics of representation in the colonial territories. The outcome for such assumed ethnicities varied. The British Liberal government gave Indian Muslims a special political status in 1909, with far-reaching effects for the history of the subcontinent. It was too weak to do the same for the Egyptian Copts. In the Malay archipelago and in Fiji, however, special administrative commissions were created to set Chinese and Indians apart from Malays and indigenous Fijians. The French rulers did much the same with immigrant Indians and Chinese in Indochina, while in Indonesia, the Dutch created special customary codes which were supposed to reflect the legal traditions of their different "peoples." Even the Americans in the Philippines built on the earlier Spanish ethnic categories of administrations, distinguishing Malays from Chinese and from indigenous Filippinos.

The Eurasian empires of Russia and eastern Europe stood somewhere between the old Asian and Middle Eastern empires and the newly industrial societies of the Atlantic in their treatment of minority groups and sub-nationalities. The Russian Empire certainly operated very much like the British in India as far as the inhabitants of its central Asian territories were concerned. Special administrative areas were marked out. Councils of elders and Islamic jurists were set up. A kind of "reverse" millet system was held in place, in which Muslims played the same role as Christians within the Ottoman Empire. But the Russian and Austrian empires faced the considerable problem that, very often, their non-Russian and non-German populations were amongst the richest and most powerful of the whole empire. The Russian rulers had to accommodate the interests and identities of Germans, Lithuanians, and Jews, as well as Tatars, Kazakhs, and other central Asians. Too vigorous assimilation would spark them into political activity; too little assimilation and administrative intervention might allow the development of "states within states."

Even in western Europe, cultural and religious differences inherited from the older, more plural political and religious orders of the eighteenth century sometimes reappeared towards the end of the nineteenth century as the new middle-class electorates redoubled the pressure to assimilate to a national pattern. Better communications, the statistical, categorizing mind-set of the state, and, above all, suspicions of minorities generated during wars were responsible for making self-styled peoples more aware of their past and their future potential. Irish nationalism developed a stronger mass base, and one which was predominantly Roman Catholic, partly in response to Protestant attempts at assimilation after 1815. In turn, Protestant Unionists stressed their English and Scottish roots and Protestant heritage. Legends about difference were elaborated into a history of the "Kingdom of Ulster" and its later contribution to Britain and its empire. Late-nineteenth-century continental Europeans began to define themselves with reference to similar ethnic identities: Basques, Bretons, Corsicans, and inhabitants of the Alto Adige all came to resent the pressures of the nation-states into which they had been incorporated, often quite recently.

The case of the Jews was different. By the 1870s most Jews across the European continent had been formally assimilated into the civic orders of the emerging states; they were no longer ghettoized. This had happened during the Napoleonic empire over much of northern Europe, and after 1848 in Italy. In the case of France and Germany, increased marriage of Jews to Gentiles and the rise of reformist religious traditions which downplayed differences in life-style between Gentile and Jew pushed forward a piecemeal assimilation. A symptomatic Jewish saying of the time was "Be a Jew in your home and a man outside."[32] But assimilation had gone only so far. Most Jewish communities continued to be endogamous. Thousands of old-style Jewish communities continued to guard their distinct and separate lifestyles. These stretched from Algeria and Libya, through Poland and Russia, or south by way of Yemen, to Cochin in India and southwestern China. Powerful movements for the revival of faith and culture were also on the move, and these challenged assimilation in a different way. Alongside these traditional communities and assimilationist tendencies, there emerged the Zionist movement for a separate Jewish homeland which first took fire at a delegate congress in Basle in 1897.

ILLUSTRATION 6.2   Assimilation, separatism, or exclusion? Jewish scholars debating.
Painting by Josef Suss, c.1900.

Amongst Gentiles, especially in central and eastern Europe, the symbol of
the Jew as a commercial parasite as well as a "killer of Christ" became,
ominously, a touchstone of nationalism. Anti-Semitism, once a localized phenomenon of religious hatred and commercial rivalry, as in 1848, was now
annexed more closely to the narrative of nationalism in large multiethnic cities.
This transformation was to make European Jewish populations yet more vulnerable during the twentieth century. War exacerbated the fear of the enemy
within. Though Jews in Russia and Austria had assimilated quite quickly into
Christian society in the first half of the century, the strains of urbanization and
the rise of capitalist production marked them out as targets for those who had
failed to benefit. War and international tension hardened hostility against them.
It was particularly after Russia's defeat by Japan in 1905 that conservative
Russian politicians and bureaucrats gave the head to pogroms against the
empire's Jews. At the same time, ideology was important. Whereas Budapest's
Jewish population was 23 percent of the total in 1900, it was in Vienna, where
they were no more than 7 percent that anti-Semitism was most virulent.
German nationalism was harder and more suspicious of "outsiders."[33]

In western Europe, hatred of the "internal enemy" proved to be the under-
side of the new nationalism. Alsatian Jews moved to Paris after the defeat by
Germany in 1871, making the community more visible. But it was in the

1890s, as rivalry with Britain and Germany grew, that anti-Semitism really took off. It was fueled by works such as Edouard Drumont's *La France juive* ("Jewish France"), published in 1886, and reached its peak with the wrongful prosecution of the military officer Dreyfus for treason. Dreyfus was an Alsatian Jew.[34]

This sharpening of the sense of ethnic difference and mini-nationalisms in response to the growth of majoritarian nationalism occurred even in the Americas. In Canada, the Catholic Frenchness of Quebec was enhanced in the later nineteenth century as the country emerged as a federated dominion within the British Empire. Immigrants to the settler societies of South America also tended to retain the language and culture of their homelands to a great extent. The United States, however, was rather different. It was a nation of immigrants, and there was no "national homeland" to claim to defend. The USA was a state that did not rest on an ethnic sense of nationalism. The earlier domination of Protestants from the British Isles had been diluted. After the 1848 famine in Ireland, millions of Catholic Irish joined the earlier generations of Protestant settlers from that country. Up to 20 million Russians, Poles, Germans, and Italians crossed to the USA in the years between 1850 and 1914 as steamship travel made the journey less hazardous. Amongst these immigrant communities, the memories, culture, and, for a time, languages of their European homelands survived. Ethnicity underlay voting patterns to some extent. But these ethnic groupings never became so politicized as to impede the immigrants' assimilation into what was now conceived of as an American nation.

The reasons for this throw light on the hardening of attitudes to minorities and racial discourses in many parts of Europe. The federal government remained relatively weak in the United States, so the status of any given group of immigrants, apart from Asians, did not become subject to national debates or definition by a centralized state. State governments and local communities handled the processes of immigration, settlement, and assimilation through the extension of the English language. Because the United States did not have an established church or even now a dominant Protestant identity, religion never became an issue beyond the local level. The richness of land and natural resources meant that labor was almost everywhere in short supply, so that none of the European-style conflicts over control of land, credit, or economic access became entrenched. Social mobility was rapid, and where, as in the cities of the east coast, a hierarchy seemed to be emerging, settlers could always move on to less hierarchical and individualistic societies. Class and ethnicity never became implicated with each other to the same extent as in the Old World.

This, of course, applied mainly to the European population. As elsewhere in the world, the United States saw a hardening of racial boundaries between people of European descent and non-Europeans. Indeed, Americans had been pioneers of racist and eugenic theorizing. After 1860, the immigration of Chinese, Japanese, and Indians was specifically restrained. By the 1890s, black slavery had been replaced by segregation on the basis of color. In practical terms, emancipation, by increasing political and economic disparities between blacks and whites in the South, had made the race barrier more contested and more important. Hunger for land pushed American "first nations" further back into impoverished reservations. Chinese, Japanese, and, occasionally, Jewish immigrant laborers were subject to well-orchestrated campaigns of discrimination, especially after the mid-1890s. In this respect, the United States did, in fact, mirror the racial histories of the British "white dominions." For it was in the later nineteenth century, too, that Canadian Amerindians and Maori and Aborigines in Australasia were penned down and restricted in their access to civil society. In South Africa, the contest between the British and the Afrikaners was accompanied by the gradual destruction of the remaining black free farmers and a pervasive campaign to exclude blacks from the skilled work force.

This section has shown that the creation of harder boundaries between "majority" and "minority" populations was the mirror image of the creation of the nation itself. It was, therefore, in the later nineteenth century, when the urge to build nations was running strongly, that internal boundaries between supposed ethnicities were also reinforced. The "divide and rule" tactics of European colonial empires were one extreme example of a more general phenomenon. Yet the state could not have secured this perception of difference without the active aid of the leaderships of these assumed ethnicities. So-called minorities saw themselves as mini-nations, even when they did not intend fully to separate from the wider society, as for instance in the case of most Jews. Their leaderships created histories, legends, and languages for them which mirrored the larger projects of the nation. Some of these groups were to secure homelands for themselves in the course of the twentieth century. Some continued to fight for a homeland well into that century. Others were to suffer persecution and even extermination.

IMPERIALISM AND ITS HISTORY: THE LATE NINETEENTH CENTURY

The last two sections of this chapter turn, first, to the projection of late-nineteenth-century nationalism abroad through imperialism and, then, to the internationalization of global linkages. Many areas of modern historiography are rather undertheorized – that is to say, historians have provided a good deal of evidence and argument but find it difficult to discern principles by which their material could be ranked in a hierarchy of relative importance, and hence understood. That is not true, however, of the later nineteenth century, for which "theories" of nationalism and of imperialism are legion. It is striking, though, that in recent times debates about these two phenomena, which were so clearly linked in the minds of contemporaries, have drifted apart. European historians study nation-states and, more recently, those excluded from or pushed to the margins within them. Imperial historians consider the origins of empires. The historians of non-European nations analyze the effects of imperialism and propose theories of non-European nationalism, which at present often revolve around the question of how nationhood was represented through gendered symbols, ceremonies, and literary themes.

Rather than looking for the origins of nationalism in imperialism, or vice versa, it is better to regard them as being in a long-standing relationship with each other. Imperial expansion forced the leaders of states to consider the substance of the nationality they claimed to embody. Equally, the experience of imperial expansion sharpened patriotic identities, amongst both the conquerors and the conquered. European expansion in the later eighteenth century had been one force by which groups on the periphery of the old nationalities had been incorporated into the emerging states of Europe. The Corsicans who became rulers in France and Napoleon's empire, and the Scots and Anglo-Irish who led the armies of the British Empire, provide examples of this process. At the same time, expansion often gave a sharper edge to the dynasty-led patriotisms of the old order in the areas invaded by imperial armies. For example, Spanish patriotism became sharper and more popular as a result of Napoleon's invasion. The British occupation of Ceylon after 1818 and the Dutch crushing of the Javanese resistance of 1825–30 began to forge a lineage for patriotic resistance against the colonial power in both these colonized societies, remembered and elaborated by later generations of peasant rebels and nationalists.

DIMENSIONS OF THE "NEW IMPERIALISM"

It does seem that the imperial expansion of the period after 1870, like the intensity of its competing nationalisms, was of a different order from that of the previous period. This was the age of the "new imperialism," when most of sub-Saharan Africa was seized by Europeans.[35] Beginning about 1878, the French strengthened their hold on the coastal territories of West Africa, while its colonial army pushed into the arid lands of the western Sudan. In 1882, the British occupied Egypt and, by 1898, they had conquered the upper Nile valley. Meanwhile, they had also consolidated their hold on central, South, and East Africa, outflanking the two small independent Afrikaner republics, the Orange Free State and the Transvaal. After Japan's defeat of China in 1894–5, a new European struggle for territory and influence broke out on the China coast. When European and American expeditionary forces invaded China to quell the Boxer Rebellion in 1900, it was quite clear that nothing but mutual rivalry prevented a partition of China along the lines of the partition of Africa. Lord Curzon, viceroy of India, complacently foresaw the possibility of a British protectorate on the Yangzi river garrisoned by Indian troops. The tsar's lieutenants strengthened their grip on central Asia.

This was a period, too, when existing imperial polities made good their claims on outlying dependencies: the Dutch in the Indonesian archipelago, the Brazilians in the interior rain forests, and the Russians in central Asia. King Leopold of the Belgians decided to enter the fray by making the Congo a great agricultural storehouse and reserve of forced labor for his country.[36] Germany, secure in its new-found military dominance in Europe, acquired Tanganyika, German West Africa, and a colony in New Guinea. Pushing out from the subcontinent, the British Indian empire reinforced its informal influence in the Persian Gulf, Afghanistan, Tibet, and north Burma. The British domination of the Malay Peninsula was consolidated, and its sultans brought to heel. Even the Ottoman Empire, now a semi-European state, began to build modern administration in the Tigris and Euphrates valley and in southern Arabia. Tellingly, the Ottoman administrations used translations of British Indian military and administrative manuals in their government of southern Arabia.

What needs to be explained, then, is the velocity and ferocity with which the European powers snapped up the remaining independent territories in Eurasia, Africa, and the Pacific, even when their absolute economic value may have been relatively limited and the danger of provoking competitive wars even greater.[37] What also needs to be explained is the eager participation in this imperial carnival of the new Japan and, briefly and more ambivalently, the USA, two powers which had themselves emerged as a consequence of struggles against imperial control.

The new imperialism of the later nineteenth century has been put down to a variety of causes. Notable among the explanations are Marxist-Leninist economic arguments, which suggest that big capitalist combines, having extracted super-profits in Europe now began to redivide the resources of the world by armed force.[38] Other historians, Marxist and non-Marxist, implicate financiers, who allegedly tried to make the world safe for foreign investment by expanding European territorial control to the rest of the world.[39] Another variant of the economic argument emphasizes the importance of "men on the spot," such as cotton-traders, mine-owners, or traders in palm oil, in pressing governments to intervene and create safe areas for their exploitation of native resources and labor.[40] The famous arguments of Robinson and Gallagher, by contrast, stressed the significance of crises on the "periphery."[41] These crises, notably in Egypt and South Africa in the 1870s, were said to have undermined the existing native economic collaborators who serviced an expanding Europe, so convincing the "official mind" in the European capitals of the need to take direct territorial control. Some bravely old-fashioned historians still insist on the primacy of diplomatic maneuvering amongst the European powers in the rush to "divide and rule." Others argue that what should really be studied are the consequences of the partition of Africa or the Pacific for native peoples, not the aims of the white conquerors.

All these arguments seem to have some force at different places and at different times in the history of the new imperialism. It is probably fruitless to seek for one overarching explanation. There do, however, appear to have been some general *preconditions* for the surge forward of European territorial control and informal influence over non-Europeans. To repeat, one general point, which seems obvious but has sometimes slipped from sight, is that the new imperialism was closely related to the more strident European nationalism which was considered earlier in this chapter. This may be an old-fashioned argument, but it does not mean that it is wrong. Imperialism and nationalism were part of the same phenomenon. Nationalism and conflict in Europe made states more aware of their competitors abroad and more inclined to stake out claims and prefer their own citizens. The partition of Africa was, indeed, partly a preemptive exercise, by which national governments attempted to steal a march on their rivals by claiming tracts of territory which might at some time in the future become economically or strategically important.

Critically, however, European governments were in a much stronger position to project their power overseas than they had been in earlier generations. Rapid-firing guns and battleships opened up an even greater military distance between Europeans and indigenous peoples. New medicines protected imperial troops more effectively. The telegraph made communications between metropolis and colony infinitely easier.[42] Technology made it possible to achieve what many earlier empire-builders had only dreamed of. But the desire had to be there as well as the means.

There is, then, much truth in the old claim that the machinations of the Concert of Europe, the high councils of the European powers, encouraged the partition of Africa and battles for concessions in Persia and the Pacific.[43] British preeminence was on the decline, and new European powers were asserting themselves.[44] The promotion of national prestige and an intense desire on the part of statesmen and soldiers to advance the interest of their own countries provided a motivation. The French invasion of West Africa and the western Sudan from 1878 to 1898 was justified by reference to a dozen petty wars of local trade and the ever-present fear of Muslim jihad. Yet trade and local defense were not really the motive. The French Overseas Army wanted to achieve domestic recognition and international glory in an atmosphere still darkened by France's defeat by Prussia in 1871.[45] After 1880, by contrast, the newly united Germany was determined to achieve status as an arbiter in Europe by adjusting its overseas conflicts. The blueprint for the partition of the remaining parts of Africa not yet staked out was drawn at the Berlin Congress of 1884, when Bismarck, the German chancellor, held the balance of power between Britain and France. Inevitably, the creation of putative spheres of national interests in Africa, in the Pacific Ocean, and on the China coast after 1896 encouraged nation-states to actually lay hold of their claim, lest others move in on it. The invasion of China during the Boxer Rebellion of 1900 by European, American, and Japanese armed forces provides a good example of competitive imperialism.

It is undoubtedly true, as proponents of the idea of economic imperialism argue, that there were side benefits from the African partition. Locally based European and even indigenous business firms were able to achieve greater security, as did the British entrepreneur Cecil Rhodes, in central southern Africa. Indigenous labor could be coerced and controlled more easily to produce staple cash crops cheaply in areas subject to direct European control, as King Leopold predicted in the Belgian Congo. Debts incurred by indigenous regimes could be paid off more quickly, as in the case of Britain's occupation of Egypt. The cotton-growing lands of central Asia conquered by Russia after 1860 provided a valuable supply of raw material for Russia's industrialization. The threat of the collapse of world commodity prices in the 1870s added to the sense of crisis in the overseas world. This set governments and economic interests at each other's throats. It was helpful to firms operating in West Africa to have the support of colonial governments.[46]

Despite these considerations, however, the economic benefits of the second age of global imperialism were always less tangible than those of the first, in 1780–1820. The grand orchestrators of the new imperialism were not international capitalists, as Lenin averred, but national governments which encouraged the commercial interests of their own citizens to preempt rival mining, telegraph, railway, or commodity companies. Southern African gold, for instance, was vital to the strength of the British currency. This predisposed British governments to search for political stability in southern Africa and, if necessary, to secure it against Dutch settlers or German rivals by armed force. Yet this does not mean that some malign cabal of international financiers sitting in dark, smoke-filled rooms in London took the British into the South African War of 1899–1902. Rather, a kind of coalition of metropolitan

ILLUSTRATION 6.3 Queen Victoria as seen by a Nigerian carver. Late nineteenth-century effigy in polished wood, Yoruba, Nigeria.

interests and "men on the spot" in the Cape Colony and Natal emerged. These men decided, wrongly as it turned out, that the conquest of the Transvaal and the Orange Free State was the solution to what they saw as problems of labor control, high taxation, and the lack of firm administration in these states. Economic imperialism was more often the handmaiden of agents of the national state than the underlying motive force of territorial expansion.

This line of argument seems even more convincing when we consider the imperialism of smaller, later-formed nation-states. Whatever dubious benefits in the longer run may have accrued to Italy from its capture of North African and Ethiopian fastnesses, Italian empire was the dream of the right-wing nationalist governments of Francesco Crispi and Agostino Depretis. These politicians were attempting to consolidate their influence in a still half-formed Italian state during the 1880s and 1890s. Given a slight Marxist twist, this is also the burden of the assertion that Bismarck's imperial ambitions in Germany were the result of "social imperialism." On this argument, Bismarck used imperialism in Africa and the Pacific as a way of "burning off" class tensions which had arisen during Germany's rapid industrialization. While it is difficult to locate the political mechanism which makes this model work, most historians would agree that Bismarck used overseas expansion as a tool of internal state building and did not see empire as an economic necessity for Germany *per se*.

In the same way, Japan, which seized Taiwan and attacked China in 1894, following a conflict over Korea, viewed empire as both a protection for, and an inevitable extension of, the national empire founded in 1868. Rival factions of military and naval officers, rooted in the half-assimilated Choshu and Satsuma domains of the earlier era, vied with each other in their desire to pursue an oceanic or a continental plan of territorial aggrandizement. Japanese traders and peasant settlers were greatly advantaged in Korea and Taiwan by the country's imperial expansion. All the same, this was essentially a nationalistic project. As one Japanese statesman opaquely put it, when urging the extension of Japanese power to mainland Asia, "If the sun is not ascending it is descending . . . If the country is not flourishing it is declining. Therefore to protect the country well is not merely [to prevent] it losing the position it holds, but to add to the position it does not hold."[47]

Japan did, in fact, have powerful competitors to fear. The Russian expansion across Siberia and into north China had clearly been motivated by a desire to strengthen its territorial and economic grip in the Far East. Even in cases of the new imperialism, where economic interests seem to have been paramount, the promotion of national prestige was a critical consideration.[48] For instance, King Leopold may have benefited handsomely from his rape of the Belgian Congo when he occupied it in the 1880s. His plan could only have worked, however, in an era of intense national competition between the larger European powers. Leopold's aim was a gamble to aggrandize the king of the Belgians and to earn his small country more respect in the wider world.

There is a second sense in which nationalism itself should be seen as the key component of any theory of late-nineteenth-century imperialism. Heightened

European nationalism was one trigger. Another was the contemporaneous growth of national feeling among colonized people or people threatened by colonial expansion. The British occupation of Egypt in 1882 was itself precipitated by the Egyptian national movement of 1879–81. The blatant financial exploitation of the country by representatives of the European bond-holders after 1876 transformed Muhammad Ali's earlier state-sponsored patriotism into a vigorous nationalist movement under Colonel Urabi.[49] The British government was tutored by its local agents to regard this as a threat, not only to the security of credit in London, but also to its whole strategic position on the route to India, which was dependent on the Suez canal.

In a rather similar way, the Boer patriotism of Dutch African settlers, founded on Calvinism and patriarchy, was transformed by British pressure into something much more akin to an Afrikaner nationalism, long before the onset of the South African War of 1899. A host of men on the spot, adventurers, and commercial interests conspired to bring East and Central Africa under European domination after 1878. But the desire of Britain and its agents to get ahead of the Afrikaner republics in their race to exploit the lands to their north remained an important stimulus to the seizure of territory.

Even in territories already held by Europeans, imperial rule became more vigorous and interventionist in response to the rise of colonial nationalism. In this sense, too, the "new imperialism" was as much the consequence as the cause of nationalism. Proconsuls and administrators such as Curzon in India, Cromer in Egypt, Milner in South Africa, and Sarrault in French Indochina, all governed their territories in the 1890s or 1900s with the aim of heading off, diverting, or suppressing demands by the educated intelligentsia for greater freedom and political representation. In turn, all four administrators goaded local politicians into more vigorous opposition, terrorism, and armed resistance. Further east, the expansion of Dutch rule, outward from Java to the islands of the archipelago, such as Sumatra, was prompted in part by Islamic and local resistance on the fringes. Only in retrospect did these newly pacified territories yield the prospect of profitable plantation agriculture and logging contracts.

In summary, when historians investigate the expansion of European power in any one area of the extra-European world, they commonly find a variety of metropolitan or local interests which were held to cause or legitimate intervention. In order to explain why the late nineteenth century saw a speeding up of empire building, large claims have been made for the importance of world economic crisis, the interests of capital, the need for agricultural raw materials, or the clamor of local commercial interests. Certainly, new technologies had come into existence, which held out the hope of exploiting the interior of vast continents. But this does not altogether explain why European governments resorted to territorial and land grabbing so determinedly, and on such a large scale. A more powerful general argument arises out of the concurrence of the new phase of imperial expansion with the full emergence of the European, American, and Japanese nation-state and the rise of extra-European national movements. Claims had to be staked out quickly, or else others might occupy them.

A WORLD OF NATION-STATES?

A key feature of the nation-state – for some analysts, *the* key aspect of the nation-state – was not its intrinsic nature or its claims and demands on its own population. It was instead the fact that the nation-state operated in a world populated by other, similar nation-states and imperial provinces, and this gave further impetus to the pressure for political uniformity across the world. The looser connections of the old, overlapping ecumenes and their circles of honorific exchange and trade diasporas, dubbed "archaic globalization" and discussed in chapter 1, were gradually eroded. In their place arose an international system driven by cooperating or conflicting national political economies. After about 1815, the European state and Western colonialism began to impose a new pattern of internationalism on the old world order. The nation-state increasingly dominated global networks. It imposed its system of more rigidly bound territories, languages, and religious conventions on all international networks.

Yet it is important to keep in mind that the older patterns of globalization persisted strongly under the surface of the new international order. Links created by pilgrimage, older patterns of connection created by the universalizing empires of the past, and even the consumption of precious and exotic items continued to remain important. More than that, these links both facilitated and subverted the new international order. This point will be elaborated first.

THE PERSISTENCE OF ARCHAIC GLOBALIZATION

When we consider how international networks were structured in the nineteenth century, the unintended consequences of older-style links as much as the policies of the leaders of the national states remain crucial. Why, for instance, after two savage and destructive wars, and despite widespread British support for the Confederacy during the Civil War, did the United States and Britain drift together in the course of the nineteenth century? International relations specialists have usually viewed this question from the perspective of "reason of state." Yet prevailing old connections were equally, if not more, important. Even after the American Revolution and the war of 1812–14, lawyers on both sides of the Atlantic continued to cling to the old lineages of common law. Old-established Protestant churches renegotiated their links and mounted an evangelical offensive across the globe. The old literary culture, which arose at the time of Shakespeare, continued to be discussed and reinterpreted in journals and books sold on both sides of the Atlantic. Before 1848 or even 1870, transatlantic links of marriage and emigration remained very similar to what they had been during the "peopling of America" in the seventeenth and eighteenth centuries. The massive export of coolies from China, Japan, and India and laborers from East and West Africa across the nineteenth-century globe extended older patterns of internal and inter-regional migration and slave trading, even as they were subjected to new forms of commercial control.

Archaic links of religion, economy, and bodily practice also continued to underpin the new international order of the nineteenth century in the economic sphere. Classic Marxist and liberal theories of economic change have emphasized the rationality of expanding capitalism. On this theory, the aim of Western expansion was to seize resources and subordinate labor. This is true in great measure. As we have seen, in the early nineteenth century much of the globe became a vast agricultural hinterland for western Europe. This occurred before mass industrialization, even in Britain. Still, many features of older global economic links persisted and remained formative in these new systems. Archaic globalization had been partly driven by the desire to acquire the exotic, to collect rarities, and to transform one's moral status and substance. That desire did not abate in the nineteenth century. If fans and exotic spices had proved lucrative items of global trade in the seventeenth century, ostrich feathers and Japanese pottery continued to flow to the European and American markets. Rhinoceros horns, sea slugs, and birds' nests were still prized in Chinese markets. Despite growing moral campaigns against it, opium in various forms remained a vital trade in Asia and continued to reach Europe and the Americas in various forms.

One particular item of international trade still proved to be greatly resistant to conventional analyses of supply and demand. Large populations, especially in Asia, consumed gold, a key item of international trade, because of its charismatic qualities as a transformer of status and even health. After 1860, gold may well have been mined through capitalist forms of production and labor control in Australia, California, and southern Africa. Its markets, however, responded to quite different rationales of prestige and family consumption. Throughout the nineteenth century and even up to the 1980s, gold consumption in India and the Middle East was highly price-inelastic. That is to say, Indians, Arabs, and others continued to import huge quantities of gold for jewelry and familial saving, regardless of its price on the international market. Anthropologists have shown how gold operates as a universal, honorific currency in India, independently of the market.[50] Until recently, the accumulation of gold bangles and other ornaments was an important tactic for preserving the financial viability of women in their husbands' families. Gold was also believed to protect, strengthen, and purify the bodily humors of the wearer. These archaic principles of consumption continued to bulk heavily in the ledgers of the "gentlemanly capitalists" of the modern world.

The global marriage patterns of the nineteenth century also preserved some archaic features. In general, anthropologists have examined the structure of marriage patterns within small societies. Social historians have tended to consider the marriage practices of particular national aristocracies. What happened in the nineteenth century, though, was a massive expansion of global hypogamy, of men taking women of perceived lower status. This often entailed marriage across boundaries between distinct cultural or assumed racial groups. It was once said that by the 1830s sexual relations between British men and Asian women were a thing of the past. There is certainly evidence of a slow imposition of racial boundaries in marriage and sex in India in the course of the nineteenth century. But this should not be overstated. The Anglo-Indian community may generally have been formed before 1820. But large Anglo-Chinese and Anglo-Burmese and Dutch-Indonesian communities came into existence after 1860. They played a dominant role in commerce and the service economies of much of southern and eastern Asia. The ancient practice of Muslim travelers contracting temporary marriages with foreign women continued to pin together the Arab, Indian, and Muslim East throughout the nineteenth century. It later became important as a network of sentiment which helped link pan-Islamic movements worldwide. Mixed-race community formation remained common in the Americas, even though what became known as "miscegenation," race mixing, was gradually limited by bourgeois, nationalistic, and racialist ideas in English-speaking North America.

Archaic conceptions of kinship continued to act as powerful formative influences on the European and American worlds themselves. The global links of European royal families – the Bourbons, Hohenzollerns, Saxe-Coburgs, and others – became a strategic network for the prosecution of private diplomacy in the later nineteenth century.[51] At the same time, the practice of aristocratic hypogamy, downward marriage, in northern Europe was to provide a vital resource for declining estate-owners after the onset of the great agricultural depression of the 1870s. British aristocratic families welcomed American heiresses. The case of the Churchills and the Curzons, whose families both acquired "new blood" and new wealth by bringing in American heiresses, are only the best-known examples of this. Old Spanish, Portuguese, and French property-owners kept their estates solvent by bringing over women from wealthy colonial backgrounds in Brazil, Cuba, and Mexico. All these archaic connections were transformed within the new capitalist structures of the world economy. Yet all of them reflected the traditions and strategies of an earlier period. Modern eugenic theories about racial vigor merely validated older conceptions about manipulating bloodlines.

It is now easier to see how this type of archaic global network did, nevertheless, become a set of international connections over a relatively short span of the nineteenth century. Much has been written about the growth of the nation-state and its alter ego, the imperial state, after 1850. Less attention has been paid to the process by which global links were themselves reconstructed by, or in relationship to, the system of nation-states. These older patterns of global interactions persisted. But they were increasingly represented in terms of national essences and controlled by nation-states.

FROM GLOBALIZATION TO INTERNATIONALISM

Chapter 1 suggested that global links in the old world were determined by ideologies and bodily practices. Before the nineteenth century, the ideologies of universal kingship and universal religion had been dominant. The critical point of change after 1800 was the way in which writers, jurists, and politicians across the world borrowed and adapted theories of individual and states' rights to their own use. Intellectual history remains very European- and American-centered. It is important to consider the ways in which Asians and Africans took up and used rights theories. Imperial expansion was obviously a key determinant of this. The apparatus of the European state and its territorial rights over space and citizens was exported to the fluid, segmented world of Asia and Africa. The idea of a universal Chinese, or Ottoman, or even Catholic Christian empire became redundant. European nationalists and colonial patriots began instead to assert their rights as individuals or representatives of cultures in the language of these appropriated theories. In the 1830s, Ram Mohun Roy, the Bengali reformer, argued in London that the *rights* of the Mughal Empire, now perceived as a state rather than as a universal polity, had been violated by the English East India Company. The defeat of China during the opium wars ultimately forced the Middle Kingdom to claim not superiority but merely equal territorial and economic rights under the law of nations. The ideological landscape of the modern international world was seen as a dialogue or concert of equal political entities which claimed uniform rights. Equally, the universalizing tendency inherent in newly diffused theories of individual and group rights began to create networks beyond the nation-state. These constituted a kind of embryonic international civil society.

Other aspects of global ideology were also transformed in the nineteenth century. Religions still remained global in their aspirations, as chapter 9 will show. Increasingly, though, they tailored their activities, forms of bureaucracy, and appeal to the nation-state. Later-nineteenth-century Christian missions were national missions. The revived Catholic Church of the late nineteenth century spoke a universal language, but its bureaucracies paralleled those of the nation-state, and its appeal was particularly strong among submerged nationalities in Poland and Ireland, for instance. Equally, pan-Islamists dreamed of a universal caliphate. Yet their political method was to empower submerged or embattled Muslim nations. Race theory, which became dominant at the end of the nineteenth century, purported to be a global historical theory. Yet its implications were almost everywhere worked out in the language of the nation-state. For instance, French racial theorists worried about the enduring characteristics of the "Teutonic" and "Latin" races, but generally their concern was whether a mixture of these two elements would weaken or strengthen the French nation and its state. In this the ideologies of race differed from the tactile, embodied system of archaic castes, which was discussed in chapter 1.

The global connections of the Old World were also created by the movement of peoples. During the late nineteenth and early twentieth centuries, such movements were increasingly regulated by state surveillance and by the control of flows of migrants. Antislavery measures by the British and later French governments created a new system of checks and treaties in international waters. Colonial governments controlled the flow of indentured laborers both inside and outside their territories. From the regulation of transatlantic emigrant ships by the British and American governments in the 1820s, through the quarantine regulations of the great cholera epidemics of the 1830s and 1840s, states acted more and more insistently to control the international traffic in free migrants. The doctrine of free trade struggled for some decades with this urge to increase state regulation. By the end of the nineteenth century, however, fears of racial decline and panics about the movement of foreign criminals or agents had handed victory to state surveillance. One aspect of this was the imposition by the United States after about 1890 of more rigid controls on immigrants, particularly "Asiatics" and Jews. This culminated in the National Origins legislation of 1924. This type of legislation defined more clearly the "essence" of the state, but it also determined the nature of international links.

In the same manner, older and looser links of global trading gave way to more formal commercial conventions between nations. This was true even in the days of free trade before the 1870s. But as political and industrial leaders sought to protect their economies by tariff agreements, the nation-state inevitably became the key actor in an international economy. This led to increasingly formal trading arrangements. The old system of honorary consuls or consultation by local rulers with the headmen of "guest" merchant communities was replaced by networks of commercial consulates and international economic treaties. The growth of the Western-dominated world economy in the course of the nineteenth century, therefore, produced a paradox. On the one hand, the movement of capital became more complex. Long-range direct investment meant that businessmen from many different countries worked together to form and invest capital. On the other hand, states became increasingly worried by such flows of capital and attempted to control the firms and their capital. During the Anglo-Boer crisis, for instance, British politicians panicked over the way in which international firms were supposedly perverting the course of international stock markets and capital flows were strengthening. At the same time, national controls on the location and use of capital became stronger with the development of the national patent and the idea of the national head office.

Thirdly, at the level of bodily practice, global links were now conducted in a different way from the earlier hierarchical cosmopolitanism. Assumed racial groups were increasingly physically separated. Europeans in the East gave up the practice of using Indian and Chinese wet nurses for their children. In the course of the nineteenth century, they rejected non-European dress and foods.[52] The process, never complete, also affected Asians and Africans. By the 1920s and 1930s, Hindu nationalists were mounting campaigns to expel Muslim body servants from their households and to prohibit their women from visiting Muslim holy men and healers. This is a good example of the way in which archaic boundaries of pollution were "nationalized," as it were, over the long nineteenth century. Yet more rigid nationalization demanded a complementary internationalization at the level of the body. In the international public sphere, males were more and more constrained to wear

English topcoats and top hats while they spoke, ate, drank, and deported themselves in a French style. Growing international uniformity went alongside growing conflict between closely defined nation-states.

INTERNATIONALISM IN PRACTICE

Three examples will help us to chart this process of the nationalization of earlier global connections at different levels of theory and practice. This chapter ends with the case study of a state institution, the passport, and an international voluntary association, the Red Cross. Finally, the chapter will examine a critical international conference, the World Parliament of Religions, held in Chicago in 1893.

Until recently, little work has been done on that preeminent tool for controlling international boundaries, the passport. But the history of the passport clearly indicates the transition between global networks of emigration and the internationalism of the nation-state. John Torpey's *The Invention of the Passport* filled a gap in knowledge as far as Europe is concerned. In the eighteenth century, elite traders and nobles moved readily across much of Europe. It was the poor and the peasantry who were tied to the land and needed papers to move around. The external passport was a royal letter, a boon which was conferred on great nobles, clerics, and others, royal protection and a request that they would not be hindered by the petty officials of another king's realm.

In Europe and the Americas, the passport became a tool of external political surveillance only during the French Revolution, when governments tried to control the movement across their borders of political agitators, or in the case of the French Republic, reactionaries and royalists. Fear of revolution continued to spur the development of passport offices and agencies throughout the nineteenth century. The 1848 revolutions and the aftermath of the revolutionary Paris Commune of 1871 saw panic attempts to extend the system even to ordinary people. Otherwise, between 1815 and 1850, there was a general move to relax controls both over internal movement and over emigration beyond states' borders. It was only during the later nineteenth century, and in response to fears about the consequences of labor mobility, that further, more rigid controls on movement across national boundaries were imposed.

The Asian world saw a similar process, but its roots were somewhat different. In Asia, too, great kings had given subjects charters for travel in India – they were called *parwanas*, leave to pass. At the local level, movement was controlled through recognized leaders and headmen. Villagers on the move do not seem to have been forced to carry papers as they were more often in Europe and China. Still, the books of the village accountant gave elites an indirect control over labor movement. In India, the expansion of the passport system to encompass ordinary merchants and travelers was at first a consequence of monopoly building by the European companies who were deeply jealous of their European rivals. The Dutch and English East India companies kept meticulous records of all foreign European subjects in their territories, fearing that they would institute competitive commerce. Asian states faced with this aggressive imperialism of monopoly instituted countermeasures, limiting foreign merchants and personnel to particular points and controlling their own subjects' relations with them. The eighteenth-century Chinese state trading corporation, the Cohong, was a good example of this. All foreigners in Canton were forced to carry accreditations from their assigned merchants.

Political fear rapidly replaced commercial jealousy after 1800. By 1830, the authorities in south India were arresting merchants from the Middle East "who were travelling without passport."[53] They feared purist Muslim teachers and other religious emissaries spreading anti-British messages in volatile port cities. In its turn, however, the imposition of passports opened up queries about who was and who was not a British Indian subject.[54] European imperial governments asserted their rights to protect or control the external movement of their subjects. Indian merchants overseas became subjects of British India, rather than guest foreigners. This was a critical point in their transformation into subjects of a nation. By contrast, some contemporary merchants of the Arab and Chinese diasporas were able to secure foreign nationality in European enclaves in order to avoid Chinese or Ottoman taxation or land law.[55] In this case, the passport as an international device was being used to subvert, rather than strengthen, the emerging nation-state; but in either case nationality had become the point of reference.

The Red Cross, the second case study, provides an example of the way in which the religious ideal of humanitarian aid and of bodily help for the wounded was nationalized. Originally a response by Henri Dunant to the horrors of the battlefield of Solferino during the unification of Italy, the Red Cross organization soon became associated with Switzerland as a nation-state.[56] The Red Cross itself was not so much a Christian or an international symbol as the obverse of the Swiss flag. Since 1880 the central organization has always been heavily Swiss. The subordinate bodies of the Red Cross were built around different national committees. This nationally based international organization has pressed national governments to create international conventions on the laws of war. Yet the tension between the national and the international has always existed under the surface. In the 1880s and 1890s the symbolic unity of the organization was breached when enraged Ottoman Muslims attacked Red Cross volunteer doctors serving on battlefields because they were wearing a Christian symbol. This forced the organizers to allow the Red Crescent to be adopted in Muslim countries. During the Balkan wars after 1911, Indian Muslims organized in defense of the Ottomans through a specifically Indian Red Crescent Organization.[57] More recently, the state of Israel has tried to insist on the use of a red Star of David in its own sphere.

The example of world religions yields a final example of the shift from archaic globalization to the internationalism of the nineteenth century. This is a theme which will be taken up more fully in chapter 9. Its Christian organizers intended the World Parliament of Religions of 1893 in Chicago to celebrate humanity's global quest for religious experience. They hoped to

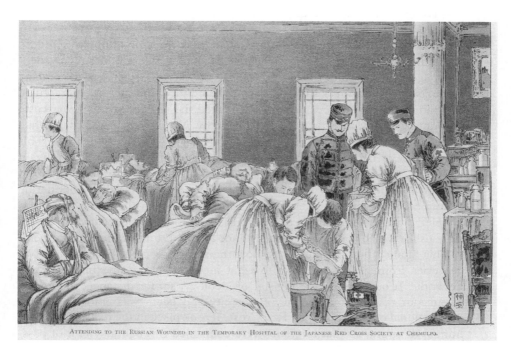

ATTENDING TO THE RUSSIAN WOUNDED IN THE TEMPORARY HOSPITAL OF THE JAPANESE RED CROSS SOCIETY AT CHEMULPO.

ILLUSTRATION 6.4 Red Cross in action: Japanese nurses attending to Russian wounded in hospital of Japanese Red Cross at Chemulpo in the Russo-Japanese War.

mitigate hostilities between different religious traditions. The context for the meeting was the rise of anti-Semitism, increased Protestant–Catholic hostility, and the Western fear of pan-Islamism. From the beginning, however, the organization of the conference was dogged with controversy over the status of national religious bodies. In the tense political situation of the period, it was found possible in many cases to allow only the representatives of specifically national churches to "represent" religions.

Though uninvited, the Bengali seer Swami Vivekananda arrived in Chicago and, by force of character, became the *de facto* Indian representative.[58] He achieved three things by his passionate speeches to the parliament. First, he managed to encourage Americans to see Hinduism as a powerful international force. He did this by ignoring the divisions between its sects and pointing to the ancient Hindu civilizations of Southeast Asia and the diaspora Hindus of South Africa and the Caribbean. He deplored the bodily practice of Western nations, their slaughter of living souls to feed their greed. He recorded his horror at the daily massacre of the sacred cow, which he saw in the Chicago stockyards. Most significantly, Vivekananda firmly welded the notion of Hinduism to the claims of Indian nationalism, contrasting the materialism of Western nations with the spirituality which he proclaimed was the essence of Eastern nations – above all, India. His moral dominance of the parliament was celebrated by many in India as the precise moment when Indian nationhood was recognized as a force in its own right, separate and superior to British imperialism.

On his return, Indians hailed Vivekananda as the embodiment of India's spirituality as a nation. A few years earlier, he had wandered the subcontinent as a pilgrim in search of traces of God, like the sacred travelers of the archaic globe. Now, his devotees subordinated caste, culture, and sacred geography to the nation. Indian princes personally dragged the chariot of this lower-caste renouncer, bodily inverting the old hierarchy. Vivekananda was meanwhile serenaded with the triumphal march from Handel's *Judas Maccabeus*. This music had itself been composed as a celebration of the fusion of religion with the once-and-future nation by an old German patriot resident in Britain. A Calcutta daily newspaper wrote: "India celebrated its conquering champion. All sections of Hinduism came together to thank the American people."[59] In this way, India came increasingly to be associated with Hinduism, a shift which was of great importance for the future of the subcontinent.

This final section has suggested how the shift took place over the last two centuries from global networks to what increasingly became inter-national networks. It occurred in the register of ideology; so, for instance, the notion of succour to the wounded in Christianity and Islam was embodied in an international organization, the Red Cross. It took place in the register of actual human diaspora, so that migrants were controlled through a system of passports determined by their nationality. It also happened in the register of bodily practice. Indians, notably Gandhi, came to believe that vegetarianism and abstinence should be a defining feature of the future Indian nation. This last register, the register of bodily practice, formed the link between the ideological and the material through the consumption and transformation of commodities. The strategic collection by people of the exotic and health-giving made way increasingly for the consumption of uniform commodities, modes of dress, and forms of deportment which were the markers of national status in the international arena. Paradoxes and conflicts emerged. The Japanese elites, for instance, asked themselves whether their modern nationality was best served by wearing European frock coats in international arenas or by adapting their traditional garments as a "Japanese" formal suit.

CONCLUSION

This chapter as a whole has attempted to bring together the historical writing on nationalism, imperialism, "internationalism," and subordinate ethnic groups for the later nineteenth century. The rise of exclusive nationalisms, grasping and using the powers of the new and more interventionist state, was the critical force propelling both the new imperialism and the hardening of the boundaries between majority and assumed "ethnic" populations across the world. Nationalism itself took on more competitive and well-defined forms as a consequence of the wars, rebellions, and international conflicts of the mid-century. These strengthened, for instance, an American, and even a

Canadian, sense of nationality, which had been developing before the mid-century. In Europe, the emergence of two new nation-states, Germany and Italy, and the humiliation of two others, France and German Austria, tipped the balance of the continent toward diplomatic and military competition both inside and outside its borders. The unification of Japan, yet more vigorous British imperial rule in South Asia, and a European offensive in the Middle East brought into existence new nationalist movements among the elites and commercial people of Asia and Africa. In turn, these began to deploy new forms of publicity to press their claims for self-rule on the colonial governments. Imperialism and nationalism reacted on each other to redivide the world and its people.

The mid-century wars had themselves arisen from a variety of causes: uneven economic growth, the relative deprivation of peasant and artisan populations, the drive for modernization of leading elite groups, and the slow diffusion of ideas of popular sovereignty from the earlier democratic revolutions. In accounting for the onward rush of claimants to nationhood in this critical period of time, however, the dominant influence was the experience and memory of mass conflict itself. The state, urbanization, and print capitalism all played a part, but war was the origin of nationalisms, just as nationalisms caused wars. Nationalism in turn reformulated the old, looser links of global diasporas and ideologies which had linked the eighteenth-century world. Even when conferences or congresses claimed to represent universal principles, they were now structured increasingly by the participation of nation-states. After the 55 years from about 1815 to 1870, when free trade was the order of the day, economic protectionism on national lines was more and more apparent as the century drew to an end. While flows of international trade, labor, and capital grew exponentially, nation-states sought vigorously to control and direct them to their own ends.

There is a paradox, then, in this picture of the rise of the nation-state and its imperial surrogate. Statesmen may well have conceived nations as monolithic and authoritative entities, but people saw the nation as a guarantor of rights, privileges, and claims on resources. When states failed to deliver on these implicit pledges, especially if they were ruled by foreigners, people came to demand them even more vociferously and aggressively. So it was that the triumph of the nation-state also saw the emergence of a plethora of voluntary associations, reform societies, and moral crusades, now increasingly organized at both a national and an international level. The antislavery associations and clubs of liberal reformers which existed in the early nineteenth century were now joined by thousands of new bodies claiming to speak in the name of, among many others, Indians, Irishmen, socialists, women, and indigenous peoples. The socialist First International was only the most radical of these. The next two chapters deal, first, with the lineaments of the state itself and, then, with the body of political thought which informed its leaders and its radical critics.

PART III

STATE AND SOCIETY IN THE AGE OF IMPERIALISM

[7] *MYTHS AND TECHNOLOGIES OF THE MODERN STATE*

THE next two chapters (7 and 8) consider at world level some of the institutions, ideologies, and economic changes which, according to contemporaries and many modern historians, reshaped the world of the nineteenth century. They consider the rise of the "modern state" and the ascent of liberalism and science. Chapters 9 and 11, by contrast, examine some features of life in the nineteenth century: namely, religion, powerful monarchies, and landed hierarchies, which many contemporaries considered to have been on the wane in the face of these supposedly irresistible forces for change. Paradoxically, what these latter two chapters stress is the manner in which religion, monarchy, and hierarchy were able dramatically to reinvent and modernize themselves in the 50 years before 1914.

The state, in the most general sense, is an important actor in this book. Well before industrialization or the emergence of the new city had become formative forces at world level, it was the triumphs and tribulations of the states of the eighteenth century, and their revolutionary and imperial successors, which determined much of social life and the pattern of globalization, as chapters 3 and 4 showed. In the process of operating at a global level and adapting to new ideas and technologies, European states and a few non-European states began to become more uniform and, at the same time, more competitive.

DIMENSIONS OF THE MODERN STATE

What, then, is meant by the "modern state," and how did it differ from the great eighteenth-century polities which were examined in the first chapter of the book? By the late nineteenth century, most regimes throughout the world were attempting to control closely defined territories by means of uniform administrative, legal, and educational structures. They wished to mark out with maps and surveys the extent of their resources and tax and utilize them in a coherent way. Earlier states had sometimes been intrusive and demanding, but only in specific areas of life, and only at certain places and times. By contrast, the modern state aspired to a monopolistic claim on its subjects' loyalties. Modernizing states were jealous of trans-territorial affiliations, whether of religion, ethnic connection, or old dynastic connection, which had characterized the old order. They attempted to abolish the rights or, sometimes, the disabilities of special categories of subjects who claimed superior status, or alternatively were condemned to inferior status, under law or government. These changes involved a growing uniformity in that the state became more cohesive. The old distinction between the king's establishment and resources and the government tended to be abolished. The state became located in a particular place, rather than moving around wherever the king went. Court factions became political parties, attempting to seize the levers of government rather than the king's favor. Yet the state also became more functionally complex, with different departments and expertises separated off within it.

The need to organize citizens for large-scale war as conscripts, or to tax them in order to develop better military technology, was an important incentive to simplify and strengthen state structures. The contemporary sociologist Michael Mann has noted that most early bureaucracies were staffed by soldiers.[1] Yet, in addition to being a military and financial steamroller, the state was also an idea. It represented an aspiration for complete power and territorial sovereignty, whether in the name of "the people," or "the nation," or despite them. The state as a concept had a life of its own which cannot simply be reduced to class interests or military exigencies. From Victorian British empire-builders to the modernizing military leaders of Ecuador and Peru, the idea of "civilization" embodied ideas about ordered, technological society and the perfectibility of the human individual. These ideas appealed to conservatives, liberals, radicals, and socialists alike, though in very different ways.

Throughout the nineteenth-century world, much state building was top-down, the "project" of dominant elite groups. This was particularly true in the European colonial empires and also in societies such as Japan, China, and Ethiopia, where indigenous elites became convinced that the powerful state was the only thing which stood between them and the extinction of "their" civilizations. But there was another form of state building which should not be lost sight of. Governments were also teased into expansion by the explosion of local disputes which they alone could mediate, or by the demand for services which they alone could supply. A good example of this bottom-up state building is provided by the demand from small farmers and local businessmen in the United States from the early nineteenth century onward that the federal government intervene to provide reasonable pricing of, and access to, railroads and credit facilities. In the same way, commercial interests in continental Europe and even in the United States began, about the same time, to demand government intervention to create protectionist tariff barriers in order to foster local businesses and services. This is not to suggest that the state, as Marxist theorists of the 1960s used to argue, was no more than an organ for the interests of the bourgeoisie. Yet it does remind us that the state was a resource, though one predominantly commanded by the relatively privileged, as well as a military and financial incubus pressing down on society "from above."

In general, then, this book is skeptical of the exaggerated claims that many recent historians have made for the overwhelming, steamroller-like nature of the domestic and colonial state in the nineteenth century. This leviathan was more characteristic of the twentieth century. All the same, the rise of the modern state during this period was a remarkable phenomenon. The Napoleonic and anti-Napoleonic state of the revolutionary years was almost a freak development. The ideologies, ambitions, and reach of rulers outgrew their strength, to be sharply deflated after 1815. The real turning point was the period 1850–70. Now, the modern state benefited from rapid industrialization, new armaments, and an aggressive edge honed by fear of revolution and the fire of nationalism. This was the period when Bismarck's Prussia, the Second French Empire, and the British colonial state in India moved into higher gear, fortified by a new scientific and professional culture.[2] That the triumph of this entity was long delayed in most parts of the world does not detract from its importance.

The chapter goes on to examine the geographical spread of the nineteenth-century state, the manner in which it related to its precursors, its tools and resources. Before doing so, it is important to consider the strengths and weaknesses of historians' (and anthropologists') approaches to the modern and colonial state, since it is now an explanatory factor that is often airily invoked by them to explain all and every change.

THE STATE AND THE HISTORIANS

Fifty years ago, historical writing on the English-speaking world and its empires had little to say about the state as such. The historical tradition founded by the nineteenth-century Whig historian T. B. Macaulay had much to say about representative government and the growth of freedoms, but much less about the development of the state's powers. His younger relative, G. M. Trevelyan, the most celebrated early-twentieth-century English historian, appeared to exclude politics as a whole from his social history of England. On both sides of the Atlantic, the liberal tradition in political thought, discussed in the next chapter, was suspicious of or hostile to the growth of the state. It was thought to be something slightly sinister, which "continental" Europeans had invented. Instead, Americans, Britons, and inhabitants of the old British dominions were said to possess constitutions, party politics, and governments which were managed by civil servants. This tended to limit the interest of modern historians. Even in the dependent territories of the British Empire, where historians acknowledged the existence of colonial government, the civil, military, and lawmaking dimensions of European power were kept separate in historical discussion, just as they had been formally separated in the ideology of British rule itself.

Continental Europeans, especially Russians and Germans, however, had been talking about the state for a long time, though many of them also believed that it was a dangerous phenomenon. Theorists and philosophers could hardly avoid it. As de Tocqueville noted, the eighteenth-century French monarchy had tried unsuccessfully to manage the state as a vast extension of the king's body, as an "estate" in the older, Renaissance sense of the term. The revolution had temporarily divorced the state from the will of any incumbent power-holder. After 1789, the state as a philosophical idea had developed a life of its own, as the embodiment of the general will. The Jacobins used that idea to override all individual rights in the course of the Terror. In Germany, the swelling of central and local bureaucracies in the nineteenth century caused the new professional philosophers, historians, and sociologists to pay much attention to the state, with Hegel himself in the vanguard. In the Prussian theory, the state was a rational institution standing above the selfish interests of society. The king, rather than being divinely empowered, was the state's supreme servant, and therefore the embodiment of reason.[3] Hegel wrote weightily of the state as a philosophical idea, not a precious gift from God to rulers:

> In contrast with the spheres of private rights and private welfare (the family and civil society), the state is from one point of view an external necessity and their higher authority; its nature is such that their laws and interests are subordinate to it and dependent on it. On the other hand, however, it is the end immanent within them, and its strength lies in the unity of its own universal end and aim with the particular end of individuals, in the fact that individuals have duties to the state in proportion as they have rights against it.[4]

Turning this on its head, Marxists argued that the state was the engine of the class power of the bourgeoisie. For Max Weber, the state was on the whole a benign, impersonal entity which guaranteed civil order and progress. Its rise signaled the decline of mystical obsessions and dangerous forms of political charisma. Even in Russia, where so much real authority lay with local estates, orders, and assemblies, political theorists in the German mold and administrators, many of whom were also Germans, speculated about the need to strengthen the tsars' autocracy and curb these local baronies. Meanwhile, French and German orientalists and historians also made great strides in analyzing the forms of the traditional state, particularly in China. The work of the American sociologist Talcott Parsons was influential in Chinese studies as they developed in the course of the twentieth century. The old centralizing bureaucracy of China seemed almost the opposite of the local and rights-based constitution of the United States.

It was not until after about 1960, however, that historians of the English-speaking world also began widely to emphasize the workings of the state in their own past. The rise of sociology, the visibility of the contemporary welfare state, and Marxist ruminations about the bourgeois order began to have an impact on the way history was written. In the 1980s, John Brewer summarized the trend in his book *The Sinews of Power*.[5] There he argued that the state had been missed in British historical writing, not because it was weak but because it was so strong and successful. The tax-gathering and war-making functions of the British state in the eighteenth century were streamlined and effective by comparison with the clumsy and venal continental states. It was for this reason that, though initially less wealthy and populous than France, Britain had been able to fight and win a more or less continuous global war between 1688 and 1820. Meanwhile, historians of labor also began to perceive the state as an organ of class domination. To the radical English historian E. P. Thompson and his collaborators and followers, this was reflected in the homicidal eighteenth-century criminal code fixated on the gallows and in the repressive policing of landed property, early industrial strikes, and political demonstrations.[6]

It was not only the academic left that changed its mind. In the 1960s, liberal and nationalist historians also discovered the history of the British state. It had long been obvious that in its colonial and foreign policy Britain had attempted to develop a more authoritative and centralized system than was apparent in its internal affairs. The Colonial Office had begun to try to legislate for the whole empire as early as 1809, while such efforts at rationalization had little effect on domestic governance until after Prime Minister Peel's reforms of the 1840s. In the 1960s, Oliver MacDonagh, considering the impact of English government on the Irish and, later, Australians, wrote about the growth of the state in nineteenth-century Britain. He was struck by the way in which British governments managed emigration to America, Australia, and New Zealand.[7] Working on the other end of the nineteenth century, the next generation of social historians, such as Jose Harris, analyzed the beginnings of the counting and classifying of people through the British and Irish censuses and the significance of income tax and of basic social provision.[8]

After the 1960s and the experience of the Vietnam War, historians of the European colonial empires also began to summon up a powerful and intrusive entity, the "colonial state," to explain distortions which were introduced into the societies of Africa and Asia by European government. By the 1990s, several American historians and anthropologists had attributed quite general cognitive and operational principles to the colonial state. Bernard Cohn wrote of the colonial state and "its forms of knowledge."[9] The trend was neatly summarized by James Scott in his *Seeing Like a State* (1999), which explained the psychology of the supposedly enlightened and improving projects pioneered by both European and colonial states. His examples of how administrators imbued the state with an urge to order and control, almost a mind of its own, ranged from forest conservancy in eighteenth-century Germany through to the eugenic project of producing perfect human beings at the end of the nineteenth century.[10] Meanwhile, the powerful influence of the French philosopher Michel Foucault began to be registered. He was less concerned with the organization of government itself than with the discourses and practices of a widely diffused state power, which he called "governmentality."

Even in American domestic history, where the story of the expansion of freedom through the action of courts and political parties continues to hold sway, economic and social historians have charted the buildup of state regulation of burgeoning industry. This became clear toward the end of the nineteenth century, with the rise of the Progressive Movement, which attempted to harness federal state power for the benefit of citizens rather than big industrial combines. In 1982 Stephen Skowronek entitled a book *Building a New American State*. After the 1890s, he argued, the USA, like Britain, began to introduce state-distributed social benefits for its citizens, though some time after Bismarck's Germany and even Britain's dominions had ventured down this path. Small as the American colonial empire was, Skowronek believed, the problems that the occupying power faced in the Pacific, the Philippines, Cuba, and Puerto Rico required a more professional and centralized army. He noted that despite opposition from the locally organized national guard and state governors, an Army War College was established in 1901, and the strength of the professional standing army was increased.[11] Presidents Theodore Roosevelt (1901–9) and William Howard Taft (1909–13) both combined a desire for administrative reform with an interest in America's position in the outside world. Taft himself had been governor in the Philippines. By the 1990s, therefore, the state was very much part of the agenda of historians of the USA, though what, precisely, was meant by the state remained in doubt.

PROBLEMS IN DEFINING THE STATE

The pre-1960s British and American historical writing which focused on constitutions, the common law, party politics, and local government found it difficult to see the connections between these different entities, let alone the way in which they represented the interests of dominant elites. By contrast, the state has now become a critical area of study, and the present chapter agrees that the state did grow in ambition, if not always in effectiveness, in the course of the nineteenth century. There are, however, dangers in the prevailing view, particularly prominent in the work of James Scott and the new imperial history, that sees the modern state as a homogeneous and all-seeing entity. In methodological terms, the emphasis on the state often involves a problematic reliance on certain categories of sources. Historians generally work with state documents. The argument becomes circular. It is very easy to assume that states are therefore responsible for any and all social change.

Secondly, in making broad assertions about the growth of the state as an entity, historians can easily ignore periods which do not fit this pattern. For instance, in the case of the British state, the Anglo-French wars at the beginning of the nineteenth century and the national and imperial self-strengthening after 1885 brought about an appreciable expansion of central government activity. But in between these peaks was a long period when the expenditure of central government actually fell as a percentage of GDP.[12] Similarly, in Germany, the post-Napoleonic search for a romantic union between state and people encouraged statesmen, for a time at least, to devolve power to local corporate bodies. Even at the height of what has been seen as William II's autocracy after 1890, the imperial German government often seemed to be a pitiful thing, not only tossed about at the mercy of princely and local jurisdictions, but frightened of German public opinion.[13]

In the United States the peaks of government activity were lower, and the troughs were deeper. For some time after independence, a substantial body of opinion (the so-called anti-federalists) opposed any regulation of local assemblies, let alone taxation managed by central government. Even that most famous of American political institutions, the presidency, might not have come into being. Some of the founding fathers distrusted the "monarchical principle" so much that they wished instead to have a kind of conciliar executive, perhaps like the French Directory of the 1790s, though shorn of most of that body's powers, too.[14]

In none of these cases can we assume, however, that governance and control did not exist at all. What they suggest is that the organs of the state in this wider sense were diffused across society. It is clear, though, that "statishness" could take a variety of forms in the nineteenth-century world. This is the reason why some historians and social theorists, following the lead of Michel Foucault, now speak of governmentality in preference to state regulation. Others, especially anthropologists, go further, arguing that for many people even in the contemporary world, the state is not so much a hard fact as an idea. The state is "out there," and its mythical power can be magicked into existence and appropriated by anyone from a gang boss to the leader of a charismatic religious movement.

These are useful theoretical developments. A whole range of authorities, increasingly speaking the language of the state, is what many of the world's populations experienced in the nineteenth century, rather than the pressure of the state as a monolithic incubus. For even where the state was not present, local magnates, commercial bodies, and political movements increasingly counted, catalogued, and kept records. Cecil Rhodes's mining and land companies in southern Africa were probably more state-like than many contemporary governments. They organized labor, surveyed resources, and produced maps. As Jean Comaroff has pointed out, the missionaries were the nearest thing to a colonial government that many southern Africans had experienced before 1914.[15] Millenarian movements deployed the language of state power. The Taipings, for instance, represented themselves as the Heavenly Kingdom of the Eternal Peace, and American Mormons established state-like regulations for the righteous government of Utah.

Outside continental Europe and Japan, too, the rise of the state was far from being a linear process. In late-eighteenth-century Iran, the power of the Shia Muslim clerics actually increased, and that of the government diminished. This was because the prevailing tribal-based regimes, including the incoming Qajar rulers in Persia, were regarded as merely secular authorities and were believed to be devoid of the religious charisma which had inhered in the earlier Safavid emperors.[16] In cases such as this, the state was more like a set of diverse and competing interests, and its stability waxed and waned over time. Even in the case of the European colonial state, which had more clearly defined claims and greater coherence, this did not always lead to greater effectiveness. In British India and French North Africa, it is easy to overstate the importance of colonial authorities. Throughout the nineteenth century, the colonizing powers had cognizance of only a tiny proportion of judicial decisions in these societies, and had much less of a grip on their revenues than they liked to believe. Their head counting and ethnographic surveys often had little practical impact, being less a guide to government than a hobby of scholar-administrators. Whole areas of the European colonial world, albeit divided by international treaties and maps into neat provinces, remained in the grip of greedy European financial interests, popular revolt, resistance to central authority, and the power of local chieftains until the very beginnings of decolonization itself in the 1940s. The administrators of the colonial state in many parts of Africa in the mid-twentieth century could be easily accommodated in a single small hut.

The myths of today's historians about the power of the state often do no more than echo the aspirations of nineteenth-century rulers. They have replaced myths which were current in the 1960s and 1970s about the growth of working-class consciousness. This chapter tries to distinguish some broad patterns of change in the claims, resources, and symbols of the state at the international level. In many places and at some periods, the state did indeed expand its powers and authority mightily. Elsewhere, and particularly outside Europe, the tiger was paper, and the lion's corpse simply produced honey for ruthless entrepreneurs or local warlords. What was important, rather, was the charisma of the idea of the state.

Initially, then, we can distinguish a number of different forms of "statishness" outside the centralized state, best exemplified in early-nineteenth-century Europe by France and Prussia. First, there was the situation where state power was quite widely diffused amongst local ruling groups, as in nineteenth-century Britain or the United States. Secondly, there were cases where the formal organs of the state were confronted with a powerful "other," which replicated its functions within society. This was the case in many Muslim and some Buddhist societies, where Islamic law or the Buddhist monkhood continued to operate as a veritable counter-state. Sometimes these institutions cooperated with the secular authorities, and sometimes not. Thirdly, there were cases where almost the whole function of government had been absorbed by powerful corporate bodies such as the Hudson's Bay Company in the Canadian northwest or the European African companies. Fourthly, throughout much of Africa, Asia, and the Pacific, power continued to lie in the hands of lineage heads or members of age-sets, and the chief or king remained an agent of their will. Fifthly, and finally, there were family-based mobile peoples for whom state power was little more than a dream of once-and-future kings.

THE MODERN STATE TAKES ROOT: GEOGRAPHICAL DIMENSIONS

The conventional view of the rise of the modern state, along with nationalism, discussed in the previous chapter, is that it took place in Europe. The new forms of administration and control were then exported to the rest of the world by the agency of imperial rule, or through imitative borrowing, as in the case of Japan. This "diffusionist model" still has much force. But it presents only a partial picture. There were several different varieties of modern state in western Europe and North America, and they had by no means established their dominance even by the end of the nineteenth century.

As far as the world outside Europe was concerned, some early modern monarchies had already begun to adapt to changing economic and demographic conditions and become more interventionist before European power expanded in the later eighteenth century. The Tokugawa regime in Japan before 1868 and the Mughal Empire provide examples of this type of polity. The forms of government they established provided a basis onto which the newly imported European styles could be grafted. This does not mean that these polities evolved seamlessly into modern, Western-style states. What it does mean, though, is that there already existed groups of families who were used to working for a public authority beyond a particular dynasty. These could sometimes be recruited into colonial bureaucracies or states modeled by indigenous reformers on Napoleon's France or Bismarck's Germany. For instance, throughout East Asia there were systems of policing and watch and ward based on groups of households, villages, and town quarters. These continued to function even during the decades of decentralized government under the Tokugawa and Qing. Institutions of this sort were revamped and used as the local level of government by modernizing regimes after 1870. Similarly, the cash-based land revenue systems common over much of Muslim and Indo-Muslim Asia and North Africa in the early modern period provided a basis on which colonial or semi-colonized independent governments could build new forms of taxation and surveillance in the course of the nineteenth century.

It was not only archaic institutional structures, but also archaic ideologies, which could be annexed and transformed by the modern state. Most of the old empires had concepts of "the barbarous." In Vietnamese, for instance, the term for savage was "Moi," a word which was applied to tribal hill people who resisted ethnic Vietnamese domination long before the boundary between Moi and Vietnamese was closely defined by French colonialists.[17] Just as the modern state was most effective where it built on some indigenous apparatuses of extraction or coercion, so it took up and transformed older notions of civilization and barbarism under the powerful impetus of European ideas of race and civility. Over large parts of the world, an important function of the state was to seize, conquer, and domesticate entitlements to land which had once belonged to native peoples. While Americans, for instance, viewed federal government with extreme suspicion on its internal frontiers, they were only too happy to see the US army garrison and federal marshals expand their external ones.

As the first chapter noted, Asante, in West Africa, has long been regarded as a particularly sophisticated form of precolonial African state. In the eighteenth and early nineteenth centuries, Asante rulers had systematized their tribute system to such an extent that historians regularly describe it as a "bureaucracy." Even though some of the wealth of Asante was derived from the Atlantic slave trade, the state's nobility also participated in the more archaic style of North African slaving system and exported gold and other local products to the market. This polity was resilient enough to survive the abolition of the British slave trade in 1807. Even if Asante disintegrated in the later nineteenth century, in response to internal conflict and further British pressure, it had a remarkable track record.[18] The shifting lineage- and age-set-based societies found in sub-Saharan Africa and parts of Southeast Asia, by contrast, were less amenable to centralized control by modernizing rulers. At the utmost extreme, Afghanistan and Abyssinia both had states, with rulers, foreign policies, and diplomatic relations by the end of the nineteenth century. But in both cases, most of what mattered to people in these societies was still carried out by local magnates, village elders, *mullahs*, or Christian priests.

A second point that must be made about the diffusionist model is that insofar as it works, diffusion worked in both directions. This again points to the value of a global perspective on social and political change. Much to the horror of liberal domestic statesmen,[19] forms of state power and government, initially developed to meet the specific needs of the colonial power and sometimes adapted from the methods of indigenous governments, could be repatriated. For instance, the professional civil service was developed first in British India and the colonial territories, and then imported back into Britain. Anglo-Indian forms of famine management, or mismanagement, and forensic techniques, such as fingerprinting, were adapted for Ireland and Britain respectively. The Mughals did not use fingerprints, but they did have systems for describing individuals' characteristics which were adapted by the British rulers and then imported back to Britain itself. Russian historians, for their part, have argued that experience on the fringes of empire swelled the state and its agencies of force to a huge size, squeezing out the empire's sickly civil society in the Russian heartlands. Even in peacetime, the nearly three million cossacks on Russia's imperial frontiers were supposed to provide 600,000 men and horses which might be used to secure compliance in the empire's capital or western provinces.[20] Visionaries of the future of the French state and nation often looked to the colonizing population of North Africa to provide the necessary infusion of true grit and bureaucratic rationality into what they saw as an enfeebled and declining domestic population.[21]

THE CLASSIC TYPES OF EUROPEAN STATE

In the early and mid-nineteenth century, recognizably modern forms of state power were grouped in certain broad geographical sectors. This section deals with the geographical expansion of the European state. Its classic features were centralization, the taxation of incomes, and its association with the idea of an armed citizenry. In Europe, the development of military state forms in one country had a knock-on effect amongst its neighbors. Fortified with the Napoleonic Code, centralized administration, and the experience of raising millions of men for a 20-year war, France was the point of origin in the European sector. But all the European regimes which had been touched by the Napoleonic wars were reconstituted to some degree. After 1815, the Austrians who ruled northern Italy retained much of the system of departments, districts, and communes which Napoleon's acolytes had established in 1802.[22] In Germany, military mobilization was the initial spur, but even after the war, many of the reconstituted German states of 1789 continued a process of rationalization and developed larger bureaucracies. The German pattern of state modernization retained its federal features, however, even after the creation of the German Empire in 1871. In Spain, politics during the mid-century was consumed by a long battle between parliamentary liberals and Carlist "reactionaries." The politicians involved, whether they espoused the will of the sovereign national assembly or the cause of king and Church, all tended to expand the role of the central administration and swell the number of bureaucrats. The steel framework of the system rested on the control exercised by the minister of the interior over the various municipal governments around which so much of Spain's national life revolved.[23] In Russia and Austria, centralized civil services expanded rapidly in the course of the nineteenth century, though often in conflict with regional and local powers representing cliques of nobles.

To this pattern, as was suggested, Britain, the British dominions, and the United States provide something of a contrast, though for rather different reasons. Formally, the power of central government was much less developed in these cases than in continental Europe. Even during the wars of the eighteenth century, traditional institutions of local governance coped with the new demands put on them without expanding very much.[24] Public debate was dominated until late in the century by liberal theorists who despised state intervention. This means, though, that the state was decentralized – that it worked through the manifold organizations of civil society and local representation – not that it did not exist at all. Though the size of its central bureaucracy did not expand greatly, nineteenth-century Britain managed to raise huge sums of money in taxation and to maintain large and efficient naval forces – a sure sign of the presence of "statishness" or "governmentality," if not of a centralized state.[25] In the dominions, the state became quite active in organizing emigration and providing welfare after 1870, much more so than in Britain. But the work of government there was still done largely by local governments, while the union of Australia did not even occur until the twentieth century. In the United States, the federal government was not even able to enhance its tax-raising ability, except during the Civil War and in the years immediately before the First World War. The US armed forces remained highly decentralized throughout the century. All the same, particularly at state level, the attenuated organs of American government were "bulked out" by a whole range of legal and voluntary institutions which acquired the characteristics of "statishness" or "governmentality," in the sense that they counted and categorized citizens and applied common principles of improvement and civilization.

Elsewhere on the American continent, political leaders attempted to emulate the continental European model, with only a limited degree of success. Where Spanish or Portuguese Crown rule had once been present and powerful, as in the Valley of Mexico, the Brazilian seaboard, or the coastal plains of Chile and Peru, military-dominated regimes emerged after independence. The Mexican revolutions of 1864–7 and 1911–15 created significant powers for national leaders, as did the European revolutions. In the hinterland, the politics of the Creole magnates and Amerindian village leaders constantly impeded the development of centralized power.

While Britons and Americans may have been ambivalent about the state at home, they generally sought to export it to their colonial possessions and spheres of influence abroad. In the Pacific, it suited traders, missionaries, and naval captains to have a strong central authority where previously rather loose notions of ritual dominance or "high kingship" had prevailed. Local rulers eagerly sought the stamp of legitimacy. In the 1830s and 1840s "King George" of Tonga proclaimed his dominance, cooked up a national flag which incorporated the British union flag, and began to levy taxation on people he now deemed to be his subjects.[26] Later in the century in the western Sudan, French officials seeking to create protectorates among indigenous kings effectively introduced the notions of territorial control and regular taxation for the first time.

HYBRID EURASIAN STATE FORMS

These last were cases where the Western state form was exported lock, stock, and barrel. Yet there were other areas, as the first section implied, where that form combined or contended in a variety of ways with indigenous state forms which were already quite strongly marked and in the process of autonomous development. The second sector in which more centralized state forms developed rapidly in the nineteenth century, therefore, was in South and East Asia. Two basic forms existed. Over much of East Asia, a Chinese-style mandarin administration with formally trained and selected bureaucrats already existed. The big Asian states had already responded to the need for taxation and to combat internal revolt and external pressure by creating a relatively dense set of state institutions at local level in at least some parts of their territories. Though formally more military in character, the Japanese "feudal" regime also retained a strong presence at village level and used literate instruments of government. Chinese and Japanese authorities sometimes attempted to control labor movement by insisting that villagers on the move carry written papers with them, for instance. In Persia and South Asia, Persianate, Indo-Islamic bureaucracies had also emerged. Because these were less homogeneous societies, the bureaucrats generally had less purchase in local society. Big landed magnates or tribal leaders with their own administrations fragmented the power of the royal centers. But even here, precolonial administrators counted the number of households, and sometimes different professions and castes, by means of censuses.

ILLUSTRATION 7.1   The state's lower rungs: A Chinese district headman, Wei Hai Wei, c.1909. Photo by A. H. Fisher.

It was, however, the expansion of the European empires which stimulated the rapid development of modern state forms in the whole arc between Persia and Japan. The new kingdoms that sprang up between 1780 and 1820 all attempted to combine indigenous forms of rural taxation, or farming out of revenue, with the war-making capability and capitalist avarice of contemporary Europe. The more successful of them recast the old relations between lord and peasant, or old bureaucracy and peasant, to create a land revenue fund for development. To one degree or another, Ranjit Singh's Punjab (1801–39),[27] the truncated kingdom of Burma after 1826,[28] Vietnam, and Thailand[29] all attempted to develop more formal bureaucracies, modern armies, regular censuses, and territorial surveys. In each case, they drew on and developed a pool of service families which had experience of serving European or Asian governments. To a large extent, too, they were all responding to the pressure put on them by the East India Company's own hybrid polity, which taxed and counted like a western European state, but allowed many social functions to be monopolized by groups of indigenous administrators and landlords.

Warfare, indeed, provided a crucible from which state forms emerged. Even before the end of the British attack on China in 1842, the Chinese were beginning to appropriate Western technology. Eighteenth-century Qing rulers had appreciated the gun-casting skills of the Jesuits. The urgency to create a state and an army to match the British and other powers was clearly understood by at least some at the court by the 1860s. Recent historians have begun to argue that the late Qing state did not make too bad a job of combining the authority of the old mandarinate with new European military and fiscal methodologies and of expanding the purview of the mandarinate.[30] The British general, George Gordon, was employed by the Qing to fight the Taipings. The problem for the Qing, however, was that they lost direct control of the huge resources of agrarian China and were forced to fall back on the relatively limited resources of maritime customs income. With rather greater success, the last Tokugawa Shoguns sent emissaries to the United States and Europe in the 1850s to study the techniques developed by Western nations. Caught between the eastern borders of the expansive European state in the form of Russia and the western borders of the British Indian state, King Nasir-al Din Shah of Persia (1848–96) created a small standing army and a Russian-officered cossack brigade, besides trying to establish an administrative college.[31] Here the tsarist and British Indian empires were his models, but he also drew on earlier traditions of Persian statehood, attempting to secure a regular income from peasant and nomad.

THE MODERNIZED MUSLIM STATE AND ITS OFFSPRING

The final broad sector in which the aspiration to create modern states spread with bacillus-like speed in the early nineteenth century was the "central" Islamic world and northern and eastern Africa.[32] Here again, a hybrid form developed. This was a composite of the kind of authoritative rulership embodied in the notion of the Byzantine-Islamic sultanate with Western ideas of despotic "improvement." The types of reformed Ottoman administration which spread across this sector had somewhat different features from the East and South Asian states discussed earlier. First, religious institutions, whether the formal learned classes (*ulama*) or Sufi mystical lineages, were welded into the structure of the hybrid state in this sector, rather than remaining in uneasy cooperation and contention with it. The new bureaucracies retained a distinctly Islamic spirit. Secondly, rulers attempted to foster peasant ownership and production. This was not always the case further east. Thirdly, the state continued to rely heavily on direct control of merchant groups through systems of provisioning.

The central Ottoman provinces had always been quite closely governed, following the Roman or Byzantine model, though central power waned somewhat in the eighteenth century. By 1800, the Ottoman Empire was weary of defeat by a Russia itself only partially reformed. Its rulers decided to try to modernize their more distant Arab and Balkan provinces. First-hand experience of the new sea power of the French and British during the Napoleonic wars forced a small number of administrative reformers to consider rebuilding the whole apparatus of state and army to preserve the independence of the empire. The consequent reforms of Sultan Mahmud II (1808–39) abolished many of the old juridical, military, and administrative forms of the state. In particular, the reformers swept away the janissary corps and tried to make the office of the chief religious dignitary of the empire a bureaucratic post.[33] It was, however, that nominal lieutenant of the sultan, Mehmet Ali, or Muhammad Ali, viceroy of Egypt, who pushed the process forward fastest. Muhammad Ali destroyed the old Mamluk corps of "slave-rulers" and seized their lands, which he transformed into a fund for military and political development. He built up military and administrative colleges, using French exemplars, and formed a new, European-style military corps. As far as he could, Muhammad Ali tried to incorporate Islamic juridiction into his own administrative courts. He and his successors tried to extend these new forms of the state to the Hejaz coast of Arabia, the Levant, and deep into the Sudan.[34] As noted earlier, his regime also tried to develop cotton as a state crop.

Egypt's attempt to surge forward had a knock-on effect on its neighbors. Defeated by Egyptian armies in 1848, an Abyssinian provincial governor, Tewodros, succeeded in imitating Egyptian military techniques and fought his way to the throne in 1855. He then followed Muhammad Ali's plan, seizing the lands of nobles and the Church and augmenting his tax base.[35] Over the next few decades, this advance of the state in northern Africa was significant, though easily reversible. To the west, in the North African Mahgreb, the sub-Ottoman regional powers also began to imitate Muhammad Ali's policy of state building. The exercise became one of survival when the French invaded Algeria in 1830. The Algerian leader, Abd al-Qadir, mobilized his followers among the Qadariyya Sufi sect to resist invasion. But he also built up a disciplined and well-armed modern fighting force of 5,000 men, with which he staged a long resistance to French power.[36] The rulers of Tripoli and Morocco took note and followed suit. In Tunisia, Khayr al-Din Pasha emulated the Tanzimat reforms and introduced a centralized state bureaucracy.[37] All these leaders resumed a pattern of state building that had already occurred in a piecemeal way in the eighteenth century. Yet now the model was clearer, and the need for self-protection much greater.

In Muslim West Africa, the state crept forward in alliance with elite literacy and the spread of purist Islam. This was illustrated in the career of Hajj Umar, teacher, reader, and state-builder, whose state later came into conflict with the French. The importance of books and literacy for this emerging Islamic society and government was very clear. A chronicler recorded:

> On one occasion, the village of Jegunko burned and three rooms full of [religious] books were destroyed. While this was going on Umar grieved and wanted to die in the fire himself. He did not care about the property that was being burned, it was only the manuscripts that mattered ... Umar entrusted himself to God. He sent his younger brother's son to Timbuktu with a considerable amount of money and paper to have new ones made.[38]

CLAIMS TO JUSTICE AND SYMBOLS OF POWER

The remainder of the chapter considers the claims of the modern state, its resources, and its administrative tools, in order to assess where and why it developed most successfully. One area where the state grew in ambition was in its theoretical and legal claims on the world's populations and in the range of symbols it was able to deploy. To an extent unequalled even in the Eurasian military despotisms of the eighteenth century, the nineteenth-century public authorities claimed to be able to create and enforce statuses which were regarded as embodied or innate under the old regime. The Declaration of the Rights of Man was more often than not a declaration of the rights of the state, which then attempted to regulate and control in new ways. Starting from first principles, the right to life or death, and other severe punishments, is the most fundamental of human issues. After 1780, the state worked internationally to wrest the right of awarding life or death from petty principalities, local jurisdictions, and tribal groups. By making all the inhabitants of "its" territory subjects on a common footing, it attempted to erode the differences of status and honor which had been critical to the old regimes. In fact, control of justice and punishment had everywhere become an issue through which the state sought to define its own rights. Local and community forms of arbitration and vengeance were increasingly denounced as illegitimate and outside the pale of civil society by theorists of the state. So the feud, the duel, and the moral vengeance of the crowd, which had been normal features of the workings of most societies even as late as the previous century, were stigmatized and criminalized.

In the Muslim world, great license had traditionally been left to local headmen or clerical courts in the administration of justice according to Sharia. Kin groups could decide whether to demand death or not in cases of murder and other heinous crimes, and in the more remote areas there was little room for the ruler's judgment at all. Following the second great wave of Ottoman "reorganization" after 1839, referred to above, centralized judicial systems claimed much more control and began to eat away at the jurisdiction of local courts. The new civil code remained Islamic in spirit, but a European-style Ministry of Justice was given responsibity for its implementation. In Egypt, the khedival administration instituted courts of judicature along French lines.[39] As the century progressed, these courts, along with those established by European pressure to try their own citizens and dependants (in the so-called capitulations), gradually eroded the competence and the fees of the Islamic judiciary. This created a tension between secular and theocratic interpretations of the national state, which already split Middle Eastern nationalisms before the First World War.

The state's new claims were equally far-reaching in the Muslim, Hindu, and Buddhist societies now directly ruled by Europeans. Here colonial administrators sought to assert their monopoly of the right to judgments of life and death and to significant punishment. Communities were gradually denied the right to decide whether they would pursue blood price in cases of murder, while lesser punishments such as flogging and amputation were disallowed in favor of hanging, transportation, or imprisonment, which were deemed more acceptable penalties for "civilized" people. The Islamic codes operated by European rulers in their territories widely eliminated the room for compromise and special adjudication which had been possible in the earlier systems. In British India, these changes also significantly affected the judicial status and self-image of the Hindu subjects of the former Mughal Empire. Rulers had often acted in the spirit of the ancient Hindu lawgivers, who had forbidden the passing of the death penalty on Brahmins. Hindu communities had often practiced female infanticide and, more rarely, the custom of widow burning on the funeral pyre of the husband. Both these were practices the British government sought to stamp out, declaring them abominations to a proper society.[40] In Japan, likewise, the Meiji regime of the 1870s stepped in to rationalize the punishments which had formerly been handed out by local judicial bodies in the domains of the great magnates.[41]

States also tried to intervene more frequently to bend to their will civil customs revolving around marriage and inheritance. Nineteenth-century administrators preferred clear lines of descent, ruling out of court adoptions of which they did not approve in noble families, and in the case of the British world insisting on the right to primogeniture. In some administrative systems, local customary law was apparently upheld, but even here it was codified and brought into more rigid conformity with the broader legal structures. In the East Indies, the Dutch evolved a complex system of *adat*, or customary law, which engaged the learned labors of the orientalists of Leiden University.[42] But *adat* was neither traditional nor customary, because it removed much of

ILLUSTRATION 7.2   The "colonial state" in undress: The British governor of New Guinea on tour, 1876. Photo by J. W. Lindt.

the independent judgment which had been allowed to the old-style jurists and imposed strict rights and penalties on different groups.

In Europe, the states of the seventeenth and eighteenth centuries had already fought hard to crush the judicial rights of local groups and magnates, especially in matters of life and death. Even here, the nineteenth-century administrators and jurists set out a plan for rationalization and reform. The Napoleonic Code and its imitations throughout Europe sought to provide common rights and duties, pains and penalties, for all subjects.[43] The rights and disabilities of different groups were stripped away. The clergy widely lost their immunities, though this happened very slowly in Russia and southern Europe. Jews were made citizens, and the rules which consigned them to ghettos after dusk and forbade them to own land or vote were widely removed. In Britain and Ireland, legal reform after 1830 was accompanied by a rather slower concession of rights to hold office to Jews, Roman Catholics, and non-Anglican Protestants. As people became legally subject to identical claims and possessors of identical rights in regard to the state, they increasingly needed a large body of trained lawyers to service their disputes. The lawyers in turn became the double of the state, working within civil society to facilitate and legitimate its claims.

As Michel Foucault famously argued, systems of regulated imprisonment formally replaced more public and often more brutal punishments which had prevailed in the old regime.[44] Removal from society replaced savage punishment within it over much of the world. Increasingly, states enacted through decree or by pushing legislation through assemblies legal forms which stigmatized and punished certain types of behavior which were regarded as anti-social – among them, abortion, infanticide, homosexuality, the holding of arms without license, cruel sports, bigamy, and the excessive consumption of alcohol in the working week. In all these matters, administrators were expressing a general desire to civilize and manage their own and their subject populations. Yet, in these very legal and increasingly public pronouncements on law and morality, they were also asserting their own right to intervene in areas which had been seen as the purview of the local church community and parochial public opinion in earlier days.

This section must conclude with a further caution. Enactment and aspiration were not the same as enforcement. In many societies, the state simply did not have the strength or the single-mindedness to enforce its newly trumpeted claims to a monopoly over violence. Equally, local communities, magnates, and religious authorities continued to deny the legitimacy of the state to intervene. Despite the lofty imaginings of Hegel, the German Reich was never able to obtain equality for its Jewish citizens.[45] Across the world, justice was still dispensed outside the control of government officials. There were assassinations and boycotts of those deemed wicked landlords in Ireland, the murder of witches in many parts of the world, and the lynching of blacks who were accused of violating white honor in the southern states of the United States. In important areas, the rights of the state and its claims hardly expanded at all. In China as late as 1900, the imperial bureaucracy, branded by some as distant, Manchu, or a pawn of the Western powers, had lost power to local gentry, regional commanders, and even to secret societies. Local elites handed out appropriate punishments where the populace demanded it; the Boxer rebels of 1900 killed priests and other Europeans. These foreigners were held to have violated the norms of proper society with impunity because of the recent weakness of the central regime. In the United States, a society which seemed to have prospered without a strong central regime, the states of the Union maintained very considerable rights to regulate their own lawmaking and lawgiving through to the present day. Justice remained local, despite occasional interventions by the Supreme Court. Here, state power, already fractured by the division between federal and state government, president, Congress, and the courts, was fiercely resisted in the name of community and liberty and sometimes put to good use by local bosses.[46] The idea of centralized government never lost the stench of corruption which had hung around it since the time of the colonial governors.

In former European colonial territories the state, though quickly forced into service by nationalist elites, still carried the taint of being a foreign, white imposition on local, self-governing communities. This is a cry that contemporary radicals and communitarians have taken up with renewed vigor. In the Islamic world, the old religious and judicial institutions of Sharia, divine law, were not, finally, replaced by the modern state, but survived alongside it. The claims of religion periodically submerged an only partly legitimate state. This situation has been seen in its most radical form in the case of Iran, where the Qajar and later Pahlavi (post-1927) dynasties failed to secure more than partial legitimacy in the eyes of their subjects. Over much of the rest of the world, including parts of southern and eastern Europe and Africa, the institutions of the state have continued to be tossed about on the surface of a sea of shifting lineage alliances and assertive local magnates. The paradox of the state was this: it always stood above classes, local powers, and factions, yet it could always be penetrated and appropriated by them.

THE STATE'S RESOURCES

Despite these illuminating and important exceptions, however, the state was potentially in a more powerful position in the world in 1914 than it had been in 1780. By the later date, it could widely deploy more men, more authority, more resources, and more destructive power against its own citizens and against other states than it had done earlier. It had, in many areas, though not all, gained a more effective control of reserves of manpower and money. It was able to deploy new symbols to enforce its authority, and it had created larger and more efficient bureaucracies, archives, and survey departments to aid it in these tasks. Above all, the state was now regarded as an embodiment of the nation, and the nation or race was assumed to be the key actor on the world stage. Ironically, of course, the argument was a circular one, for states had as often created nations as vice versa, an issue alluded to in the last chapter.

It is important not to underestimate the power of the Eurasian states of the eighteenth century, as the first chapter noted. But the great international humiliations of proud states in the eighteenth century were as nothing to their almost daily embarrassments in governing their own territories. As King Louis XVI found at the cost of his head, the French monarch could not control his own capital city, from which abuse and ridicule of his regime had poured almost daily since 1783. Though finally safe from civil war, the British Hanoverian monarchy could still see its capital city ablaze and its parliamentarians under siege during the anti-Catholic Gordon Riots of 1780. Despite the modernization of Catherine the Great of Russia, peasant and cossack revolt stopped Russian rule dead for years over much of its vast land mass. Asian states, which had never been forced to create the same degree of internal surveillance or resource management as the Christian bigots and military plunderers of early modern Europe, were even worse placed. Insurgent Jat peasant leaders regularly looted the heart of the Mughal Empire within 20 miles of the imperial throne even under as great a ruler as Aurangzeb (1658–1707).

There had been a significant change by 1900. Most states in the Western world and most colonial regimes were able to tax, control, and exploit their own territories, most of the time. A change of government did not necessarily lead to a long-term and sustained collapse of order and security. The 1871 Commune and the 1917 Revolutions in Russia arose from exceptional and massive military conflicts, not from an endemic instability or lack of resources. Indeed, 1917 should be seen as a sudden rupture in a pattern of gradually increasing and effective governance, not as it once was, as the culmination of inexorable social conflicts. It quickly saw in the emergence of Bolshevik government the installation of an even more centralizing and resource-hungry state. Even in the case of China, where mid-twentieth-century historical writing saw a collapse of the state, most authorities would now see a strengthening of local elites. State power became more diffused. It did not disappear. The 1911 Revolution came relatively suddenly in the context of drought and panic about epidemics.

How and why had the state come to acquire new resources? We should not be squeamish about this. Much state building across the world remained, as it always had been, a massive act of plunder. Canny entrepreneurs and commission agents followed military invaders, and it was they who often helped root the state. Despite their grandiose claims to be advancing "civilization," the French revolutionary authorities and the British colonial governments in early-nineteenth-century India were based on the appropriation of money and land rights. Their British, French, Italian, and Indian collaborators had an interest in obscuring this.

One answer to the question of why the state grew, therefore, must be that it was now better armed. Its military resources were greatly improved by the world wars of 1780–1820, and later scientific advance improved them further.

Earlier smaller-scale advances in military resources had benefited local magnates and rebels almost as much as centralized states. Matchlocks could be purchased by local war bands, popular levies, or peasant leaders. Barons and local rajas could construct fortresses to the designs of the French architect Vauban. After 1800, however, it was big states which monopolized military advances. Huge capital and organization were required to build and deploy ironclad battleships, heavy artillery, and chemical shells. Military reform provided a breach through which many different sorts of advocate of state power could swarm. The need to modernize armed forces set in chain changes in the form of the state. Ruling groups had to strengthen their bureaucracies and taxation systems. Reformers with agendas for civilian improvement pointed up the need for better-educated and healthier subjects.

The capacity of the state, initially of the European state alone, to deploy a wholly new level of military power was revealed fairly early in the nineteenth century. By 1820, the British had developed the iron steamship. It was quickly put into use in the British Empire, where steamboats patrolled the river Ganges, helping the development of the cotton export economy and later, during the 1857 rebellion, keeping Britain's main artery of military supply open. A spectacular example of the use of steam power and new naval guns occurred during the Anglo–Chinese opium wars of 1839–42 and 1856–61.[47] Quite apart from the logistical advantage which this gave to the British, it was the complete helplessness of Chinese armies in the face of this projection of Western technological power which helped to undermine the authority of the Qing regime. Similar political effects were brought about in Japan, where the Americans and British both used naval guns to force open Tokugawa ports to their trade and diplomacy. For all the inaction of the late-nineteenth-century colonial state in India or French North Africa, we must not forget that a large-scale disarming of the local population did occur between 1840 and 1880. Huge numbers of "unlicensed weapons" were seized by the authorities in both regions.

"Internal pacification" of this sort occurred in the heart of European nations, and not just on the colonial peripheries. In Ireland in 1798, for instance, the British armies instituted a "white terror." Their columns destroyed villages, killed livestock, and resorted to summary executions. In 1831, the relatively backward Russian armies completely destroyed the movement for Polish autonomy. Mass purges, confiscations of land, and quarterings of troops, reminiscent of Napoleon's era, were used to suppress open dissent for another 17 years.[48] Extraordinary force was used by the French authorities against the workers of the Paris Commune of 1871, even by comparison with the violence of the 1790s and 1840s. The new, rapid-firing rifles could kill hundreds within minutes, and city streets were now built to give an adequate line of fire. Of course, the new military resources of the state did not always work in its interests in the short term. Bigger and better-equipped armies sometimes meant bigger and better-equipped mutinies. Alexander I of Russia, for instance, garnered much grief from the military colonies on which he settled the millions of men who had been mobilized during the Napoleonic war. The veterans resented the tsar's attempts to micro-manage every detail in the colonies and took up arms against him on several occasions. Nevertheless, the balance of military might generally seems to have shifted in favor of the state and against its local opponents.

Critical changes in communication helped states to deploy this new military and political power. The electric telegraph helped defeat the Indian mutineers and the Zulu braves. In the war against the Sudanese Khalifa in 1898, the British general, Herbert Kitchener, would have suffered the fate of his head-strong predecessors, who rushed into the desert to defeat, if he had not built a railway to Khartoum and then dragged his fleet of transports along the Upper Nile with steamboats. The American Union clinched its victory over the South in the Civil War because its powerful advanced navy could blockade Houston and Galveston, the southern cotton ports. It is well known that the development of railway communications contributed to the speed of mobilization during the First World War. But the military benefits of rail transport were already in evidence in the mid-century European wars, when the Prussian victories against the Austrians and the French were owed in part to their rapid deployment of men and heavy artillery by rail. Railways also eroded the internal autonomy and difference of old regional groupings within large states.

The point is partly that the power of the state, still so unformed in the eighteenth century, was greatly enhanced by the development of new military resources and techniques. The converse is also true. It was, centrally, the exigencies of new forms of warfare that forced the state to intervene, husband its economic power, and generally trench more deeply into society. One military historian writes: "An adequate defence system in the new age required not only the military training of the entire male population but also expenditure on strategic railways; the accumulation of huge stocks of war supplies; and the maintenance of a high birth-rate and a high level of education."[49]

In Britain an unexpectedly poor performance in the mid-century Crimean War against Russia had consequences for military organization and the working of government itself. Regiments were amalgamated, new forms of training were introduced, and a professional War Office was created where, previously, a seventeenth-century institution, the Horse Guards, had very often blocked all movement towards change. The loss of life from disease and on the battlefield resulted in the creation of a new nursing profession and gave a great impetus to medical research on civilian as well as military populations. But the ripples from this and other military humiliations spread outward into the working of the Treasury and the public accounts.

In the same way, the Prussian state was galvanized by the need to create a mass conscript army, and the French government became yet more centralized in the aftermath of the defeat of 1870–1. It was probably in the non-European world, however, that the forms of the state were most dramatically and rapidly changed by military exigency. As early as 1842, the Chinese rulers were found to be experimenting with the building of British-style steamboats and modern cannon. Following the devastation of their country by the Second

ILLUSTRATION 7.3   The state's resources of power. The site of the construction of the Aswan Dam, Egypt, 1902–6.

Opium War and the Taiping Rebellion, the Qing regime embarked on an attempt at instantaneous modernization during the so-called self-strengthening movement of the 1870s. Prince Kung created a new military board. Li Hongzhang, the Chinese governor in Canton, followed suit, attempting to build up his own arsenals and shipyards. The point is that this was a dynamic process. New resources had to be found so that the state could fund these innovations. Given its lack of fiscal purchase in the countryside, the regime sought resources from the revamped Maritime Customs service. This, the first completely modern bureaucratic institution in China, required for its functioning that the Chinese adopt a different attitude to international affairs, diplomacy, and the negotiation of foreign loans.[50]

The same process of military-led state building can be seen in the case of Japan. Defeat and humiliation by the barbarians in the 1850s and 1860s required the building of new model armies and navies. Yet the finance to make this possible could only be found by revamping the whole system of internal taxation and the privileges inhering in it. The new rulers of Meiji Japan revoked the fiscal privileges of the samurai. The state pensioned them off on fixed stipends and assimilated their perquisites into the state's exchequer. The new government also measured and registered the land, instituting a national tax system.[51] These moves ended the decentralized

269

patrimonial style of state structure which had held sway in Japan since the Middle Ages. Peasant, samurai, merchant, and daimyo all became Japanese subjects, even though the old statuses continued to have purchase in the negotiations of social life.

Late as it came, and patchy as were its results, industrial developments also signally aided the expansion of the state in complex ways. The problem for rulers across Eurasia in the eighteenth century had been their lack of resources. After 1850, though, the proceeds of industrial production, in the form of greatly increased moneys from taxes on income, licenses, and trade, gave the state a large new cache of resources. These were easier to tax than fractious landholders and peasantry who often resisted or ran away when tax collectors came in sight. Japan provides a case in point. In the 1970s and 1980s, free-market economists used to argue that state-led industrialization might actually have impeded the pace of Japanese industrialization. Be that as it may, the Japanese state's modernizing effort could never have maintained its spectacular pace without external security and external plunder. Rapid military modernization and the building of an industrial infrastructure allowed Japan to defeat and extract huge resources from its Chinese neighbor in 1895. Later, that same military spurt paved the way for success against Russia, the one enemy which might have derailed its whole dash to great power status.[52]

Population expansion during the eighteenth and nineteenth centuries helped many states, though this was less true of the Chinese Empire. Only the expansion of population, which followed the domestication of plague and better standards of nutrition, could have allowed Napoleon to field his huge armies. Britain could not have afforded both to deploy her own substantial forces and to man essential industries and food-producing agricultural production in the early nineteenth century without population growth.[53] In colonial territories, a burgeoning and impoverished peasantry provided recruits for imperial armies, while at the same time producing the rent with which the government maintained them and the seasonal labor which satisfied its commercial allies amongst plantation owners.

Rapid urbanization and growing international trade provided much easier pickings. Once cities were properly policed and controlled, tax-gatherers could go about their work with impunity. By the end of the nineteenth century, cities such as London, Paris, and Boston, which had sustained orgies of rioting a century before in the face of quite minor and indirect taxes on gin, absinthe, or tea, were quieter. They were even prepared to stomach direct income taxes, provided some small part of the proceeds was spent on crime control, health, and education. Resources from trade and industrial production were also much more transparent to the state than had been the resources of countrymen and local usurers in the old regime.

Of course, there was no steady growth of the state's resources in all fields of the world economy. For much of the century, the doctrine of free trade meant that governments, led or coerced by the dominant British, forswore heavy taxation and control of trade. The elaborate system of commercial and trade regulation of the eighteenth century was abolished by consent in northwestern

Europe. It was blown apart by British and French gunboats in China and the Ottoman Empire and North Africa. Partly as a result of the economic recession of the 1870s and 1880s, the division of the world into trading blocks only began again after about 1890. Yet the state's withdrawal in this one area was merely a tactic. Governments sought an increase in overall wealth, particularly their own, by means of the doctrine of free trade. The overall burden of indirect taxes continued to rise.

THE STATE'S OBLIGATIONS TO SOCIETY

The erratic, but distinct, growth of the claims and resources of the state in the course of the nineteenth century brought in its train comparable obligations. Particularly after the 1850s and 1860s, the state had to do more for its subjects in order to justify itself. Of course, one should not underestimate the extent to which older forms of state, both in the West and outside, had acknowledged obligations to their subjects. Though their writ was quite circumscribed in some areas, earlier Chinese, Islamic, and Indo-Islamic regimes had been expected to encourage the digging of wells, give relief and control supplies in times of famine, and consume the fine products of different regions. Flood control and fire control in old wooden cities were typically activities which in East Asia brought together subjects and rulers in societies of mutual cooperation. These decentralized forms of succoring continued in Europe, where governments were general overseers of a variety of forms of poor law or public charity, which persisted into the early years of the nineteenth century. In Prussia before the 1850s, the royal government indirectly supported its subjects by giving financial privileges and remissions of tax to Protestant organizations which supported orphanages, educational institutions, and food handouts to the poor.[54]

There was, however, a distinct change in direction after about 1850. Experience of the mid-century wars, outlined in chapter 4, encouraged governments to draw out more resources from their territories. Yet they also had to intervene and placate their fractious citizens. At the very least, in order to guarantee the reproduction of resources and military strength, many governments were concerned that their citizens should be disease-free, reasonably educated, and properly fed. For their part, wealthy and powerful citizens who were subject to increasing direct and indirect taxation demanded something back in return. Social programs legitimated the flow of wealth from individuals to government. At the other end of society, the explosion of working-class militancy in new industrial cities or peasant rebellions in the overtaxed countryside demanded palliative measures. After the hungry 1840s, elites became uneasily aware that older patterns of seasonal misery had been replaced by "structural" poverty in town and country. This was poverty that persisted for generations or more. Much of Asia and Africa, too, seemed to have fallen into almost total impoverishment, relative to the rich white lands. People permanently trapped at the bottom were fodder for indigenous rebels, socialists, or anarchists.

Some room has to be left, finally, for the independent activities of individual reformers, who roused a growing public to the belief that government ought to intervene to improve the moral tone of society or adjust its skewed distributions of wealth. This was the age when Lord Shaftesbury campaigned to end child labor in Britain and when American abolitionists campaigned unceasingly for government action to end slavery. And across the world, reformers sought to end the burning of Indian widows, ritual cannibalism in the Pacific, the binding of Chinese women's feet, and the discontinuance of customary practices of inheritance, which were regarded as contrary to God's law in Islam. These reformers inevitably looked to the newly empowered state to achieve these objectives and so strengthened its claims to be the dominant actor in society, over and above the mosque, the church, or the local magnate.

What were the areas in which the state intervened? Famine relief and public health were obviously central. In the first flush of power at the beginning of the nineteenth century, the new European and American states and the colonial regimes springing up in Africa and Asia were often fired by notions of laissez-faire. Society would organize itself better if the state refused to intervene, it was argued. During the famines in Scotland, Ireland, and India during the 1830s and 1840s, the officials of the British Empire were in fierce dispute about the extent to which the government should intervene to provide food or relief works to the starving. Some believed, in a parody of the ideas of Thomas Malthus, that famine was God's way of checking the growth of population and should not be interfered with.

Even in the early part of the century, though, there were some areas in which administrators just could not turn a blind eye. The cholera epidemics that ravaged all parts of the world in the 1820s and 1830s brought about the introduction of rules for quarantine and internal barriers to stop the spread of the disease. The threat posed to international shipping and the passage of labor from continent to continent by unscrupulous operators led to the regulation of emigration and conditions of work on ships. Governments intervened to prevent slavery, infanticide, ritual crime, and practices which were thought "abhorrent to mankind." Later epidemics of cholera and bubonic plague, which swept across the world after 1890, also redoubled the pressure on governments to quarantine, control, count, and vaccinate their populations.[55]

Prussia, France, and the northeastern states of the United States led the way in government-sponsored systems of popular education. This was an outgrowth of the ideas of the Enlightenment about improvement. The need for an educated nation for military purposes combined in these cases with a philosophical commitment to popular enlightenment nourished by libertarian or Protestant Pietist ideas. By the mid-century, however, most European and many non-European states had invested in education. In addition to the military impetus, so clear in the case of Egypt or Japan, for instance, sectional rivalries also provided a rationale for expanding primary education.

The French Republic and the new Italian regime introduced state education to limit the power of the Catholic Church. In England, the Anglican Church lobbied for an extension of educational provision precisely because Dissenting and Roman Catholic interests had been so active in promoting schools.

By 1880, even in those areas where the state had receded, withdrawn, or faltered in the earlier decades, the notion that the government should provide for the welfare of its subjects was becoming widely accepted. During the 1880s, the German Reich under Bismarck introduced pensions, national medical provision, and the right to education.[56] State insurance for ill or disabled workers was coupled with stringent efforts to control Communist "conspiracy."[57] Prussia had long been in the vanguard of public education, but the chancellor's policy was clearly also a move in the long battle over the allegiance of urban working-class and small-farming groups, which Bismarck was fighting with his socialist and Catholic political rivals. The result was the famous system of social insurance which gave basic pension and health provision to citizens. The welfare state came much later in Britain. It happened only after the revival of urban conservatism in the 1880s and the rise of the Labour Party put pressure on Prime Minister Lloyd George's Liberals to distinguish themselves from their enemies.[58] In fact, in the British Empire, it was in the colonies of European settlement that the idea of "cradle to grave" state provision was first introduced. In the case of New Zealand and Australia, progressives sought change in order to make their societies more equal and distinguish them from what were seen as the class despotisms of the old European states.[59]

State provision in the fields of health and education, let alone pensions, was hardly on the agenda at all in European colonies in Asia and Africa, where life expectation scarcely crept above 35 years of age. Here laissez-faire stinginess was reinforced by the notion that natives naturally died like flies. There were minor advances. By the end of the nineteenth century, British India had a famine code; India, French Algeria, Indochina, and the Dutch East Indies had made a halting beginning in the provision of primary education. The colonial government was attempting to establish its own system of education to supersede "native" educational institutions, which had been connected with religious authorities and survived on the charity of great magnates. To some degree this reflected the colonial state's need for skilled manpower; but the rise of colonial nationalism also made it an issue of legitimacy for even the most uncaring colonial regimes. A similar pattern emerged in Asia and Africa's semi-independent regimes. Stung by the taunts of Western-educated "progressives," the late-nineteenth-century rulers of China began to establish an imperial school system after 1900. In the Ottoman Empire, Egypt, and Japan,[60] ruling groups became critically aware of the power and resources of their European enemies. They began to establish their own academies, schools, and systems of health care, concerned that otherwise they might lose the allegiance of the restive young or the working class of their growing cities.

TOOLS OF THE STATE

In order to rule and organize resources, the state clearly had to know what it was ruling and who its neighbors were. From the later Middle Ages, European states had begun to map out their territories, partly because the boundaries between them were so complex and contentious. The Ottomans had followed suit. By 1600, the sultans even possessed maps of the Atlantic coast of North America based on European examples which their agents had collected. The Mughals, the Chinese, and the reformed royal despots of early-nineteenth-century Thailand and Vietnam[61] also began to map their territories, often depicting the empire as a territory defined by roads which spiraled out from the imperial center. These were not as complete or as geographically accurate as the European maps. This was a sign not so much of Asiatic backwardness as of the relative unimportance of closely delimiting territory in Asian statecraft. For many of the great kings of Asia and North Africa had large, skilled bureaucracies. These were proficient in the creation and preservation of large bodies of data which could be passed on in written form or by officials who memorized them.

For Europeans, the late eighteenth and early nineteenth centuries were the high age of mapmaking. At this time, mapmakers began to try to project a more precise sense of space. Before this, two-dimensional measurement had been rough-and-ready. Now, after about 1750, there were practical reasons why new tools began to be available to governments. The great expansion of navigation during the century had encouraged naval captains to record coastlines and coastal peaks with much greater precision. The steady improvement of navigational instruments had made this possible. On land, the later stages of the military revolution had involved the development of much more sophisticated forms of artillery and fortresses built to direct accurate fire. Siting cannon required military officers to have a much more geometrical understanding of a landscape, so as to avoid dead ground and to estimate a clearer line of sight.

The links between warfare and mapping by the state were startlingly represented in the mapping efforts of the French and British states and empires. In France, Napoleon's École Polytechnique drew together a huge range of mathematical and cartographical skills for civil and military purposes. It built on material collected by the French Académie Royale and the topographical maps of the country which had been made after 1744. Standardized French place-names were often substituted for those in regional patois in the course of this exercise. This effort was later expanded to Corsica. During Napoleon's occupation of Egypt, the land was surveyed, and the results were published in the *Carte topographique de l'Égypte* (Paris, 1825).[62] Britain's national mapping project was, and still is, called the Ordnance Survey, clearly indicating its origin in planning for artillery warfare. After the Catholic rebellion in the Highlands in 1745, Scotland was carefully mapped. In the later eighteenth and early nineteenth centuries, Ireland was also mapped. In many areas of the west of Ireland, this was the first time that representatives of the British state had penetrated into the countryside at all. The high point of the whole enterprise was the great Trigonometrical Survey of India, which completed its work between 1818 and 1840 under the direction of Sir George Everest, after whom the Himalayan peak was named. The survey involved the use of a large Indian staff and took British officers into parts of the countryside where they had never been before.[63]

While the origins of the idea of surveying may have been utilitarian, its consequences worldwide were both symbolic and practical. At a symbolic level, the progress of the survey through the countryside represented the triumph of Western science and technology and the final establishment of British dominion. Gaelic place-names were rendered into English, and Indian place-names were standardized and entered into gazetteers. At a slightly later date, the American authorities began a similar process of mapping and codifying the plains and mountains of the west. Again, indigenous names were often supplanted by Anglo-Saxon ones, marking the claims to ownership of their new masters.

In Asia, as in Europe, the newly energized states which emerged from the Napoleonic wars and contemporary world crisis demanded an exact delimitation of their territory. Indians came to understand this; some indigenous rulers tried to impede the surveying work, while mobs sometimes attacked and demolished the trigonometrical towers. At the same time, native voices were able to enlist and put to use maps as symbolic and practical resources. By the 1840s, books written by Indians were seeking to demonstrate the boundaries of India or of the Hindu sacred realm. Geography was an important part of the early nationalist ideology. Meanwhile, in the heavily taxed countryside, Indian plaintiffs and defendants in British courts made use of the large-scale maps which were generated out of the original survey. Much the same thing had happened in Ireland. Here the Gaelic literati associated with the survey published their own antiquarian and historical works, which praised old Irish civilization and language and helped imbue the diminished post-famine population with a sense of pride in their nation. In those parts of Asia and North Africa which remained independent or semi-independent, indigenous rulers also began to create maps which drew on local representations of the body politic, but also slowly brought European techniques of measurement to bear on them. By the 1820s or 1830s, the rulers of Burma and Thailand had had relatively accurate maps of their territory drawn. Li Hongzhang again encouraged the preparation of detailed maps of south China.

The states' efforts to map their territories were widely accompanied by attempts to enumerate, categorize, and assess their populations and resources. Most early modern kingdoms had resorted to periodic household censuses, whether this was to locate resources to be taxed or to count labor which kings might require. Descriptions of subdivisions had long existed, in which local literati praised their home province and wrote about its cities, men of religion, famous local dynasties, and products. What happened in the nineteenth century was that censuses, descriptive gazetteers, and formal archival procedures became more precise and also more widespread. China probably

STATE AND SOCIETY IN THE AGE OF IMPERIALISM

possessed the oldest system of district gazetteers in the world. In the thirteenth to seventeenth centuries, these had been produced in order to help officials in their relations with local elites. In turn, the literati used the gazetteers to show how important were their home places and what contribution they had made to the empire. During the seventeenth and eighteenth centuries, new gazetteers were produced, which bore the mark of the central state and its interests more obviously. Even as the Chinese government fragmented in the nineteenth century, so new editions were produced for the use of the provincial regimes and foreign entrepreneurs. In the Ottoman Empire and other parts of the Islamic world, the old form of *kaiyfyat*, or local description, was easily adapted to create gazetteers for modernizing officials.

Gazetteers, local handbooks, maps, and censuses were both symbolic statements and practical tools for the nineteenth-century state. What they represented was public and governmental knowledge. It was at this same period that the state asserted its control over the archives and collections of papers which ministers and other public officials amassed while in office. Previously, such officials had usually decamped with their papers at the end of their term of office. But just as states now insisted that officials were not to accept presents or bribes while in office, so they also insisted on the distinction between official and private information.

If the state was to have trust in its officials, it needed to train them itself. The development of a professional and trained civil service and an efficient police was another important theme of the nineteenth century. Of course, fine officials and administrators had existed in all the great kingdoms of the early modern era. Yet these men usually saw themselves as personal servants of the ruler; their terms of service were not fixed, their training was diverse, and their ideologies various. Perhaps only the Roman Catholic Church in the West and the Chinese Empire with its sinicizing vassals in the East possessed anything which could reasonably be called bureaucracies, unified by common principles and training, and serving the institution rather than the king.

The nineteenth century saw the expansion of bureaucracy as the state swelled and became more intrusive. In Germany, Austria, and France, the first half of the nineteenth century saw the emergence of a civilian state from under the shadow of military officialdom. Historians have come to see this as part of the broad pattern of "professionalization" which they discern in education, the sciences, and the medical world. Prussia introduced a codified career structure for civil servants in 1873, as a consequence of experience during the French war. "Modern" subjects of study became increasingly significant in the curriculum. Japan, which followed hard on the German precedents, introduced an examination system for promotion in 1882. At a lower level, the role and training of the police also underwent a considerable change. In Italy by the time of the First World War, the officer class among the police was expected to have a degree in law or forensic medicine. In France, by contrast, the inheritance of Napoleonic bureaucracy actually seems to have made it harder for politicians of the Third Republic to press through reform measures after 1870. This was true to an even greater extent in China, where proponents of the scholar-gentry system, with its memorized tests in the Confucian classics, fought a rearguard action against change. The classical inheritance was finally defeated in 1905, when the 1200-year-old examination system was abolished, because it was "an enemy and hindrance to the school system."[64] This was a reference to private academies increasingly teaching modern subjects which had flourished under the patronage of the provincial intelligentsia since the 1870s. After the turn of the century, Japanese advisers were brought into China with greater frequency to establish academies and professional training schools. In this way French and German models were modified and transferred from one Asian society to another.

Britain and America were also somewhat late in the move to the creation of professional civil servants, because of aristocratic suspicion of state officials in the one and democratic suspicion of them in the other. America, however, came to realize it needed a merit-based system, not least because a large percentage of federal income came from customs revenues on the eastern seaboard, which needed expert and uncorrupt handling. The federal government civil payroll swelled from 53,000 in 1871 to 256,000 in 1901.[65] The Pendleton Civil Service Act of 1883 created a civil service commission which set academic standards for entrants. All the same, the older idea persisted that non-elected officials were dangerous, and civil service positions remained part of the electoral "spoils system." President Theodore Roosevelt, arch-proponent of an efficient state, tried to push for further reform in 1903–4, but even in 1914, the question of whether civil servants were agents of the state or agents of political parties remained unresolved. In Britain, likewise, the hold of aristocratic patronage had been loosened, and a meritocratic system of examination had been introduced. Yet the training of civil servants remained archaic, and they continued to be drawn from a narrow range of upper-middle-class families with access to Oxford and Cambridge universities.

As in several other respects, government was more modern in Britain's eastern colonial empire. Officials had needed to be trained to oversee the complex systems of taxation and judicial arbitration which had been inherited from the earlier Indo-Muslim governments. The East India Company set up a training school in languages and political economy at Haileybury in 1809, which was far in advance of anything in domestic government. After the civil service reforms of 1856, British recruits into the Indian Civil Service were taken from among graduates of Oxford, Cambridge, and Trinity College, Dublin, and were trained in languages and political economy before being sent to the subcontinent. This became the model for the British territories. The University of Leiden served the same function for Dutch government in the East and spawned a distinguished line of oriental scholars.

STATE, ECONOMY, AND NATION

The nineteenth century is commonly thought of as the age of laissez-faire, when the state acted as "night watchman" and only intermittently and

Table 7.1 Government servants

a. Civilian personnel at all levels (thousands)

Date	Austria	Great Britain	France	Prussia-Germany	United States
1760	26	—	—	—	—
1850	140	67	300	55	—
1910	864	535	583	c.1000	1,034

Source: Mann, *Sources of Social Power*, vol. 2, pp. 804–10.

b. Civilian personnel at central state level (thousands)

Date	Austria	Great Britain	France	Prussia-Germany	United States	India
1760	10	16	—	—	—	—
1850	72	40	146	32+	26	—
1881	—	—	—	—	—	580
1900	297	130	430	—	239	—

Source: Mann, *Sources of Power*, vol. 2, pp. 804–10; *Census of India, 1881*.

c. Military personnel (thousands)

Date	Austria	Great Britain	France	Prussia-Germany	United States	India
1760	250	144	460	150	—	—
1850	318	197	390	173	21	230
1900	230	486	620	629	126	c. 500[a]

[a] Including princely armies.
Source: Mann, *Sources of Power*, vol. 2, pp. 804–10; *Census of India, 1881*.

reluctantly intervened in the economy. Only after about 1890 did protectionist pressures build up, so that even in Britain the cry for imperial preference was voiced. This view is based largely on a reading of British, British imperial, and American history, and even here it is rather partial. We have already noted that over much of the world the modern state was designed precisely to create an economy which could support a technologically efficient military power. Governments moved to improve agricultural production, hoping to raise more taxes and avert scarcity, the great enemy in war. This was true even of regimes which had not traditionally intervened in production very deeply. In Danubian Bulgaria, for instance, Midhat Pasha, one of the great Ottoman governors of the nineteenth century, encouraged agriculture and patronized the Christian peasantry.[66]

In some ways the modernizing efforts of Peter the Great in early-eighteenth-century Russia anticipated rulers in the nineteenth century who turned to the regulation of customs and investment in industry. Russia, in fact, was the first of the "developing countries." Famously, the German customs union of the 1830s was intended to form an economic solidarity which would make political union more likely. Contemporary Egypt, the Ottoman Empire, Iran, China, and Japan all strove mightily to concentrate resources to invest in modern industrial and especially military-industrial factory production. Where these moves failed in the medium term, as they did in China, the Ottoman Empire, and Iran, it was partly because they were aborted by the intervention of the powers, especially Britain, which were averse to the industrialization of the peripheries, as chapter 8 shows. At the same time, the Ottoman and Chinese cases also indicate that indigenous regimes might restrict industrialization to preserve their own power. The Qing court clipped the wings of the provincial viceroys because it was worried about the buildup of their armies and navies. Where indigenous attempts at industrialization succeeded, as in Japan, new industrial enterprises were sold off to entrepreneurs, resulting in the role of state intervention being underplayed by historians.

Even in the case of Britain and America, state power was both overtly and covertly used to promote economic integration and industrial growth, well before the protectionist wave at the end of the nineteenth century. Throughout the British Empire, governments used their power to keep markets open and tariffs low; this was a perennial complaint of the first generation of nationalist politicians in India, Egypt, and even latterly in Ireland. But positive action was taken by the state in specific cases. The colonial governments in South and Southeast Asia, including French and Dutch ones, intervened throughout the later nineteenth century to create forest reserves and to limit the access of indigenous people to valuable resources of timber. The generally tight-fisted colonial governments inaugurated canal schemes and provided legal and financial backing for schemes of railway development. Above all, colonial governments and the great powers, operating through banks and financial treaties, worked to manipulate currencies and reserves of gold and silver in their own interest. British control of South Africa's gold reserves represented a major aspect of her stake in the African continent, for instance. It also gave the Bank of England and the British Treasury a huge international economic advantage during periods of war, especially after 1914.[67] Even in the United States, where there was an even greater ideological distrust of state intervention in the economy, the federal government was quite active in providing subsidies to railroad companies and for the improvement of harbors and other infrastructure projects.

Apart from this, there were many ways in which the relatively lightly governed states and dominions of the English-speaking world intervened, or were increasingly compelled to intervene, in the management of economies. Governments provided legal infrastructures and promulgated private laws which paid particular attention to the organization of economic activity. They established institutions to promote the flexible operation of the free-market economy at home and abroad. The most notable of these were central banks of issue, whose purpose was to assure the stability of the national currency, guarantee the gold convertibility of paper money, and to organize a secure system of short-term credit for the economy. Governments in these lightly ruled territories also guaranteed the viability of transport and telegraphs, and at the end of the century, the introduction of the electric telegraph. Finally, of course, the expansion of European empires and of the informal spheres of military and political influence of the great powers contributed to the growth of a global economy in which long-distance direct investment by entrepreneurs spread to Asia, Africa, Latin America, and Australasia. While nationalists and liberal historians have argued about where the benefits from such investment accrued, there is no doubt of the importance of these new international financial links, or of the key role which the state played in forging them, at least initially.

At this point, we can return to an issue broached in the previous chapter: the relationship between state and nation. In Hobsbawm's formulation, the state created the nation, rather than vice versa. Yet it did not do so in a vacuum, and in some cases the nation created the state. Living traditions of language, law, religion, political ethics, and deportment made it easier for the state or for aspirant state-builders among colonial nationalists to claim that they represented a nation or a would-be nation. This contention between state and community about the boundaries of the nation continued into the twentieth century. It is true that the new bureaucracies helped solidify this more potent sense of nation in many ways. They created geography textbooks which showed the boundaries and divisions of the state to the young, and promulgated novels and histories which standardized languages and created a long, and sometimes largely fictitious, lineage for states. Schools in Catholic Ireland began increasingly to teach the ancient Irish language and Celtic myths. American school textbooks emphasized the ideals of the War of Independence more vigorously after the Civil War. In India, more problematically, school textbooks sanctioned by British rulers began to inscribe a particular "Hindu" view of history from which Muslims were largely excluded as foreign invaders. Passbooks, military service, rituals of state and nation, public statues of nationalist heroes, and great commemorative buildings attempted to achieve the same standardized patriotism in more subtle ways.

Historians have often tried to have their cake and eat it. They like to argue that the peasant, the tribesman, the woman, or the working-class man have "autonomy." Yet, when it comes to emotions like patriotism or nationalism, of which they disapprove, that agency is denied to ordinary people who are deemed to be dupes of the elites or automata easily stamped with the mark of state power. In fact, nationalism and patriotism also drew on more profound desires and aspirations, outside the purview of the state, which had in earlier times often been attached to family, clan, or religious group. Wars started by states certainly reinforced and generalized these sentiments. So too did people's wider experience of the turbulence of modernity. Patriotism, jingoism, and inter-communal hatred often proceeded from the people and influenced otherwise cautious statesmen, rather than vice versa. This was true in England even in the eighteenth century, when the celebration of imperial victories was as often directed against the government as much as promulgated by it. It was demonstrated again in nineteenth-century Japan, where "Deep Ocean" and "Nanyang" (Southeast Asia) societies were founded by ordinary samurai to promote overseas expansion and imperial greatness, even when the Meiji leaders were extremely skeptical of the wisdom of such policies. Popular anti-Semitism similarly bent and buckled the policies of the growing state in Germany and Austria. The modern state and nationalism remained in fevered dialogue throughout the century to 1914. Nationalism was not simply a sentiment forced on hapless and naive peoples by wicked power-brokers or greedy capitalists.

A BALANCE SHEET: WHAT HAD THE STATE ACHIEVED?

Earlier sections argued that it was not in all societies and at all times that the claims and resources of the state grew steadily in the course of the nineteenth century. In the Anglo-Saxon world and in China, above all, central government

ILLUSTRATION 7.4 Internal exile: Russian prisoners on their way to Siberia. A lantern slide for teaching the horrors of despotism, late nineteenth century.

as such remained relatively small and constrained, and even contracted in some respects between 1815 and the end of the nineteenth century. This does not mean, however, that the growth of professional administration suffered to the same degree. In Britain, organs of local government and societies associated with the metropolitan elite continued to develop the apparatus of paid secretaries and administrators throughout the period. Local school boards and other decentralized institutions did the same in the United States. "Governmentality" expanded, even when the state as such did not.

In China, too, local officials developed their own staffs with expertise in irrigation, taxation, and transport, for instance. Here, where central administration suffered both a loss of legitimacy and a loss of revenue during the Taiping and Nien rebellions of 1850–70, the tax base increased later in the century, with healthy sums coming in from internal and external customs duties. As Hans van de Ven has recently argued, it would be wrong to think as some historians once did that the Chinese government was in a state of decline between the mid-century rebellions and the Communist revolution of the twentieth century.[68] The powerful regional viceroys of the post-Taiping era established their own links with the landed gentry clans which had provided the administrators of the Qing dynasty. There were even moves under Prince Kung in the 1870s, and again after China was defeated by Japan in 1895, to reform the central financial administration of the empire and give its officials a modern education rather than one in the Confucian classics. These Chinese self-strengtheners had noted that other societies as conservative as the Japanese, and even the British, were embarking on the same process, in order to face the common problems of international trade, diplomacy, and warfare.

It might be thought, too, that large areas of political life remained relatively untouched by the growth of the power and the claims of the state: international contacts, religion, and socialism, for instance. But even where this was so, the mark of the state was very much in evidence, as the close of chapter 6 suggested. The international telegraph treaties, the expansion of the Red Cross and Red Crescent societies, the arrangements for exploration and preservation of the Arctic and Antarctic continents, all of which came to pass between 1900 and 1914, indicate the global interests of elites. Yet all of these arrangements started from the assumption that nation-states were the key players. Scientific and scholarly interchange which in the 1780s had proceeded through informal and personal links between gentlemen-scholars were now created by alliances of national academies and scientific societies. The rise and self-organization of the great "world" religions, discussed in chapter 9, were not immune from these pressures. It is true that many people owed allegiance to a religious tradition which lay outside, and was sometimes even hostile to the claims of the state within whose boundary they lived. Yet the revived agencies of Roman Catholicism, pan-Islamism, and Confucian nationalism generally took care to acknowledge and work with the national organs of the confessional group within which they operated. Even socialist activity at a world level was constrained by the representation of interests of specific national socialist leagues. The total collapse of the illusion of international socialist brotherhood in 1914, when socialists too went to war with each other, made this very clear. The modern state drove forward the great simplification of the form of ruling groups, the notion of sovereignty, and the aims of governance which were noted at the beginning of the book.

Where the triumph of the modern state was less sure was on its inner frontiers. Parochial powers and cultures still retained their influence, particularly where train and telegraphic communications were poorly developed and literacy was low. It was not only Christ, in the words of the popular saying, but the Italian government, which stopped at Eboli, the southern Italian town legendary for its pagan lawlessness. Throughout much of the world, the state remained perched atop segmentary political systems, its magistrates and governors effective only insofar as they could find influential allies amongst clan heads and tribal elders. The revolts that occurred at the end of the First World War over the Middle East, central Asia, Afghanistan, and Africa are sometimes represented as periods of anarchy when the state "broke down." More often than not, however, they simply reflected the emergence into view of the vital play of local political accommodation and conflict which had been obscured in the historical record by a thin patina of state power. At the other end of the spectrum of social change, the vigorous entrepreneurial communities of the United States and of some industrial cities in Europe were already seeing a retreat of the state. Local associations, voluntary societies, and private initiatives were taking over the social functions which government had quite briefly acquired. That was to be the pattern of the later twentieth century, though the decades of war and depression between 1900 and 1950 were to slow the pace of change immeasurably.

What was certain, above all, was that during the nineteenth century the sound and fury, the *éclat* of the state, spread widely across the globe, whether its local forms were powerful or not. The paraphernalia of flags, drilling soldiers, uniforms, and rituals of rule were taken up by power-hungry people, even in societies remote from the new centers of global government, and even by religious or charismatic movements which claimed a higher purpose than mere worldly dominance. This universal mimicking of the power and charisma of centralized authority began to anger a few intellectuals. It turned some of them into anarcho-syndicalists, who lauded the virtue of the ungoverned community. It transformed others, such as John Ruskin, Leon Tolstoy, and Mohandas Karamchand Gandhi, into apostles of the life of the simple artisan or peasant.

[8] THE THEORY AND PRACTICE OF LIBERALISM, RATIONALISM, SOCIALISM, AND SCIENCE

THIS chapter and the next concern ideas and ideologies. Liberalism, socialism, and science were potentially revolutionary sets of ideas, which many contemporaries and later historians believed had transformed the nineteenth-century world. The chapter argues that all of them were dramatically recast as they passed from continent to continent, often losing their revolutionary character. If anything, as chapter 9 shows, it was the competitive development of the great religious systems which did more to shape the mental life of the period.

Across the nineteenth-century world, intellectuals and politicians argued from complex philosophical positions for individual liberty, the sovereignty of the people, and for a redistribution of wealth and power. Established political and religious authority came under unprecedented attack from liberals, radicals, socialists, and spokesmen for the natural and social sciences, now organized into professions. These intellectual challenges gained momentum where they flowed in the direction of the social and economic developments discussed in earlier chapters. Intellectual movements, however, were more than simply a reflection of social change. They both represented it and determined its direction.

CONTEXTUALIZING INTELLECTUAL HISTORY

The history of political and social thought in the late eighteenth and nineteenth centuries is an exceptionally vibrant area of study. But it suffers from two major weaknesses. First, many intellectual historians continue to equivocate on the question of how to relate intellectual history to social and political history, for the good reason that this is an enormously difficult enterprise. Secondly, the history of political thought remains resolutely centered on

Europe and North America. If the rest of the world is considered at all, historians tend to assume that there occurred a relatively simple process of diffusion in which the doctrines of Western thinkers were slowly spread across the world to those elite members of non-European societies who knew European languages. An exception to this rule is the history of science. Historians of science have recently found much more room for the dynamic role of Asians, Africans, and other non-European peoples in the creation of the hybrid bodies of learning by which global society understood the natural world. They have also been quite successful in explaining how preexisting assumptions and styles of intellectual training guided people's reactions to new scientific ideas coming to them from the West. Western ideas gained currency in part because they were a reflection of Western military and economic power. They were imposed by colonial regimes through schooling systems and public debate. Even in these cases, however, intellectual domination was not a simple process. Western ideas and languages of debate were subtly altered, adjusted, and set to new purposes by indigenous writers and intellectuals.

This chapter builds on and generalizes approaches which are drawn mainly from the history of science. It aims to account for the reception or rejection of radical concepts derived from the learned and political worlds of Europe with reference to the intellectual formation of different societies across the world. Liberalism, socialism, and science quite clearly spread initially from Western sources, but they widely mingled with and were empowered by ideas derived from indigenous rationalistic and ethical traditions. The chapter also considers how intellectuals and activists in Asia, Africa, and Latin America created radical ideologies for change which spoke directly to their own condition, without a similar degree of indebtedness to Western ideas. These discussions are continued in the examination of "world religions" in chapter 9. Most important, the chapter shows how new sets of ideas became politically influential and contributed to changes in society. It shows how, for instance, administrators influenced by hostility to "feudalism" brought about significant changes to the power of landed magnates, and how the development of the idea of science led to the emergence of new types of social organization in "professions."

THE CORRUPTION OF THE RIGHTEOUS REPUBLIC: A CLASSIC THEME

In order to understand these changes, it is important to appreciate that in the seventeenth and eighteenth centuries there were already ideologies and political languages that operated at a global level, to which people of different major civilizations had contributed. The second chapter of this book pointed to some of the forms of debate and investigation which continued to absorb the energies of indigenous intellectuals in the Indian, Islamic, African, and East Asian worlds until the very point of Western intrusion. One preoccupation was the form of the "righteous republic" and the dangers to good government posed by corruption and tyranny. This was a widespread theme throughout Eurasia, Africa, and the Americas. Recent developments in the historiography of Western political thought have made it easier to see linkages and analogies in global political thought during the age of revolution and the first period of worldwide imperial expansion.

Until the 1960s, Western political theorists tended to see the American and French revolutions and the emergence of British radicalism after 1800 as intimately connected to the rise of what C. B. Macpherson called the doctrine of "possessive individualism."[1] This clutch of doctrines, clearly originating in the European-Atlantic world in the writings of the Enlightenment thinkers John Locke, Adam Smith, David Hume, and the French and German *philosophes*, stressed the primacy of the rational individual. It validated the need for the individual's pursuit of his own interest, especially in relation to the workings of economic life. Since the 1960s, however, intellectual historians have partly changed their views. They now portray much of the critical thought of the revolutionary age, which was once seen as distinctly modern, as the last flowering of a much earlier political tradition.

The moral and ethical dimensions of the thinking of those pioneering theorists of the market, Adam Smith and his French coeval the marquis de Condorcet, have been reestablished.[2] Bernard Bailyn[3] for American history and John Pocock[4] for the history of the Atlantic world in general, among others, have traced back the tradition of "civic republicanism," through the "Commonwealth" divines of the seventeenth-century English Civil War, to the learned men of Renaissance Italy, and, indeed, to classical times. This tradition still flowed strongly in the eighteenth century. It influenced the way American colonists thought about royal colonial government before and during the War of Independence. It also influenced the thinking of English, Scottish, and Irish radicals as they attempted to limit the powers of the Crown and the overblown aristocracy after 1714. These ideas, however, bore a family resemblance to political programs and ideologies common across Europe, as they were all derived from classical and Renaissance sources modified by Christian ethics. In the later eighteenth century, for instance, the "liberator" party in Holland[5] and the Genoese and the Florentines, who wished to tame princely tyranny by the restoration of a virtuous republic, stood in the same broad tradition of thought.

Pocock and Bailyn argued that thinkers in the civic republican tradition emphasized the importance of the patrimonial household, rather than the market, and highlighted the obligation of the individual citizen and of the republic to pursue virtue. In the civic republican tradition, the enemies of virtue were corruption and luxury, particularly the corruptions and vices of the royal court and its mercenary hangers-on. In the British and North American world, this tradition was associated with what Pocock called the "country party," which opposed the tyranny and idolatrous religion of the "court party." Rather than being the harbingers of a free market, commerce, the tradesman, the usurer, and the hoarder were figures of detestation to American and to many French radicals.

The contemporary interpretation has the virtue of putting late-eighteenth-century thought in a longer perspective. For instance, hatred of corrupt government, overweening bureaucracy, and the dishonesty of the market was to remain a constant element in American political thought throughout the nineteenth century, even when free-market liberal individualism had become the dominant ideology for both Democrats and Republicans. Other recent writers have also emphasized the conservative features in the thought of the so-called revolutionary age, especially in America. Historians accept that the American founding fathers wished to sever religion from the state. Yet, they argue, this was to preserve the godliness of the local community, not a tactic to promote modern "secularism." In a similar vein, David Brading, writing in 1991,[6] discerned an older tradition of "Creole patriotism" working within the movement to Latin American emancipation from Spanish rule, even when the early liberal economists were constantly on the lips of the leaders of opinion. Figures such as the mercy-giving Mexican Virgin Mary, Our Lady of Guadalupe, and a myth of descent from the old Aztec Empire were prominent symbols of this tradition. Creoles, such as Fray Servando Teresa de Mier, the Dominican theologian and patriot,[7] based their case on an ideology of righteous conquest and summoned up the spirit of the land in their support. These were themes which sit uneasily with modern liberal political theory based on individual rights of property.

Recent writers, such as François Furet,[8] have also been less certain of the radical modernity of the ideological origins of the French Revolution than they were a generation ago. No one doubts that Rousseau's concept of the social contract and Voltaire's radical anticlericalism gave the revolutionaries powerful ideological justifications for their decisions to assail the monarchy and the Church. Yet analysis of the popular fêtes and festivals which accompanied revolutionary outbreaks has shown how widely ordinary people subscribed to leveling, communitarian ideologies which can be traced back to the seventeenth century. The French Revolution is no longer necessarily seen as the triumph of the bourgeoisie or of middle-class, market-oriented virtues. Except in the revolution's earliest and most violent stages, Christianity also remained influential in the thought of early-nineteenth-century French radicals, who believed that the ideal society envisaged in the Bible would come into its own again after the revolution. The virtues of community, rather than the state or the market, were an important element in the ideologies of many of the other European revolutionaries and their pupils in European colonies. Insofar as historians can recover popular mentalities, it seems that a similar mixture of communitarian and simple Christian doctrines was pervasive in them. They provided a common political language for elites and ordinary people.

Since the 1970s this skepticism about radical intellectual ruptures has spread to historians of the nineteenth century, too. Gareth Stedman Jones reinterpreted the "language of politics" of nineteenth-century British radicalism to reveal an eighteenth-century tradition of civic republicanism, which was, again, anti-court and hostile to taxation and swollen central government.[9] The English Chartist radicals, who demanded popular representation in the 1840s, were aware of the doctrines of immediate revolution promulgated by the French Communist Louis Blanc and the new formulations of German socialism being honed by Karl Marx. Yet English radicalism continued to look back to its communitarian, provincial, and Christian Nonconformist origins. Historians of the British dominions have shown how the ideas of the Chartist reformers of the 1840s about community, land, and justice influenced early associations of miners and small farmers in their battles with mine-owners and colonial governments in Australia during the 1860s. In their turn, German and Scandinavian liberalism as often bore the imprint of Lutheran ideas of the Christian community as it reflected an emerging ideology of capitalist individualism.

RIGHTEOUS REPUBLICS WORLDWIDE

This reevaluation of political theory and its representations in Europe and its former American colonies is an important development for the writing of global history. It has the effect of diminishing the distance between Western ideas and the major strands of non-European political thought. It makes it easier for the analyst to perceive implicit connections and analogies between the ideological origins of the European and American revolutions and events such as the 1868 Meiji "restoration" and the emergence of Indian, Chinese, and Egyptian nationalism or anti-colonialism, as will be shown below. The intellectual leaders of these Asian and Middle Eastern movements also mixed elements from modern Western radicalism and theories of human rights with claims to defend ancient traditions of community and the honor of the land from the rising tide of global commercialization, most powerfully manifested in the Atlantic economies.

Indeed, ideas not dissimilar to European traditions of civic republicanism existed in many world societies. Anthropologists, for example, have shown how precolonial Africans used ideologies of good kingship to justify the overthrow of wicked and ineffectual rulers. John Peel has demonstrated this particularly effectively in the case of the West African Yoruba, a people who recorded their struggles to maintain a harmonious society and wise kingship through bardic myths which stressed the role of the honorable householder.[10] Wise counsel, care for the toiler, and the desire to be ruled by virtuous patriarchs were, quite understandably, the social goods sought by intellectuals in all agrarian and early commercial societies before industrialization. In contrast, what was perceived as corruption, although it was understood differently in the various traditions, seems to have been a cause for dissent and even revolt almost universally.

In Japan, as chapter 1 suggested, violation of the rights of the "noble peasant" by a corrupt court, which had diverged from the norms of the classic Confucian writings and their respect for the ancestors and the workings of nature, was a potent theme. Ogyu Sorai, probably the most influential thinker of eighteenth-century Japan, attacked samurai corruption and merchant violations of the moral economy. He saw this as a way of safeguarding the regime.[11] Later, in the late eighteenth and early nineteenth centuries, dissidence against the Tokugawa dynasty gradually coalesced around such themes. Western-derived themes of modernization, science, and efficiency certainly gave greatly added strength to the legitimacy of the leaders of the 1868 coup in Japan. Yet the Japanese "revolution" and "renaissance" were rooted in these older ideas, particularly as they related to the ethnic myth of divine monarchy and good rulership. In Hindu and even Muslim India, by contrast, the elite and popular understandings of corruption took on a more immediate, bodily sense through the notions of purity and pollution. The pollution of the land and the domain of the good householder by the British and their vile habits served as a constant theme in colonial patriotism and later nationalist movements. Early local orators of the Indian National Congress continued to employ this sort of language, even after liberal political economists, such as Dadhabhai Naoroji, Britain's first Indian member of Parliament, ransacked British official papers to put together technical economic arguments for the protection of nascent Indian industries and other self-consciously modern arguments for political autonomy.

The connections between Euro-American civic republicanism and patriotic communitarianism elsewhere are not merely implicit, but explicit, in the case of the Muslim world. The doctrine of holy war, the "lesser *jihad*," was always at hand for rebels and resisters of European rule. Yet it was sparingly and carefully used. Instead, much early Muslim nationalist and pan-Islamic thought harked back to the medieval Arab and Persian moralists' attempts to reconcile Aristotle's civic morality with the Prophet's norms of the godly life. These had been expressed in the medieval ethical literature of the Islamic world (in the *akhlaq* tradition).[12] One feature of what might be called the "Ottoman renaissance" of the seventeenth century was the translation of Aristotle into the Ottoman language. Many editions of his works were printed in the nineteenth century. Nineteenth-century Arab, Persian, and Javanese[13] thinkers argued that Western invasion and corrupt forms of indigenous governance spread the evils of bad counsel, usury, the violation of men's homes, and the dishonoring of women. Here one can glimpse a direct, if distant, connection between the archaic European traditions of civic republicanism and the political ethics of an extra-European society. Aristotle was common to both civilizations. As in the thought of American patriots, so too, some traditions of Islamic thought, especially within its Shia branch, held that since religious authority was eternal, it should be protected from the intrusion of the state.

Aristotle even came late to China, through Jesuit interpreters in the seventeenth century. Chinese literati moved quickly to translate and disseminate it. Robert Wardy has shown how, far from being misunderstood or distorted on the procrustean bed of conceptual and linguistic difference, rendering it into Chinese sometimes actually expressed the sense of the Greek original more effectively.[14] It was in the nineteenth century, though, that Chinese reformers began to cite Aristotle's *Ethics* and *Politics* more widely.

The international spread of Euro-American liberalism, socialism, and science across the world after 1815 is not really in doubt. In many contexts these foreign ideas made people see the flaws in their own societies quite differently, as did Marxist doctrine in the twentieth century. Yet their reception, appropriation, and use were subtly determined by the continued vitality of such earlier ethical and political traditions, not only outside but also within Europe. In Europe, for example, socialism incorporated these earlier themes. The recent work of some historians and social scientists seems to suggest that the real difference between European and non-European political thought lay in the matter of religion. According to this argument, Europeans developed a secular tradition of progressive political thought, whereas Asians and Africans fell back on the past and on the purity of their religion when they came to think about their future. This distinction is definitely too stark. European intellectuals were almost everywhere influenced by religion. Secular liberals such as John Stuart Mill continued to work within a Christian humanist tradition, even if they denounced credulity and the Church. Even Marxists took over the structure of earlier millenarian thought. By the same token, much of what has traditionally been classified under the rubric of "religion" in Islamic, African, and Asian thought bore quite directly on everyday life and politics. That non-European traditions of political thought were steeped in religious ideology does not mean that they were simply manifestations of an unchanging "religious mentality." They reflected instead a notion of the good governance of one's own passions, the household, and, in consequence, the polity. Thus some Islamic liberals in nineteenth-century Egypt appealed to the early days of the Prophet's reign in Medina, which they pictured as a sort of representative government.

THE ADVENT OF LIBERALISM AND THE MARKET: WESTERN EXCEPTIONALISM?

That said, it is important not to go to the other extreme by underestimating the novelty of certain emerging features of European intellectual life in the seventeenth and eighteenth centuries. The notion of generalizable individual rights and the emphasis on the "hidden hand" of the market in this Western tradition seems indeed to presage something strikingly new. These truly radical ideas, too, found a niche in a world beginning to experience new forms of state power. In many important ways, the rapid expansion of the international market and of European empires required people across the world to adapt these new intellectual tools for their own use. What is needed, then, is an approach to global intellectual history which leaves room for innovative political thought, yet stresses the resilience of old ideas of good government and proper deportment in emerging social and political movements. The first section considers some of the novel political ideas which were emerging in Europe under the old regime. It goes on to show how, in their application to issues such as exploitation of the land, management of trade, political representation, and scientific practice, these ideas were modified and even neutralized by older ideologies and local discourses.

As noted in chapter 1, most world civilizations gave rise to forms of debate, argument, and empirical observation which stand comparison with the emerging scientific rationalism of western Europe. Islamic thinkers of the eighteenth century laid much stress on the rational sciences, while the late Qing period saw a concerted move toward empirical observation of man and the natural world in China. The Western radical philosophical tradition from the time of the Renaissance scholars René Descartes and Francis Bacon onward seems, nevertheless, to display some quite distinct features. These were both intrinsic to its thought and generated by its reception and context.

The philosophical tradition, foreshadowed by René Descartes in France and pioneered by John Locke and David Hume in England, became influential in Europe and America. It emphasized the importance of the individual's "desire to see for himself in the light of what is reasonable evidence." Except, perhaps, in the case of Hume, this argument was originally intended to offer rational proofs for Christian belief. In effect, however, it tended to undercut the authority of tradition, priesthood, and monarchy. It made redundant, even if it did not directly challenge, the Christian and humanist elements in the civic republican tradition discussed earlier. For Hume, in particular, religion was the preserve of those "who demand certainty when probability only is to be had." This tended to undermine the claims of secular powers to be based on religious sanction. Rulers could hold power only conditionally, if human beings could deal only in probabilities. In a more abstract style, Immanuel Kant (1724–1804), writing in the 1780s, urged that individual liberty must be the unconditional basis of all proper rational judgment. Though his connection with Voltaire and the French *philosophes*, let alone the French revolutionaries, was quite remote, many people during the revolutionary years associated Kant with the assault on religion and despotic monarchy.

Equally, rational analysis of the "facts" of society led Adam Smith and his French coeval, Condorcet, to conclude, following Hume, that the market should allow the free play of the interests of morally independent individuals. State and tradition should not impede the market, and the bars, obstructions and imposts, which all the nations of Europe and none more than England have put on trade should be removed, as Hume put it. Economic relations emerged ideally as a sphere in which the virtuous self-interest of all was practically adjusted, rather than one where ethical or semi-religious norms of right and obligation were imposed from above.[15] This is not to say that either Smith or Condorcet or their immediate followers believed that economic activity was amoral. On the contrary, moral individuals could only be free individuals, and this extended to economics as well as politics and belief.[16] Still, the idea of moral and economic "independency" was a striking one. If "economy" was emerging as a concept potentially disconnected from the idea of political and theocratic paternalism, so too was "society" in the work of the Italian thinker Giambattista Vico and the science of sociology that he inspired.[17] The idea of "society" as an abstract entity existing beyond local sociability at a national or even global level was a revolutionary one.

None of these traditions of thought, to repeat, were inherently anti-religious or anti-monarchical in origin, even though Hume himself was a radical skeptic. Most of the descendants of these thinkers among the liberal, utilitarian, and even socialist writers and public men of the nineteenth century remained formally Christian and honored kings. But, at the very least, God was removed very far from the workings of the natural and human worlds in these theories. The seventeenth-century French cleric and philosopher the abbé Bayle, for instance, thought that a society of atheists could function perfectly decently without the need for any belief in God. This intellectual erosion of the validity of sacred traditions of government and the supernatural was, pushed to its extreme, potentially annihilating. Indeed, it became so in the later scientific Marxist tradition.

This was apparently not the case in the empirical and rationalist traditions of other world societies, not, at least, until they were influenced by Western ideas. Outside western Europe, even in the orthodox Christian lands of eastern Europe and the Near East, older cosmological ideas continued to encapsulate domains of rational and empirical argumentation. In none of these other civilizations did a significant number of thinkers render the idea of God's saving intervention so thoroughly redundant as in eighteenth-century Europe. Abstract Buddhist thought, it is true, enshrined a highly technical and philosophical form of anti-theism. Radical Islamic Sufism sometimes toyed with a reversal of the common Muslim statement of belief, changing "There is no god but God" into "There is no God." Yet there was relatively little in the way of a political or ethical debate around the notion of atheism or agnosticism. Nor did thinkers apparently construct an abstract conception of human "society" beyond and outside the community of believers or the harmonious communion of man and the living world. Generally, too, outside western Europe, benign change was still envisaged as an attempt to return to a golden age of the past, even where great virtuosity was employed to smuggle in innovation under this rubric.

In parts of western Europe, by contrast, public men brazenly trumpeted the virtues of the future and of a complete rupture with the past. In his book on the British Enlightenment, Roy Porter has highlighted the conviction of Locke, Hume, and their followers that they were ushering mankind into a new and glorious age of reason, which made all earlier thought redundant.[18] When radicals in Bengal adopted the notion of "society," a dispassionate community of interacting interests, they also adopted the same linguistic and conceptual shift that their European exemplars had pioneered between Machiavelli and Vico. The word *samaj*, which meant "assembly" or "gathering," took on this striking new sense.

The continuing distinctiveness of the Western liberal tradition lay not only in its intellectually revolutionary character, but in the context of thought and in the social processes in which it was located. While Confucian, Islamic, and

Indian public debate were notable for their acerbity and contentious character, the eighteenth-century European and American philosophers displayed a greater tendency to contradict and overthrow previous authorities as a matter of pride and argue their case completely anew. Debaters in the Sanskrit, Pali, and Confucian traditions generally attempted to reconcile and make relevant to their arguments older authorities, rather than completely reject them, as happened increasingly in western Europe. The "animal spirits" of these radical philosophers, like those of the military and naval entrepreneurs and proto-industrialists with whom they mixed, encouraged them to think that they could change history. That change was to be a secular change reflected in human minds and through them in the enlightenment and wealth of whole societies. Man was not only the measure of all things, but it was he who created his own salvation on this earth. The idea that Divine Providence acted directly on humanity continued to resonate with large sections of the population. It even informed some of the economic theories of the early nineteenth century, which saw periodic economic crises as the judgment of God on sinful nations.[19] Now, however, a potentially independent body of thought and sentiment stood beside the older tradition of rumination on God's will and purpose.

One act of exceptional intellectual endeavor can soon, however, lead on to others. As these western European ideologies were received in other parts of the world, they, too, were transformed by acts of thought equally creative and revolutionary in their impact as those of Locke or Montesquieu. The Indian reformer Raja Ram Mohun Roy, for instance, made in two decades an astonishing leap from the intellectual status of a late-Mughal state intellectual to that of the first Indian liberal. Some themes of the old Muslim-Aristotelian tradition were present in his thought. He insisted, for instance, on the importance for the British of good political counsel, justice, and consultation with Indians. He also inherited and selected from Hindu religious traditions, especially in the way in which he recast old theistic ideas within Hinduism to construct a world of old Indian monotheism to which its people must return before they could achieve political autonomy. Here, he independently broached themes that were being simultaneously developed in Europe by Garibaldi and Saint-Simon. As an economic liberal, he argued for free trade as vehemently as contemporary English liberals, because he believed that this would destroy the corruption of the East India Company. While some modern Indian historians see Roy as a conservative, he developed the first constitutional theory of resistance in modern Indian history. In 1832, contrasting the effects of British misgovernment in America, he drew attention to the case of Canada and, by extension, India.

> The mixed community of India, in a like manner [as the Canadians] so long as they are treated liberally, will feel no disposition to cut off its connection with England, which may be preserved with so much mutual benefit to both countries. Yet, as before observed, if events should occur to effect a separation . . . still, a friendly and highly advantageous commercial intercourse may be kept up

between two free and Christian countries, united as they will be by resemblances of language, religion and manners.[20]

What was most remarkable about Roy, however, was his dispassionate concern for other peoples around the world. He wrote with feeling of the cause of the Italian and Spanish revolutionaries of the 1810s and of the Irish. All peoples, he believed, should have local forms of political representation which were appropriate to their characters. At the apex of their international influence, none of the vaunted "great thinkers" of the Western intellectual tradition, by contrast, were entirely able to rid themselves of the assumption of Western racial superiority or to think creatively beyond the bounds of the European world.

The remainder of this chapter will follow the reception and modification or rejection of the classic ideas of liberalism, socialism, and science, both in Europe and North America and in the world outside. At every point, the form of the intellectual or scientific sensibility which emerged from these

ILLUSTRATION 8.1 Liberalism globalizes: The Indian reformer Raja Ram Mohun Roy, c.1832. Book plate, 1870s, Calcutta.

encounters was molded by the preexisting and developing ethical and political traditions, which have been discussed. They also reflected the political and economic circumstances of their different societies and the degree of their subjection to Western imperialism. The survival of indigenous rulers, mercantile magnates, and the trajectory of the "industrious revolutions" which they had undergone also proved important determinants of intellectual change.

The chapter will show how indigenous ideas of good government and the impetus of Western liberal thought worked in practice to effect social change. Neither a "diffusionist" nor an "endogenous" explanation of intellectual and social change is satisfactory. What is required is a blending and transcending of both. Again, while postcolonial critics can "provincialize Europe" in significant ways and show that non-westerners were able to parody and subvert new ideas,[21] it is pointless to deny that intellectual traditions can be, and often are, ruptured by novel and dangerous ideas. Europe and its former American colonies in the late eighteenth and early nineteenth centuries were particularly fecund in such ideas for a time. In the same way, the vibrancy of their civil societies was, at least temporarily, of a different order from the ferment of debate in emerging public spheres elsewhere in the world.

LIBERALISM AND LAND REFORM: RADICAL THEORY AND CONSERVATIVE PRACTICE

The ideas of liberalism, nationalism, secularism, and the self-determination of peoples were closely connected, in that they all presupposed the action of autonomous individuals singly or in groups. A new language of politics was created by the French and British thinkers of the eighteenth century, and its practical implications were made clear in the first libertarian spring of the American and French revolutions. As obvious or even hackneyed as this theme may seem, the writings of contemporaries leave no question of the carrying power of such ideas. Young people, not just in western Europe and North America, but across the world, woke up and saw their situation afresh. The movement of Russian liberal nobles in 1825, which was dedicated to securing a constitution from the autocratic tsar, reflected this ideological tumult. The reformist nobles invoked older notions of the virtuous republic alongside the rights of man, the checks and balances of the American constitution, and the glorious tableaux of radical nations under arms, which they had recently glimpsed in Naples, Portugal, and Spain.[22] One of their key intellectuals declared:

> This divine law was decreed for all men in equal measure, and consequently everyone has an equal right to its fulfilment. Therefore the Russian people is not the property of any one person or family. On the contrary, the government belongs to the people and has been established for the good of the people and the people does not exist for the good of the government.[23]

In a very different context, Ignacio Altamirano (1834–93), the Mexican Indian radical, urged his countrymen to "love the patria and consecrate themselves to science," singling out the ideals of the French Revolution as a permanent goal for Mexico.[24] As early as 1795, some French-speaking Ottomans had been alerted to the ideas of the revolution by the *Gazette française de Constantinople*. By 1837, Sadik Rifat Pasha, an Ottoman ambassador to Vienna, was writing about the relationship between "liberty" and classical Islamic notions of justice.[25] The works of John Stuart Mill became a bible for Latin American liberals in the 1850s and 1860s. In Brazil, the abolitionist Joaquin Nabuco stated: "I am an English liberal . . . in the Brazilian parliament."[26] The Meiji reformers of the 1870s secured copies of the life of George Washington. Low-caste western Indian reformers of the 1850s read Hume, Voltaire, Tom Paine, and Gibbon.[27] Munshi Abdullah, the first modern writer of the Malay world, drew on Western liberal themes and Muslim notions of enlightenment when he attacked the ignorance and corruption of the Malay rajas in the 1820s.[28]

What empowered the political ideologies which arose around the ideas of liberalism and improvement was the way in which they could be applied to contemporary problems. They addressed a wide range of social conflicts and dilemmas which faced critics of the old order around the world in the aftermath of the world revolutions and the decline of the old empires. They could also reinvigorate and sharpen the older discourses on good government. At a global level, none of these ideas was more important than the liberal thinkers' skepticism about the embodied hierarchy of priests, nobles, and kings, and, in particular, their hostility to the control by these authorities of the land and the labor of the peasantry. Ironically, though, in the course of their attack on embodied hierarchies, these thinkers and their political disciples thought in terms of a new sort of hierarchy. This was a hierarchy of races and cultures distinguished by their degree of enlightenment, the perfection of their commerce, and the freedom of their markets in land and labor.

Among the targets of liberal thinkers and statesmen throughout the nineteenth century, therefore, were great feudal estates, or *latifundia*. In Europe, Central and South America, and the Caribbean, huge estates had remained in the hands of old noble families or had been created by land grants from the Crown or the sequestration of church properties in the case of Protestant countries. Colonial governments overseas, such as those of the Dutch and English East India companies, were also tempted to "stabilize" society by conceding lordship over the land to indigenous aristocracies or farmers of revenue. The commercial growth of the eighteenth century had actually benefited many of these holders, at the expense of their undertenants or peasant occupiers. Whereas earlier thinkers in many traditions believed that a powerful and honorable landowning class helped to maintain social stability, many later liberal thinkers asserted that large privileged landlords were a prop of tyranny and a heavy burden on agricultural productivity. These ideas were powerfully articulated in the eighteenth century by Adam Smith and other political economists, especially in Scotland and France. These authors asserted that, as with other forms of monopoly, a monopoly in land impeded the development of a market in land, strangled efficiency, and gave rise to moral and political corruption by perpetuating dependence and servility. In the French playwright Beaumarchais's (and Mozart's) *The Marriage of Figaro*, it was Count Almaviva's status as a great landowner that allowed him to insult his servants and abuse his female dependants.

British liberals and radicals also targeted landed power, though most eighteenth-century continental European thinkers would have regarded the country as immune to the worst depredations of "aristocrats." In Britain the younger sons of nobles were classed among commoners, so that while huge estates persisted through the nineteenth century, the caste-like status of the landowning class apparent in pre-revolutionary France or Russia in the eighteenth century was never so obtrusive there. All the same, the malign electoral influence of large proprietors and their jobbery and control over local council bodies provided one of the main impetuses behind the campaign for the reform of Parliament and later Liberal campaigns for agrarian reform. Radical agrarian liberals in the 1870s used the image of the farmer with "three acres and a cow" as their ideal of an appropriate agrarian order for the highland parts of Britain. In Ireland, where large estates were overwhelmingly in Protestant hands, the attack on landlordism had a sharper edge. In Daniel O'Connell's great campaigns of the 1820s and 1830s for Catholic emancipation, the land issue always lay in the background. Later, John Stuart Mill joined Irish publicists in denouncing the "superstition of landlordism" and argued that all fixed tenants should be given permanent rights to the land.[29] By the 1880s, the swell of agrarian unrest made the compulsory purchase of absentee estates and their distribution among the largely Catholic peasantry an absolute condition for Ireland's continuance in the union with Britain, even if this was secure only in the medium term.

In North America, the huge acreage of land available to be divided up and farmed made the consolidation of a hereditary landed class much more difficult. But American and Canadian radical publicists were always on the look-out for dangerous concentrations of landed power. In Canada, the conflict between peasant-farmers and crown land agents provided a rallying cry for the French rebellion of 1838. During the fierce American debates over slavery, abolitionists consistently argued that the slaveholders' estates were not only morally corrupt but also economically inefficient. The argument was just as fierce in South America. Here, horrified eighteenth-century European travelers reported on the oppression of the Mexican and Peruvian Indians by the owners of the great *haciendas*, or estates, and the periodic savage revolts which the system encouraged. Equally hostile was the view taken by reforming Spanish officials of the later eighteenth century who had been influenced by Adam Smith and denounced the feudal system of the Spanish peninsula as vigorously as its bastard offspring, the *haciendas* of the New World.[30] Throughout the nineteenth century and right up to the Mexican Revolution of 1911, radical politicians in Mexico and Latin America set out to break up by legislation large concentrations of land held by the Church and magnates.[31]

They had a point, because the petty military dictatorships which rose and fell throughout the region were generally supported by venal alliances between big estate owners and commercial magnates in the cities.

A radical overhaul of landed society along liberal or, later, socialist lines proved nearly impossible for nineteenth-century regimes to achieve, however. This was for both practical and theoretical reasons. In practical terms, the more centralized and intrusive governments which developed unevenly across the globe in the nineteenth century were caught in a dilemma. The reforming bureaucrats in St Petersburg, Berlin, and Calcutta were very keen to stamp hard on the little kings of the areas who impeded their attempts to tax, to raise armies, and to assert their juridical rights over ordinary citizens. The tsarist rulers moved heavily against the Polish landowning class, seeking to strip them of their privileges of taxation and jurisdiction over their tenants. Equally, the British authorities in south India warred down the region's petty "fort-holding" warrior-kings in several campaigns in the early nineteenth century. Still, none of these new governments was really strong enough to collect taxes, raise men of military age, or control local outbreaks of dissidence without the help of landowners and chieftains "on the spot."

The usual result of these ideological and practical tussles was a pact between the liberal bureaucrats of the state and the smarter of the local power-holders. The landowners were trying to maximize profits by turning themselves into big local agro-businesses or efficient tax-collectors. This happened to Prussian junkers, Mexican *hacendados*, and Javanese *regenten*. Entrepreneurial landed interests like this needed the governments to put in roads, railways, and canals for them. Equally, the administrators needed the support of the big landowners, provided they could be persuaded to reform sufficiently to head off peasant revolt and the hostility of the urban dwellers. In many cases, the result was that agrarian reform was often desultory. So, for instance, Spanish liberals and moderate Catholic critics of the establishment deplored the poverty of the peasants on great estates in the south of the peninsula and the drift of vagrants to the towns or to the Americas. Yet nothing much was done by the Spanish government until 1907, when weak land legislation was passed which provided a little capital for resettlement and half-hearted measures of protection for tenants against landlords.[32] Here, as in Central and South America or southern Italy, conditions on the estates hardly improved over the course of the nineteenth century.

Ideological issues, however, were as important as practical ones here. On the one hand, the rural reformers opposed large estates on the grounds of corruption and monopoly. On the other hand, most liberal spokesmen were also sure that society could progress only if a general rule of law was maintained by which the state and elected governments were also bound. The influential works of the eighteenth-century French agrarian thinker Charles de Secondat de Montesquieu, continued to hang over this debate in the nineteenth. The notion of the need for security of property for "improvement" was as powerful as the objection to the concentration of ownership. Nineteenth-century thinkers, outside the ranks of the socialists, were extremely reluctant to confiscate property, since the title to property was itself seen as the first and greatest of "human rights." For liberal political theory was based on the idea that rights, particularly rights concerning land, predated government and in a sense provided the basis of society.[33] Though some of these rights theories were now on the rocks and under assault from utilitarians to the left[34] and conservatives to the right, they still provided much of the reforming program of governments throughout the European world and its dependencies. In France, however strong the revolutionary tradition remained in other respects, the right and the moderate left in the nineteenth century agreed on the sacredness of property. The nobility lost their status and privileges before the law, but they discreetly retained much of their land or sold it off, as in Britain and Germany, to rising commercial men, administrators, or railway companies.

In the colonial world, the philosophical arguments in favor of property were buttressed by European administrators' assumptions that native peoples responded naturally to a despotic form of government and social organization. Consequently, great landlords – little kings in their own localities – were the main guarantors of social order. Since early Asian and African liberals in these societies were often themselves from a petty landlord background, they also tended to argue that propertied people "represented" the respectable classes of the emerging nation. The earliest pressure groups to arise in colonial India were bodies such as the British India Association, a body of liberal landlords with connections among Calcutta lawyers. Before 1914, little was heard in the Indian National Congress about land reform. In the same way, Egyptian nationalist spokesmen worked together with big landlords and village notables in the anti-colonial movements of the 1880s and 1890s.

There was another side to the adjustment between liberal political theories about the nature of land rights and the practice of governing agrarian societies. The idea that property was the basis of civil government applied only to forms of property which seemed to nineteenth-century rulers to be subject to proof and also "useful" to the idea of improvement. Nomads, herdsmen, hunter-gatherers, or even peasants who moved around frequently or indulged in practices such as "slash and burn" cultivation were a nuisance to colonial states and other emerging political authorities which wanted regular taxation. Here, the exclusionary dimension of liberal political theory could be invoked as legitimation for the suppression or expropriation of "difficult" people of this sort. The idea of "no-one's land," or *terra nullius*, had emerged in Protestant battles with Catholic opponents who claimed that the pope had awarded them lands across the globe. Later, however, it informed intellectuals and administrators who believed that native peoples in various parts of the world had no notion of property, or did not deserve property even if they believed it was theirs, because they managed it badly. Australian settlers used this intellectual weapon against Aborigines, Americans against Amerindians, and Russian settlers against the hunter-gatherers and fishing peoples of Siberia. It merged with what became a common understanding of history in the early nineteenth century: that human development went through "stages," and that without property or settled cultivation, human populations were scarcely human at all.

This was another case in which liberal political theory tended to reinforce older ideas and give them a new, lawyerly and intellectual stamp of approval. God, it had once been said, gave land to "chosen peoples." At the beginning of the century, the Boers in southern Africa and American settlers justified their colonizing treks with this idea. At the end of the century, Zionists were elaborating it to legitimate settlement in the Holy Land. Spokesmen for colonization shifted easily between this sort of archaic ideology and the ideas of English lawyers and Scottish economists, which gave them a new theoretical basis. Even non-European rulers employed their own versions of the language of "barbarism" in their bids to secure land from native peoples who used nature in ways of which they did not approve, as chapter 12 suggests.

FREE TRADE OR NATIONAL POLITICAL ECONOMY?

Free trade was another key doctrine of nineteenth-century liberals, and it raised similar dilemmas. Once again Adam Smith and the French *philosophes* of the eighteenth century, notably Condorcet and François Quesnay, had provided the theoretical basis for the assault on all sorts of trade monopolies and protectionism. The basic economic doctrine insisted that free trade made it possible for producers and consumers to specialize in doing what they were best at, so increasing the total volume of both production and trade. This would ultimately ensure the best possible distribution and use of resources, and the liberation of humankind from corrupting economic and moral "dependency." These ideas struck at the roots of earlier systems of protection, such as the British Navigation Acts, which assumed that there was only a finite volume of real wealth in the world and that governments ought, therefore, to ensure that their citizens had the largest share of it. As with the objection to landlordism, however, the Enlightenment thinkers also objected to the moral depravity which seemed to accompany the activities of monopoly companies and trades. Later generations of economists jettisoned much of the complex ethical and political argumentation with which the Smith generation hedged around "free trade." This held that it was sometimes just and moral for governments to intervene in land or labor markets. It was, however, this brutal "Smithianism," rather than Adam Smith's views, which often found its way into the manuals of practice of governments, particularly in the British Empire.[35]

→ Free trade and its wider application, laissez-faire, understood as a desire to "keep government out of the economy," spread from Britain to much of continental Europe, the southern USA, and Central and South America in the course of the mid-nineteenth century. It is important not to date its victory too early. The words "free trade" may sometimes have been uttered by politicians and theorists of the European empires and continental European states before 1830. But the dominant philosophy remained the idea of royal monopoly. This was the more so because, for Smith himself, free trade was the best "default position." Even in theory, war and national interest might justify the continuation of some monopolies. Increasingly after 1830, however, states and empires, European and non-European, which tried to maintain protectionism came under pressure. As chapter 4 showed, the British applied these policies with force to the Chinese, the Ottomans, and the governments of Latin America. The European chartered company, a state-guaranteed monopoly, went out of favor rapidly after 1780. Not only were these old monoliths thought to threaten liberty and suppress commercial endeavor at home, they had also proved themselves venal and despotic abroad. In 1773 Americans threw the tea of the East India Company into Boston harbor. Thereafter successive British administrations sentenced the company to death by a thousand cuts.

While the assault on domestic monopolies was broadly popular, the other side of the coin, which demanded free entry into other peoples' markets, provoked massive opposition from those under assault. The theoretical and political reaction to free trade was not long in coming. As early as the 1830s, the German economist Friedrich List had begun to argue against uncontrolled free trade. Its proponents, he implied, had forgotten that, as a global phenomenon, free trade would inevitably damage the economies and livelihoods of numerous national systems of political economy. It was all very well for the British, whose eighteenth-century commercial efficiency was increasingly supported by the great savings created by industrial production. But in a country like Prussia or Piedmont, free trade would only wipe out local manufacturers and squander existing national resources.

That argument was patchily taken up in Latin America, southern Europe, and throughout the non-European world. Statesmen and theorists in these societies instinctively knew that protection was an essential tool for the maintenance and enhancement of the life and property of subjects. Chinese and Indian literati could draw on ancient treatises of political economy which urged magistrates to seal grain warehouses and prohibit exports in time of famine, practices vigorously opposed by the eager political economists among colonial officials and consular representatives. So, in many societies, a kind of economic nationalism actually predated the birth of organized nationalist agitation against European rule and penetration. For example, there was a clear line of thought linking the principles of the state corporation, the Cohong, which had controlled China's external trade in the eighteenth century, and the attempts by magistrates in coastal China in the 1860s and 1870s to exclude European traders and products – particularly, of course, opium. Equally, the insistence of Mughal statesmen that kings and nobles should consume the produce of their territories, in order to provide for the livelihoods of their peoples, gave a traditional and emotional charge to the demands of early nationalists for protection from British or other European imports. Indian economic nationalists were able to draw from these sources in order to propagate these views among ordinary people. They also made increasing use of List and Mill, because political ideologies had to be seen to be "modern." The ideas of Mill on liberty, including economic liberty, were always hedged around with the proviso that our liberty must be called into question when it impinges on the liberty of others.

Implicitly, this left room for a more plural approach to the question of the proper form of government, and placed some restrictions on the vigorous pursuit of a free market. Mill may himself have stated that non-European peoples needed European government to bring them to enlightenment. But his more abstract musings in *On Liberty* and *Representative Government* also provided arguments which colonial intellectuals could deploy against this idea. In Indochina during the 1890s, Gilbert Thieu adapted protectionist ideas from List and his followers, ostensibly to argue against Chinese economic dominance in his homeland, but in fact to challenge the French colonial free-trade system.[36]

By the 1870s and 1880s, therefore, liberal and left thought throughout the world was fiercely divided on the issue of state regulation of trade and the economy. Even in the home of free trade, Britain, powerful protectionist lobbies were developing on both sides of the political spectrum by this time. For the development of the global economy, especially after mid-century, had exposed British producers themselves to the stiff winds of competition from other newly industrialized countries or countries where labor costs were lower. Though their arguments were not taken up seriously until the twentieth century, some liberals and conservatives began to argue for a tariff regime that would protect the whole British Empire against foreign economic competition.

REPRESENTING THE PEOPLES

If the liberal wave fragmented on issues of political economy, the idea of the representation of the people and individual political rights, which lay at its heart, also introduced great tensions into political theory and practice. The arguments of Locke's *Two Treatises on Government* for the ultimate sovereignty of the people were intended to demolish the arguments of earlier theorists who had perfected the idea of the divine right of kings. His aim was to lay to rest the philosophical disagreements which had set factions in the British church and state against each other in between 1640 and 1715. The notion of popular sovereignty matched the idea that the common law of England was accessible to all free men. Yet Locke and the other pragmatic philosophers of eighteenth-century England were much less radical when it came to the form of that representation. Most seem to have accepted a narrow franchise and the need to discipline the excesses of "democracy" with a concept of representation of major interests, especially landed interests, in the body politic. The long career of the unreformed British Parliament and its tiny electorate, which remained minuscule until it was expanded significantly in 1867, was a consequence not only of vested interests, but also of philosophical doubts. Popular sovereignty did not mean popular government. Indeed, the experience of the

French Revolution, eloquently denounced by Edmund Burke, turned opinion against a rapid extension of the franchise. Liberal and conservative thinkers differed not in their degree of fear of uncontrolled democracy, but simply in the degree to which they were prepared to allow popular representation at all.

The problem was more acute in parts of the world which had felt the pains of the French and American revolutions directly. Eighteenth-century French theorists had also articulated a theory of popular sovereignty. Yet, during the revolution, the electoral process had been usurped by the Jacobin state and used to harass enemies and destroy them and their property. The idea of the popular will was deeply suspect to liberals such as Alexis de Tocqueville, who, though admirers of American representative government, believed that class and religious divisions in Europe made full popular enfranchisement difficult to achieve in the short term.[37] The problem would not go away. During the revolutions in France and across the rest of Europe in 1789–93, 1830, and 1848–52, ideologues and radical politicians argued incessantly for popular sovereignty to be matched with a full adult male franchise. In the German states and in the USA, one further wholly disenfranchised section of the population began to make its voice heard. Women, too, attempted to seize for themselves a much more public political role, especially in the shadow of the 1848 revolutions.

The great statesmen of emerging European nationalisms, such as Cavour and Bismarck, were very cool to an idea which they believed would aid their socialist or Roman Catholic clerical opponents. Yet here again, the very late development of the adult male franchise, let alone women's suffrage, across Europe also reflected philosophical doubts amongst the political leaderships. Moderate liberals believed that a stake in property or commerce was an essential qualification for exercising political judgment. On this view, people had to be economically independent in order to exercise independent judgment. They had to hold property or real wealth in their own hands. In Britain, proposals to create universal male suffrage were delayed until 1884 by the specter of Louis Napoleon's "dictatorship" in France, which had conceded universal male suffrage by 1848. Even where relatively full franchises had been created by the 1890s, powerful checking and balancing mechanisms were put into place. In Britain, again, the House of Lords, which represented mainly the landed interest, retained a veto over legislation until 1911.[38] Arguably, this was no mere constitutional anomaly, but a reflection of the elite's widespread and continuing belief in hierarchy and the collegiate nature of the body politic. In Germany, the complex constitutional structure gave considerable influence to the princes and to state bureaucracy, limiting the role of the relatively broad electorate. Here the Enlightenment idea, enunciated by Hegel and demonstrated by the historian Leopold von Ranke, that the state stood above society, adjudicating its conflicts, existed in unresolved tension with the concept of individual political rights.[39] At the other end of the spectrum, the conservatism of the Russian bureaucracy, even after the revolution of 1905, was reinforced by the fear that anything approaching mass democracy would result in social revolution.

The USA, the Netherlands, Scandinavia, and some British dominions were the only societies to achieve adult male suffrage relatively painlessly in the course of the nineteenth century. In the USA, broad electorates for freemen in the colonial period laid the basis for a fairly widespread move toward adult male suffrage by the 1810s and 1820s. This, however, should be seen as in many ways a conservative tactic, in full accord with the ideas of civic republicanism which were discussed earlier. An adult male franchise was a check on arbitrary government, though it was not explicitly mentioned in the constitution. Yet the danger of tyrannical democracy was to be avoided by the delicate system of checks and balances which the constitution had put in place. It was obvious, too, that this was full enfranchisement only for Americans of European extraction. During the Civil War, northern aspirations were concentrated on the abolition of slavery itself, rather than on attempts to improve the civil status of blacks. Even as late as the 1890s and 1900s, southern state legislatures representing white propertied interests succesfully blocked the implementation of an adult male franchise for millions of former slaves. The same type of argument was used for the "negro's" incapacity for rational decision making as was used against the industrial working class, field-workers, and women in mid-nineteenth-century Britain.

While the forces of conservatism remained strong, the conflict within liberalism between the ideals of universal rights and the idea of "moral independence" limited its capacity to effect real political change. This became particularly clear when it came to non-white populations. In the colonial world, the authorities had created a few, limited local councils. Yet even advanced liberals, headed by John Stuart Mill himself, broadly denied the capacity of Indians, Chinese, or Africans to rule themselves, on the grounds that their domestic life was defective, and that centuries of oriental despotism had inured them to autocratic rule. This was a view they inherited from eighteenth-century writers. Native self-rule could only follow on from native enlightenment over the longest possible term. The most radical European reformers, such as Allan Octavian Hume, founder of the Indian National Congress, resorted to the fiction that Indians were fit for self-rule because they were "Aryans," honorary whites, in a sense. Where the British introduced tiny non-European electorates, as in India and Egypt, and the Caribbean after 1883, these were seen as adjuncts to the mechanisms of taxation, or sops to rising nationalist opinion, rather than as schools for self-government. The New Zealand measures after 1867, which gave seats in Parliament and, later, voting rights to some Maori, seem to be a partial exception here. Yet these Maori were seen as a civilizing agency for their less tractable brothers.[40] In general, a rigid system of representation of native interests was preserved, and only the propertied or aristocratic classes were allowed to exercise the very limited powers conceded. Religious categories were also built into the electorate in several British and French colonial territories to ensure the representation of different interests, causing indigenous politicians to complain of policies of "divide and rule."

In French-ruled territories, a few coastal African settlements and Caribbean peoples had been enfranchised as French citizens during the revolutionary period. Little attempt was made to extend this privilege to the mass of the indigenous population of Indochina or Africa as they came under colonial control after 1870. The idea that people had to achieve a level of "civilization," in this case French civilization, was used to scotch any idea of the universal right to political representation until well into the twentieth century. French colonial settlers saw to it that the barriers to French citizenship for non-white people were very high indeed.

At the same time, the reception of ideas of popular sovereignty in the non-Western world during the nineteenth century was highly ambivalent. Most African, Asian, and Pacific societies possessed traditions of advisory councils which presented the "sense of the people" to the rulers or bureaucracy. These indigenous intellectuals were as wary of popular representation through individual votes as their European contemporaries. Nakae Chomin, for instance, was the nearest Japan ever came to a full-blooded liberal, and he hated the authoritarian features of the Meiji constitution. Yet, when he came to argue for a popular, elected assembly in 1887, he mixed Rousseau with Confucius and veneration of the emperor, stating through the mouth of a character in a parable: "I would simply establish constitutionalism, reinforce the dignity and glory of the Emperor and increase the happiness and peace of all the people below."[41] In themselves, individual "rights" could never be enough to ensure right government in Japan, he surmised. The emperor and his ministers would have to remain the ultimate arbiters of the fate of the Japanese people. Kang Youwei in China urged a similar case during the "hundred days" reform movement of 1898.[42]

In Islam, the whole body of believers acted, technically, as a consultative and arbitrational body of last resort (the *shura*). Yet, as in the older European traditions, great weight was given to certain types and conditions of people. This, too, tended to work against the idea of electoral majoritarianism. Clerics among Muslims, like Brahmin priests and monks among Hindus and Buddhists and gentry-people in China, were all held to have a consultative weight which far exceeded that of the ordinary male subject, in that they embodied the virtue of ancient constitutions. If the fount of justice was the sultan himself, many thinkers were uneasy with any institution which compromised his God-given duty. In the Ottoman world, the Bey of Tunis introduced a constitution and an advisory council in 1861, but it was speedily revoked. Ottoman "parliaments" waxed and waned throughout the latter part of the century. But they were regarded with suspicion by conservative intellectuals and many ordinary people, as nests of privilege compromising good government. Ottoman subjects officially became "citizens" in 1869. In practice, they remained dependent on the sultan's servants.

Indeed, most Middle Eastern and Asian liberals were themselves very cautious reformers.[43] While the first generation of nationalist politicians in the 1870s and 1880s may have called for broad electorates and representative politics under the influence of Mill, Paine, and Voltaire, many influential people shied away from the consequences. Copts, Middle Eastern Christians, and Indian Muslims feared the domination of Middle Eastern Muslims and

Hindus. In India, Muslim leaders such as Sir Sayyid Ahmad Khan provided ammunition for complacent colonial officials by arguing that Muslims would inevitably be disadvantaged by any extension of the franchise in local government to the wider population, as this would create an inbuilt Hindu majority. Those of low caste and low class were refused all standing because they were thought almost literally to embody depravity.

Women were excluded from political competence almost universally. While this is usually seen as the result of immovable male prejudice, it is also the case that political principles were thought to be involved. Women, by virtue of their social role, were not capable of independent judgment. British reformers in 1867 balked at a female franchise, mainly because it might create political divisions within families between husbands and wives, as Jane Rendall showed.[44] By contrast, it is revealing that some of the earliest women's franchises were adopted in European frontier territories. The American state of Wyoming adopted one in 1869, Utah in 1870, New Zealand in 1893, and South Australia in 1894. It was not predominantly classical liberal theories of individual rights, but the notion that women might be able to "govern" semi-civilized men for the benefit of the family that appears to have tipped the balance in these borderlands.[45] Elsewhere, the notion of female rights and duties was often espoused by male nationalists. But these activists were still quite unwilling to make any concession to women as individuals. The position of Muslim reformers illustrated this very well. In Egypt, Qasim Amin wrote of "the emancipation of women" and said that Muslim treatment of women violated Islamic beliefs. He was vigorously attacked.[46] The reformer Rashid Rida wrote "A Call to the Fair Sex," in which he claimed that women were better treated in Islam than in Western societies and had unspecified political rights. But when a woman in one of his audiences said that women should be able to mix with men on a freer basis, Rashid Rida denounced her as an apostate.[47] These reformers were mainly concerned with the rights of subject populations and of nations, not those of individuals.

For much of the nineteenth century, therefore, the theoretical principles of liberalism had only a limited purchase on the practice of politics, except in the realm of middle-class property relations. After the failures of 1848–51, many intellectuals turned to pessimistic philosophies of rejection of the social order, violence, or nihilism.[48] Liberalism's practical victories were limited, too. Most governments moved to enhance order by removing at least some of the abuses on the land, though huge dependent peasantries survived in eastern Europe and the colonial world. Outside the United States and western Europe, the electorate remained very small everywhere until 1914. Even in Germany, constitutional provisions were used to negate popular power. Yet, while examples such as these indicate that the more radical principles of liberalism were intrinsically and externally limited, it does not mean that it was wholly stillborn as a creed. Liberalism and the notion of individual rights undoubtedly influenced the aspirations and vision of the future held by millions of people. The goal of an imagined liberal society was a more powerful social force than the practice of liberalism.

SECULARISM AND POSITIVISM: TRANSNATIONAL AFFINITIES

Underpinning ideas about orderly government, representation, and the creation of wealth, the nineteenth century saw a much more general shift in the ideals and beliefs of ruling groups throughout the world. One important development, as noted earlier, was the rise of philosophical belief systems which were anti-religious, or at least highly skeptical of the existence of God, or gods, with which humans could communicate in any way at all. Religions, in the broadest sense, remained strong and even expanded their influence during the period. This was no age of non-belief, as will be seen in chapter 9. Yet large areas of thought were increasingly insulated from the direct influence of older beliefs about salvation and the purpose of creation. Religious postulates were themselves increasingly subject to the test of empirical verification and historical proof. The French and Scottish philosophers of the eighteenth century had already prefigured an age of reason, from which superstition was banished. In the great Asian and African societies, traditions of learning had developed which also stressed empirical verification and observation, especially in fields such as astronomy and agriculture. This process went much further in the nineteenth century, as more ordered forms of useful knowledge became, ultimately, "science." The old "productive harmony" between religion and knowledge began to decline.

In the course of the nineteenth century, these more ordered constructs of empirical thought were mainly generated in the great centers of European and American learning. From here they were spread throughout the Western world by journals and learned societies, but simultaneously they were diffused to the wider world through colonial expansion and new media of communication. In the course of this diffusion and reception, the meaning and social significance of concepts such as science, reason, and empirical verification were greatly modified, often blending with preexisting ideas in still-vigorous indigenous systems of thought. These modern concepts often came to carry unintended new meanings for people, whether within or outside Europe and North America.

One of the best examples of this process concerns the ideas of the French thinker Auguste Comte (1798–1857), who developed the philosophical theory of positivism.[49] According to Comte, human thought passed through an early theological period dominated by religion to a period when deep metaphysical speculation was the vogue. Following this, mankind would pass into an age of positive thought, freed from speculation and dominated by scientific and historical verification of known fact. Positivism therefore provided a theory of knowledge, a philosophy of history stressing the idea of progress, and a methodology of science. By the 1840s, many important thinkers throughout Europe had absorbed some positivist ideas. Positivism also provided a convenient philosophical gloss for the new human sciences of social statistics, sociology, and anthropology. It contributed to the tendency to see human history not as a religious or ethical journey to salvation, but as a complex of impersonal forces. This trend was taken up in the sociology of another important French thinker later in the century, Emile Durkheim. Durkheim famously argued that the phenomenon of suicide represented not the result of individual moral or ethical failings, but was a consequence of the rootlessness created by urban industrial society. When a society worshipped God, it was worshipping itself – that is, religion was "functional" to the workings of society and had no meaning outside it. Later, Marxism presented a parallel evolution to Comte's positivism, again stressing the role of impersonal forces in history and society.

Yet the direction of the positivistic enterprise also underwent a series of radical transformations as it spread across the world. As far as its dedicated supporters in France were concerned, it was already in the 1850s becoming a "religion of humanity," complete with quasi-divine services, calendrical ceremonies, obeisances to the Supreme Being, and rules for moral conduct. Positivism in France, in fact, began to replicate the forms of French Roman Catholic belief, while in Britain it looked more and more like an austere Protestant sect, partly approved by such worthies as J. S. Mill. Outside Europe, positivism was overtaken by an even more ironic fate. In India, it proved a serviceable set of values for those Hindus who objected to the old priestly hierarchy but wished to see India's supposedly ancient caste order preserved. Initiates did not lose caste or marriage connections, as they did when making the more radical social break to Christianity or the hybrid Hindu Unitarianism of the Brahmo Samaj (Society of the Supreme Being). In a ceremony which would have startled and perhaps disappointed Comte, initiates took his works down to the sacred river Ganges and read texts to devotees on its banks as the old priesthood did with the sacred Sanskrit texts.[50]

In Russia, by contrast, positivism was taken up as a weapon against "feudalism" and tsarist autocracy, losing much of its philosophical underpinning and becoming a "counter-culture" religion. In Japan, the intellectual Nishi Amane (1829–97) used positivism in a campaign against the Tokugawa regime, which he described as a type of feudalism and therefore bound to succumb to the coming age of reason. In Mexico and Brazil, similarly, Comte's ideas were deployed against great landholders and the Church. One disciple wrote of his influence: "We have wrested the sceptre from the Spanish monarch, but not from the Spanish spirit." Comte was to help break the chains of that old thinking. Ironically, it was the notion of scientific and technical modernization which was the cherry that Latin American leaders picked from Comte's basket. Several of them went on to become, or support, modernizing military autocrats in the later nineteenth century.[51]

THE RECEPTION OF SOCIALISM AND ITS LOCAL RESONANCES

Positivism was a product that found a small niche in the intellectual market only among dedicated intellectuals and other odd characters. Socialism was a different matter. Marxian socialism regarded itself as scientific. That is to say, Marxists believed that history was ruled by unchangeable laws. These could be ascertained by empirical observation, and their outcomes were predictable. This was an analogy made by many of the early socialists themselves, especially as Marx's theories became common currency after the publication of *Das Kapital* in 1867. One contemporary wrote that Marx "gave science the same importance as Darwin's theory, and just as the latter dominates the natural sciences, so Marx's theories dominate the social and economic sciences."[52]

There is some truth in this analogy. In both social and scientific thought, the early part of the nineteenth century saw great accumulations of ordered data. Throughout the world, governments collected data about the condition of the peasantry and the urban poor. Early statisticians speculated about disease and nutrition. Thomas Malthus came close to positing a purely materialistic theory of the growth and death of human populations, but most nineteenth-century social theories retained semi-religious notions about grace and corruption in them. Both Darwin and Marx were important, in that they attempted to develop iron laws of development independent at all levels of the workings of providence. In the one case, the most adaptable species survived; in the other, the actual producers of wealth would ultimately capture political power.

Socialism, however, was a vague and heterogeneous concept in the nineteenth-century world. Its enemies and its proponents both had an interest in exaggerating its influence and its unity. Much of the thought commonly designated "socialist" at the time was millenarian rather than scientific in form. It drew on the great tradition of apocalyptic visionary thought which dwelt at the margins of the imaginings of the good society which were discussed at the beginning of this chapter. Unlike later left-wingers, many of the first generation of socialist thinkers were Christians, seeing in Christ the original communitarian, sharing philosopher. The strength and vitality of these earlier traditions in different societies go a long way to explain why and where more "orthodox" socialist and Communist ideologies became rooted amongst intellectuals and the general populace. This development was not welcomed by Communist ideologues. Marx and his more rigorous followers had come to see religious belief as a force which dulled the worker's sense of his own deprivation and alienation; it thus detracted from true "class consciousness." Equally, millenarian visions of the coming of a just society were dangerous to Marxists, because they ignored the iron laws of history and seemed to suggest that revolution could come before the appropriate material conditions for it were in place.

Socialist thought, however, rapidly developed in a series of subcenters, each with its different intellectual culture. France, home of the first modern revolutions, nurtured an insurrectionist form of socialism. This was apparent in the idealistic extremes of Jacobinism, and later in the visionary ideologies of some of the leaders of the Paris Commune. The insurrectionist tradition was particularly associated with Auguste Blanqui, who believed in the efficacy of revolutionary putsches and the immediate redistribution of property to the poor.[53] The views of Blanqui and his followers were in many ways closer to those of the anarchists of the late nineteenth century, such as the Russian Mikhail Bakunin, than they were to the scientific socialists of Germany. Both groups of theorists tended to believe that the state would disappear once a benign rule of property had been established. Such opinions seemed appropriate in early-nineteenth-century France and Russia, where labor laws were particularly hostile to working-class associations. They also drew on local traditions of romanticism and religion. Marx himself had not altogether ruled out conspiracy and *coups d'état*. Yet the emphasis in his later works lay much more on the autonomous development of class struggle. The ideas of Henri de Saint-Simon represented another dimension of this French millenarian envisioning of society. Saint-Simonians expected to achieve progress as a result of the enlightened rule of philosopher-kings, who would put in place an international rule of reason and humanity and abolish the corruptions of inequality.[54] In effect, they awaited a heaven on earth without the Christian God. Marx's language and patterns of German Communist organization certainly influenced the French left wing. Generally speaking, though, neither Marxism nor constitutional socialism working through trade unions had much purchase in France before the 1920s.

Formal socialist parties were slow to develop in Britain and the British dominions, for similar reasons. Here, however, it was the old tradition of Nonconformist and community-based religiosity which blocked Marxism, rather than the idealizing of insurrection. Thinkers and activists on the left of British politics before the 1890s tended to look back to an idealized era of guild-like work and labor, in which the artisan and the field-worker owned his tools and his plot of land. It is not surprising that romantic intellectuals, such as the art historian John Ruskin, were in the forefront of the movement to create labor leagues. British socialists idolized Cromwell and other seventeenth-century anti-monarchists. They also lauded the British radicals of the late eighteenth and early nineteenth centuries. Typically, the English managed to create a kind of "feudal socialism." An English edition of the first volume of Marx's *Capital* did not appear until 1887. If foreigners were read at all by ordinary members, they were most likely to be "patriots" such as Mazzini, Garibaldi, and the heroes of the 1871 Commune, not German socialists.[55] The British Labour Party itself, when it emerged after 1900, assimilated into its purportedly socialist agenda many of the ideas of Christian good works. It inherited the dislike of the high-spending state which had been strong in British radical movements as early as the seventeenth century. It was to be a radical extension of the Liberal Party, rather than a new political force standing outside the British tradition.

None of this was very surprising in light of the origins of Marx's own thought. Even in Germany, what was to become the Marxist-Leninist phalanx emerged from a local intellectual background in which people envisioned an ideal future of reason and benevolence.[56] Initially, this too had more in common with contemporary Christian Pietist revivalism than it did with empirical scientific theory. As late as 1843, Marx himself was writing that his aim was the "reform of consciousness," and the idea of the alienation of the worker from his person and the withering away of the state represented latent millenarian traces in his doctrines. By locating this revolutionary "consciousness" in the proletariat, and insisting that social and economic change had to precede a more general moral change, Marx began the process of making Hegel's idea of the onward march of the idea of reason and emancipation through history an economic science.

The 1848 revolutions led to neither the dominance of the bourgeoisie nor the rapid transition to the dictatorship of the proletariat which Marx had prophesied. Instead, the scientific legitimacy which Marx had given to a future without the state and without private property proved to hold a lasting appeal for the political wings of the organized working-class movements which emerged in central European cities after 1860. Radicals might plan the imminent collapse of the "bourgeois" state. But trade union leaders in the united Germany, Belgium, parts of northern Italy, and even belatedly in Britain could plan to achieve more pragmatic advances in workers' rights while using the rhetoric of scientific socialism to give weight to their cause. Despite the irredeemable factionalism of Communist and socialist parties, leagues, and conventions, the specter of an international labor movement did much to frighten governments and landowners into making small concessions.

Outside its central European heartland, the situation was similar. The reception of the wider doctrines of socialism also remained dependent on various preexisting patterns of belief in the possibility of a better life among intellectuals and ordinary people. In Russia, the socialists who made the running in the 1905 revolution appealed as much to traditional notions of peasant community as they did to the modern factory proletariat. Russian socialism even displayed some affinities with the thought of the Old Believers. This was an Orthodox Christian sect which had never really come to terms with the modernizing ideologies gripping Westernized Russian intellectuals since the time of Peter the Great. The biggest socialist party in Russia was, in any case, the non-Marxist Social Revolutionaries, who owed allegiance to an older romantic tradition of dissidence among intellectuals. In India and China, where socialism achieved little visibility at all before 1914, it was also annexed to the ideology of community values and opposition to the market. In rapidly industrializing Japan, again, the type of socialism which appealed to intellectuals stressed the moral and ethical distortions in a society where the laboring poor seemed to be growing in numbers. Japanese socialist rhetoric was not easy to distinguish from that of the "agrarianist" critics of modern change who harked back to the ideal village, with its communal patterns of labor in the rice fields.[57]

In China, too, the young radicals who began to espouse Marxism in the dismal 1890s fell back on the traditional denunciations of corruption and the oppression of the poor which had echoed in the Taiping and Boxer rebellions. They thought that what they believed to be the growing "power of the rich", people outside the quasi-Confucian moral community, could be halted by strikes, as had apparently been the case in the tsarist autocracy.[58] Here, as in Italy or in revolutionary Mexico, agrarianism, socialism, and populist conservatism developed in the same breeding grounds as what was later to be called "fascism." In China, though, new political ideas were also subtly adapted to prevailing doctrines. Hu Hanmin, an early collaborator of Sun Yatsen, wrote of socialism in 1905:

> Not all collectivist theories may be applied to China in her present state of development. But in the case of land nationalisation we already have a model in the "Well-field" system of the Three Dynasties [a very early form of joint holding and irrigation of land] and it should not be difficult to practice something indigenous to our racial consciousness in this period of political change.[59]

There is no doubt that the leading ideas of liberalism, secularism, and socialism implied major intellectual ruptures with all past traditions. This was because the ideologues in these traditions deliberately sought new principles of political legitimation and consciously rejected all past authorities in a manner that was very rare in the early modern world. Up to about 1700, those seeking radical change argued that the ideal republic had been corrupted or that the king was receiving bad counsel. After this date, the claim was increasingly heard that the people alone, and in the present, could constitute all legitimacy anew. In their translation into the popular discourse of both European and non-European societies, however, these ideas also underwent a change. They were conjoined with, and drew strength from, older languages of political ethics and righteous popular outrage, in particular, millenarian Christian, Buddhist, and even Hindu ideas, which predicted the coming of a better life.

SCIENCE IN GLOBAL CONTEXT

An important aspect of many versions of liberalism, positivism, and communism was their belief that they were scientific. The link between nineteenth-century science and political thought has been rather obscured by the way in which historical study has been split into "intellectual history" and "the history of science" in the twentieth century. Comte and Marx both saw human society as an organism evolving through the application of developmental laws. This was an idea which appealed to the emerging discipline of anthropology, most of whose early theorists posited the organic evolution of races-cum-cultures. Herbert Spencer, the most influential liberal political theorist of the late nineteenth century, was an evolutionist before Darwin. He believed in the universality of "natural causation." Societies, like plants or fish, evolved from the simple to the more complex, as a result of natural selection. Unlike Comte, Marx, and Durkheim, however, Spencer in his later years was a radical individualist and a strong proponent of laissez-faire. Government intervention, he believed, undermined individual initiative, which was the wellspring of progress.[60] Despite these differences, science was as influential in the mind-set of the nineteenth century as religion had been during the Renaissance.

Science itself was perhaps the most radical of the new philosophies which purported to transform the globe. As with liberalism and positivism, science also reacted in complex ways to the varied intellectual traditions and lived circumstances of the thinkers who espoused it. Yet, during the nineteenth century, scientific and technological establishments became distinct social formations, as important in their way as classes, economies, and religions. There had, of course, been men of science in many cultures before the nineteenth century. In Europe, China, and the Islamic worlds, bodies of them had achieved remarkable honors and access to royal power. But it was only quite late in the nineteenth century that science became a body of knowledge substantially distinct from what became the humanities, law, and theology. By then, science had developed an internal intellectual coherence and a set of causative principles which were broadly accepted by large bodies of professional practitioners. Those practitioners could now directly influence the policies of governments in the realms of public health or military and environmental planning. Increasingly, colonial governments and ruling groups in the extra-European world also came to establish their legitimacy by appeals to scientific knowledge that reinforced more traditional claims to maintain justice and public tranquillity.

There were three broad stages in this construction of professions and systematic knowledge. The first saw the rapid accumulation of huge archives of data about natural phenomena, which could be classified into types and families, whether in the realm of geology, geography, medical statistics, or botany. The classic case was that of the Swedish biologist Carolus Linnaeus, who organized plants and animals into a huge scheme of living things. As Richard Drayton showed with reference to botany, this phase had its origins in the Renaissance and reached its apogee in the eighteenth century.[61] The second phase saw a search for the evolutionary principles and patterns of historical change which underlay these systems, whether these were in the spread of diseases, families of animals, or mankind itself. This phase was coterminous with the ideological shift which occurred during and after the French Revolution.[62] A further stage in the creation of historical laws for science occurred in the mid-nineteenth century. The publication of Charles Darwin's *Origin of Species* in 1859 remains a pivotal date in this shift of emphasis. Historians of science have set Darwin in the context of other evolutionists and have tried to cut him down to size in other ways. But those among them with scientific training still insist that it was the particular predictive power of Darwin's formulation which gave his work its lasting significance. Finally, at the end of our period, leading scientific thinkers were beginning to challenge and modify the naturalistic categories, essences, and developmental schemes which had been delineated in this second stage. Some scientists began to argue that uncertainty was a feature of natural processes.

The first stage, the massive accumulation and categorization of data about natural phenomena, had begun in the early modern period and speeded up in the eighteenth century. Observations of the heavens, the mapping of geological strata, the beginnings of archaeology in southern Italy and the Egyptian desert, the listing of the variety of species as a consequence of Pacific expeditions or journeys in search of the source of African rivers: all these developments reflected the inquisitive burrowings of Enlightenment scholars and travelers.[63] The systematic organization of data and creation of categories and connections were the work of a small number of great synthesizers during the global convulsions of 1790–1813. Goethe and Alexander von Humboldt, the German geographer and sociologist, for instance, stood at the center of a huge web of taxonomical speculation, creating analytical tools for subjects as widely separated today as geology, botany, and perceptual psychology. In the field of linguistic analysis, the East India Company judge William Jones and the later German Sanskrit scholar Franz Bopp (1791–1867) were similar great synthesizers. They sought to describe the elements that made up historical languages, to class them into groups, and then perceive connections between them. Explorers to Africa and Asia, such as Mungo Park, who "discovered" the source of the Niger, and William Moorcroft, who crossed the Himalayas into central Asia, transformed the data on which geography was to be formed. The Pacific was drawn into the context of Asia by linguists and early anthropologists.[64] Governments had come to believe that they had a role in discovering new facts and felt that they would gain both honor and resources from doing so.

Outside Europe, these great collections were often built on data supplied by indigenous intellectuals and administrators. Asian and African rulers and intellectuals had also built up huge archives of data as the powers of governance and world trade expanded across the world after 1500. European medical advances drew on the pharmacopoeia and herb collections of Chinese and Indian specialists, and the embodied knowledge of African and Native American healers. Indian Brahmin grammarians provided the great word treasuries out of which European theorists of language began to derive their historical genealogies. Expeditions within Africa, represented to Europeans as "discoveries," were guided, fed, and supported by local people with deep knowledge of the ways of animals and the lay of camping grounds. Pacific peoples and Canadian Inuit contributed their skills in animal tracking and their knowledge of the currents of the waterways. In many cases, European and American explorers merely expropriated their knowledge and then used it to deprive them of their lands, fish, and animals.

This flood of natural-historical description was driven by men perceived as heroes of science, giants of the romantic world, of whom Goethe was the most famous. Their findings were sometimes suffused with more ancient ideas that all being was organized in a great chain from the highest to the lowest. Governments, however, soon became involved and were very active after about 1760.[65] The culmination of this enterprise was the scientific expedition of scholars from the French Academy whom Napoleon sent to Egypt in 1798 to collect the relics of ancient Egyptian civilizations and chart the Egyptian world. This was the largest government "research project" to date. In Britain from the 1780s to the 1820s, Sir Joseph Banks organized and collated, through the Royal Society of London, a web of observers and explorers drawn from the medical doctors of the Royal Navy and the East India Company, which also took the form of a national science project. Military and naval surgeons were mines of information. However, the state and the political establishment by no means had a monopoly of scientific data collection or knowledge creation. Radical politicians and anti-hierarchical evangelical movements contributed signally to the growth of scientific knowledge. They also built it up into usable bodies of theory which supported their wider ideological aims. In the Pacific, missionaries, with their own teams of native informants, acted as invaluable observers of human and natural forms. They used their findings to proclaim the inexhaustible nature of God's bounty and the imminence of salvation. Likewise, science not only validated the establishment, it was also drawn upon by its opponents. "Scientific" theories such as phrenology,[66] positivism, and the liberationist ideas of Saint-Simon were invoked to validate political radicalism in Britain and on the European continent, especially during the political eruptions of the 1840s.

By the 1840s, when the railway, the telegraph, and the steamship had hugely improved the global exchange of information, fixed scientific bureaucracies were coming into being. Professional scientists and scientific departments of government became increasingly prominent. Descriptions of natural products and manufactures were being made for all parts of the world. Sir Roderick Murchison, imperial explorer and geological engineer, had pioneered dozens of expeditions and fact-finding missions in Canada, Africa, and South America. He was invited to Russia by the imperial authorities to work with Russian scientists in the search for coal and iron ore in the newly absorbed territories of Asiatic Russia. Kew Gardens in London, the Prussian Botanical Gardens, and their equivalent in Paris stood at the center of a series of comprehensive surveys of living things made by a growing army of professionals. Military mining schools had often made the most important findings in chemistry, physics, and geology, but now universities, first the newer and more dynamic centers such as Edinburgh and Hamburg, later Paris, Oxford, and Bologna, began to teach the new natural history. By the latter half of the century, large industrial companies had begun to establish their own research departments, especially in Germany and the United States. Science became more than simply an accumulation of ordered information. It became an engine of human perfectibility, a force of history. This was to change humankind's material conditions and even its spirit. Governments called on science to legitimate themselves as often as they called on God.

Yet, at this point a series of intellectual shocks began to transform what had been rather static, genealogical sciences into disciplines that not only assigned to nature principles of development but also placed humankind itself firmly in the field of science. The science of political economy, evolving since the seventeenth century, had already begun to posit laws governing human activity. Now the immemorial action of nature's laws began to become clear. Darwin's austere theory of natural selection through survival of the fittest was the first of these shocks. It was adapted to, and provided a principle of change for, many fields, from anthropology to natural religion. Above all, it asserted historical development, rather than providential intervention, as the cause of all change. Darwin remarked:

When I view all beings not as special creations, but as the lineal descendants of some few beings which lived long before the first bed of the Silurian system was deposited, they seem to me to be ennobled .... Hence we may look forward with some confidence to a secure future of equally unappreciable length.[67]

Darwin entered the popular consciousness in Britain and throughout the world because of the public controversies his work generated. His theories were vigorously assaulted by churchmen and theologians, who believed they would undermine the biblical and moral account of creation. But not all churchmen were as worried. Some believed that Darwinism might still be compatible with God's underlying plan for creation. In the longer term, though, the amoral nature of Darwinism proved quite difficult to square with an ethical understanding of the natural and human world. The later discovery of germs and the development of the study of life cycles of diseases provided the same kind of shock to the life sciences. By 1900, a theory of the expansion of the universe and of the making of the earth's crust had posited similar teleologies of development for cosmology and geology.

Darwin himself had a profound influence on the human sciences. Herbert Spencer adapted some of his theories to explain the development of human

ILLUSTRATION 8.2   Darwinism in dispute: Charles Darwin and an ape. Cartoon by unnamed artist, in *The London Sketch Book*, 1872.

societies through the "survival of the fittest." Spencer was taken up in turn by Chinese, Indian, and Arab intellectuals. These men feared for the organic health of their own societies, yet hoped that weak nations, like endangered species, might finally adapt and survive. Japan's *risorgimento* provided them with a glimmer of light.

Mid-twentieth-century accounts of the history of science married a history of the triumph of Western rationalism to the emergence of Western economic domination across the world. Historians believed that scientific thought began with the ancient Greeks and ascended through the European Renaissance to reach its apogee in the modern age, when it was diffused to the rest of the world through imperial universities. Some scholars still believe that the Greek, and hence Western, contribution was unique. The Greeks, it is said, developed the idea of "scientific egotism," of science as the act of individual will challenging hierarchies and traditional knowledge by the application of proofs. For these scholars, and for much of the scientific profession itself, Western "exceptionalism" is still a respectable idea. An early "European" lead in the organization of useful knowledge and theory seemed to have allowed the West massively to extend its advantages over the rest of the world in the course of the nineteenth century. Certainly, it was in the later nineteenth century, especially in German universities, that scientific knowledge finally became formalized into subjects distinct from metaphysics and religion, with its own rules of procedure. In the same way, sociology became a formal discipline, especially in France, and economics was developed as a class of knowledge separate from the study of moral sentiments, above all in Britain and the United States.

Yet this position was challenged, first by non-Western intellectuals and later by radical scholars across the world. Even in the nineteenth century, the spokesmen of extra-European movements for religious and political reform had begun to argue that Asian and African peoples had anticipated most of what became supposedly Western scientific knowledge. Indian religious reformers asserted that the Hindu scriptures contained references to artillery and mechanical engines, for instance, while Islamic modernizers pointed to the West's dependence on the ideas of the medieval Arab astronomers. The idea that science was a unique product of Western rationalism had already begun to rankle with European radicals caught up in the movements for decolonization in the early twentieth century. Joseph Needham, the leftist historian of Chinese science, who began writing on this subject in the 1930s, was one such.[68]

By the end of the twentieth century, the idea of Western scientific exceptionalism was under more corrosive attack. Adopting an extreme position, some historians and theorists argued that much of the Western scientific canon was itself merely a discourse of power, with no more capacity to predict physical events than Persian astrology or Zen Buddhism. Science was merely socially "constructed." Certainly, some of the self-styled scientific movements of the late nineteenth century – race theory, cranial and nose measurement, and even theosophy – fall into this category. Irrationalist movements in literature, philosophy, and the arts developed a huge head of steam as 1848 blighted hopes for an earthly paradise, and industrialization seemed to make the poor in Europe ever poorer.[69] Conversely, as chapter 2 observed, the great non-European societies had all developed forms of empirical observation and ways of categorizing useful knowledge well before European sciences influenced them. By this standard, even Needham was trapped in a diffusionist model of scientific advance. He simply reversed its polarities by arguing that scientific knowledge had passed from China to the West, in order to restore the energy and pride of Chinese science.

If we want to describe the emergence of scientific thought at a global level during the nineteenth century, the following propositions seem acceptable in the midst of this fraught and now rather politicized debate on the nature of scientific endeavor and the relationship between science and colonialism. Complex human societies everywhere had developed rational systems of thought and ways of applying technologies to production. The early expansion of industrialization and the creation of professions in Europe and North America, however, had given specialists there a substantial lead in the creation of general systems of scientific thought which legitimated themselves internally, rather than through recourse to theological or cultural arguments. Euro-American economic expansion also allowed physical, chemical, and biological discoveries to be applied to routine mass production more rapidly. When non-European societies began to experience rapid urbanization, state formation, and industrialization, they, too, rapidly found ways of borrowing from the Western centers, as well as adapting aspects of their own, older systems of useful knowledge and rational investigation to create indigenous scientific thought.

In some parts of the world, and in some areas of scientific endeavor, non-Westerners quickly narrowed the gap and established viable and intellectually independent research institutes. In the Ottoman Empire, for instance, Rifaa Tahtawi, who had been educated in France during the 1830s, wrote a geographical and social study of France in Arabic. Back in Egypt, he was instrumental in the founding of the School of Languages which translated more than 2,000 works, adapting them to an Arabic audience as they proceeded.[70] In China, the Kiagnan Arsenal did a similar job. Old-style literati and new nationalists both helped to spread knowledge of new scientific practices adapted to local uses. The political leader Sun Yatsen and his friend Che'n Chih, who had medical training, wrote about the use of fertilisers in a Chinese context, for instance.[71]

Medical science is an area of particular interest because it is so central to the well-being of people and the functioning of governments, armies, and industries. Japan's adoption of scientific thought is a good case with which to illustrate these points. Early modern Japanese society was, in the first place, notably receptive to ideas from abroad. Far into the past, Japanese rulers, nobles, and Buddhist sages had sent missions to China to investigate and report back changes in the thought and practice of the Chinese scholar-gentry. "Dutch" learning was absorbed equally eagerly through the Dutch East India Company's trading station at Nagasaki. As early as 1777, a translation was made of a Dutch anatomical treatise. The important point is that this Dutch medical lore was then validated by standards of empirical observation which reflected the methods used to validate texts and methodologies amongst contending groups of Confucian scholars. This "positivism which insisted that all hypotheses be validated"[72] made it much easier for Japanese to accept the Western scientific ideas which they observed during the many missions to the West dispatched by the Tokugawa and Meiji governments after 1854. It also provided a basis on which Western teachers and engineers could build when their numbers in Japan increased after the Meiji restoration of 1868.

Two other features of the Japanese case are important. First, Japanese society, like that of Korea and China, was well attuned to the rapid dissemination of useful knowledge by block printing. This had been the case even in the eighteenth century, when Edo boasted as many bookshops as London or Paris. New printing technologies were adapted with alacrity and spread new regimes of thought very fast indeed. That classic paean in praise of useful, practical knowledge, Samuel Smiles's *Self-Help*, sold about 250,000 copies in Britain and America in the later nineteenth century. The Japanese edition sold a million copies and was still being republished in 1920. Secondly, the very rapid development of professional bodies of scientists, engineers, and other experts in Japan seems to owe something to the transformation of loyalty to a "feudal" master, the *bushido* ethic, into a notion of professional service to the national public. Japanese patriots of the mid-nineteenth century were quite clearly ashamed that their scientific, technical, and medical knowledge was demonstrably inferior to that of the Western barbarians and moved vigorously to correct this. They were successful quite early. By the end of the nineteenth century, Japanese scientists were making original, world-class contributions to the sciences. Seismology, the science of earthquakes, for instance, was an area in which Japanese researchers such as Sekiya and Omori developed a new body of knowledge, working alongside American collaborators based in the country, for whom Japan seemed an ideal laboratory.[73]

The importance of local literati and existing systems of knowledge in the adoption of Western medical ideas in Japan and China is very clear. The resulting medical theories and practices often remained hybrid, reflecting their dual origin. Much the same was true of Indian and Arabic medical sciences, which also retained their influence and were even reinvented as a consequence of contact with Western medical thought and practices. The old Indian systems of ayurvedic medicine came under investigation. This was based particularly on the use of herbs and minerals, but was supported by routines of meditation, ritual purging, and prayer. This body of learning was the butt of increasingly violent denunciation by the British medical specialists and Indians of the East India Company's military medical services in the course of the early nineteenth century. Yet Western medicine was too uncertain in its results and sometimes failed in the face of cholera and bubonic plague, both scourges of the Indian Empire. The result was an emerging dual system of scientific endeavor. On the one hand, the Indian intelligentsia took up and adapted aspects of Western scientific knowledge with alacrity. The medical colleges at Calcutta and Madras proved successful and innovative. On the other hand, for many people, the revived traditional system of medicine was associated with bodily purity, being unpolluted by dubious Western substances.[74]

In time, the revival of indigenous medical lore and practice became associated with cultural and political revival. This also occurred in the case of the traditional Islamic-Greek systems of medicine amongst Indian Muslims and throughout the Muslim world. Modernizing rulers and colonial officials established medical services and medical professions, drawn increasingly from Western-educated local people. At the same time, unani and ayurvedic medical colleges were founded, drawing on the older Arabic or Sanskrit traditions. Parallel sets of licensed indigenous practitioners emerged. Medical knowledge drawn from Sanskrit or Islamic and ancient Greek sources was standardized and organized along the lines of Western medical knowledge. Standard forms of pills and remedies were introduced. They were advertised in vernacular newspapers and sold through recognized outlets in the bazaars. As with religious thought and practice, indigenous medicine survived and increased in scale, while at the same time bearing the imprint of its European models. Ordinary people were canny enough simply to seek help from anyone who offered any hope of cure or relief from pain and disease, often trying Western remedies and, when these failed, falling back on traditional forms. Such hybrid systems also began to appear in Africa, where traditional-style healers and cult leaders adapted some aspects of missionary teaching and of Western medical practice to protect and maintain the validity of their own forms of learning.

PROFESSIONALIZATION AT WORLD LEVEL

Examining this process, it becomes clear that, as in the case of nationalism and the state, the "diffusion model" cannot be employed without considerable modification. Indigenous intellectuals were building up bodies of theoretical and applied science across the nineteenth-century world at much the same time. Scientific and learned professions emerged rapidly in many societies, just as did professional administrators and commercial people with global interests. It is best to think in terms of professional scientists emerging in linked and global networks, rather than of diffusion of science from the "West" to the "East" and the "South." For a start, what was the "West"? It is important to remember that growth of a regular body of medical science and a system of professional practitioners was occurring in Asia, Africa, the Pacific, and South America at more or less the same rate as it was in Europe and North America. In eighteenth-century Europe, physicians, surgeons, and apothecaries operated as caste-like bodies of experts, much as the elite physicians of the Chinese, Indian, and Islamic worlds. Yet in all these locations, most healing activity was still down to cunning women, philanthropic local magnates, men of religion, or traveling experts in vaccination, bleeding, acupuncture, or herbal remedies. The European Enlightenment had certainly put a premium on rational knowledge and discounted sin or luxury as the origin of disease.

Asian, Islamic, and African systems also had their rational medical sciences and descriptions of disease. In all these societies, including European ones, magical and moral elements continued well into the nineteenth century. After all, in the late-nineteenth-century West, consumption, a disease of the lungs, was still associated with overactive sexuality and hysteria.

Thus professional and regulated medical knowledge and practice arose from the efforts of all these human communities to grapple with broader historical conditions. High medical science spread from Edinburgh to the more isolated parts of England at more or less the same pace as it spread from England to India and China and out into the hinterlands of Calcutta and Shanghai. Overseas travel and warfare were themselves forcing houses of medical and other scientific knowledge. The Edinburgh medical schools borrowed from Leiden. But Edinburgh and, later, Dublin were successful in turn because their graduates, English, Irish, and Scottish, could be assigned to posts in the army, the East India Company, and especially the navy, which were all grappling with the problems of overseas service, poor health, and poor morale. Some of the most important discoveries were consequently made on the colonial frontier and with the help of indigenous medicines and indigenous assistance. This had been true of the quinine developed to control fever by American Indians. It was true in the eighteenth century of the adaptation of inoculation methods of the Ottomans by European doctors. French medical practice was greatly improved by the experience of mass warfare in Russia and Egypt. Napoleon's military hospitals developed some of the first methodologies of surgical practice. Later in the century, the discovery of the malaria vector by Sir Ronald Ross was a clear response to the dangers of the tropical environment. He was signally helped by his Indian research workers, especially Muhammad Bux.[75]

In the later nineteenth century, this process of standardization and professionalization in medicine went ahead with even greater speed. By the 1850s, most European countries had legislation in place to control access to medical practice through academies or colleges. Local healers and unorthodox practices were spurned and ignored, even if many poor people still resorted to them. Systems of medical knowledge were now more and more likely to treat populations as a whole. The discovery of germ theory was undoubtedly a scientific breakthrough, however uneven and sometimes unsuccessful were the therapies based on it. It was acceptable to the new medical hierarchies, because it appealed to the disciples of Lamarck, who had begun to delineate species, and Darwin. Diseases had a natural life span and development of their own. The fittest germs survived and prospered in whole human populations, which also had their own patterns of generation, expansion, and sometimes exhaustion. There was no need to invoke God, or even the particular humoral and physical features of the individual.

The great German and French scientists of the later nineteenth century illustrate how this process of professionalization and regularization of knowledge occurred in the context of social and economic development. Louis Pasteur (1822–99), the French chemist, was the son of a tanner. Some of his major scientific findings in the study of germs arose from problems associated with French agriculture and local industry. He investigated diseases of wine and beer, epidemics among silkworms and rabies, all of which affected agricultural labor. Pierre and Marie Curie, who led the world in studies of radioactivity, were awarded the Nobel Prize. Founded by an arms magnate, the prize marked the pinnacle of the new hierarchy of international scientific endeavor.

Governments now had to pay for hospitals and the treatment of their own populations. They also found the new theories and the newly ordered professions congenial. They were increasingly aware of the danger to trade, military manpower, and public order presented by diseases. The diseases of the poor could be treated by improving hygiene, sanitation, and education. The provision of better housing and water supplies also made working-class districts and backward rural areas more accessible and transparent to the state for the purposes of taxation, military recruitment, and political control. The great expansion of public health facilities in Paris, for instance, followed fears aroused among the middle classes by experience of the revolutionary Commune of 1871.

Much the same was true in the colonial and semi-colonial world. Public health schemes were underfunded and small-scale here, of course. They were mainly concerned with the health of European soldiers and other European residents. Florence Nightingale, British nurse and reformer, argued that the health of the British soldiers in India could only be improved if the health of ordinary Indians was of concern. In the last years of her life she went further, arguing that the British government of India itself had to be reformed before either of these desirable changes could take place. Public health systems in China, Egypt, and South America also came into being as a result of pressure from expanding European and American business populations in these countries. Modern historians have come to argue that the imposition of modern medical and psychiatric systems on the world's population was a manifestation of the desire by the state and the bourgeois to control and categorize. They did not embody any general truths beyond this context. This position is too instrumental. It is true that some of the "sciences" held in high regard by nineteenth-century people – for instance, phrenology (the measurement and classification of skulls) and various types of racist and physical measurement schemes – were purely fictional constructs. It is also true that Victorian whites were too keen to lampoon peasant and folk medicine, which sometimes had the capacity to cure disease. Yet the empirical findings of some contemporaries resulted in real and quantifiable advances in medical knowledge which did, for instance, lead in time to the control of malaria, tuberculosis, syphilis, and diphtheria. Even if they appealed to the regulating and categorizing instincts of contemporary administrators, these imperfect medical advances cannot be written off as mere discourses of power.

CONCLUSION

What, broadly, were the changes wrought by the confrontation of older schemes of knowledge and political virtue with liberalism, socialism, and science in the nineteenth century? At the level of leadership and institutions, greater uniformity was apparent at the world level. Even where public men insisted on the value of older understandings of the physical and human world, these were now increasingly presented in the form of the knowledges of the European Enlightenment. They spread through academies, associations, and print media in similar ways. Chinese, Indian, and Arab medicine each had its own teaching institutions and textbooks. This phenomenon was not limited to self-proclaimed rational knowledge. It affected religion, too. As chapter 9 argues, Roman Catholic thought was similarly recast to meet the challenges of the newly invigorated Protestant heresies and Islam, and it consequently adopted a polemical and expository style like theirs. One particular aspect of uniformity was the way in which specialists increasingly claimed a historical genealogy for their great teachers and bodies of learning. In the human and natural sciences considered here, and also in the analysis of religious texts and legal systems, the idea of historical evolution was widely accepted.

Western liberalism, socialism, and science had left an indelible imprint on most human communities by 1914. In the process, intellectuals and popular audiences the world over had rapidly transformed their meanings into a variety of doctrines, often very different from their exemplars. The diffusion, reception, or rejection of these ideas depended on many different circumstances. In the colonial world, the nature and extent of the education system was one factor. More generally, new ideas took root where ruling groups decided to promote them as badges of legitimacy and so lay claim to their own versions of modernity. For instance, the Meiji elite of Japan used modern knowledge and scientific techniques as a way of symbolizing their own status as radical, but still Japanese, renovators of the constitution. Liberals in Hungary appropriated Emile Durkheim, in part because he seemed to argue against the religious basis of political power in the Austro-Hungarian monarchy.

Yet the extent to which learned people could do this depended, in turn, on how far these new ideas could be accommodated and understood within earlier systems of rational thought, ethics, or political ideology. New ideas were likely to be more persuasive when they could be formulated within existing reasoning practices and appeared to complement indigenous concepts. Social Darwinism and "race theory" found a fertile audience in many societies, for instance, because they fitted into existing schemes of ethnic ranking. Race theory provided a gloss for existing local forms of discrimination. These were as varied as North American ideas of productive competition, Hindu concepts of purity and pollution, Confucian ideas of refinement, and Japanese concepts of divine descent. In this way, race theory and social Darwinism were not only appropriated but also transformed in different world contexts.

In general, later historians saw liberalism and science as antagonists of the great world religions. Both this chapter and the next suggest that there is good reason to query that claim. Liberalism inherited much from the idea of spiritual equality before God. Scientific thought and practice were often grounded in the idea of discovering God's bounty. Equally, as chapter 9 will show, many aspects of nineteenth-century religion were themselves phenomena of modernity, even though priests and preachers spoke of ancient truths.

[9] EMPIRES OF RELIGION

MANY contemporaries and some historians have seen the nineteenth century as an age when science and secular thought eroded religious belief or began to push it to the margins of social life. This chapter takes a different view of the religious experience of the nineteenth century. More even than a period when liberalism or the concept of class rose to power, the nineteenth century saw the triumphal reemergence and expansion of "religion" in the sense in which we now use the term. The chapter first considers the views of contemporary intellectuals and modern scholars about the fate of religion in the nineteenth century. It then examines the global linkages and conflicts which brought about the reformulation of doctrine and authority. This was seen in all "world religions" during the period.

Many of the historical processes discussed earlier in the book aided the expansion of these reinvigorated religions. The new, more aggressive European states and empires, alongside insurgent non-European nationalisms, often promoted religion as their badge of identity even when they spoke of liberalism and science. Those middling people who benefited from industrious revolutions, whether Muslim, Christian, or Hindu, promoted their own faiths, because piety and respectability went together. Again, the emerging world of print and the public sphere promoted religions as much as abstract philosophical or political beliefs. These propositions did not always, however, seem self-evident either to contemporaries or to later historians.

RELIGION IN THE EYES OF CONTEMPORARIES

During the revolutionary years, many writers were very sure that older forms of religious belief were declining throughout the world, and some of them welcomed this. The tone was set by the French *philosophes*, who looked forward to an age of reason when superstition and priestcraft would be banished from the realms of rulers animated by pure reason. Insofar as the

ILLUSTRATION 9.1   Lourdes: Pilgrims at the Grotto. Lithograph by unnamed artist, c.1885.

men of the Enlightenment were able to imagine peoples outside Europe and its American colonies at all, it was to approve of those civilizations where they thought idolatry and "enthusiasm" were at a minimum. Voltaire and other rationalist thinkers believed that China was a society of philosopher-kings. Others saw the Islamic world as the seat of a transcendent rational religion, devoid of priestly hierarchy, which seemed to mirror their own belief in a remote and impersonal deity. The English historian Edward Gibbon, for example, professed to believe that Islam was superior to Christianity, because it was less prone to "superstition."

The philosophers' more radical disciples among the French, European, or Haitian revolutionaries were more often anticlerical than irreligious, but in their public rituals they frequently sought a clean break with the traditions of the Church, as well as the monarchy. The founding fathers of the American constitution divorced religion from the state by disestablishing the Church. Some of them, such as Thomas Jefferson, spoke the language of philosophical skepticism. The new French regime of 1793 invoked the "Supreme Being," temporarily abolishing God and the Christian feast days.[1] In the first flush of their victory, the French revolutionaries followed a vigorous policy of de-

Christianization, disrupting religious services and encouraging priests to marry. The international spread of revolution was sometimes accompanied by the burning of churches and monasteries. Napoleon, for his part, was contemptuous of the intricate venality of the old Catholic Church. The Italian republics which mushroomed after his invasion of the peninsula in 1796 happily sequestered church property. But more cautious counsels soon prevailed even among those inclined to be suspicious of religion. In 1797, northern Italy witnessed a vigorous anti-French reaction. Crowds in town and country attacked the French and their collaborators with the cry of "Viva Maria!" on their lips. Hundreds of miracles were reported from across revolutionary Europe.[2] Napoleon rapidly came to realize that he could not abolish Catholic belief, while the pope soon came to the conclusion that much of the church land sequestered after 1789 would never be returned. This paved the way for the Concordat of 1801 between Church and the French imperial state and, in the long term, a Catholic revival and the strengthening of the authority of the papacy across the Roman Catholic world.[3]

The liberals and radicals who wrote and lectured so profusely throughout the nineteenth century, however, continued to be ambivalent about religion. On the one hand, many of them had philosophical objections to "superstition" and "priestcraft," which they associated with organized religion. On the other hand, they tended to appreciate the role of belief in disciplining the poor and guaranteeing social stability. John Stuart Mill, whose influence extended well beyond Britain and English-speaking countries, wished to remove religion from the realm of politics and relegate it to the domestic world. Toleration of divergent beliefs and even of non-belief, he argued, was the essential guarantee of civil society. Like his ancestors in the British radical Protestant tradition, he associated emotional religiosity with superstition and backwardness. Attitudes on the left hardened later. Saint-Simon and Mazzini tried to envision an abstract, rational deity who loved secular "progress." The latter wrote to his clerical opponents: "Your dogma humanises God; our dogma preaches the slow, progressive humanisation of man. You believe in grace; we believe in justice."[4] The more materialist Marxists and socialists of the years after 1848 held, according to their own scientific doctrines, that religion was "false consciousness," and therefore a declining force. The people would no longer require the opiate of religion when true working-class self-consciousness emerged from social contradictions. Yet this secularism was more common among the leaders than the followers. One apocryphal working-class radical of the Paris Commune of 1871, for instance, insisted that he was an atheist at the same time as he proclaimed his faith in the Virgin Mary. This was a fairly typical pattern. Even where religious belief was attenuated or in decline amongst elites, the masses remained devout.

Intellectuals drawn from the rich of the European-dominated coastal cities of Asia and the Middle East also challenged religious institutions and anticipated the decline of certain older forms of belief and ritual within their own societies. Sometimes they pressed into service ideas derived from the West. If apparently successful Western societies had stripped away the more objectionable features of priesthood and superstition, should they not also do the same? In the context of European imperialism and arrogance, however, this was a risky tactic. Instead, most Indians, Japanese, and Chinese who wished to press for social and intellectual change insisted that they were confronting modernity with religious sensibilities derived from an indigenous past.

Across the Asian world, Hindu, Buddhist, and Confucian reformers of the nineteenth century emphasized the rational and philosophical elements in their religious inheritance, condemning superstition, mindless priestcraft, and magical beliefs. Here again, they brought to bear many Western-derived liberal sensibilities, but they rarely did so in a void. It is true that some of the firebrands among the radical Calcutta college students of the 1840s who called themselves "Young Bengal" deliberately feasted on cow's meat and alcohol in order to offend and deride their elders. Yet most contemporary intellectuals drew on rationalistic traditions and philosophies which had long been present in their respective religious traditions. The so-called Hindu Unitarians gathered in the Brahmo Samaj insisted that the true religion, as propagated by the ancient sages, had always been a monotheistic doctrine, like Christianity or Islam.[5] Though they were influenced by Christian ethics and Islamic monotheism, the Brahmos emphasized a much older strand within Hinduism which posited the existence of a supreme deity beyond and above the outward forms of "polytheism." They believed that this pure faith had been corrupted by the Brahmin priesthood during the middle ages of Indian history. Religion, to them, was a system of reason, and most of its outward forms should be purged and controlled. The leader of Buddhist revival in Ceylon in the 1870s and 1880s, Anagarika Dharmapala, employed a similar tactic when he urged his coreligionists to return to the ancient faith of the people, which he alleged had been corrupted, in this case by alien Hinduism and Christianity.[6] These reformers came up with divine hybrids which looked quite a lot like the rational providence espoused by Mazzini, Saint-Simon, and Mill.

This pattern reappeared in the Islamic world. Here modernizing intellectuals such as the Indian, Sayyid Ahmad Khan, and the Egyptian scholar, Muhammad Abduh, pioneered a new type of critical historical study of Muslim religion and its key doctrines.[7] They challenged conservatives by arguing that human reason, being God-given, could and should replace an abject dependence on textual authority. At one level, they were obviously responding to the impact of "scientific" ideas originating in the West. At another, they were drawing on and refashioning earlier schools of Muslim thought. As in Europe, the rethinking of religious belief was accompanied by renovations of religious organization. The emerging modern political leadership in the Ottoman Empire and its provinces sought to bring under control the religious authorities and their large holdings of lands and money (the *waqfs*). They claimed that the secular ruler, tracing his right to the Prophet himself, had always disposed of religious endowments for public religious welfare.

Despite this evidence of adaptation, however, nineteenth-century historians and cultural critics often continued to portray their own age as an age of growing godlessness. The romantic English and German historians who studied the Middle Ages deplored the tearing apart of the seamless web of ancient Christian civilization. They believed that medieval religion had been deeply woven into the fabric of the community. The English art critic and moralist John Ruskin savaged the art of the European Renaissance for lacking creative authenticity and displaying outward signs of the decline of faith.[8] This was not surprising. The justifying ideologies of the great movements of religious revival in the nineteenth century in most faiths stressed corruptions of the present time. For them, the past had always been better.

THE VIEW OF RECENT HISTORIANS

For much of the twentieth century, modern historians of Europe and the extra-European world followed the lead of these vocal contemporary activists and writers. They saw the "long" nineteenth century as an era when religion, if not in retreat, was bleeding away before it succumbed to the fatal diseases of modernity. What Owen Chadwick called the "secularisation of the European mind"[9] and, by extension, the secularization of minds influenced by Europe, has been a pervasive theme in British and European history. Historians almost unconsciously enlisted the weighty authority of Max Weber, the greatest social theorist of the early twentieth century, in support of the argument that the world had been progressively "demystified," that belief in miracles and the supernatural was on the wane. For these historians, mob attacks on churches during the revolutionary upsurges signaled the turning away of the people from religion. The apparent decline in church attendance in some parts of industrializing Europe during the second half of the nineteenth century was seen by the social historians of the 1970s as further evidence that urbanization and industrialization were incompatible with religious observance.

Because, until very recently, Marxist or materialist historiography was a powerful tradition within the European academy, this view retains its potency. But even in America, where it was much more difficult to argue the case for a decline in religious observance, historians appeared content for many years to see church history and the history of religion separated off into their own specialist ghettos. Later, after the 1980s, when postmodernist approaches surfaced within historical writing worldwide, their emphasis on the protean and transgressive in decentered narratives tended to direct attention away from "orthodox" religion in its dominant forms. Historians were inclined to concentrate on localized millenarian movements and subaltern challenges to elite religions, rather than doctrine and ecclesiastical organization.

Many Third World intellectuals were also convinced that the modernization of societies inevitably led to the decline of religion. Indian Marxist historians writing in the 1960s and 1970s, such as Bipan Chandra[10] and Irfan Habib, largely ignored religion in their analyses, except when it was manifested as pathological "communalism," or interreligious conflict. Meanwhile, Chinese and Japanese Marxists followed the master in seeing religion as an "opiate of the people," a distraction from class consciousness. This is one reason why the resurgence, in the 1980s and 1990s, of Islam, orthodox Judaism, and evangelical Christianity outraged and took so many contemporary secular and left-wing historians unawares.

THE RISE OF NEW-STYLE RELIGION

In reality, the great religions staged a remarkable resurgence after 1815. In the process, they transformed themselves and the societies within which they worked. Of course, religious authority made a series of pacts and concordats, often on poor terms, with newly vigorous states and empires. In Brazil, for example, the Catholic Church was disestablished after the republic was declared in 1889. In France, the Church was permanently embattled during the long years of the Third Republic after 1871. In Britain, the ancient rules that disallowed Dissenters and Roman Catholics from taking degrees at Oxford or Cambridge universities were finally abandoned. Churches withdrew from pointless and perhaps unwinnable battles with ascendant liberal and scientific ideas in some cases, and were symbolically defeated by them in others.

Yet religious authorities widely made tactical retreats in order to conquer new areas of cultural and social life. "Secularization," in fact, was only one small part of the reconstruction from within of the religious sensibility and of religious organization. It was the fly in the wheel, not the wheel itself. Almost everywhere the world religions sharpened and clarified their identities, especially in the later nineteenth century. They expanded to try to absorb and discipline the variegated systems of belief, ritual, and practice which had always teemed beneath the surface in the earlier ages of supposed religiosity. Their leaders reached outward to encompass great areas of decentralized spirituality, especially in Africa, the Pacific, and on the inner frontiers of Asia and the Americas, which had never been in their purview previously. In the process, the great world religions invaded areas of social and family life which had previously been policed by tribal elders and custom, rather than fixed religious codes. The constant complaints of revivalists about the decline of religion, the rise of secular mentalities, and the ignorance of the heathen or working people should therefore be seen not as statements of historical "fact." They were, instead, means of mobilizing increasingly assertive religious authorities and the Christian, Muslim, Hindu, and Buddhist publics to which they spoke.

A critical aspect of this revival of religions was that it was happening on a global scale. It has always been clear that Judaism, Islam, Hinduism, and Buddhism reformulated themselves partly in response to vigorous missionary assault from Christians in the age of European empires. Within the Christian world, even Roman Catholicism was forced to reevaluate its doctrines and practices in the early nineteenth century in reaction to the growing secular power of Protestants and their imperialist evangelization. A less obvious point is that Christian religions themselves were irrevocably changed by the

ILLUSTRATION 9.2   God's Word: London Missionary Society School, Torres Strait, S.W. Pacific. Photo by A. C. Haddon, 1888.

experience of proselytizing and propaganda wars outside Europe. Forms of missionary publication and preaching developed in Asia, Africa, and the Pacific were rerouted back to the European and American continents in the guise of missions to the poor. American Baptists, for example, founded one of their earliest general conventions in 1814 in order to support the mission of Adoniram Judson to Burma. Later, other conventions were established to coordinate domestic charity and evangelism at a national level. The first tentative beginnings of Christian interdenominational cooperation also came about in the Asian and African mission fields where non-Christians could so readily deride Christians as being unable to agree even amongst themselves. In Asia, those same American Baptists and Congregationalists found no alternative to cooperation with the better-supported British Baptists already established in India and with the East India Company's government.

In many theaters of Christian evangelization, indeed, it was the prior expansion of Islam which forced the Christian reaction, rather than vice versa. Similarly, within the Islamic world itself, it was struggles with heterodoxy and unbelief on the fringes, in places such as northern Nigeria, the Sudan, and the Dutch East Indies, which fed back into and revivified the organization and theology of the center. As mentioned earlier, the eighteenth-century purist preacher from impoverished central Arabia, Abd al-Wahhab, made the mosques of Istanbul and Cairo shake. Global history here, as elsewhere, reveals a pattern of causation invisible to national or regional specialists or specialists in one religious tradition.

This chapter will emphasize what historians and anthropologists continue to call "world religions." In our period, religious people interpreted this to mean "advanced religions," as opposed to more "primitive" or "animist" religions. Such evolutionary ideas are, of course, out of date. Here the term is meant to convey no more than that these forms of faith were, to one extent or another, global in their reach; they were able to travel over distances and between cultures. This was because they had some form of written scripture, a tradition of preaching, and congregational or public worship. Even Hinduism and Confucianism, families of religious belief and practice which put less emphasis on the duty of preaching than Islam and Christianity, had the capacity to bring groups at their geographical margins into a kind of communion of ritual.

The category "world religion" far from exhausts the repertoire of human spirituality, however. There existed other, community-based religious traditions which rarely expanded by making converts. To this category belonged north Indian Sikhism, Judaism, and those versions of Orthodox and Syriac Christianity which were located in Russia, the Middle East, and India. Religious traditions of this sort traveled when their adherents migrated. But they were rarely propagated beyond the bounds of delimited regions and ethnicities, though all three of these faiths had at one time been more expansive. Secondly, there were cults *within* religions. These, again, were less likely to "travel." In this category were the practices of ancestor and spirit worship, and the "old" religions within the Chinese and Japanese worlds called Daoism and Shintoism. Other examples were esoteric practices, such as Shakti[11] within Hinduism, for instance, and some of the locally rooted cults of Catholic Christianity. Such cults provided access to spiritual energy for groups of adherents who would still have considered themselves members of the wider, doctrinally complex world religions.

Yet even these regional faiths and cults within religions came to feel the organizing and categorizing power of the world religions. For example, Orthodox Syriac Christians began to edit and print their own scriptures when they came under pressure from Catholic or Protestant missionaries attempting to convert them. Similarly, by the 1870s, Sikhs in India began to insist, "We are not Hindus" and to formalize their doctrines when apostles of revived Hinduism attempted to claim them for themselves.[12] As the Japanese moved abroad in search of trade and empire, they began to try to propagate their essentially domestic cult, Shinto, in these new territories.

Finally, over large parts of Melanesia, Polynesia, Africa, and the Native American world, were to be found a profusion of non-verbal, non-text-based, and non-congregational forms of spiritual experience which took the form of initiation into "mysteries."[13] All these represented a form of spirituality wholly different from the world religions, in that their rationale was secrecy and individual experience, not preaching and conformity. There is no doubt that these divergent forms of human religious belief and practice were still changing, developing, or dying out in the long nineteenth century, according to their own inward logics. What makes the era unique, however, was the extent to which this whole spectrum of spirituality was profoundly influenced, and sometimes transformed, by the expansion of the world religions. Many of these differing forms survived, resisted, or even flourished, but very few were completely untouched by the rising empires of religion.

MODES OF RELIGIOUS DOMINION, THEIR AGENTS AND THEIR LIMITATIONS

Like the other major social formations of the period – the state and capitalism – expanding religions accessed and exploited the underlying changes in technology and sentiment which characterized the period. Religious authorities expanded and rationalized the bureaucracies and training institutions which they had inherited from the eighteenth century. They made full use of the new opportunities for travel and communication. Benedict Anderson has emphasized the importance of new, far-flung communities of readers indirectly joined by print in the creation of the nation, as noted in chapter 6. Yet the "imagined communities" of print readers developing around the idea of nation were nowhere near as large as the audiences subject to the huge outflow of printed books, pamphlets, Bibles, Qurans, and Buddhist *jatakas* (tales of the life of the Buddha) directed to the potential faithful. Religious literature was at the forefront of the print revolution as it expanded beyond the European, American, Chinese, and Japanese elites. Religious instruction became more widely institutionalized, with the expansion of mosque schools, Hindu and Buddhist temple schools, and Christian Sunday schools. These institutions generally took off at a far faster rate than secular training institutes, let alone the limited efforts of working men's associations or international congresses of bearded radicals teaching the doctrines of class struggle. Nineteenth-century religious art and architecture, with their sentimental Christian saints and gaudy, over-painted Hindu or Confucian temples, now seem rather vulgar. But religious buildings and art grew with a vigor unseen since the Renaissance in the Christian world or the great age of the seventeenth-century Persian Safavids and Mughals in the Muslim world.

Religions expanded "down" into particular societies by imposing uniformity. At the same time, they expanded geographically. The new authorities colonized and made use of earlier communities of believers and practices of worship, attempting to submit them to new disciplines. In Christendom and Islam, authoritative clerics increasingly attempted to whip into line the religious orders and Sufi mystical brotherhoods respectively, which were suspected of practicing heterodoxy or saint worship, and so detracting from the unity of God. Even in the decentralized world of Hindu practice, religious authorities tried, not always successfully, to bring bodies of *fakhirs*, renouncers of the world, within the purview of temple-based religious practice. The threat from Western encroachment and aggressive neighbors encouraged rulers in Southeast Asia and the Far East to establish more uniform and governable religious authorities. Kings in Buddhist realms had always "purged" the monasteries from time to time. But in Thailand, Burma, and Tokugawa Japan, this was accompanied, in the century after 1760, by novel attempts to direct and control the monkhood.[14] In the 1830s and 1840s, under Chinese and European pressure, the rulers of Vietnam strengthened the Confucian institutions of their kingdom and introduced the purest Chinese rituals.[15] In China, the embattled monarchy also tried to reassert its authority with the help of conservative Confucian bureaucrats, though this merely appears to have exacerbated religious dissent. In all the main religious traditions, pilgrimage became more popular, and the authorities seeded with it a more uniform pattern of religious belief. By the middle of the century, therefore, public religious practice had quite widely taken on new institutional forms across the world.

The chapter now moves on to examine some of these changes in greater detail. Proceeding by theme, rather than by religious tradition, allows us to appreciate that many of these changes were cumulative and interrelated at a world level. For instance, the emergence of a more authoritative set of recorded beliefs, a scripture as it were, amongst Buddhists in Ceylon, Burma, and Japan, reflected a general engagement by leading monks with changes in the contemporary world. At the same time, the experience of encountering Christian scripture in a polemical mode, as it spread across the colonial world, also convinced Buddhist teachers that they too needed a defined set of dogmas with which to compete in the almost Darwinian struggle for survival between world religions.

When we speak of the rise of religion during the nineteenth century, however, it is important not to ascribe all agency to priesthoods and intelligentsias. On the contrary, among the most powerful agents in the building up of these more uniform religious practices were ordinary people of the "middling sort." These included schoolmasters, government clerks, and small tradesmen, who saw standardized religious observance as part of a more general struggle to assert their worth and respectability and to find common ground with each other. In European societies, the expansion of Protestant Pietism or Catholic orthodoxy was the project of the German artisan, given new status by the expansion of a local industrial city, or the Irish laborer in Dublin, Liverpool, or Sydney, who associated religion with education and the aspiration to nationhood. In Italy, small shopkeepers in major towns formed associations to elect Catholic representatives to local bodies.[16] Equally, lower government servants and small farmers were strongly represented in the revival of Islam, Buddhism, and Hinduism. Prosperous small farmers in Japan attached themselves to the state-sponsored Shinto shrines which were vigorously patronized by the new Meiji regime.

In many societies, women were also important bearers of orthodoxy or orthodox practice, as nuns, schoolmistresses, or reformers within the home. Elsewhere, women and the control of women was an important theme in the teaching of male religious reformers, who associated disorderly sexuality with heterodoxy, "syncretism," and deviant religious practice. Conversion or the introduction of new piety accorded with the interests of powerful men in local societies. Even what Europeans and Americans regarded as their greatest Christian triumph, the evangelization of Africa, was carried out very often by other Africans. In West Africa, the elite of the Krio people of Sierra Leone were among the first to receive British-style education. It was Krio pastors and missionaries, not British ones, who did much of the pioneer preaching in adjoining parts of West Africa.[17] In Melanesia and Polynesia, again, it was local people who did much to spread Christianity after the initial Western contacts had been made.[18]

So the "victory" of more orthodox forms of belief and of colonizing religions, notably Christianity and Islam, was nowhere achieved without the agency of local people. Nor did they make much headway unless they were compatible with existing beliefs at some level. No more than the nation-state, Western liberalism, or science could the world religions accomplish an easy hegemony. For instance, most studies of the spectacular rise of Christianity in Africa south of the Sahara and in the Pacific during the nineteenth century have emphasized that Christian belief flourished only where it worked with the grain of social change in Africa itself.[19] No doubt the appearance of European and American missionaries was important, as was European settlement and colonization, in dramatizing the power of Christianity. Yet Christianization proved particularly successful where rising African rulers or Maori chiefs felt the need to "capture" the charisma of a well-known Christian missionary and "convert" on their own terms. Christian doctrine was most successful where it subtly adjusted to African predilections, coming closer, for instance, to the African ideal of the healing cult and abandoning its European medieval emphasis on sin and redemption. In the Pacific, it was the heroic genealogies of the Old Testament, rather than the peaceful words of Jesus Christ, that particularly appealed to warrior-chieftains in the process of becoming entrepreneurs. In New Zealand, differences among Christian denominations often reflected existing divisions between different Maori subgroups: Maori here used a variety of Christian confessions to preserve and enhance their own identities.[20] In many areas of South and Southeast Asia, Islam spread where it met the need of merchants and people on the move to seek out communities of trust, where common practices and beliefs could create a moral bond between strangers.[21]

Yet these were not simply matters of social practice. Beliefs were equally important. The world religions found it easier to spread and consolidate their position where existing ideas of divinity were compatible with them. Asian scholars have emphasized that Islam often filled the space once occupied by Buddhist notions of a universal realm of belief and righteousness, or *dharma*. Christianity often moved more easily into African or Polynesian societies which already had some sense of a high god or a world spirit.

In other words, we should ask, with Susan Bayly,[22] not only why Africans, Amerindians, and Australasians converted to Christianity, but also how

Christianity was converted by Africans, Amerindians, and Australasians. Obviously, too, it would be wrong to assume that the process of standardization was by any means complete or even half-complete by 1914. On the contrary, local spirit cults, forms of witchcraft, white magic, and shamanism persisted, or even expanded, across much of the world, often in response to the inroads of world religions. Where Christian or Muslim missionaries seemed to have successfully propagated their faith in authoritative scripture and congregational worship, they were sometimes horrified to find wholly unorthodox millenarian movements springing up amongst their converts. What *can* be said, however, is that most of these decentralized patterns of belief and practice had been touched by changes which tended toward greater uniformity both within and between religions.

FORMALIZING RELIGIOUS AUTHORITY, CREATING "IMPERIAL" RELIGIONS

The first priority for religious leaderships attempting to build and propagate their message was to establish, or reestablish, clearer lines of authority. Only then could doctrine be organized and dealings with the state and with apostles of secularism be made effective. This was no easy task. The ancien régime in religion, as in politics, had involved a loose and overlapping set of jurisdictions and claims to legitimacy or succession to the Prophet, St Peter, or the Buddha. In the case of "Hinduism," it is doubtful if a religion existed in this conventional sense at all. Even in the case of Islam, which was a faith with an ancient inheritance of formalized doctrine, local jurists could propagate decisions (*fatwas*) which were wildly contradictory of each other. This added further complexity to a situation in which Sunni and Shia, mystic Sufism and intransigent monotheism, were already locked in dispute. These ancien régime complexities were further confounded by the impact of the global crisis of 1780–1820 and the new doctrines it unleashed.

Paradoxically, the establishment of firmer lines of spiritual authority and the bureaucratization of belief were made easier by religion's partial expulsion from the political domain. As we have seen, the nineteenth century witnessed a widespread decline of the political authority of the major religions. Over much of the world, the state dominated by a single religious confession struggled and declined. In the United States, religion was formally severed from government, and the First Amendment protected religious plurality.[23] The revolutionaries, after all, had suspected that the resurgent British Empire had been intending to impose on them an Anglican Settlement, or even Roman Catholicism. Liberty of religion was therefore an essential basis of the Republic. This liberty allowed religion to be associated, not with authority, but with community. The founding fathers themselves argued that a secular state would preserve and enhance religion in the small community, not discourage it. Consequently it become a powerful force for social transformation. In Britain, the Test Acts and other legal disabilities suffered by Catholics,

Dissenters, and Jews were reluctantly removed in the course of the century. The same was true in many of the north European Protestant countries. This allowed all these heterodox faiths to compete with the Anglican, Lutheran, or Calvinist establishments in order to expand and develop among the urban working class.

On the face of it, again, Roman Catholicism fared even worse in its relations with the secular authorities than the Protestant churches. The Italian *risorgimento* had destroyed the pope's political influence by 1870 and locked up his power in Vatican City. The revolutionary inheritance in France, buffeting against the role of the Church, finally accomplished its de-linking from the state between 1902 and 1905. This was when Catholics lost control of large areas of education, marriage, and social policy, with many monks and nuns decamping to Italy and Belgium.[24] Within the broad enclave left to them, however, the religious authorities throughout Europe, particularly those closely linked to the papacy itself, were able to greatly expand their moral and social influence. The churches were able to offer guidance, support, and hope to people whom the state could hardly reach. Indeed, as implied above, the very fact that religious authority was now further separated from state power made it easier for priests, mullahs, and preachers to become guardians of the poor and protectors of "true" spiritual values. It is doubtful that the Roman Catholic Church in France could have staged a powerful revival after 1870 if it had still been implicated in the privileges of the aristocrats and had levied its own taxes.

In the dominated, non-European world, the advent of European or, as it was often regarded, Christian government seems to have accomplished the same outcome even more drastically. The indigenous law officers who had previously tried cases according to Islamic law, or the pandits and Buddhist monks who advised rulers, were now subject to British, French, and Dutch colonial officials. Their jurisdiction was apparently secularized and formalized into colonial law codes. Even in parts of the non-European world where European influence was indirect, religious authorities seem to have lost much of their power. In Japan, the Meiji patriots of the 1870s remained suspicious of Buddhism, which they saw as a prop to the old regime. They therefore suppressed or ignored the Buddhist sects and concentrated instead on building up a state religion around the old indigenous belief system, Shinto, which they linked to the cult of the emperor in Tokyo.[25] In China, Kang Youwei came to the conclusion that "Confucianism" was the Chinese religion, as Christianity was the religion of the West. He wanted to create a nationwide network of educational institutions and to make local shrines into temples for the worship of the "immortal sage," Confucius. This was an important strand in the abortive "hundred days" reform movement of 1898, which briefly rocked the dynasty.[26] The reforming potentates of the Ottoman Empire sought much more direct political control of the learned Islamic classes and the mystics, especially the Bektashi and Mehlevi orders, which had been close to the now-disbanded janissaries.[27] They insisted that men loyal to the state should head the religious hierarchy and often discreetly pilfered the money and lands of religious institutions in the course of a kind of Muslim reformation.

While this is all true, such assaults by the state and secularists on the world religions acted as a pressing call to action for their leaderships. Religion had now to define itself against its competitors, perhaps for the first time. By being partly expelled from the workings of politics and the state, it had to create its own sphere of transcendental religious value. In the process it transformed itself. Now that the colonial governments had directly or tacitly refused their obligations as protectors of indigenous religions, Hindu, Buddhist, and Muslim laymen had to come forward to fill the gap in economic and political support for "religions in danger." The Delhi teacher Shah Abd al-Aziz, for instance, argued that now the Muslims had lost political power over much of Asia, they would have to reform themselves from within in order to save the faith.[28] And the impetus for reformation was not simply the result of external pressures. The new media of the nineteenth century and the emergence of an educated middle-class public inevitably revealed dramatically the existing fractures within religious practice and belief. The conflict between the different sects within Islam was deepened by the new opportunities for transmitting ideas over long distances and by the pamphlet and newspaper wars that erupted in particular localities. As much the largest entity, Sunni Islam emerged as a more coherent and organized religious community at a world level. But so, too, did the smaller sects, the Shias and Ismailis.

So, across the world, ways were found of creating more authoritative religious structures. The Protestant churches in Europe, North America, and throughout the British Empire instituted a series of doctrinal commissions and congresses which made Anglican, Baptist, and Congregational traditions worldwide churches with similar organization and doctrine for the first time. The large Anglican Communion abroad achieved degrees of independence from the British state, first in 1783 when the Americans broke away, and increasingly in the dominions after 1850. But periodic conferences of priests and lay people at Lambeth Palace in London after 1867 instilled a surprising degree of common purpose, laying the issue of authority to rest.[29] American denominations, too, began to operate at a national level after they were disestablished in the states in the generation after independence. Even where churches were plagued with conflict, as over the issue of slavery, they organized more tightly. Facing the threat from northern abolitionists, for instance, the Southern Baptist Convention moved after 1845 to tighten its organization.[30]

In the Roman Church the change was more dramatic. The Vatican bureaucracy was broadened and widened; the training of priests was centralized in Rome. Catholic universities sought to propagate a more unified curriculum. Most epochal was the decision of the General Council of the Roman Catholic Church in 1870 to promulgate the doctrine of Papal Infallibility. It was already believed that the Church in Council could not err. Now the Pope's considered judgment on matters of doctrine and practice was held to be in direct accordance with the will of Christ. Originally, the Council had the modest objective of reorganizing pastoral duties, and no direct engagement was intended with modern doctrines.[31] Yet Infallibility was to prove a serviceable weapon in the Vatican's suppression or disciplining of what were thought to be heterodox and dangerous ideas, many of them hybrid ones, such as Christian socialism or Christian liberalism. It was also designed to bring to heel over-mighty bishops who had been particularly prominent in the eighteenth century. Better and more centralized training also allowed the Church to reestablish its authority worldwide. As a tide of state secularism, positivism, and Protestantism swept through Latin America after the 1870s, the Vatican turned to the offensive and sent large numbers of European priests to the spiritual war fronts in Brazil and Argentina.

Islamic leaderships were no more able than Christian ones to finally resolve old and deep sectarian splits within their world communities. Yet within the major traditions, much more uniformity was created. In India and Southeast Asia an eighteenth-century curriculum for religious schools and universities, the Dars i-Nizamiya, was spread widely in the nineteenth century. The famed teaching mosques of the Islamic world became more important, too, with larger numbers of theology and philosophy students from around the world traveling for education to the great mosque in Cairo, al-Azhar. Just as improved communications made it easier for bishops' and missionary congresses to meet, so Islamic scholars found it easier to travel and sit at the feet of famed scholars, so giving a greater uniformity to their own teaching so.[32] Ironically, the intervention of the state, both colonial and semi-independent, tended to firm up Islamic jurisdiction in those areas which were left to it after the state's intervention. In seeking a stable form of "Islamic" law administered by recognized lawyers and judges, the European powers widely entrenched more orthodox and scripturally "correct" forms of personal and property law than had existed earlier.

In the Hindu and Buddhist worlds, where authority had often been even more decentralized, these same pressures also led to a search for authority and uniformity. As the colonial authorities withdrew from the direct management of religious institutions in India or overseas Indian communities, it was educated laymen who took over the management of charities and religious endowments and of pilgrimages. By the later nineteenth century, neo-orthodox Hindus, devotees of the "eternal religion," or "faith of our fathers" (*sanatan dharma*), were gathered into Hindu associations which comprised temple priests and pontiffs of the major temple shrines, as well as English-educated lawyers. These met in regional and all-India voluntary associations and attempted to offer authoritative pronouncements on the position of "Hindus" on matters of law, custom, and politics.

In Ceylon and Burma and on the China coast, Young Men's Buddhist associations also emerged as a modern source of social authority, sometimes in tension with the monks. The British colonial state played an important part in this. Defining Hindu priests and renouncers as the equivalent of "churchwardens" and "abbots" in English practice, it sought their advice on matters of custom and law through the court system and in urban representative

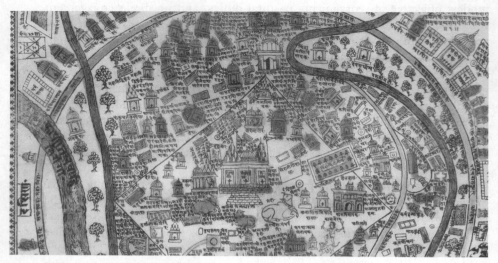

ILLUSTRATION 9.3   Pilgrimage of grace: Block-printed pilgrim's map of the Hindu holy city of Benares, showing temples and the river Ganges, 1903.

institutions. Craving authoritative pronouncements on religion, the European colonizers empowered a variety of functionaries who had previously been servants and ritualists of the community, rather than its guides or spiritual shepherds in a Christian sense. Thus religious authorities of wider and more uniform competence were created in a system which had often been more decentralized and contested under the old regime. Religious authority also became more open. A lay public, linked by associations and journals, could influence and be influenced by it.

In the very different conditions of European and American Jewry, some similar changes can be glimpsed. On the one hand, the decline of traditional exegesis and rabbinical authority in fast-moving diaspora communities encouraged the emergence of "reformed" congregations in which ordinary lay people took a greater role in the management of synagogues. On the other hand, state intervention and legislation on religious trusts encouraged uniformity across religions, so that chief rabbis, Anglican bishops, moderators of Protestant Dissenting churches, and Catholic cardinal-archbishops came subtly to resemble each other more closely.

FORMALIZING DOCTRINES AND RITES

Another, related process that helped produce "imperial religions" in the nineteenth century was the formalizing of the rites and philosophies of Asian religions into something more like the belief structures of Judaism, Christianity, and Islam. In other words, not only was there a search for religious authority, but the resultant authorities came to be seen as guardians of discrete, coherent bodies of doctrine. These changes partly reflected the spread of European and American "ways of knowing," which privileged consistency, uniformity, and empirical proof. Partly, too, it reflected the need for ruling groups in these societies to reestablish their claims to authority in the face of changes which were global and not merely Euro-centric in origin. In the eighteenth-century Chinese Empire, for example, what came to be called Confucianism remained a set of classical texts considering issues of ethics and duty, transmitted by great teachers. It was venerated by emperors and gentry-administrators, in the same way perhaps as Aristotle's or Plato's philosophical teachings had been revered in the classical West. It was not really a religion. Over the centuries, however, and partly under the influence of Buddhism, the diversity of Confucian material was turned into a "doctrine" by court intellectuals.[33] Jesuit missionaries, searching for a key to Chinese beliefs, also saw it in this light and began to compare it, usually unfavorably, with Christianity.

This process proceeded further in the nineteenth century, when Protestant missionaries, especially the Reverend James Legge, further refined the notion of Confucianism. He regarded Confucianism as a system of "un-religion," but nevertheless sought the authentic words of the sage and a usable canon.[34] This fixing and formalizing of the Analects of Confucius and other parts of the tradition into a Chinese system of belief was beginning to be important to the Chinese elites, too. They needed to see themselves, and be seen, as authoritative exponents of a cultural tradition, now that their embodied status as scholar-gentry was under assault. As internal dissidence and external pressure grew on China after the 1850s, imperial bureaucrats began to propagate a particularly conservative version of orthodox Confucian belief and practice, insisting on the closure of the country to foreign commercial and spiritual influences. Similar developments occurred in Vietnam after 1802, when the reorganized kingdom itself instituted a fully Confucian bureaucracy and inveighed against "heterodox beliefs," which included Buddhism, Christianity, and even the more colorful versions of the region's own spirit religions.[35]

Some Chinese were no doubt influenced by the terms of the debate about the characteristics of "true religions" set up by Christian missionaries and propagated in mission schools along the China coast and among overseas Chinese communities. They felt they needed a morally authoritative religion with strong ethical norms, with which to fight off the alien doctrines of the Christians. For Kang Youwei, Confucius became the "uncrowned king," a common Christian description of Jesus.[36] Others, such as the first great Chinese nationalist leader, Sun Yatsen, felt that China needed a religion representative of her ancient culture if she was to stand tall once again among nations. By the 1890s, the China coast and the Nanyang (Southeast Asia) had spawned hundreds of societies for the propagation of an entity called "Confucianism." In other words, what had once been seen as a set of precepts for garnering virtue and ordering society now became a religious essence of the Chinese people.

Over the same period, what is now called "Hinduism" was undergoing a parallel transformation. Of course, modern Hindu nationalists and the first generation of Indian scholars of the nineteenth century who analyzed their own religious traditions endorsed the view that there had always been something called Hinduism. They needed it in their battles against the equally fixed entities of Christianity and Islam. But there is much doubt about how far we can assume the existence of anything so homogeneous before the nineteenth century. At best, "Hinduism" in 1780 was a huge extended family of systems of belief, philosophies, rituals, and techniques for harnessing esoteric power, which were recognized by insiders and outsiders as having something in common. Authoritative religious structures certainly existed, and millions of people venerated the sacred books, the Vedas. But authority tended to be localized and specific to certain Indian communities, while only a tiny minority read, and even fewer understood, the Vedas. Muslims acknowledged something they called "Hindu," though this appears often to have been a geographical rather than a religious term, derived as it was from the geographers' term for the river Indus ("Sindhu"). Some precolonial Muslim rulers in India sought to make legal distinctions between their Muslim, Christian, and "Hindu" subjects. Yet, viewed from the inside, this was still a shifting and ambivalent category. Most so-called Hindus would have recognized themselves as worshippers of a transcendent deity (sometimes called Brahman) or of one particular form of God, such as Lord Vishnu or Lord Shiva. But many people away from the great temples – dwellers in forests, marshes, and scrub – would have worshipped divinities who had only the most distant relationship to these great gods.

During the nineteenth century, however, Hinduism, like Confucianism, took on a much more closely defined form. In part, again, this was because the colonial administrators and courts used the terms and delivered judgments in what they thought of as Anglo-Hindu law. In part, it was because people within the Hindu family began to group themselves together under pressure from the aggressive outsiders who attacked the religion as false. Swami Dayananda, a vigorous reformer who founded the Aryan Society (*Arya Samaj*), went further, arguing that Hinduism was the true ancient religion of all mankind, and that it had been a monotheistic religion without a priesthood.[37] In its most perfect form, however, it had been located on the sacred soil of India. This notion, which appealed increasingly to all shades of Hindu opinion, was, of course, very acceptable to an emerging nationalist sentiment. Indian religious men with more traditional beliefs than Dayananda similarly began to highlight certain moral precepts in the vast corpus of Sanskrit mythology and learning, to produce authoritative texts which came to represent creeds and catechisms.

Parts of the address of divine Krishna to king Arjuna in the ancient epic the Mahabharata became a virtual creed for many Hindus, and the mythical warrior-king Ram became a moral exemplar for men, comparable with Jesus. Notions of "sin," "goodness," and salvation, of religiously informed sexual propriety and of philanthropy, were emphasized in Hindu and Buddhist ritual systems, where they had previously been of less relevance or had possessed different spiritual implications. At one level, again, this attempt to create a "Hindu church" reflected the impact of Christianity as the religion of the British colonizer. Hindus needed an accessible tradition and a feeling of historic worth when faced with the humiliation of foreign rule. At the same time, it spoke of the need to legitimate changing social codes in an era when law and the valuation of the individual were changing across the world. The search for homogeneous religions to reflect national or racial essences was not a feature only of the directly colonized world. In Russia, Slavophiles, opposing Westernization, tried to refine the notion of Slavic Orthodox Christianity. In Ethiopia, Coptic bishops began to collect and organize ancient religious texts.

The Christian churches also followed a trend toward greater uniformity of doctrine in many cases, though both authority and doctrine had been more clearly defined in this tradition. Anglicanism was itself a rather loose alliance of British, colonial, and American bishoprics. Its doctrines were internally contested, bearing witness to its birth as a political, as much as a spiritual, movement. Still, the periodic influence of ecclesiastical conferences and a common education system for clergy created a surprising degree of doctrinal cohesion. Careful editing of the Bible and the Prayer Book promoted a similar end. In the Roman Church, the rise of papal authority and ecclesiastical centralization were bound up much more closely with doctrinal orthodoxy. Pope Pius IX promoted the Syllabus of 1864, which outlined a number of errors in doctrine. Throughout much of the nineteenth century, the teaching of what was called "neo-scholasticism" preserved the uniformity of doctrine.[38] It was not until the early years of the twentieth century that the Church faced a modernist theological movement which sought to give wider scope to the interpretation of scripture and church tradition. Even the Orthodox churches of Greece and the Slavonic lands began to respond to pressures of liberal intellectuals and foreign Christian churches by establishing clearer forms of liturgy and doctrine.

THE EXPANSION OF "IMPERIAL" RELIGIONS ON THEIR INNER AND OUTER FRONTIERS

The creation of firmer centers of authority and more easily grasped essential doctrines and rites among the world religions gave force to their geographical expansion and their deeper penetration into societies where formal religion was only surface-deep. In the European and North American worlds, elites took over from the priesthood in trying to spread formal practice across the emerging nation-states. They targeted, first, heterodox and minority groups within their own bodies politic. For example, in Pietist Germany during the early nineteenth century, missions based on university cities such as Halle gave special attention to converting the German Jewish population. British Protestants, meanwhile, turned to the equally difficult and ultimately counterproductive task of converting Roman Catholics, not only in the great English industrial cities and in northern Scotland, but even in Ireland itself. Secondly, evangelical Christians based in north European and east coast American cities sent missions out into the slums of the developing industrial cities or the deep countryside to bring the word of God to the poor. No doubt their initiative derived from an uneasy sense of their social and political vulnerability to political movements from below or from crime motivated by poverty and desperation. External missionizing among Asians and Africans had drawn attention to "Satan's dwellings" at home. In Protestant northern Europe, the "colonization" of the urban working class by religious denominations was at best partial and patchy. Still, churches did establish themselves in all urban localities as a visible presence. They also played a major role in the expansion of mass education. In Britain, a religious census in 1851 shocked the faithful by showing how many of the working classes had drifted away from religious observance.[39] Strenuous efforts were made to build more churches and to draw these people back in. Contemporary Pietist Lutherans in Germany adopted a similar program.

This was more than a simple effort at social control. The evangelicals were also attempting to define themselves as Christian citizens, to "atone" for their own luxury and sin, as one of the key ideas of the period had it. A third target of expanding religion, then, were ruling groups and "middling people" in Europe and North America who had themselves lapsed from Christian practice altogether or had left their original faith. With the re-foundation of the great Catholic orders, such as the Society of Jesus and the creation of new ones such as the Marian order, the Roman Church followed suit in putting an emphasis on internal regeneration. Resolute attempts were undertaken to make country people purify their faintly unorthodox saints' cults. In areas of Protestant political domination, such as Ireland and the united Germany, movements of reform were often counter-strikes against aggressive preaching by the "heretics." In Spain, Italy, and Latin America, the Catholic Church had taken a battering during the revolutionary period. The assaults of liberals and socialists in the course of the nineteenth century forced it onto the offensive, bringing about a "re-Catholicization" of the upper and middle classes in Spain and determined efforts to bring the poor back into the Church.[40]

One important dependent group of people within the Euro-American world, who received close attention from the expanding religious communities, were slaves. In the eighteenth century, slave-owners in the Caribbean and the Americas had been intensely suspicious of attempts to convert their chattels. This attitude was no longer respectable in the next century, and vibrant Christian cults of resignation and protest spread across the plantations. Here the greatest change was registered in the United States. Before the Civil War, the Afro-American population, both slave and free, had had a kind of affiliate status in many of the white churches of the southern and western states. In the countryside, a submerged form of black church in its own Babylonian exile had served to promote a sense of community and a desire for change.[41] Many white churches in the southern states still clung to the doctrine that slavery could be justified by the Bible, while, on the other hand, religion provided powerful themes for the abolitionists during the prelude to war.

The consequence of the defeat of the South and of slave emancipation was a massive growth of organized religion among Afro-Americans. In the towns, blacks seized control of their own churches. In the countryside, the submerged slave church emerged into the light, creating its own preachers and ecclesiastical disciplines. The church became "the first social institution fully controlled by black men in America."[42] These new black churches, with the Baptists in the forefront, were particularly important in fostering educational institutions and literacy among the 90 percent of southern black adults who were illiterate in 1860. Ex-slaves thirsted to read the Word of God for themselves. Decentralized, community-controlled churches had always been critical institutions in the westward expansion of the American republic. As in other parts of the world, the later nineteenth century saw a social deepening and consolidation of organized religion. In the case of the American South, however, this deepening tended to institutionalize racial division. Most blacks withdrew from the white churches in which they had previously been second-class associates, constantly reminded of the "legitimacy" of slavery.

These patterns of internal consolidation were accompanied by a vast expansion of missionary activity overseas and among non-Christian peoples, as European power spread over the globe. The outstanding examples of the mass expansion of the world religions in the nineteenth century can be found in Africa. But, ironically and to the chagrin of Christian officials and missionaries, Islam was widely the winner.[43] The expansion of formal Islamic belief and practice into sub-Saharan Africa, especially into what is now Nigeria, occurred in the late eighteenth and early nineteenth centuries.[44] Critical here, as they had been in central and south Asia in the thirteenth and fourteenth centuries, were the mystical Sufi orders and, especially in north and central Africa, the Qadariyya and the purist Sanussiya orders. The idea that secret knowledge of Islam was passed down in pupil-teacher families and made immanent in the charisma of the tombs of great teachers proved an attractive one for the leaders of great north African lineages. Emerging dynasts developed close relationships of patronage with learned men who had prayed at the Arabian holy places and had been initiated into a Sufi order. Sometimes, marriage relations developed between the military families and the learned ones. The authority of Sufi teacher and warrior-king therefore reinforced each other in developing north African state systems. The kings spread Islamic norms in their territories, while new adherents to the kingdom were initiated into the Sufi orders. Merchants also benefited from the creation of new communities of trust and the growth of political security. Movements of Islamic consolidation consequently spread into southern Sudan and along the Arab-influenced trade routes of central and east Africa. The community of Islam was serviceable to new networks of merchant trust and to the proprieties of newly settled townsmen. Islam also provided the benefits of spiritual and moral assurance in a world still troubled by random occult violence and physical depredation.

The Fulani Jihad, or "war of conversion" of 1800–20, which led to the foundation of the Sokoto Khilafat, or Islamic state, in what is now northern Nigeria, was the most dramatic of these movements of Islamic consolidation and expansion.[45] In this region there had long existed a delicate balance between townsmen and cultivators of the Hausa ethnic group and the Fulani

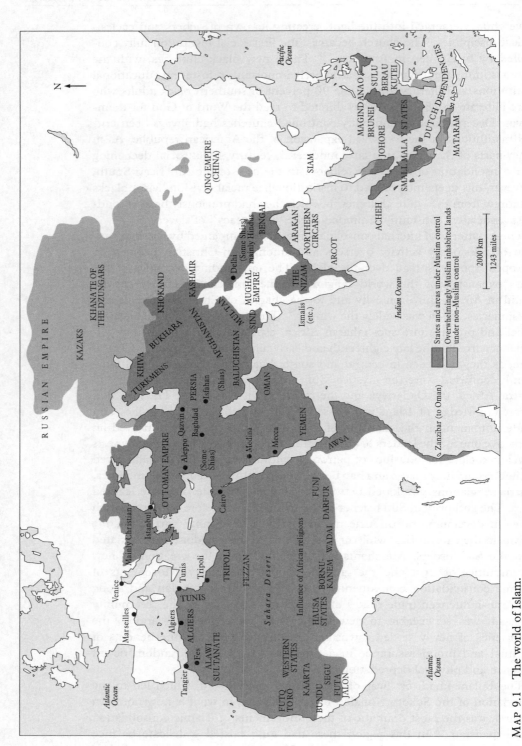

MAP 9.1 The world of Islam.
Source: Amira K. Bennison, in A. G. Hopkins (ed.) *Globalization in World History* (New York, 2002), pp. 82–3.

ILLUSTRATION 9.4   A Maulvi preaching at the end of the feast of Ramadan, Algeria, 1905. Photo by C. J. P. Cave.

herdsmen whose wealth lay in the herds of cattle which they sold to the cultivators. The Fulani were warriors as well as cattle-keepers, and they "offered" protection to the settled people, sometimes becoming local rulers. About 1800, restless Fulani leaders received the message of Islam from a teacher, Dan Fodio, who had been on pilgrimage to Mecca. The spread of the Islamic message reflected a much wider movement of revival which flowed through the Middle East and north Africa in the eighteenth and early nineteenth centuries. This brought young men from distant parts of Africa to Rabat, Cairo, and Mecca, and sent them back to their place of birth to teach more orthodox forms of Islam. Yet the establishment of the Khilafat was empowered by a general political and social change. After 1800, aspiring Fulani leaders were rapidly displacing Hausa magnates and settling as a local aristocracy amongst the townsmen and farmers of the region. The incoming Fulani lineages created a relatively strong centralized state. This became the guardian of Islamic norms and established local Muslim judicial officers, who regulated custom and patterns of inheritance. The rulers of Sokoto thereby created one of the only sub-Saharan states ruled by written laws rather than by the will of kings.[46]

Christian expansion was almost as spectacular in nineteenth-century Africa. Christian missionary activity and the conversion of African kings and their nobles had a very long history here. Coptic Christians had helped bring about the conversion of Ethiopia in the early centuries of the first millennium. In the mid-sixteenth century, Portuguese missionaries had registered some success in converting to Christianity African courts along the west coast, where trading and hence cultural links with the European world held out advantages. The decline of these court centers early in the following century had resulted in a widespread reversion to African cults, but Christianity remained a tenuous presence around the factories and slave ports on the coast. The Christian missionary effort in Africa, as in much of the rest of the world, revived again immediately after 1800.[47] Much of it was based in the colony of former American slaves in Liberia, and of British ones in Sierra Leone. On the west coast, Roman Catholic "barefoot" Capuchin friars were often the first in the field. Meanwhile, in southern Africa, Christianity had already been established by the Boer farmers who had inhabited the Cape since the 1640s. Some of their freed slaves from the African or the Malay world provided an early pool of Christian converts. When the British occupied the Cape permanently after 1806, the pace of conversions among Africans picked up. Dutch and British missionary societies began competitively to convert local Khoisan, Xhosa, and ultimately Zulu peoples; or rather, these local peoples began to see profit and value in attaching themselves to one or more mission stations. African Christians and people of mixed race became missionaries to other African people.

Outside coastal West Africa and the Cape, where Christianity was already being built around mission stations and native converts, conversion in the first half of the nineteenth century followed its earlier ambivalent and shifting patterns. Here the "conversion," or at least acquiescence, of warrior-leaders and tribal elders was generally the first stage. These men often brought in missionaries to strengthen their own access to divine power and legitimacy. Sometimes one clan or group "converted" to Christianity as an act of political defiance against other groups. Elsewhere, on the fringes of the still-young European townships, conversion sometimes went along with the settlement of formerly nomadic or "predatory" groups and the development of the market. This distantly echoed the form of conversion to Islam. Changes in religious practice of this sort were often very incomplete from the missionary point of view, hardly representing "conversion" in the biblical sense at all. Indigenous peoples might accept the broad supremacy of the Christian God as a supreme deity, but continued their local magical and healing cults. As on the fringes of other expanding "imperial religions," mixed or syncretic cults were very common. Preachers arose who invoked the Christian God but also worshipped the ancestral spirits and called up occult forces. The boundaries between Christianity and what the missions called "paganism" were very permeable.

After about 1860, however, the pace of the expansion of Christianity increased dramatically, and conversion itself seems to have changed form.[48] In part, this was the result of developments in Europe and the Americas. It went along with the rise of nationalism and the global spread of the scientific and manufacturing economy. Improved drugs against tropical diseases made it possible for Europeans and Americans to spend longer in Africa. As mining, palm oil, and coffee companies began to exploit Africa in earnest, missionaries followed in their wake. The missionaries sometimes irritated the ruthless entrepreneurs, but others saw the merit of having a docile, Christian work force. Eager, dedicated evangelists from all the Christian denominations flooded into Africa as communications improved and the great powers began to occupy large sectors of the continent. It has been estimated that there were as many as 100,000 European missionaries in Africa by 1900. Chiefs still played a major part in these changes, symbolically capturing the potency of the missionaries. For instance, the Barotse chief, Lewanika, patronized a series of missionaries to demonstrate his royal power and benevolence.[49] To all intents and purposes, he used these men as tools of power and carefully controlled their impact on his people. However, as the schools of the mission stations began to produce more and more young men educated in European languages, the process became self-reinforcing. Christian education conferred literacy, and literacy in turn conferred power and economic status. Christianity began to become an avenue for social mobility, so that young men outside the bounds of the tribal leaderships became new focuses of power in their communities. This was a process that the missionaries found hard to direct. Even before the First World War, independent African churches with their own preachers had begun to emerge. Conversion began to change in form, too, during this phase. Settled systems of Christian education left less room for the persistence of older cults or forms of syncretism. The newly educated young men policed the boundaries of their new religion, seeking decisively to put behind them the "errors" of their ancestors.

Similar changes occurred in other parts of the world. In the Pacific, the Maori, Polynesian, and Melanesian populations went through a parallel cycle of settlement, increased awareness of the power and value of literacy, and formal conversion to Christianity. Initially, as in Africa, the new faith more often confirmed than undermined the social order. Chiefs in Fiji and Tonga, for instance, confirmed their political status and links with the dominant British power by inviting in Christian missions and encouraging conversion.[50] Yet the speed of conversion in the Pacific and New Zealand suggests that a much wider range of forces was at work to attract people to Christianity besides purely political aims: fascination with the new, including trade goods like tobacco, eagerness for travel, the desire to read, and genuine spiritual interest. The Maori chief Temorenga wrote to the Reverend William Yate of the Church Missionary Society:

> Remember, that it was Temorenga, who sat in your veranda at your house-door, and told you all about native men's ways. Do not forget who I am, and what I have said to you. Bring out one, two, three, perhaps more Missionaries to go to the Southern Tribes, that there may be no more fighting between us here and them there . . . . Let the men, who carry the fowls for you on board the man of war, carry me back one fig of tobacco, as my pipe is empty. Go in peace, Mr Yate; so says Temorenga at Manawenua, his residence, where he sits.[51]

A parallel pattern occurred in North and South America as the frontier of European settlement expanded. In the United States, Christianity triumphed decisively over the surviving tribal cults when the First Nations were penned into reservations after 1850. In Central and South America the invasion of indigenous scrub and forests by farmers and loggers expanded the frontiers of Christianity to newly settled Amerindian communities, especially in the Central American hinterland and along the Brazilian river systems.

In all these cases, colonial power broadly gained in the medium term from the spread of Christianity. It provided colonizers with intermediaries who shared some of their preconceptions and helped create accessible and disciplined labor forces. In the longer term, however, Christianized populations, or populations feeling the pressure of missionizing foreigners, began to turn some Christian beliefs against the colonizers. The Judaeo-Christian theme of the "chosen people" was used by the first generation of native rights activists in the Pacific during the 1880s and 1890s to argue that the appropriation of Maori and Fijian lands by British and, later, Indians should stop. The same theme was used to empower Afro-American churches in the southern United States, as they struggled to achieve the status of citizens promised during the Civil War. Some interpretations of the equality of all peoples before God provided good ammunition for native intellectuals writing against the segregation and racial exclusiveness that became a powerful ideology toward the end of the century. This reaction was not simply a feature of the colonized world. Christian themes were pressed into service by radicals everywhere, and the very expansion of the world religions helped new political leaderships find common cause with pious peasant-farmers and working-class activists. Even Communism inherited and used themes derived from a Christian ethic. The great Communist hymn, the "Internationale," composed by a Frenchman at the time of the Paris Commune, spoke of salvation, but on this earth, and of a saviour, who was not Christ, but the worker himself.

This rapid pace of Christian evangelization was not matched in the Islamic world and the great Asian societies, however, despite the increase of European power there after 1800. Neither Catholic nor Protestant missions had much effect on Indian, Chinese, or Japanese societies, if we think mainly in terms of "conversion." This was largely because the hierarchies of the religions of these countries were powerful and literate, and they quickly began to fight back and "write back" against Christianity, using print media and movements of proselytization themselves. In part, though, it was because Christianity did not confer high status. Christians in the Eastern world had long been perceived as slaves, conquered serfs, despised businessmen, or half-breed crews of fornicators and alcoholics. Conversion conferred no particular educational or economic advantage which could not be acquired by education without conversion, often within complaisant, or unduly hopeful, Christian institutions.

Perhaps the most important point, however, was that the Asian religions rapidly took up Christian missionaries' methods of preaching and evangelization. In some senses indeed, they became proselytizing religions for the first time. By 1900, the Hindu orthodox had begun to establish purifying associations (*shuddhi sabhas*), which tried to "reconvert" to Hinduism lower-caste and "tribal" groups who had become Muslim or Christian in recent times. Of course, the idea of conversion in Hinduism, or even the idea of a unified Hinduism itself, was quite recent in origin. This went along with the slower and older process of ritual consolidation by which Hindu priests, ascetics, and text-readers moved among tribal and low-caste people, gradually attaching them to more orthodox rites and forms of worship. In the case of the Arya Samaj, the Aryan Society, a self-consciously modern form of Hinduism, "evangelical" activity extended to denouncing other world religions and sending missions to Indian communities abroad in places such as Fiji, Mauritius, and the Caribbean. The society's preachers and publicists consciously imitated the aggressive form of Christian preaching and printing and ridiculed the inconsistencies and dubious logic of the Christian scriptures. Toward the end of the nineteenth century, students along the China coast and in Southeast Asia followed suit and began to found organizations such as the already mentioned Young Men's Buddhist Associations, which were directly modeled on the YMCA and played a significant role in the origins of Chinese nationalism. In all these revivalist movements, the newspaper and printed pamphlet played an important role in confirming the integrity of believers.

These empires of religion, reforming and consolidating themselves, had much in common with the national states on which so many histories of the period have concentrated. They also sought more unified, central authorities. They spawned larger bureaucracies. They tried to prevent syncretic cults drawing on different religions, just as the national states were uneasy with citizens who displayed loyalty to one or more polity. Like the nation-states, they also benefited from the massive step forward in the technology, the density of communications, and the human race's control over its natural environment. We now consider in more detail three typical features of the era: the expansion of religious travel, or pilgrimage; the harnessing of print media; and the worldwide increase in religious building. In all these developments, the processes of uniformity were working at world level.

PILGRIMAGE AND GLOBALIZATION

Human beings have always been religious nomads. In all the great religions, the wanderer in search of religious experience has always had a place. Pilgrimage to Jerusalem, Mecca, Lord Shiva's Benares, or the places associated with the life of the Buddha were all firmly established by the turn of the first millennium of the Christian Era. The armed pilgrimage, crusade, or "lesser" jihad also emerged early in the Christian Era. But until the turn of the nineteenth century, pilgrimage of any sort was hazardous and costly. Devotees and members of religious orders already separated from their families and from the agricultural cycles went on pilgrimage. So too did the rich, who could afford to leave their lands and businesses in the hands of stewards. Ordinary people, of course, did go in

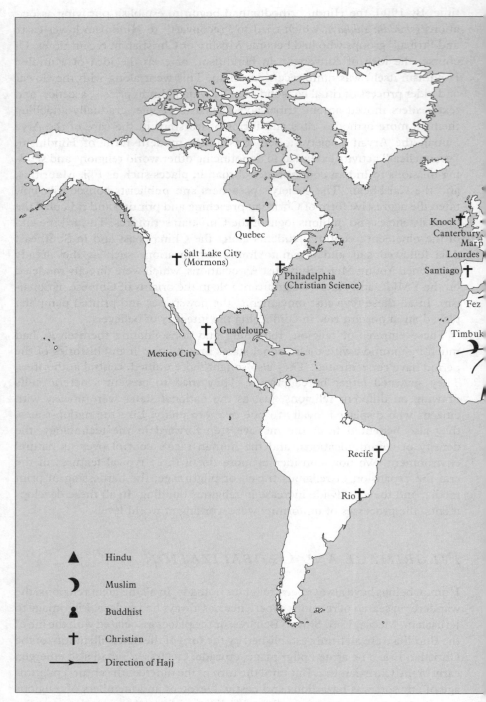

MAP 9.2 Major religious centers in the nineteenth century.

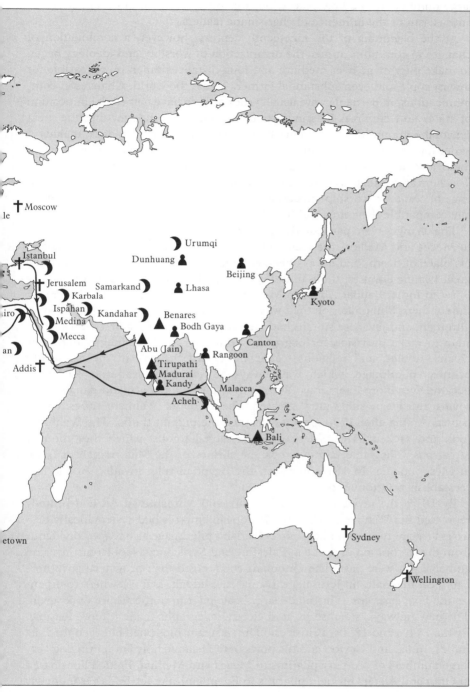

MAP 9.2 (*Continued*)

large numbers to the holy places, but this often reflected unusual periods of enthusiasm or the influence of charismatic leaders.

At the beginning of the nineteenth century, however, a combination of changes in communications, the organization of worship, and ideology began to make pilgrimage over medium and long distances much more feasible for townspeople and even substantial farmers across the world. Changes in communications, in particular, are usually supposed to have helped the imposition of states and empires. It is important to remember, though, that the great spiritual communities also secured advantages from such changes, making it easier for normative and authorized versions of religious belief and practice to mold and accommodate themselves to the sensibilities of ordinary people. Teachers and texts passed to and fro along the pilgrimage routes. The experience of common worship encouraged people to standardize and make mutually compatible their rites and beliefs.

The changes were particularly apparent in the domain of Islam. Pilgrimage to Mecca and Medina, the scenes of the Prophet's revelation, and Jerusalem, his place of death, had always been enjoined on Muslims. In the days of the great Islamic empires, thousands of people had passed through ports such as Surat in India, Bandar Abbas in Mesopotamia, Bandar Acheh in Sumatra, or the southern Philippines on their way to the holy places. The Mughal, Safavid, Ottoman, and Javanese sultans had regarded it as one of the first duties of the state to make provision for pilgrimage. But pilgrims were mainly rich merchants, nobles, and religious teachers. Toward the end of the eighteenth century, pilgrimage, which was always at risk from seaborne predators, became ever more dangerous. By sea, the "pirate" menace and danger from roving European ships grew greater. The revolt of Wahhabi tribesmen in central Arabia after 1730 greatly disrupted the pilgrim traffic. The Wahhabis took and sacked Mecca, destroying its sacred tombs, which they thought idolatrous. The same fate overtook the shrines of the Shia branch of Islam in Mesopotamia. In 1811, however, the Egyptian ruler invaded Arabia and reestablished Ottoman power.[52]

By 1815, the revived Ottoman Empire and Muhammad Ali had brutally repressed the Wahhabis, while the European empires had systematically destroyed free port-kings and corsairs. Overland pilgrimage also reaped dividends from the restoration of peace in Palestine and Syria once Napoleonic invasion and civil war were past. The Ottomans encouraged their provincial governors and local magnates in Jerusalem, Damascus, Jiddah, and elsewhere to organize the Hajj caravans. This made large-scale pilgrim traffic secure once again. The new railways, steamships, and electric telegraphs made it more feasible. By the 1840s and 1850s, British and Dutch steamships plied between the East Indies, India, and Ceylon and the ports of the Islamic holy land, bringing very large numbers of ordinary pilgrims to Mecca and Medina. French lines based in Oran and Algiers brought pilgrims to Egypt en route for Jiddah from newly conquered North and West Africa. The fact that the costs of transport and the length of passage had been greatly reduced meant that middle-class people could take the Hajj for the first time. A new way of organizing the pilgrimage and tending to pilgrims was developed. The Ottoman authorities and the local Arab dynasties took their role as guarantors of the Hajj increasingly seriously as the nineteenth century wore on. Snouck Hurgronje, the famous Dutch oriental scholar, made a study of the pilgrimage from Indonesia in the 1880s. He observed the careful organization of middlemen, preachers, doctors, and pilgrim-mentors which encouraged a huge growth in pilgrimages from Indonesia in the late nineteenth century.[53]

Ideological changes both confirmed and resulted from these processes. While it was an uneven process, the slow spread of forms of Islam which were more scripturally orthodox increased the attractions of pilgrimage to Mecca and Medina. For instance, the jihads in northern Nigeria in the 1820s and 1830s, which established the Sokoto caliphate, also encouraged more "Nigerians" to conform to the dictates of Islam, including making the Hajj once in their lifetime. In turn, the thousands of people who saw the sites of the Prophet's life with their own eyes took back the sense of blessing to their own distant communities. Pilgrimage increased people's own status in society. They were revered and called "Hajji," emblazoned their houses with texts and, sometimes, maps of the pilgrimage. This encouraged others to make the journey. The expansion of pilgrimage advanced the new emphasis on the Prophet's person as exemplar of the perfect life which was a feature of Islam in many societies during this period. Practices and ideas common at Mecca and Medina, such as homilies on the life of the Prophet, were taken back to Africa, India, Indonesia, and southwest China. The famed teachers of nineteenth-century Islam became known across a broader and broader range of the Islamic world. A more unified vision of Islam was, therefore, both an encouragement to pilgrimage and a consequence of it. In time, the new awareness of the community of the Islamic world provided the groundwork for the so-called pan-Islamic political movements in the second half of the nineteenth century.[54]

One aspect of the rise of nineteenth-century pilgrimage was the manner in which it elevated even further the importance of particular pilgrimage centers. So in Hinduism, the cities of Benares, Gaya, and Allahabad in north India emerged as the preeminent centers to visit in search of salvation, whereas earlier, other regional centers had been regarded as almost equally sacred. To some degree this reflected improvements in communications, but an element of competition also set in here. Muslims sometimes called Benares (Varanasi) the "Mecca of India," and Hindus seem to have assented increasingly to this idea. Yet this does not mean that smaller centers were unimportant. On the contrary, one feature of the expansion of normative religion was the co-option and even creation of local centers of devotion and pilgrimage by religious authorities. A few of the Muslim reformers of the nineteenth century were actively hostile to Sufi mystics and their local cult places, but most urged the pious and learned to become initiated in the Sufi brotherhoods in order to direct and discipline these scenes of local worship.[55]

In the nineteenth century, Roman Catholic pilgrimage to Rome also expanded greatly as a result of the improvements of internal security in Europe and the growth of the railways. The revived Catholic Church, strengthened by its "Babylonian exile" during the Napoleonic wars, used pilgrimage to Rome to spread its devotional message by adapting the secular modes of tourist promotion for religious purposes. But faced with rumors of the growth of socialism and secularism, it also made deliberate attempts to build up centers of local folk devotion at strategic points. Some of the chosen sites had been renowned since the Middle Ages. These included the great basilica of St Anthony at Padua. Whereas Padua had then been the resort of the Venetian aristocracy, by the later nineteenth century large numbers of ordinary pilgrims from all over Italy and later Spain, Portugal, Poland, and Spanish America began to come to seek the saint's healing intercession.

More Roman Catholic places of pilgrimage developed in the later nineteenth century, because after mid-century the popes made more saints, and places associated with some of these, renowned for miracles, became sites of pilgrimage. Pope Pius IX, who started the trend, distrusted intellectuals and had spent his early years close to the common people. He promoted the cult of Mary, promulgated the doctrine of the Immaculate Conception, and felt an affinity for popular cults. But the beatification or sanctification of popular miracle-workers and teachers also had a clear political context. The Church had come under pressure with the rise of secular forces in France after the fall of Napoleon III and in Germany with Bismarck's long struggle with the Catholic Church during the so-called *Kulturkampf*, or culture wars. So the promotion of popular cults became a way of counterattacking the secular trend from below. Some sites were wholly new and here none was more important than the great shrine of Lourdes in southern France (see illustration 9.1).[56] The rise of the cult of Bernadette, the young woman who saw visions of the Virgin, was initially a popular phenomenon. It was local people who believed in the promise of salvation she had revealed to them. Then, "during the French conflicts over religion and clericalism, the pilgrimage to Lourdes became a catholic political demonstration."[57] After the separation of Church and state in France in 1907, the day of the miraculous appearance to Bernadette was declared a feast day for the whole Church by the pope.

Similar local cults and pilgrimage cycles were promoted in other lands where the Roman Church faced powerful enemies, notably at Knock in Ireland and at Marpingen in Germany. Yet even where politics did not form the background, the blessing of local cults by the Church helped to control and form movements of popular religion, and thus to create greater homogeneity of belief and practice. In Velanganni in southern India, the church of Our Lady of the Snows, a popular site of pilgrimage for the local Portuguese-speaking Christian maritime community, was promoted by a more active papacy. In Central and South America, revolutionaries and reactionaries alike sought papal benediction and authorization for pilgrimages which had grown up around specifically American versions of the Virgin Mary, some of which were venerated at shrines close to pre-Columbian cult centers.

In many major religious traditions, in fact, pilgrimage to places of spiritual power, great and small, became increasingly accepted as a form of worship in its own right. Moreover, the spiritual journey, self-sacrifice, and joy experienced gave the pilgrim a special form of individuality, which he or she could share with others. It became a form of self-expression and gave rise to printed accounts of travels in many languages.

PRINTING AND THE PROPAGATION OF RELIGION

The anthropological historian Benedict Anderson popularized the view that rapidly developing techniques of printing and the proliferation of books and newspapers helped create new, imagined national communities. However, what was true for the nation was equally true for religion in the more uniform pattern that it now came to assume. In many parts of the world, notably in the Middle East, southern Asia, and Africa, printing had made little headway before the beginning of the nineteenth century. In eastern Asia, ancient techniques of block printing had long existed, and these had been used to diffuse religious and ethical literature. But the coming of movable type from Western sources nevertheless opened up whole new possibilities for the easy production and cheap distribution of literature. Even in the Western world, the nineteenth century saw great advances in printing techniques, making possible mass publishing of books. Newspapers, a hobby of the elite in the eighteenth century, hugely increased their print runs, so that by the later nineteenth century, syndicated information was made available through newspapers with print runs of over a million, controlled by "press barons" in Europe and North America.

Religious books, pamphlets, and newspapers formed a very large category within this expanding world of publishing. The Bible itself was, of course, the single most published book in all the Protestant countries of Europe and North America. The early nineteenth century saw a great surge in the publication of missionary and religious journals. It would not be an exaggeration to say that the breach in the English-speaking world caused by the American Revolution had been largely healed by 1830, and that linked missionary activities within and outside the purview of the British Empire were a critical reason for the rapprochement between them. While the great national newspapers of Europe are remembered, it is also important to acknowledge that publications such as the Anglican *Church Times* were among the most important of all newspaper publications. Though the Roman Catholic liturgy remained in Latin, and the possibilities for mass publication of the Vulgate were limited, Catholic publications achieved a degree of uniformity and diffusion which was unknown before 1789. The papal journal *Osservatore Romano*, founded in 1871, achieved a special status as the authoritative voice of the Church. This explosion of print helped smaller sects, too. In 1885, the first edition of the *Christian Science Journal* appeared in Boston. Here, religion and science, the two great concerns of the age, came together in the context of print.

ILLUSTRATION 9.5   The Muslim Boys' School at Famagusta, Cyprus, 1909. Photo by A. H. Fisher.

To a greater or lesser extent, the great scriptural texts and propaganda tracts of other world religions went through a similar transformation. By 1870, the Arabic Quran was being published very extensively in Cairo, Alexandria, Damascus, and Istanbul.[58] But in the south and southeast Asian worlds, the transformation was even more significant. In India, the Quran, which had earlier been translated from Arabic into Persian, was made available for the first time in Urdu, a vernacular tongue, by purist reformers in the 1840s. A Malay edition of the Quran appeared shortly afterwards. Moral and ethical teachings of the faith were also published and widely disseminated from this date onward. Early newspapers in Arabic, Persian, Urdu, and Malay filled their pages with sermons, pious articles, and scriptural stories.

In the Christian, Jewish, and Muslim cases, preprint and early print religious texts had already achieved a degree of uniformity. There was something much more like an authorized version of Scripture and tradition available to most branches of the Christian Church and of Islam. What happened as a result of the changes in communication during the nineteenth century was the creation of an even greater degree of uniformity and popular penetration of versions of religious texts. This occurred not only through movements of conversion at home and abroad, but because conflicts over doctrine, between Catholic and Protestant, or between Sunni and Shia Muslim, Ahmadiyya and Bahai, also sharpened up doctrinal discipline. In the case of Hinduism and Buddhism and the other Indian religions (such as Sikhism, Jainism, and Zoroastrianism), the process was even more radical, at least as far as the content of "doctrine" was concerned. In one sense, one could say that Hindu and Buddhist doctrine were actually created in the nineteenth century, mainly as a consequence of the print revolution. Previously, a massively complex and even contradictory bundle of hallowed traditions had existed. Print allowed Hinduism to be arrayed in textual form in one single bookcase. It also allowed texts to be more easily translated and subjected to the new scientific and historical types of analysis which were alluded to in chapter 8.

RELIGIOUS BUILDING

Religions have always created sacred landscapes which memorialized the appearance of divinity on the soil and provided places where believers could gather together and re-create their sense of community. Religious building has also long been a way in which rulers or groups of aristocrats and magnates announce their own status and power, calling attention to their piety and self-sacrifice for the community. Nineteenth-century men and women set out with even greater vigor to sanctify their landscapes. Islam already had what was perhaps the most systematic organization of religious building. The presence of a congregational mosque, local neighborhood mosques, and public baths for ritual purposes was itself an important indication of the existence of a Muslim community. From the days of the Prophet onward, when Muslim rulers conquered new lands, they constructed great mosques, announcing God's sovereignty and, through it, their own. As an era in which Islam spread very fast, especially in the continent of Africa, the nineteenth century saw the construction of many new mosques. Alongside rulers, newly wealthy trading people constructed religious buildings and hospices for pilgrims and the poor, especially perhaps when they were connected with European-dominated commerce and were trying to preserve their reputations in the eyes of their coreligionists.

Among Muslims, the chief change in the nineteenth century, apart from the simple global expansion of mosques, was the beginnings of the trend toward architectural conformity. The Arabian and Ottoman styles of domed mosque architecture won out over the much more heterogeneous set of styles which had characterized the earlier period (see illustration 9.6). In particular, the

Arabian form spread into West Africa, southern India, and the Malay Peninsula and Indonesian archipelago, where local forms of walled compound and wooden hall had previously been prevalent. This change was another aspect of the growing uniformity of doctrine and practice which was discussed in the previous section. If rulers had made pilgrimages to the holy places, they wanted the mosques they patronized to look more like those they had seen in Mecca, Medina, or Karbala. If they had not been there, they wished to copy and re-create the ideal buildings they saw in block prints or imagined from travelers' tales.

The nineteenth century was also perhaps the most important period of church building in Christian history since the High Middle Ages. New construction techniques and scientific progress helped make this possible. Fervent faith and the rolled-steel joist reinforced each other. Philanthropists and rising businessmen built new churches and cathedrals in the industrial districts and burgeoning middle-class suburbs to signal piety and progress. Religious toleration also had the effect of redoubling the number of churches, as newly enfranchised Catholic communities in northern Europe built on a huge scale. Massive Roman Catholic and Dissenter edifices began to rear up in competition with older Protestant churches in English, Irish, American, and German cities to signal the end of earlier discrimination. In much of the English-speaking and German world, there was a conscious return to the

ILLUSTRATION 9.6 The "Muhammadan temple," or Nagore Dargah, Singapore, c.1880.

style of the Middle Ages. The Gothic style recalled the supposedly seamless Christian communities of the undivided Christian world and spoke to that nostalgia for a social order untroubled by class or consumerism which was mentioned in chapter 8. Sometimes the results were dire, as in the clumsy attempts of the architect Viollet-le-Duc to make the real Gothic buildings of Paris yet more gothic,[59] so endangering their stylistic integrity.

This spread of religious edifices also happened in the overseas world. Wherever Europeans conquered or held influence, from the China coast to southern Africa, they built large churches where previously timid and anxious communities of indigenous Christians had built only modestly. If many colonial governments in Asia were extremely wary of encouraging conversion amongst non-Christians, this did not prevent expatriate communities from announcing their dominance and the supremacy of their own religions in less direct ways. French Indochina was seeded with churches on the pattern of the church of Saint-Sulpice or Notre-Dame in Paris. Anglican churches began to rear up among the golf links of India's, Burma's, and Malaya's European retreats and hill stations. Here it was not only Christians who gained new self-confidence. Newly wealthy Hindu and Buddhist communities invested huge sums in the construction of temples in cities long dominated by mosques or in overseas settlements where Hindus had previously been a small and harassed minority. These temples, like the Christian churches, were stylistic throwbacks. They summoned up visions of the great Hindu temples of the eleventh to thirteenth centuries. But if concrete and rolled steel gave these new structures greater stability, the art that decorated them was garish and mundane by comparison with that of those great buildings.

All these architectural developments were an aspect of the new urbanism which chapter 8 has shown was so prominent in the later nineteenth century. The city life-style set the tone for the whole society in a way that had not been true even in the eighteenth century. Consequently, religious authorities redoubled their efforts to be central to urban life through the provision of great sacred buildings.

Religious building illustrates well a central concern of this book. There was growing uniformity of styles and social functions across the world and across religions. The West was not the only center of diffusion. The Arabic mosque style, the late Qing Confucian temple style, and the tenth-century, central Indian style of Hindu temple achieved a dominance parallel to that of the Gothic church. It was not even that this diffusion of these styles always represented a reaction to the expansion of Christendom. The opposite was often the case. Christian communities built new edifices to display their piety to Muslim, Hindu, or Buddhist neighbors.

RELIGION AND THE NATION

The nineteenth century was a period when religious texts, oleographs, printed copies of the Bible and the Quran, and small devotional objects and amulets, often now mass-produced, penetrated deeply into everyday life. The landscape was scattered with new religious structures, and millions more people made long voyages and treks to experience the community of religious belief. Religious education was formalized and expanded across most of the world, and the shrines of saints, Sufis, and local deities were annexed more firmly to the wider world of abstract religious norms. If, then, this was an era of demystification, as Max Weber termed it, it can only have been so in a very specialized sense. It may be that some forms of magic, magicians, shamans, and fetish objects lost power, that ghosts retreated into the world of romance, and that everyday things lost their power to convey malevolence or benediction. Yet this was only so among the small international middle class. Elsewhere such rationalization had not proceeded very far. Meanwhile, religions as formal structures of authority and belief had made enormous advances. They stood up to the emerging nation-state, and in most parts of the world, if not in Europe, they were still powerful when the nation-state began to fray and fragment toward the end of the twentieth century.

As significantly, many modern nationalisms were themselves heavily influenced by emerging religious solidarities of the type discussed here and, by the same token, helped shape them. The leadership and the formal agenda of national movements might well speak in terms of liberalism, secularism, or economic justice, but in the popular mind religion and the demand for nationhood were more closely paired. Religion provided a rallying cry for Spanish patriots and Russians fighting Napoleon. In Russia, one of the most powerful ideologies proved to be pan-Slavism. This was a heady amalgam made up of romantic nationalism, reaction to Western "materialism" and "individualism," and, above all, a devotion to the Orthodox Church and its temporal defender, the tsar. Unlike the case of Roman Catholicism or Islam, the Orthodox Church did not witness a deep revision of doctrine or ritual in the course of the nineteenth century. There were, it is true, some proselytizing movements in the Caucasus and central Asia, designed to prevent people from "relapsing" into Islam. But these were on a small scale. Instead, the Church became a symbol of nationality. Numerous intellectuals and artists rode to its defense as a kind of mystical embodiment of the soul of the Russian people. In the Balkans, the old Orthodox Christian ecumene of the Ottoman Empire was broken up into a series of national churches. A new Church of Greece was founded in 1833 after national independence. Later, in 1870, a Bulgarian Church emerged. As Mark Mazower notes, "Religion became a marker of national identity in ways not known before."[60] Religious leaderships were more closely tied to national projects. Yet, at the same time, they were given the leeway to proselytize in regional languages and to standardize and discipline peasant religion in a way that had not happened under the Ottoman governors.

The cases of Ireland and Poland, both dependencies of larger, composite states during the nineteenth century, show how a sense of religious discrimination and religious pride could energize popular nationalism or resistance. The poet Kazimierz Brodzinski (1791–1835) seemed to sum up the experience for both submerged motherlands. He wrote, referring to the 1795 annexation and partition of Poland:

> Hail, O Christ, Thou Lord of Men,
> Poland, in Thy footsteps treading,
> Like Thee suffers, at Thy bidding
> Like Thee, too, shall rise again.[61]

Religion and patriotic identities reacted in explosive ways. In 1879, for instance, when Austrian troops entered Bosnia as part of the peace treaty which ended the war between Austria and the Ottomans, there occurred a major popular revolt which was given force by religious solidarity. It might have been expected that the tough mountain Muslims would revolt, but so too did the Orthodox Christians of this old Ottoman province. Neither group wanted to be dominated by Austrian Roman Catholics. Revived religion, as much as ethnic or linguistic nationalism, was to keep the Balkan crisis simmering until 1914 and, indeed, to the present day. Again, in Egypt and Muslim India, the demands for national independence which emerged in the 1880s were strengthened and given shape by the sense that religion was in danger. And religion could, of course, fragment a drive for national self-determination as often as unite it.

CONCLUSION: THE SPIRITS OF THE AGE

Historians of ideas have come to realize in the last generation how deeply religion influenced the supposedly secular ideologies and sciences of the nineteenth century. For instance, early nineteenth-century economics and demography in Protestant nations were influenced by the idea that periodic economic downfalls were a sign of God's punishment, for which the peoples had to atone. Much liberal, and even socialist, thought continued to reflect deep-rooted ideas about justice and community which were of Christian origin. When Hindus, Muslims, and Buddhists adapted such ideas to their own circumstances, they also tinctured them with religious sensibilities. The social thought of non-Western elites was everywhere suffused with religious ideas about good government and divine justice. So it was with science. Christian missionaries were pioneers of scientific collection and categorization, especially in Africa and the Pacific, as they sought to display God's bounty to humankind through his creation. The Christian squabble with Darwin has obscured the *modus vivendi* to which religious people and scientists generally subscribed. Equally, Hindu and Muslim intellectuals sought to prove the verity of their own sacred texts by showing that they were replete with scientific wisdom. They saw no conflict between science and religion.

One final point should be made. This chapter has argued that the years after 1815 saw the expansion and consolidation of the great world religions. In retrospect, this process is as important as, if not more important than, the theme of the rise of nationalism or liberalism, which has so often dominated studies of this period. It would be wrong, however, to imagine that uniformity in religious practice, let alone belief, ruled unchallenged across the globe in 1914. On the contrary, the religious experience of many people, rich and poor, remained ambiguous, fractured, or insurgent. Some parts of the world, such as the Brazilian and African rain forests or the uplands of Papua and New Guinea, had hardly seen a Christian missionary by 1914. In large areas of forest, desert, and mountain in Asia, local shamans and forms of spirit cult persisted more or less untouched by Hinduism, Buddhism, or Islam. Here, people's religious experience was not of organized, congregational worship involving words and beliefs, but of flashes of mystical spiritual strengthening which altered the individual consciousness.

By contrast, there were regions where people had apparently passed beyond conventional religion altogether. Western intellectuals toyed with spiritualism, theosophy, Eastern religions, and even devil worship. The French seer Allan Kardek provided a modern justification for groups of spiritualists across the French-influenced world from Indochina to Brazil who searched for a universal religion for mankind. Odd beliefs lurked in dark corners. The British diplomat Lord Frederick Hamilton gave an example of a not-untypical incident which took place at the high point of the "Christian revival" in London, the world's most powerful city:

> [A] se"ance took place at the Pantheon in Oxford Street, in either the [eighteen] "forties" or the "fifties" . . . . A number of people had hired the hall, and the Devil was invoked in due traditional form. Then *something* happened and the entire assemblage rushed terror-stricken into Oxford Street, and nothing would induce a single one of them to re-enter the building.[62]

Whereas skepticism, diabolism, and messianic cults in the Christian tradition go back at least as far as the Roman emperor Julian, atheism, which was a vigorous devotional cult itself, spread across the Western world in reaction to these very processes of religious consolidation. Babi-Bahai universalism, defeated in Iran in the 1840s, spread all over the world and made a particularly good showing in Chicago and other US cities. Likewise, the Ahmadiyya sect, regarded as idolatrous by many orthodox Muslims, exploited the print medium very effectively and maintained its following across the world. Asians, Africans, and Latin Americans continued to revere local cults, despite the injunctions of more powerful and more meddlesome priests and schoolteachers. Some of the greatest subaltern revolts of the century were infused with messianic religious themes, which outraged orthodox leaders. Millenarian Buddhism and syncretic Christianity were the ideologies that challenged the Confucian order of the Chinese Empire. Muslim jihad movements confronted both Muslim rulers and foreigners throughout the century. Christian messianism played a role in the 1848 rebellions, the Boer Great Trek, and the Mexican Revolution.

What can be said, though, is that across a much vaster area of the globe, among the rich, the middle class and the poor, the claims of the great standardizing, world religions were much more widely known and acted on in 1914 than they had been in 1789. Even many of the local heterodox, messianic, spiritualist, and shaman-led movements mentioned above now defined themselves with reference to the dictates of the world religions. They adapted some of the forms of the papacy, the techniques of Protestant evangelization, or the temple architecture of "high" Confucianism. The same can be said of the new, hybrid spiritual movements which developed among members of the international middle classes of the later nineteenth century, who claimed that a new age of spirituality was dawning. For instance, the Irish, American, Australian, British, and Indian theosophists of the 1880s were adepts of a self-consciously global and intellectual tradition; they were not representatives of an embattled "little tradition" of the locality. The idea of the "coming teacher," which was purveyed by theosophy, was clearly post-Christian, and theosophists borrowed liberally from Hinduism and Buddhism in their vision of a universal human spirituality. The French cabinet ministers of 1905 who resorted to the Ouija board to contact the spirits were post-Christians, not survivals from a pre-Christian "world which we have lost." As with the charisma of the nation-state, so with the teaching of the Christian Bible, the Torah, or the Quran, many more now knew of them, if only very distantly.

[10] *THE WORLD OF THE ARTS AND THE IMAGINATION*

THE international reach of the nation-state and the great world religions was a dominant feature of the period from about 1860 to the First World War. Over this period, the workings of industrial capital further empowered the dominant European governments, while the growth of communications broadened religious community. As chapter 11 will show, these modern forms often reproduced themselves by maintaining, or reinventing, older forms of hierarchy or representations of power. This chapter, however, turns to the working of the human imagination in the arts and literature. The arts, too, often registered the direct influence of the nation, religion, imperialism, and capital. The processes of uniformity worked strongly to produce an international art market, art history, museums, and an international artistic sensibility, which transformed the older schools and traditions across the world. Yet, at the same time, the extraordinary power, complexity, and variety of the artistic imagination threatened continuously to subvert these trends. A century which began with the Spanish painter Francisco Goya's lurid nightmares of war and revolution ended with Japanese sculptors modifying the style of the French master Auguste Rodin, while Indian modernists borrowed Japanese techniques of color and brushwork.

ARTS AND POLITICS

First, then, the arts, architecture, and literature worldwide did quite often directly reflect the dramatic changes in political and social life which have been charted in this book.[1] Artists, architects, and novelists became active agents to a degree unparalleled before in the creation of new polities and social sensibilities. In the 1860s Giuseppe Mazzini summed up the conventional contemporary view of the relationship between art and the emerging nation: "Art is not the caprice of one individual or another, but a solemn historical pageant or a prophecy.... Without Fatherland and Liberty we could perhaps have prophets of Art, but not Art itself."[2] Richard Wagner's music dramas became, for many, an embodiment of a sense of German-ness which represented the new, united nation. Alessandro Manzoni not only anticipated the new united Italy, but, in his novels and letters, he generalized a particular version of Tuscan Italian into something like a national language for the new nation.[3] The funeral in Paris in 1885 of Victor Hugo, author of *Notre-Dame de Paris* and *Les Misérables*, was held on an almost Napoleonic scale, and boulevards and streets were named after him across the French Empire. As the first non-Western recipient of the Nobel Prize for literature in 1913, Rabindranath Tagore became a national icon for India, while at the same time he envisioned a powerful sense of yearning for the lost village community which informed the ideology of its embattled urban intelligentsia.

As in so many other dimensions of thought, commentators on art in this period turned to history in order to understand the evolution of their own times. In the work of the German-Swiss scholar Jacob Burckhardt and his contemporaries, we see the emergence of the first academic art history. Ancient China and Renaissance Europe had long known scholars who wrote on the history of artists and built up collections. Yet, in his desire to depict the origins of the Italian Renaissance, Burckhardt was also celebrating the rise of bourgeois individualism in his own time.[4] The Italian artistic figures whom he and his contemporaries brought to life, such as the silversmith Benvenuto Cellini and the "universal" Renaissance man, Leon Battista Alberti, reflected the desire of the nineteenth-century world to throw off tradition and create a new domain of the imagination as much as to re-create the world of the fifteenth and sixteenth centuries. Meanwhile, European and American scholars reached overseas in their attempt to delineate the development of the art and literature of other world civilizations. Here they interacted with Asians and Africans deeply concerned to laud the virtues of their own art and literatures, which were now seen increasingly as embodiments of national genius.

HYBRIDITY AND UNIFORMITY IN ART ACROSS THE GLOBE

Over and above this active engagement of artists and historians of art in making history, more fundamental changes were at work in both the arts and literature: globalization and, later, "internationalization" and the tendency towards contested uniformity. As late as 1750, most societies possessed highly distinctive artistic traditions, both elite and popular. Artists working in these traditions wished to represent symbolically patterns of belief and understandings of kingship. Representations of the life of the Buddha or Christ and stylized carvings of verses from the Quran, for instance, marked the presence of the divine in everyday life. While these traditions had interpenetrated and borrowed from each other to some degree, they remained distinct and were animated by different ideologies and aesthetics with deep lineages in the past. The systems of representation within them remained quite coherent. Even in western European art, where the symbols of paganism jostled with those of Christianity and picaresque depictions of everyday life, the symbolic vocabulary was relatively limited and was easily recognizable by ordinary people as well as intellectuals.

By 1900, these traditions had been transformed, often at a deep level. A host of new, often opaque symbols had been added to the repertoire of Western art and literature. At the same time, new media of representation had made possible an explosion of popular forms of art and performance. According to many observers, too, the great independent aesthetic traditions of the non-European world were on the point of death, succumbing to European academic painting, European styles of architecture, and the European novel. Thus the Anglo-Ceylonese art critic and nationalist Ananda Kentish Coomaraswamy believed that the most devastating blow inflicted by the Western world on Asia was not economic ruin, but the vulgarization and destruction of artistic traditions which had breathed the essential truths of Hinduism, Buddhism, and Confucianism.[5] These predictions of cultural extinction were probably exaggerated. Non-European arts and literatures maintained their vitality, often in hybrid forms. These borrowed and appropriated European ideas and techniques, rather than simply falling victim to them. Popular art, music, and drama flourished, even where high courtly and religious art had been much reduced.

Conversely, African, Asian, and Polynesian motifs and styles invaded European painting, sculpture, and decorative arts after 1880. For instance, the Anglo-American painter J. M. Whistler spread the fashion for the so-called hawthorn jar which was modeled on the imperial Kanxi blue-and-white style. A little later, Paul Gauguin was deeply influenced by the subtle color coding he saw in the French Polynesian islands, while the young Pablo Picasso adopted African themes and colors at the beginning of a lifetime of eclecticism.

There is no doubt, though, that the high traditions of art in many of the great non-European societies had declined, along with their great patrons and artisanal traditions. Even in Europe, the art of princes, popes, and potentates, which had existed in a clear lineage from 1300 onward, dissipated and atrophied between 1800 and 1900. This is readily apparent to a visitor to the Vatican Museum, one of the world's greatest collections of European art. At the end of the visit, he or she emerges from the glorious profusion of Christian and classical images of the sixteenth to eighteenth centuries into a worthy, but desperately humdrum, gallery of "modern Christian art." This in itself is an interesting reflection of the transformation of religion discussed in the last chapter. The art of the nineteenth-century "empires of religion" was popular, mass-produced, and, arguably, second-rate. Even the century's great buildings – the new mosques, neo-Gothic churches, and neo-Hindu temples – were products of rolled-steel joists and more mechanical building techniques. In many parts of the world, religion as royal and aesthetic cult had been ignored or totally uprooted.

In 1799, the last year of the Qian Long emperor, the imperial potteries and numerous small potteries across China, Korea, and Vietnam were still producing large quantities of fine porcelain for the court and the scholar-gentry, as well as for export. Since the wisdom of the past was the most highly valued of qualities, elaborate copies of the typical artefacts of earlier dynasties were still being made for newly rich patrons who could not afford the originals. Some change had been registered, of course. The blue-and-white or pink-and-white styles had gradually become more elaborate, displaying myriads of small figures and slightly gaudy patterns which would have displeased earlier connoisseurs. The seventeenth-century imperial summer palace had incorporated features introduced by the Jesuits, who advised the court on matters of astronomy and the measurement of time. European techniques and motifs began to appear. Yet the Jesuits were still ultimately present on imperial sufferance, and, against their wishes, they worked in the service of Confucian principles and purposes. The lineage of culture in art and literature was still clear and largely indigenous. Equally, in Europe, the imports of the Dutch and English East India companies had brought Chinese and Indian designs, fabrics, and porcelains to the *palazzi* of Florence, the *hôtels* of Paris, and the country houses of Britain and Ireland. Here, however, they were set within aesthetic patterns still dominated by the inheritance of the Renaissance "Romanizing" architect Palladio and his designer contemporaries. What was happening could still be understood in terms of what chapter 1 called "archaic globalization." People searched for the exotic to display themselves as great collectors and savants within a particular cultural tradition.

By 1914 much of this had changed. The Chinese imperial summer palace had been destroyed by the British in 1860. The imperial palace itself was systematically looted by the invading allied armies in 1900 during the Boxer Rebellion, its contents finding their way to museums in London, Paris, Washington, and Tokyo. Already, in the last years of the regime, decorative arts once reserved for the imperial house had begun to be made for the market. For instance, the beautiful dragon-emblazoned gowns worn by the royal family were made available to wealthy Chinese and foreign individuals.[6] Many of the great imperial porcelain factories were closed down by the nationalist government after 1911. Old families of artisans continued to produce porcelain, metal- and lacquer-ware, just as old literati families continued to write traditional forms of poetry and prose. Yet the cohesion of this cultural style had vanished with the high bureaucrats and the court which once maintained it. European-style artefacts were in demand among the middle classes of the port cities, and Chinese entrepreneurs built hotels and palaces in the neo-Gothic and neoclassical styles which could be seen everywhere from Florida to Nice.

Meanwhile, cheap European imitations of the florid styles of late Qian Long porcelain were being produced throughout Europe and the United States. Not only the great patrons, but a whole visual aesthetic had apparently crumbled in less than a century. It had been widely replaced by flows of hybrid objects, part European, part Chinese, moving along trade routes to the living rooms of the rising international middle classes. As early as the 1820s, for instance,

Indian merchants in Calcutta bought huge mass-produced Chinese vases and displayed them alongside imported copies of European Renaissance statues in Carrara marble.[7] Later, Sindhi merchants traded Chinese and Japanese mass-produced artefacts to British and French consumers in the cities of North Africa.[8] Markets in artistic creations had existed for generations, particularly in Europe, the Middle East, and China, but they had been limited to small classes of gentry and aristocratic connoisseurs. Now the market was much larger, more predatory, and international.

The decline of high art and architecture had occurred in many other parts of the world. The sacral and royal art of the old political centers had been destroyed or discontinued following European invasion. The bronzes of the West African kingdom of Benin had found their way to the British Museum after a punitive expedition in 1897.[9] When the British restored the Benin monarchy in 1914, court ritual resumed, but the beautiful tradition of bronze casting which had persisted since the fifteenth century was never to be fully revived. The throne and regalia of the kings of Burma had also gone to London after occupation in 1886, only to be returned at the time of independence in 1948. More importantly, the rationale for the production of the prized artefacts of these old royal and sacral worlds had begun to dissipate. When the sultans began to wish to portray themselves as modern constitutional monarchs after the Tanzimat reforms, they moved from the Topkapi Sarai and installed themselves in neoclassical palaces on the other side of the Golden Horn. The ancient potteries of Iznic closed down as the palace eunuchs were dispersed and the dervish orders were expelled from politics. In all these cases, connoisseurship and craftsmanship survived in scattered form, but the unities of the old civilization were lost.

Even in Europe, this happened to some degree. Napoleon's expansion across Europe saw the looting of pictures, sculpture, and literary artefacts on a scale that matched that of the British in Asia and Africa. Eighty percent of the art treasures of Venice were pillaged and found their way to France and other parts of northern Europe, mostly between 1796 and 1815. The guilds of craftsmen, which had nourished the traditions of popular art in Italy, were closed down, being viewed as reactionary in the days of revolutionary populism.[10] It is true, of course, that the royal and ecclesiastical art of eighteenth-century Europe, with its sentimental saints and plush cherubs, has come to be seen by many modern art historians as the embodiment of ancien régime decadence. Yet this art, and the literature associated with it, remained embedded in a tradition. The Venetian painter Canaletto or François Boucher, his French contemporary, were much closer in technique and the spirit of their aesthetic to the classicist architect Palladio and the mannerist painter Guido Reni in the sixteenth century than they were to the French impressionist artists of a mere 80 years later. In the nineteenth century the art treasures of Italy's declining aristocracy and churches continued to spill outward to northern Europe and America. East coast American millionaires had Venetian palazzi transported across the Atlantic brick by brick and rebuilt in their home towns.[11]

LEVELING FORCES: THE MARKET, THE EVERYDAY, AND THE MUSEUM

These massive changes related to the function and valuation of art in society. Yet inward changes of the spirit of artistic representation were also at work. By 1914, a great deal of elite and popular art was "commodified." It was no longer designed for a known religious or aristocratic patron, but for the market. Art became increasingly a value in itself, separate from the idea of encouraging worship or conveying charisma. It is useful to expand on this point for different societies.

In most civilizations, the creation of art had been in an important sense an aspect of religious devotion. Painting a miniature of a great Sufi saint, a Tantric Buddhist cosmology, or a Russian icon was deemed a religious act on the part of the artist, while a glimpse of the work was held to help concentrate the spiritual insight of the viewer. The production of small representations of deities, the Buddha, or the Christian saints served the same function for poor, devout people across the world. The religious artisans who made these small objects were also artists in an important sense. They, too, were disciplined by a subtle aesthetic. In Japanese Shinto, there existed a hierarchy of gods of nature, the *kami*. Popular *Noh* plays were often based on their shrine legends, while other *kami* of forge and kiln literally embodied themselves in the famous samurai swords and pieces of pottery produced by rural master craftsmen.[12] In some African societies, by comparison, almost everyone carved wood. Carving was an aspect of the creation and maintenance of community identity. Making images fixed the powerful natural and supernatural forces which bound together human generations, their ancestors, and their descendants. Amongst the Yoruba, for instance, metal blades, axes, and spears were made not only for their use value, but also as channels of communication with the ancestors.[13]

The same was true of classic musical performances. Even in Western music, where royal and popular celebratory functions developed early, the work of J. S. Bach and the eighteenth-century Venetian composers played a specific role in a tightly controlled ritual calendar which ordered the life and religious performances even of the poor. In Asia, the Indian *raga*, or sitar composition, and the Indonesian gamelan band were intended to evoke devotional or magical states. In Burma, closely choreographed drama and dancing accompanied the numerous *pwes*, or ritual performances, many of which were designed to calm and enlist the help of the powerful local spirits, the Nats.

To use again the words of Max Weber, "art" in the nineteenth century was partially demystified. Indian and Russian miniature artists turned more and more to producing works for lay patrons, and the mystical dimensions of representation were drained away by the pull of the market. The makers of Persian carpets found buyers distant from the great mosques and houses of aristocrats who desired religious and totemic symbols to be incorporated in their commissions. Those Indian and African craftsmen and artisans who

survived the onslaught of mechanization and Christianity increasingly produced "art" rather than religious or totemic artefacts. Their consumers were
as likely to be expatriate European residents as the guardians of temples and
royal altars. In western Europe, art and music also became increasingly
secular. Paradoxically, the expansion of religion as doctrine and practice
discussed in chapter 9 was marked by its slow withdrawal from the realm of
art. Devotion was instead reflected in the factory production of religious
trinkets.

The precipitate collapse of aristocratic patrons meant that Italian artisans
sold products with machine-made components to a growing north European
tourist market. Much of Verdi's music was diffused throughout Europe at city
and village band concerts, which reflected new forms of uniform sociability in
the new nation. It must be remembered, of course, that, despite Weber's hope
and belief, the state and the market themselves became imbued with a kind of
religious awe. A bravura 1890s picture or statue of King Victor Emmanuel II
of Italy may have stirred the patriotic fervour of the viewer. But it was not
intended to improve his soul in quite the same way as a picture of St Mary
Magdalene in the eighteenth century, even when the earlier picture had been
painted in the self-consciously charming style of the Venetian Giovanni Battista Piazzetta.

Mechanization itself had a considerable effect on the international production and circulation of the arts. An early example of this was the rapid
elimination of the artisan textile industries of South Asia and even the as-yet
uncolonized Middle East. The decline of Indian handicrafts, however, was
matched by strenuous attempts of British and, later, Belgian and German
textile-makers to use and adapt the styles and symbols of the old indigenous
producers. The Indian shawl had been a pledge of royalty and a sign of the
wearer's aristocratic merit. By the 1830s, Scottish industrialists in Paisley,
near Glasgow, had begun to mass-produce Indian styles, and these were
then sold on a global market for shawl products.

Mechanization, however, did not always wipe out arts and crafts. In some
cases, it helped to perpetuate them or make them more viable. Scandinavian
woodcrafts, for instance, gained a new lease of life from the development of
machine tools. The chemical and mineral dyes and factory-manufactured
glass of the early Industrial Revolution were used by British Pre-Raphaelite
painters and craftsmen. What became know as the Arts and Crafts Movement
in Britain, its dominions, and empire was, therefore, a Janus-faced phenomenon. Taking their lead from the art critic John Ruskin, artists of this school
sought to recover the devotion and techniques of medieval craftsmen,
spurning the European Renaissance, let alone modern industrialism.[14] At
the same time, many of them used the products of the Industrial Revolution,
and their clients and admirers were to be found in the new middle-class towns
that sprang up in the aftermath of industrialization rather than among the
sturdy and pious artisans depicted in Ruskin's art histories.

A further broad change which occurred in all these different arenas and
across the continents was the growing alignment of art with the modern and

the quotidian. Increasingly, the themes of operas, the plots of novels, and the representations of paintings reflected incidents in modern everyday life rather than the doings of saints, kings, and mythological heroes of the past. Genre paintings of flower-sellers and peasants had long existed in European art, but they did not constitute the central theme in the art of their time as did, for instance, did Henri de Toulouse-Lautrec's depictions of café society, bar maids, and prostitutes. Revealingly, some of Toulouse-Lautrec's most famous prints were in a style which imitated the bold colors of Japanese block prints. Outside Europe, novelists such as the Hindi writers of the 1880s began to chart the trials and tribulations of the contemporary middle classes, rather than the doings of Hindu gods and great Muslim kings of the past and their consorts.[15]

The location of art changed, too. At an international level, the nineteenth century saw the rise of the museum. Great collections such as those of the Louvre in Paris and the Metropolitan Museum of Art in New York were matched by smaller museums established by colonial or semi-colonized regimes in Hanoi, Batavia, Bombay, and Cairo. The "high" art of the old order, which had been looted and redistributed, often found its way to these collections. "Museumization," as the specialists call it, was not wholly destructive, of course. The arrival of Egyptian antiquities in Paris after Napoleon's invasion created a surge of demand for objects with sphinx's heads or feet and antique obelisks. Some of the workmanship was very fine. In the colonial world, the display of Khmer Buddhas in the museums of French Indochina encouraged local craftsmen to paint and carve in new ways. Art's context was now as likely to be the museum and the market as the temple or palace.

The remainder of the chapter will take up some of these themes: secularization, obsession with the present, and nationalism, in different spheres of art and literature. Some notes of warning should be sounded. First, it is not intended to suggest here that all the art forms of the nineteenth century can be reduced to simple reflections of social or political processes. Artistic creation had some origins quite outside the political world. So, for instance, the classical themes associated with revolutionary virtue after 1789 had already been given a great impetus by purely scholarly discoveries in the ruins of Roman Pompeii. Art was responsive to much more than simple political imperatives. The world of the imagination remained autonomous of politics to a remarkable degree. With the emergence of early abstract painting and atonal music, around 1900, it can be argued that European and American artists were able to liberate themselves from conventional life to a greater extent than was possible in the days of closed political and religious ideologies. The collapse of artists' guilds and the decline of the long artistic apprenticeship in the course of the nineteenth century gave new freedoms. Yet the point can still be made that even the most abstract and least conventional forms of artistic endeavor were seen by the end of the nineteenth century as social and political "movements" seeking self-cultivation in this world rather than benefits from the supernatural world.

Secondly, the argument about growing global uniformity and the decline of the cultural integration of art is not intended to suggest any slackening of the creativity on the part of artists, particularly popular artists. Many traditions of popular art and craft production survived, or even expanded, despite the general poverty of the artisans. Photography as an art form globalized with astonishing speed after its discovery in France in the late 1830s. By 1860, there were Indian, Chinese, and North African artist-photographers, many of whom pioneered new techniques. The end of the century also saw the birth of jazz, the ultimate hybrid, intercultural popular music, along with that greatest of modern popular art forms, the cinema. The cinema developed almost contemporaneously in Paris, Cairo, and Shanghai.

THE ARTS OF THE EMERGING NATION, 1760–1850

Nineteenth-century art had many faces. Intimate devotional art persisted in parts of Catholic Latin America, in the form of Russian icon painting and in the paintings of the north Indian hills depicting the life of the god Krishna. Paintings of mountains, waterfalls, and country towns reflected the interest of the age in the sublimeness of nature and the persistence of human community. Yet state patronage for artists remained critical. Consequently, a common theme across the world was the representation of the new forms of political power, and especially of national state and empire. Even in the late eighteenth century, depictions of the splendors of royal courts or famous victories had begun to represent the glory of proto-nations as much as that of kings. Frescoes in Versailles showed the victories of France worldwide, while paintings in Vauxhall Gardens, London's pleasure park, represented the triumphs of Britain's military heroes in Canada and in Europe. British governors of Bengal and Indian regional rulers both employed traveling European artists, notably Johannes Zoffany, to present themselves in a good light in the complex factional politics of the emerging British Empire.[16] Meanwhile, the country seats of the great Venetian aristocratic families along the Brenta Canal displayed, with pathetic exaggeration, the Republic's dwindling trading importance by means of frescoes of the statuesque female figures of Asia, Africa, and America bringing commerce to the Most Serene Republic.[17]

This shift from the representation of dynasties and aristocratic military heroes to more abstract embodiments of state and nation, became much sharper after the French Revolution. Depictions of the American Continental Congress as a "parliament of reason" had already anticipated this trend in a limited way. Imaginings of the French revolutionary people, or its embodiment, the secular goddess Marianne, wearing the Cap of Liberty, initiated a school of revolutionary art which persisted into the age of the Communist states of the twentieth century. Brutus, slayer of the tyrant Caesar, and his family were particularly attractive to this revolutionary school of artists, who looked back to the Roman Republic rather than the Roman Empire.[18] Modern scholars have also noted that the allusion to Brutus's wife, Portia, symbolically anticipated the widespread relegation of women to domestic space even in this age of violent change.

The most notable protagonist of the revolutionary style of symbolizing the state through a vision of classical virtue was Jacques-Louis David (1748–1825). This artist's famous picture of the death of the Montagnard leader Marat was complemented by his sensuous portrait of the dying boy Bara, child-victim of the counterrevolution. Yet the universalizing intention of the revolution was most splendidly visualized in Anne-Louis Girodet's 1797 portrait of the black Haitian revolutionist Jean-Baptiste Belley, seen on the cover of this book. Belley, in the dress of a member of the French Assembly, leans against a bust of the abbé Raynal, eighteenth-century proponent of colonial reform and enlightened Christianity. Belley himself intervened decisively in an assembly debate of 1794 to secure the temporary abolition of slavery.[19] Again, by transforming the classical nude and the scene of classical virtue into icons of modern revolutionary virtue, painters and sculptors in this school provided a visual grammar for international revolution.

These artists also charted and faithfully represented the transition from revolution to Napoleon's autocracy. Jean-Auguste-Dominique Ingres's first painting of Napoleon as First Consul still showed him as an embodiment of

ILLUSTRATION 10.1   Revolutionary heroism: *The Death of Joseph Bara*, a nineteenth-century version of David's vision. Painting by Jean-Joseph Weerts, 1883.

revolutionary republicanism. Within a decade he, along with David and Girodet, was depicting Bonaparte as universal emperor (see illustration 3.2). In one striking painting which verges on the subversively grandiose, Napoleon appears enthroned and holding scepters. He is pictured as a hybrid of the classical Jupiter, the Roman emperor, and Charlemagne, king of the Franks.[20] This monumental vision of the First Empire was also seen in architecture and sculpture, symbolizing the overblown state of the age of revolutions. The Venetian sculptor Antonio Canova made huge classical nudes of Napoleon, one of which was later purloined by the duke of Wellington for his house in central London. Another still stands outside the Palazzo Brera in Milan. Over the next generation, Canova's classical mythological forms found wide currency in parts of Europe influenced by revolutionary sensibility, where the new administrative elite wished to distance themselves from the rococo excesses of the ancien régime. Likewise, Ingres's portraits of the administrators, postal officials, and military governors of Napoleonic Italy are reminiscent of those of Britain's colonial governors in the wartime period. They stand forth as representatives not of a dynasty or an aristocracy, but of an emerging state and an enlightened bureaucracy.

The *éclat* of this state rang in the ears of all nineteenth-century regimes, as chapter 6 suggested. The art which was deemed appropriate to it was influential well beyond the European borders. The new rulers of independent Latin America looked to the French revolutionary hero as their visual model. In some representations after his death, Simon Bolivar became the Brutus or even the Napoleon of the Spanish American Revolutions. With less plausibility, the Mexican dictator Santa Anna – he of the leg – had himself portrayed as Bonaparte. Yet in Mexico, classical Rome was anomalously mixed with the symbols of the ancient Central American regimes in the iconography of independence. For, despite their intention of subordinating the labor of the Amerindians as vigorously as their predecessors among the royal governors, the Creole leaders still wished to claim a legitimacy which went back to a time even before the Spanish kings and Roman emperors, and was firmly rooted on American soil.[21]

Because of the Islamic prohibition on representations of the human figure, the enlightened despotisms of the nineteenth-century Middle East followed these patterns only hesitantly. It was quite late that the square of the citadel in Cairo was adorned with a bronze statue of the triumphant Ishmael Pasha, son of Muhammad Ali, who had put down the Wahhabi threat in Saudi Arabia. Instead, the age of the Tanzimat in Istanbul and its dependencies displayed its modernity with French military uniforms, classical barracks designs, and European-style furniture, rather than with large portraits. One exception within the Islamic world was the development in Persia of the huge form of the Qajar portrait out of the earlier miniature tradition. One luminous portrait of Fath Ali Shah, the first of the Qajar "new monarchs," shows him standing holding a scepter in what many believe is a clear allusion to Ingres's portrait of Napoleon in state mentioned above.[22] The artist retained traditional Persian style and symbols, however. He endowed Fath Ali with a long and lustrous black beard, an indication of wisdom and potency in the father of his people.

In France, the artistic center of Europe after Napoleon's invasion of Italy, painting and other visual arts provide revealing evidence of the contradictions of legitimacy during the period of the restored monarchy, which was discussed in chapter 4. Even if a political version of eighteenth-century absolutism could be restored to Europe in 1815, the iconography of the old regime was irrevocably shattered. After 1830, the problem was partially resolved when a historical version of revolution once again became the official aesthetic, following the declaration of the July monarchy in 1830. Themes such as the "Apotheosis of Napoleon," the "March of the Marseillaise," and the "Departure of the Volunteers of 1792" were brought together in the new public art with representations of contemporary events, notably the revolutions of 1830 and the rise of the new Napoleon in the years 1848–52.[23]

The conventions of public art which emerged from the revolution proved equally useful in the high age of European imperialism. British artists depicted great Indian durbars, or royal gatherings,[24] while Theodore Géricault showed French conquerors receiving the obeisance of North African chiefs during the conquest of 1830–40.[25] The themes of European visual art proved serviceable to empire in other, subtler ways, too. Romantic and sublime depictions of landscapes and people emerged out of a new reflection on the relationship between man and nature in literature and science which rejected the formalism of the old regime. The romantic hero might sometimes be a political martyr, but his relationship with the new state forms was generally more nuanced and indirect. Great nations, like great artists and poets, were invested with a particular power and virtue. Romanticism and nationalism were related, but the Romantic artists often scorned the world of politics and men altogether. George, Lord Byron, for instance, could hardly be depicted as a man of the British establishment, but his passionate poetry and philhellenism made him a hero of the Greek revolution and gave him the status of a national icon for the new nation after his death.

A good deal of the art generated by the European conquests across the world from 1760 to 1840 was distantly, but only very indirectly, related to projects of Western dominion. Géricault and Eugène Delacroix depicted their North African chieftains as noble, romantic warriors on white horses, the embodiments of ancient – indeed, anachronistic – virtue. On a smaller scale, the British artists who made prints of the Indian interior dwelt on the ruins of great kingdoms and their picturesque modern denizens. Members of the Daniell family, for instance, painted Xhosa male figures in South Africa and picturesque views of the China coast, as well as their better-known series on India.[26] Sometimes these were accompanied by condescending commentaries on these lands and peoples. Many scholars have suggested, therefore, following the works of the postcolonial polemicist Edward Said, that these techniques merely tended to reinforce the "otherness" of non-Europeans and acted as a form of negative triumphalism of the West.[27] There is some truth in this. The French expedition to Egypt had revealed a great ancient civilization, which understood well the importance of centralization and public works. Implicitly, then, dwelling on this past greatness reminded contemporary Europeans of their own heroic destiny to raise the degraded modern descendants of the pharaohs or the ancient Indian kings. Yet ambivalence characterized the whole enterprise. In making Asians and Africans "other," European artists were often also harking back to the European preindustrial age and invoking themes of chivalry and heroism which they feared the industrial age would erase. Delacroix and Géricault painted the avatars of modern France, her great feudal monarchs, and ancient popular festivals in the same manner in which they pictured sheikhs and the women of the harem. They seemed to long for a past which had now sadly become "the other."

In America, the same ambivalence characterized the art of the new republic, reflecting the tense issue of the relation between the whites, the Amerindians, and the slave population. In the early days of the republic, a "creolizing" tendency, similar to that seen in Spanish America, allowed the figure of America to be envisaged as a Native American woman. Later, however, "America" or "Columbia" became a classical figure, typical of European visions of the goddess of the nation.[28] This ambivalence continued to haunt American depictions of their continent. Over the first half of the nineteenth century, many images were created to laud the great project of the expansion westwards and the heroic acts of settlers in facing down the attacks of Native Americans. A famous painting of the slaughter of a heroic pioneer woman by raiding braves[29] is reminiscent of academic and popular paintings which showed British women about to be massacred by the Indian sepoys in 1857[30] and the struggles of white frontiers-people in the Zulu wars (see illustration 10.2). At the same time, equal numbers of paintings continued to represent the noble Amerindian warrior, nostalgically reflecting on the "death of the native," as indigenous populations were rapidly herded into reservations. In Australia before about 1860, Aboriginal peoples were scarcely noted at all beyond the realms of early ethnography. Instead, artists painted the exotic landscape and the quality of the light in a mode which seemed often to validate the idea that this was an "empty land."

Ambivalence also characterized the way in which artists envisioned popular action during the age of revolution and imperialism. "The people" were viewed with circumspection of the sort that surrounded "the native." The most outstanding proponent of this theme was the Spanish painter Francisco Goya (1746–1828). Originally a court artist who memorialized the statesmen and popular characters of Spain's interrupted Enlightenment, Goya painted a famous series of images of "The Disasters of War" and of the massacres of 1808 which accompanied uprisings against Napoleon's rule in Spain. This sequence foreshadowed depictions of the heroic people in 1848, the Paris Commune of 1871, and the Russian Revolution of 1905. Yet, in view of Goya's early espousal of the revolution, it is ironic that he showed French imperial troops massacring the populace of Madrid which was rising for king and Church.[31] Goya's shift in allegiance reminds us that Beethoven wrote the "Eroica" Symphony for Napoleon, only later to rescind its dedication to the

ILLUSTRATION 10.2   Art and the savage: *The Death of Jane McCrea*. Painting by
John Vanderlyn, 1804.

emperor in disgust and pen "Wellington's victory." Later in the century, the
same Wagner who composed the opera *Rienzi* in celebration of the radical
republicanism of 1848 became the court composer, as it were, of German
state-based nationalism. In this way, the ambivalent and contradictory attitudes of contemporaries to the enlightened nation-state, imperialism, and
popular revolution were sharply illustrated in the work of artists.

Following the mid-century wars, the relationship between art and nation
seemed to develop in two different directions. First, formal academic and
official art continued to depict iconic moments and figures in the creation of
the new nations. The declaration of the German Empire in 1871, the debates
of the Third French Republic, and the person of the enlightened tsar all had
their painters. The decorative arts responded to new political movements and
also to industrialization. Jean-Baptiste Carpeaux (1827–75) made sculptures of

Napoleon III, which were then miniaturized and sold to Bonapartist supporters in their thousands.[32] Outside Europe, the leaders of the new Japan and, ultimately, the Chinese nationalists and Young Turks all had themselves pictured in the appropriate modernized dress of frock coat or Prussian military uniform. The late Qajar portraits show not lush beards symbolizing the fecundity of the dynasty or the jewelry of the great conqueror Nadir Shah, but stiff men in formal European coats with only the tarbush to indicate their identity as Islamic kings of Persia.[33] Nationalists in India tried to revive the Indian artistic tradition which had lapsed and fragmented after the decline of the post-Mughal courts. They used Indian and even Japanese styles to depict ideal figures such as Mother India or the great figures of the Hindu mythological past. Notable here was Raja Ravi Varma, who adapted the naturalistic techniques of British academic painting to the Hindu epics.[34] His representations were taken up by the lithographic printers of the bazaars and spread to ordinary families in hundreds of thousands of copies, forming modern India's image of her deities and of the land itself. His still-popular images visually complemented the speeches of nationalist leaders and the novels of Rabindranath Tagore.

ARTS AND THE PEOPLE, 1850–1914

The art of the later nineteenth century came to reflect the emerging nation and its troubles in a less symbolic way. After about 1850, history painting in most Western countries began to decline in significance and quality. The nation was now to be represented less through the charismatic moments of its own past, and more through the lives of ordinary people in the great industrial towns or in the declining countryside. This shift left a visual space in which critiques of modernity, industrialism, or even the nation itself could flourish. Many artists came to identify themselves quite closely with the socialist critics of what they saw as the bourgeois order. The French movement for artistic liberation which culminated in the first great Impressionist Exhibition in Paris in 1874 seems at first sight to be totally apolitical. It is true that Edouard Manet (1832–83), Auguste Renoir, and Edgar Degas were much further from the centers of political power in the Third Republic than David and Géricault had been in earlier generations. But these artists were also making political statements in the broadest sense. They refused to accept the long guild-like artistic training which even the most radical of their predecessors had undergone. They gloried in the complex, the odd, the exotic, and the transgressive. Whereas the dominant tradition of the century had created a heroic and historical art for the middle-class public and its state, the modern art which emerged after about 1870 was concerned to negate, question, or deconstruct what was taken for granted in middle-class life.[35]

This did not take place through an obviously political imagery, but through a depiction of ordinary people and places, of harmonious colors and abstract shapes, which were supposed to speak to popular amity and a future utopia. Vincent van Gogh (1852–90), the emblematic artist of the late nineteenth

ILLUSTRATION 10.3 *The Meal.* Painting by Paul Gauguin, 1891.

century in Europe, wrote of himself and an artist friend: "Neither you nor I meddle with politics, but we live in the world, in society and involuntarily ranks of people group themselves." His aim was to paint the abstract essence of these ranks of people. Paul Gauguin, by comparison, went outside Europe to French Tahiti to critique the values of the bourgeois by exploring the value of the "other." His paintings of an idealized, sensual island world differed in spirit from many earlier depictions of the non-European exotic, because Gauguin identified with his subjects and sought in them his own best instincts rather than barbaric and archaic forms of life which had disappeared in Europe (see illustration 10.3).[36] Finally, with the emergence of cubism after 1907, following Pablo Picasso's *Les Desmoiselles d'Avignon*, Western art seemed to be moving into a phase as radical and iconoclastic as its anarchistic and Communist movements.[37]

OUTSIDE THE WEST: ADAPTATION AND DEPENDENCY

As for the art of the world outside Europe and the Americas, the picture was, literally, mixed. Revealingly, Japanese visual culture seems to have fared best in a world increasingly invaded by Western artistic forms. This was in part because its popular painting and artisan lithographic tradition remained dynamic and adaptive on the eve of direct European intervention in the country. Katsushika Hokusai (1760–1849) started his career by portraying scenes of the "floating world," the courtesans and actors of the early Edo period. Later, he developed his own style, which blended Japanese and Chinese traditional themes with European romantic styles.[38] Like his contemporaries in science and surgery, he was able to gain access to examples of Western painting through the "Dutch learning" diffused from the port of Nagasaki. The advanced state of Japanese commercial block printing and the European craze for japanoiserie in the later nineteenth century helped achieve international fame as a well as a national status for Hokusai. His 36 scenes of Mount Fuji and *The Great Wave* are probably the best-known works of non-Western art of the nineteenth and twentieth centuries. Later Japanese painters came to terms with Western academic art, and some painted the collusion between tradition and industrial modernity in a way which paralleled the work of contemporary French artists. One famous picture of a young girl in a kimono, standing on a bridge and looking into the far distance along the railway lines, is a striking example. It was exhibited at the 1900 exhibition in the Grand Palais, Paris. Thus the traditional art of Japan, along with its political culture, made an easier transition to modernity than elsewhere, largely because of its own strengths. The old style of depicting everyday urban and rural life in popular prints seemed appropriate to a developing nation with its own strong sense of patriotism. Traditional

ILLUSTRATION 10.4   The character of the land: Boatmen crossing the Tamagawa River, Musashi Province. Print by Katsushika Hokusai.

potteries also adapted to new styles and Western demand, just as Chinese forms and the Chinese tea ceremony had been adapted to a Japanese vision several hundred years earlier. An art school was established in Japan in 1880. Among its earliest products were a series of bronzes of naked Japanese women in the style of Rodin.[39]

To a lesser extent, traditional styles of block printing and miniature painting in China, Korea, and India reacted to lithography and mass consumption after 1860. As late as 1900, Chinese artists continued to adapt block printing to new circumstances. One pro-Boxer artist produced a whole set of prints depicting mythical defeats of the Japanese and Western powers by imperial armies.[40] A similar form of adaptation took place in Vietnamese block printing, which quickly developed satirical anti-French themes.[41] In many areas, how-ever, native styles of painting, stone carving, wood carving, and pottery making declined in quality and respect even among their own people during the second half of the nineteenth century. Little of value was made to replace the Turkish Iznic styles, for instance. The art schools of British India, started under the impetus of the British Arts and Crafts Movement, produced little more than trinkets for the Western market, as Coomaraswamy bitterly noted. Only in more remote regions, such as Kutch and north Gujarat, which were insulated from the market, or "tribal" areas did vibrant popular art continue to develop.[42] Yet, rather than being the popular reflection of a broad regional artistic culture, these arts and crafts were increasingly seen as "ethnic sur-vivals." In the longer run, they or their Pacific and African equivalents wereto become dangerously dependent on the Western tourist market and local sponsorship by the national state.

ILLUSTRATION 10.5 Exporting the classical tradition: Elementary drawing class, the Mayo School of Art, Lahore, India, 1909. Photo by A. H. Fisher.

ARCHITECTURE: A MIRROR OF THE CITY

The rise of that contested global uniformity was even more apparent in the field of architecture and the modeling of cities. In the first half of the century, buildings that mirrored the spirit of the historical and classical pictures of a David or a Delacroix represented the power of the new national state. They reflected claims to an antique lineage of reason. This was the message of the Capitol in Washington, the Pantheon in Paris, and the great modernized classical buildings of St Petersburg. A variant on this in the British world was the neo-Gothic palace and later railway station which, ironically, reflected a nostalgic desire for the old world of Christian amity, feudal virtue, and social order in the midst of industrialism. Barry's Houses of Parliament became the model for thousands of similar structures in England, and ultimately for neo-Gothic hotels and town halls across the empire in the great commercial boom towns such as Bombay, Melbourne, and Victoria, British Columbia. As noted, some non-European rulers moved out of their Ottoman, Manchu, or Mughal-style palaces in order to capture the charisma of modernity in neoclassical buildings, which often incorporated indigenous features in a purely superficial manner. The Dolmabace palace in Istanbul, which marked the early-nineteenth-century reforms, and the palace of the Raja of Mysore, built in the 1820s to inaugurate the "ancient Hindoo constitution" after the end of the Muslim interregnum in 1799, were examples of this. In some parts of the East, hybrid styles of architecture emerged. In the North Indian kingdom of Awadh (Oudh), its semi-independent kings constructed religious and secular buildings in the first half of the nineteenth century which merged eighteenth-and nineteenth-century classical with Iranian and Mughal themes.[43] Generally, however, it was the European-style elements which won out, even if surface decoration remained "Saracenic." The rolled-steel joist made it possible for powers across the world to build larger and more European-style structures.

After 1850, indeed, more grandiose attempts to remodel urban and architectural space were widely in evidence. Within a few days of the *coup d'état* of Louis Napoleon in 1852, plans were set afoot to wholly remodel Paris, now a city of one and a half million people. Baron Georges Haussmann began to construct new water and sewerage systems and to plan huge new boulevards which erased many of the old quarters, now represented as pits of disease and sedition. The aim was as much to absorb hundreds of thousands of unemployed laborers as to represent the *éclat* of the new, undemocratic, but modern order. As Edouard Manet showed in his *The Barricade* of 1871, these new streets were put to exemplary use by the state in the mass executions which followed the Paris Commune.[44] The basilica of Sacré-Coeur, which was built over the killing-ground, represented the reaction of Catholic bourgeois France in its sensational gothicism.

The example of Paris was followed elsewhere in the world, where straight streets, boulevards, and opera houses were built in profusion to symbolize the new order and the triumph of the royal yet bourgeois culture. Rome was given its massive and overbearing monument to the Risorgimento, the memorial to Victor Emmanuel II, who died in 1878. In the early nineteenth century, the tsars embellished and developed the classical city of St Petersburg, appearing less often in medieval and orthodox Moscow. However, as Timothy Mitchell has shown, some of the most dramatic changes in urban life were effected in Cairo and Alexandria.[45] Here the khedives rigorously pursued policies of modernization which began the destruction of many of the old quarters and also began to enact a redivision of urban life which concentrated the rich in well-protected suburbs and swept aside the poor into specially designated areas. In many parts of the dependent world, as also in Japan and China, it was indeed colonial subjects who initiated policies of drainage and improvement. These projects separated them off from the lower classes of their own society in a manner which had not been common in the medieval-style cities of the past. At the turn of the twentieth century, some of the greatest architectural expressions of the domination of the state were still being constructed by colonial rulers, even when, or possibly because, they were beginning to feel the first winds of national self-determination. Sir Herbert Baker's plans for the monumentally ordered New Delhi were being put into effect before the First World War.[46] In South Africa, the subordination of the black population and the uneasy truce between the English-speaking and Afrikaner populations was memorialized in the construction of the neoclassical buildings of Pretoria.

Yet, as in the world of the visual arts, the century cannot be summed up only in the buildings of state, the bourse, and revived religion, however powerful these were. Not only the pride of local communities, reflected in the great town halls of the industrial north of England or New York's early skyscrapers, but the imaginings and vision of particular communities outside the purview of the state and capitalism found their expression in building. This was the era of the great Mediterranean and Alpine resorts, where the joys of urban living were conjoined with a new romanticism about the beach, the sun, and the mountains. This was the era of the artists' settlements and model housing colonies in which those reacting against industrial modernism and trying to establish utopian communities still invested their energies.

TOWARDS WORLD LITERATURE?

It was after 1850, too, that the world's literatures became more uniform and, at a superficial level, more Westernized. As late as the end of the eighteenth century, the dominant forms remained the mythological epic, the fable or moral tale, the romance, and the devotional poem. Each of these genres was to some degree constrained by the dominant religious and ideological systems of the societies for which they were written, and this is what gave world literature its variety.

These different forms allowed plenty of scope for innovation, and where, as in western Europe, China, and Japan, this was allied with highly developed printing trades, authors could reach large popular audiences. In the highly variegated and sophisticated literature of China and Japan, there existed a whole variety of styles of writing, from romantic and erotic tales, through detective stories, to tales of the deeds of ancient kings and "social bandits." Each of them, to one degree or another, reflected the nature of ancient wisdom and the consequences of the decline of virtue and proper conduct. The same was true of the genre of "city thrillers" in the seventeenth- and eighteenth-century Ottoman Empire. In South and Southeast Asia, epic remained the most revered form, and the great Hindu tales, the Mahabharata and the Ramayana, provided a pattern on which were modeled later representations of heroism and good kingship. For instance, in the eighteenth-century western Indian tale of "Pabuji," the eponymous hero imitates many of the great deeds of these ancient heroic exemplars. But he also saves sacred cattle from the depredations of the "Turk," thus indicating the epic's adjustment to the more recent history of Muslim rule in the subcontinent.[47] Folktales, such as the *kissas* of the Punjab, however, spoke to the trials and tribulations of ordinary people, but these lay figures are designated by caste names and endowed with the supposed characteristics of the different castes. Thus one depicts a long war of wits between Mrs Penny-Pinching-Khattri (a commercial group) and Mrs Solid-Friendly-Jat (a farming community).[48] In West Asia and North Africa a whole literature had developed out of Sufi devotional practice, which could represent at once erotic fantasies and higher spiritual truths. This was the genre which Edward Fitzgerald brought to the attention of the West in his rendering of the "Rubaiyat" of Omar Khayyam, which achieved great popularity in the later nineteenth century.

Much of the world's literature remained oral in form, though sometimes bards and balladeers created written versions of stories as *aides-mémoire*. Where contemporary Europeans and later scholars have preserved these stories, they also appear to be responsive to the present, while at the same time adjusting contemporary observations to regional styles of epic or fabulous narration. East African storytellers, for instance, alluded to the coming of the Arabs and the Portuguese, but these events were added to the structures of the ancient legends of heroes, which thus became a kind of palimpsest.

Even in western Europe, the inheritance of the classical past and its forms continued to constrain artistic expression. Racine and Corneille, the dramatists of the French old regime, still used the form of the classical Greek comedy in their plays of men and morals; Alexander Pope adopted the form of the classical epic in his satirical *The Dunciad*. But in the course of the eighteenth century, writers and dramatists began to transcend the structure of the classical writings in a parodying, self-aware manner which was unusual even by the standards of China's ironic and sophisticated literature of everyday life. In particular, the novel emerged as a powerful new form. Though the revolutionary character of the European novel has probably been overstated by literary critics, it does mark itself out in form from even the most biting and satirical of the older forms. The novel was designed to live in the present. It was built around stories of everyday life less dominated by classical archetypes, though often using them. Novels were intended to amuse, frighten, and titillate, but they also became political tracts, implicitly denouncing the folly of the estab-lishment and satirizing the doings of the great. In both Britain and France, bawdy novels and stories, like contemporary printed cartoons, became a way of challenging the status quo. In Russia, in the hands of Lermontov, Dos-toevsky, and Tolstoy, the novel became a great parable of present social follies, opening the way for a new society.

As in the world of the visual arts, the revolutionary era let loose a huge range of new energies which were directed to seeking a utopian future or individual fulfillment, or equally to blocking it off. Goethe, universal man of the era, searched in his later imaginative writing for a way in which the romantic and the sublime could be represented so that the contemporary political conflicts could be seen reflected in the grandeur of nature. With the old order breaking down, revolutionary and romantic poets of the German school began to write epics which lauded the nation as a community of sentiment seeking fulfill-ment. At the same time, they depicted the hallowed terrain, the sublime mountains and rivers on which that nation would one day reign supreme. In a similar vein, Byron, one of the most influential writers of the era, forged his sense of the restless romantic desire for personal freedom together with a universal commitment to national freedom. This brought him to his death in Missolonghi in 1824, as the first Greek War of Independence against Ottoman authority began in earnest.

In dark contrast, the first age of global imperialism which accompanied and underpinned the Atlantic revolutions saw a grand immolation of the literary inheritance of much of the non-European world. The libraries and manuscript collections of Delhi and of Jogjakarta and Sulu in Java were destroyed, while the brief Napoleonic intervention in Egypt was accompanied by a wholesale dispersal and sale of manuscripts. Later, the classics of imperial China were looted from Beijing. Obviously, too, the European settler advance in the Americas, Australasia, and southern Africa saw the destruction of the oral traditions of many First Nations. This was because the people themselves were destroyed, infected, or demoralized to an extent only paralleled during the great Spanish conquests of the Americas three centuries before.

Yet this era also saw the beginnings of adaptation and a degree of creativity in some societies. Much of this lay in the realm of non-fiction prose writing, of course. The traditional form of newswriting and recording of great events in the Arab and Islamic world, for instance, was adapted to charting the rise of Europeans. Al Jabarti wrote the *Annals of Napoleon in Egypt* as Ghulam Hus-sain Tabatabai and other Indian writers wrote histories of the degenerate era of "the Moderns," many of which included literary and poetic reflections on their peoples' travails. But some writers adopted old styles of lament on the wickedness of the age to the new cataclysm. Thus, for instance, the golden age of poetry and prose writing in the rapidly developing North Indian literary language, Urdu, was the very period when the poets witnessed the decline of the old empire and the rise of upstart and wicked people. They mused on "the last phase of an oriental civilization" and the age "when the face of the heavens was changed."[49] In the Southeast Asian world, Munshi Abdullah virtually invented a new Malay literary language in the 1820s and 1830s, conjoining observation of peoples and places in the region with a "new language of politics" which belabored the autocracy of the sultans. As the tide of Western expansion swept on towards China and Japan, literary men as well as statesmen adapted the melancholic and dramatic styles of their classical literature to ponder the onset of brutal modernity.

The beginnings of a new style of literature in the world outside Europe, lauding the suppressed nation and criticizing modern society, coincided broadly with a shift in European literature towards a new type of social realism which depicted ordinary people rather than sublime journeys and melancholic or picaresque heroes. In North America, the emerging sense of national culture was given powerful impetus by the novels of Mark Twain, who memorialized the old, paternalistic relations between white and black races just at the point where they were about to undergo a fundamental rupture. Longfellow and his contemporaries painted a verdant picture of the variety of the American landscape, which matched American mid-century landscape watercolors. In western Europe, the new literature was announced in the novels of Charles Dickens, Thomas Hardy, and Charles Baudelaire. The new French social novelists echoed quite closely the popular history associated above all with Jules Michelet, chronicler of France's social revolutions. The aim in fiction and non-fiction alike was to give an accurate picture of the people not as an abstraction, but as networks of individuals with character, personal loves, and tragedies. Here, in these less idealized and romanticized portraits of communities and nations, inequalities of wealth and power were freely depicted. While Dickens's characters were remembered for their depiction of English national rituals, such as Mr Pickwick's plum-pudding Christmas, the criminality and oddity of mid-Victorian social life were also on display, notably in the character of Scrooge. Perhaps the most romantic version of "the people" was found in Russian literature. As in painting and music, so in poetry and the novel, the Russian intelligentsia moved away from French models and the worship of rationalism to an investigation of the "soul" of the people through the life of the peasant. The work of Nikolai Gogol (1809–52) set the trend here, with its dislike of the west and its reverence for popular Orthodox Christianity.[50] The move from the novel of history and heroes to the depiction of people as heroes of everyday life, reflected the changes in contemporary pictorial art. In a subtle way these novels and short stories continued to embody the development of the sense of the nation and its essential characteristics, though in a less grandiose and transparent manner.

These socially realistic novels were important, not only because they displayed the form of communities and nations in the round, but because in several countries they were the crucible for a new, more truly national language. So Alessandro Manzoni's novel of love and marriage in Habsburg-ruled Lombardy, *I promessi sposi*, was as remarkable for its representation of Catholic virtue and patriotism among ordinary people as for taking the final step from Dante's Tuscan Italian to the modern Italian language of today. By contrast, in

Ireland, the great novels of James Joyce later in the century pioneered a subversive literary sensibility which nevertheless gave a powerful dynamic to a specifically national literature.

These European novelists and short-story writers created new literary sensibilities, but within the novelists' tradition which had been emerging for more than a century. Outside Europe and the Americas, the emergence of realistic prose writing and the novel was a much more dramatic development. In India as early as the 1840s, the Westernized Parsi community of Bombay had established a theater for which tickets were sold on the open market, an epochal change in the form of cultural patronage. Late-nineteenth-century novels in Urdu did have a short genealogy going back to the tales and *kissas* of the eighteenth century. But when Hindi novels began to be written on modern themes and in a realistic style in the 1870s and 1880s, this marked a significant breakthrough. Not only was this a new form of social comment, it was also written in a language which was consciously being formed for the promotion of national integration. Individuals such as Harish Chandra of Benares and Kartik Prasad Khattri lampooned the follies of modern society, turning their ire on the miserliness of the Indian commercial magnates but also criticizing the British government in fairly direct terms. The great Bengali writer Bankim Chandra Chatterjee created a literary and national sensibility as profound as that of Manzoni and his contemporaries, revealing an Indian spirit broken by the humiliations of colonialism, but also glimpsing its own future modernity. The high literature of the novelists was matched by an effusion of popular "farces" and dramatic works which caricatured the Bengali middle class, especially those who aped what were thought of as Western mores and sexual habits. In Egypt, where the emergence of modern Arabic was very much the creation of newspapers, a generation of nationalist critics and authors such as Salama Musa had emerged by 1914, claiming to represent a united nation, but also popularizing a fluid, standardized language.

None of these forms, of course, wholly destroyed the traditions of popular literature, drama, music, and storytelling which existed in most societies through to the onset of mass television broadcasting in the later twentieth century. These forms remained vital, sometimes cannibalizing and adapting the characters and themes of the new, Western-derived world literature. What it did mean was that the reading matter of educated people across the world was rapidly converging in style, while at the same time it became more distant from these popular forms and was less and less influenced by them.

CONCLUSION: ARTS AND SOCIETIES

By 1914, the language of symbols in Western art was infinitely more varied, contradictory, and opaque than it had been in 1780. By mid-century some strange influences were beginning to be felt. The French sculptor Emmanuel Fremiet (1842–1910) mixed romanticism, gothicism, and science. One of his sculptures, *Gorilla Carrying off a Woman*, echoes the contemporary debates over Darwinism.[51] Outside architecture, the classical style had widely been abandoned. Impressionism, pointillism, primitivism, and early forms of abstract art all jostled with more traditional academic styles at the 1900 Paris Universal Exhibition.[52] Gustav Klimt's strange melting harpies rubbed shoulders with upstanding lions and "monarchs of the glen" in the conservative style of Sir Edward Landseer. But generally, where classical symbols retained their potency, it was often the most unsettling and uncertain ones. In Paris, the severed head of John the Baptist was widely on display in a variety of paintings in different styles. Richard Strauss was soon to write an opera on this theme, charged with themes of weird sexuality. His music had also begun to break away from the classical norms of tone and scale. James Joyce, the Irish novelist, and his contemporaries were similarly on the point of rupturing the narrative style of the novel.

Though the analogy is an attractive one, art historians and literary historians are now somewhat skeptical of arguments that link contemporary artistic unease with Heisenberg's Uncertainty Principle or Sigmund Freud's psychoanalysis and "discovery" of the unconscious mind. What is more certain is that the relatively stable, guild-like structure of late-eighteenth-century art and letters and the abundance of ecclesiastical, aristocratic, and royal patronage, which once maintained it, had vanished. This allowed space for the burgeoning of styles and artistic themes which were more experimental, at once both more political and less public.

Complexity was accompanied by greater global uniformity. In many societies, Western styles and forms had pushed elite non-European high arts and literature to the margins, or at the best subordinated them to the status of crafts. Only Japanese and, to a lesser extent, Chinese arts largely escaped this fate, and even they were showing alarming signs of kitsch. The decline of patronage, mechanization, and the drive for modernity in education had accomplished what great destroyers such as Genghis Khan and Tamberlaine had failed to do. Asia, Africa, and the Pacific were to produce fine artists in the twentieth century, but almost all of them would now paint Western art in indigenous styles, or at best a hybrid style, rather than indigenous art. Hybridity, of course, does not equate with decline. In Europe and outside, it often gave a new surge of dynamic power to artistic creation. Yet the symbols were mixed, the traditions entangled, and the high art of court, temple, and church lost its integrity. Art had, in fact, changed its function quite dramatically. Artistic creation was driven less by the religious faith and values of the great patron or the small learned class, than by a large, impersonal and increasingly international market. People still had recourse to works of art, or created works of art, to contemplate or embody the spirits. Yet many now made, collected, or displayed them solely as marks of personal status or in pursuit of secular enlightenment.

To set against this sober conclusion is the vitality of the popular arts at the end of the nineteenth century. The great movements of people and ideas which characterized the period, along with its technical innovations, had created a unique context for their development. Rail travel had made the diffusion of popular theater in West and East more possible than ever before. In Europe and North America, the magic lantern and early cinema were reaching out into country towns. Chinese, Vietnamese, and Burmese popular operatic and dramatic groups moved around the villages telling stories of the heroes of the past and subtly spreading opposition to colonial governments. Techniques of lighting and new musical instruments made the traditional rendering of the Indian epics in the small towns and villages more spectacular than ever before. If missionaries wiped out the ancient war and marriage songs of the Maori and other Pacific peoples, they spread across the region new styles of popular hymn singing. Welsh hymns were heard in the Chin Hills of Burma and were adapted to their new environment. In Western societies, the music hall spread rapidly as a money-making enterprise among the crowded residential areas of the new working class. In Britain at least, music hall drama provided a creative and versatile counterpoint to the rather staid tradition of classical theater. Almost everywhere, popular writing exploded massively with the diffusion of the printing press. Popular Arab detectives and Xhosa lovers populated a vast range of cheap chapbooks which spread as widely in society as once had devotional hymns or Dutch Bibles. Finally, at the end of the century, the cinema staged its dramatic denouement, not only in Paris and New York, but in Bombay and Cairo. Not all this effusion of creativity could be attributed to popular agency, of course. It was usually shrewd businessmen who saw the potential in the popular market. But, to differing degrees, the

ILLUSTRATION 10.6   A Malay gamelan band, 1880s.

success of these new or modified art forms reflected active choice by working people, and it sometimes reflected their own creative involvement in making culture.

PROSPECT

Art-historical writing is particularly unilinear, because we know visually "what happened." The outcome of all this was Pablo Picasso, Gropius, and James Joyce, modernists who, in the twentieth century, broke down the conventions of art, architecture, and literature respectively. But if we had stood in an art museum or a public place about 1900, there would still have been much to remind us of the old order. Tsars on horseback in white uniforms still populated the exhibition rooms of the 1900 Paris exhibition. Sir Edwin Lutyens, the British architect, still created country houses for the landed gentry. Peasants across the world still bought block prints which visualized their own particular local deities and patrons. The next chapter turns to the perpetuation of hierarchy in the context of modernity.

PART IV

CHANGE, DECAY, AND CRISIS

[11] *THE RECONSTITUTION OF SOCIAL HIERARCHIES*

ACCORDING to many nineteenth-century intellectuals, rational modern government, liberalism, science, industrialization, and the new urbanism had unleashed changes which made their era distinct from all previous ages. Earlier chapters have severely qualified this judgment. Liberalism remained an aspiration in 1850 and was on the defensive by 1900. The reception of science was determined to a significant extent by preexisting patterns of intellectual activity. Industrialization and the new city were slow in coming to much of the globe. Surprisingly, perhaps, the most dynamic social force of the era was religious belief, which many intellectuals felt, or hoped, was progressively losing its influence over the century after 1789.

This chapter examines more broadly the persistence and rebuilding of the types of social hierarchy which had characterized the old order. By "hierarchies" are meant forms of social and economic domination and subordination which are justified by ideologies of honor, embodied worth, or divine dispensation. The old regimes were by no means all monarchies, of course. In the cases of Venice, Hungary, and the Netherlands, for instance, ancient republican forms had survived the era of enlightened despots. In many non-European societies, titular chiefs were dependent on councils of tribal elders. Even in these cases, though, the system itself was hierarchical, generated out of old-style oligarchic values. This was a major reason why Napoleon, a new republican state-builder, hated the old-style republicans of Venice, with their ranks and orders and closed confraternities.

The chapter considers gender subordination, slavery, serfdom, the gentry class, and monarchies. It argues that the survival of these social forms and dependencies was not simply a matter of historical "continuity." Instead, the people of the nineteenth century preserved and embellished these features of the old order precisely because they were useful or valuable to them in an era of change. The need to reconcile arguments about continuity or change, and about the dissolution or reconstitution of hierarchies, becomes clearer if we first examine the contradictory narratives which historians have constructed over recent years.

CHANGE AND THE HISTORIANS

Until the late 1970s, most histories of nineteenth-century Europe still saw their narratives as attempts to explain why the revolution came to Russia in 1917, or why Nazism emerged in the 1920s, or why the Labour Party came to power in Britain, for instance. Historians of Asia and Africa espied the beginnings of nationalism in cow-protection movements in India in the 1890s and invulnerability cults in Africa in the 1900s. This remained a thoroughly "whiggish" historiography, in which social processes were believed to have an end inherent in themselves. Then, in 1981, the American historian Arno Mayer published a work on European history entitled *The Persistence of the Old Regime*.[1] He argued that what was striking about the modern European state system in 1914 was not the rise of democracy, the rise of labor, or the progress of modernity, but how little these supposedly irresistible forces for change had actually eroded the apparently immovable objects of imperial systems, aristocracies, and the hierarchical subordination of peasant to lord. In fact, Europe in 1914 was more like Europe in 1789, before the French Revolution, than it was like Europe in 1945. It was the wars of the twentieth century, Mayer implied, not the wordy social movements and shallow economic changes of the nineteenth century, which really brought the modern world into being. He thus distanced himself from a series of arguments about the consequences of the French Revolution, first proposed by de Tocqueville, which became the assumption on which the Marxist, social, and labor historians of the twentieth century founded their work.

Mayer's work caused less debate than it might have done, partly because the argument was overdone, and partly because the mood in history writing was already changing.[2] Ironically, and by no means logically, the decline and later collapse of the Soviet Union and European Communism after 1989 seemed to throw into question the whole narrative of historians who had put revolutionary change or even the rise of democracy at the top of their agendas. Since the 1990s, by contrast, much has been written about the politics of courts, the role of religion, and the persistence of the old order into the later nineteenth century.

There is apparently much to be said for a view of continuity during the nineteenth century in Europe. In the south and the east of the continent, far less than a third of the population lived in cities in 1900. Many of the rural dwellers remained pathetically dependent on lords and seigneurs as share croppers or as tenants-at-will. Travelers in the mid-nineteenth century did not need to go much beyond the boundaries of France itself to realize that the French Revolution had not done much to change the relationship between lord and peasant. Even in Britain, Belgium, and northern Germany, where industrialization had proceeded more rapidly, the expanded electorate was still dominated by great magnates, and supposedly democratic politics was subject to periodic monarchical intervention. Lord Salisbury, descendant of one of Elizabeth I's great courtiers, and a cohort of big landowners dominated the British government in the 1890s and continued to command great social deference in their constituencies. After Queen Victoria's death in 1901, the new monarch, Edward VII, took a closer interest in government policy.

This was a widespread pattern. Following the defeat of the Italian armies by the Abyssinians at Adowa in 1896, King Umberto proceeded to undermine his ministers and assert his personal authority.[3] As late as 1907, Nicholas II of Russia arbitrarily and unconstitutionally changed the newly inaugurated electoral law and invoked the authority "delegated to him by God."[4] Elsewhere, conservative peasantries remained remarkably tenacious in the face of rural capitalism. Even in the United States, some of the great colonial era families, such as the landowners of the Chesapeake Bay area, had preserved their lands and position after the abolition of slavery. In the Deep South states, meanwhile, slavery was a mere generation away, and the emancipated black population continued to subsist as sharecroppers, increasingly subject to a color bar which excluded it from schools, churches, and urban spaces in the towns.

If we look outside Europe, the argument seems to gain even more plausibility. Indeed, it can be suggested that the stasis in Europe was in part the product of the annexation to itself of a huge extra-European hinterland which could only be governed by force and conservatism. At the beginning of the nineteenth century, empire-builders had argued that their brutal conquests paved the way for the rise of civilization, trade, and humane government in erstwhile barbarous states. Asia and Africa would be transformed by Christianity, utilitarian government, the doctrine of the rights of man, and perhaps by American freedoms. The situation in 1900 hardly seemed to bear out these predictions. The urban population throughout the British and French empires in Asia and North Africa remained stubbornly stuck at about 10 percent of the total, barely changed from the precolonial figure, and standards of living may even have fallen over the previous century. Anecdotal evidence collected by the first generation of Asian and African nationalists asserted that many once-prosperous bodies of peasants and artisans were actually worse off and more dependent on magnates than they had been in 1800.

Colonial government had apparently neither improved people's lot nor ushered in a more rational system of politics. Far from bringing in modern administrations, colonial rule had perpetuated the rule of a host of archaic potentates: sultans, *marabouts*, rajas, and Hawaiian chiefs. In British and French Africa, respectively, Lord Lugard and Marshal Lyautey gloried in the system of "indirect rule" in which the paraphernalia and personal justice of the precolonial systems survived.[5] Natives, they thought, responded to arbitrary and despotic regimes. Christianity, let alone education, was the harbinger of anarchy unless very carefully handled. Throughout the colonial empires, slavery died a very prolonged death. It was still extant in Cuba and the Spanish Caribbean in 1898, when the Americans and Spanish went to war.[6] Elsewhere, slavery had been formally abolished, but systems such as indentured labor, tribal labor reserves, apprenticeship, and domestic servitude simply replaced it.

Even in the semi-independent and independent states of the non-European world, the ancien régime seemed to survive in all its vigor. If anything, recent historical writing here also supports the thesis of "distorted continuity." From 1900 to the 1980s, for instance, most commentators and historians regarded the Qing Empire of the later nineteenth century as a hopeless case. It was no more than a hollow crown, rendered impotent by the real power-holders in China, the local landlords, provincial governors, and Western powers perched in the treaty ports. This view is in the process of being reappraised. The fall of the Qing dynasty in 1911 now seems less of an inevitability, as Hans van de Ven argues.[7] After the mid-century peasant rebellions, the empire had been more successful in self-strengthening than it might appear. Even after the Boxer Rebellion, great regional militarists, notably General Yuan Shikai, still worked for the survival of the regime.[8] The events of 1911, when the empire finally fell, represented short-term financial crisis which got out of hand. Deference to the imperial house remained strong throughout society. Confucian China was alive and well in 1900; its complete demise could not have been predicted.

In a similar manner, the Ottoman Empire has been subject to a thorough-going reevaluation in the last two decades. Historians now see it as a viable, sophisticated system for adjusting ethnic and religious disputes, rather than a bear pit of nationality problems. The "Sick Man of Europe" was the victim of Western medical imperialism. Ottoman patriotism survived well into the twentieth century amongst Arab and even Greek subjects of the empire.[9] It might even have survived the First World War had the Committee of Union and Progress, a group of young officers who attempted to reinvigorate the regime, not chosen the wrong side. Japan's modernization is held to have been successful only because the great barons and samurai warrior classes retained atavistic values of loyalty to the imperial house. This great act of modernization, paradoxically, imposed yet further burdens on the middle and poorer peasantry, benefiting only the rich.[10] Moreover, semi-independent clan-based zealots in the Imperial Navy were already purposively pursuing a plan of imperial conquest in mainland Asia, which was to culminate in the implosion of the empire itself. Japanese modernization was only skin-deep.

Historians keep themselves in a job by overthrowing received wisdom once a generation or so. This is a task which can usually be achieved quite simply, because all historical writing is a question of assigning emphasis. Historians of labor and socialist writers 30 years ago could reasonably point to the massive growth of industrial cities and the world division of labor which occurred in the nineteenth century. But, just as reasonably, today's historians can point out that most people on earth in 1900 were peasants, as they had been a hundred years before, and that their standard of living and the systems of subordination under which they labored remained broadly similar, if they were not actually deteriorating.

One way past this impasse is to ask not only what changed and what did not change over this century, but *why* certain older practices, political structures, and hierarchies – meaning systems of subordination legitimated by cultural values – were allowed to survive. What did these older systems continue to offer in an era when it is difficult to deny that there was already quite sharp population growth, the rise of industrial capitalism, democracy, and the modern state? This chapter tries to give an answer to this by examining the realms of urban and rural labor, aristocracy, and monarchy. Part of the answer is that politicians and elites selected the older systems for survival precisely because they still helped to hold together a world of relationships which were becoming more uniform yet also more complex. At the same time, not all these survivals can be explained in "functional" terms. Sometimes, hierarchies and apparently redundant beliefs survived or were reconstituted simply because people valued them.

GENDER AND SUBORDINATION IN THE "LIBERAL AGE"

Before looking at wider social formations, it is instructive to look at a more basic building block of human society: the family and the relationship between the genders. Many historians and social scientists from the socialist Friedrich Engels to the present day have seen inequalities in gender relations as the essential foundation of all other forms of inequality and subordination in society. What, broadly, was the effect of the changes discussed here, the somewhat hesitant rise of the state, capitalism, and liberalism, on relations between men and women? One persistent assumption in the mid-twentieth-century literature on modernity was that the older extended family system, which supposedly prevailed over much of the world outside Protestant northern Europe and North America, would break down in the face of economic change. This in turn would lead to a rise in individualism and a more equal relationship between men and women.

It must be said that formal analyses of family structures do not point to massive changes in gender relations. Most historians of the family, looking from the outside, see few major changes in the structure of the family across the world in the course of the nineteenth century. The dominance of the large extended family in early modern Asia has probably been exaggerated. Equally, the dominance of the small "nuclear" family in Europe, and especially in northern European societies such as Denmark, England, and Holland, has probably been exaggerated, too. This is because non-kin, residential "helpers" of families have not been taken into account. When these assessments are corrected substantially, and families are seen as ad hoc assemblages of people as much as biological units, rapid changes are less easy to perceive between the early modern period and the nineteenth century.

Where change did take place in European family structure, moreover, it often worked to entrench more deeply existing inequalities between men and women. For example, much labor in nineteenth-century mines, factories, and commercial farms, whether in tsarist Russia or in southern Italy, was casual peasant labor. As these capitalist enterprises developed, they took male labor away from the sphere of domestic family labor for long periods.[11] This inevitably increased the pressures on women, particularly on women carrying or nurturing children who were left at home. The men did not remit much of the money they earned to their families and often fell into debt. The women not only had to look after the children, but also to earn money or grow food in the absence of their male partners or relatives. Women's health consequently declined. In other industries, such as Chinese and Indian tea gardens, women constituted much of the labor force because they were supposed to be able to work more rapidly with their hands. The paltry wages they earned were all remitted to male members of their families in the home districts, if the money had not already been stolen by male overseers and contractors.

Things were not changing very fast even for elite Western women. In 1784 the Scottish judge, Lord Kames had intoned in regard to the woman's role: "To please her husband, to be a good oeconomist and to educate her children are her capital duties each of which requires much training. . . . The time a girl bestows on her doll is a prognostic that she will be equally diligent about her offspring."[12]

In the following two generations, garnished with references to religious devotion, education, and physical health, that saying could be taken to reflect the attitudes of male reformers and intellectuals across the world. No doubt some significant gains were registered by elite women in Western societies over the century or so before 1914. Rising incomes and better communications in western Europe and North America allowed aristocratic and middle-class women some subtle influence in politics and patronage. Electorates, however, were only very slowly expanded to include women. Some states of the USA had female franchises in the late nineteenth century, but most not until the Constitutional Amendment of 1920. Women over the age of 30 only achieved the right to vote in Britain in 1918,[13] and this happened later in France and Italy. In Australia, New Zealand, and Canada, more radical provisions had created full female suffrage. Continental Europe lagged behind on the franchise, but powerful forces for women's emancipation had been stirred, and women played a fuller part in other aspects of public life. For instance, women could take full degrees at the University of Paris, as did Marie Curie, the physicist, long before they could do so in England. By the turn of the century, elite women were achieving a degree of independence in regard to marriage, the ownership of property, and the use of leisure. Capitalism was beginning to adjust to the idea of women as an important group of consumers to be cultivated.

Women's historians, however, have rightly queried the actual substance of many of these formal changes. There is no doubt that women remained excluded from most forms of male employment. Female suffrage did not really mean that women were given a significant political voice, even though the nation was usually represented as a female entity, and women were allowed to take part in "polite" political enterprises such as abolitionism or in religious and charitable activity. Rising living standards for the lower middle classes often allowed men to withdraw women from trading or working in the public sphere, where at least they had had some chance of operating as independent agents or building up personal savings. Working-class women of the supposed "labor elite," who were forced to work in the textile and other industries on both sides of the Atlantic, were subjected to poor working conditions and paid only a fraction of what their male co-workers were paid. Employers often found ways of channeling female wages back to men.

Women of all classes and races remained the victims of male understandings of disease and childbirth which subtly classed them as inferior mentally and physically. It was in the nineteenth century, after all, that doctors came widely to treat "hysteria" as a particularly female disease connected with the womb. In fact, an important aspect of the rise of the medical profession was the emergence of gynecology, a male speciality controlling women's bodies. The old midwives, wet nurses, and "wise women" of the past were increasingly spurned and even turned into criminals by "respectable" people in many parts of the world.

The advance of Western women was, to say the least, unsteady before 1914, and in many ways science and industrialism allowed men to maintain a patrimonial hold over women's bodies and minds rather than undermining male dominance. It is even more uncertain that non-Western women made much of an advance in the nineteenth century. In many respects, indeed, their status and life expectations may well have declined. It is very doubtful that the precolonial legal order in many societies gave much of a role to women property-holders in fact. But colonial regimes, concerned to raise revenue and create acquiescent pools of military and civil labor, tended to entrench the status of male family heads in their new codes of law, making male control more rigid at the very least. There were, of course, celebrated moral offensives by missionaries, European women, and colonial reformers to improve the lot of women in many of these societies. Institutions such as the American Zenana Mission, a mission to the women's quarters, sought to educate and liberate women from what were thought of as the restrictions of the Indo-Islamic and Middle Eastern family. These reformers tried to spread education, Christianity, and hygiene to women secluded in Hindu and Muslim families. Women's education became a mantra for European colonial powers when they sought to justify imperialism to skeptical domestic opinion. There were celebrated campaigns, also apparently on women's issues, against female infanticide and infant marriage in India, forced concubinage and foot binding in China, and genital mutilation in Africa. Yet these were more often discursive offensives by Europeans against "depraved natives" than sustained efforts to improve women's lot. The Indian Age of Consent Bill of 1882, outlawing child marriage, was less concerned with the well-being of young girls than with "raising the physical, moral and mental status of the native" and stopping "evils which sap national vigour and morality."[14] More significant, perhaps, were indigenous efforts at reform. The purist reformers of the nineteenth century, notably Mohamed Abduh in Egypt, emphasized the importance of female education, though in a strictly segregated form. Likewise, the Meiji reformers built on late-Tokugawa developments to establish a school system, which by 1890 was educating about 35 percent of school-age girls, by comparison with 70 percent of boys.[15]

Whatever the effects of these local reformers' initiatives, however, wider socioeconomic changes do not seem to have helped women much – perhaps the contrary. Famine and disease fell unequally on females, and demographers have glimpsed a family survival tactic in the figures which indicate excess mortality among women. Women and children remained preeminently the pathetic victims of the great famines which swept China, India, and parts of north and central Africa throughout the century. If some moves toward "respectability" may have aided women, most others actually restricted their movement. Over much of Asia and Africa, rural magnates removed women from view and restricted them to the home as family income grew.

Paradoxically, then, social and economic change may well have had the effect of restricting the independence of women, rather than enhancing it amongst both elite and poor, though for different reasons. In this microcosm of human society, one can see the wider paradox that vaunted modernity may in some respects have re-empowered hierarchy. More than this, the very possibility of keeping women's labor, child-rearing capacity, and skills subordinated may well have been an important and unspoken force for the preservation of other helot classes, especially slaves and peasant bondsmen.

SLAVERY'S INDIAN SUMMER

The reinforcement of subordination certainly seems to be a valid theme for the lowest reaches of the world's labor system. The first half of the nineteenth century may indeed have been the heyday of the slave system, even if the slave trade came increasingly under scrutiny. One reason why slave-owners and slave-traders were able to stave off the growing attacks of abolitionists in the eighteenth and early nineteenth centuries was that practically every set of legal or religious traditions in the world gave it some degree of legitimacy. In the European case, Aristotle and Roman law notoriously accepted slavery as a natural condition, while the Church Fathers had nodded and winked in its direction. Islamic and Buddhist traditions, among others, also accepted forms of deep social dependency which bore family resemblances to the European slavery of the classical world. Both were formally egalitarian religious systems, but many Muslims held that those captured in war could be made slaves, while Buddhists invoked the law of *karma*, or "cosmic retribution," to justify slavery. Far from losing power in the nineteenth century, classical systems of law and normative codes were widely reinvented, sometimes providing justification for the proponents of slavery. So, for instance, after 1760, the revived

Burmese kingdom of Ava propagated a form of classical Hindu-Buddhist law which appeared to bind many classes of people into deeper dependency.[16] In Brazil and Cuba, where plantation slavery survived well into the 1880s,[17] a reinvigorated Roman Catholic hierarchy continued vigorously to justify it with Aristotle's arguments, even though this subsequently became increasingly embarrassing for the Vatican.

Above all, racial difference was invoked by white Europeans and Americans, and to a lesser extent by Asians and Africans, to justify slavery. In the eighteenth century and before, it was often claimed that the Bible had condemned black Africans to inferiority and slavery. In the nineteenth century, some commentators used the new racial "sciences" to justify the continuation of slavery and other forms of labor bondage. Here, as in other areas, the effect of the rise of the doctrines of social and economic liberalism and emancipation can be greatly exaggerated.

Yet plantation slavery on the American and Caribbean model was a different system from the family and farm dependency more common in the European classical world and across contemporary Islamic lands. In many ways it could be seen as an aspect of early modern capitalist enterprise rather than as an ancient survival. It was to a large extent, therefore, the economic value still inhering in the slave system for plantation-owners, traders, and states which promoted its survival into the later nineteenth century.

The figures which have been assembled by historians of the slave trade are quite striking. P. E. Lovejoy calculated that 6,133,000 slaves were transported from Africa across the Atlantic between 1701 and 1800, and a further 3,330,000 between 1801 and 1900. If one were to take the period covered in this study, 1780–1914, it is probable that the total number of West Africans captured and uprooted over the "long" eighteenth century (c.1680–1780) and the "long" nineteenth century would not be very different.[18] Ironically, the 1780s, the very era of the supposed breakthrough into modernity and enlightenment, appears to have been the all-time peak of slave trading. Equally, slave taking by Arab traders and states from East Africa and in Southeast Asia may actually have increased towards the end of the eighteenth century.[19] So the British abolition of the slave trade in 1807 should not be assigned too much importance in the history of worldwide slave trading. Even in British territories, slave holding continued until 1834–8, and its consequences for much longer.[20] On islands such as Jamaica, where gang working continued into the 1830s, as compared with the system of tasking individual slaves which was more common in the USA, rebellions and savage punishments also persisted into the "age of reform" of the 1830s. Indeed, black rebels in the West Indies were treated like slaves for more than a generation after the British emancipation. In the former Spanish and Portuguese territories of the New World, slavery persisted for another generation or more. Moreover, Brazil, not the Caribbean, was the most important destination of African slaves in the period 1780–1830.

Consequently, the British Parliament's decision to abolish slave trading also had little impact on Africa itself for a generation or more. Britain might use legal means to ensure that its own citizens could not trade, but its only weapon against foreigners was to station naval vessels off the West African coast and intercept slave ships in order to free the slaves. The Spanish and Portuguese merchants who traded with the main slave destinations, Cuba and Brazil, developed sophisticated systems to evade British patrols. If anything, the profits from the trade were now much greater, so the trade moved and reformulated itself, rather than dwindling away. Civil war in African kingdoms in the early nineteenth century and the tenacity of the African elites, especially in the kingdoms of Asante and Dahomey and other West African states which grew prosperous from slavery, also helped to perpetuate it. The West African "legitimate" export trades remained quite small until the 1850s or 1860s, and agrarian production was volatile; earnings from the slave trade were among the few sources of income to maintain emerging aristocracies and trading magnates. Some authorities have also argued that the long-term effect of the Atlantic slave trade on Africa was to increase slavery, especially female slavery, within African society, thus further naturalizing slave export, as it were. It is likely that the British abolition of the slave trade actually increased the number of slaves in West Africa and helped produce a more deeply stratified society. Revolts by slaves against their African masters encouraged African kings to continue with ritual killings, which warned criminals and terrorized slaves.[21]

In the New World, to which so many of the African slaves were dispatched, economic needs determined the survival of slavery to a similar or greater degree. The basic point was that the small white population did not believe that any other system would guarantee the continuation of viable production. In the British West Indies, the Napoleonic wars coincided with a period of great profitability for the sugar industry, as neighboring French colonies were disrupted by the effects of the French Revolution and slave revolts on Haiti and elsewhere. When the sugar economy took a downturn after 1815, it was already evident that the existing slave population was not reproducing itself very quickly because of disease and overwork. This made the labor of existing slaves even more essential and accounts for the fierce resistance of the plantation-owners to British calls for the termination of the whole system, as abolitionist political pressure built up again in the late 1820s. It also explains why after the final abolition of 1834–8, the owners sought to impose a system of "apprenticeship" on former slaves, which was in some ways as exploitative as the earlier formal slavery.[22]

Over much of Spanish and Portuguese America, the same conditions prevailed. Labor was generally scarce, and before 1840, immigration from Europe could meet only a small proportion of the continent's needs. Yet the sugar economies of both Brazil and Cuba were flourishing in the early nineteenth century as European and American demand for tropical produce expanded. A million and a half African slaves were landed in Brazil before British pressure forced the end of the trade in 1850. Brazil's hesitant moves toward the final abolition of slavery in 1888 resulted as much from the need to attract free labor from Europe, where slavery was unpopular, as from any growth in humanitarian sentiment.[23] On Cuba, which remained a Spanish colony until the end of the century, slavery was not ended until 1886, and vestiges of it remained in the form of bonded labor until the twentieth century.

The culture of slavery and dependence was about more than simple economics. It was also a system of hierarchy. Slaveholding was also a life-style. Being a master required slaves, and the servile dependence of human beings on the master was as essential a badge of status for the tropical plantation-owner as the consumption of tropical goods were for contemporary bourgeois families in Europe. In the British Caribbean before abolition, the defense of slavery went hand in hand with the defense of proud colonial assemblies which resented the attempt of ministers or Parliament to tell them what to do. Attempts by the home government or British governors to ameliorate slavery were seen as an attack on property and on the rights of "freeborn Englishmen." In Brazil, Emperor Peter I's attempts in the 1820s to placate the British by banning the slave trade produced a patriotic reaction from deeply conservative rural magnates. In Cuba, continued loyalty to the king of Spain by the leading magnates was intertwined with a fierce philosophical defense of slavery. In the southern states of America, most resoundingly, defense of the old federal constitution became a rallying cry around which slave-owners could mobilize.

The most striking example of the persistence of slavery was, indeed, in the southern states of the United States, for that "peculiar institution" survived in a society which was self-consciously modern and had proclaimed itself in 1776 the home of the rights of man. Here, too, slavery was found useful to an emerging capitalist economy. At the same time, the social systems which emerged around it were also underpinned by ideologies and social values which proved resistant to the lure of modernity. A generation of outstanding historians of the 1960s and 1970s, led by Stanley Engermann, Robert Fogel, and Eugene Genovese, painted the picture in detail.[24]

Slavery in the South had arisen, as everywhere, from a deficiency in the supply of labor. The emerging American society needed to buy industrial manufactures from Europe, and particularly Britain. Tobacco from the upper South and rice from the lower South made up a large part of the American export trade with Europe and the Caribbean. African slaves had been brought in in huge numbers as slave plantations spread from Virginia westward and southward. The discovery of the cotton ginning machine in 1793 gave a huge boost to the crop, which was dispatched in large quantities to fuel Britain's Industrial Revolution and, later, that of the northern states. Thus, while the northern states abolished slavery between 1774 and 1804, the number of slaves in the South expanded from 700,000 in 1790 to about four million in 1860. In the early decades of the nineteenth century, cotton represented about 60 percent of US exports.

Fogel and Engermann argued that slavery persisted because it was a relatively efficient system of production, certainly more productive than the small free-labor farms of the North. Though the South lagged behind the North in industrial growth, it was not the stagnant semi-colonial slum which contemporary abolitionists and many later historians depicted. Slavery, they argued, was more diverse, less brutal, and allowed more social mobility to the slaves than was once believed. This seemed to be supported by the fact that slave populations continued to grow naturally after the transport of African slaves was banned in 1808. Most surprising, slave standards of living and life expectation appear to have been better than those of the post-emancipation black population, though some black historians dissented from this view. Economic historians in the 1990s continued to produce evidence that slavery was perfectly compatible with – indeed, enhanced – early industrial production.[25]

The importance of the economic motivation for slavery seems to fit well with the one case where slavery seems to have declined somewhat: in the cities, not only in North America, but elsewhere. Both in the cities of the American South and in Cape Town, urban slavery declined before the institution itself came under direct assault. The urban slave population in the American South declined from 22 to 10 percent of the population between 1800 and 1860. Legislative interventions and economic needs for the free movement of labor seem to have brought about this situation. But its effects do not seem to have radiated to the rural hinterlands, where slaveholding was still profitable.

In the United States, too, the economic reasons for the continuation of slaveholding were complemented by powerful social and ideological ones.[26] Eugene Genovese, in particular, argued for slavery's cultural role and was less convinced of its economic functionality. For slave-owners, the plantation seemed to represent an idyllic world of rural community, where the master could play biblical patriarch or classical philosopher-king to his liking. One slave-owner told a British visitor: "We want no manufactures; we desire no trading, no mechanical or manufacturing classes." Even if slaveholding was somewhat less efficient than free labor, it was thought to avoid the vicious class conflict and anomie of North American and European capitalism. Self-serving as this was, there seems to be some evidence that American slave populations could adjust to bondage and survive a "social death" which gave them no civil or even domestic rights.[27] Some historians have argued controversially that brutality and violence were less pervasive than might be thought. Religion and family affection survived hardship. Slave rebellions did occur in America, especially in the early years of the nineteenth century, but they were less horrible in their consequences than contemporary ones in Jamaica, Haiti, San Domingue, and Brazil. This was no doubt in part because the slave populations made up less than half the total populations of the southern states and were hence more readily controlled. But it was also because southern slave-owners realized that the recurrence of abuses would ultimately undermine the whole system.

The intertwining of economic and cultural aspects of slavery was just as much in evidence in the Islamic lands, Asia, and the Pacific, where various forms of domestic and field bondage also survived late into the nineteenth century. Large numbers of Africans continued to be exported from both East and West Africa to the Middle East and the Persian Gulf. Under the Tanzimat reforms in the Ottoman Empire, the importation of slaves was formally banned. Yet in outlying areas, such as Arabia and North Africa, slaveholding and trading persisted until the First World War and after.[28] Ruling groups in East Africa, such as the Yao people of what is now Kenya, continued to export captured people. Cities such as Timbuktu in the northwest and Mombasa on the east coast retained their prosperity into the later nineteenth century on the profits of this trade.

The continuation of Ottoman–African slavery reflected not so much a proto-capitalist commercial demand, as in the case of Brazil or the southern United States, but a more pervasive lack of labor. Both North Africa and the Middle East had suffered serious epidemics in the early part of the century, and their populations seem to have been more or less static over the whole century. In addition, slaveholding within the family was a sign of status in many of these societies. Here, "slavery" was a blanket term for a spectrum of statuses, rather than the absolute condition it represented in the USA. It was quite common for slaves to be given a degree of autonomy and recognition within households. The children of slave mothers and free fathers often became powerful freemen themselves within Arab and Ottoman society. This became a feature of Atlantic slavery only quite late in the history of the institution, as the effects of Christian missionary activity began to be felt. One cannot assume either that "slavery" in these contexts was always regarded as an unmixed evil by the societies from which the enslaved were taken. It could sometimes be seen as a justified extension of a more local traffic in people. As late as 1930, when the president of Liberia banned the pawning of children under a League of Nations convention, it was reported that:

> In sections of the country where it had been a custom for generations for natives to pawn their children away to neighbouring tribes, the chiefs declared that their main sources of income had been removed and they did not see how they are going to get the silver to pay their hut taxes if they cannot pawn their children to the tribes nearer the coast.[29]

A less visible system of slavery persisted, or even expanded, in India and in Southeast Asia, despite the belated efforts of the British and later the Dutch to suppress it. Here the Islamic form of slaveholding, brought to South Asia in the Middle Ages, merged with the practice of Hindu caste. However, slaves in these societies were not treated very differently from bonded laborers on the land or lowly domestic servants, with the important exception that they and their children could be bought and sold. Here again, lack of labor in some areas and the felt need for great men to be surrounded by dependants and servitors played their part. Many women, especially within the great Muslim households of South and Southeast Asia in the nineteenth century, were effectively slaves.[30] The peculiar form of the trusted slave-eunuch was also a feature of South and Southeast Asian courtly circles until around 1850. When in Egypt and India, the British intervened to emancipate domestic slaves, there were complaints from indigenous intellectuals that this merely threw whole classes of people, especially women, into poverty or prostitution.

Even after the end of formal slave trading and slave owning across the world, the system of indentured labor represented another form of deep bondage which could take its place, creating in the words of Hugh Tinker, who was himself quoting Lord John Russell, the mid-nineteenth-century British prime minister, a "new system of slavery."[31] Within the Asian and African societies of the nineteenth century, there existed particular districts or regions which, year after year, produced armies of "coolies" or indentured laborers for public works, plantations, and mines. These people were often drawn from Aboriginal or "tribal" populations. This system could easily be adapted to supply the needs for labor overseas. Between the 1830s and 1912 (when the British government limited the transport of indentured labor from India following a campaign by nationalists and humanitarians), a further four million or more Indians, Malays, Sinhalese, Chinese, and Japanese were carried across the world to work as laborers. Though technically freemen, so bound were they by the terms of their indentures and the debts which they owed to their employers, that their situation gave rise to abuses on the same scale as slavery itself.[32] Indians from Bihar and the south were sent to the sugar islands of the Caribbean, Mauritius, and Fiji. By 1914, 250,000 poor Indians had been imported into Guiana, 134,000 into Trinidad, and 33,000 into Jamaica.[33]

ILLUSTRATION 11.1 A new system of slavery? Tamil coolie labor on Malayan rubber estate, early twentieth century.

Emboldened by the knowledge that Indian laborers would take near starvation wages and Burmese would not, British and Indian entrepreneurs had also begun to take large numbers of Indian coolies to Burma before the First World War. They were accommodated in dormitories in Rangoon and other cities so filthy that they made American slave quarters seem like model townships. Large numbers also went to Natal and Cape Colony, where, in the 1890s, they found their great champion in the young M. K. Gandhi. Chinese and Japanese laborers were taken to Southeast Asia, the Pacific, and North and South America, where they played a major role in the building of the railways and the development of the mining industry. The transcontinental railways of both the United States and Canada were built by indentured laborers, for example. Their situation was often one of abject dependency. Here again, economic interest may have brought the system into being, but in cultural terms it also represented a form of patriarchal atavism backed by ingrained judgments of racial worth. In the tropical colonies and former colonies, people of European race could act out myths of antique domination, as Gilberto Freyre, the Brazilian historian, brilliantly argued.[34]

The transformation of slavery in the course of the nineteenth century had consequences for the representation of race in academic and popular discourse. In turn, these representations reinforced the idea of African, or even Chinese, racial inferiority and the availability of such people as a labor pool. In the early modern worlds of Asia and the Atlantic, the idea that black people were lowly beings in the human family was very common. God (and Aristotle) had selected them for slavery, and their skin color seemed almost to embody their original sin. Even the Chinese appear to have naturalized this idea in their thought, though it was, naturally, the yellow rather than the white races which embodied reason and refinement in their schema. Such ideas began to go out of fashion in the nineteenth century, as biblical and other creationist ideas lapsed, and black people themselves began to reject the idea of sin. In the United States and western Europe, former slaves, such as Gustavus Vassa and Mary Prince, began to write of their sufferings in terms which suggested to white society the need for its own redemption. In place of old ideas of sin and expiation, however, a new vocabulary of biological racial backwardness and perfection came into use. Inherent racial qualities were used to explain the primitive nature of the African or Aboriginal, the despotic lethargy of the Chinese or Arab, and the freedom of the white races. In a world where African slavery lived on, but other groups of "lazy natives" had to be corralled to work for white masters down mines or in plantations, these ideas also proved temporarily serviceable. A hierarchy of human beings made legitimate by the Bible was easily replaced by one apparently supported by the most recent scientific theories.

As in the case of women's dependence, slavery's persistence tended to perpetuate other forms of dependency by strengthening despotic and warlike tendencies within Africa. Some demographers have argued that slavery may have reduced Africa's population by up to a half in the long term,[35] through deaths in Africa[36] and the exportation of people. Whatever the technical debates around this subject, slavery must, therefore, have contributed to some significant degree to the wider dependency of Africans as a whole within the emerging world economy.

THE PEASANT AND RURAL LABORER AS BOND SERF

When Sir Charles Metcalfe, previously governor-general of India, became governor of Jamaica in 1839, the former slave population of the island seemed to him infinitely better fed and more prosperous in appearance than the Indian peasant, staggering under the weight of rent and land revenue payments. In the nineteenth-century world, many peasants and rural laborers remained as poverty-stricken and dependent on their lords or state bureaucrats as slaves, though they were technically free. Here again the hierarchies typical of the pre-1789 order seemed to have been perpetuated or even deepened by the emergence of industry and the modern state. This section considers why that should have been the case.

Throughout the nineteenth century, reformers trumpeted the need to improve the lot of the rural masses of the world, and many believed that the expansion of world trade, enlightened colonial administration, or at least pressure on the Ottoman or Qing governments, for example, might improve their state. Twentieth-century experts such as the Dutch economist Hermann Boeke[37] argued that a "dual economy" came into existence in the nineteenth century. The progressive and dynamic force of European and North American capitalism and industrialization simply could not penetrate rural societies in which irrational practices and forms of tenure continued to hold back development. Since the 1950s, historians and "world systems theorists" have argued precisely the contrary case. Economic expansion, industrialization, and imperialism in the rich northern heartlands of Europe or the Americas served only to impoverish tributary dependencies both inside and outside the European world. Underdevelopment was not a natural state, but a state created by the very motors of capitalist development and imperialism themselves. This was the so-called dependency theory associated with André Gunder Frank[38] and developed as a historical model by Immanuel Wallerstein.[39] From this perspective, Mexico was "underdeveloped" by the expansion of the United States. Ireland's peasantry suffered from famine and dispersal across the English-speaking world as a consequence of the industrial growth of Britain and the ideologies of free trade which came in its wake. In Africa the population was stunted by the devastation of the slave trade, only to be subjected to a new bondage by the expansion of the so-called legitimate trade in commodities such as cocoa and palm oil destined for the industrializing ports of western Europe. Such forms of rural economic dependence, it was argued, were also strengthened and legitimated by concepts of racial and religious backwardness, which were given a new scientific tinge by evolutionist theories.

This picture is somewhat overdrawn, but it does help to remind us that the progressive elimination of the peasantry by industrialization and urbanization and its transformation into a class of prosperous owner-occupier farmers happened only unevenly and was limited to some particularly dynamic economies. Eugene Weber's celebrated book *Peasants into Frenchmen*[40] charted this process which was clearly happening in some parts of western Europe and Central or South America. In areas such as northern and eastern France, powerful forces were acting to bring this about. They included rapid economic growth, the strenuous activities of both secular and religious bodies in promoting education, and the interventions of a powerful state, fortified by republican hatred of rural privilege. Even so, when France suffered from an acute labor shortage, as it did seasonally during the southern harvests and with great severity during the First World War, thousands of France's tributary peasants were brought in from Algeria and Indochina to top up numbers. The peasants of the Third World were drafted in to fill the depleted ranks of European peasantry. These "peasants" never evolved into "Frenchmen," except briefly when needed as cannon fodder during wars. This Third World situation was visible in southern Europe too. In Italy[41] and Spain and much of eastern Europe, the state had hardly even begun to touch the huge mass of rural poverty, malnutrition, and malaria before the end of the nineteenth century. The only way out was by emigration. Impoverished Italian, Spanish, Portuguese, and German peasants flooded across the Atlantic to Brazil and Argentina, in particular after 1848. Irish, Russians, Scandinavians, and Germans made the voyage to North America.

Why were these deep relationships of dependency between peasant and lord or peasant and state reproduced in the nineteenth century? The argument that European growth helped hold down living standards elsewhere works well for many areas of the incipient poor colonized "south" which became raw material exporters to the rich "north." This is clear if one examines the figures for the distribution of profits from some of the great nineteenth-century cash crops, such as raw cotton, hides, jute, cocoa, and palm oil. In all these cases, it was the overseas shippers, insurers, carriers, and vendors in Europe and North America who took the vast proportion of "value added" to a quantity of produce in world trade. Local African, Asian, or South American merchants, let alone the peasant-producers, got only a very small percentage of the profits. On the other side, developing economies were forced to buy in at high cost the machinery for processing these agricultural raw materials. Thus the terms of trade were very much to the disadvantage of the "south" throughout the nineteenth century, and actually deteriorated as more relatively poor areas became producers of basic export crops.

Yet there were other forces working to reinforce relative poverty and the lord–peasant hierarchy in the countryside. Population pressure was one reason why rural people continued to fight for existence throughout the century. A generation ago, under the influence of Fernand Braudel and the *Annales* school of French social historians, demography was the starting point of all rural history. Now, culture and the state are more evident in historians' analyses, while much demographic history has separated itself off as a rather arid subdivision of mathematics. Still, it is impossible to ignore the growing weight of numbers as a factor depressing farmers' and laborers' living standards, especially during a period when economic growth rates worldwide were barely keeping up with population expansion. This was a vicious circle. Populations grew, not mainly because death rates were falling, but because farmers wanted to make sure that there were enough hands for the future, insuring themselves against periodic famines and disease. The more peasants there were, the weaker their bargaining power in relation to lord and state. In the latter part of the century, for example, rising population and falling wages pushed Latin American peasants into debt bondage, thus increasing their vulnerability to big landlords and state labor service.[42] Growing population also meant that landowners were less at risk from peasant migrations than they had been earlier. People could no longer find better conditions by moving on to sparsely populated areas, because these, too, were now filling up.

Despite the enormous setback to China's massive rural population, brought about by its mid-century wars, the population increased from something like 300 million in 1790 to about 450 million in 1914.[43] Better nutrition and the relatively long period of peace terminated by the Taiping Rebellion of 1850 played a part, but the search for security mentioned above was more critical. People needed children as an insurance for old age. Over the same period, the Egyptian rural population expanded from about 3 million to about 15 million people,[44] and that of Java on the same order. This was exceptional, but in most parts of the rural world population rose by more than 50 percent over the century and a quarter. With little possibility of growth in the area of cultivation, plot sizes fell, and farmers had to work harder and more ingeniously to satisfy the demands of the state and elites as well as to provide for their own subsistence. The less developed parts of Europe saw similar problems. In Austria-Hungary, population growth was very fast before 1848, and in Hungary this persisted into the later nineteenth century, causing "severe pressure on the land"[45] and explaining, in part, the social and political tensions between the two kingdoms.

Periodic calamities, such as the famines in Ireland in the 1840s, in India in the 1830s, 1870s, and 1890s, and in China and Africa in the 1880s, or the ravages of cholera and plague in the latter part of the century, held back even faster growth. Many economic historians argue that the very fact that these rural hinterlands were now tied into the world economy by railways and steamships put them at a disadvantage in periods of scarcity.[46] Food could be shipped out more easily by grain-dealers to benefit from high prices. In the later nineteenth century, therefore, many of those still living on the land in Europe seemed barely to moved forward in the course of a century, despite emigration to the towns and abroad. Imperialism and the expansion of international trade had exposed those living outside Europe to the vagaries of external economic shocks and the yet more vigorous extraction of their economic surplus. These conditions combined with a long inheritance of local overpopulation and periodic starvation.

Another set of pressures which affected the world's peasantry derived, as implied in chapter 7, from strengthening of the state, whether this took the form of an indigenous or a colonial government. The "military revolution" of the seventeenth and eighteenth centuries had made it easier for the state and propertied people to police and extract wealth or labor from the countryside. For instance, the post-Ottoman and semi-colonial regimes in Egypt coerced huge amounts of compulsory peasant labor to construct irrigation systems and the Suez Canal during the nineteenth century.[47] In Japan, the Meiji regime actually increased the tax burden on the poorer sections of the rural population in its desperate push to modernize. Moreover, it was strong enough to collect these taxes. The deeper trenching of the state into peasant incomes was made much worse in the early part of the century by the widespread lack of silver currency which followed the closing of silver mines by the Spanish American revolutions. People in the Asian countryside were generally paid in copper cash or other local currencies for their produce. Yet they had to pay their taxes in silver. This meant that they needed to sell more and more produce in order to keep up their revenue and rent payments. Later in the century, deflation was replaced by inflation. This affected peasant-farmers who needed to buy items on the market.

Emerging regimes and social groups seem to have needed to deepen subordination to proclaim their honor. Capitalist economics was not the only force

ILLUSTRATION 11.2 Britain's surviving peasants: Ploughing with camels on the banks of the Nile, c.1902. Photo by Donald MacLeish.

at work. Here the experience of Tokugawa Japan is instructive, for this was a society little affected by the West until the 1850s, and one which still operated largely within an East Asian trading system. Herman Ooms has shown how the outcaste workers and peasants of Japanese society (the *kawata*) actually came to experience broader and more systematic forms of subordination and discrimination in the late eighteenth and early nineteenth centuries. These populations of leather-workers, killers for meat, and scavengers suffered from the bar of pollution, as did similar groups throughout East and South Asia. They had always lived in special, segregated hamlets away from other villagers, and had found marriage partners and companionship only within their own groups. Yet, as the Tokugawa system of government became more intrusive and regularized over this period, the *kawata* were subjected to more and more legal penalties which bound them to service of their masters among the prosperous owner-occupier peasants and put new restraints on their free movement. Evidently, labor needs were one of the considerations here. Yet, in his analysis, Ooms puts more stress on the role of the state in extending subordination. Officials of the Tokugawa regime and Japan's "feudal" domains desired to categorize, exclude, and degrade these groups almost as a principle of pure power. The language of caste, ritual purity, and pollution was here broadened out to something more akin to the racism of Europe or the Americas. When in the 1870s, the new Meiji modernizing elites took power in Japan and abolished many of the old privileges and perquisites of the aristocracy and samurai warrior caste, the *kawata* were freed from formal legal restraints. Yet they remained despised and discriminated against, "much like American blacks"[48] after their own emancipation in the 1860s. Ooms's argument echoes that of Genovese for the persistence of slavery and dependency in the American South.

Examples of the re-creation and strengthening of social hierarchies like this can be multiplied across East and Southeast Asia, where communities of leather-workers, charcoal-burners, scavengers, and the like were treated similarly. Southern and eastern Europe had their gypsies. As we will see, native peoples in the white dominions of the British Empire and the United States came to suffer similar disabilities, ravaged in addition by alcoholism and disease. The most striking comparison, however, can be made with the low castes of India, the so-called untouchables and those of very low peasant status. Here again the rise of the state and the ethos of the elites in the immediate precolonial and early colonial periods seems to explain the expansion of the phenomenon of ritual subordination better than any purely economic imperative. In eighteenth-century India, the skills of tracking, gold panning, leather working, and similar professions seem to have conferred some advantage on low castes and outcastes in the mobile world of entrepreneurship and warfare. The Indian historian David Washbrook wrote of the eighteenth century as the "Golden Age of the Pariah," the South Indian version of the "untouchable." Even at this period, however, we see some of the new aspiring rulers of the era, keen to assert their high ritual status within Hinduism, passing ordinances which restricted the movements of the low castes. They imposed different and harsher legal penalties on them, or even excluded them from temples and religious rites.[49]

Far from being age-old, many facets of India's caste system are of relatively recent origin.[50] British colonial rule often further deepened these tendencies. British administrators tended to adopt the high-caste and Brahmin definition of custom, because they were advised by high-caste subordinates. The classical texts they used in their judgments often prescribed penalties for the low castes which were not previously put into operation. New landed and clerical groups emerging in Indian society in the nineteenth century, stripped by colonial dominion of real power or the ability to show prowess through martial valor, maintained their ritual superiority and, by the same token, the subordination of others. As landlords, they needed to discipline labor, and the rhetoric of degradation proved useful here, too. Washbrook writes of a pervasive "traditionalization" of Indian society in the first half of the nineteenth century.[51] By this he means that, far from breaking down old, irrational status relations, colonial government helped to re-create them.

THE PEASANTS THAT GOT AWAY

There were, however, important exceptions to the rule of the perpetuation of rural poverty and dependence through the course of the nineteenth century. As chapter 4 argued, without the emergence of rich peasant elites in some areas, or the transformation of peasants into farmers, it is difficult to see how the nineteenth-century world could have achieved even the fragile stability it did achieve between the waves of war and rebellion. For instance, improvements in communications and techniques of cultivation did work to offset these burdens and make it possible for some bodies of peasants across the world to improve their economic position over the period. Better irrigation and well-technology and the spread of iron ploughs improved levels of productivity. Those who did best were specialist agrarian producers living near big, industrializing cities. Even as early as the sixteenth century, many features of classic peasant life had disappeared from England and Holland with the growth of a huge market in London, Amsterdam, and other cities. After the French Revolution, peasants in France and northern Italy released themselves from seigneurial dues, consolidated holdings, and began to produce for big consumer cities. Even in Italy, where 58 percent of the population still subsisted on agriculture in 1911, high productivity and a good mix of crops allowed the Po valley peasantry to prosper by exporting to the new Italian cities and to central Europe.[52] Cotton, the great symbol of the century, was a very volatile crop, but the peasant-entrepreneurs of western India and the more substantial peasantry of lower Egypt improved their status at the expense of their poorer neighbors in the latter part of the century.

Legislative intervention did improve conditions in some parts of the world, even though it failed to live up to the aims of the liberal reformers. Farmers in northern Europe, Ireland, and the British dominions achieved greater security of tenure in the course of the nineteenth century. Colonial governments in French North Africa and Indochina and in British Asia and southern Africa made limited moves to recognize tenant rights in the aftermath of sporadic rural revolts. In general, however, these regimes were too reliant on the power of landholders to contemplate radical land reform. Agrarian society in Russia stood, as usual, somewhere between the Asian and European models. At the end of the eighteenth century, Russia's serfs were subject to innumerable local legal codes and seigneurial and state demands. Government hardly penetrated into the locality, and local bodies decided all important issues. As with the Celestial Emperor or the Sublime Porte, so the Tsar of all the Russias functioned not as a supreme administrator but as a symbolic court of final appeal and guarantor of impartial justice. The level of urbanization, about 9 percent, was reminiscent of the great Asian societies and did not even match the levels of southern Europe. The 90 percent of the population who paid the head tax were a lower caste, subject to corvée labor and military service. Divided between clergy, Slav, non-Slav, and guest community, social ordering was similar to the millet system of the Ottoman Empire. The so-called reforms of the eighteenth-century enlightened despots had served largely to regularize and reinforce subordination and the obligations of different groups, as had the contemporary Japanese reforms.

On the other hand, Russia also had a small cosmopolitan bureaucracy, looking with interest at developments in the German states and galvanized into action, first by the Napoleonic and then the Crimean wars. The abolition of serfdom, however, was postponed until 1861, and even then not accompanied with any serious expansion of individual rights.[53] Echoing the thoughts of many a British or French colonial administrator or American slave-owner, a Russian bureaucrat rejected reform on the grounds that the peasants' "capacity to reason is in a child-like state." Change would risk rebellion, undermine the state's fiscal resources, and threaten the rights of the landholders who helped stabilize society. When the emancipation of the serfs did finally come, it was pushed through by a vigorous central elite against the wishes of numbers of bureaucrats. While some of the measure's proponents wished to modernize society, others wished simply to strengthen the basis of the tsarist autocracy by managing social change. With a new European order rapidly forming, it was vital for conservatives to make significant concessions in order to hold off more radical reforms.

However, despite Russia's slow modernization and the growth of a few pockets of modern industry, large parts of the old society of orders and particularistic estates survived until it was brutally uprooted by the revolution and Stalin's terror. Agrarian conflicts continued to smoulder beneath the surface of Russian society. After emancipation, peasants remained determined to destroy what remained of aristocratic privilege and also resisted attempts by their more successful members to split off from the community as a kind of prosperous yeoman class. By 1914, peasants owned most of the land. The introverted and suspicious world of the peasant commune (the *mir*) was set against the callous regimes of the remaining big noble estates, many of which became economically less viable in the later nineteenth century. In some regions, strikes, peasant desertions, and arson were endemic. These conflicts blazed out of control in 1905, when the state was weakened by military defeat.

At the broader level, therefore, the end of the nineteenth century widely saw governments seeking to stabilize land-owning peasantries in the interest of both political order and food production. The Russian chief minister, Stolypin, trying to stabilize landed society in European Russia and the Ukraine, had very much the same idea as late Ottoman governors in Iraq, Syria, and the Yemen. These men wanted to confer land rights on peasants and reduce their tax burden in order to boost agricultural production. Some colonial governments, in the Indian Punjab and the Mekong Delta, for instance, did the same. Liberal reformers in southern Italy, Sicily, Spain, and Mexico were simultaneously working to benefit peasant owners rather than the great estates. On this model, peasantries would not be eliminated, but they would be improved.

WHY RURAL SUBORDINATION SURVIVED

Let us now return to the question with which this section started: why did the conditions of peasant life remain roughly comparable in the course of the nineteenth century, despite large-scale economic changes and a pervasive rhetoric of hostility to rural privilege? A large part of the answer seems to lie in the fact that the existence of tributary peasantries was economically expedient and conducive to their status for the elites and governments of the new commercial and industrial economies. Peasants, in turn, were still in a weak position to resist these demands. Political coercion and the pressure of their own numbers forced peasants to market their crops. Yet poor, undereducated, and politically unsophisticated rural people were unable to extract much of a bargain in return for feeding the urban and industrializing areas. Peasants, even less than industrial workers, had generally failed to create long-term associations which might give them greater political clout, though Russian populist reformers and Bengali intelligentsia were beginning to work amongst them by the 1880s. Karl Marx, a shrewd observer of his times, whatever the demerits of his prophecy, noted memorably that the peasantry were like a "sack of potatoes." He meant that they had weight, but little capacity for cohesion, because they were generally concerned with obtaining property rights to their family farms and were not inclined to act on behalf of any subjective "class interest." Urban dwellers could afford to tolerate the relative inefficiencies of peasant farming because of the political benefits it conferred on them. Richer, more self-confident peasants on the road to becoming commercial farmers would bid up the cost to an industrializing society, as Joseph Stalin found to the detriment of the Soviet *kulaks*, the supposed peasant magnates, two decades into the following century.

This consideration again reminds us of some of the merits of global, as opposed to national or regional, histories. Forms of peasant labor in the outlying areas of Europe, Asia, and Africa should be regarded as central and not simply peripheral to the industrializing economies of the Atlantic world. The anthropologist and historian Alan Macfarlane argued persuasively that "English individualism" arose out of a decline of the English peasantry in the early Middle Ages.[54] If we look only at the lands within 200 or 300 miles of London, peasantry indeed disappeared from the story of English society and economy. Yet Britain at the point of "takeoff" of industrialization had the largest tributary peasantry in the world, in Highland Scotland, Ireland, India, and Africa. This was a peasantry that not only provided the agricultural raw materials for British industry and its international balance of trade, but also filled the ranks of its overseas armies. Domination of the world's peasantries did not create the Industrial Revolution, but it did help to underpin the social and political power of industrializing Britain and its wealthy dominions, Australia, Canada, New Zealand, and South Africa. Much the same is true of the Netherlands, whose population had made the transition from peasant to Dutchman as early as the fifteenth century, but benefited greatly from getting Javanese peasants to produce crops at a knock-down rate through the so-called Cultivation System after 1825. King Leopold of the Belgians took the hint and tried to set up something similar in the Congo in the 1880s and 1890s. Even the United States, home of the archetypal free, politically self-conscious, improving farmer had its own tributary peasant economies on a small scale. After the collapse of the slave system, it set up lucrative and unequal relations with the poor peasant economies of the Caribbean, Latin America, Polynesia, and the Philippines, though, except in the case of sugar and tropical fruit, these relationships were of little economic significance to the USA itself.

The global approach also helps to contextualize the still small, but increasingly important, industrial working class which was emerging out of the more mobile elements of the peasantry in many societies. As chapter 5 noted, neither in the more developed nor in the less developed economies were urban workers simply "peasants in disguise." Even casual workers soon developed their own politics and their own social organizations in the work place and in the city quarter. On the other hand, the relative poverty of the peasant and agricultural laborer meant that industrial managers could keep wages low. A factory job, however poorly paid, seemed attractive in comparison to the grind of agricultural labor and the misery and debt which followed bad seasons. Many industrial managers were able to rely on badly paid casual labor, because, in a recession, workers could always rely on some support from their rural kin or even go back to the countryside until conditions improved. Poverty and dependency in town and country tended to reinforce each other.

THE TRANSFORMATION OF "GENTRIES"

In addition to these economic and military reasons for the survival of the peasantry, we should consider the extraordinary capacity of the gentry and the landholding classes to remodel themselves. Gentleman-landlords throughout the world had the knack of retaining and reproducing their economic and political controls over country people (and often over urban people as well). In addition to their economic clout, they were able to continue to call up those sentiments of respect and subordination which recalled the social attitudes of a much earlier period. Looked at from the perspective of 1789, or the great peasant revolts in Russia and Asia, however, the persistence of gentry and nobility needs some explanation. The revolutionary rhetoric of those years, denouncing hereditary privilege, customary payments, and the arbitrariness of aristocracy, seemed to carry all before it. It is worth considering this, in order to appreciate how thoroughly rural hierarchies needed to be revamped.

These "gentry" classes varied greatly in their size and in the nature of the social power which they could mobilize in order to re-create their authority. Over much of the English-speaking world, landlord classes possessed the great advantage of the rule of primogeniture, by which the eldest son inherited the family property. This had the effect of maintaining, rather than fragmenting, the economic power of landed families. For instance, in Virginia and the Carolinas, old slaveholding families managed to hang on to prestige and power even after the abolition of slavery, because they could plough continuing profits from the land into emerging local industrial enterprises. By contrast, the Russian and Chinese gentry, or even the Cape Dutch landed families, had no such rule and often saw their landholdings fragmented generation by generation. Yet embodied status, complex systems of family alliance through property-holding women, or dominance of local political institutions allowed gentry classes of this sort to perpetuate themselves. When, as in the case of Hungary, the gentry continued to dominate a powerful regional assembly which dated back to the feudal order, it had a good chance of fighting off centralized state building and maintaining its political role.[55] Britain, where a gentry class with primogeniture dominated representation in an old assembly, had one of the most stable hierarchies of all. The gentry were able to absorb the shock of rapid economic change and ultimately to concede power to the middle and working classes while maintaining much of their wealth and prestige intact.[56]

CHALLENGES TO THE GENTRY

At the beginning of the period, however, the outlook for castes of landowners looked rather poor. During the French Revolution, ferocious vendettas were unleashed against proprietors great and small. In Britain during the 1790s, "the gentlemen were thoroughly frightened" by the specter of rural violence, though it was only really in Ireland in 1798 that a full-scale peasant revolt came about. Even so, there was enough agitation against mechanization by poor farmers and rural laborers to give rise to the myth of retribution from the fire-setter "Captain Swing" in the slump after the end of the Anglo-French wars. Again, nineteenth-century Russian and Polish novels denouncing the effete and corrupt aristocracy found numerous echoes outside Europe throughout the century. In Russia, where serfdom was given a new lease of life until 1861, there remained uneasy memories of the peasant revolts of the 1670s, 1700s, and 1770s, among landholders who contemplated even the mildest of constitutional movements. Anti-landlord rhetoric flared up even in the Americas. Their revolutionaries had warned incessantly that the continuation of British or Spanish control would bring into being a rich, corrupt aristocracy like that of the home countries. Where the control of the British Crown persisted, even in Canada, where land was plentiful, that same fear lay behind the revolts of the later 1830s both in the English- and French-speaking parts of the country. Though the 1848 revolutions in Europe started in the industrializing urban centers, landholders throughout central and eastern Europe feared that rural explosions would rock their power.

The great Asian and North African peasant groups seemed even more likely to explode and throw off the more obnoxious forms of landlordism. From the 1830s, British India was convulsed by a series of revolts, some of which mixed social discontents with millenarian Islamic themes, as did the Faraizi movement in Bengal, which concerted land leagues against proprietors and indigo estates from the 1840s to the 1870s. Others, like the movements in the North Indian plains during 1860s and 1890s, specifically vented the grievances of tenants against landlords, moneylenders, and the colonial state which supported them. Rural revolts were also common throughout the old Ottoman lands and northeastern Africa, especially on the "thirsty" fringes of the arable land, where impoverished cultivators were expected to pay both state land tax and dues to a variety of landlords and tribal overlords. In Morocco, the Rif region regularly erupted in anti-French and anti-landowner revolts after 1870, while Abyssinian peasants rose against their lords whenever crop failures depressed their incomes.[57]

ROUTES TO SURVIVAL: STATE SERVICE AND COMMERCE

The widespread persistence of gentry and landlord power in the context of periodic rural rebellions throughout the world therefore needs further elaboration.[58] This chapter has already suggested that peasant production was a convenient, socially gratifying system for urban elites. But how were they able to fight off the challenge of periodic rural rebellion? The answer seems to be that the people with rural properties were able to hedge their bets, investing in a variety of new forms of political power associated with the growing state as well as in small pockets of commercial agriculture. In many societies, they were also able to reinvent their legitimacy, claiming now to be the true bearers of national tradition in the modern world, rather than a survival of the old.

This section first examines the survival of one of the oldest and most distinctive gentry categories in the world, the Chinese "scholar-gentry," or *shen-shi*. The Chinese gentry was composed not of a small number of "men of broad acres," but of a large population, perhaps 2 million strong, holding lands and other agrarian rights collectively. Organized by clan around private temples, schools, and religious organizations, the gentry was a status group as much as a landholding class. Gentry clans trained their young men for imperial service. Once secure in official posts as magistrates or members of the Qing central administration, the gentrymen could then use their salaries to purchase new lands and rights, while at the same time reaching out for the support of the local gentry in the districts to which they were assigned. As the classic study of Ping-ti Ho established, by the early nineteenth century, gentry-people were adept at making money from China's sophisticated and expanding internal trade system, despite the disdain expressed in Confucian teaching for trade of all sorts.[59] They acted as local tradesmen and moneylenders to the peasantry. Increasingly, they benefited from the loosening grip of the central administration after the 1790s, pocketing in the form of fees and perquisites much of the surplus produced by a peasantry increasingly forced to subsist on smaller and smaller plots of land.

In turning themselves from a status group within the old imperial system to something like a class of rural magnates, the gentry laid up long-term problems for China. They failed to keep the all-important drainage and irrigation systems intact or made their own illegal dykes: an imperial gazetteer of Hunan noted in 1881 that "not one single dyke remains here, neither official, people's nor illegal."[60] Ecological problems of soil desiccation were added to those of overpopulation. Yet for nearly 200 years, the gentry managed not merely to cling on to their power, but to enhance it.

Not surprisingly, given growing social inequality and regional ecological decline after 1800, the gentry found themselves targets of Buddhist millenarian and sectarian movements of protest. In the great Chinese tradition of righteous resistance associated with the so-called water margin, good or "social" bandits were expected to fight for the people against "evil gentry" and "local bullies." So it was that in the 1850s and 1860s the first phase of the Taiping Rebellion against the Qing government seemed to make gentry-people its target. There were resounding cries to seize and redistribute gentry land through a sacred treasury. Yet the rebellion was not an uncomplicated peasant movement against an agrarian hierarchy. Many of its leaders were dissident gentrymen influenced by an amalgam of millenarian Buddhism, Daoism, and Christianity, which they learned from the coastal mission stations. There was also a strong element of inter-ethnic conflict, with incoming northerners of the Hakka group at odds with locals. Proletarian elements, laid-off tea porters, river pirates, and stragglers from the armies, defeated by the British in the opium wars, also played their part.

Growing anarchy brought about a reaction, and it was the gentry who took the initiative at the local level. The Taiping movement itself became more conservative in its later stages, hoping to draw the gentry to its side. More and more gentry began to rally to the side of the imperial forces; or, rather, gentry-people used imperial power and their leadership of the old system of local militias as a mask behind which to reassert their own interest. They rebuilt the local defense forces (the *baojia*) and protected people against bandits and stragglers. During the later Nien Rebellion of the 1870s, gentrymen organized resistance to the bands of rebel raiders. Not only did they benefit from the peasants' need for protection, they also cashed in on residual loyalty to imperial institutions and a sense that order and harmony had to be restored. Gentry clans who had lost numerous members through warfare and insurgency surreptitiously introduced non-elite marriage partners into their clans. They helped restart agricultural operations in devastated areas by making loans to peasant headmen. They took over and used lucrative new taxes on internal trade imposed by the government to pay for its military effort. They staffed the offices and armies of the Chinese provincial governors who now really ran the country for the distant court in Beijing. Finally, they proved adaptable in adjusting to the new opportunities for internal and export trades which came with the steamship and the telegraph.

Yet this was not merely a matter of economic survival. The ethos of the gentry and of obeisance to them persisted, deeply ingrained within Chinese domestic life and socialization. A former gentryman remembered the old extended family home in the 1900s:

> In the prayer room against the wall, facing the entrance, stood a big black altar. It was the *shen tang*. Its fancy wood-carving was inlaid with bone. On the black wood of its upper half there was a column of five golden hieroglyphics. They represented 'The Sky', 'The Earth', 'The Emperor', 'The Ancestor', 'The Teacher'. This column rested on a sixth hieroglyphic which read 'The Altar.' On both sides of this main column which we call *tung-li*, hung two small strips of cypress wood. . . . The names of the ancestors of the three nearest generations were traced on these strips.[61]

While the later nineteenth century was once associated with the "fall of the Chinese empire," more circumspect historians now write, therefore, of the emergence of new elites from among the ranks of the old scholar-gentry class.[62] What is striking is how this revivified gentry class was able to present itself as guardians of the dynasty and even the emerging Chinese nation against divisive internal forces and the depredations of foreign barbarians. This theme of the persistence of the gentry helps to explain the extreme vehemence of the Communist campaign against them in the 1940s.

The nearest equivalent to a gentry in Japan was the samurai "caste."[63] In the ancien régime, they had differed from the Chinese gentry in several important respects. Their ethos was that of a warrior rather than a learned status group. They operated a system something like European primogeniture, in which the eldest son inherited the family property. Before 1868, the samurai were split up among the domain lords, the so-called feudal barons of the Tokugawa period. In the nineteenth century, they encountered vigorous but different challenges to their position. In 1868, samurai from the outer, coastal domains, which were challenged most directly by Western incursions, took the lead in rallying to the regime, rather as the Chinese gentry did in the Taiping era. However, the new centralized state that emerged from the Meiji

ILLUSTRATION 11.3   The last mandarin: A graduate of the Chinese examination system, about the time of its abolition, Wei Hai Wei, 1909. Photo by A. H. Fisher.

"restoration" took away the "feudal" privileges of the samurai and commuted them to stipends and later to government bonds. This was more drastic than anything that happened to European landed aristocrats during their own revolutions. Many samurai families successfully negotiated this sharp transition. They staffed the new imperial bureaucracies, the growing army and navy. Some of them cleverly invested their stipends and bonds in new, prospering enterprises, emerging alongside members of merchant firms (*zaibatsu*) as leaders of businesses. Even if the basis of their power in the social hierarchy had been transformed, the principles of deference still remained strong, and peasants and merchant-class people still looked up to the samurai. This was not least because they successfully captured and embodied the sense of national pride which permeated the politics of the Meiji era.

In both China and Japan, substantial elements within the old "gentries" managed to perpetuate themselves through the turmoil of the later nineteenth century. Across the colonial world, however, the trend was even clearer. Colonial governments usually discovered that they needed what they called "leaders of the people" to maintain their local control and bring in the revenue. Wherever they were reasonably adaptable, the old aristocracies managed to switch from military activities and rent receiving into trades in the export staples with which the colonial powers financed their rule. In the East Indies after 1830, younger and poorer aristocratic lineages, the *priyayi*, supplemented their rural control with local political offices in a Dutch version of indirect rule.[64] Berber chieftains, specially selected by the French, exported food products to France from Algeria. Village *sheikhs*, or small landowners, in Egypt financed the raw cotton trade to northern Europe, but also clung to their older status as servants of the state and pious Muslims, by military service and enrollment in the great urban mosques. In the Yoruba areas of West Africa and in Dahomey, old warrior aristocracies which had played a signal part in the slave trade went into the production of agricultural produce for northern Europe after 1830. They fought off the challenge from peasant-proprietors by investing in large palm oil estates, which they manned with slave labor.[65]

One general development which could be skillfully used, or abused, by the rural propertied people to maintain their power was the introduction of simpler and more saleable land rights.[66] Colonial officials found the complex, overlapping tenurial systems of the old regimes irritating and diffuse. They longed for the simplicity of Roman law or English common law. Very widely, therefore, they vested landlords with powers to coerce those beneath them and buy and sell unified land rights on the land market which had not existed in that form before colonial rule. For instance, India's landholders, *zamindars*, did well at the expense of both the state and their own tenants throughout the course of the nineteenth century. Judging that they had alienated too many landlords before 1857, the Indian Mutiny-Rebellion made the British yet more cautious and conservative.[67] They decided that India was a feudal society and invested their favorites with the trappings of Scots barons and English squires. Courts of Wards were established to manage the estates of those earlier described as "parasites on the land," while they were turned into English gentlemen in chiefs' schools.

MEN OF FEWER "BROAD ACRES" IN EUROPE

Some of these considerations operated in Europe too, so that in 1914 many old families who had not frittered away their fortunes in casinos or bordellos retained their influence. In some cases, though, the casinos and houses of ill repute actually helped them to survive. The Italian landowners had lost land and status to wealthy bourgeois during the Napoleonic period. But intermarriage and a subtle osmosis of status from aristocracy to wealthy middle class created an *amalgame*, an amalgated ruling class that survived through to the Fascist era of the twentieth century across much of the country.[68] The "springtime of peoples" of 1848–50 administered another shock to the landed elites, but many found ways to survive. The princes of Monaco lost their feudal right to tax orange and lemon trees in Provence after the 1848 revolution. Undeterred, they brought in a German gambling expert to set up a casino for them. Rail connections with France and investment by Napoleon III, the "Bonaparte of industry," helped to restore their fortunes. As the wealthy and famous came to holiday in Monaco in greater numbers at the end of the century, the princes became richer and richer. The Prussian landowners made the same leap from landlordism to capitalism and bureaucracy on a larger scale. They provided officers for the new model army created by the German Empire and then lent to the new imperial state. At the same time, they were helped by economies of scale to produce foodstuffs in massive volumes for the industrial cities of the Rhineland and the Ruhr. In western Europe, great landowners became the core of the new plutocracy if they had urban property or coal mines, or went into industry.

In Russia, a few well-connected landed families of the eighteenth century had got a grip on the new public offices created by the reforms of Peter the Great and Catherine the Great. They retained their prominence throughout the nineteenth century, even while many fellow aristocrats fell into the cycle of debt and decline so lugubriously described by so many of Russia's great nineteenth-century novelists. Russian historians have debated whether rural Russia in the late nineteenth century was bound to descend into a new period of peasant wars, or whether agrarian capitalism was giving a new stability to some parts of the countryside. The jury on this is still out. What is clearer, though, is that, even in Russia, agrarian change was speeding up, and that some landed families were finding new prosperity and career avenues. Whether in Italy, Russia, or Prussia, the embodied schemes of gentlemanliness characteristic of the old order were now being transmuted into the professions of the nation-state. Members of the old gentries were all becoming "samurai" in the service of the new state. By the same token, men from the middling and merchant orders were emulating their style. For example, German naval captains, drawn from the new wealth of the Rhine and the Ruhr, began to sport dueling scars in imitation of those acquired by the old landed junker class of East Prussia. The junkers themselves, meanwhile, were going into agro-business. The growing spending power of the social elites allowed them to accumulate large establishments of personal and domestic servants from the city and country working classes. At the same time, it is worth noting that gentry were able to perpetuate their power, in part at least, because some of them were able to stand aside from their direct sectional interests and promote wider schemes for improvement. Members of the English and German gentry, in particular, were in the forefront of movements to improve the health and status of rural and urban laborers.[69]

In Britain in 1900, less than 1 percent of the population owned 80 percent of the land. The influence of the great territorial aristocrats had largely survived industrialization and the widening of the adult male franchise. The politics of deference and class still worked in their interests. The more hard-nosed among them invested in or inherited estates in the new urban centers, held large portfolios in the City of London,[70] and benefited handsomely from bishoprics, governorships, and colonelcies in the empire.[71] Until 1911, the territorial aristocracy held the emerging British democracy in a tight headlock through the mechanisms of the House of Lords. Even in France, this more discreet breed of gentlemanly capitalists emerged from beneath the shadow of the guillotine, tending its estates in the Loire or Brittany. New wealth, particularly Jewish wealth, assimilated to the style of the European aristocracy with ease, populating the hunting fields, the spas, and the hotels or casinos of the Côte d'Azur. As David Cannadine has recently insisted, the British also exported their notions of class dominance to the empire, securing for themselves a lavish life-style of servants, balls, and hunts which very few of them could have maintained at home.[72] Once again, the inheritance of empire rushed in to confirm the relative social stasis at home. The East and the West met, not only in manly friendships, but also in gaudy and conspicuous display. Perhaps it was only in Ireland that the gentry faced economic and social pressures comparable with their peers in eastern Europe or Russia. And like their equivalents there, they too became imperial soldiers and administrators, or fell into a Chekhovian indolence.

Across the world, then, many aristocracies and gentries were able to perpetuate or reconstruct their power. Partly this was because they were the traditional warriors and adapted quickly to the new ways of deploying force. Even where they were not, as in the case of China, gentries remained important in putting down peasant rebellion and staving off external invasion. Many gentries also invested their money well, selling their lands to railway companies and putting it in colonial railway or mining schemes, for instance. As supposed embodiments of chivalry, they also reinvested their inheritance of status, becoming among the most passionate proponents of the new nationalism and imperialism. Even where gentry-people faced economic decline and social conflict, as in Russia and in other parts of eastern Europe after the 1880s, they could not be written off. The devastation caused by the First World War cannot be seen as a straightforward consequence of the agrarian conflicts of the late nineteenth century.

SURVIVING SUPREMACIES

The final section considers the survival of monarchy itself. This, again, needs some explanation. At the beginning of the period, a revolutionary wave was sweeping Europe and the Americas, while expatriate European, Asian, and African intellectuals denounced the corrupt and impious sovereigns of these regions throughout the century. The survival of monarchy not only implied the maintenance of centralized royal courts, it also helped to shore up a whole host of special jurisdictions, corporations, and privileges which drew their legitimacy from kings. To some extent, these survivals put a break on the process of growing social and political uniformity which was a feature of nineteenth-century globalization. Yet, in a more subtle way, monarchs, courts, and royal corporations also played a functional role in nineteenth-century society, and thus aided the very processes they seemed on the surface to impede. Monarchies and courts are also interesting in their own right. A new generation of social historians, less concerned with grand, teleological narratives, has begun to examine royal courts as a type of social drama, revealing much about the societies they supposedly epitomized.

A convention of historical literature through into the 1980s was to regard nineteenth-century monarchies as survivals of the ancien régime, gaudy extravaganzas, bound to fail. At the extreme end of the spectrum, the Ottoman and Qing monarchies were placed in the terminal ward of history, viewed as patients on the point of succumbing to the virulent plague of emerging Arab, Turkish, or Han Chinese nationalism. Even semi-constitutional monarchies, such as the Austro-Hungarian or the German imperial systems, were seen as slightly ridiculous hangovers, tripping along to the music of Johann Strauss and Richard Strauss, respectively. Historians viewed the German imperial monarchy with particular disfavor, not only because of its complex relations with the provincial *Länder*, but because of Kaiser William II. William was seen as a near-pathological figure. His supposed blend of arrogance and weakness combined with a nasty, and supposedly peculiarly German, habit of giving political power to mentally unstable despots. Such historians often found license for this in the writing of contemporaries. The Russian reformer Sergei Witte wrote of his conservative enemy Trepov, who had resigned his position as governor-general of St Petersburg: "It was quickly evident that, far from having lost power by giving up all his provincial posts for the comparatively lowly one of palace commandant, he had become even more powerful, answerable to no-one, an Asiatic eunuch at a European court."[73]

Since 1980, however, that has begun to change. Historians have become interested in the perpetuation of charismatic royal power and in the role of the nineteenth-century courts as scenes of complex ritual. Cultural historians have examined them as sites of cross-dressing, homosexuality, or the playpens of powerful women, such as the Empress Dowager or Queen Victoria. Historians' recent rejection of the progressive teleologies of nationalism and socialism has also implied that it was only the experience of defeat in war which brought down these imperial edifices, which otherwise seemed to demonstrate considerable resilience.

What should be stressed is that these monarchical systems, with their ill-assorted mishmash of charismatic authority and populism, of ritual and base privilege, of intrigue and leadership, were valuable to nineteenth-century polities in many ways. In other words, they were useful to the political forces trying to mediate an increasingly complex society. The cases of Louis Napoleon and Kaiser William II illustrate this well. Louis Napoleon, earlier regarded as a mountebank figure and even as a precursor of the democratic authoritarianism of twentieth-century Fascist leaders, was actually an extremely successful political actor who could play many parts. Through family and the symbols of empire, Napoleon III could hark back to the tradition of the First Empire and stand as the leader of the army, now increasingly involved in imperial expansion. As Louis Napoleon, victor of elections in 1848 and a plebiscite in 1851, he could claim to embody the popular republican tradition. As an anointed monarch, he could calm the fears of the conservatives, promote France's Catholic mission in Mount Lebanon and Indochina, and calm the fears of the Church and the Catholic nobility, which had survived the revolution. As new man, he could promote industrial and commercial development.[74] His only mistake was to go to war with the Prussian army.

The Austro-Hungarian monarchy seems actually to have strengthened after its defeat by Prussia in 1866. The Austrians had to concede virtually equal status to the Hungarians, and the two ruling groups were able to play off against each other leftists and the smaller nationalities in the empire. Emperor Franz Joseph managed to keep his two-horse barouche trotting along even after 1900, as nationalist pressures grew stronger throughout Europe. Again, it was war which finished off the dynasty.[75]

For his part, Kaiser William II was able to act as a central point of stability for different interests. By astute manipulation of the press and acquiescence in the views of elected politicians, he could serve the interests of the new middle classes of Germany's industrial cities. As commander of the forces and descendant of Frederick the Great, he was the symbolic leader of the junkers of east Germany and their brothers and sons in the imperial army. As emperor of Germany, he could pacify the interests of the states and regions, both Catholic and Protestant, which had seemed locked in battle at the time of Bismarck. Arguably, the kaiser not only dropped the pilot, but found a better chart. Again, only defeat in war spelled his doom. If anything, the imperial house was more popular and politically effective in 1913 than it had been in the 1880s.[76]

The survival and refurbishment of the Japanese monarchy might, on the face of it, seem to represent some deep atavistic and religious feeling among its subjects. To what extent this was true is difficult to know. Certainly, though, the Meiji statesmen also saw the throne as a supremely *useful* institution. The leading statesman, Ito Hirobumi, addressed the Privy Council in July 1888 about why the monarchy retained so many powers in the revised constitution. It was, he said, because neither democracy nor religion could provide the "axis of the state" in Japan as they did in various European countries. Democracy was too new to Japan, and the Shinto religion too inchoate, to serve this function. He went on: "In Japan it is only the imperial house that can become the axis of the state. It is with this point in mind that we have placed so high a value on imperial authority and endeavored to restrict it as little as possible in this draft constitution."[77]

This cannot really be said of either the Russian or the Chinese monarchies. These regimes faced crippling problems of legitimacy and political control. Even in these cases, though, many historians would agree that the monarchies retained considerable reserves of support right up to their last days. They continued to appeal to gentry and peasant, and acted as a final arbitrator between different contending nationalities in their huge realms. While it seems clear that neither the Qing nor the Romanovs would have survived much beyond 1905 as autocratic rulers, their complete disappearance from the scene could not really have been predicted.[78]

The real parallel with late-imperial Germany was not imperial Russia, where autocracy, though still powerful, clearly displayed signs of brittleness after the revolution of 1905. It was Britain. In Britain, as is well known, the royal ritual of coronations, parades, and state openings of Parliament became more elaborate and more beautifully choreographed as the century wore on. Queen Victoria emerged from the unpopularity that plagued her after the death of Prince Albert to become the Great White Queen. The queen was the pinnacle of a class and status system. She also appealed to a conservative and imperialist working class. Meanwhile, she was friend of Indian princes, confidante of a be-kilted Scottish footman and turbanned Indian orderlies, and putative mother of Maori and Canadian chiefs. As Supreme Head of the Anglican Church and Empress of India, she could act as a point of reference and a channel of political influence for a range of assorted bailiwicks, corporate bodies, and arcane aristocracies, which would have put the Qian Long emperor to shame. At the same time, Victoria could represent a discreet modernity. She represented the triumphs and tragedies of the English Christian family. She promoted industry at the time of the Great Exhibition of 1851. The queen was among the first to use a double-needle telegraph to communicate with her distant subjects, though the machine was modestly cased in a classically pillared antique wooden box.[79]

ILLUSTRATION 11.4 High noon of empire: The king-emperor and queen-empress in the Red Fort, Delhi, 1911.

Considerations like this seem even more pertinent if we examine the great states of the Middle East and Asia. The monarchy which consistently received the worst press was the late Ottoman dynasty. The last powerful sultan, Abdul Hamid II, was once portrayed as a hennaed degenerate, presiding over the ludicrous ritual of court and harem in the gaudy, overblown new palaces on the Bosphorus. Yet the Ottoman Empire survived until 1922, partly because of the sultanate, not despite it. The sultans were also khalifas, viceroys of the Prophet on earth. Far from waning as the nineteenth century wore on, Muslims felt embattled by the Christian powers, and across the world many of them turned to the spiritual unity of the Khilafat. Distant Chinese Muslims listened to the words of Istanbul during the crisis of the Boxer Rebellion. Even in Egypt, where political leaders sometimes voiced a desire for the return of the Khilafat from Ottoman to Arab hands, the sultanate served as a useful court of appeal against the arbitrariness of the occupying British power.

As anti-Turkish and anti-Islamic rhetoric became more intense among the Western powers, the sultanate was able to draw on the themes of Islamic holy war to counteract it. In 1914, the sultan declared *jihad* against Britain, France, and Russia. At the same time, the sultanate had never been rigorously Islamic. It mediated between Sufi mystics and Islamic teachers; between Sunni, Druze, and Shia. If the end of the empire saw ferocious massacres of Balkan and Armenian Christians, it was not primarily because they were Christians, but because they were seen as rebels and dissidents against the regime itself. For these reasons, some historians, Jewish, Turkish, and even Arab, see the late Ottoman Empire as a Golden Age, a "long peace" before the horrors of twentieth-century ethnic conflict in the Middle East. Different religious confessions, tribal coalitions, and language groups jostled together with each other, but did not fight. In general, the sultan's officers were able to adjust the peaceful play of interests. Only Western attack, culminating in the First World War, brought to an end this Ottoman summer. While this view may rather underplay the emergence of indigenous regional and patriotic identities,[80] it does highlight the fact that the imperial system and its local governors could play a constructive, and not merely a coercive, role in mediating local conflicts until well after its supposed historical "sell-by date."

CONTINUITY OR CHANGE?

Historians think that they are at their best when challenging orthodoxy. Because the historians of the mid-twentieth century so firmly stressed the transforming role of industry, empire, science, and the rise of labor, those writing since about 1970 have vigorously dissented. They have insisted on the persistence of the old order internationally. This chapter has been written as an attempt to begin to bring these two positions into dialogue with one another, since both can be supported by powerful, but different, historical evidence. It is still possible to hold that industry, the expansion of European empires, the diffusion and co-option of new ideas wrought epochal changes in

ILLUSTRATION 11.5   Before the deluge: Tsar Nicholas II and Tsarina Alexandra, 1913.

international life between 1780 and 1914. As the final chapter will show, there is a particularly good case to be made that the speed of social change and industrialization quickened significantly after about 1890 across the world. Yet it is the case that many older forms and representations of power and sovereignty were peculiarly resilient in the face of change. This was because they continued to perform useful social, political, and emotional functions in the midst of the changes brought about by industrialization, imperial expansion, and the rise of the state. The old supremacies bent in the face of these changes and reconstituted themselves in relation to it. Paradoxically, therefore, these continuities were empowered by change itself.

[12] *The Destruction of Native Peoples and Ecological Depredation*

PREVIOUS chapters have shown how, between 1780 and 1914, governments across the world became more like each other. They created sharp territorial boundaries and defined their subjects against foreigners. They worked to build streamlined patterns of government which bypassed many older forms of power and privilege. They created centralized armies and efficient tax systems. This growing political uniformity across the globe was matched, rather later, by a growing economic uniformity built around the demands of industrial capital. Despite enormous differences in wealth within and between countries, a much higher proportion of the world's population had been incorporated into the international capitalist economy by the end of the century. As peasants, these vast populations produced cash crops for export. As industrial workers, they kept the factories manned. As commercial and professional people, they traded, educated, or litigated within the context of this new world.

The patchy convergence of the state and the economy towards a norm also tended to produce a greater similarity in society and life-styles across the world. This present chapter, however, examines the fate of a variety of human communities which were pushed to the margins, and sometimes completely destroyed by such changes. The previous chapter suggested that some apparently old forms of social organization and life-style not only survived, but were actively promoted by the forces of modernity. That was much less the case for what this chapter calls "native peoples." These were often judged to stand in the way of progress, and their survival was widely in doubt as late as 1890.

WHAT IS MEANT BY "NATIVE PEOPLES"?

Native peoples, as defined here, include groups without a well-defined state structure, pastoralists, nomads, forest-dwellers, and fisher-peoples, those who were often gathered together in early anthropological works as "primitive tribes." The definition of these groups cannot be very precise, since there was still much intermarriage and cultural interchange between them and the more settled peoples and the subjects of states. For example, in Southeast Asia, some of the so-called tribal peoples, such as the Karen, Kachin, and Shan, settled among the ethnic Burmese peasantry and became peasants, indistinguishable from them except in matters of dress and social custom. Other tribal people became more completely "Burmese" through a process of marriage, induction into orthodox patterns of Theravada Buddhism, and the Burmese language. Yet others remained distinct as hill-dwellers and reinforced this distinction by an early conversion to Christianity during the 1820s and 1830s. Africa also provides many similar examples of shifting cultural boundaries. In West Africa, the relationship between the Fulani nomadic people and the Hausa town-dwellers was complex and many-sided. Urbanized Fulani provided dynasts and Islamic teachers for the settled population as well as a substantial part of the urban poor. There were also more isolated social groups, such as the peoples of Melanesia and the deep Amazon, who had had little contact with outsiders over hundreds of years, and for whom "first contact" with whites or other settlers in the nineteenth century represented an extraordinary cultural trauma.

Not all such societies were subordinated and ravaged by firearms, alcohol, and disease in the course of the nineteenth century. The Tasmanians and many east coast Australian Aborigines were either hunted down or driven away. But there are examples of Hawaiian and Maori chieftains who preserved something of their independence and separate culture by adapting their entrepreneurial skills to Western demand. Sometimes they provided labor service as guards. Sometimes they became workers, making trophies and curios which appealed to the acquisitive Western desire for exotic objects. What can be said is that small cultural groups which were not centrally involved in intensive peasant commodity production came under unprecedented political, cultural, and demographic pressure where previously they had been able to bargain with residents of the settled domains or early representatives of European and American power. The "cultural terms of trade" moved decisively in favor not only of white societies of European origin, but more generally of all settled societies producing a permanent agricultural surplus or industrial artefacts.

The total numbers of such peoples were relatively small in 1780, probably not more than 4–8 percent of the world's population. But the beginning of the end of the ancient variety of mankind's culture and life-styles is a development of symbolic importance, especially as it was so often accompanied by massive ecological changes: the felling of forests, the exhaustive fishing of rivers and oceans, and the ploughing up of prairies. It was only in the second half of the twentieth century that the full moral and environmental implications of these changes became evident. Nation-states now apologize for their treatment of "native peoples" and seek to repair the ecological damage of 200 years of ravaging and destruction. Whereas violent climatic change was once blamed on divine anger, it is now put down to the human race's destruction of its

environment and its extirpation of peoples who, in the more optimistic interpretations, interacted with nature on nearly equal terms.

Two prime causes of the "near-death of the native" in many locations
across the world were the impact of European imperialism and the headlong
expansion of European forms of government across America, Australasia, the
Pacific, and eventually Africa. A related cause was the continuing "internal
colonialism" of indigenous polities, now strengthened by the adoption of
Western weapons and forms of communication. It was, for instance, the
Muslim viceroys of Egypt who, from the 1820s, pushed their power into
southern Sudan, bending the local Nilotic African peoples to their will.
They deployed European-style armies, but the desire for domestic slave
labor and Islamic versions of the discourse of barbarism and civility created
some continuities with the great premodern Muslim empires.

The imposition of European-derived definitions of absolute property rights
drove staked fences across formerly limitless hunting grounds and herding
lands. The imposition of scientific forestry created patterns of uniformity
where there had previously been variety in the relations between man and
the forest. Yet imperialism and colonization were only one, often violent
dimension of much more general developments which saw the nation-state
and the capitalist economy conquering and transforming its own internal
frontiers. Here, as much weight must often be put on the growth of population
and improvements in communications than on any deliberate policy of standardization, extirpation, or assimilation. Across most of Europe, for instance,
this was the period when many hill-farming, fishing, and herding communities
were settled, tempted away to labor in cities, and disrupted by the agents of
the state, the national church, or the modern education system. The progress
of uniformity challenged the Lapps and the Gaelic fishing communities of
northern Scotland and western Ireland, as much as it did the Cree Indians of
Canada or the Maori of New Zealand. It saw the extirpation of the Cornish
language, severe damage inflicted on the Gaelic, Irish, and Welsh languages,
and the near-assimilation of the Occitan language of southern France. This
took place within the same span of years as the destruction of the Cham
Muslim culture in what was to become French Indochina and the decimation
of the Native Americans of the east coast of the United States.

EUROPEANS AND NATIVE PEOPLES BEFORE C.1820

In the nineteenth century the opening and settlement of new lands became
gradually more aggressive and destructive for their original inhabitants. This is
not to say that there were no examples of aggressive settlement before that
date. Significantly, the English, the leading colonizers of the nineteenth century, had a long history of what we would now call "ethnic cleansing" of
nomadic, pastoral, and forest peoples in their earlier patterns of colonization.
English settlers in Wales and Ireland had often appeared intolerant of the

continuing presence of the original population, and attempts were still being made in the nineteenth century to force Gaelic place-names and naming patterns into the Anglo-Saxon mold. On most Caribbean islands, seventeenth-century settlers had driven away or killed the indigenous population of Carib, Arawak, and Taino peoples, though some survived on Dominica and St Lucia, and mixed or maroon populations remained significant.[1] In the New England colonies in the seventeenth and eighteenth centuries, there had also been many examples of virtual ethnic wars when colonists attempted to annihilate or expel members of the Amerindian nations with which they came into contact. The African slave trade, of course, showed these instincts turned to more mercenary purposes. The English notion of private property, its intensive methods of agricultural production, and, later, Protestant intolerance and aversion to intermarriage appear to have been factors here. In the New England colonies, for instance, Indian defeat was often followed by a period of social demoralization when the native peoples were split up and gradually reduced to the status of vagabonds or poor dependants. As a French observer noted of Massachusetts Indians in 1780, "In a few years their territories were surrounded by the improvements of the Europeans, in consequence of which they grew lazy, inactive, unwilling, and unapt to imitate or follow any of our trades and in a few generations ... totally perished."[2]

Some Scandinavian populations exhibited a similar intolerance toward indigenous Balt and Lapp peoples of their northern territories, while on the fringes of Russian Orthodoxy, where it met Mongol and Islamic peoples, savage wars of extermination and expulsion had also long taken place, but so too had intermarriage. The eighteenth-century Russian conquest of the lands stretching south towards the Khanate of the Crimea involved the settlement of Russian and Christian colonies amongst the shifting tribal societies of the region. It was only in the early nineteenth century that ethnic expulsions began in some parts of the western Caucasus. Spanish, Portuguese, and even French settlers in the Americas and the Caribbean were equally violent, though more inclined to take women from indigenous populations, giving rise to a much larger *mestizo* or *métis* population in their new areas of settlement. In all these cases the relatively moderating effects of the presence of Catholic priests and especially members of the Jesuit order, who took care to preserve their subject indigenous populations, offers another important explanation of the difference in outcome. By the end of the eighteenth century, however, there was not a great deal to distinguish British from French treatment of native peoples in Canada or the Caribbean.

In a rather different way, Chinese, Japanese, and Ottoman expansion on what were to become their inner frontiers displayed an uncompromising character similar to that of the English, though the aim was generally cultural assimilation or subjugation rather than outright extermination. The unique features of Chinese civilization were clamped on the country's "animist" neighbors, most obviously through the Chinese characters and the Confucian rites. Japanese expansion in the eighteenth century had all but assimilated the independent Ainu people of Hokkaido Island. In the Ottoman Empire, the idea that shifting hill-farming communities and nomads should, where possible, be settled and drawn into the dominant society was already prevalent before the end of the eighteenth century. The clash between the official idea that these people were troublesome "mountain Turks" and the indigenous identity that these peoples claimed as the non-Turkish and non-Arab Kurds, as well as their assertion of sovereignty over lands, pointed forward to more modern conflicts. Kurdish revolts against Ottoman governors broke out between 1770 and 1840.

These examples of early modern wars of settlement were, however, the exception rather than the rule before the mid-nineteenth century. Across much of the world, expansive agricultural and commercial societies had accommodated and used the tribal, nomadic, and hunter populations they encountered. For one thing, the power of the premodern state was often not sufficient to permanently man and control a "barbarian watch." Indeed, it was often the "barbarians" themselves who were called on to mount these watches against their less amenable relations. Secondly, the forest and nomadic polities had much to offer the rulers of the settled lands politically. Tribesmen provided mobile cavalry, sappers, and miners for siege warfare and other elite praetorian corps for these rulers. Traditionally, the shahs of Persia had recruited much of their armies from moving peoples such as the Bakhtiari. The Qajars themselves were, after all, a conquering Turkish dynasty. Even expanding European powers had achieved something similar. Italian states drew on Albanian fishing people for their Mediterranean galleys. Scottish Highlanders from poor farming and fishing communities served in the British armies from the mid-eighteenth century. At one extreme of this process were the warrior-nomads who, over the course of a generation or two, became great rulers of the settled in their own right. These included the Timurids who ruled India, the Manchurians who ruled China, the Armenian dynasty which presided in Baghdad, the Bedouin Saudi rulers who slowly became kings of the Arabian peninsula, and the Fulani cattle-keepers who established the Sokoto caliphate in West Africa.

Thirdly, these peoples provided important economic services. Everywhere from Russia to North Africa, nomads moved grain and other goods across the map, while providing skins and animals for the commanders and peasants of the settled. In the Indian, Chinese, and Southeast Asian societies, medicinal herbs and other produce harvested by the people of the forests played a critical role in the cultivation of well-being of the wider population. Elephants and teak were hugely valuable products.[3] Finally, though they certainly perceived them as "other," the people of the plains and the settled lands did not regard tribal peoples as primitive and savage in the way that they came to be viewed after about 1820. Islamic teachers regarded them as good material for forging into converts on the pattern of the Arabian Bedouin, originally brought to Islam by the Prophet. The forest and the fastness also played an important part in the life of the great religions, which venerated wanderers who left city life for distant places. Tribesmen were still believed to harbor shamans with particular knowledge of the supernatural.

During the long nineteenth century, however, these societies were penned in, ravaged, and subjected to expanding farming populations and the agents of the modern state. It was in the age of revolution and expansion from 1780 to 1820 that the first inroads were made, though the tribal peoples continued to provide useful services for the new powers. The deluge came between 1830 and 1890 when the massive expansion of settler populations from Siberia through Australasia and southern Africa to the Americas expropriated native peoples' lands and forests to a large extent. Finally, after 1870, their remaining populations were visited by the agents of the state and of moral improvement. They were increasingly forced to adopt the dress, life-styles, and religion of the dominant populations, or they were corralled off into reservations and special homelands to be exploited as pools of labor for capitalist farms and mines. The next sections consider these two periods of change.

NATIVE PEOPLES IN THE "AGE OF HIATUS"

During the Napoleonic wars and the first age of global imperialism, the military and demographic balance had not shifted decisively against native peoples. In North America, the British had continued to cultivate relations with the Five Nations Iroquois which had been presaged during the Seven Years War and the War of American Independence. British North America's Indian Department, run by the famous Anglo-Irish Johnson family, maintained careful practices of gift giving with the major Mohawk and other Amerindian leaders. They recruited young warriors into their mobile units, and British officers even married into native society and adopted some of its customs. Contemporary conflict with the much larger settler population of the new American Republic gave the British a diplomatic advantage here. But in the Midwest, the Americans too continued to use the skills of native people to prosecute the fur trade, even though the Indians were removed and dispossessed with particular English thoroughness behind the frontier. Native scouts made a considerable contribution to the speed and success of the American and Canadian expansion into the central plains.[4] Since James Cook's voyages, the Indians of the northwestern coast had made similar links with the small, naval-supported British and American fishing and fur-trading posts. The massive Chinese demand for luxury furs made of them a lucrative commodity which could initially, at least, benefit both the whites and the Indians of the Pacific coast.

This pattern was repeated in other contexts. In southern Africa, the Dutch and the British recruited Khoikhoi, or "Hottentot," herdsmen and farmers into their militia to police the frontiers of European settlement.[5] The release of trade goods and weapons into the interior may have indirectly added to the major changes taking place in contemporary African societies. The Mfecane, the rise of the Zulu warrior-state to the north of the Cape colony and in Natal, seems in part to have reflected a response to European disturbances on the coast. On the other hand, the European governments on the Cape had begun to restrict native land and to hammer Africans into a useful work force.[6] More clearly, the first stage of European influence in New Zealand a generation later saw the shrewd Maori chiefs and entrepreneurs of the Bay of Islands region learning new techniques of warfare and emerging as a dominant force across the North Island and even invading the South Island.[7] The cost in lives was enormous, as equally matched tribal wars were outbalanced in the 1830s and 1840s by an infusion of Western weapons. So, too, as American and British influence gradually penetrated the Hawaiian Islands, the fate of its indigenous peoples was mixed. While rates of death from disease rose dramatically, well-placed chieftain families were able to make fortunes from the sale of sandalwood and other exotic produce which was bound for both European and Chinese consumer markets. These notables spent their wealth on exaggerated versions of feasting and royal consumption, with which they had traditionally marked themselves out from commoners.

Meanwhile, as Russian armies and colonies of settlement moved further into Siberia and pushed into the western Caucasus, some local chieftains also made compacts with the invaders, supplying food, timber, and specialist soldiers. In all these areas, native peoples were still able to sell military skills and their services as trackers as they congregated around new forts and trading posts.

Even on the fringes of the British Indian Empire and in Southeast Asia, tribal, nomadic, and forest people continued to play an important part in the consolidation and expansion of empire. Nomadic grain merchants (banjaras) continued to service the British armies in India into the 1840s. Warren Hastings's friend, Augustus Cleveland, attempted to create an armed force out of the hill people of northeastern India, while later, in the western hills and forests of the Bombay presidency, the Bhil foresters were organized into a special Bhil Corps in the early years of the century. The most famous example of all is provided by the Gurkha warriors of Nepal. These mountain farmers and herders nearly defeated the British in the war of 1814–16. Impressed by their military skills, the British increasingly drew on the Gurkhas for fighting manpower. By the same token, Gurkha Nepalis became increasingly dependent on income from overseas service as the population rose in the high valleys. This pattern was acted out elsewhere in European Asia. The Dutch, for instance, had already begun to recruit from the forest communities of the Moluccan Islands when they suppressed the 1825–30 resistance movement in Java. As the French became established in Cochin China in the early nineteenth century, they also began to recruit people from the tribes on the Cambodian border. These policies, adopted pragmatically, later became useful in the ethnic politics of colonial government, setting the scene for the inter-communal clashes of the later nineteenth and twentieth centuries.

Here the Europeans were merely extending and intensifying policies which Asian kingdoms had long adopted. The Muslim kingdoms had all been adept at giving hill men and foresters the task of patrolling the mountain passes and jungle fringes. Even as late as the 1790s, when the Chinese Qian Long emperor invaded Szechwan, his commanders were careful to incorporate and reward nomadic leaders by giving them imperial positions. On the Burmese frontier, the same Chinese armies tried to enlist non-Burmese, Chinese, and Shan peoples of the mountains as a counterweight to the Burmese kings. As the lineaments of the state became clearer after the mid-century rebellions, however, the pressure built up.

THE WHITE DELUGE, 1840–1890

Already, and even before 1840, European expansion in the Americas, Australasia, and Eurasia had put a different order of strain on native peoples. The postwar colonial governments all sought to raise revenue. Nomads and hill and forest tribals who paid little in the way of taxes were of little economic value and potential sources of tension if they continued to assert their right to raid and tax the settled. Fierce local skirmishes between settlers and Australian Aborigines over land rights in the hinterland of Sydney and the continuing wars of extermination along the borders of the American expansion were typical of the period. The American president, Andrew Jackson, introduced a "removal policy" whereby tribes which were thought to be holding up the march of Western civilization were relegated to areas of distant and, usually, poor land.[8] This was the forerunner of the wholesale policy of creating native reservations later in the century. In Canada, British authorities veered between removals of a Jacksonian sort on a small scale and botched attempts at assimilation.

The decisive change came with the expansion of settlement after 1840. The next ten years was the decade when total emigration to the Americas rose nearly 40 percent. By this date, British emigration to east and south Australia was also speeding up. A great wave of European settlement spread on the back of the steamship, the railway, and the voracious desire for gold, becoming a deluge by the 1870s. The Russian equivalent, in south Siberia, only really took off after 1890, but it had entailed similar consequences by the 1930s.

This great influx had serious consequences for native peoples everywhere. Different forms of treaty relationship between European and American governments and indigenous people – or a lack of them – imposed different patterns and time periods on expropriation. In some respects, the colonial governments in Canada and New Zealand were slower than the Americans to seize native land. But, ultimately, expropriation was general. Particularly significant was the land hunger which drove the European surge. Most of the settlers saw themselves as arable farmers. Their aim was to occupy and fence in land which they could then pass on to their children, something that many of them had not been able to do in Ireland, Poland, southern Italy, or the landlord terrain of Greater Russia. The rush for private property in land affected native peoples in many ways, both directly and indirectly. It sometimes eliminated the areas of temporary settled agriculture which were important in the flexible life-styles of native peoples who combined small-scale crop production with migration and living off the forests or prairies. Elsewhere, it impeded the movement of livestock, both domestic and wild, on which they lived. Their food dwindled as the buffalo, bison, kangaroo, and wildebeest retreated before the white man's settlement. In the islands of the South Pacific, the goal was not only land but also the whale, whose blubber and oil had become an important commodity in the early stages of the industrial and industrious revolutions. Predatory settlers, including of ex-seamen, beachcombers, and traders, invaded New Zealand and the islands of the southwestern Pacific, spreading venereal disease, mumps, chickenpox, and graft. In time, the evangelical captains of the British Navy and the missionary societies introduced their own benignly lethal notions of civilization and benevolence to indigenous peoples, who were resettled around white-painted Christian churches.

Across the world, the sheer propinquity of white agriculture and trade damaged many communities irremediably. Many succumbed to disease, others to alcohol. Yet others were torn away from their original societies to act as poor daily workers, alive, but mere serfs. Quite often, sheer violence eliminated them from the face of the earth. This was the period when the last inhabitants of southern Argentina were exterminated by Spanish and other southern European settlers. In Florida, Native American peoples were driven back into the swamps of the interior as white settlers colonized the arable strip along the coast. In South America, successive governments of Chile, for instance, did their best to clear their central tracts of the so-called Araucanian Indians, tough mobile farmers and fishermen who resisted the pressure to "improve" their agriculture. In Tasmania, much of the original population was systematically wiped out by the intolerant British settlers, having been literally hunted to death. Native peoples sometimes responded to these events by taking part in apocalyptic religious movements. Sometimes, as in southern Africa and among Amerindians, they killed their animals or destroyed their villages and belongings. The white deluge seemed to signal the end of the world, so these peoples felt the need to acknowledge its coming.

It was after the 1840s, too, that land hunger in the United States finally tipped the balance against coexistence with indigenous peoples. The constant outbreak of wars with Indians propelled state authorities in the Midwest into the policy of creating reservations. The Indian peoples were pushed onto more and more marginal land. They were effectively walled off, not only from their old hunting and grazing grounds, but also from the dynamic parts of the new national economy. Reservations and the railroads contributed to a 50 percent drop in the native American population between 1850 and 1890. The federal governments of the revolutionary era hated corporate property; consequently, Indian tribal land rights had widely been abolished in law. It was, however, with the expansion of railways and settlement one or two generations on that these rights were actually extinguished on the ground. In Latin America, where indigenous peoples had clung to their old life-styles in the high valleys and forest margins, the 1840s to 1870s saw a similar painful retreat.[9] The expansion of rubber production in Brazil in the mid-nineteenth century saw white settlement pushing up the river Amazon and driving away or transforming the Indian populations it encountered.

THE DELUGE IN PRACTICE: NEW ZEALAND, SOUTH AFRICA, AND THE USA

This critical change will be briefly illustrated in three different locations: New Zealand, southern Africa, and the United States. In New Zealand, or Aotearoa, white settlers had established whaling stations on the Bay of Islands, which lies on the tip of the North Island, as early as 1796. Maori people provided the ships with food and supplies and, being entrepreneurial people, some chieftains became rich on the proceeds and built up a formidable power. At the same time, Christian missionaries from Europe and Australia established themselves at several points in the country. Here, as in many parts of Africa, indigenous people seem quite successfully to have incorporated those parts of the Christian message which they found appealing and useful. Maoris, for instance, created lineages for their aristocracies from the genealogies of prophets in the Old Testament.[10] After 1840, international competition and the arrival of European colonies of settlement impelled the British Crown to assert its sovereignty over the islands.

The Treaty of Waitangi of 1840, which many of the participating native chiefs do not appear to have understood, let loose a rush of land purchase and appropriation by white settlers and the government. Maori peoples, fearing the loss of land, livelihood, and the charisma of their chiefs, were pushed into revolt. The Maori managed to fight the British and the settlers to a standstill between 1865 and 1873. But though some native land rights were recognized, and convert Maori played a small part in the government of white New Zealand after 1870, the damage was already done. In 1842, the white population was about 2,000, and the indigenous population about 80,000, whereas the New Zealand Census of 1896 recorded a white population of 700,000 and a Maori one of about 40,000. Disease, warfare with Europeans and other indigenous people, and the consequent social disruption had heavily tipped the balance of ethnic power in favor of the *pakeha*, or whites.[11]

Southern Africa saw a very similar pattern, in which an early violent coexistence was replaced by white settler domination. Some of the British administrative actors in the story were indeed the same. White settlement had begun in Cape Colony much earlier. By 1795 a white population of about 20,000 dominated a slave population (black and Asian) of about 25,000 and a Khoikhoi native population of about 15,000, which had been severely reduced over the previous 150 years. In the early years of the nineteenth century, British troops supported the efforts of the still mainly Dutch settlers to drive out Bantu-speaking peoples from the best lands. Until the 1840s, relatively strong Xhosa polities acted as something of a block on settler and colonial expansion. Thereafter, however, Europeans quickly established their domination. The export of European wars and rivalries overseas made British governments more ruthless in the prosecution of their strategic interests. The steamship, telegraph, and leaps forward in medicine and techniques of war had opened up an even wider gap in power and resources between European and African. Since they had little history of urban living, the peoples of South and East Africa, unlike those of West Africa, found it more difficult to adapt to cities. They were allowed into white towns as menial workers, and those that had adapted were increasingly segregated. As with the Australian Aborigines, it was the hunting populations of San, or Bushmen, who were worst affected by the loss of control over the land.

As communications improved, so the numbers of settlers increased. Between 1873 and 1883 alone, 25,000 arrived and, attracted by the lure of diamonds and gold as well as land, pushed aggressively into the interior. British governments, determined to retain their control over the growing settler societies, decided that this was incompatible with the continuation of fiercely independent African polities. The Zulu kingdom was finally broken in 1881. To the north, the Ndebele people, settled in present-day Zimbabwe, were gradually penned in and finally defeated after a bloody revolt in 1896–7. The dissolution of the kingdom led to "landlessness, to cultural disorientation, to personal anomie" as thousands of white settlers poured into these new lands. In the Matopo hills of present-day Zimbabwe, Africans struggled to create a vibrant peasant economy after the war. Adepts of the great god Mwali, who had played an important role in the revolt, "blessed the corn of a large number and received gifts."[12] But white farming, missions, and colonial administration could not be halted in their steps. By 1914, hundreds of thousands of southern Africans had become laborers in mines or on the estates of white-owned farms. Far from initiating a period of land reform, as some Africans had hoped, the war for control between the British and the descendants of Dutch settlers from 1899 to 1902 simply confirmed the racial division

ILLUSTRATION 12.1   Shilluks repairing their boat on the White Nile, early twentieth century.

of labor. Thousands of Africans were uprooted and resettled in labor camps, where they died of disease, though the story of the death of Afrikaners in the first "concentration camps" is better known.

Some Maori, Ndebele, and Zulu peoples, who lived in centralized polities, put up fierce resistance to the Europeans, fortified by a sense of patriotism and commitment to their land. More decentralized polities with shifting settlement patterns tended to succumb more slowly to piecemeal settlement, disease, alcoholism, and slow cession of their lands. This latter pattern seems to have held true in the case of the native peoples of Canada, whose resistance was further weakened by malnutrition brought about by over-hunting of buffalo. When native rights were extinguished across the southern prairies in 1871–7, tribal elders were mollified by the provision of desperately needed medical supplies and food, as well as overawed by the disciplined violence of the Royal Canadian Mounted Police.[13] Dependency eroded their tribal autonomy as readily as violence. But further south, in the American states of the Midwest and Southwest, armed conflicts between settlers and native peoples continued with ferocity until the 1880s. Native American polities in the great plains were both more powerful and more centralized than those in the colder climates of the north. This was because of the abundance of animals and natural produce, represented above all by the great herds of bison which populated the prairie.

Here, in the central and western states of the United States, the whole drama of defeat and dispossession was played out in its most dramatic and most publicized form. In the eastern states, the alternating conflict and coexistence between the white settler population and the Native Americans, which had characterized the years of the fur trade and the Anglo-French wars, came to an end much earlier. During the age of revolutions, the young republic had already militarily defeated and driven off the majority of the tribes. The Iroquois, who had long played a mediating role between whites and native society, were dispossessed or migrated off into Canada, where there was less pressure of settlement. The defeat of the more powerful, buffalo-hunting peoples of the great plains, however, was more or less coterminous with the defeat of the native polities of New Zealand and the subjugation of southern and eastern Africa.

During the early nineteenth century, the US federal government had held settler, mining, and ranching interests in check to some degree. The Indian Office had sent agents to deal with peoples such as the Sioux and Cheyenne and had tempted them into treaties which set aside some land for settlement, but allowed native chiefs unfettered control over large areas of the interior. The native peoples, who had adapted to horseback warfare with firearms, remained powerful enough to defeat white troops and farmers on occasion, as General Custer learned to his cost. The emerging pattern here of treaties, followed by the settlement of white resident agents among the tribes and sporadic local conflict, was not unlike the one which was played out between whites and Xhosa in Africa. It even bears distant comparison with the activities of the political service of British India among the tribal groups of the northeast.

The break-in of the white population came with the rapid expansion of the railroads in the 1850s and the sudden explosion of immigration as the steamship lines brought more and more Europeans to North America. In addition, the convulsions of the Civil War sent both defeated Confederate forces and the agents of the triumphant North into the Indian reservations. By about 1880, once the US army had overcome the final resistance of the peoples of the great plains, the question of what to do with the "Red Man" became pressing. Contemporary theories of the "civilizing mission," as famously expressed by the pen of Lewis Henry Morgan, one of the first professional anthropologists, claimed that total cultural assimilation was not only possible, but desirable. Missionaries, state schoolmasters, and doctors labored until the early years of the new century to assimilate Native Americans into white society. The spirit of individualism was encouraged, and tribespeople were given the right to buy allotments in the formal tribal reservations.

This policy of "assimilation" to "Aryan civilization" was gradually abandoned, however, in the early years of the twentieth century. The authorities' attempts to force Native Americans into the mold of a common citizenship were frustrated by the Native Americans' own desire to maintain their own customs and by their resistance to the time discipline and acquisitive individualism of the wider society. Observers began once again to decide that "the Native American race was distinctly feebler, more juvenile than ours."[14] Left in a limbo and subject, like blacks and Chinese immigrants, to a newly "scientific" version of racist segregation, the Indians entered the twentieth century subject to detribalization, impoverishment, and alcoholism, unrolling now at an even faster pace.

RULING SAVAGE NATURES: RECOVERY AND MARGINALIZATION

Such brutal dispossessions were accompanied by local and piecemeal social changes brought about by Western missionary effort, which later generations of native rights spokesmen were to see as no less disruptive of indigenous lifestyles. Roman Catholic missions had long been active in evangelizing the unsettled tribal people of Central and South America, the southeast and southwest African coasts, the Philippine Islands, and parts of Indonesia. In these areas the local church, along with the plantation-owner's house, had emerged as centers of economic and cultural exchange. Generally speaking, indigenous high gods had been displaced by versions of southern European Catholic Christianity, but life-cycle rites and ceremonies connected with the harvest continued to bear the mark of indigenous systems of belief. In some parts of Mexico and Peru, the Jesuits and other orders had achieved considerable economic and political power. By the later eighteenth century, the pace of Catholic missionary activity throughout the world had slowed down. In different ways, the regimes in China, Japan, and Southeast Asia had worked to limit the impact of Christian evangelization by closing their countries to missions. The viceroys of New Spain in the last days of the empire were jealous of their power, and the Jesuits were expelled from French and Spanish territory after 1760. In the African kingdoms adjoining the Portuguese settlements, factional struggles and dynastic changes had reversed earlier formal gains in Christian confessions. In many parts of the world, the period saw a revival of syncretic forms of rite which earlier missionaries and priests had done their best to suppress. Islam, and even Sanskritized versions of Hinduism, also made gains amongst unsettled tribal peoples in their respective geographical zones, which were to become northern Nigeria or Assam in eastern India.

Protestant churches initially did little to fill the gap left by the slackening of Roman Catholic activity among native peoples. Both from theological conviction and because of the indifference or hostility of the secular authorities, Dutch and English churches concentrated on bringing the "Good News" to their own people and did not work amongst non-Europeans. Even on the frontiers of North American settlement, township authorities were very hesitant to irritate people of First Nations peoples by promoting Christianity. Slave-owners in the South and the Caribbean regarded evangelization as too dangerous for labor control.

All this changed rapidly from the beginning of the nineteenth century. The settlement of freed slaves in Sierra Leone and Liberia by the British and Americans respectively, powered by the moral drive towards abolitionism, initiated mission activity in many new areas, including West Africa. The emergence of a Protestant missionary public in the United States, Britain, and Europe after 1800 provided personnel and funds for a large evangelizing effort. This drove missionary settlements deep into the American and Canadian hinterlands, and particularly to areas inhabited by what were regarded as "primitive peoples," who were thought to be less resistant to change than peasant indigenes. Protestant missionary efforts in education and social "improvement" picked up throughout the British Empire, registering considerable success in the new Pacific and Australasian territories. Important here was the interest taken in the issue after 1832 by the reformed British Parliament, which established a Committee on the Aboriginal Peoples of the British Empire. The revival of French imperial activity after 1815 and the reorganization of the Church after the ravages of the Napoleonic onslaught also signaled a reemergence of Roman Catholic activity in overseas missions, which were soon active among the "tribes" of highland Indochina and West African forests.

At first the new mission activity adapted to the changes in indigenous politics. Chiefs and headmen sought to capture the charisma of the missionary and the Book to enhance their authority. Whole communities converted to gain access to what they thought of as new knowledge and power. New, hybrid communities developed around mission stations, their sense of identity expressed through a melding of local traditions with the notion of a "chosen people" drawn from Scripture. In this period, missions sometimes actually acted as a counterweight to the growing rush of white settlement. British Dissenting missionaries fulfilled this role in the hinterland of the Cape Colony and in the Pacific, where they were sometimes, if only temporarily, able to put a brake on the greed of the settlers. In Brazil, revived Roman Catholic missions attempted to protect the native peoples of the Amazon from depredation as the pace of logging and deforestation was stepped up after 1850.

Later, however, during the age of dispossession and military conquest, Christian conversion and the adoption of hybrid European life-styles and customs became the only resort for many among the First Nations people who were suffering from alcoholism, disease, and punitive regulation. Whole communities of Maori, Pacific Islanders, and Australian Aborigines converted as one way to secure a menial stability within the colonial system. The alternative was revolt and resistance, which also often appropriated and turned back Christian ideas against Europeans. Such was the so-called King Movement revolt in New Zealand in 1868[15] and the revolts against the Spanish in the northern Philippines in the 1870s. Even in the case of American Indian tribes who resisted the US or Canadian authorities, Christian millenarian ideas were sometimes woven into their ideologies. Native peoples always came out the worse from these conflicts. So almost everywhere the trend was towards the abrading of indigenous social patterns by European and missionary activity, at its most devastating in the mid-nineteenth century.

Missionaries believed that by implanting the virtues of methodical cash crop production, time discipline, and regular, Western-style marriage, they would avert any possibility of return to the old rites. Not only were cannibalism, human sacrifice, and inter-tribal wars suppressed, but polygamy and indigenous religion and forms of dress were severely discouraged. In some cases in the Pacific region, the transformation from inter-tribal war and ritual cannibalism to Methodism took a mere 20 years. The price was high. The removal or radical reorganization of the older tribal polities cut free many young men. Some adapted to the new dispensation as field laborers, domestic servants, or artisans around the white settlements. This redoubled the burden on women left in the villages who had to bring up children and also grow food for the residual settlements. But in many cases, the young men drifted off to a life of vagabondage or crime, filling the jails of the new settlements and feeding the racism of the European settlers. Neither assimilation nor reservation, but widespread demoralization, was the longer-term result.

These inroads into the variety of human cultures and life-styles were not simply the preserve of the new areas of European settlement. Across the world, homogenization and settlement picked up their pace in the early nineteenth century. The expansion of the ethnic Chinese and Japanese populations eliminated the political structures of the remaining tribal groups in Taiwan, the South Chinese mountain ranges, and Hokkaido island quite rapidly between 1820 and 1880. Ethnic Vietnamese settlers moved into the lands of the Moi, or tribal peoples, literally "savages," as population grew in the late-eighteenth and nineteenth centuries. Vietnamese shamans sometimes symbolically propitiated the priests and gods of the tribal peoples. Yet the land was lost, and the indigenous discourse of civility and barbarism accommodated itself quite well to the interests of the few white officials present. Indian farmers invaded the Dang forested areas of western India over the same period, disrupting the old tribal structures.[16] The Santal revolt in Bengal in 1856 saw the final destruction of tribal independence there. Meanwhile, British and American missionaries worked amongst the Nagas, Shan, and Kachin of the Indian and Burmese mountain ranges. Demographic and cultural pressures were so intense that many at the end of the nineteenth century spoke of the "death of the native." The world was to be the possession of the dominant white races and their clients among industrious Indian, Indo-Chinese, Chinese, and Arab peasantries.

Yet this final immolation, ultimately, did not occur. By the last 20 years of the nineteenth century, the situation had stabilized somewhat. The last major wars between native peoples and Europeans had been fought, and indigenous peoples, battered and restricted, began in some cases to learn techniques that made possible their longer-term survival, at least as the poorest relations within the world economic system. Christianity, and other global religions, gave them a language through which they could articulate a notion of rights. Religion blunted the edge of racial or cultural domination. The ruthless exploitation characteristic of white expansion sat uneasily with the language of religious paternalism which suffused much of its politics. The emergence of the scientific professional described in chapter 8 also played its part. The sciences of living beings, natural history, and anthropology intervened to class native peoples and rare animals as specimens, and this afforded them a degree of protection. Some of the European officers who policed the special jurisdictions that had been created for these small populations were trained anthropologists who argued for their seclusion from the modern world. As "living fossils," such peoples surely needed conservation as much as the physical objects and natural history specimens preserved in museums.

Some native peoples, such as the Maori, gained a little respite from being classed as "Aryan" or descendants of other "high" races in the imaginative schemes of civilizational and racial categorization developed by European thinkers.[17] Native rights champions came forward to plead for larger reservations, the protection of grazing, hunting, or fishing rights, and the protection of indigenous shrines. Acculturation had gone so far that, as in New Zealand and among the Tuareg of the desert fringes of French North Africa, local chieftains educated in European languages were able to petition and challenge the agents of the state. Some even sat in councils and representative institutions by the end of the nineteenth century.

In general, too, the modern state, whether colonial or independent, was more likely to protect and maintain native rights and life-styles than the settler populations. These states began latterly to wish to preserve forests, rivers, and other resources for their own use. They were suspicious of the greed and aggression which they saw all along the white settler frontier. This so often embroiled hard-pressed administrations in frontier or tribal wars that they could ill afford. To some degree, colonial- and national-level administrators

ILLUSTRATION 12.2 Dance of the Eland Bull: Kalahari "bushmen" (San or Ko), early twentieth century.

had also imbibed liberal ideas of progress, protection, and "trusteeship." They sought to count, classify, and section off native populations which they had been taught were their special responsibility. Often, of course, these efforts at preserving the tribesmen had as bleak an impact on them as whole-sale assimilation and subordination, because it cut them off from opportunities in the new economy. Some, like the Australian Aborigines, were so weak politically and so unadaptable to the norms of settler society that their decline into poverty and alcoholism continued unabated.[18]

Yet, aided by the young science of anthropology and political resistance from some native peoples, the administrators at the end of the nineteenth century did begin to call a halt to the mass expropriation and destruction of tribal peoples. Many native populations stabilized at a low level and began to protect more effectively some proportion of their rights over their traditional lands. Finally, it should be emphasized again that this severely limited survival was not primarily the work of chiefs and the administrators of the modern state. It also bespoke the adaptability of the tribal people themselves. Some began again to find a niche for themselves in the new economy and society. They became guides and trackers for the hunting parties of European settlers and visitors who insisted on plunging into the forests and high plains in order to slaughter big game. They adapted their traditional religious and domestic art to provide curios for the first generation of European tourists and the growing demand in Europe and America for exotic objects. In New Zealand, some tribes continued a lucrative trade in shrunken heads, which had become a valuable commodity in the European market for native artefacts. Others sought to exploit the produce of their forests and wild places, bringing skins, beeswax, honey, and medicinal plants and animal products to sell in the markets of the settled peoples. In other cases yet, tribal and marginal peoples continued to provide troops for colonial and national armies. As the First World War approached, the British began again to recruit native peoples in numbers. They called to the colors Fijians, Indian Naga tribesmen, and Kachin, as well as Karen and Chin levies for their frontier colonial wars. On the northwest frontier of British India, Pathan tribesmen were recruited to fight their cousins in the hills and to overawe the people of the plains. The French and the Dutch recruited North African Tuareg and Moluccan forest-people into their respective colonial armies. The Russians created a Caucasian mountain division, the so-called Savage Division, which rose to bloody fame in the First World War.

There was, however, little halt to the depredations of nature which accompanied this widespread expropriation of native peoples. It is naive to believe that such peoples were the world's "first conservationists." They ruthlessly hunted, poisoned, and laid waste whale and fish stocks, herds and forests. Still, their tools were simple, their population numbers small, and their

ILLUSTRATION 12.3   Exterminating the wild: A colonial officer with tusks, 1905. Photo by Ernst Haddon.

veneration of nature encouraged its regeneration. The ideologies of the settlers from the wider society, however, taught them to exploit and exterminate. The Industrial Revolution gave them the iron tools, machines, and firearms to plunder the natural world to an unprecedented degree, even at the same time as they were classifying and investigating it.[19] The fur-bearing and meat-bearing animals of the Russian steppes and the American prairies were all but exterminated between 1780 and 1914. Fish and whale stocks were massively reduced in the southern oceans. Teak forests throughout the world were cut down to provide wood for European shipping. Less valuable timber was plundered for railway sleepers and pit props for mines. Sometimes the disastrous results were already clear by the time of the First World War. Deforestation had led to erosion and flooding in vulnerable parts of India and China, adding to the problems of overpopulation and falling agricultural yields. As early as the 1830s and 1840s, natural historians and administrators were alarmed by the progress of what they called "desiccation," the drying out and ruining of the soil, especially in the dependent European empires.[20] The lessons of conservation, like the lessons of international dispute resolution, were not yet learned even 100 years after the end of the period.

[13] CONCLUSION: THE GREAT ACCELERATION, c.1890–1914

THIS final chapter returns to the big themes of the book: the multi-centric nature of change in world history, the growth in contested uniformity and functional complexity across the world, the growing velocity of international connections, and the rise of Western dominance and challenges to that dominance. First, however, the chapter considers the acceleration of political and economic change which occurred in the two decades before the outbreak of the First World War. Industrialism, democracy, and non-European nationalism seemed finally to be making their long-heralded breakthrough in this era of self-conscious modernity.

PREDICTING "THINGS TO COME"

V. I. Lenin and his revolutionary contemporaries believed that the years after 1890 had seen a dramatic speeding up of social and economic change, and that this signaled the terminal phase of capitalist society. The socialists saw evidence of this in the persistent rumble of strikes throughout the industrializing world and the rash of diplomatic crises which occurred after 1890. Many of these crises were conflicts between imperial powers over spheres of influence in the extra-European world, so late capitalism and imperialism were regarded as partners in crime. Lenin revised his views in 1916, in his work *Imperialism*, which sought to account for the coming of the First World War. He developed the argument that capitalism had indeed moved into a new and final phase of monopoly and imperialism after 1890. But he was forced to concede that it had also bribed the working class to take part in this violent redivision of the world's resources. Most socialists abandoned working-class brotherhood in 1914 and enlisted behind the European states' war aims.

Many liberals and conservatives, too, were affected by a kind of millennial panic around 1900, glimpsing "things to come" which terrified them. J. A. Hobson, the British liberal, feared that a malevolent alliance of state power

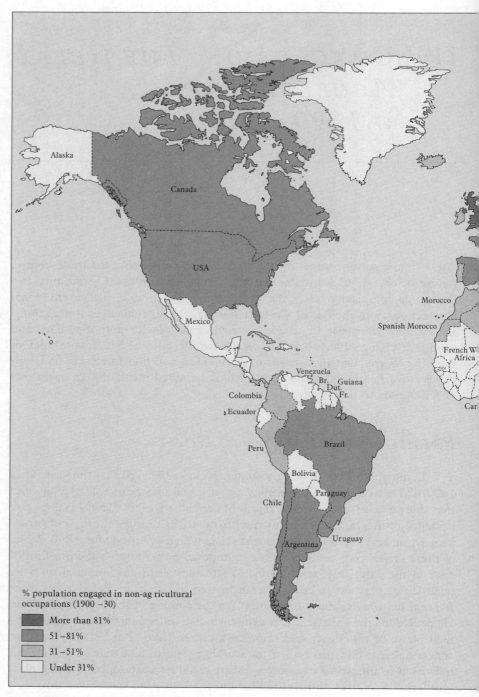

% population engaged in non-agricultural
occupations (1900–30)

More than 81%

51–81%

31–51%

Under 31%

MAP 13.1   The industrial world, c.1900–30.

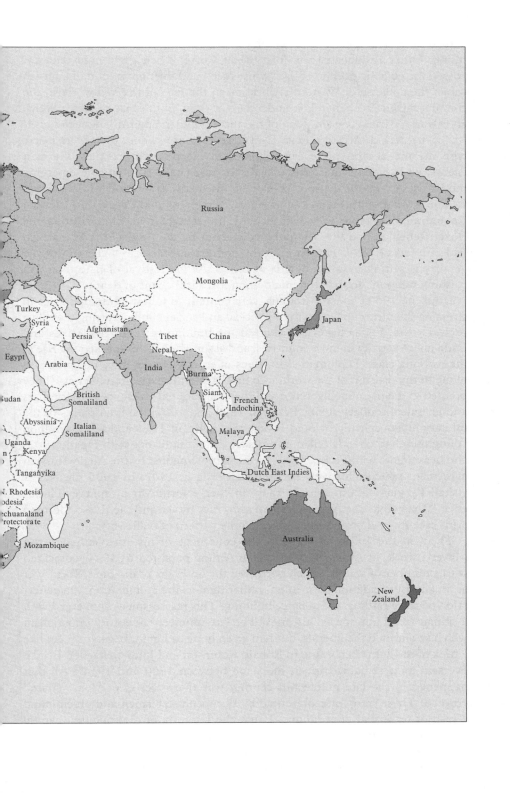

and commercial rapacity in the colonies would distort and destroy the constitution. Other European seers foresaw far worse. Their nightmares encompassed the eugenic decline of the "white race" and the domination of a Jewish cabal; the collapse of Western civilization in the face of the Yellow Peril; the rise of a mixed-race, anarchist underclass or even, in the case of H. G. Wells, an extraterrestrial invasion. One of the most popular English-language novelists of the period, Arthur Conan Doyle, wrote stories whose plots were heavy with the menace of exotic evil, signaled in the plots of orientals, German agents, and criminal masterminds. As the last chapter noted, the emerging modernist art of the period, shown in the Paris Exhibition of 1900, was woven through with themes of violence, perversity, and decay. In Calcutta, Rabindranath Tagore was disturbed by the slaughter in China during the Boxer Rebellion and the death of civilians during the Anglo-Boer War which had erupted in 1899. He wrote of the coming apocalypse: "The sun of the century is setting today in clouds of blood. At the festival of hate today, in clashing weapons sounds the maddening, dreadful chant of death."[1]

Until the 1960s, most historians were content to follow contemporaries in stressing the inexorable growth of political and social conflict during these last prewar years. Labor historians charted the buildup of industrial strikes and trade union activity in most countries, and assumed that this marked the rise of the working class. Diplomatic historians of strictly conservative pedigree also wrote of the division of the world into blocks and the escalation of crisis. They pointed to the rise of belligerence and the international arms race in battleships and chemical artillery shells. Between 1898 and 1907, the final pieces of the military alliances which would ravage the world in 1914 and kill 20 million young men had already fallen into place. Britain's alliance with Japan (1902) and her entente with France (1904) were complemented by the Anglo-Russian agreement which effectively partitioned Persia in 1907. In 1905 the Kaiser visited Tangier and threatened France in "her" North African sphere of influence. Meanwhile, the Anglo-German arms race by sea and the Russo-German arms race by land ominously confirmed the pattern of bellicosity.

Then, in the 1970s and 1980s, the consensus of histories shifted. Arno Mayer's work, insisting that the ancien régime persisted to 1914, coincided with a number of studies which portrayed the outbreak of the First World War as an almost accidental happening, rather than as the culmination of a generation of sabre rattling and alliance building. This reassessment converged with a similar trend in imperial histories. The late-nineteenth-century imperialism which so alarmed the liberals, but had given hope to Lenin, began to seem like a trick of the light. According to Ronald Robinson and John Gallagher, British overseas aims remained much the same between 1800 and 1914.[2] All that happened in the late nineteenth century was that a series of "local crises" erupted. These were misrepresented by European statesmen and precipitated a rash of territorial annexations. Later, the interests of metropolitan capital came back into the picture of imperial expansion in the guise of the "gentlemanly capitalism" thesis of Peter Cain and A. G. Hopkins. But these historians also seemed to suggest that little dramatic change occurred in the aims or structure of capitalist imperialism in the later nineteenth century.[3] The City of London and allied financial centers appeared to be pursuing the same policies of making the world safe for capitalism as they had pursued since the early nineteenth century.

Colonial nationalism before the First World War also became a "paper tiger," or straw man. According to Anil Seal and several of his pupils, Indian nationalism before 1914 was no more than the demand for jobs and offices of a "microscopic minority."[4] Elie Kedourie refused to acknowledge that Arab nationalism had any real lineage at all before the First World War.[5] It was a wartime creation of the chancelleries of Europe. This trend of argument continued. To a later generation of leftist Indian historians, the ideology of Indian nationalism was mainly a "derivative discourse" voiced by inert imitators of the West,[6] a line of argument which increasingly found an echo in the work of historians of China and Japan. Skepticism among economic historians about the impact of industrialization, even as late as 1914, sustained the view that the First World War itself was a war fought predominantly with agrarian resources, at least during its first three years. Later, Richard Price further elaborated the argument for continuity in the case of Britain.[7] Though he acknowledged that there was some change after 1890, Price's view was that the "long eighteenth century" lasted more or less until the end of the nineteenth century. Throughout this period Britain remained a localized, little-governed society, in which the politics of deference remained much more important than the politics of class.

THE AGRICULTURAL DEPRESSION, INTERNATIONALISM, AND THE NEW IMPERIALISM

This lurch by historians from stressing hectic change to postulating comparative immobility probably reached its outer limits in the 1990s. Chapter 11 agreed that there were indeed many apparent continuities in political and economic form across the nineteenth century, especially if we take a global perspective. These continuities, however, occurred when and where the institutions, economic forms, and ideologies of different societies had adapted to, or were compatible with, the rise of the nation-state, expanding international trade and the growing density of international communications. Peasantries and old elites in Asia, Africa, and southern Europe persisted throughout the century. Some forms of government remained reminiscent of the old order. Yet there were substantial shifts in relations of power and profit at a global level, which the proponents of stasis tend to underplay. In particular, the international terms of trade turned sharply against all the major societies of Asia and Africa after 1820, even if they temporarily advantaged the raw materials producers of Latin America, the southern USA, and Australasia. Capital formation and railway building did usher in a new economy after the 1840s, even if industrialization as such was quite localized in its effects. State forms were widely becoming more uniform, while the growth of professions and urbanization created more complex and analogous social groupings, though the effects of these changes were restricted initially to a relatively small number of cities and their hinterlands. The idea of citizens' rights became a global phenomenon, with new leaders across the world envisaging national self-determination. In important ways, too, changes outside Europe and North America intruded more and more on the politics and economies of what had now become the "core" of the world economy.

Even if the historians' arguments over continuity and change remain relatively evenly balanced up to about 1890, there is very good reason to think that change ought to win out decisively in any analysis of the years thereafter. Many people of the time, contemplating the speed of change between 1890 and 1914, were convinced that this age was the crucible of modernity and represented it as such in political discourse, art, and literature. One important solvent of the old order, biting deeply into it by 1890, was the social consequence of the great agricultural depression of the 1870s and 1880s. The mid-century expansion of agricultural production in the Americas, Australasia, and southern Africa had caused the prices of basic grain and other commodities to fall dramatically. By the last decade of the century, 15 years of price depression in agriculture had begun to register itself in quite significant changes in social hierarchies across the world. The fortunes of European landed families had taken a downturn, often forcing them into an alliance with new wealth. In Britain, 80 of the 100 wealthiest families in the country in 1910 now owed their fortunes to manufacturing, not to landed income. This was the age when the heirs of Queen Elizabeth I's nobles began to marry the daughters of bankers, mill-owners, or even, in extremity, Americans. In Germany, the landed classes became increasingly dependent on investment in industrial shares and military and political office, though the agricultural protectionist regime which the empire maintained afforded them better protection than their English peers enjoyed. Businessmen and bankers rapidly increased their political power in relation to the landed classes in most European countries. In Russia, the gentry fared particularly badly. In Italy, severe agrarian crisis fed into political instability in the mid-1890s, but it was from this very time that the country's industry began to expand rapidly, changing the composition of its elite. To an equal extent, the expansion of New World agriculture had put huge fortunes into the hands of urban financiers and commodity traders in Chicago and the east coast cities of North America. A further quite severe downturn in the United States' economy in 1893–7 had drawn together a number of rather disparate opponents of big business and big farming. They were to open up the practice of American politics and goad forward the pretensions of federal government in the so-called Progressive Era.

The character of commercial power itself was changing quite fast by the outbreak of the First World War. Technical change flowed around the world. The Pathé film company was founded in 1900. Marconi completed his wireless experiments in 1902 (see illustration 13.1). Blériot crossed the Channel by air in 1909. The motorcar began to appear on roads around the world.

ILLUSTRATION 13.1   Communicating modernity: Guglielmo Marconi sending a transatlantic radio message, 1902.

The structure of industry shifted in line with the appearance of these icons of modernity. The old British pattern of gentlemanly capitalism was being modified by a new form of business culture, especially in Germany and the USA, which increasingly divorced ownership from management. In addition, many of the greatest family fortunes of the twentieth century were consolidated in the 1890s or the new century's first few years: the Fords, Carnegies, and Gettys, and in Europe the Krupps, Gulbenkians, and Nobels. In Germany, particularly, the application of advanced science to manufacturing production moved ahead very fast in the chemical, defense, electrical, and, later, motor industries. In Japan, the great mining and smelting entrepreneur Furukawa Ichibe became the richest man in the realm. Even in India, where the landholding elite held on by ratcheting up customary demands from the peasantry and currying official favor, there were some signs of change. Industrial magnates such as Tatas and G. D. Birla began to build their textile fortunes and challenge the dominance of British expatriate firms. The knowledge base of industry changed. The application of scientific research to business opened up new possibilities for innovation. In 1892, the American company General Electric was founded and set about producing a range of commercially viable dynamos. In 1900, it founded an industrial research laboratory on the German model, and two years later Du Pont, the chemical company, followed suit.[8] At the same time, the global capital market appears to have become

Table 13.1 Number of universities in different parts of the world (approximate numbers)

Region	1875	1913
North America	360	500
South America	30	40
Europe	110	150
Asia	5	20
Africa	0	5
Australasia	2	5

Source: Hobsbawm, *Age of Empire*, p. 345.

Table 13.2 Accelerating emigration from Europe to other parts of the world, 1871–1911 (millions)

Dates	Total immigration from Europe in these years to all parts	To the United States	To Canada	To Argentina and Brazil	To Australia and New Zealand	To other regions
1871–80	4.0	2.8	0.2	0.5	0.2	0.3
1881–90	7.5	5.2	0.4	1.4	0.3	0.2
1891–1900	6.4	3.7	0.2	1.8	0.4	0.25
1900–11	14.9	8.8	1.1	2.45	1.6	0.95
1871–1911	32.9	20.5	1.9	6.15	2.5	1.7

Source: Hobsbawm, *Age of Empire*, based on A. M. Carr-Saunders, *World Population* (London, 1936).

more integrated and more speculative. Massive flows of money went into dubious schemes, such as West African gold mining or cornering copra supplies in the Pacific. Scientific and technical training in universities increased, and new flows of labor migrants serviced advanced industries in northern Europe and North America.

When Lenin wrote about imperialism being "the highest stage of capitalism," he was speaking about the redistribution of wealth and resources within continental Europe as much as in European colonies as such.[9] Here his case was a much more convincing one, particularly if we look at the great enterprises which started up in the 1890s and 1900s. The French Trans-Siberian Railway and the German Berlin–Baghdad Railway projects showed international capital working on a yet larger scale. After 1890, the Western powers and their bankers began to intervene more purposively in the Ottoman Empire. The sultan, like his Egyptian deputies, had built up huge debts to Westerners. The latter now began to take over and manage parts of territories to secure interest payments. The grandiose schemes of Rhodes in southern Africa and battles between large European companies backed by their respective governments in Persia, China, and the Ottoman Empire, suggest that political conflicts were being deepened by economic rivalries. To a much greater extent than during the mid-years of the nineteenth century, consulates carefully monitored and tried to preempt the commercial advances of their rivals. In 1895, for instance, the European powers and Japan set about squeezing the life out of China in response to the weakening of its integrity after the war with Japan. A few years later, the French ambassador personally intervened with Lord Salisbury, the British prime minister, when it was rumored that Britain was about to offer China a huge loan in exchange for unilateral economic concessions.[10] Were capitalists following the state in these cases, or was the state following the capitalists? Where modern historians continue to differ from Lenin is that they emphasize the political, and even cultural, origins of these apparently economic conflicts. There was no master plan for German domination of the world, of course, but German foreign policy was permeated by a sense of international mission, to displace the greedy Anglo-Saxon empires of trade and exploitation with a supposedly more cultural German peace.[11]

The political map was also being inexorably redrawn as new centers of power emerged rapidly. Bismarck's careful and consistent foreign policy was replaced after 1890 by the more ambitious, global strategy of Kaiser Wilhelm II. Germany began its career as a naval power and challenged the British position in the Ottoman Empire. It created a small fleet in the China seas and avidly sought a coaling station and harbors on the China coast. Later, after 1905, the Kaiser attempted to intervene in North African politics and also threatened Britain's century-old influence in Istanbul. Germany's growing political clout was matched by its capacity to outsell Britain in many of her old colonial and overseas markets, especially Latin America, China, and the Middle East. It is not surprising that even the British came to question the doctrine of free trade which had served them so well since 1815, and there was vigorous talk of imperial preference in the Conservative Party. The relative decline of Britain was measured not only in the embarrassments of the South African War, in which she was initially outmaneuvered by a small population of armed farmers, but in the field of heavy industry too. By 1890, American and German production of iron and steel had overtaken Britain's. France, the other major European power of mid-century, also seemed to be fading. Conflict between Catholics and secularists, between the army and the left, seemed to become even more bitter in the 1890s. The French worried about their declining birthrate and the rise of a belligerent Germany across their frontiers.

America – temporarily – began to exert greater influence internationally. In 1898, she went to war with Spain, ousting her from Cuba and Puerto Rico, and converted the Philippines into an American colony. Theodore Roosevelt, lauding American aims in Cuba, articulated in 1902 the stark contradiction in American attitudes toward overseas influence which was to dog it throughout the rest of the twentieth century. He demanded a treaty which would put US interests in a favorable position in Cuba:

ILLUSTRATION 13.2 Pan-Islamism in action: Indian Muslim leaders Muhammad and Shaukat Ali take ship in defense of the Ottoman Khilafat and the holy places, c.1911.

Not only because it is enormously in our interest to control the Cuba market and by every means to foster our supremacy in the tropical lands and waters south of us . . . but also because we should make all our sister nations of the American continent feel that we desire to show ourselves disinterestedly and effectively their friends.[12]

The events in China in 1900, following the so-called Boxer Rebellion, also pointed toward the birth of this multinational, but more dangerous, world. When confronted with a nationalist upsurge in Egypt in 1882, Britain had occupied this province of the Ottoman Empire and had asserted her right as the dominant power. In 1900, however, the defeat of the Chinese Empire led to what the Americans called an "open door" policy. European powers and the Japanese were allowed to force concessions out of China, while the Americans sought to use their enhanced power to avert its partition or total subjugation to the Europeans. US missionaries, publicists, and newspapermen around the world began to articulate the views of a more vigorous American public opinion about international politics.

Most extraordinary of all in upsetting the older consensus was the rise of Japan, which defeated China in 1894–5 and went on to humiliate the Russian Empire ten years later. In the meantime, Japan, already entrenched as a colonial power in Taiwan, expanded into Korea and established in that country an imperial administrative system distantly modeled on the British Empire.[13] The psychological significance of the rise of Japan and its successful competition with European powers should not be underestimated. Throughout the non-European world, nationalist leaders, newspaper editors, and even ordinary people suddenly saw that Western dominance was neither inevitable nor everlasting. In Indian villages distant from the battlegrounds of Mukden and Tsushima, where the Russians were defeated, newborn babies were given the names of Japanese admirals. Nationalist artists in Calcutta began to adopt Japanese techniques and sensibilities to mark themselves out from European influences. In French Indochina, Phan Boi Chau inaugurated the "look to the east" movement which was to take many young people to Tokyo, where they mingled with expatriate Chinese, Korean, and Indian students.[14] Even in distant Abyssinia, buoyed up by its own recent victory against the Italians at Adowa in 1896, the country's first social scientist urged his countrymen to look to the Japanese example of modernity. In stark contrast was the gradual buildup in the United States and its Pacific territories of opposition to Japanese immigration and racialist legislation against it. By 1914, the rhetoric of Japanese self-consciousness and expansionism had taken on a bitter tone.

Also important in magnifying and amplifying the sense of change and conflict was the revolution in communications which was now fully in place. The globe was newly linked by telegraphic communication, and this allowed governments, interest groups, and radicals to concert their action at a world level. Between 1900 and 1909 the volume of press traffic on the telegraphs trebled. At the same time, mass publishing had come into its own. While it is doubtful that "new imperialism" and national conflicts overseas were caused by a populist ground swell, organized public opinion certainly gained greater political weight as a consequence of its manipulation by press comment. British Empire opinion was rallied against the Boers by *The Times* at the same time as American opinion was being mobilized against the Spanish by William Randolph Hearst's newspapers. His famous telegram to his correspondent in Cuba summed up the evolving relationship between media and politics: "You furnish the pictures and I will furnish the war."

The surge of radical nationalism over much of the non-European world between 1900 and 1910 also reflected the new speed of international communications. Chinese, Indians, Egyptians, Indochinese, and Irish began to make analogies between their own plight and that of other nations. They began to meet together in conferences in London, Paris, and Chicago, as socialists, pan-Africanists, students, and journalists. Ministries and government officials were bombarded with protests over the telegraph, and, at least to begin with, they were forced to take some note. The contemporary language of race war and conflict between species exacerbated the sense of international tension. War correspondents reporting on small conflicts and local rebellions could project themselves directly into the drawing rooms and onto the breakfast tables of Europe and the USA.

THE NEW NATIONALISM

Nationalism was already on a rising path after 1860. Yet 1890–1940 was to be the age of hyperactive nationalism. In the most economically developed provinces of Russia and Austria-Hungary, minority-language nationalism evidently began to develop a mass base from the turn of the century. In Ireland, Sinn Fein, which emerged as a popular political party, capitalized not only on poverty and social conflict in rural society, but also on the expansion of Catholic education and self-confidence, which had been gathering pace since the 1880s.[15] A sense of nationhood also developed rapidly in Britain's colonies of settlement, in part because of disillusionment with Britain's leadership during the South African War. Nationalism in the non-white Asian and African colonies and semi-colonies remained largely the preserve of educated urban elites and pockets of businessmen before the First World War. Even here, however, there were important new departures after 1890. Limited educational development and the expansion of communications had given ideologies of liberation and development a new, harder edge. In the Dutch East Indies, the "ethical policy" of native development announced by Queen Wilhelmina in 1900 encouraged Chinese and, latterly, Muslim liberals to demand local self-rule. A number of short-lived self-improving societies were superseded in 1912 by Sarekat Islam (the Islamic Union), which was to be the main vehicle for anti-colonial nationalism and Indonesian economic protectionism against Chinese business until the 1930s.[16]

In Egypt and India, nationalists began to demand immediate independence, and in both territories authoritarian British rulers created a climate in which small numbers of young intellectuals turned to terrorist violence. Lord Curzon's partition of Bengal in 1905, which damaged the interests of the Hindu intelligentsia of Calcutta and the landlords of east Bengal, sparked an outpouring of anger in a province which had pioneered the idea of a national political economy.[17] In Egypt, a massacre of villagers by British troops in 1906 marked the end of Lord Cromer's proconsulship and the beginnings of mass demonstrations against British occupation. In French North Africa, a new generation of pan-Islamic radicals demanded citizenship from the French and looked to the Turkish revolution of 1908 as their model. Stripped of honor and influence, the scholar-gentry of French Indochina also turned to revolutionary violence. Before the heir to the Austrian Empire fell to the bullet of a Serbian extremist in 1914, a significant number of European colonial officials had met a similar fate.

To the south of the African continent, the long-standing cultural and religious divisions between British and Boer settler were deepened by an unsuccessful attempt by the British to assert control in 1881. Boer separatism became in the 1890s something more like an intransigent settler nationalism fortified by religious fervor and a new sense of the separateness of the Afrikaans language. Paul Kruger, the president of the Transvaal state, who was to fight the British for a second time in 1899, emphasized the centrality of language and religion. He told Boer children in 1893: "If you become indifferent to your language, you also become indifferent to your forefathers and indifferent to the Bible."[18]

Among the most striking events, however, were the two revolutions which brought new, Western-educated professionals and soldiers within sight of power in the Ottoman and Chinese empires. As chapter 10 suggested, it is easy to exaggerate the backwardness of the late Qing and Ottoman administrations, just as it is possible to overestimate the degree of change which occurred outside the major cities in the aftermath of the "Young Turk" revolution of 1908 and the Chinese revolution of 1911. But both were sharp reactions to the apparently inexorable expansion of European and American economic and political influence around the world. The Chinese professional groups finally abandoned their allegiance to the Manchus when a new system of extraterritorial control biased towards Western railway companies and other concession-holders appeared in the offing. The Manchu dynasty was seen to have failed ultimately in its duty to protect the country, despite significant attempts to promote change since the Taiping Rebellion. Overseas Chinese trading communities and discontented young men in the coastal cities who had often been exposed to Christian education joined hands to rid themselves of "Manchu barbarity." Yet even before 1911, an epochal intellectual change had taken place. The imperial reform edict of 1901, after the Boxer Rebellion, had concluded that certain principles of morality were immutable, whereas methods of government had always been mutable. To improve those methods, a scrutiny of both Chinese and Western governmental patterns would be necessary. This was an astonishing concession to "barbarian knowledge."

In Istanbul, the relentless pressure of Russia and Austria in the Balkans drove the young military leadership to radical reform as an act of national self-strengthening.[19] Since the attempt to transform a universal empire into a modern state had failed, radicals argued that there was no alternative to rapid and violent modernization. The new rulers who thrust aside the sultan were largely of Turkish-speaking and eastern Balkan extraction, rather than Arabs. Initially, at least, some of them began to advocate the Turkish language. In turn, this raised urgent questions about what it now meant to be an Arab, a Syrian, or an Egyptian. These two coups were of the deepest symbolic importance. The Qing had ruled as absolute monarchs in Beijing since the 1640s, the Ottomans in Istanbul since 1453. The Qing dynasty was now replaced by a republican regime, while the once-despotic Ottoman sultan became more like a constitutional monarch. Many observers both within and outside the Ottoman Empire and China believed that modernity had finally conquered what were regarded as stubbornly conservative states. The pan-Islamic movement which had slowly burgeoned in all the major Muslim societies under colonial rule was given a huge fillip by this demonstration that Muslims, too, could be modernizers. When Istanbul went to war with the Balkan powers again in 1913, young Muslim activists in all parts of the world, from Indonesia to Algeria, sprang to her assistance.

THE STRANGE DEATH OF INTERNATIONAL LIBERALISM

Even when we turn to internal national politics and social change across the world in 1900, a quickening of pace and boiling up of tensions since 1890 is evident. In most European countries, the earlier dominance of upper-class liberals and free-traders had given place to a politics now more sharply polarized between conservatives and leftist radicals. In Britain, the Liberal Party was now being ground to pieces between the upper millstone of urban, popular conservatism and the lower one of the rising Labour Party. Though historians have pored long over statistics in trying to disprove the existence of the phenomenon, it does seem that after 1893 a distinctively working-class Toryism came into being. The defection of Joseph Chamberlain, self-proclaimed champion of the industrial cities, from the Liberal Party to the Tories, protectionism, and imperialism partly reflected the interests of a newly enfranchised urban electorate. The moderate, reforming socialism of the British Labour Party also finally began to make headway in elections after 1896, and some trade union socialists began to be elected to Parliament.[20]

In France, the battle between liberal anticlerics and Catholic conservatism was highlighted by the Dreyfus case, in which the army made a scapegoat of a Jewish liberal. In 1902, the French left, led by Jean Jaurès, scored its greatest win since its future had been blighted by the Commune. Even in the United States, which largely avoided political extremism except in regard to the black population, some members of the Republican Party became more nationalistic. Both Democrats and Republicans of the North conjured up a popular backlash against big business and growing disparities of urban wealth, in the form of the Progressive Movement, which sought to strengthen government in the face of big business and moved away from classic liberalism. After 1900, too, the American reformist philosophy of "progressivism" began to transform itself into something more like European social democracy, a political movement concerned to ameliorate the effects of rampant capitalist development through the imposition of measures of social security and controls on the doings of the big corporations. Not only long-term proponents of the "bigger state" such as Theodore Roosevelt, but also liberal Democrats, such as the future president Woodrow Wilson, envisaged an increased role for federal government, as John A. Thompson has shown.[21]

In the Western democracies, these attacks on liberal parties and moves away from classic liberal doctrines did not, of course, imply a repudiation of the principles of representative government and a free press. On the European fringes, however, the situation was more dangerous. In 1895, the anti-Semite, Catholic extremist Karl Lueger was elected mayor of Vienna. The 1905 Russian Revolution failed, but in the process stirred vicious rightist reaction and gave the revolutionary left a clear model. Other European and American societies under great strain showed similar developments. A study of Milan has shown that small shopkeepers, under attack in a period of economic conflict from a rising socialist movement, began to look to the right as their protector after 1905.[22] In Mexico, pent-up agrarian conflict and a fierce sense of national betrayal brought about one of the most violent rural revolutions of the century. The new progressive elite, which took power in the country in 1910, ultimately compromised with the rural magnates, who contrived to cling on to their power. The shock imparted to the Spanish American world was permanent.[23]

It is not surprising, then, that contemporary Marxists and their followers among modern historians saw in these events the flexing of the muscles of organized labor and a more worrying phenomenon, the emergence of a lower-middle-class populist reaction against labor, taxation, and foreigners. Clearly, there was a quite rapid spurt of industrialization and urbanization right at the end of the nineteenth century. These social and economic changes coincided with the development of new instabilities in the international political order. Where we have to be careful, though, is in assuming that either of these developments led straightforwardly to intensified social conflict, and therefore to international war. It is as plausible to see the working classes and lower middle classes fighting hard to secure their position as "stakeholders" in a new distribution of global wealth. The onset of world revolution was, as previous chapters suggested, a powerful ideological artefact, rather than a depiction of historical reality.

Equally, there is some evidence that the international situation was beginning to stabilize by 1908 and that only a series of massive miscalculations by the powers brought about the final standoff of 1914. It is even possible that, without the impact of the First World War, the tsars' servants and the European empires might have bought off enough of their commercial and educated subjects to stagger forth into a new era. The Ottoman Empire might not have imploded but for the fact that it picked the wrong side in the war. Separatist nationalism among Arabs and even Asia Minor's Greeks was by no means dominant in 1914. Yet to doubt that the social and political trends of the 1900s led inexorably to the First World War and the age of mass colonial nationalism does not require one to deny the reality of contemporary social conflicts and the rapidity of social change.

In 1900, politics and society also appeared more polarized outside the Western world. In many societies, both colonial and semi-independent, indigenous versions of liberal politicians held sway in 1860, and even in 1880. We have already noted the lurch into "extremism" and terrorism in Egypt and India around the turn of the twentieth century. This itself reflected a much deeper shift in attitudes to politics and society. Liberalism was in retreat there, too. The language of politics was increasingly inflected with ideas of race and race war. In the Chinese Boxer Rebellion of 1900 and the swing of Japanese conservatives to "pure" indigenous values in the 1890s, we glimpse a much more robust and acerbic dismissal of the West than had been common before. The Indian seer Aurobindo Ghose, the Buddhist preacher Anagarika Dharmapala of Ceylon, and the polemicists of pan-Islamism throughout the Muslim world to one degree or another rejected liberal nationalism. They favored violent change but staked their claim not on individual rights, but on the word of God and the promptings of the blood. These themes were likely to resonate amongst an increasingly restive peasantry and an alienated working people forced into the wretched conditions of the colonial and semi-colonial industrial cities.

The old style of polite liberalism may have declined, but radical movements for the securing of rights for working people, "natives", and women appeared all over the world. Improvements in communications and the fruits of a general expansion of educational provision after 1870 seem to have provided the initial stimulus. Pan-African Congresses proliferated after 1900. The movement for the abolition of indentured labor throughout the European empires became more radical. In New Zealand, Maori associations demanded the redress of their wrongs more frequently, while at the same time enlisting to fight for the British Empire in the South African War.[24] Similar movements began to spring up in Canada and the USA. It was often in the cultural sphere that these changes first manifested themselves. As noted, women had not widely acquired the vote by 1914. Yet the spread of the notion of rights and general economic expansion thrust women into the public arena during these years. Sarah Bernhardt, the actress, became a public figure in Paris. Marie Curie followed her deceased husband as Professor of Physics at the Sorbonne in 1906.[25] In Tokyo, the publication of the Chinese serial *The Journal of Natural Principles* signaled the fact that the attack on the remaining old regimes would be closely allied with the struggles of workers, peasants, and women.[26] There thus began the struggle between radical socialism and ethnic and religious revivalism for the allegiance of the masses which has shaped much of the twentieth century and seems to have ended with the decisive victory of ethnicity, religion, and nationalism over the left.

Again, none of this meant that the coming of mass nationalism or the collapse of the reinvented old order was in any way predetermined. In 1912 and 1913 some of the most pressing nationality problems in the Balkans, western Europe, and Iran seemed to have been temporarily resolved. It is possible, too, that ruling groups in town and country might have reformed in the face of rapid social and political change, to give the elements of continuity in the "long nineteenth century" a new lease of life. In Britain, Asquith's government might have made a final successful effort to solve the Irish question. The British administration was apparently in the process of defeating the "extremist" threat in India and Egypt, at least in the medium term. The Russian government might have been able to bury leftist insurrectionism and rightist reaction in a new wave of wealth-creating industrialization. What can be said, however, is that the rapidity of political and social change was throwing governments off balance more and more often. The fading of the Ottomans, the Qajars (1909), and the Qing and the near-collapse of the tsarist and Austro-Hungarian regimes over a short period of time only seems unremarkable by comparison with the cataclysms which were to follow in 1917–19.

Lenin's view that what we are calling here the "great acceleration" after 1890 was rooted in the uneven development of capitalism at a global level still has something to recommend it, even though his longer-term predictions now seem misplaced. The Germans were worried about the political threat from a huge, unevenly developing Russia. The British feared the growing commercial might of Germany. A great political and economic rift in the core of the world economy – Britain, France, Germany, and the United States – was generalized by swirling tensions in its outer reaches – Russia, the Balkans, and the Ottoman Empire. The mechanization of agriculture in the "new Europes" of the Americas, southern Africa, and Australasia had altered the balance of class forces at home, bringing into being the "age of anxiety." New forms of large-scale capitalist production and organization of resources faced governments and societies with stark problems of social inclusiveness and social provision. The international deployment of the technology of warfare and of capital converged with a sharper understanding amongst non-European peoples of the reality of their exploitation in the international economic and political system. Yet economic differentials were themselves only measures of a wider disillusionment among intellectuals and ordinary people in Europe, Africa, and Asia alike. Most political activists now came to believe that the liberal civilization born of the compromise between revolution and hierarchy in 1815, and recalibrated around 1870, had failed. If Western intellectuals and artists such as Émile Zola, Leon Tolstoy, and Richard Wagner could so roundly condemn the worthlessness and corruption of their own civilization, how much more dramatic were the diatribes of Mohandas Gandhi, Aurobindo Ghose, and Mohammad Abduh, who saw it as an affront to God, not simply a perversion of man?

SUMMING UP: GLOBALIZATION AND CRISIS, 1780–1914

It is now time to return to some of the general issues raised in the introduction. First, what is the use and value of the global approach to historical change adopted in this book? World history is no more than one among many ways of doing history. Its profile has risen in recent years, for several reasons. After 1970, in North America and Australasia, university foundation courses in European civilization began to seem out of date to educationists in societies increasingly aware of their multicultural origins. In Europe, imperial histories – the nearest thing to global history taught there – also began to look anachronistic. The result was that scholars of empire increasingly tried to reinvent their subject as a kind of international social history of power, race, class, and culture. Scholars of national and regional history, meanwhile, became international historians. The historical profession needed a new way of making analogies, comparisons, and connections, because teachers realized instinctively that the subject had to be taught at a broader level than through the medium of national history, or even international diplomatic history.

These institutional changes were reinforced by changes in public attitudes, as a new interest in "globalization" challenged old national histories and area studies. The change registered itself quite widely. Domestic British historians, for instance, became alert once again to the way in which the slave trade and colonialism contributed to the growth of the British economy from the seventeenth to the nineteenth centuries, even if there is much disagreement about their quantitative implications. The formerly inward-looking English historical profession revised the way in which it saw English identity by expanding its interests to Ireland, Scotland, Wales, and the British beyond the seas. Writers reconsidered the way in which the experience of empire, the model of the American struggle over slavery, and the closeness of revolutionary and "dictatorial" France has shaped the British "national character" and constitution. The new British history saw Britain not as an antique organic entity, but as a construction of global as well as regional forces.

Historians of the extra-European world also began to "rescue history from the nation," in the words of Prasenjit Duara,[27] and consequently to highlight global connections that existed in earlier periods. Scholars of China, for instance, realized that the Qing court's closure of the country in the early modern period was no reason to neglect the great importance of China's "American-style" frontiers in Southeast Asia or central Asia. Here, in the offshore trade emporia and borderlands, war, wealth creation, and new cultural contacts helped shape the form of China's domestic society throughout the early modern period and on into the nineteenth century. The Qing Empire was a Manchu Empire as well as a Chinese one. The Chinese business classes were state-builders over much of Southeast Asia.

At a wider level, writers such as R. Bin Wong and Kenneth Pomeranz have rewritten the history of Western economic exceptionalism by using new data and arguments from China.[28] If, in terms of economic growth, what distinguished Europe from China before 1800 was only its intensive use of coal and the existence of a vast American hinterland to Europe, then a lot of cultural baggage about inherent European political superiorities looks ready to be jettisoned. A significant result of this is that the concept of globalization has itself been revised to take account of Chinese-centered or, equally, Islamic forms of universalism and globalization.

One aim of a world history such as this book, then, is to clarify and to probe those connections and analogies between the histories of different parts of the world.[29] This has become urgent now that regional and national historians increasingly incorporate studies in comparative historiography into their own work. World history at its best does not aim simply to tell a very general story, the virtue of which is that it is less Euro-centric than the old Western civilization courses. It also acts as a corrective to revised regional and national histories. It is a heuristic discipline which asks the question: What happens if we blow down the compartments which historians have made between this region and that region, or between this subdiscipline of history and that one? Global history points to broader connections and probes the assumptions that lie behind the narratives which regional historians construct. All historians are world historians now, though many have not yet realized it.

Of course, the aim of increasing historians' alertness to global or international connections and comparisons should not lead to the creation of a completely homogeneous picture. It should not try to elide all difference and resolutely to relativize all important trends in economies and societies. Undoubtedly, the world of the eighteenth and nineteenth centuries was more interconnected than today's historians have allowed. Yet some differences were truly irreducible. Many societies and states were "exceptional" to some degree. Some intellectual constructs were unique to particular societies and particular periods. The point is to find out why these special circumstances existed, and not merely base judgments of exceptionalism on assumptions or prejudices.

GLOBAL COMPARISONS AND CONNECTIONS, 1780–1914: CONCLUSION

This book has argued against Western exceptionalism, but also against complete relativism. It concludes that northwestern Europe was, in some significant areas, more economically, intellectually, and politically dynamic than the rest of the world at the end of the eighteenth century. Its "great divergence" from Asia and Africa after that date was not simply the result of the "failure of the rest," or even its access to coal and the Americas. It also resided in an egotistical buoyancy of philosophy, invention, public debate, and, more dismally, efficiency in killing other human beings. That point has only been made by considering Europe in the context of "the rest." It has been argued only after full weight has been given to those forms of public debate, commercial acumen, and patriotic resistance which were common in Asia and Africa, even during the eighteenth century, and which were later enlisted to empower its own nation creation and intellectual modernities.

To take another example, it is difficult to doubt that free access to land and labor, alongside a decentralized constitution, which put much weight on individual judgment, did, after all, make the United States of America "exceptional" in the world of the nineteenth century. American exceptionalism has been the founding mantra of the still-isolationist American historical profession. Yet, at the same time, American history must be studied comparatively. Many of its supposedly exceptional features can also be seen at work throughout the nineteenth century in Britain and, even more so, in its settler dominions. America continued to receive and to refashion ideologies and sensibilities derived from Europe over these years. In its history of internal colonization and treatment of American Indians and African slaves, the American elites charted a path very similar to that of contemporary European empires and their overseas expatriates, and for similar reasons, both intellectual and practical.

These are broad historiographical conclusions. This book has also had the more precise purpose of analyzing world history in the nineteenth century. History is, ultimately, about change over time. This account has attempted to isolate and analyze major turning points at a global level during the long nineteenth century. The first four chapters showed how sets of world events during given historical periods were related to each other in origin and impacted on one another over time. It is taken for granted in today's world that events far from the centers of the world economy can impact with extraordinary force on the economics and politics of those centers. Regions which are apparently peripheries in contemporary global society, such as the west bank of the river Jordan, the high valleys of Afghanistan and Kashmir, and the drug-growing lands of Colombia, can become, if only briefly, centers from which new, powerful historical changes are unleashed. Yet, insofar as it has been written at all, the history of early modern globalization has usually been written in terms of "the rise of the West."

Here, I have followed those few historians, such as Jack Goldstone,[30] John E. Wills II, and specialists on the Muslim world, who have insisted on the multicentric nature of globalization in the early modern world and its persistence into the nineteenth century and beneath the surface of Western hegemony. Europe and its American colonies may already have had a competitive advantage in several areas as early as 1750. They may have been able to exploit their own and others' industrious revolutions in local production and consumption most effectively. But this does not mean that all significant change was initiated there. The origins of change in world history remained multi-centered throughout. We need not so much to reorient world history as to decentralize it.

Chapter 3 suggested that the first tremors in the global commercial and political system which announced the coming of the global "age of revolutions" were registered in Mughal India and Safavid Iran, rather than in France or even in the American colonies. Thereafter, Asian and African events played a primary, not merely a subsidiary, role in propelling forward the global "wreck of nations" and the state forms which shaped the age of revolutions. The French defeat in Egypt in 1800–1 limited the options of the Napoleonic Empire and indirectly contributed to its defeat in Europe 15 years later. Conversely, the slave revolutions in the Caribbean in the 1790s preserved the impetus of the revolutions in Europe by consuming huge quantities of British money and manpower. This allowed the outward spiral of revolutionary conflict, not only in Europe, but also in the extra-European world, as far as the Cape of Good Hope, Java, and the China coast.

The extra-European origins of the modern "European" and "American" worlds can also be seen in the domain of economics. Competition from Indian textiles at a world level was one of the main triggers of the British Industrial Revolution. African consumer demand and taste helped to sustain it. Non-European knowledge and techniques continued to play an important part in the development of European science, philosophy, and industrial change throughout the nineteenth century.

The book argues that it is now possible to write a global history of ideas, one that also stresses the multi-centered origins of ideological production. The participants in the revolutionary events of 1780–1820 understood them in the context of philosophical traditions which were very different from each other, at least initially. But there were many common features and interconnections. British radicals, French and Haitian Jacobins, and even Dutch "liberators" on the Cape of Good Hope adapted and appropriated the language of the rights of man to their particular struggles. The contemporary South Asian understanding of "revolution," the Arabian Wahhabi idea of "renovation," and the Chinese theme of the ending of the "Mandate of Heaven" seem to come from quite different traditions of thought. Even in these cases, though, it would be wrong to contrast Western radical secularism too sharply with the supposedly cyclical, religious time of the East or Africa. The thinkers of late eighteenth-century Cairo, Delhi, Beijing, Edo, and Sokoto were also grappling with philosophical and ethical issues which arose from common global modernities of that era. These thinkers also pondered the problem of the corruption of office, the loss of legitimacy by kings, the decline of community, and the sudden collapse of livelihoods. As chapter 2 suggested, the Atlantic reformer Benjamin Franklin and the Indian religious and social critic Shah Wali-Allah were employing radically different religious assumptions and philosophical methods. Yet both men were confronting a set of linked modernities, and it makes little sense to relegate Wali-Allah to the ranks of "religious revivalists," while assigning Franklin to the ranks of secular modernizers. Neither category works very well.

This type of global, interactive analysis of political and economic conjunctures remains a useful historical tool even for the nineteenth century, a period when Europe had risen to worldwide dominance. During the 1990s, historians began charting the global implications of the 1848 rebellions. But this book has argued that the impulses generated by the "springtime of peoples" in Europe met and mingled with the consequences of two other global events with extra-European origins. The Taiping Rebellion and its consequences in East Asia and beyond was no less dramatic as a world-historical event than the American Civil War, the wider impact of which has received curiously little attention, even from American historians. The combination of these world crises profoundly affected the emerging new nationalism of Europe as well as reconstructing the nature of European dominance in Asia and Africa.

A further important example of the multiple and interconnected origins of global change arises in the case of the so-called new imperialism of the later nineteenth century. Chapter 5 accepted the argument that intensified rivalry between the great, technologically armed European powers was a critical reason for the great leap forward of European empires after 1870. The new nationalism and the "new imperialism" of the 1870s were two sides of the same coin. The most powerful forces of globalization became international-ized. Formally uniform nation-states became the biggest players on the world stage, subordinating flows of goods, peoples, and ideas to their control.

The new imperialism was also a conjunctural phenomenon, however. It arose from the collision of different types of causation. Robinson and Gallagher long ago argued that the great expansion of European territorial control in Africa and elsewhere was caused by the eruption of "local crises." Where their analysis was self-limiting was in their failure to see that these annexations were not the result of weakness and corruption in failing "native government." That was simply to echo the Victorians' own cant. Instead, patriotic self-assertion in Egypt, India, and parts of western and southern Africa was the cause, and not simply the consequence, of the more rigorous interventions and annexations by imperial powers in the late nineteenth century. It was the growing sophistication and coherence of movements of resistance to Western domination in the non-European world which created a new, contentious phase in European history. To a significant extent, then, it was change away from the apparent centers of the world economy, in the supposed African and Asian "peripheries," which galvanized the metropolitan centers into action, modernization, and conflict.

Finally, this adjusted perspective fits well with emerging interpretations of the First World War. The "great acceleration" – the dramatic speeding up of global social, intellectual, and economic change after about 1890 – set loose a series of conflicts across the world which quite suddenly, and not necessarily predictably, became unmanageable in 1913–14. This was undoubtedly a European Great War. Yet it was also a world war and, in particular, a world-wide confrontation between Britain and Germany. As many contemporaries acknowledged, this was a war which had its roots in Mesopotamia and Algeria, Tanganyika and the Caucasus, as well as on the Franco-German and German-Russian frontiers. In one sense, Lenin was right when he argued that the First World War was an "imperialist war." Economic, political, and cultural rivalries in the Balkans, Asia, and Africa were central causes of a conflict which was international in character. Yet these were not simply diplomatic crises between European powers. Instead, these struggles repre-sented the unresolved conflicts of more than 100 years of uneven social change during which the leaderships of old multiethnic polities, within and outside Europe, attempted to reorder themselves in the face of economic and political decline and the emergence of mass politics.

WHAT WERE THE MOTORS OF CHANGE?

There are some things missing, however, from a multi-centric, global history of connections and interconnections which charts the buildup of chaotic waves of events. The first is a consideration of origins. What were the root causes of change? The second missing element is the question of power. Who came to hold power in the nineteenth century, how did they use it, and how were people affected by it?

Since the late eighteenth century itself, historians and theorists have been arguing about the origins of the striking changes of the long nineteenth century, which they understood as the highroad to modernity. Some of these commentators viewed change as the inevitable playing out of deep forces in human society and the human mind. According to Hegel and, in a different way, Comte, they represented the culmination of a world-historical process in which human consciousness became free and sovereign. Ernest Gellner,[31] for his part, saw the period as one of a breakthrough to modernity, signaling the emergence, again, of a novel consciousness about the relationship of man to history. According to different varieties of socialist historians, from Karl Marx to Immanuel Wallerstein and Eric J. Hobsbawm,[32] this was the age when capitalism emerged unfettered by archaic rules about property and people to fully and finally subjugate the labor of the world. A further view, prominent since the 1980s, is that it was the dominance of the aggressive, rationalistic project of the Western intellect, manifest particularly in the counting and categorizing project of the modern state, which also provided the mainspring of social change across the colonized world.

All these arguments seem to work for some parts of the world at some periods of time during the long nineteenth century. This book has argued that, by their very nature, these forces for change must have interacted with one another. It is of little use to separate out capital, the state, or rationalistic ideology as the "prime mover." Industrialization itself only seems to have become a critical impetus to change after about 1850. But the railways and the steamship had already created powerful economic convergences across the globe even before this date. An important feature, though not the only feature of the "age of acceleration" after 1890, was the pressure generated by the rapid industrial growth of Europe, North America, and, latterly, Russia and Japan. Before this date, the socioeconomic roots of global change apparently lay more in three other types of developments. These were the rise and decline of "industrious revolutions" across the world; the effects of the "great domestication" or settlement of the world to peasant production; and, thirdly, the great expansion of seaborne commerce which linked together these discrete phenomena over the oceans.

The book has argued that Euro-American "industrious revolutions" and their non-European analogues were low-level but persistent changes which operated beneath the din of battle and state formation. The reorganization in local societies of labor, production, and consumption was accompanied by more settled patterns of daily life, rigorous timekeeping, and exploitation of low-level advances in artisan industries and resource use. Internally, these patterns of change saw the emergence of local banks and moneylenders, chains of local shops in new bazaars, and literate service classes. Externally, they quickened the pace of inter-regional and global trade. The beneficiaries of the European industrious revolutions consumed the products brought in by Asian trading companies and the sugar and tobacco of the slave plantations. Analogous populations in Asia powered Chinese overseas trade, not only in bird's-nests, sandalwood, and sea slugs, but also in raw cotton, tea, and opium.

These reorderings of society were, at root, changes in life-style and values, as well as economic changes. They reconstituted local hierarchies and made it possible for the middling sort of people to persuade the poor and dependent to adopt their styles of life. The local elites which emerged often wanted to institute a purer, more regular life-style. This promoted a kind of global "methodism" in the broadest sense of the term. Besides Methodism in Britain and the United States, these aspirations to godly respectability encompassed German Pietism, Spanish neo-Catholicism, Krio Anglicanism in West Africa, Chinese New Sect Buddhism, and the "Duties," or Faraizi, movement among Indian Muslim farmers in the productive delta of east Bengal. Changes of this sort also contributed to the growth of governmentality at the local level. These industrious and methodical people wanted to use local forms of the law and state authority to control vagabonds, wanderers, and pastoralists, and to assert their own rights to land and market access. They wanted drainage, running water, local education, and disease control. This encouraged the slow and uneven development of "statishness" or governmentality in the broadest sense. It was the "third revolution" alluded to in chapter 3, powerfully registered in the European and English-speaking overseas worlds, but finding analogies and connections globally. Thus Samuel Smiles, the Victorian apostle of self-help, became a "noble tradesman" and a "noble peasant" in his Japanese guise and recorded his most lasting successes in that country.

While godly and industrious revolutions provided a base level of change, the *Birth of the Modern World* has described the role of the autonomous and domineering aspect of increasingly centralized national and imperial states. These states constantly intervened in, and often interrupted, such longer-term patterns of social change. Quite often during the eighteenth and nineteenth centuries the principle of power seems to have cut loose completely from its social moorings. Nadir Shah, the two Napoleons, the Zulu high kings, King George of Tonga, and the European conquerors of Africa after 1870 were pure manifestations of power and the urge for dominion. Yet the book has implied that they, too, must be located in the context of changes in society, technology, and ideology. The state-builders were a product of the second age of the "military revolution." They exploited and responded to situations where the costs of armaments and military manpower ran way ahead of the capacity of states to fund them. They adapted and used the prevalent language of religious, ethnic, and national confrontation and exclusion which had been sharpened by war itself. They expanded their domineering gaze along the trade routes which had emerged as industrious and, later, industrial revolutions pulled world trade into new patterns. War and state building thereby developed a momentum of their own and brought about a brutal redivision of the world's resources. The "elephantiasis" of the European and colonial state, which had been a feature of the generation after 1780, flared up strongly in the generation before 1914.

To this extent, it is too reductionist to look for a single or even a predominant cause of global change in the long nineteenth century. If we start from capitalism and industrialization, as did the Marxist and social historians of the late twentieth century, we will inevitably find that they were the mainspring of change. If we look for the exclusive, rationalist Western state as, ironically, do contemporary historians of the "fragment," it will ineluctably seem to be the major cause of change. Instead, it is the concatenation of changes produced by the interactions of political, economic, and ideological change at many different levels that provides the key. It explains both the great divergence between Europe and non-Europe at the beginning of the century and the great acceleration of social conflict and social change at its end.

POWER IN GLOBAL AND INTERNATIONAL NETWORKS

As the last section implied, one problem with a history which charts global interconnections and the multiple origins of change is that it may find it difficult to deal with power. An emphasis on networks and connections interlinking different cultures and peoples might seem to conceal the dominant and often racialistic power of Europeans and Americans, which was the most striking feature of the era for most non-European peoples, and has remained so for many of their historians. Interconnections and networks seem to speak of dialogue and accommodation, rather than of dominance. Over and against this, interpretations of the period which stress power and dominance often seem one-dimensional. This was true of the world systems theories of the 1960s and 1980s, which sometimes appeared to do little more than chart the rise of the capitalist world system, relegating everything else to the conceptual dustbins of "periphery" and "semi-periphery." It is also true of some recent postcolonial cultural studies approaches to the nineteenth century. These replace Western economic imperialism as the key actor with the rise of white, rationalist hegemony, which is held to relegate the essence of the non-West – the values of local community and cherished difference – to a conceptual periphery. The dualism of "West" and "non-West" is reproduced in culture rather than economics. At heart, this is also a description, rather than a historical analysis. It explains something, but not very much.

This book has shown that it is possible to describe the world in the nineteenth century as a complex of overlapping networks of global reach, while at the same time acknowledging the vast differentials of power which inhered in them. I have suggested that it was, in part, the capacity of European companies, administrators, and intellectual actors to co-opt and bend to their will existing global networks of commerce, faith, and power that explains their century-long dominance. This is not so much a theory of collaboration, as one of subordination. Afghan cavalry soldiers worked for the gentlemanly capitalists of the East India Company because it was their only option if they wished to maintain honor, family, and livelihood. It was not because they understood or approved of the activities of the grasping Europeans. Chinese merchants worked under the protection of the Dutch in the East Indies. This was not because they were "selling out" to colonialism; for decades, even centuries, they had only the vaguest sense of the nature of colonial power and resources. It was because they were incorporated into a vaster system of commercial exploitation by the availability of silver, goods, and protection within the ambit of the Dutch power. It was the parasitic and "networked" nature of Western domination and power which gave it such strength, binding together, and tapping into, a vast range of viable networks and aspirations.

Outside Japan, it was some years beyond the terminal date of this book that this European dominance began to flake and decay over much of the colonial world. It did not really happen until the 1930s in India and China, the 1950s and 1960s in Africa, and the 1980s in the Soviet Empire and the Latin American world, as native and indigenist movements began to emerge. Huge differentials in income and life fulfillment between "North" and "South" persisted in the contemporary world, worsened again by disease and war. Yet Western political dominance and ideological hegemony were both highly unstable. Even at their height in the last third of the nineteenth century, they already seemed friable and vulnerable. In part, this was because popular and subaltern rebellions against exploitation erupted constantly to test the weaker forms of political and economic domination. The dominant groups could not hold onto power if popular resistance combined with powerful external critiques of those forms of domination mounted by dissident dominant groups or middling people. Even at the height of the influence of the new state, the European empire, and the dominion of capital, a myth of the popular resistance had spread out across the world. This became a political force in its own right.

Yet there were also other reasons for the friability of Western dominance and of the power of the triumvirate of royalty, capital, and land within Europe itself. Networks of patronage that secured the cooperation or acquiescence of subordinate groups may well have been able to maintain the dominance and intellectual hegemony of the new ruling groups in the medium term. But they also made possible leakages and the transfer of power and intellectual skills from those elites to the people without power. Ironically, European doctrines of power and resistance, and European techniques for mobilizing resources, combined with local ideologies outside the developed core of the world economy. They created powerful hybrids which began to subvert European dominance.

This kind of *transference* happened for a number of different reasons in different domains. In the economic domain, the very nature of capitalist accountancy and economic rationality constantly sought to "off-lay" costs to more impoverished parts of the world. It was cheaper to employ Sicilians, Corsicans, Irish, Algerians, Indo-Chinese, or Filippinos in the armed forces and administrative structures of the colonial territories than Frenchmen, Americans, and so on. Asians and Africans were recruited into the organs of governmentality and developed new skills. In the political domain, domestic political conflicts in Europe and the USA acted constantly to fracture dominance and hegemony. They provided small but important possibilities for self-assertion by elite colonial nationalist politicians and, eventually, for a wider range of spokesmen from disadvantaged peoples. For instance, the political battles between Catholic right and republican left in France, between Liberals and Conservatives in Britain, or between Protestants and Catholics across the religious realm, created rhetorical openings and ideological contradictions. Indigenous activists were quick to notice and exploit them, denouncing missionaries for ignorance and administrators for hypocrisy.

In the realm of ideas, the unintended consequences of domineering imperial expansion were quite apparent. If these connections caused colonized intellectuals to create tame, "derivative discourses," it also gave them the opportunity to dissect Western ideologies, to emphasize their inconsistencies, and to construct potent, hybrid species of ideas which appealed both to local audiences and to the wider world. The pan-Islamic teachers Jamal al-din al-Afghani and Muhammad Abduh achieved such a successful cross-breeding. Again, Gandhi's marriage of Ruskin's aesthetics and Tolstoy's communitarianism to the indigenous discourses of *swadeshi* (home industry) and the "good artisan" produced a strong hybrid which kept the British morally on the back foot until independence in 1947. Co-option into the imperial system also created new connections. Before the beginning of the twentieth century, relatively privileged and by no means racially blind Irish nationalists had begun to recruit Indian and Egyptian spokesmen into their battles for home rule within the British Isles. This "internationalized" these nationalisms and handed their ideologists new examples and analogies.

In a harsher and more dramatic way, the conflicts between the European powers created diplomatic and military "windows of opportunity" through which Asian, African, and Latin American leaders could march their troops. The new Japan, for instance, exploited the long duel between the Russian and British empires. In turn, the idea of "Asia for the Asians" encouraged the Japanese navy to cultivate support among colonized Asian peoples in its struggle with the imperial army.

In this way a proper understanding of the global networks of politics, commerce, and ideology can illuminate both the exercise of dominance of

Western imperial domination and the prefigurings of its fragmentation, which had already become apparent before 1914.

CONTESTED UNIFORMITY AND UNIVERSAL COMPLEXITY REVISITED

In addition to considering the origin of global changes in the nineteenth century, this book has also tried to show how they affected the way in which mankind lived and organized itself. One of the key themes of the book is how, over a relatively short span of 140 years, the variety of social, economic, and ideological systems across the world was significantly curtailed and how a much greater uniformity become apparent. At the same time, and paradoxically, most human societies demonstrated a much greater complexity within these limits.

THE STATE IN UNIFORM

This was most obvious in the case of the nature of the state. Many of the complex forms of sovereignty which had existed in 1780 had been amalgamated, snuffed out, or rendered purely ceremonial. Malay or German princelings, for instance, continued to exist in 1914, but administrators had now mostly bundled them into federations and other regional-level entities. They had attempted to prescribe very precisely how the powers of such princes related to those of their neighbors and to the authorities above them. Historians have traditionally viewed this as a top-down change whereby the national or imperial state moved to snuff out the earlier diversity in the interests of military and financial efficiency. Yet more important, as Max Weber would have argued, was the vaunted spirit of rationality which moved within these new political structures. Whether representative government or liberal ideology had successfully rooted themselves or not, the aims of the administrator and the accountant had prevailed.

In 1780, most societies had been ruled by bodies of nobles, clerics, or classically trained judges. By 1914, several Chinese cities had public accounts and accountants. Systems of policing and municipal auditing had been established across the Ottoman Empire, and South American cities were ruled by city councils of lawyers, rather than royal governors or their successors, the big men or caudillos. All countries, even Afghanistan, had instituted types of census, and the majority had tried to impose direct income taxes, replacing the cesses and land taxes of earlier eras. Conversely, people now generally expected something from the state in return, over and above protection and honor, which were mainly what the rulers had provided 140 years earlier. Now even colonial territories, where millions had died of starvation in the course of the nineteenth century, had their "famine codes" to preserve life, however ineffective in practice these may have been. The idea of national primary and secondary education had taken root everywhere, even if the majority of agriculturalists could not afford to let their children attend school on a regular basis.

A pervasive theme in the historical and anthropological literature since the 1980s has been resistance to the state, especially to states run by foreigners. Most writers in this vein would wish to draw attention to the persistence of multiple identities, to everyday resistance against landlord or administrator, and to the myriad of rebellions still occurring in 1914 in cases where new administrative structures or levies were thought to violate moral economies. Certainly, the recruiting sergeants of 1914–16 were to encounter resistance and rioting widely across Africa, Egypt, and Indochina. Even in the European war, men did not sacrifice themselves to the guns and bayonets as cheerfully as the older patriotic histories made out. The fact, nevertheless, that as many as 50 million young men could be mobilized, counted, equipped, fed, and thrown into battle from all corners of the globe for four years remains powerful evidence of the reach of communications and the moral and material force of the modern state.

In the 1780s, "resistance" had been part of a game of blind man's buff with the rulers, a matter of bargaining, struggling, falling out of favor at court, and coming back into favor again. Even peasant revolts were not one-sided things, because lords ultimately needed peasants to plant their fields. Peasant "desertions" or strikes as often brought an abatement of taxation or forced labor as they did village burning and execution. By 1914, the pattern of peasant and, even more, of working-class agitation was powerfully marked by the abstract rules and structures of the state. National peasant parties and leaderships had emerged to politicize protests which had earlier been resolved by lordly bounty or savage and condign punishment.

'FAITHS' IN CONTENTION

Another related social process discussed in earlier chapters was the consolidation of a concept of religion. This ensured that the theory and practice of religiosity across the world were slowly converging on common norms, especially among the more privileged. Of course, faith and the expectation of divine intervention are human attributes which are the least likely to display uniformity. Throughout our period, and especially in the run up to the year 1900, a huge variety of localized cults and decentered and mystical beliefs flourished even in long-Christian societies. The rise of a traditional shaman, the monk Rasputin, in Orthodox, modernizing Russia is only the most striking example of this. Far from turning to agnostic rationalism, anti-religious leaders throughout Europe and the Americas turned to alternative religions. Theosophy remained powerful and influenced the development of abstract art. Christian Science achieved great influence on the east coast of the United States at the very time of the United States' second scientific revolution.

Theosophical societies and Freemasons' lodges flourished; esoteric practices and forms of magical divination sprang up even in supposedly regulated religious communities such as those in Islam. It is commonly thought that austere, text-based Islam triumphed decisively over Sufi esoteric religion with the onset of modernity. But in fact, throughout North Africa and Southeast Asia, Sufism continued to spread along the lines of migration and established itself with as much vigor as the formal teaching schools in new Muslim communities. In sub-Saharan Africa, the rise of the Christian religion had come about precisely because the new religion fitted into the hierarchies and mediated between the divergent beliefs of existing local healing cults. Worship, to use modern jargon, remained radically decentered.

The point, therefore, is not that religious worship and belief had become rigidly homogeneous. It is that even these decentered manifestations of the religious had to contend more regularly with, and stake out their position in relation to, a set of assumptions about what religions ought to be which were everywhere becoming more uniform. Elite believers, teaching schools, and missionaries were proclaiming rules of conduct and belief which were now widely diffused. Even isolated populations in areas such as Melanesia or South America which had only recently come into contact with world religions witnessed spiritual movements which adopted the congregational worship and the uniform rituals typical of Islam and Christianity. The great religious systems, too, were now more clearly delineated, more authoritative with their followers, and often more bureaucratic in character. In fact, they had come to resemble states and empires, just as states and empires had become inured to enforcing patriotic belief as if it were a spiritual commitment. Chapter 9 suggested that the Roman Catholic Church emerged from the mid-century crisis with a stronger internal hierarchy. As radicalism, socialism, and that suspect hybrid, Christian socialism, became more vigorous immediately before the First World War, so the Vatican and the national hierarchies came together more vigorously to challenge and suppress deviations they did not approve of. There were severe conflicts with secularizing authorities in South America, France, and Germany between 1900 and 1920. In Poland, meanwhile, revived Catholicism proved to be a critical determinant of the spread of the nationalism which was to sever the country from Russia and Germany after the world war.

Colonial nationalisms and Chinese resurgence also called on religious traditions in their fight against foreigners, and this often served to make Islam, Buddhism, and Hinduism more coherent, if more embattled, entities in the minds of their followers. In India, the years before the First World War saw the rapprochement of modernized Hinduism in the form of the Aryan Society and neo-traditional Hinduism in the form of Societies of Ancestral Religion. Both these traditions had created more regular scriptures to face down the Bible and the Quran. But it was on the pan-Hindu symbol of Mother Cow that they grounded their common aims. Similarly, pan-Islamism was officially sponsored by the Ottoman Empire during its last stand between 1907 and 1917. The international preaching of the heirs of Sheikh Jamal al-din al-Afghani also tended to give the faith a more resolute, proselytizing, militant face. The nationalism stirred by the approach of war in Protestant Europe and North America saw a return to religion among many ruling-class people. This paralleled the Christian revival which had unfolded since the 1880s in the great working-class cities. Internal and external missionizing went hand in hand. In Britain, the new antislavery movement against the abuses of the Belgian Congo after 1890 was sponsored by Baptist and Methodist churches among the lower middle class and respectable working class. It became the biggest moral reforming movement of the end of the century, comparable to the antislavery movement at its beginning.

The growing uniformity of the claims of religion as doctrine and arbiter of practice often came into conflict with the disorganized and unstructured pattern of human belief in the supernatural. The merging of the claims of religion and state to the mind as well as the body of the subject added to the pressure on minority groups. Thus the period before the war saw unrelenting pressure on Jewish minorities in Russia and eastern Europe, even though social change was tending to assimilate them. Before 1914, harmonious social relations between Muslim, Jew, and Armenian Christian were also decaying. The pogroms and genocides of the years after 1930 were not, of course, inevitable consequences of these developments. The experience of war and depression were critical here. Yet some of the intellectual and bureaucratic tools of mass murder had already been forged before 1914.

A GLOBAL ECONOMY AND INTERNATIONAL CAPITAL

A further area where this book has charted a growing uniformity in social processes is the world economy. In terms of the means of production, the agrarian, nomadic, and forest-dwelling societies which were prevalent in 1780 had themselves been uniform. Yet the social relations of production, the variety of what was produced, and the multitude of small semi-autonomous ecological zones had fractured this uniformity into a massive, tessellated pavement. By 1914, much of this variety had been eroded. Over large areas, nomadic, hunter-gatherer, and slash-and-burn societies had been totally uprooted. In some cases, as in the Pacific and the Americas, populations had been slaughtered by white invaders and reduced by disease in a broader replay of the devastation of the *conquista* of the sixteenth century in Spanish America. Elsewhere, as in South and East Asia and parts of Africa, former nomads and "tribal" people had been forced to settle either as poor sharecroppers or penned in to become a pool of migrant labor. The final rash of wars of resistance by the world's native peoples had come between about 1850 and 1880, when Bengali Santals, Maori, Sioux, Ndebele, and Canadian Métis had battled a white invader now fortified with that most deadly of weapons, the railway. Yet a brushfire of revolt was still continuing in the first years of the twentieth century as scientific forestry and race-based policing swept in to administer the *coup de grâce*. There was a major tribal rebellion in central India in 1899, a year after the Khalifa's last stand at Omdurman in the Sudan; in the 1900s the French faced the Rif revolt, and the Germans the Maji Maji revolt in Tanganyika. Certainly, the elements of balance between peasants and the state that represented them, on the one hand, and the hunter-gatherers and nomads, on the other, had been significantly altered, to the detriment of the latter by 1914. These peoples were widely relegated to the care of anthropologists and curio collectors.

Peasant society itself was significantly different from what it had been in 1780. Only famine and poverty remained always present. However, famine and poverty had changed their shape, too, as absolute food scarcities created by drought or flood gave way to artificial scarcities caused by a collapse of entitlement to food in a market dominated by cash. By 1914, the area of the peasant world dominated by cash crop and animal-producing regimes importing their own food had grown greatly. The railway expansion of the 1860s and 1870s had been followed by a consolidation of big agricultural produce buyers. In the first years of the twentieth century, huge areas of new grain production were coming on stream in Russia, Argentina, and the Midwest of the United States. Landlordism had been transformed from a semi-feudal regime of extra-legal rights and dues into a massive agro-business as the global economy pulled out of the depression of the 1870s and 1880s. The great increase of telegraph lines and world shipping after 1900 had brought prices across the globe much more closely into alignment.

The uniformity expressed itself most forcefully in the industrial realm. There was a surge in the pace of industrial production from the 1890s into the 1910s. This reflected the transformation of the United States and Germany into the world's first corporate capitalist societies, alongside a growth in iron and steel and textile production in poorer societies. Count Witte's Russia began to "take off" in the 1890s, as cheap produce from the Ukraine and Siberia fed its industries. As part of its military industrialization project, Japan's industrial production passed 1 percent of world industrial production for the first time in 1897. Asian entrepreneurs in Bombay, Shanghai, and Alexandria began, for the first time, to claw back some of the internal market in textiles lost to foreigners. London and New York, the great financial centers of the world, took delivery of huge sums of speculative capital as investors sought new sources of profit. As diplomatic rivalries among the great powers heightened after 1898, national and imperial governments sought forcefully to advance the interest of national banks, industrial firms, and economic migrants. The fact that Britain and France were increasingly losing out in traditional spheres of economic interest to Germany, the United States, and Japan certainly helped to raise the tension in southern Africa, the Far East, and the Middle East.

THE NEW PROFESSIONS AND INTERNATIONAL PUBLIC OPINION

The rise of the state, the generalization of the concepts of religion and nation, and the steady expansion of the capitalist economy had thus given the world an outward appearance of greater uniformity by the beginning of the twentieth century. On the other hand, societies had become more complex and more varied within these broad boundaries. In 1780, a tiny group of lords, priests, and men of the pen had dominated a large number of agricultural workers and artisans. By 1914, the picture was much more complex. Perhaps 100 million people across the world were industrial workers, deploying different types of skills which were complementary to each other rather than broadly comparable. Large numbers of professional bodies of specialists had emerged. These were common across the globe, but the picture in itself was more varied. In China, the descendants of the old mandarin class were now lawyers, account-ants, newspaper editors, surgeons, pharmacists, and university lecturers. Gen-teel origins had now to be complemented with bodies of specialist knowledge and access to regulated bodies of specialists. Men still read the sayings of the Prophet, the Analects of Confucius, or the Greek and Latin classics to stock their minds, but their training required them to master bodies of new, sup-posedly objective knowledge in a large range of subfields.

If the state and the nation had grown massively in their claims and preten-sions over the period, the means of deploying power had become more complex and more conditional. Eighteenth-century regimes had all used subtle ways of influencing the opinion of their most important subjects. They had memorialized themselves as universal kings, protectors of religion, embodiments of the land, or perfecters of science. In western Europe and the American colonies, where print media were used on a wide scale, bodies of aristocrats vied for power within royal administrations and used the tools of public criticism, ridicule, satire, or subterranean whispering to undo their enemies. But even in the Asian and African realms, well-tried forms of debate among the elites could legitimate or undermine rulers. Despots, whether enlightened or oriental, were never as absolute as their caricatures suggested. By 1914, however, 100 times as many newspapers were printed as had been printed in 1780, in a huge variety of languages. A mass book-publishing industry had also emerged, and this defeated even the most assiduous of censors.

The emergence of the public in the late eighteenth and early nineteenth centuries was the particular interest of the German sociologist Jürgen Haber-mas, and the concept of a public has been used very widely by historians since the 1960s. The most recent generation has been somewhat skeptical of this "grand narrative" of the emergence of a body of critical comment "between" state and society, but commenting on both. To some writers, the most striking thing was who was excluded from the public: women, the poor, ethnic minor-ities. To them, the public has seemed to be no more than verbiage thrown up by the bourgeois elite to hide and reflect its power. The appearance of criticism was a mere ploy. To others, the public never existed. All there was, was a din of distinct but mutually unintelligible discourses. Ultimately, the appearance of debate merely co-opted and silenced the people without power. This political confidence trick was played to its utmost in the so-called democracies, where powerful vested interests simply appeared to limit their power in response to the wishes of the electorate. A widely recognized problem with the formulation of Habermas and his followers was that the notion of a public, like that of nationalism, is analyzed as if it moved from west to east and south. It was another of those great gifts of Europe and North America to the rest.

Whatever the problems with the concept of public opinion and the mobilized public, the emergence of articulated representations of something which politicians saw as "public" or "national" opinion was undoubtedly a feature of the nineteenth century. Despots were never absolute. They had always been subject to the opinion of the men of religion, the administrators, and the rumors of the markets and bazaars. Yet a huge variety of rumors and special pleading by vested interests was now capable of being represented through newspapers, books, and organized public meetings in all the world's major societies. Even where elections were pro forma rubber stamps for the state, tsar and kaiser needed to manipulate and control the thing represented as "public opinion" in a way that their ancestors did not. Even colonial governments, mouthing platitudes about their trusteeship of subject races, had to bow to "native opinion" from time to time. By 1916, the viceroy of India had abandoned the opium trade and modified the system of indentured labor in response to demands from Indian and Chinese intelligentsia as well as European liberals. Kaiser William of Germany in the same years had to placate the Liberal and Social Democratic newspapers which were attacking his foreign policy. Rather than being a mentally unstable tyrant, he appears in recent work as a ruler desperately trying to stay afloat in the currents of a powerful public opinion.

This greater complexity, within the trend to worldwide uniformity, seems characteristic of the intellectual life of the beginning of the twentieth century. In 1780, powerful bodies of received wisdom formed the context for ideas within all the world's societies. Scholars and administrators in China trying to innovate empirical methods of observation were obliged to show that their work merely reinvented aspects of Confucian classical thought. When Islamic scientists attempted to come to terms with new cosmological theories from Europe, they had to validate change by recourse to the notion that "Greek science" had always played its part in Islamic thought. Over the last generation, historians have tended to argue that the breakthrough to modern sensibilities was an ambiguous and partial one even in the West. Despite the philosophical revolution of the Enlightenment, most thinkers in western Europe and the Americas tended to argue that they were reviving the classical patria or pushing forward the gift of reason which God had given to mankind. In other words, most thought still sought the perfection of tradition. As John Pocock reemphasized, whatever its revolutionary consequences, the train of thought which nurtured the founding fathers of the United States was a grander version of the old Whig dislike of the big state and the corrupt court which continued to lurk in the British localities.

Ironically, the discovery of history as the essential mode of explanation for all phenomena, natural and human, was the most revolutionary change of the nineteenth century. Contemporary ideologies were broadly historicist and increasingly evolutionary. By binding the world to a notion of history, thinkers also envisioned a future history, the progress of species, mankind, race, nation, or religion. Scholars outside the European scientific and philosophical academies found little difficulty in creating a historical legend for their own culture. For Hindus, Lord Rama, who had been a luminous presence in scripture and landscape, became an actual historical figure. Likewise, for Ethiopians, the legendary figure of Solomon became the actual founding father of a historical past. Vigorous indigenous schools of scriptural criticism, dynastic archaeology, or medical teaching imposed Western methods of representation on non-Western traditions, living and invented. Around the turn of the century, racial-historical theorizing reached its apogee. Many theorists foresaw a coming "race war" in which by no means all predicted a victory of white Aryans. Indian philosophers turned the survival of the fittest on its head in predicting the survival of the most spiritual.

Yet there were already signs that the consensus which had shifted in the course of the century from ordering man and nature to tracing their genealogies was beginning to break up. It is almost a commonplace that from the 1890s a number of developments in both science and the humanities were sowing a new sense of doubt, though their full social consequences were not realized until after the cataclysm of the 1914–18 war. Liberalism increasingly found itself under assault from revolutionary socialist tendencies which argued for immediate class war, even before the objective and rational conditions for it had come into being. Friedrich Nietzsche argued that the individual will could break through the conventions of organic growth and change in society. Sigmund Freud "discovered" the human unconscious. The notion of uncertainty was creeping into the mathematical end of the sciences. These changes were dramatically illustrated in the arts, where atonal music, cubism, and impressionism were subverting the traditional patterns of academic figurative painting and the dominance of harmony in music. Gauguin, Klimt, and Picasso began to dislocate the classical inheritance of Western art.

Outside Europe, the reaction to historical and evolutionary thought often took the form of a rejection of what the West had claimed it stood for and a reversion on the part of intellectuals and politicians to reworked traditional forms of political practice and belief in the sacred: the aristocratic Bushido cult in Japan, worship of the terrible goddess Kali in India, and pan-Slavic spiritualism in Russia. On the surface, many of these forms seemed traditional or indigenous – the revival of the sleeping spirits of the East and of Africa, as some western commentators saw them. In fact, they clearly displayed the impact of the modernities which had been unleashed by the unified state and by the experience of industrialization. Many perceived the "Decline of the West," well before Professor Oswald Spengler began to write his book of that title. The result was an extraordinary complexity of ideological positions. Whereas in 1750, intellectuals could be assigned to a few broad schools of thought which reflected on the past in different but mutually comprehensible ways, this was no longer the case by 1900. Proponents of ancient religion who rejected modernity jostled with neo-conservatives who recognized the role of modernity, but had reshaped their own traditions to confront it. Within the modernist camp there existed a whole range of political and religious opinions, from revolutionaries and atheists to liberals and theological pragmatists.

On the one hand, it is the huge variety of ideological positions taken up and vehemently supported in print and public meetings across the world in 1900 which is so striking in comparison with 1780. There may have been theological nihilists in India at the earlier date, but by 1900 there were Indian atheists. Japanese scholars may have wept over the destruction of nature in 1780, but by 1900 there were Japanese ecologists and conservationists. Some Americans may have been interested in what they thought of as Oriental religions in 1780, but by 1900 there were white American Bahais. On the other hand, this vast variety of movements, ideologies, and sensibilities now adjusted increasingly to an international set of norms about meetings, voting, finance, communication, and the presentation of ideas. Even among the poor and those most distant from the springs of the Western capitalist world, more spontaneous and traditional forms of debate and social organization were increasingly influenced by, and molded to, the patterns of middle-class action.

AUGUST 1914

This book has put considerable weight on the development of the national state and the emergence of a globally linked economy in the course of the nineteenth century. Yet this uniformity, as we have seen, paradoxically,

ILLUSTRATION 13.3   The storm gathers: A sea-plane on the Nile, 1914.

produced its own complexity. The very linkages which created these new pervasive entities also empowered people across the world who wanted to direct, limit, or oppose them. Many of these were associated with left-wing and trade union movements, but not all. Even before 1914, international conferences were convened in vain attempts to call a halt to the arms race. Pacifist societies spread fast amongst the *fin-de-siècle* intelligentsia, and the Red Cross organization had worked since the 1870s across national borders to try to alleviate the suffering of victims of war. Even national statesmen, however, had dimly begun to perceive that cooperation across the boundaries of national states was essential simply to secure their own interests. International law developed fast in the 1900s, and several treaties were enacted which sought to control access to the deep oceans and Antarctica. The Greenwich Meridian had finally been accepted as the world's temporal reference point, despite vigorous opposition from the French, who had nominated Paris. International rules increasingly governed the movement of ships and river traffic which passed through several national territories. Late experience of bubonic plague and cholera, along with various forms of animal disease, had forced medical men across the world to come together and put in place international rules for public health. Amidst the mass slaughter of game in Africa and Asia which accompanied the high summer of imperialism, a few organizations arose to protect animals and conserve the environment, though it was in general only official agencies concerned with hard cash that succeeded in this.

The tragedy was that the international links that might have prevented the descent into destructive competition, and ultimately to war, were not strong enough to resist the catastrophic conjuncture of August 1914. As the great guns opened up in that month, people in many countries began to experience similar patterns of scarcity, conscription, death, and disease. In turn, and out of this carnage, were to emerge fierce new ideologies which stressed even more vigorously the worldwide uniformities of class or race or nation-state. This book has charted a number of key themes, particularly the role of organized violence in creating global and international linkages, the multi-centered nature of the origins of trends in world history, and the way in which crises and responses to those crises across the world were interconnected. The First World War and its aftermath were to demonstrate these themes in action yet more dramatically.

NOTES

INTRODUCTION

1   Arjun Appadurai, *Modernity at Large: Cultural Dimensions of Globalization* (Minneapolis, 2000).
2   Fernand Braudel, *Civilisation matérielle, économie, capitalisme xve–xviiie siècle* (Paris, 1979).
3   Linda Colley, *Britons: Forging the Nation 1707–1837* (London, 1992).
4   Catherine Hall, *Civilising Subjects: Metropole and Colony in the English Imagination 1830–67* (Cambridge, 2002).
5   Geoffrey Hosking, *Russia, People and Empire, 1552–1917* (London, 1997).
6   Dominic C. B. Lieven, *Empire: The Russian Empire and its Rivals* (London, 2000).
7   R. Bin Wong, *China Transformed: Historical Change and the Limits of European Experience* (Ithaca, NY, 1997).
8   Kenneth Pomeranz, *The Great Divergence: China, Europe and the Making of the Modern World Economy* (Princeton, NJ, 2000).
9   Wang Gung Wu, *The Chinese Overseas: From Earthbound China to the Quest for Autonomy* (Cambridge, Mass., 2000).
10 Joanna Waley-Cohen, *The Sextants of Beijing: Global Currents in Chinese History* (New York, 1999).
11 Michael C. Meyer and William H. Beezley (eds), *The Oxford History of Mexico* (Oxford, 2000), pp. 380–93.
12 Hew Strachan, *The First World War*, vol. 1 (Oxford, 2001).
13 Eric J. Hobsbawm, *The Age of Revolution; The Age of Capital; The Age of Empire; The Age of Extremes* (London, 1988–98).
14 Perry Anderson, "Confronting defeat," *London Review of Books*, 24, 20 (17 Oct. 2002).
15 For an initial discussion and references, see Patrick Joyce, "The return of history: post-modernism and the politics of academic history in Britain," *Past and Present*, 158 (Feb. 1998), pp. 207–35.
16 The most recent body of writers stressing the people and their resistance is the Indian Subaltern Studies Collective, which has been influential among Latin American historians. For the debates surrounding their work see Vinayak Chaturvedi (ed.), *Mapping Subaltern Studies and the Postcolonial* (London, 2000).

17 S. N. Eisenstadt, *Modernisation, Protest and Change* (Englewood Cliffs, NJ, 1966).

18 Ernest Gellner, *Plough, Sword and Book: The Structure of Human History* (London, 1988).

19 Alan Macfarlane, *The Riddle of the Modern World: Of Liberty, Wealth and Equality* (Basingstoke, 2000).

20 David Landes, *The Wealth and Poverty of Nations* (London, 1998); *idem, Favourites of Fortune: Technical Growth and Economic Development since the Industrial Revolution* (Cambridge, 1991).

21 "Spirit capture: the native Americans and the photographic image," *International Herald Tribune*, 25–6 Aug. 2001.

22 R. C. Cobb, *Death in Paris: The Records of the Basse-Géole de la Seine* (Oxford, 1978).

23 The role of the state in this process was studied in the work of Norbert Elias (tr. Edmund Jephcott), *The Civilizing Process:* vol. 2: *State Formation and Civilization* (Oxford, 1994).

24 Emma Tarlo, *Clothing Matters: What to Wear in Colonial India* (London, 1998).

25 Ismail Hami, cited by Bernard Lewis, *The Emergence of Modern Turkey* (London, 1961), p. 231.

26 Hasan Kayali, *Arabs and Young Turks: Ottomanism, Arabism and Islamism in the Ottoman Empire 1908–18* (Berkeley, 1997), p. 63.

27 E. M. Collingham, *Imperial Bodies: The Physical Experience of the Raj c.1800–1947* (London, 2001).

28 "Newspaper," in *Encyclopaedia Britannica*, 13th edn (London, 1911), vol. 19, pp. 19–20.

CHAPTER I OLD REGIMES AND "ARCHAIC GLOBALIZATION"

1 John Komlos, *Stature, Living Standards and Economic Development: Essays in Anthropometric History* (Chicago, 1994).

2 Marshall G. S. Hodgson, *The Venture of Islam: Conscience and History in a World Civilisation*, 3 vols (Chicago, 1974).

3 Joseph Fletcher, "Turko-Mongolian tradition in the Ottoman Empire," in I. Sevcenko and Frank E. Sysyn (eds), *Eucharisterion*, vol. 1 (Cambridge, Mass., 1978), pp. 240–1.

4 Pamela Crossley, *A Translucent Mirror: History and Identity in Qing Imperial Ideology* (Berkeley, 1999), compares China with Peter Burke, *The Fabrication of Louis XIV* (New Haven, 1992).

5 W. Beik, *Absolutism and Society in Seventeenth-Century France: State Power and Provincial Aristocracy in Languedoc* (Cambridge, 1988).

6 I. M. Kunt, *The Sultan's Servants: The Transformation of Ottoman Provincial Government 1550–1650* (New York, 1983).

7 Burton Stein, *A History of India* (Oxford, 1998); but see John F. Richards, *The Mughal Empire* (Cambridge, 1995), and Irfan Habib, *The Agrarian System of Mughal India (1556–1707)* (Bombay, 1963); Sugata Bose and Ayesha Jalal, *Modern South Asia: Culture, Political Economy* (Delhi, 1998).

8 Jonathan Spence, *The Search for Modern China* (New York, 1990), pp. 112, 144, 157.

9 Evelyn S. Rawski, *The Last Emperors: A Social History of Qing Imperial Institutions* (Berkeley, 1998).

10 Ivor Wilks, *Asante in the Nineteenth Century: The Structure and Evolution of a Political Order* (Cambridge, 1975).

11 P. J. Bakewell, *A History of Latin America* (London, 1997), pp. 282–3.

12 Spence, *Search for Modern China*, pp. 165–70.

13 William Doyle, "The Union in a European context," *Transactions of the Royal Historical Society*, 6 ser., 10 (2000), p. 168.

14 Lieven, *Empire*, p. 204; Richard Pipes, *Russia under the Old Regime* (London, 1974), p. 204.

15 Lieven, *Empire*, p. 171.

16 Crossley, *Translucent Mirror*.

17 Kunt, *Sultan's Servants*; private communication from Prof. Kunt.

18 D. H. A. Kolff, *Naukar, Rajput and Sepoy: The Ethnohistory of the Military Labour Market in Hindustan 1450–1850* (Cambridge, 1986).

19 Rawski, *Last Emperors*.

20 Leonard Blussé⁀, *Strange Company: Chinese Settlers, Mestizo Women and the Dutch in VOC Batavia* (Dordrecht, 1986).

21 Timothy Brook, *The Confusions of Pleasure: Commerce and Culture in Ming China* (Berkeley, 1998).

22 John Iliffe, *Africans: The History of a Continent* (London, 1995), pp. 62–127.

23 A. G. Hopkins, *An Economic History of West Africa* (London, 1973).

24 Donald Denoon and Philippa Mein-Smith with Marivic Wyndham, *A History of Australia, New Zealand and the Pacific* (London, 2000), pp. 9–33.

25 Hamid Algar, *Religion and State in Iran 1785–1906* (Berkeley, 1969).

26 John T. Alexander, *Autocratic Politics in a National Crisis: The Imperial Russian Government and Pugachev's Revolt, 1773–5* (Bloomington, Ind., 1969).

27 Jan de Vries, *The Dutch Rural Economy in the Golden Age 1500–1700* (New Haven, 1978).

28 I have tried to develop the concept of archaic globalization more fully in A. G. Hopkins (ed.), *Globalization in World History* (London, 2002), pp. 47–73.

29 James L. Hevia, *Cherishing Men from Afar: Qing Guest Ritual and the Macartney Embassy of 1795* (Durham, NC, 1995).

30 Denoon et al., *History of Australia*, pp. 43–4.

31 See, e.g., Firdausi, "Shahnamah" painted for the Emperor Akbar, c.1595, Add. MSS 12208, ff. 280b, British Library, London, where Iskander (Alexander) meets the Brahmins in a Persianate landscape, recalling his earlier meeting with the Greek sages.

32 e.g., Moorcroft Papers, MSS Eur D 251, ff. 300–39, Oriental and India Office Collections, British Library, London.

33 See, e.g., "Akhlaq-i-Jalali" (tr. W. F. Thompson), *The Practical Philosophy of the Muhammadan People* (London, 1836), esp. introduction.

34 J. G. A. Pocock, *The Machiavellian Moment: Florentine Political Thought and the Atlantic Republican Tradition* (Princeton, 1975).

35 Napoleon famously stated that in Egypt he was a Muhammadan and that he would return the Jews to the Temple; for Tone, see Theobald Wolfe Tone (ed. R. Barry O'Brien), *The Autobiography of Theobald Wolfe Tone* (London, 1893), vol. 2, p. 303.

36 This, of course, is not to say that much local and even some inter-regional trade in archaic Eurasia was not generated by the more pragmatic exchange of basic food and other commodities, merely that long-distance transactions were particularly influenced by the exchange of charismatic items of this sort.

37 Appadurai, *Modernity at Large*.

38 Glyndwr Williams and P. J. Marshall, *The Great Map of Mankind: British Perceptions of the World in the Age of Enlightenment* (London, 1982).

39 Nigel Leask, "Francis Wilford and the colonial construction of Hindu geography," in Amanda Gilroy (ed.), *Romantic Geographies: Discourses of Travel, 1775–1844* (Manchester, 2000), pp. 204–23; C. A. Bayly, "Orientalists, informants and critics in Benares, 1790–1860," in Jamal Malik (ed.), *Perceptions of Mutual Encounters in South Asian History, 1760–1860* (Wiesbaden, 2000), pp. 172–210.

40 Cf. M. C. G. Saiz, *Las castas mexicanas: un genero pictorico americano* (Mexico City, 1989).

41 F. Dikotter, *The Discourse of Race in Modern China* (London, 1992).

42 Sanjay Subrahmanyam, "Du Tage au Gange au xvie siècle: une conjoncture millénariste à l'échelle eurasiatique," *Annales*, 1 (Jan.–Feb. 2001), pp. 51–84.

43 Pomeranz, *Great Divergence*.

CHAPTER 2 PASSAGES FROM THE OLD REGIMES TO MODERNITY

1 These issues will be addressed in John F. Richards, *The Unending Frontier: Environmental History in the Early Modern Centuries* (Berkeley, 2003).

2 Bakewell, *History of Latin America*, pp. 262–3.

3 Iliffe, *Africans*, pp. 97–126.

4 Maurice Bloch, *Ritual, History and Power: Selected Papers in Anthropology* (London, 1998).

5 Denoon et al., *History of Australia*, pp. 41–2.

6 Ibid., p. 86.

7 Jan de Vries, "The Industrial Revolution and the industrious revolution," *Journal of Economic History*, 54 (1994), pp. 240–70.

8 Jan de Vries and Adriaan van de Woude, *The First Modern Economy* (Cambridge, 1997).

9 Hans Joachim Voth, *Time and Work in England 1750–1830* (Oxford, 2000).

10 This is brought together in Pomeranz, *Great Divergence*.

11 Evelyn S. Rawski and Susan Naquin, *Chinese Society in the Eighteenth Century* (New Haven, 1987).

12 Francesca Bray, *Technology and Gender: Fabrics of Power in Late Imperial China* (Berkeley, 1997), p. 82.

13 Conrad Totman, *A History of Japan* (London, 2000), pp. 246–57; T. C. Smith, *The Agrarian Origins of Modern Japan* (Stanford, Calif., 1959).

14 Prasannan Parthasarathi, *The Transition to a Colonial Economy: Weavers, Merchants and Kings in South India* (Cambridge, 2000).

15 J. R. Perry, *Karim Khan Zand* (Chicago, 1979).

16 André Gunder Frank, *ReOrient: Global Economy in the Asian Age* (London, 1998); cf. Jack Goody, *The East in the West* (Cambridge, 1996).

17 Kenneth Pomeranz, "Rethinking the late imperial Chinese economy: development, disaggregation and decline 1730–1930," *Itinerario*, 24, 3/4, (2000), pp. 29–75.

18 C. A. Bayly, "South Asia and the great divergence," *Itinerario*, 24, 3/4 (2000), pp. 89–104.

19 Sevket Pamuk, *The Ottoman Empire and European Capitalism, 1820–1930* (Cambridge, 1987).

20 Pomeranz, *Great Divergence*.
21 Mark Elvin, *The Pattern of the Chinese Past* (London, 1973).
22 P. K. O'Brien (ed.), *The Industrial Revolution in Europe*, 2 vols (Oxford, 1994).
23 A. G. Hopkins, "Asante and the Victorians: transition and partition on the Gold Coast," in Roy E. Bridges (ed.), *Imperialism, Decolonisation and Africa: Studies Presented to John Hargreaves* (Basingstoke, 2000), pp. 39–42.
24 Sevket Pamuk, *A Monetary History of the Ottoman Empire* (Cambridge, 2000).
25 Pipes, *Russia under the Old Regime*.
26 K. N. Chaudhuri, *Asia before Europe: Economy and Civilisation of the Indian Ocean from the Rise of Islam to c.1750* (Cambridge, 1990).
27 N. A. M. Rodger, "Sea-power and empire, 1688–1793," in P. J. Marshall (ed.), *The Oxford History of the British Empire*, vol. 2: *The Eighteenth Century* (Oxford, 1998), pp. 169–83.
28 Niels Steensgaard, unpublished paper, Leiden, 1994.
29 Dominic C. B. Lieven, *Nicholas II* (London, 1993), p. 10.
30 He wrote a pamphlet, "A la nation artésienne": Doyle, "Union in European context,", p. 176.
31 E. A. Wrigley, *People, Cities and Wealth: The Transition of Traditional Society* (Oxford, 1988).
32 Adrian Hastings, *The Construction of Nationhood: Ethnicity, Religion and Nationalism* (Cambridge, 1997), p. 101.
33 Ibid.
34 T. C. W. Blanning, *The Power of Culture and the Culture of Power* (Oxford, 2001).
35 Dennis Showalter, *The Wars of Frederick the Great* (London, 1996); Hagen Shulze, *The Course of German Nationalism: From Frederick the Great to Bismarck 1763–1867* (Cambridge, 1982).
36 John A. Davis (ed.), *Italy in the Nineteenth Century* (Oxford, 2000), p. 8, citing E. Galli della Loggia, *L'identità italiana* (Bologna, 1998) and A. Schiavone, *Italiani senza Italia: storia ed identità* (Turin, 1998).
37 Dr C. M. Clark, personal communication.
38 Kathleen Wilson, *The Sense of the People: Politics, Culture and Imperialism in England, 1715–1785* (Cambridge, 1995).
39 Brian Allen, in C. A. Bayly, *The Raj: India and the British 1600–1947* (London, 1990), pp. 29–31.
40 Lieven, *Empire*, p. 163, citing C. Ingrao, *The Habsburg Monarchy 1619–1815* (Cambridge, 1994), p. 191.
41 Joanna Waley-Cohen, "Commemorating war in eighteenth-century China," *Modern Asian Studies*, 30, 4 (1996), pp. 869–99.
42 M. Roberts, "Beyond Anderson: reconstructing and deconstructing Sinhala nationalist discourse," *Modern Asian Studies*, 30 (1996), pp. 690–8.
43 Totman, *History of Japan*, pp. 219–20.
44 Henri Terasse, *Histoire du Maroc, des origines à l'établissement du protectorat français* (Casablanca, 1950).
45 Hastings, *Construction of Nationhood*, pp. 155–6.
46 Iliffe, *Africans*, pp. 173–80.
47 J. B. Peiris (ed.), *Before and After Shaka* (Grahamstown, 1983); J. D. Omer-Cooper, *The Zulu Aftermath* (London, 1966).
48 Thomas McCarthy, *The Critical Theory of Jürgen Habermas* (London, 1984).
49 Most recently, Peter Clark, *British Clubs and Societies, 1580–1800: The Origins of an Associational World* (Oxford, 2000).
50 Benjamin Franklin, *Autobiography*, Everyman edn (London, 1906).
51 Landes, *Wealth and Poverty of Nations*.

52 Mervyn Hiskett, *The Development of Islam in West Africa* (London, 1984), pp. 156–71.

53 S. A. A. Rizvi, *Shah Walli-allah and his Times* (Canberra, 1980).

54 J. S. Grewal, *The Sikhs of the Punjab* (Cambridge, 1994).

55 Spence, *Search for Modern China*, pp. 60–3.

56 Ibid., p. 62.

57 Ki-baik Lee (tr. E. W. Wagner), *New History of Korea* (Seoul, 1986), pp. 236–8.

58 Totman, *History of Japan*, pp. 259–72.

59 Chaudhuri, *Asia before Europe*.

60 Janet Abu Lughod, *Before European Hegemony: The World System AD 1250–1350* (New York, 1989).

61 Anthony Pagden, *The Lords of All the World: Ideologies of Empire in Spain, Britain and France c.1500–c.1800* (New Haven, 1995); David Armitage, *The Ideological Origins of the British Empire* (Cambridge, 2000).

62 Spence, *Search for Modern China*, pp. 300–2.

CHAPTER 3   CONVERGING REVOLUTIONS, 1780–1820

1   Michael Lienesch, *New Order of the Ages: Time, the Constitution and the Making of Modern American Political Thought* (Princeton, 1988).

2   John Stuart Mill, *Autobiography* (1873; repr. London, 1949), p. 53.

3   See C. A. Bayly, "The first age of global imperialism 1780–1830," in Peter Burroughs and A. J. Stockwell (eds), *Managing the Business of Empire: Essays in Honour of D. K. Fieldhouse* (London, 1998), pp. 28–43.

4   M. Ricklefs, *A History of Modern Indonesia since 1300* (London, 1993).

5   David Morgan, *Medieval Persia 1040–1797* (London, 1988).

6   John F. Richards, *The Mughal Empire* (Cambridge, 1995).

7   Philip A. Kuhn, *Soulstealers: The Chinese Sorcery Scare of 1768* (Cambridge, Mass., 1990).

8   Stanford J. Shaw, *Between Old and New: The Ottoman Empire under Selim III 1789–1807* (Cambridge, Mass., 1971).

9   Geoffrey Parker, *The Military Revolution: Military Innovation and the Rise of the West, 1500–1800* (Cambridge, 1988); Jeremy Black, *European Warfare 1660–1815* (London, 1994).

10 D. B. Ralston, *Importing the European Army: The Introduction of European Military Techniques and Institutions into the extra-European World 1600–1914* (Chicago, 1990).

11 John Rule, *The Vital Century: England's Developing Economy 1714–1815* (Harlow, 1992), p. 276.

12 Black, *European Warfare*.

13 Bakewell, *History of Latin America*, pp. 280–93; D. A. Brading, *The First America: The Spanish Monarchy, Creole Patriots and the Liberal State 1492–1867* (Cambridge, 1991), pp. 467–91.

14 Emma Rothschild, "The East India Company and the American Revolution," unpublished paper, Centre for History and Economics, University of Cambridge, 2002.

15 R. R. Palmer, *The Age of Democratic Revolution*, 2 vols (London, 1959, 1964); Hugh Brogan, *The Penguin History of the USA* (London, 1999), pp. 110–85.

16 See Marshall (ed.), *Oxford History of the British Empire*, vol. 2, introduction; C. A. Bayly, *Imperial Meridian: The British Empire and the World 1780–1830* (London, 1989).

17 "De l'influence de la révolution d'Amérique sur Europe" (1786), in A. Condorcet O'Connor and M. Arago (eds), *Oeuvres de Condorcet* (Paris, 1847–9), viii. 19, cited in Emma Rothschild, "Globalisation and democracy in historical perspective," unpublished paper, Centre for History and Economics, University of Cambridge, 2000.

18 William Doyle, *The Origins of the French Revolution* (Oxford, 1988).

19 D. Sutherland, *France 1789–1815: Revolution and Counter-Revolution* (London, 1985).

20 Martin Lyons, *Napoleon Bonaparte and the Legacy of the French Revolution* (London, 1994), pp. 229–43.

21 Stuart Woolf, *Napoleon's Integration of Europe* (London, 1989); Geoffrey Ellis, *Napoleon: Profiles in Power* (Harlow, 1997).

22 Woolf, *Napoleon's Integration of Europe*, p. 183.

23 L. Bergeron, *Banquiers, négociants et manufacturiers parisiens du directoire à l'empire* (Paris, 1975), pp. 156–8.

24 C. L. R. James, *The Black Jacobins: Toussaint L'Ouverture and the San Domingo Revolution* (London, 2001); Michael Duffy, *Soldiers, Sugar and Seapower: The British Expeditions to the West Indies and the War against Revolutionary France* (Oxford, 1987).

25 Bakewell, *History of Latin America*; Kuhn, *Soulstealers*, pp. 5–25.

26 Iliffe, *Africans*, pp. 173–6.

27 "Declaration and resolutions of the First Continental Congress," 14 October 1774, in *Documents Illustrative of the Formation of the Union of the American States* (Washington, DC, 1927), p. 5.

28 Robert Darnton, *The Forbidden Best-Sellers of Pre-Revolutionary France* (London, 1996); cf. Keith Baker, *Inventing the French Revolution: Essays on French Political Culture in the Eighteenth Century* (Cambridge, 1990); Mona Ozouf, "L'Opinion publique," in Keith Baker (ed.), *The Political Culture of the Old Regime* (Oxford, 1987), pp. 419–34; Colin Lewis, "Pulling teeth in eighteenth-century Paris," *Past and Present*, 166 (2000), pp. 100–45.

29 Blanning, *Culture of Power*, develops this theme for France and for Europe more widely.

30 Lynn Hunt, *Politics, Culture and Class in the French Revolution* (Berkeley, 1984).

31 François Furet and Mona Ozouf, *Dictionnaire critique de la révolution française* (Paris, 1988).

32 Spence, *Search for Modern China*, pp. 110–16.

33 Sugito Genpaku, "Nochimigusa," cited by Takeuchi Makoto, "Festivals and fights: the law and the people of Edo," in James L. McClain et al. (eds), *Edo and Paris: Urban Life and the State in the Early Modern Era* (Ithaca, NY, 1994), p. 385.

34 Totman, *History of Japan*, pp. 271–2.

35 Anand A. Yang, *Bazaar India: Markets, Society and the Colonial State in Bihar* (Berkeley, 1998), pp. 53–111.

36 Grewal, *Sikhs of the Punjab*.

37 Carter V. Findley, *Bureaucratic Reform in the Ottoman Empire: The Sublime Porte 1789–1922* (Princeton, 1980).

38 Ibn Bishr, cited in R. Bayly Winder, *Saudi Arabia in the Nineteenth Century* (New York, 1965), p. 13.

39 Stuart Woolf, *A History of Italy 1700–1860* (London, 1979), pp. 255–65.

40 e.g., William H. Sewell, *Work and Revolution in France: The Language of Labour from the Old Regime to 1848* (Cambridge, 1980).

41 Gamal el-din el-Shayyal, "Some aspects of intellectual and social life in eighteenth-century Egypt," in P. M. Holt (ed.), *Political and Social Change in Modern Egypt* (London, 1968), pp. 117–32.

42 J. Tulard (ed.), *Dictionnaire Napoléon* (Paris, 1987), p. 451.

43 Woolf, *Napoleon's Integration of Europe*.

44 Williams and Marshall, *Great Map of Mankind*.

45 Matthew Edney, *Mapping an Empire: The Geographical Construction of British India 1765–1843* (Chicago, 1997).

46 Richard Drayton, *Nature's Government: Science, Imperial Britain and the "Improvement" of the World* (London, 2000).

47 Ranajit Guha, *Towards a Rule of Property for Bengal* (The Hague, 1963).

48 James J. Sheehan, *German History 1770–1866* (Oxford, 1989), pp. 470–84.

49 Denoon et al., *History of Australia*, p. 107.

50 Giuseppe Mazzini, *Ricordi autobiografici di Giuseppe Mazzini con introduzione e note di Mario Menghini* (Imola, 1938), p. 7.

51 Cited in Orlando Figes, *Natasha's Dance: A Cultural History of Russia* (London, 2002), p. 72.

52 Khaled Fahmy, *All the Pasha's Men: Mehmed Ali, his Army and the Making of Modern Egypt* (Cambridge, 1997); cf. Afaf Lutfi al-Sayyid Marsot, *Egypt in the Reign of Muhammad Ali* (Cambridge, 1984).

53 Cf. C. A. Bayly, *The Origins of Nationality in South Asia: Patriotism and Ethical Government in the Making of Modern India* (Delhi, 1998), pp. 63–97.

54 Spence, *Search for Modern China*, pp. 143–52; Mark W. McLeod, *The Vietnamese Response to French Intervention 1862–74* (New York, 1991), pp. 13–21.

55 Gordon S. Wood, "The significance of the early Republic," in Ralph D. Cray and Michael A. Morrison (eds), *New Perspectives on the Early Republic* (Urbana, Ill., 1994), p. 14.

56 Ibid.

57 Denoon et al., *History of Australia*, pp. 100–1.

58 Alan Atkinson, *The Europeans in Australia: A History*, vol. 1 (Oxford, 1997).

59 Leila Tarazi Fawaz, *Merchants and Migrants in Nineteenth-Century Beirut* (Cambridge, Mass., 1982).

60 Robert Ilbert (ed.), *Alexandrie entre deux mondes* (Aix-en-Provence, 1988).

61 Denoon et al., *History of Australia*, pp. 82–3; for southern Africa, see Norman Etherington, *The Great Treks: The Transformation of Southern Africa 1815–54* (London, 2001).

CHAPTER 4 BETWEEN WORLD REVOLUTIONS, C.1815–1865

1 Charles Tilly, *Coercion, Capital and States AD 900–1992* (Cambridge, Mass., 1992), p. 165.

2 Bakewell, *History of Latin America*, pp. 385–408.

3 Alexis de Tocqueville, *The Old Regime and the French Revolution* (New York, 1955).

4 S. A. A. Rizvi, *Shah Abd al-Aziz: Puritanism, Sectarian Politics and Jihad* (Canberra, 1982).

5 Spence, *Search for Modern China*, p. 144.

6 B. R. Tomlinson, in Andrew Porter (ed.), *The Oxford History of the British Empire* (hereafter *OHBE*), vol. 3: *The Nineteenth Century* (Oxford, 1999), pp. 52–73.

7 Yrjo Kaukiainen, "The improvement of communications in international freight markets c.1830–1870," in Hiram Morgan (ed.), *Information, Media and Power through the Ages* (Dublin, 2001), pp. 137–52.

8 William L. Cleveland, *A History of the Modern Middle East* (Boulder, Colo., 1994), pp. 64–75; Roger Owen, *Cotton and the Egyptian Economy: A Study in Trade and Development* (Oxford, 1969); al-Sayyid Marsot, *Egypt in the Reign of Muhammad Ali*; Fahmy, *All the Pasha's Men*.

9 K. N. Chaudhuri, in Dharma Kumar (ed.), *The Cambridge Economic History of India*, vol. 2 (New Delhi, 1983), pp. 874–8.

10 Douglass C. North, *The Economic Growth of the United States, 1790–1860* (Englewood Cliffs, NJ, 1961).

11 Bakewell, *History of Latin America*, p. 443.

12 Ricklefs, *History of Modern Indonesia*.

13 Woolf, *History of Italy*, p. 263.

14 P. Elphick and H. Giliomee, *The Shaping of South African Society 1600–1850* (London, 1983).

15 Denoon et al., *History of Australia*, pp. 127–8.

16 Cf. Akintola J. Wyse, "Britain's African junior partners: a re-examination of the role of the Krio in nineteenth-century West Africa," in Bridges (ed.), *Imperialism, Decolonisation*, pp. 3–24.

17 George R. Taylor, *The Transportation Revolution 1815–1860* (London, 1951).

18 Sheehan, *German History*, pp. 466–85.

19 Laven, in Davis (ed.), *Italy*, ch. 2, and M. Meriggi, *Amministrazione e classi sociali nel Lombardo-Veneto 1814–48* (Bologna, 1983).

20 Marjorie Harper, in Porter (ed.), *OHBE*, 3, pp. 73–100; Dudley Bains, *Emigration from Europe 1815–1930* (Basingstoke, 1991).

21 David Northrup, in Porter (ed.), *OHBE*, 3, pp. 88–99; see also Robert L. Irick, *Ch'ing Policy towards the Coolie Trade 1847–1878* (Taipei, 1982).

22 Rajat Kanta Ray, "Asian capital in the age of European domination: the rise of the bazaar, 1800–1914," *Modern Asian Studies*, 29, 3 (1993), pp. 449–554.

23 Hugh Tinker, *A New System of Slavery: The Export of Indian Labour Overseas 1830–1920* (London, 1974).

24 Nigel Worden, *The Making of Modern South Africa* (Oxford, 1994); A. du Toit and H. Giliomee (eds), *Afrikaner Political Thought*, vol. 1 (Berkeley, 1983).

25 Denoon et al., *History of Australia*, pp. 130–6; C. Saunders and I. R. Smith, in Porter (ed.), *OHBE*, 3, pp. 601–4.

26 Cormac O'Grada, *The Great Irish Famine* (Dublin, 1989); Christine Kinealy, *This Great Calamity: The Irish Famine 1845–52* (Dublin, 1994).

27 W. A. Speck, *A Concise History of Britain 1707–1975* (Cambridge, 1999), pp. 78–80; Eric J. Evans, *The Forging of the Modern State: Early Industrial Britain 1783–1870* (London, 1983).

28 F. List (tr. S. Lloyd), *The National System of Political Economy* (London, 1885).

29 Miklos Molnar, *A Concise History of Hungary* (Cambridge, 2001), p. 169.

30 Ronald Robinson and John Gallagher, "The imperialism of free trade," *Economic History Review*, 2, ser. 6, 1 (1953), pp. 1–15; D. C. M. Platt, *Finance, Trade and Politics in British Foreign Policy 1815–1914* (Oxford, 1968).

31 Davis, in Davis (ed.), *Italy*, p. 247.

32 Owen, *Cotton and the Egyptian Economy*.

33 J. Y. Wong, *Deadly Dreams: Opium and the Arrow War (1856–60) in China* (Cambridge, 1998).

34 Lyons, *Napoleon Bonaparte*.
35 John Cannon, *Parliamentary Reform 1640–1832* (Cambridge, 1973).
36 T. C. W. Blanning and Peter Wende, *Reform in Britain and Germany, 1750–1850* (Oxford, 1999).
37 Raymond Carr, *Spain, 1808–1939* (Oxford, 1966), pp. 129–46.
38 Molnar, *Concise History of Hungary*, pp. 168–9.
39 Cited in J. P. T. Bury and R. P. Tombs, *Thiers 1797–1877: A Political Life* (London, 1986), p. 34.
40 Cited in John F. Coverdale, *The Basque Phase of Spain's First Carlist War* (Princeton, 1984), p. 274.
41 Hosking, *Russia, People and Empire*.
42 Stanford J. Shaw, *A History of the Ottoman Empire and Modern Turkey*, vol. 2: *Reform, Revolution and Republic: The Rise of Modern Turkey 1808–1975* (Cambridge, 1975), pp. 43–56.
43 C. A. Bayly, *Indian Society and the Making of the British Empire* (Cambridge, 1988), ch. 4.
44 Spence, *Search for Modern China*, pp. 145–8; James M. Polachek, *The Inner Opium War* (Cambridge, Mass., 1992).
45 John Keep, *Soldiers of the Tsar: Army and Society in Russia 1462–1874* (Oxford, 1985), p. 275.
46 Christophe Charle, *Social History of France in the Nineteenth Century* (Oxford, 1994), p. 169.
47 J. Stuart Anderson, *Lawyers and the Making of English Land Law 1832–1940* (Oxford, 1992).
48 Thomas R. Forstenzer, *French Provincial Police and the Fall of the Second Republic* (Princeton, 1981), p. 226.
49 F. Calderon de la Barca, *Life in Mexico* (Berkeley, 1982), p. 462, cited in Bakewell, *History of Latin America*, p. 385; cf. pp. 391–3.
50 Spence, *Search for Modern China*, pp. 165–93; Franz Michael and Chang Chung-li, *The Taiping Rebellion: History and Documents*, 3 vols (Seattle, 1966–71).
51 J. F. Cady, *The Roots of French Imperialism in East Asia* (Ithaca, NY, 1954), pp. 103–18.
52 Thant Myint-U, *The Making of Modern Burma* (Cambridge, 1999).
53 C. A. Curwen (ed. and tr.), *Taiping Rebel: The Deposition of Li Hsiu-ch'eng* (Cambridge, 1977), pp. 79–80.
54 Barbara D. Metcalf and Thomas R. Metcalf, *A Concise History of India* (Cambridge, 1994); Bayly, *Indian Society*, ch. 5; E. T. Stokes, *The Peasant and the Raj* (Cambridge, 1979).
55 Peter Carey, "Waiting for the Ratu Adil: the Javanese village community on the eve of the Java War," *Modern Asian Studies*, 20, 1 (1986), pp. 55–137.
56 Jonathan Sperber, *The European Revolutions 1848–1851* (Cambridge, 1994).
57 Sheehan, *German History*, p. 659.
58 Sperber, *European Revolutions*, p. 123.
59 D. Kertzer, in Davies (ed.), *Italy*, pp. 188–91; Roland Sart, in ibid., pp. 92–8.
60 Norman Davies, *God's Playground: A History of Poland*, vol. 2: *1795 to the Present* (Oxford, 1981), p. 35.
61 Sperber, *European Revolutions*, pp. 203–38.
62 Miles Taylor, "The 1848 revolutions in the British Empire," *Past and Present*, 166 (2000), pp. 146–81.
63 Brogan, *Penguin History of USA*, pp. 315–45; W. R. Brock, *Conflict and Transformation: The United States 1844–1877* (Harmondsworth, 1973); Peter J. Parish, *The*

American Civil War (London, 1975); C. Vann Woodward, *The Origins of the New South* (Baton Rouge, La., 1951).

64 Brian Holden Reid, *The Origins of the American Civil War* (London, 1996), pp. 368–95.

65 P. K. O'Brien, *The Economic Effects of the American Civil War* (Basingstoke, 1988).

66 Eugenio F. Biagini, *Gladstone* (Basingstoke, 2000), pp. 59–60.

67 Speck, *Concise History of Britain*, pp. 86–7.

68 Denoon et al., *History of Australia*, p. 33.

CHAPTER 5   INDUSTRIALIZATION AND THE NEW CITY

1 Peter J. Cain and A. G. Hopkins, *British Imperialism*, vol. 1: *Innovation and Expansion 1688–1914* (London, 1993).

2 Martin Wiener, *English Culture and the Decline of the Industrial Spirit* (Harmondsworth, 1981).

3 P. K. O'Brien and Ronald Quinalt (eds), *The Industrial Revolution and British Society* (Cambridge, 1993).

4 Alfred D. Chandler, Jr., *Scale and Scope: The Dynamics of Industrial Capitalism* (Cambridge, Mass., 1990), p. 7.

5 Ibid.

6 A useful overview is provided in P. K. O'Brien, "The reconstruction, rehabilitation and reconfiguration of the British industrial revolution as a conjuncture in global history," *Itinerario*, 3/4 (2000), pp. 117–34.

7 Roderick Floud and Deirdre McCloskey (eds), *The Economic History of Britain since 1700*, vol. 1 (Cambridge, 1994).

8 Parthasarathi, *Transition to a Colonial Economy*.

9 Pat Hudson, *The Industrial Revolution* (London, 1992); P. K. O'Brien and Leando Prados de la Escosura (eds), *The Costs and Benefits of European Imperialism from the Conquest of Ceuta (1415) to the Treaty of Lusaka (1974)*, special issue of *Revista de Historia Economica* (Madrid, 1998).

10 W. W. Rostow, *The World Economy: History and Prospect* (Austin, Tex., 1978), pp. 51–3.

11 North, *Economic Growth of the United States*.

12 Chandler, *Scale and Scope*.

13 Sheehan, *German History*, pp. 501–4.

14 Ibid., p. 740.

15 Robert Tombs, *France 1814–1914* (London, 1996), p. 399.

16 Rostow, *World Economy*, pp. 52–3.

17 Bakewell, *History of Latin America*, pp. 404–5.

18 Roger Owen, *The Middle East and the World Economy 1800–1914* (London, 1981).

19 Pomeranz, *Great Divergence*.

20 Spence, *Search for Modern China*, p. 218.

21 See, e.g., William T. Rowe, *Hankow: Conflict and Community in a Chinese City 1796–1895* (Stanford, Calif., 1989).

22 Rostow, *World Economy*, pp. 52–3.

23 Smith, *Agrarian Origins of Modern Japan*.

24 Totman, *History of Japan*, pp. 314–37.

25 These were bodies of supposed ethnic Manchus, who had effectively become military pensioners by the nineteenth century. In some ways they resembled the Ottoman janissaries before their abolition.

26 B. R. Tomlinson, *The Economy of Modern India 1860–1970* (Cambridge, 1993).
27 R. S. Chandavarkar, *The Origins of Industrial Capitalism in India* (Cambridge, 1996).
28 C. A. Bayly, *Rulers, Townsmen and Bazaars: North Indian Society in the Age of British Expansion* (Cambridge, 1989).
29 Denoon et al., *History of Australia*, p. 142; cf. p. 89.
30 Sheehan, *German History*.
31 A classic study for England is Gareth Stedman Jones, *Outcast London* (Oxford, 1971).
32 Eric Foner and Olivia Mahoney, *Reconstruction: America's People and Politics after the Civil War* (New York, 1995).
33 Pipes, *Russia under the Old Regime*, pp. 360 ff.
34 Chandavarkar, *Origins of Industrial Capitalism*.
35 Bakewell, *History of Latin America*, p. 427.
36 Chandavarkar, *Origins of Industrial Capitalism*, pp. 212–18.
37 Figes, *Natasha's Dance*.

CHAPTER 6   NATION, EMPIRE, AND ETHNICITY, c.1860–1900

1 A very insightful summary of the important British literature on the subject can be found in John Breuilly, "Historians and the nation," in Peter Burke (ed.), *History and Historians in the Twentieth Century* (Oxford, 2002), pp. 55–87.
2 Cited by B. Jelavich, *A History of the Balkans*, vol. 2: *Eighteenth and Nineteenth Centuries* (Cambridge, 1983), p. 197.
3 Hastings, *Construction of Nationhood*.
4 Blanning, *Culture of Power*.
5 His most recent synthetic work is Anthony D. Smith, *Nationalism and Modernism* (London, 1998).
6 Ernest Gellner, *Nations and Nationalism* (Oxford, 1983).
7 Lieven, *Empire*, p. 183.
8 E. J. Hobsbawm, *Nations and Nationalism since 1780* (Cambridge, 1990).
9 John Breuilly, *Nationalism and the State* (Manchester, 1993).
10 Benedict Anderson, *Imagined Communities: Reflections on the Origin and Spread of Nationalism* (London, 1991).
11 Sperber, *European Revolutions*, p. 97.
12 See the valuable essay by Robert Wiebe, "Imagined communities: nationalist experiences," *Journal of the Historical Society*, 1, 1 (Spring 2000), pp. 33–63.
13 François Furet and Jacques Ozouf, *Reading and Writing Literacy in France from Calvin to Jules Ferry* (Cambridge, 1982).
14 J. P. Parry, "The impact of Napoleon III on British politics 1851–1880," *Transactions of the Royal Historical Society*, 6 ser., II (2001), pp. 147–75.
15 Molnar, *Concise History of Hungary*, pp. 206–12.
16 Lieven, *Nicholas II*, p. 12.
17 Engin Deniz Akarli, *The Long Peace: Ottoman Lebanon 1861–1920* (Berkeley, 1993).
18 Kayali, *Arabs and Young Turks*.
19 Charles Tripp, *A History of Iraq* (Cambridge, 2000), pp. 27–9.
20 Fahmy, *All the Pasha's Men*.

21   David Landes, *Bankers and Pashas: International Finance and Economic Imperialism in Egypt* (London, 1958); Ilbert (ed.), *Alexandrie.*

22   Juan R. I. Cole, *Colonialism and Revolution in the Middle East: Social and Cultural Origins of Egypt's Urabi Movement* (Princeton, 1993).

23   Amira K. Bennison, "Muslim universalism and Western globalisation," in Hopkins (ed.), *Globalization in World History*, pp. 88–9.

24   J. Ayo Langley, *Ideologies of Political Liberation in Black Africa, 1856–1970: Documents on Modern African Political Thought from Colonial Times to the Present* (London, 1979).

25   Robert W. July, *The Origins of Modern African Thought: Its Development in West Africa during the Nineteenth and Twentieth Centuries* (London, 1968), p. 218.

26   Bayly, *Origins of Nationality in South Asia.*

27   Paul A. Cohen, *History in Three Keys: The Boxers as Event, Experience and Myth* (New York, 1997).

28   J. Y. Wong, *The Making of a Heroic Image: Sun Yatsen in London 1896–7* (London, 1986).

29   Ernest Gellner, "Do nations have navels?," *Nations and Nationalism*, 10 (1996), pp. 366–70.

30   Maya Shatzmiller, *The Berbers and the Islamic State* (Princeton, 2000); Michael Brett and Elizabeth Fentress, *The Berbers* (London, 1996).

31   Harjot Singh Oberoi, *The Construction of Religious Boundaries: Culture, Identity and Diversity in the Sikh Tradition* (Delhi, 1997).

32   Cited by Davies, *God's Playground*, p. 254.

33   Molnar, *Concise History of Hungary*, p. 229.

34   Maurice Agulhon, *The French Republic 1879–1992* (Oxford, 1993), pp. 68–70.

35   A concise survey of these issues is Andrew Porter, *European Imperialism 1860–1914* (London, 1994); for a more extended discussion see *OHBE*, 3, especially Colin Newbury, "Great Britain and the partition of Africa 1870–1914," pp. 624–50.

36   The best general treatment of non-British expansion in Africa which also deals with the British is H. L. Wesseling, *Divide and Rule: The Partition of Africa 1880–1914* (Westport, Conn., 1996). This work stresses European rivalries and warfare.

37   Roger Owen and Bob Sutcliffe, *Studies in the Theory of Imperialism* (London, 1972), remains a valuable collection.

38   The best general treatments remain D. K. Fieldhouse, *Economics and Empire* (London, 1984) and Norman Etherington, *Theories of Imperialism: War, Conquest and Capital* (London, 1984).

39   Notably, Cain and Hopkins, *British Imperialism*, vol. 1.

40   e.g. Alexander Scholch, *Egypt for the Egyptians* (Ithaca, NY, 1981); Arthur Keppel-Jones, *Rhodes and Rhodesia: The White Conquest of Zimbabwe 1884–1902* (Montreal, 1983).

41   Notably in Ronald Robinson and John Gallagher, with Alice Denny, *Africa and the Victorians: The Official Mind of Imperialism* (London, 1963); W. Roger Louis, *The Robinson and Gallagher Controversy* (New York, 1976).

42   Daniel Headrick, *The Invisible Weapon: Telecommunications and International Politics 1851–1945* (New York, 1991); *idem, The Tools of Empire: Technology and European Imperialism in the Nineteenth Century* (New York, 1981).

43   Wesseling, *Divide and Rule.*

44   Ronald Hyam, *Britain's Imperial Century, 1815–1914: A Study of Empire and Expansion*, 3rd edn (Basingstoke, 2002).

45   A. S. Kanya-Forstner, *The Conquest of the Western Sudan: A Study in French Military Imperialism* (Cambridge, 1969).

46   Hopkins, *Economic History of West Africa.*

47 Cited in W. G. Beasley, "Japan and the West in the mid-nineteenth century," offprint, *Proceedings of the British Academy* (London 1969), p. 83.

48 C. Coquery-Vidrovitch, *Le Congo au temps des grands compagnies concessionnaires* (Paris, 1972).

49 Cole, *Colonialism and Revolution*.

50 Cf., e.g., Helen Ward, "Worth its weight in gold: women and value in northwest India," unpublished PhD dissertation, University of Cambridge, 1999.

51 C. M. Clark, *Kaiser Wilhelm II* (London, 2000).

52 Collingham, *Imperial Bodies*; Charu Gupta, *Sexuality, Obscenity, Community: Women, Muslims and the Hindu Public in Colonial India* (Delhi, 2001).

53 e.g., "The Magistrate of Trichinpoly asks the Madras government what action should be taken in the case of a Greek named Jacob Lucas and a Persian Himes Ebba Usuf who had been arrested for travelling without passport": Board's Collections, vol. 1685/64431, Oriental and India Office Collections, British Library, London.

54 The parallel process, of using the fingerprint as a method of internal surveillance, has been recently tackled by Radhika Singha, "Settle, mobilize, verify: identification practices in colonial India," *Studies in History* (Delhi), 16, 2, n.s. (2000), pp. 151–98.

55 Stanley Fisher, *Ottoman Land Law* (Oxford, 1919); I thank Professor Leila Fawaz for this reference.

56 This is mostly based on Caroline Moorehead, *Dunant's Dream: War, Switzerland and the History of the Red Cross* (London, 1998).

57 Mushirul Hasan, *A Nationalist Conscience, M. A. Ansari, the Congress and the Raj* (New Delhi, 1987), chs 6–8.

58 *The Life of Swami Vivekananda by his Eastern and Western Disciples*, 2 vols (Calcutta, 1981); Vivekananda, *Chicago Addresses*, 16th impression (Calcutta, 1971).

59 Romain Rolland, *Ramakrishna the Man God and the Universal Gospel of Vivekananda* (Calcutta, 1960), p. 103.

CHAPTER 7   MYTHS AND TECHNOLOGIES OF THE MODERN STATE

1 Michael Mann, *The Sources of Social Power*, vol. 2: *The Rise of Classes and Nation States 1760–1914* (Cambridge, 1993).

2 Drayton, *Nature's Government*.

3 Gregg Kvistad, *The Rise and Demise of German Statism: Loyalty and Political Membership* (Oxford, 1999).

4 G. F. Hegel (tr. T. M. Knox), *Hegel's Philosophy of Right* (1821; Oxford, 1952), p. 161.

5 John Brewer, *The Sinews of Power: War, Money and the English State 1688–1783* (London, 1989).

6 E. P. Thompson, *Whigs and Hunters: The Origin of the Black Acts* (London, 1975); V. A. C. Gattrell, *The Hanging Tree: Execution and the English People 1770–1868* (Oxford, 1994).

7 Oliver MacDonagh, *Patterns of Government Growth 1800–1860: The Passenger Acts and their Enforcement* (Aldershot, 1993).

8 Jose Harris, *Private Lives, Public Spirit* (Oxford, 1993); also Martin Daunton, *Trusting Leviathan: The Politics of Taxation in Britain 1799–1814* (Cambridge, 2001).

9   Bernard S. Cohn, *Colonialism and its Forms of Knowledge: The British in India* (Princeton, 1996).

10 James C. Scott, *Seeing Like a State: How Certain Schemes to Improve the Human Condition have Failed* (New Haven, 1998).

11 Stephen Skowronek, *Building a New American State: The Expansion of National Administrative Capacities 1877–1920* (Cambridge, 1982), pp. 214–15.

12 P. Harling and P. Mandler, "From fiscal-military state to laissez-faire state, 1760–1850," *Journal of British Studies*, 32, 1 (1993), pp. 1–34.

13 C. M. Clark, *Kaiser Wilhelm II*.

14 Brogan, *Penguin History of the USA*, p. 209.

15 Jean Comaroff, *Body of Power, Spirit of Resistance: The Culture and History of a South African People* (Chicago, 1985).

16 Cleveland, *History of the Modern Middle East*, pp. 108–9; Nikki R. Keddie, *Roots of Revolution: An Interpretative History of Modern Iran* (New Haven, 1981).

17 Oscar Salemink, *The Ethnology of Vietnam's Central Highlanders: A Historical Contextualisation 1850–1930* (London, 2002).

18 Hopkins, "Asante and the Victorians."

19 Miles Taylor, *The Decline of British Radicalism 1847–1865* (Oxford, 1995).

20 Hosking, *Russia, People and Empire*.

21 See, e.g., C. Soleillet, *L'Avenir de la France en Afrique* (Paris, 1876).

22 Davis (ed.), *Italy*, pp. 54–61.

23 Carr, *Spain*, pp. 98–9, 370, 477.

24 Joanna Innes, "The domestic face of the military fiscal state in eighteenth-century Britain," in Lawrence Stone (ed.), *The Imperial State at War: Britain from 1689–1815* (London, 1990), pp. 96–127.

25 Daunton, *Trusting Leviathan*.

26 Jane Samson, *Imperial Benevolence: Making British Authority in the Pacific Islands* (Honolulu, 1998), pp. 48, 65.

27 Grewal, *Sikhs of the Punjab*.

28 Myint-U, *Making of Modern Burma*.

29 David K. Wyatt, *Thailand: A Short History* (New Haven, 1984); *idem*, *The Politics of Reform in Thailand: Education in the Reign of Chulalongkorn* (New Haven, 1969).

30 M. Rankin, *Elite Activism and Political Transformation in China* (Cambridge, Mass., 1993).

31 Cleveland, *History of the Modern Middle East*, pp. 110–12.

32 The classic study remains Roderick H. Davison, *Reform in the Ottoman Empire 1856–76* (Princeton, 1963).

33 Shaw, *History of the Ottoman Empire*, pp. 30–60.

34 Cleveland, *History of the Modern Middle East*, pp. 71–5; al-Sayyid Marsot, *Egypt in the Reign of Muhammad Ali*.

35 Iliffe, *Africans*, p. 166.

36 Charles-Robert Ageron, *Modern Algeria from 1830 to the Present* (London, 1991); Jamil Abun-Nasr, *A History of the Mahgrib* (Cambridge, 1971).

37 Kayali, *Arabs and Young Turks*, pp. 21–2.

38 Cited in David Robinson, *The Holy War of Umar Tal: The Western Sudan in the Mid-Nineteenth Century* (Oxford, 1985), pp. 114–15.

39 Shaw, *History of the Ottoman Empire*, p. 439; Davison, *Reform in the Ottoman Empire*.

40 Radhika Singha, *A Despotism of Law: Crime and Justice in Early Colonial India* (Delhi, 2000).

41 Totman, *History of Japan*, p. 296.

42 Ricklefs, *History of Modern Indonesia*.

43 Lyons, *Napoleon Bonaparte*, pp. 94–103.
44 M. Foucault (tr. Alan Sheridan), *Discipline and Punish* (Harmondsworth, 1979).
45 C. M. Clark, *Kaiser Wilhelm II*.
46 Brogan, *Penguin History of the USA*, pp. 399–402.
47 Spence, *Search for Modern China*, p. 158.
48 Davies, *God's Playground*.
49 Michael Howard, in G. N. Clark et al. (eds), *New Cambridge Modern History*, vol. 11: *Material Progress and Worldwide Problems 1870–98* (Cambridge, 1963), p. 205.
50 Stanley Wright, *Hart and the Chinese Customs* (Belfast, 1950).
51 W. G. Beasley, *The Meiji Restoration* (Stanford, Calif., 1972); Totman, *History of Japan*.
52 Ramon H. Myers, Peter Duus, and Mark R. Peattie, *The Japanese Informal Empire in China 1895–1937* (Princeton, 1989).
53 Black, *European Warfare*.
54 Sheehan, *German History*.
55 See, e.g., Richard J. Evans, *Death in Hamburg: Society and Politics in the Cholera Years 1830–1910* (Harmondsworth, 1990).
56 Otto Pflanze, *Bismarck and the Development of Germany*, vol. 3: *The Period of Fortification 1880–98* (Princeton, 1990), pp. 145–84.
57 Lothar Jall (tr. J. A. Underwood), *Bismarck: The White Revolutionary*, vol. 2: *1871–1898* (London, 1986), pp. 127–9.
58 Speck, *Concise History of Britain*, pp. 135–9.
59 Denoon et al., *History of Australia*, pp. 232–8.
60 Cleveland, *History of the Modern Middle East*, pp. 126–8; Totman, *History of Japan*, pp. 298–302.
61 Thongchai Winichakul, *Siam Mapped: A History of the Geo-body of a Nation* (Honolulu, 1994); for Vietnam, see the examples in the National Museum, Hanoi.
62 Anne Godlewska, "Napoleon's geographers (1797–1815): imperialists and soldiers of modernity," in Anne Godlewska and Neil Smith, *Geography and Empire* (Oxford, 1994), pp. 31–53.
63 Edney, *Mapping an Empire*.
64 Douglas R. Reynolds, *China 1898–1912* (Cambridge, Mass., 1993), p. 113.
65 Skowronek, *Building a New American State*, p. 49.
66 M. Mazower, *The Balkans* (London, 2000), p. 37.
67 Porter (ed.), *OHBE*, 3, pp. 610–16.
68 Hans van de Ven, *Military and Financial Reform in the Late Qing and Early Republic* (Taipei, 1999).

CHAPTER 8   THE THEORY AND PRACTICE OF LIBERALISM, RATIONALISM, SOCIALISM, AND SCIENCE

1 C. B. Macpherson, *The Political Theory of Possessive Individualism: Hobbes to Locke* (Oxford, 1962).
2 Emma Rothschild, *Economic Sentiments: Adam Smith, Condorcet and the Enlightenment* (Cambridge, Mass., 2001).
3 Bernard Bailyn, *The Ideological Origins of the American Revolution* (Cambridge, Mass., 1971).
4 J. G. A. Pocock, *The Machiavellian Moment* (Princeton, 1975).
5 Simon Schama, *Patriots and Liberators: Revolution in the Netherlands 1780–1813* (London, 1992).

6   Brading, *The First America*.

7   Ibid., pp. 582–602.

8   François Furet, *Penser la Révolution française* (Paris, 1978).

9   Gareth Stedman Jones, *Languages of Class* (Cambridge, 1983).

10 J. D. Y. Peel, *Religious Encounter and the Making of the Yoruba* (Bloomington, Ind., 2000).

11 Totman, *History of Japan*, pp. 264–5; cf. Toshinobu Yashinaga, *Ando Shoeki: Social and Ecological Philosopher in Eighteenth-Century Japan* (New York, 1992).

12 Cf. Nasiruddin Tusi (tr. G. M. Wickens), *The Nasirean Ethics* (London, 1969); W. F. Thompson (ed.), *The Practical Philosophy of the Muhammadan People* (London, 1839), a translation of the "Akhlaq-i-Jalali."

13 Cf. Nancy K. Florida, *Writing the Past, Inscribing the Future: History as Prophecy in Colonial Java* (Durham, NC, 1995).

14 Robert Wardy, *Aristotle in China: Language, Categories and Translation* (Cambridge, 2000).

15 Albert O. Hirschman, *The Passions and the Interests: Political Arguments for Capitalism before its Triumph* (Princeton, 1972).

16 Rothschild, *Economic Sentiments*.

17 F. Vaughan, *The Political Philosophy of Giambattista Vico: An Introduction to La Scienza Nuova* (The Hague, 1972).

18 Roy Porter, *Enlightenment: Britain and the Making of the Modern World* (London, 2000).

19 Boyd Hilton, *The Age of Atonement: The Influence of Evangelicalism on Social and Economic Thought 1785–1885* (Oxford, 1988).

20 Ram Mohun Roy (ed. E. S. Bose), *The Selected English Works of Raja Ram Mohun Roy*, vol. 2 (Calcutta, 1887), p. 618.

21 Dipesh Chakrabarty, *Provincialising Europe* (Princeton, 1999).

22 S. Dixon, *Modernisation in Russia 1676–1825* (Cambridge, 1999), pp. 208 ff.

23 P. I. Pestel, cited in G. Vernadsky et al. (eds), *A Source Book for Russian History from Early Times to 1917*, vol. 2: *Peter the Great to Nicholas II* (New Haven, 1972), p. 514.

24 Brading, *First America*, pp. 663–4.

25 Bernard Lewis, *What Went Wrong? Western Impact and Middle Eastern Response* (Oxford, 2002), p. 51.

26 Richard Graham, *Britain and the Onset of Modernisation in Brazil 1850–1914* (Cambridge, 1972), p. 263.

27 Rosalind O'Hanlon, *Caste, Conflict and Ideology* (Cambridge, 1985), p. 83.

28 Anthony Milner, *The Invention of Politics in Colonial Malaya: Contesting Nationalism and the Expansion of the Public Sphere* (Cambridge, 1994), pp. 10–31.

29 Mill, *Autobiography*, pp. 248–51.

30 Brading, *First America*, pp. 420–41.

31 Alan Knight, *The Mexican Revolution* (Cambridge, 1986), vol. 1, pp. 96–9.

32 Carr, *Spain*, p. 418.

33 Uday Mehta, *Liberalism and Empire: A Study in Nineteenth-Century British Liberal Thought* (Chicago, 1999).

34 Eric Stokes, *The English Utilitarians and India* (repr. Delhi, 1989).

35 Emma Rothschild, "*Smithianismus* and Enlightenment in nineteenth-century Europe", unpublished paper, Centre for History and Economics, University of Cambridge, 1998.

36 David Marr, *Vietnamese Anti-Colonialism 1885–1925* (Berkeley, 1971).

37 De Tocqueville, *Old Regime and the French Revolution*.

38 Speck, *Concise History of Britain*, pp. 89–114.

39 Kvistad, *Rise and Demise of German Statism*, pp. 27–55.

40 James Belich, *Making Peoples: A History of the New Zealanders from Polynesian Settlement to the End of the Nineteenth Century* (Auckland, 1996), pp. 265–6.

41 Nakae Chomin (tr. Nobuko Tsukai), *A Discourse by Three Drunkards on Government* (New York, 1984), p. 25.

42 Luke S. Kwong, *The Mosaic of the Hundred Days: Personalities, Politics and Ideas of 1898* (Cambridge, Mass., 1984).

43 Albert Hourani, *Arabic Thought in the Liberal Age, 1789–1939* (Oxford, 1970).

44 Catherine Hall, Keith McClelland, and Jane Rendall, *Defining the Victorian Nation: Class, Race and Gender and the Reform Act of 1867* (Cambridge, 2000).

45 Denoon et al., *History of Australia*, pp. 206–8.

46 M. A. Zaki Badawi, *The Reformers of Egypt* (London, 1978), p. 90.

47 Ibid., p. 111.

48 J. W. Burrow, *The Crisis of Reason: European Thought 1848–1914* (New Haven, 2000).

49 Walter Simon, *European Positivism in the Nineteenth Century: An Essay in Intellectual History* (Port Washington, NY, 1963).

50 Geraldine Forbes, *Positivism in Bengal: A Case-Study in the Transmission and Assimilation of an Ideology* (Delhi, 1998).

51 Bakewell, *History of Latin America*, pp. 420–2.

52 G. Haupt, *Aspects of International Socialism 1871–1914* (Cambridge, 1986), p. 10.

53 S. Bernstein, *Auguste Blanqui and the Art of Insurrection* (London, 1971).

54 E. F. Manuel, *The New World of Henri Saint Simon* (Cambridge, Mass., 1956).

55 Margot C. Finn, *After Chartism: Class and Nation in British Radical Politics 1848–1874* (Cambridge, 1993).

56 Gareth Stedman Jones, Introduction to Karl Marx and Friedrich Engels, *The Communist Manifesto* (London, 2000).

57 Totman, *History of Japan*, p. 348.

58 Spence, *Search for Modern China*, p. 260.

59 Hu Hanmin, cited in Martin Bernal, *Chinese Socialism to 1907* (Ithaca, NY, 1976), p. 71.

60 For a useful summary of Spencer's ideas, see Herbert Spencer (ed. Duncan Macrae), *The Man versus the State* (1884, 1886; repr. London, 1969), introduction.

61 Drayton, *Nature's Government*.

62 James Secord, *A Victorian Sensation* (Chicago, 2000).

63 Drayton, *Nature's Government*.

64 Tony Ballantyne, *Orientalism and Race: Aryanism in the British Empire* (London, 2001).

65 Drayton, *Nature's Government*, pp. 9–19.

66 R. Cooter, *Phrenology in Europe and America* (London, 2001). Phrenology purported to classify human types according to the structure of the head.

67 Charles Darwin, *On the Origin of Species by Means of Natural Selection, or The Preservation of Favoured Races in the Struggle for Life* (London, 1859; 1920 Everyman edn), p. 449.

68 Joseph Needham, *Science and Civilisation in China*, 8 vols (Cambridge, 1965–90).

69 Burrow, *Crisis of Reason*.

70 P. J. Vatikiotis, *The History of Modern Egypt: From Muhammad Ali to Mubarak* (London, 1991), pp. 114–15.

71 John K. Fairbank and Kwang-Ching Liu (eds), *The Cambridge History of China*, vol. 11, pt. 2: *Late Ching* (Cambridge, 1980), pp. 170–1.

72 Marius B. Jansen, in Jansen (ed.), *The Cambridge History of Japan*, vol. 5: *The Nineteenth Century* (Cambridge, 1989), p. 466.

73 Watanabe Masao, "Science across the Pacific," in Ardath W. Burks (ed.), *The Modernisers: Overseas Students, Foreign Employees and Meiji Japan* (Boulder, Colo., 1985), p. 377.

74 David Arnold, *Science, Technology and Medicine in Colonial India* (Cambridge, 2000).

75 Deepak Kumar, *Science and the Raj 1857–1905* (Delhi, 1995), p. 170.

CHAPTER 9 EMPIRES OF RELIGION

1 Mona Ozouf, *La Fête révolutionnaire 1789–1799* (Paris, 1976).

2 Woolf, *History of Italy*, pp. 181–3.

3 Lyons, *Napoleon Bonaparte*, pp. 84–93.

4 Giuseppe Mazzini, *The Duties of Man and Other Essays* (c.1870; repr. London, 1966), p. 307.

5 David Kopf, *The Brahmo Samaj and the Shaping of the Modern Indian Mind* (Princeton, 1979).

6 G. D. Bond, *The Buddhist Revival in Sri Lanka* (Columbia, SC, 1988); Steven Kemper, *Presence of the Past: Chronicles, Politics and Culture in Sinhala Life* (Ithaca, NY, 1991).

7 Christian Troll, *Sayyid Ahmad Khan: A Reinterpretation of Muslim Theology* (Delhi, 1978); Jamal Mohammed Ahmed, *The Ideological Origins of Egyptian Nationalism* (London, 1960).

8 John Ruskin, *The Stones of Venice* (London, 1960).

9 Owen Chadwick, *The Secularisation of the European Mind in the Nineteenth Century* (Cambridge, 1975).

10 Bipan Chandra, *Communalism in Modern India* (Delhi, 1984).

11 A technique for harnessing spiritual power through ritual or austerities.

12 Oberoi, *Construction of Religious Boundaries*.

13 The distinctions have been elucidated by the anthropologist Harvey Whitehouse, *Arguments and Icons: Divergent Modes of Religiosity* (Oxford, 2000).

14 For a general study of Southeast Asian Buddhism, see Stanley J. Tambiah, *World Conqueror and World Renouncer* (Cambridge, 1972).

15 Milton Osborne, *The French Presence in Cochin China and Cambodia* (Berkeley, 1971).

16 Jonathan Morris, *The Political Economy of Shopkeeping in Milan, 1886–1922* (Cambridge, 1993), pp. 163, 180, 196.

17 Wyse, "Britain's African junior partners," pp. 5–8.

18 Denoon et al., *History of Australia*, pp. 104–6.

19 Comaroff, *Body of Power*.

20 Belich, *Making Peoples*, pp. 221–2.

21 William R. Roff, *Islam and the Political Economy of Meaning: Studies in Muslim Discourse* (London, 1987).

22 Susan Bayly, *Saints, Goddesses and Kings: Christians and Muslims in South Indian Society 1700–1900* (Cambridge, 1989).

23 Sidney E. Ahlstrom, *A Religious History of the American People* (New York, 1972).

24 Agulhon, *French Republic*, pp. 103–8.

25 Helen Hardacre, *Shinto and the State 1868–1988* (Princeton, 1989).

26 Kwong, *Mosaic of the Hundred Days*, pp. 105–8.

27 Shaw, *Ottoman Empire*, vol. 2, pp. 19–22.

28 Rizvi, *Shah Abd al-Aziz*.

29 E. R. Norman, *Church and Society in England, 1770–1970: A Historical Study* (Oxford, 1976), pp. 151, 144–5.

30 "Baptist," in *Concise Dictionary of United States History* (New York, 1983), p. 185.

31 Owen Chadwick, *A History of the Popes, 1830–1914* (Oxford, 1998), pp. 165–214.

32 F. C. R. Robinson, *Islam and Muslim History in South Asia* (New Delhi, 2001).

33 Spence, *Search for Modern China*, pp. 59–62.

34 James Legge, *The Chinese Classics*, vol. 1 (repr. Taipei, 1994), pp. 1–111.

35 Osborne, *French Presence in Cochin China*.

36 Kwong, *Mosaic of the Hundred Days*.

37 Kenneth Jones, *Arya Dharm: Hindu Consciousness in Nineteenth-Century Punjab* (Berkeley, 1976).

38 See David Kertzer, "Religion and society 1789–1892," in Davis (ed.), *Italy*, pp. 181–205.

39 Speck, *Concise History of Britain*, pp. 60–1.

40 Carr, *Spain*, pp. 465–7.

41 Eugene Genovese, *Roll, Jordan Roll: The World the Slaves Made* (New York, 1974).

42 Foner and Mahoney, *America's Reconstruction*, p. 92.

43 For an overview, see P. M. Holt (ed.), *The Cambridge History of Islam*, vol. 2 (Cambridge, 1970).

44 Hiskett, *Development of Islam*.

45 Ibid., pp. 158–68 and Mervyn Hiskett, *The Sword of Truth: The Life and Times of the Shehu Usuman Dan Fodio* (New York, 1976).

46 Iliffe, *Africans*, pp. 200–1.

47 Ibid., pp. 177–9.

48 Andrew Porter, "Religion, missionary enthusiasm and empire," in Porter (ed.), *OHBE*, 3, pp. 235–9.

49 Gwyn Prins, *The Hidden Hippopotamus: Reappraisal in African History: The Early Colonial Experience in Western Zambia* (Cambridge, 1980).

50 Samson, *Imperial Benevolence*, pp. 65–8.

51 William Yate, *An Account of New Zealand and of the Church Missionary Society's Mission in the Northern Island* (1835; repr. Shannon, 1970), p. 262. My thanks to Dr Jane Samson for this reference.

52 Cleveland, *History of the Modern Middle East*, p. 72.

53 C. Snouck Hurgronje (tr. A. O'Sullivan), *The Achehnese* (Leiden, 1906).

54 Obert Voll, *Islam: Continuity and Change in the Modern World* (Boulder, Colo., 1982).

55 Peter Hardy, *The Muslims of British India* (Cambridge, 1969); Barbara D. Metcalf, *Islamic Revival in British India: Deoband 1860–1900* (Princeton, 1982).

56 Ruth Harris, *Lourdes: Body and Spirit in a Secular Age* (London, 1999).

57 Chadwick, *History of the Popes*, p. 565.

58 J. R. I. Cole, "Printing in urban Islam," in L. T. Fawaz and C. A. Bayly, *Modernity and Culture from the Mediterranean to the Indian Ocean* (New York, 2002), pp. 344–64. Francis Robinson, "Technology and religious change: Islam and the impact of print," *Modern Asian Studies*, 27, 1 (1993), pp. 229–51.

59 Niklaus Pevsner, *Ruskin and Viollet-le-Duc: Englishness and Frenchness in the Appreciation of Gothic Architecture* (London, 1969).

60 Mazower, *Balkans*, p. 76.

61 Davies, *God's Playground*, p. 9.

62 Lord Frederick Hamilton, *The Days before Yesterday* (London, 1920), p. 228.

CHAPTER 10 THE WORLD OF THE ARTS AND THE IMAGINATION

1 I am far from a specialist in art history, yet art provides an essential historical source material, still largely ignored by social and political historians, especially for the nineteenth century. I have benefited greatly from important synthetic volumes, notably Stephen F. Eisenman, with Thomas Crow, Brian Lukacher, Linda Nochlin, and Frances K. Pohl, *Nineteenth-Century Art: A Critical History* (London, 1998). I have learned much from visiting galleries and museums across the world and am glad that so much visual material is now available on the worldwide web.
2 Mazzini, *Ricordi autobiografici*, p. 10.
3 Alessandro Manzoni, *I promessi sposi* (1827; repr. Florence, 1962). The novel describes peasant life under an earlier foreign domination, that of the Spanish.
4 Jacob Burckhardt (tr. S. G. C. Middlemore), *The Civilisation of the Renaissance in Italy: An Essay* (London, 1950).
5 Ananda K. Coomaraswamy, *Essays in National Idealism* (Colombo, 1910).
6 Chinese gallery, Victoria and Albert Museum, London.
7 See, e.g., the Malik Palace, Calcutta.
8 Claude Markovits, *The Global World of Indian Merchants 1750–1947: Traders of Sindh from Bukhara to Panama* (Cambridge, 2000).
9 African gallery, British Museum, London.
10 "Risorgimento" gallery, Museo Correa Venezia (apparently now permanently closed) and Musée du Louvre, Paris.
11 Notably in the Gardiner Museum, Boston, Mass.
12 "Shinto" exhibition, Asahi Shimbun gallery, British Museum, London, 2001.
13 African gallery, British Museum.
14 Andrew Wilton and Robert Upstone (eds), *The Age of Rosetti, Burne-Jones and Watts: Symbolism in Britain 1860–1910* (London, 1997).
15 Francesca Orsini, *The Hindi Public Sphere 1920–40: Language and Literature in the Age of Nationalism* (Delhi, 2002), ch. 1.
16 Brian Allen, in Bayly (ed.), *The Raj*, pp. 119–20.
17 Notably in the Villa Nazionale, Brenta.
18 Regis Michel et al., *Aux armes et aux arts: les arts de la révolution 1789–1799* (Paris, 1989). The best collection is in the Musée du Louvre, Paris.
19 Eisenman et al., *Nineteenth-Century Art*, p. 39; the picture is at the Palais de Versailles.
20 Les Invalides, Paris, Eisenman et al., *Nineteenth-Century Art*, p. 47.
21 Brading, *First America*.
22 S. J. Falk, *Qajar Paintings: Persian Oil Paintings of the Eighteenth and Nineteenth Centuries* (London, 1972).
23 Eisenman et al., *Nineteenth-Century Art*, pp. 73–5.
24 The best collections are in the Victoria Memorial, Calcutta; the Victoria and Albert Museum's Nehru gallery, London; the India Office Reading Room, British Library, London; see Allen in Bayly (ed.), *The Raj*, pp. 26–37.
25 The best collection is in the Institut du Monde Arabe, Paris.
26 Mildred Archer, *Early Views of India: The Picturesque Journeys of Thomas and William Daniell 1786–94* (London, 1980).
27 Edward Said, *Orientalism* (London, 1970); but see also John M. MacKenzie, *Orientalism, Art, Literature and Society* (London, 1995).
28 Pohl, in Eisenman et al., *Nineteenth-Century Art*, p. 146.

29   e.g., John Vanderlyn, *The Death of Jane McCrea*, ibid., p. 147.
30   Sir Joseph Noel Paton, *In Memoriam*, private collection, reproduced in Bayly (ed.), *The Raj*, p. 325.
31   Prado Museum, Madrid.
32   See the captions of the examples in the little-visited nineteenth-century Europe gallery of the Victoria and Albert Museum, London.
33   Qajar exhibition, Brunei gallery, School of Oriental and African Studies, London, 2000.
34   Tapati Guha-Thakurta, *The Making of a New "Indian" Art: Artists, Aesthetics and Nationalism in Bengal c.1850–1920* (Cambridge, 1992); Partha Mitter, *Art and Nationalism in Colonial India 1850–1922* (Cambridge, 1994).
35   Eisenman et al., *Nineteenth-Century Art*, p. 244.
36   The best examples are in the Musée du Jeu de Paume, Paris.
37   Elizabeth Cowling, *Interpreting Matisse, Picasso* (London, 2000), Tate Gallery exhibition, London, 2000.
38   Matthi Forrer, *Hokusai: Prints and Drawings* (Munich, 1991), National Gallery of Japan, Tokyo.
39   Japan gallery, Victoria and Albert Museum, London.
40   James A. Flath, "Liu Mingjie – a modern peasant? A nianhua printer's view of imperialism," in Robert Bickers (ed.), *The Boxer Rebellion* (forthcoming).
41   Nineteenth- and twentieth-century galleries, National Museum of Vietnam, Hanoi.
42   Sarabhai Museum, Ahmedabad.
43   Banmali Tandan, *The Architecture of Lucknow and its Dependencies 1722–1856*, 2 vols (Delhi, 2000).
44   Eisenman et al., *Nineteenth-Century Art*, p. 239; cf. the display on 1851 in the Musée Carnavalet, the city museum, Paris.
45   Timothy Mitchell, *Colonising Egypt* (London, 1985).
46   Robert Grant Irving, *Indian Summer: Lutyens, Baker and Imperial Delhi* (New Haven, 1981).
47   J. D. Smith, *The Epic of Pabuji: An Essay in Transcription and Translation* (Cambridge, 1991).
48   D. J. Singh, "Historical significance of Jhaggra Jatti te Katrani da," in F. Singh and A. C. Arora (eds), *Maharaja Ranjit Singh: Politics, Society and Economics* (Patiala, 1984), pp. 289–91.
49   M. Saidiq, *History of Urdu Literature* (London, 1964).
50   Figes, *Natasha's Dance*.
51   Nineteenth-century Europe gallery, Victoria and Albert Museum.
52   1900 exhibition and catalogue, Royal Academy, London, 2000.

CHAPTER 11   THE RECONSTITUTION OF SOCIAL HIERARCHIES

1   Arno Mayer, *The Persistence of the Old Regime: Europe to the Great War* (London, 1981).
2   But also because expert critiques challenged its "totalizing argument"; see Dominic C. B. Lieven, *The Aristocracy in Europe 1815–1914* (London, 1992).
3   Denis Mack Smith, *Italy and its Monarchy* (New Haven, 1989), pp. 123–5.
4   Lieven, *Nicholas II*, pp. 161–203.
5   Peter Burroughs, "Institutions of Empire," in Porter (ed.), *OHBE*, 3, pp. 173–5.

6   Franklin W. Knight, *Slave Society in Cuba during the Nineteenth Century* (Madison, Wis., 1975).
7   van de Ven, *Military and Financial Reform*.
8   Spence, *Search for Modern China*, pp. 249–56.
9   Akarli, *Long Peace*; Kayali, *Arabs and Young Turks*.
10 Totman, *History of Japan*, pp. 332–8.
11 R. O'Hanlon, in J. M. Brown (ed.), *OHBE*, vol. 4: *The Twentieth Century* (Oxford, 1999), pp. 379–98.
12 Amanda Vickery, *The Gentleman's Daughter: Women's Lives in Georgian England* (London, 1998), p. 289.
13 Speck, *Concise History of Britain*, pp. 119–20.
14 Himani Bannerji, "Age of consent and hegemonic social reform," in Clare Midgely (ed.), *Gender and Imperialism* (Manchester, 1998), p. 27.
15 Totman, *History of Japan*, p. 299.
16 William J. Koenig, *The Burmese Polity 1752–1819: Politics, Administration and Organization in the Early Kon-baung Period* (Ann Arbor, 1990).
17 Bakewell, *History of Latin America*, pp. 414–15.
18 Iliffe, *Africans*, pp. 130–1; Philip D. Curtin, *The Atlantic Slave Trade: A Census* (Madison, Wis., 1969).
19 Suzanne Miers and Igor Kopytoff (eds), *Slavery in Africa: Historical and Anthropological Perspectives* (Madison, Wis., 1977).
20 James Walvin, *Black Ivory: Slavery in the British Empire* (Oxford, 2001), pp. 259–72.
21 Iliffe, *Africans*, pp. 152–3.
22 David Watts, *The West Indies* (Cambridge, 1987).
23 Bakewell, *History of Latin America*, p. 447.
24 Genovese, *Roll, Jordan Roll*; Robert W. Fogel and Stanley L. Engermann, *Time on the Cross: The Economics of American Negro Slavery* (London, 1989).
25 Charles B. Dew, *Bond of Iron: Master and Slave at Buffalo Forge* (London, 1994).
26 Kenneth M. Stampp, *The Peculiar Institution* (New York, 1956).
27 D. B. Davis, *The Problem of Slavery in Western Culture* (Ithaca, NY, 1966).
28 Kayali, *Arabs and Young Turks*, pp. 155–6.
29 S. Holsoe, "The Vai," in Miers and Kopytoff (eds), *Slavery in Africa*, p. 299.
30 Indrani Chatterjee, *Gender, Slavery and Law in Colonial India* (Delhi, 1999).
31 Tinker, *New System of Slavery*.
32 But see D. Northrup, *Indentured Labour in the Age of Imperialism 1834–1922* (London, 1995).
33 Walvin, *Black Ivory*, p. 281.
34 Gilberto Freyre, *The Masters and the Slaves: A Study in the Development of Brazilian Civilisation* (New York, 1963).
35 Walvin, *Black Ivory*, pp. 272–8.
36 For this see Joseph C. Miller, *Way of Death: Merchant Capitalism and Angolan Slave Trade 1730–1830* (London, 1988).
37 J. H. Boeke, *Economies and Economic Policy of Dual Societies as Exemplified by Indonesia* (Haarlem, 1953).
38 André Gunder Frank, *Mexican Agriculture 1521–1630* (Cambridge, 1979).
39 Immanuel Wallerstein, *The Modern World System* (New York, 1974).
40 Eugene Weber, *Peasants into Frenchmen: The Modernisation of Rural France, 1870–1914* (Stanford, Calif., 1976).
41 For Italy, the best brief account is Davis (ed.), *Italy*, pp. 245–55.
42 Knight, *Mexican Revolution*, pp. 1, 86–8.
43 The figures are from Spence, *Search for Modern China*, pp. 94, 210.

44 The figures are from Owen, *Cotton and the Egyptian Economy*.

45 David F. Good, *The Economic Rise of the Habsburg Empire, 1750–1914* (Berkeley, 1984), pp. 138–40.

46 David Arnold, *Famine: Social Crisis and Historical Change* (Oxford, 1988).

47 Nathan T. Brown, *Peasant Politics in Modern Egypt: The Struggle against the State* (New York, 1990).

48 H. Ooms, *Tokugawa Village Practice: Class, Status, Power, Law* (Berkeley, 1996).

49 This was the case in the Maratha kingdom of Pune, for instance.

50 Susan Bayly, *Caste, Society and Politics in India from the Eighteenth Century to the Modern Age* (Cambridge, 1999).

51 D. A. Washbrook, "Economic depression and the making of 'traditional' society in colonial India, 1820–1855," *Transactions of the Royal Historical Society*, 6, 3 (1993), pp. 237–63.

52 A. S. Milward and S. B. Saul, *Development of the Economies of Central Europe, 1850–1914* (London, 1977), pp. 256–8.

53 T. McDaniel, *Autocracy, Capitalism and Revolution in Europe 1815–1914* (Berkeley, 1988).

54 Alan Macfarlane, *The Origins of English Individualism* (Oxford, 1976).

55 Lieven, *Empire*, pp. 245–6.

56 Lieven, *Aristocracy in Europe*.

57 J. McCann, *From Poverty to Famine in North East Ethiopia: A Rural History 1900–1935* (Philadelphia, 1987); A. Seddon, *Moroccan Peasants: A Century of Change in the Eastern Rif 1870–1920* (London, 1981).

58 For a classic historical sociology, Barrington Moore, Jr, *Social Origins of Dictatorship and Democracy: Lord and Peasant in the Making of the Modern World* (London, 1984).

59 Ping-ti Ho, *The Ladder of Success in Imperial China: Aspects of Social Mobility 1368–1911* (New York, 1962); Chang Chung-li, *The Chinese Gentry* (Berkeley, 1965).

60 Cited in Peter Perdue, *Exhausting the Earth: State and Peasant in Hunan, 1500–1850* (Cambridge, Mass., 1987), p. 231.

61 S. Tretiakov, *A Chinese Testament: The Autobiography of Tan Shih-Hua as Told to S. Tretiakov* (New York, 1934), p. 5.

62 The trend was set by Philip A. Kuhn, *Rebellion and its Enemies in Late Imperial China 1798–1864* (Cambridge, Mass., 1970).

63 Totman, *History of Japan*; Beasley, *Meiji Restoration*; K. B. Pyle in Jansen (ed.), *Cambridge History of Japan*, vol. 5, ch. 11.

64 Ricklefs, *History of Modern Indonesia*, pp. 120–5.

65 Hopkins, *Economic History of West Africa*, pp. 142–4.

66 Lauren Benton, *Law and Colonial Cultures: Legal Regimes in World History 1400–1900* (Cambridge, 2002).

67 T. R. Metcalf, *Land, Landlords and the British Raj: Northern India in the Nineteenth Century* (Berkeley, 1979).

68 Davis (ed.), *Italy*, p. 49.

69 Speck, *Concise History of Britain*, pp. 75–7.

70 Cain and Hopkins, *British Imperialism*, vol. 1; David Cannadine, *The Decline and Fall of the British Aristocracy* (London, 1992).

71 David Cannadine, *Class in Britain* (London, 2000).

72 David Cannadine, *Ornamentalism: How the British Saw their Empire* (London, 2001).

73 Cited in Lieven, *Nicholas II*, p. 120.

74 Roger Price, *Napoleon III and the Second Empire* (London, 1997); Tombs, *France*.

75 Molnar, *Concise History of Hungary*, pp. 243–6.

76 C. M. Clark, *Kaiser Wilhelm II*; John G. C. Röhl, *The Kaiser and his Court: Wilhelm II and the Government of Germany* (Cambridge, 1994).

77 Irokawa Daikichi (tr. and ed. Marius B. Jansen), *The Culture of the Meiji Period* (Princeton, 1985), p. 266.

78 Lieven, *Nicholas II*.

79 Exhibited at "The Victorians," Victoria and Albert Museum, London, 2001–2.

80 Cf. Ernest Dawn, *From Ottomanism to Arabism* (Urbana, Ill., 1973).

CHAPTER 12   THE DESTRUCTION OF "NATIVE PEOPLES" AND ECOLOGICAL DEPREDATION

1 Philip D. Morgan, "Encounters between British and 'indigenous' peoples c.1500–c.1800," in Martin Daunton and Rick Halpern (eds), *Empire and Others: British Encounters with Indigenous Peoples 1600–1850* (London, 1999), pp. 42–78.

2 Daniel R. Mandel, *Behind the Frontier: Indians in Eighteenth-Century Eastern Massachusetts* (Lincoln, Nebr., 1996), p. 204.

3 See, e.g., Sumit Guha, *Environment and Ethnicity in India 1200–1991* (Cambridge, 1999).

4 Olive P. Dickason, *Canada's First Nations: A History of Founding Peoples from the Earliest Times* (Toronto, 1992).

5 Nigel Worden, *The Shaping of South African Society: Conquest, Segregation and Apartheid* (Oxford, 1994).

6 L. C. Duly, *British Land Policy at the Cape 1796–1834* (Durham, NC, 1964).

7 Belich, *Making Peoples*.

8 Bruce G. Trigger (ed.), *The Cambridge History of the Native Peoples of the Americas*, vol. 1: *North America*, pt I (Cambridge, 1996).

9 Bakewell, *History of Latin America*, pp. 400, 406.

10 Belich, *Making Peoples*.

11 R. Dalziel, in Porter (ed.), *OHBE*, 3, pp. 581–2.

12 Cited in Terence Ranger, *Voices from the Rocks: Nature, Culture and History in the Matopos Hills of Zimbabwe* (London, 1999), p. 45.

13 G. Martin, in Porter (ed.), *OHBE*, 3, p. 533.

14 Herbert Walsh, 1902, cited in Frederick E. Hoxie, *A Final Promise: The Campaign to Assimilate the Indians, 1880–1920* (Cambridge, 1984), p. 193.

15 James Belich, *The New Zealand Wars* (London, 1988).

16 Ajay Skaria, *Hybrid Histories: Forests, Frontiers and Wildness in Western India* (Delhi, 1999).

17 Ballantyne, *Orientalism and Race*.

18 Denoon et al., *History of Australia*, pp. 174–5.

19 John M. MacKenzie, *Imperialism and the Natural World* (Manchester, 1990).

20 Richard H. Grove, *Green Imperialism: Colonial Expansion, Tropical Island Edens and the Origins of Environmentalism* (London, 1995).

CHAPTER 13   CONCLUSION: THE GREAT ACCELERATION, C. 1890–1914

1 I am grateful to Deep Kanta Lahiri-Choudhury for this translation; cf. "Shelidah," cited by Krishna Dutta and Andrew Roberts, *Rabindranath Tagore: The Myriad-Minded Man* (London, 1995), p. 129.

2   Robinson and Gallagher with Denny, *Africa and the Victorians*.
3   Cain and Hopkins, *British Imperialism*, vol. 1.
4   Anil Seal, *The Emergence of Indian Nationalism* (Cambridge, 1969).
5   Elie Kedourie, *The Chatham House Version and Other Middle-Eastern Studies* (London, 1970).
6   Partha Chatterjee, *Nationalist Thought and the Colonial World: A Derivative Discourse?* (London, 1986).
7   Price, *British Society*.
8   Olivier Zunz, *Why the American Century?* (Chicago, 1998), pp. 7–10.
9   Eric Stokes, "Late-nineteenth-century colonial expansion: the attack on the theory of economic imperialism: a case of mistaken identity?," *Historical Journal*, 12 (1969), pp. 285–302.
10 "Russian expansion in Central Asia," Curzon Papers, MSS F111, 700, Oriental and India Office Collection, British Library.
11 Strachan, *First World War*, vol. 1
12 Cited in Hugh Thomas, *Cuba: Or the Pursuit of Freedom* (London, 1971), p. 468.
13 Peter Duus, *The Abacus and the Sword: The Japanese Penetration of Korea 1895–1910* (Berkeley, 1995).
14 Marr, *Vietnamese Anti-Colonialism*.
15 F. S. Lyons, *Ireland since the Famine: 1850 to the Present* (London, 1971), pp. 313–27; idem, in W. E. Vaughan (ed.), *A New History of Ireland*, vol. 6, pt 2: *Ireland under the Union 1870–1921* (Oxford, 1986), pp. 111–44.
16 Ricklefs, *History of Modern Indonesia*, pp. 143–6.
17 A. L. al-Sayyid-Marsot, in Porter (ed.), *OHBE*, 3, pp. 651–64; Bose and Jalal, *Modern South Asia*.
18 Johannes Meintjes, *President Paul Kruger: A Biography* (London, 1974), p. 172.
19 Kayali, *Arabs and Young Turks*; Feroz Ahmad, *The Committee of Union and Progress in Turkish Politics 1908–14* (Oxford, 1969).
20 Duncan Tanner, Pat Thane, and Nicholas Tiratsoo (eds), *Labour's First Century* (Cambridge, 2000).
21 John A. Thompson, *Woodrow Wilson* (London, 2002).
22 Morris, *Political Economy of Shopkeeping in Milan*.
23 Alan Knight, *Mexican Revolution*.
24 Denoon et al., *History of Australia*, pp. 250–1.
25 Agulhon, *French Republic*, pp. 114–20.
26 *Cambridge History of China*, vol. 11, pt 2, p. 492.
27 Prasenjit Duara, *Rescuing History from the Nation: Questioning Narratives of Modern China* (Chicago, 1995).
28 Wong, *China Transformed*; Pomeranz, *Great Divergence*.
29 See A. G. Hopkins, introduction and "The history of globalization – and the globalization of history," in idem (ed.), *Globalization in World History*, pp. 12–44.
30 Jack A. Goldstone, *Revolution and Rebellion in the Early Modern World* (Berkeley, 1991).
31 Gellner, *Plough, Sword and Book*; cf. Macfarlane, *Riddle of the Modern World*.
32 E. J. Hobsbawm, *The Age of Empire 1875–1914* (London, 1994).

BIBLIOGRAPHY

BOOKS

Abu Lughod, Janet, *Before European Hegemony: The World System 1250–1350* (New York, 1989).

Abun-Nasr, Jamil, *A History of the Mahgrib* (Cambridge, 1971).

Ageron, Charles-Robert, *Modern Algeria from 1830 to the Present* (London, 1991).

Agulhon, Maurice, *The French Republic 1879–1992* (Oxford, 1993).

Ahlstrom, Sidney E., *A Religious History of the American People* (New York, 1972).

Ahmad, Feroz, *The Committee of Union and Progress in Turkish Politics 1908–14* (Oxford, 1969).

Ahmed, Jamal Mohammed, *The Ideological Origins of Egyptian Nationalism* (London, 1960).

Akarli, Engin Deniz, *The Long Peace: Ottoman Lebanon 1861–1920* (Berkeley, 1993).

"Akhlaq-i-Jalali" (tr. W. F. Thompson), *The Practical Philosophy of the Muhammadan People* (London, 1836).

Alexander, John T., *Autocratic Politics in a National Crisis: The Imperial Russian Government and Pugachev's Revolt, 1773–5* (Bloomington, Ind., 1969).

Algar, Hamid, *Religion and State in Iran 1785–1906* (Berkeley, 1969).

Al-Rasheed, Madawi, *A History of Saudi Arabia* (Cambridge, 2002).

al-Sayyid Marsot, Afaf Lutfi, *Egypt in the Reign of Muhammad Ali* (Cambridge, 1984).

Anderson, Benedict, *Imagined Communities: Reflections on the Origin and Spread of Nationalism* (London, 1991).

Anderson, J. Stuart, *Lawyers and the Making of English Land Law 1832–1940* (Oxford, 1992).

Appadurai, Arjun, *Modernity at Large: Cultural Dimensions of Globalization* (Minneapolis, 2000).

Archer, Mildred, *Early Views of India: The Picturesque Journeys of Thomas and William Daniell 1786–94* (London, 1980).

Armitage, David, *The Ideological Origins of the British Empire* (Cambridge, 2000).

Arnold, David, *Famine: Social Crisis and Historical Change* (Oxford, 1988).

Arnold, David, *Science, Technology and Medicine in Colonial India* (Cambridge, 2000).

Atkinson, Alan, *The Europeans in Australia. A History*, vol. 1 (Oxford, 1997).

Badawi, M. A. Zaki, *The Reformers of Egypt* (London, 1978).

Bailyn, Bernard, *The Ideological Origins of the American Revolution* (Cambridge, Mass., 1971).

Bains, Dudley, *Emigration from Europe 1815–1930* (Basingstoke, 1991).

Baker, Keith, *Inventing the French Revolution: Essays on French Political Culture in the Eighteenth Century* (Cambridge, 1990).

Baker, Keith (ed.), *The Political Culture of the Old Regime* (Oxford, 1987).

Bakewell, P. J., *A History of Latin America* (London, 1997).

Ballantyne, Tony, *Orientalism and Race: Aryanism in the British Empire* (London, 2000).

Bayly, C. A., *Imperial Meridian: The British Empire and the World 1780–1830* (London, 1989).

Bayly, C. A., *Indian Society and the Making of the British Empire* (Cambridge, 1988).

Bayly, C. A., *The Origins of Nationality in South Asia: Patriotism and Ethical Government in the Making of Modern India* (Delhi, 1998).

Bayly, C. A., *The Raj: India and the British 1600–1947* (London, 1990).

Bayly, C. A., *Rulers, Townsmen and Bazaars: North Indian Society in the Age of British Expansion* (Cambridge, 1989).

Bayly, Susan, *Caste, Society and Politics in India from the Eighteenth Century to the Modern Age* (Cambridge, 1999).

Bayly, Susan, *Saints, Goddesses and Kings: Christians and Muslims in South Indian Society 1700–1900* (Cambridge, 1989).

Beales, D. E. D., *Joseph II*, vol. 1: *In The Shadow of Maria Theresa, 1741–80* (Cambridge, 1987).

Beasley, W. G., *The Meiji Restoration* (Stanford, Calif., 1972).

Beik, W., *Absolutism and Society in Seventeenth-Century France: State Power and Provincial Aristocracy in Languedoc* (Cambridge, 1988).

Belich, James, *Making Peoples: A History of the New Zealanders from Polynesian Settlement to the End of the Nineteenth Century* (Auckland, 1996).

Belich, James, *The New Zealand Wars* (London, 1988).

Benton, Lauren, *Law and Colonial Cultures: Legal Regimes in World History 1400–1900* (Cambridge, 2002).

Bergeron, L., *Banquiers, négociants et manufacturiers parisiens du directoire à l'empire* (Paris, 1975).

Bernal, Martin, *Chinese Socialism to 1907* (Ithaca, NY, 1976).

Bernstein, S., *Auguste Blanqui and the Art of Insurrection* (London, 1971).

Biagini, Eugenio F., *Gladstone* (Basingstoke, 2000).

Black, Jeremy, *European Warfare 1660–1815* (London, 1994).

Blanning, T. C. W., *The Culture of Power and the Power of Culture* (Oxford, 2001).

Blanning, T. C. W. and Peter Wende, *Reform in Britain and Germany, 1750–1850* (Oxford, 1999).

Bloch, Maurice, *Ritual, History and Power: Selected Papers in Anthropology* (London, 1998).

Blusse, Leonard, *Strange Company: Chinese Settlers, Mestizo Women and the Dutch in VOC Batavia* (Dordrecht, 1986).

Boeke, J. H., *Economies and Economic Policy of Dual Societies as Exemplified by Indonesia* (Haarlem, 1953).

Bond, G. D., *The Buddhist Revival in Sri Lanka* (Columbia, SC, 1988).

Bose, Sugata and Ayesha Jalal, *Modern South Asia: Culture, Political Economy* (Delhi, 1998).

Bowen, H. V., *Revolution and Reform: The Indian Problem in British Politics 1757–1773* (Cambridge, 1991).

Brading, D. A., *The First America: The Spanish Monarchy, Creole Patriots and the Liberal State 1492–1867* (Cambridge, 1991).

Braudel, Fernand, *Civilisation matérielle, économie, capitalisme xve–xviiie siècle* (Paris, 1979).

Bray, Francesca, *Technology and Gender: Fabrics of Power in Late Imperial China* (Berkeley, 1997).

Brett, Michael and Elizabeth Fentress, *The Berbers* (London, 1996).

Breuilly, John, *Nationalism and the State* (Manchester, 1993).

Brewer, John, *The Sinews of Power: War, Money and the English State 1688–1783* (London, 1989).

Bridges, Roy E. (ed.), *Imperialism, Decolonisation and Africa: Studies Presented to John Hargreaves* (Basingstoke, 2000).

Brock, W. R., *Conflict and Transformation: The United States 1844–1877* (Harmondsworth, 1973).

Brogan, Hugh, *The Penguin History of the USA* (London, 1999).

Brook, Timothy, *The Confusions of Pleasure: Commerce and Culture in Ming China* (Berkeley, 1998).

Brown, J. M. (ed.), *The Oxford History of the British Empire*, vol. 4: *The Twentieth Century* (Oxford, 1999).

Brown, Nathan T., *Peasant Politics in Modern Egypt: The Struggle against the State* (New York, 1990).

Burckhardt, Jacob (tr. S. G. C. Middlemore), *The Civilisation of the Renaissance in Italy: An Essay* (London, 1950).

Burke, Peter, *The Fabrication of Louis XIV* (New Haven, 1992).

Burke, Peter (ed.), *History and Historians in the Twentieth Century* (Oxford, 2002).

Burks, Ardath W. (ed.), *The Modernisers: Overseas Students, Foreign Employees and Meiji Japan* (Boulder, Colo., 1985).

Burroughs, Peter and A. J. Stockwell (eds), *Managing the Business of Empire: Essays in Honour of D. K. Fieldhouse* (London, 1998).

Burrow, J. W., *The Crisis of Reason: European Thought 1848–1914* (New Haven, 2000).

Bury, J. P. T and R. P. Tombs, *Thiers 1797–1877: A Political Life* (London, 1986).

Cady, J. F., *The Roots of French Imperialism in East Asia* (Ithaca, NY, 1954).

Cain, Peter and A. G. Hopkins, *British Imperialism*, vol. 1: *Innovation and Expansion 1688–1914*, and vol. 2: *Crisis and Deconstruction 1914–90* (London, 1993).

Cannadine, David, *Class in Britain* (London, 2000).

Cannadine, David, *The Decline and Fall of the British Aristocracy* (London, 1992).

Cannadine, David, *Ornamentalism: How the British Saw their Empire* (London, 2001).

Cannon, John, *Parliamentary Reform 1640–1832* (Cambridge, 1973).

Carr, Raymond, *Spain, 1808–1939* (Oxford, 1966).

Chadwick, Owen, *A History of the Popes, 1830–1914* (Oxford, 1998).

Chadwick, Owen, *The Secularisation of the European Mind in the Nineteenth Century* (Cambridge, 1975).

Chakrabarty, Dipesh, *Provincialising Europe* (Princeton, 1999).

Chandavarkar, R. S., *The Origins of Industrial Capitalism in India* (Cambridge, 1996).

Chandler, Alfred D. Jr., *Scale and Scope: The Dynamics of Industrial Capitalism* (Cambridge, Mass., 1990).

Chandra, Bipan, *Communalism in Modern India* (Delhi, 1984).

Charle, Christophe, *Social History of France in the Nineteenth Century* (Oxford, 1994).

Chatterjee, Indrani, *Gender, Slavery and Law in Colonial India* (Delhi, 1999).

Chatterjee, Partha, *Nationalist Thought and the Colonial World: A Derivative Discourse?* (London, 1986).

Chaturvedi, Vinayak, *Mapping Subaltern Studies and the Postcolonial* (London, 2000).

Chaudhuri, K. N., *Asia before Europe: Economy and Civilisation of the Indian Ocean from the Rise of Islam to c.1750* (Cambridge, 1990).

Chomin, Nakae (tr. Nobuko Tsukai), *A Discourse by Three Drunkards on Government* (New York, 1984).

Christie, Ian R. and Benjamin W. Labaree, *Empire and Independence 1760–1776* (London, 1976).

Chung-li, Chang, *The Chinese Gentry* (Berkeley, 1965).

Clark, C. M., *Kaiser Wilhelm II* (London, 2000).

Clark, G. N. et al. (eds), *The New Cambridge Modern History*, vol. 11: *Material Progress and Worldwide Problems 1870–98* (Cambridge, 1963).

Clark, Peter, *British Clubs and Societies, 1580–1800: The Origins of An Associational World* (Oxford, 2000).

Cleveland, William L., *A History of the Modern Middle East* (Boulder, Colo., 1994).

Cobb, R. C., *Death in Paris: The Records of the Basse-Géole de la Seine* (Oxford, 1978).

Cohen, Paul A., *History in Three Keys: The Boxers as Event, Experience and Myth* (New York, 1997).

Cohn, Bernard S., *Colonialism and its Forms of Knowledge: The British in India* (Princeton, 1996).

Cole, Juan R. I., *Colonialism and Revolution in the Middle East: Social and Cultural Origins of Egypt's 'Urabi Movement* (Princeton, 1993).

Colley, Linda, *Britons: Forging the Nation 1707–1837* (London, 1992).

Collingham, E. M., *Imperial Bodies: The Physical Experience of the Raj c.1800–1947* (London, 2001).

Comaroff, Jean, *Body of Power, Spirit of Resistance: The Culture and History of a South African People* (Chicago, 1985).

Concise Dictionary of United States History (New York, 1983).

Cook, Chris and David Waller, *Longman Handbook of Modern American History 1763–1996* (London, 1997).

Cook, Chris and John Stevenson, *Longman Handbook of Modern European History 1763–1991* (London, 1992).

Coomaraswamy, Ananda K., *Essays in National Idealism* (Colombo, 1910).

Cooter, R., *Phrenology in Europe and America* (London, 2001).

Coquery-Vidrovitch, C., *Le Congo au temps des grands compagnies concessionnaires* (Paris, 1972).

Coverdale, John F., *The Basque Phase of Spain's First Carlist War* (Princeton, 1984).

Cowling, Elizabeth, *Interpreting Matisse, Picasso* (London, 2000), Tate Gallery exhibition, London, 2000.

Cray, Ralph D. and Michael A. Morrison (eds), *New Perspectives on the Early Republic* (Urbana, Ill., 1994).

Crossley, Pamela, *A Translucent Mirror: History and Identity in Qing Imperial Ideology* (Berkeley, 1999).

Curtin, Philip D., *The Atlantic Slave Trade: A Census* (Madison, Wis., 1969).

Curwen, C. A. (ed. and tr.), *Taiping Rebel: The Deposition of Li Hsiu-ch'eng* (Cambridge, 1977).

Daikichi, Irokawa (tr. and ed. Marius B. Jansen), *The Culture of the Meiji Period* (Princeton, 1985).

Darnton, Robert, *The Forbidden Best-Sellers of Pre-Revolutionary France* (London, 1996).

Darwin, Charles, *On the Origin of Species by Means of Natural Selection, or The Preservation of Favoured Races in the Struggle for Life* (London, 1859, 1920 Everyman edn).

Daunton, Martin, *Trusting Leviathan: The Politics of Taxation in Britain 1799–1814* (Cambridge, 2001).

Daunton, Martin and Rick Halpern (eds), *Empire and Others: British Encounters with Indigenous Peoples 1600–1850* (London, 1999).

Davies, Norman, *God's Playground: A History of Poland*, vol. 2: *1795 to the Present* (Oxford, 1981).

Davis, D. B., *The Problem of Slavery in Western Culture* (Ithaca, NY, 1966).

Davis, John A. (ed.), *Italy in the Nineteenth Century* (Oxford, 2000).

Davison, Roderic H., *Reform in the Ottoman Empire 1856–76* (Princeton, 1963).

Dawn, Ernest, *From Ottomanism to Arabism* (Urbana, Ill., 1973).

de Tocqueville, Alexis, *The Old Regime and the French Revolution* (New York, 1955).

de Vries, Jan, *The Dutch Rural Economy in the Golden Age 1500–1700* (New Haven, 1978).

de Vries, Jan and Adriaan van de Woude, *The First Modern Economy* (Cambridge, 1997).

Denoon, Donald and Philippa Mein-Smith with Marivic Wyndham, *A History of Australia, New Zealand and the Pacific* ((London, 2000).

Dew, Charles B., *Bond of Iron: Master and Slave at Buffalo Forge* (London, 1994).

Dickason, Olive P., *Canada's First Nations: A History of Founding Peoples from the Earliest Times* (Toronto, 1992).

Dikotter, F., *The Discourse of Race in Modern China* (London, 1992).

Dixon, S., *Modernisation in Russia 1676–1825* (Cambridge, 1999).

Doyle, William, *The Ancien Regime* (Basingstoke, 1986).

Doyle, William, *The Origins of the French Revolution* (Oxford, 1988).

Drayton, Richard, *Nature's Government: Science, Imperial Britain and the 'Improvement' of the World* (London, 2000).

Du Toit, A. and H. Giliomee (eds), *Afrikaner Political Thought*, vol. 1 (Berkeley, 1983).

Duara, Prasenjit, *Rescuing History from the Nation: Questioning Narratives of Modern China* (Chicago, 1995).

Duffy, Michael, *Soldiers, Sugar and Seapower: The British Expeditions to the West Indies and the War against Revolutionary France* (Oxford, 1987).

Duly, L. C., *British Land Policy at the Cape 1796–1834* (Durham, NC, 1964).

Durand, J. D., *Historical Estimates of World Population* (Philadelphia, 1974).

Dutta, Krishna and Andrew Robinson, *Tagore: The Myriad-Minded Man* (London, 1995).

Duus, Peter, *The Abacus and the Sword: The Japanese Penetration of Korea 1895–1910* (Berkeley, 1995).

Edney, Matthew, *Mapping an Empire: The Geographical Construction of British India 1765–1843* (Chicago, 1997).

Eisenman, Stephen F., with Thomas Crow, Brian Lukacher, Linda Nochlin, and Frances K. Pohl, *Nineteenth-Century Art: A Critical History* (London, 1998).

Eisenstadt, S. N., *Modernisation, Protest and Change* (Englewood Cliffs, NJ, 1966).

Elias, Norbert (tr. Edmund Jephcott), *The Civilizing Process*, vol. 1: *The History of Manners*, and vol. 2: *State Formation and Civilization* (Oxford, 1994).

Ellis, Geoffrey, *Napoleon: Profiles in Power* (Harlow, 1997).

Elphick, P. and H. Giliomee, *The Shaping of South African Society 1600–1850* (London, 1983).

Elvin, Mark, *The Pattern of the Chinese Past* (London, 1973).

Etherington, Norman, *The Great Treks: The Transformation of Southern Africa 1815–54* (London, 2001).

Etherington, Norman, *Theories of Imperialism: War, Conquest and Capital* (London, 1984).

Evans, Eric J., *The Forging of the Modern State: Early Industrial Britain 1783–1870* (London, 1983).

Evans, Richard J., *Death in Hamburg: Society and Politics in the Cholera Years 1830–1910* (Harmondsworth, 1990).

Fahmy, Khaled, *All the Pasha's Men: Mehmed Ali, his Army and the Making of Modern Egypt* (Cambridge, 1997).

Fairbank, John K. and Kwang-Ching Liu (eds), *The Cambridge History of China*, vol. 11, pt 2: *Late Ching* (Cambridge, 1980).

Falk, S. J., *Qajar Paintings: Persian Oil Paintings of the Eighteenth and Nineteenth Centuries* (London, 1972).

Fawaz, Leila Tarazi, *Merchants and Migrants in Nineteenth-Century Beirut* (Cambridge, Mass., 1982).

Fawaz, Leila Tarazi and C. A. Bayly, *Modernity and Culture from the Mediterranean to the Indian Ocean* (New York, 2002).

Ferguson, Niall, *Empire: How Britain made the Modern World 1700–2000* (London, 2001).

Fernando-Armesto, Felipe, *Millennium* (London, 1995).

Fieldhouse, D. K., *Economics and Empire* (London, 1984).

Figes, Orlando, *Natasha's Dance: A Cultural History of Russia* (London, 2002).

Findley, Carter V., *Bureaucratic Reform in the Ottoman Empire: The Sublime Porte 1789–1922* (Princeton, 1980).

Finn, Margot C., *After Chartism: Class and Nation in British Radical Politics 1848–1874* (Cambridge, 1993).

Fisher, Stanley, *Ottoman Land Law* (Oxford, 1919).

Florida, Nancy K., *Writing the Past, Inscribing the Future: History as Prophecy in Colonial Java* (Durham, NC, 1995).

Floud, Roderick and Deirdre McCloskey (eds), *The Economic History of Britain since 1700*, vol. 1 (Cambridge, 1994).

Fogel, Robert W. and Stanley L. Engermann, *Time on the Cross: The Economics of American Negro Slavery* (London, 1989).

Foner, Eric and Olivia Mahoney, *America's Reconstruction: People and Politics after the Civil War* (New York, 1995).

Forbes, Geraldine, *Positivism in Bengal: A Case-Study in the Transmission and Assimilation of an Ideology* (Delhi, 1998).

Forrer, Matti, *Hokusai: Prints and Drawings* (Munich, 1991).

Forstenzer, Thomas R., *French Provincial Police and the Fall of the Second Republic* (Princeton, 1981).

Foucault, Michel (tr. Alan Sheridan), *Discipline and Punish* (Harmondsworth, 1979).

Frank, Andre Gunder, *Mexican Agriculture 1521–1630* (Cambridge, 1979).

Frank, Andre Gunder, *ReOrient: Global Economy in the Asian Age* (London, 1998).

Franklin, Benjamin, *Autobiography*, Everyman edn (London, 1906).

Freyre, Gilberto, *The Masters and the Slaves: A Study in the Development of Brazilian Civilisation* (New York, 1963).

Furet, François, *Penser la Révolution française* (Paris, 1978).

Furet, François and Jacques Ozouf, *Reading and Writing Literacy in France from Calvin to Jules Ferry* (Cambridge, 1982).

Furet, François and Mona Ozouf, *Dictionnaire critique de la Révolution française* (Paris, 1988).

Gattrell, V. A. C. *The Hanging Tree: Execution and the English People 1770–1868* (Oxford, 1994).

Gellner, Ernest, *Nations and Nationalism* (Oxford, 1983).

Gellner, Ernest, *Plough, Sword and Book: The Structure of Human History* (London, 1988).

Genovese, Eugene, *Roll, Jordan Roll: The World the Slaves Made* (New York, 1974).

Gilroy, Amanda (ed.), *Romantic Geographies: Discourses of Travel, 1775–1844* (Manchester, 2000).

Godlewska, Anne and Neil Smith, *Geography and Empire* (Oxford, 1994).

Goldstone, Jack A., *Revolution and Rebellion in the Early Modern World* (Berkeley, 1991).

Good, David F., *The Economic Rise of the Habsburg Empire, 1750–1914* (Berkeley, 1984).

Goody, Jack, *The East in the West* (Cambridge, 1996).

Government Printing Office, Washington, DC, *Documents Illustrative of the Formation of the Union of the American States* (Washington, DC, 1927).

Graham, Richard, *Britain and the Onset of Modernisation in Brazil 1850–1914* (Cambridge, 1972).

Grewal, J. S., *The Sikhs of the Punjab* (Cambridge, 1994).

Grove, Richard H., *Green Imperialism: Colonial Expansion, Tropical Island Edens and the Origins of Environmentalism* (London, 1995).

Guha, Ranajit, *Towards a Rule of Property for Bengal* (The Hague, 1963).

Guha, Sumit, *Environment and Ethnicity in India 1200–1991* (Cambridge, 1999).

Guha-Thakurta, Tapati, *The Making of a New 'Indian' Art: Artists, Aesthetics and Nationalism in Bengal c.1850–1920* (Cambridge, 1992).

Gupta, Charu, *Sexuality, Obscenity, Community: Women, Muslims and the Hindu Public in Colonial India* (Delhi, 2001).

Habib, Irfan, *The Agrarian System of Mughal India (1556 –1707)* (Bombay, 1963).

Hall, Catherine, *Civilising Subjects: Metropole and Colony in the English Imagination 1830–67* (Cambridge, 2002).

Hall, Catherine, Keith McClelland, and Jane Rendall, *Defining the Victorian Nation: Class, Race and Gender and the Reform Act of 1867* (Cambridge, 2000).

Hamilton, Lord Frederick, *The Days before Yesterday* (London, 1920).

Hardacre, Helen, *Shinto and the State 1868–1988* (Princeton, 1989).

Hardy, Peter, *The Muslims of British India* (Cambridge, 1969).

Harris, Jose, *Private Lives, Public Spirit* (Oxford, 1993).

Harris, Ruth, *Lourdes: Body and Spirit in a Secular Age* (London, 1999).

Hasan, Mushirul, *A Nationalist Conscience, M. A. Ansari, the Congress and the Raj* (New Delhi, 1987).

Hastings, Adrian, *The Construction of Nationhood: Ethnicity, Religion and Nationalism* (Cambridge, 1997).

Haupt, G., *Aspects of International Socialism 1871–1914* (Cambridge, 1986).

Headrick, Daniel, *The Invisible Weapon: Telecommunications and International Politics 1851–1945* (New York, 1991).

Headrick, Daniel, *The Tools of Empire: Technology and European Imperialism in the Nineteenth Century* (New York, 1981).

Hegel, G. F. (tr. T. M. Knox), *Hegel's Philosophy of Right* (1821; Oxford, 1952).

Hevia, James L., *Cherishing Men from Afar: Qing Guest Ritual and the Macartney Embassy of 1795* (Durham, NC, 1995).

Hilton, Boyd, *The Age of Atonement: The Influence of Evangelicalism on Social and Economic Thought 1785–1885* (Oxford, 1988).

Hirschman, Albert O., *The Passions and the Interests: Political Arguments for Capitalism before its Triumph* (Princeton, 1972).

Hiskett, Mervyn, *The Development of Islam in West Africa* (London, 1984).

Hiskett, Mervyn, *The Sword of Truth: The Life and Times of the Shehu Usuman Dan Fodio* (New York, 1976).

Ho, Ping-ti, *The Ladder of Success in Imperial China: Aspects of Social Mobility 1368–1911* (New York, 1962).

Hobsbawm, E. J., *Nations and Nationalism since 1780* (Cambridge, 1990).

Hobsbawm, E. J., *The Age of Revolution; The Age of Capital; The Age of Empire; The Age of Extremes* (London, 1988–98).

Hodgson, Marshall G. S., *The Venture of Islam: Conscience and History in a World Civilisation*, 3 vols (Chicago, 1974).

Holt, P. M. (ed.), *Political and Social Change in Modern Egypt* (London, 1968).

Holt, P. M. (ed.), *The Cambridge History of Islam* vol. 2 (Cambridge, 1970).

Hopkins, A. G., *An Economic History of West Africa* (London, 1973).

Hopkins, A. G. (ed.), *Globalization in World History* (London, 2002).

Hosking, Geoffrey, *Russia, People and Empire, 1552–1917* (London, 1997).

Hourani, Albert, *Arabic Thought in the Liberal Age, 1789–1939* (Oxford, 1970).

Hoxie, Frederick E., *A Final Promise: The Campaign to Assimilate the Indians, 1880–1920* (Cambridge, 1984).

Hudson, Pat, *The Industrial Revolution* (London, 1992).

Hunt, Lynn, *Politics, Culture and Class in the French Revolution* (Berkeley, 1984).

Hurgronje, C. Snouck (tr. A. O'Sullivan), *The Achehnese* (Leiden, 1906).

Hyam, Ronald, *Britain's Imperial Century, 1815–1914: A Study of Empire and Expansion*, 3rd edn (Basingstoke, 2002).

Ilbert, Robert (ed.), *Alexandrie entre deux mondes* (Aix-en-Provence, 1988).

Iliffe, John, *Africans: The History of a Continent* (London, 1995).

Irick, Robert L., *Ch'ing Policy towards the Coolie Trade 1847–1878* (Taipei, 1982).

Irving, Robert Grant, *Indian Summer: Lutyens, Baker and Imperial Delhi* (New Haven, 1981).

Jall, Lothar (tr. J. A. Underwood), *Bismarck: The White Revolutionary*, vol. 2: *1871–1898* (London, 1986).

James, C. L. R., *The Black Jacobins: Toussaint L'Ouverture and the San Domingo Revolution* (London, 2001).

Jansen, Marius B. (ed.), *The Cambridge History of Japan*, vol. 5: *The Nineteenth Century* (Cambridge, 1989).

Jelavich, B., *A History of the Balkans*, vol. 2: *Eighteenth and Nineteenth Centuries* (Cambridge, 1983).

Jones, Kenneth, *Arya Dharm: Hindu Consciousness in Nineteenth-Century Punjab* (Berkeley, 1976).

Jones, P. M., *The Peasantry in the French Revolution* (London, 1988).

July, Robert W., *The Origins of Modern African Thought: Its Development in West Africa during the Nineteenth and Twentieth Centuries* (London, 1968).

Kanya-Forstner, A. S., *The Conquest of the Western Sudan: A Study in French Military Imperialism* (Cambridge, 1969).

Kasaba, Reçat, *The Ottoman Empire and the World Economy: The Nineteenth Century* (Albany, NY, 1988).

Kayali, Hasan, *Arabs and Young Turks: Ottomanism, Arabism and Islamism in the Ottoman Empire 1908–18* (Berkeley, 1997).

Keddie, Nikki R., *Roots of Revolution: An Interpretative History of Modern Iran* (New Haven, 1981).

Kedourie, Elie, *The Chatham House Version and Other Middle-Eastern Studies* (London, 1970).

Keep, John, *Soldiers of the Tsar: Army and Society in Russia 1462–1874* (Oxford, 1985).

Kemper, Steven, *Presence of the Past: Chronicles, Politics and Culture in Sinhala Life* (Ithaca, NY, 1991).

Keppel-Jones, Arthur, *Rhodes and Rhodesia: The White Conquest of Zimbabwe 1884–1902* (Montreal, 1983).

Kinealy, Christine, *This Great Calamity: The Irish Famine 1845–52* (Dublin, 1994).

Knight, Alan, *The Mexican Revolution*, 2 vols (Cambridge, 1986).

Knight, Franklin W., *Slave Society in Cuba during the Nineteenth Century* (Madison, Wis., 1975).

Koenig, William J., *The Burmese Polity 1752–1819: Politics, Administration and Organization in the Early Kon-baung Period* (Ann Arbor, 1990).

Kolff, D. H. A., *Naukar, Rajput and Sepoy: The Ethnohistory of the Military Labour Market in Hindustan 1450–1850* (Cambridge, 1986).

Komlos, John, *Stature, Living Standards and Economic Development: Essays in Anthropometric History* (Chicago, 1994).

Kopf, David, *The Brahmo Samaj and the Shaping of the Modern Indian Mind* (Princeton, 1979).

Kuhn, Philip A., *Rebellion and its Enemies in Late Imperial China 1798–1864* (Cambridge, Mass., 1970).

Kuhn, Philip A., *Soulstealers: The Chinese Sorcery Scare of 1768* (Cambridge, Mass., 1990).

Kumar, Deepak, *Science and the Raj 1857–1905* (Delhi, 1995).

Kumar, Dharma (ed.), *The Cambridge Economic History of India*, vol. 2 (New Delhi, 1983).

Kunt, I. M., *The Sultan's Servants: The Transformation of Ottoman Provincial Government 1550–1650* (New York, 1983).

Kvistad, Gregg, *The Rise and Demise of German Statism: Loyalty and Political Membership* (Oxford, 1999).

Kwong, Luke S., *The Mosaic of the Hundred Days: Personalities, Politics and Ideas of 1898* (Cambridge, Mass., 1984).

Landes, David, *Bankers and Pashas: International Finance and Economic Imperialism in Egypt* (London, 1958).

Landes, David, *Favourites of Fortune: Technical Growth and Economic Development since the Industrial Revolution* (Cambridge, 1991).

Landes, David, *The Wealth and Poverty of Nations* (London, 1998).

Langley, J. Ayo, *Ideologies of Political Liberation in Black Africa, 1856–1970: Documents on Modern African Political Thought from Colonial Times to the Present* (London, 1979).

Latham, A. J. H., *The International Economy and the Undeveloped World 1865–1914* (London, 1978).

Lee, Ki-baik (tr. E. W. Wagner), *New History of Korea* (Seoul, 1986).

Legge, James, *The Chinese Classics*, vol. 1 (repr. Taipei, 1994).

Lewis, Bernard, *The Emergence of Modern Turkey* (London, 1961).

Lewis, Bernard, *What Went Wrong? Western Impact and Middle Eastern Response* (Oxford, 2002).

Lienesch, Michael, *New Order of the Ages: Time, the Constitution and the Making of Modern American Political Thought* (Princeton, 1988).

The Life of Swami Vivekananda by his Eastern and Western Disciples, 2 vols (Calcutta, 1981).

Lieven, Dominic C. B., *The Aristocracy in Europe 1815–1914* (London, 1992).

Lieven, Dominic C. B., *Empire: The Russian Empire and its Rivals* (London, 2000).

Lieven, Dominic C. B., *Nicholas II: Emperor of all the Russias* (London, 1993).

List, F. (tr. S. Lloyd), *The National System of Political Economy* (London, 1885).

Louis, W. Roger, *The Robinson and Gallagher Controversy* (New York, 1976).

Lyons, F. S., *Ireland since the Famine: 1850 to the Present* (London, 1971).

Lyons, Martin, *Napoleon Bonaparte and the Legacy of the French Revolution* (London, 1994).

MacDonagh, Oliver, *Patterns of Government Growth 1800–1860: The Passenger Acts and their Enforcement* (Aldershot, 1993).

Macfarlane, Alan, *The Origins of English Individualism* (Oxford, 1976).

Macfarlane, Alan, *The Riddle of the Modern World: Of Liberty, Wealth and Equality* (Basingstoke, 2000).

Mack Smith, Denis, *Italy and its Monarchy* (New Haven, 1989).

MacKenzie, John M., *Imperialism and the Natural World* (Manchester, 1990).

MacKenzie, John M., *Orientalism, Art, Literature and Society* (London, 1995).

Macpherson, C. B., *The Political Theory of Possessive Individualism: Hobbes to Locke* (Oxford, 1962).

Malik, Jamal (ed.), *Perceptions of Mutual Encounters in South Asian History, 1760–1860* (Wiesbaden, 2000).

Mandel, Daniel R., *Behind the Frontier: Indians in Eighteenth-Century Eastern Massachusetts* (Lincoln, Nebr., 1996).

Mann, Michael, *The Sources of Social Power*, vol. 2: *The Rise of Classes and Nation States 1760–1914* (Cambridge, 1993).

Manuel, E. F., *The New World of Henri Saint Simon* (Cambridge, Mass., 1956).

Manzoni, Alessandro, *I promessi sposi* (1827; repr. Florence, 1962).

Markovits, Claude, *The Global World of Indian Merchants 1750–1947: Traders of Sindh from Bukhara to Panama* (Cambridge, 2000).

Marr, David, *Vietnamese Anti-Colonialism, 1885–1925* (Berkeley, 1971).

Marshall, P. J. (ed.), *The Oxford History of the British Empire*, vol. 2: *The Eighteenth Century* (Oxford, 1998).

Mayer, Arno, *The Persistence of the Old Regime: Europe to the Great War* (London, 1981).

Mazower, M., *The Balkans* (London, 2000).

Mazzini, Giuseppe, *The Duties of Man and Other Essays* (c.1870; repr. London, 1966).

Mazzini, Giuseppe, *Ricordi autobiografici di Giuseppe Mazzini con introduzione e note di Mario Menghini* (Imola, 1938).

McCann, J., *From Poverty to Famine in North East Ethiopia: A Rural History 1900–1935* (Philadelphia, 1987).

McCarthy, Thomas, *The Critical Theory of Jürgen Habermas* (London, 1984).

McClain, James L., John M. Merriman, and Ugawa Kaoru, *Edo and Paris: Urban Life and the State in the Early Modern Era* (Ithaca, NY, 1994).

McDaniel, T., *Autocracy, Capitalism and Revolution in Europe 1815–1914* (Berkeley, 1988).

McEvedy, Colin and Richard Jones, *Atlas of World Population History* (Harmondsworth, 1978).

McLeod, Mark W., *The Vietnamese Response to French Intervention 1862–74* (New York, 1991).

Mehta, Uday, *Liberalism and Empire: A Study in Nineteenth-Century British Liberal Thought* (Chicago, 1999).

Meintjes, Johannes, *President Paul Kruger: A Biography* (London, 1974).

Meriggi, M., *Amministrazione e classi sociali nel Lombardo-Veneto 1814–48* (Bologna, 1983).

Metcalf, Barbara D., *Islamic Revival in British India: Deoband 1860–1900* (Princeton, 1982).

Metcalf, Barbara D. and Thomas R. Metcalf, *A Concise History of India* (Cambridge, 1994).

Metcalf, T. R., *Land, Landlords and the British Raj: Northern India in the Nineteenth Century* (Berkeley, 1979).

Meyer, Michael C. and William H. Beezley (eds), *The Oxford History of Mexico* (Oxford, 2000).

Michael, Franz and Chang Chung-li, *The Taiping Rebellion: History and Documents*, 3 vols (Seattle, 1966–71).

Michel, Regis, et al., *Aux armes et aux arts: les arts de la révolution 1789–1799* (Paris, 1989).

Midgely, Clare (ed.), *Gender and Imperialism* (Manchester, 1998).

Miers, Suzanne and Igor Kopytoff (eds), *Slavery in Africa: Historical and Anthropological Perspectives* (Madison, Wis., 1977).

Mill, John Stuart, *Autobiography* (1873; repr. London, 1949).

Miller, Joseph C., *Way of Death: Merchant Capitalism and Angolan Slave Trade 1730–1830* (London, 1988).

Milner, Anthony, *The Invention of Politics in Colonial Malaya: Contesting Nationalism and the Expansion of the Public Sphere* (Cambridge, 1994).

Milward, A. S. and S. B. Saul, *Development of the Economies of Central Europe, 1850–1914* (London, 1977).

Mitchell, Timothy, *Colonising Egypt* (London, 1985).

Mitter, Partha, *Art and Nationalism in Colonial India 1850–1922* (Cambridge, 1994).

Molnar, Miklos, *A Concise History of Hungary* (Cambridge, 2001).

Moore, Barrington, Jr., *Social Origins of Dictatorship and Democracy: Lord and Peasant in the Making of the Modern World* (London, 1984).

Moorehead, Caroline, *Dunant's Dream: War, Switzerland and the History of the Red Cross* (London, 1998).

Morgan, David, *Medieval Persia 1040–1797* (London, 1988).

Morris, Jonathan, *The Political Economy of Shopkeeping in Milan, 1886–1922* (Cambridge, 1993).

Myers, Ramon H., Peter Duus, and Mark R. Peattie, *The Japanese Informal Empire in China 1895–1937* (Princeton, 1989).

Myint-U, Thant, *The Making of Modern Burma* (Cambridge, 1999).

Needham, Joseph, *Science and Civilisation in China*, 8 vols (Cambridge, 1965–90).

Norman, E. R., *Church and Society in England, 1770–1970: A Historical Study* (Oxford, 1976).

North, Douglass C., *The Economic Growth of the United States, 1790–1860* (Englewood Cliffs, NJ, 1961).

Northrup, D., *Indentured Labour in the Age of Imperialism 1834–1922* (London, 1995).

Oberoi, Harjot Singh, *The Construction of Religious Boundaries: Culture, Identity and Diversity in the Sikh Tradition* (Delhi, 1997).

O'Brien, P. K., *The Economic Effects of the American Civil War* (Basingstoke, 1988).

O'Brien, P. K. (ed.), *The Industrial Revolution in Europe*, 2 vols (Oxford, 1994).

O'Brien, P. K. and Leando Prados de la Escosura (eds), *The Costs and Benefits of European Imperialism from the Conquest of Ceuta (1415) to the Treaty of Lusaka (1974)*, special issue of *Revista de Historia Economica* (Madrid, 1998).

O'Brien, P. K. and Ronald Quinalt (eds), *The Industrial Revolution and British Society* (Cambridge, 1993).

O'Grada, Cormac, *The Great Irish Famine* (Dublin, 1989).

O'Hanlon, Rosalind, *Caste, Conflict and Ideology* (Cambridge, 1985).

Omer-Cooper, J. D., *The Zulu Aftermath* (London, 1966).

Ooms, H., *Tokugawa Village Practice: Class, Status, Power, Law* (Berkeley, 1996).

Orsini, Francesca, *The Hindi Public Sphere 1920–40: Language and Literature in the Age of Nationalism* (Delhi, 2002).

Osborne, Milton, *The French Presence in Cochin China and Cambodia* (Berkeley, 1971).

Owen, Roger, *Cotton and the Egyptian Economy: A Study in Trade and Development* (Oxford, 1969).

Owen, Roger, *The Middle East and the World Economy 1800–1914* (London, 1981).

Owen, Roger and Bob Sutcliffe, *Studies in the Theory of Imperialism* (London, 1972).

Ozouf, Mona, *La Fête révolutionnaire 1789–1799* (Paris, 1976).

Pagden, Anthony, *The Lords of All the World: Ideologies of Empire in Spain, Britain and France c.1500–c.1800* (New Haven, 1995).

Palmer, R. R., *The Age of Democratic Revolution*, 2 vols (London, 1959–64).

Pamuk, Sevket, *A Monetary History of the Ottoman Empire* (Cambridge, 2000).

Pamuk, Sevket, *The Ottoman Empire and European Capitalism, 1820–1930* (Cambridge, 1987).

Parish, Peter J., *The American Civil War* (London, 1975).

Parker, Geoffrey, *The Military Revolution: Military Innovation and the Rise of the West, 1500–1800* (Cambridge, 1988).

Parthasarathi, Prasannan, *The Transition to a Colonial Economy: Weavers, Merchants and Kings in South India* (Cambridge, 2000).

Peel, J. D. Y., *Religious Encounter and the Making of the Yoruba* (Bloomington, Ind., 2000).

Peiris, J. B. (ed.), *Before and After Shaka* (Grahamstown, 1983).

Perdue, Peter, *Exhausting the Earth: State and Peasant in Hunan, 1500–1850* (Cambridge, Mass., 1987).

Perry, J. R., *Karim Khan Zand* (Chicago, 1979).

Pevsner, Niklaus, *Ruskin and Viollet-le-Duc: Englishness and Frenchness in the Appreciation of Gothic Architecture* (London, 1969).

Pflanze, Otto, *Bismarck and the Development of Germany*, vol. 3: *The Period of Fortification 1880–98* (Princeton, 1990).

Pipes, Richard, *Russia under the Old Regime* (London, 1974).

Platt, D. C. M., *Finance, Trade and Politics in British Foreign Policy 1815–1914* (Oxford, 1968).

Pocock, J. G. A., *The Machiavellian Moment: Florentine Political Thought and the Atlantic Republican Tradition* (Princeton, 1975).

Polachek, James M., *The Inner Opium War* (Cambridge, Mass., 1992).

Pomeranz, Kenneth, *The Great Divergence: China, Europe and the Making of the Modern World Economy* (Princeton, 2000).

Porter, Andrew, *European Imperialism 1860–1914* (London, 1994).

Porter, Andrew (ed.), *The Oxford History of the British Empire*, vol. 3: *The Nineteenth Century* (Oxford, 1999).

Porter, Roy, *Enlightenment: Britain and the Making of the Modern World* (London, 2000).

Price, Richard, *British Society 1680–1880: Dynamism, Containment and Change* (Cambridge, 1998).

Price, Roger, *Napoleon III and the Second Empire* (London, 1997).

Prins, Gwyn, *The Hidden Hippopotamus: Reappraisal in African History: The Early Colonial Experience in Western Zambia* (Cambridge, 1980).

Ralston, D. B., *Importing the European Army: The Introduction of European Military Techniques and Institutions into the Extra-European World 1600–1914* (Chicago, 1990).

Ranger, Terence, *Voices from the Rocks: Nature, Culture and History in the Matopos Hills of Zimbabwe* (London, 1999).

Rankin, M., *Elite Activism and Political Transformation in China* (Cambridge, Mass., 1993).

Rawski, Evelyn S., *The Last Emperors: A Social History of Qing Imperial Institutions* (Berkeley, 1998).

Rawski, Evelyn S. and Susan Naquin, *Chinese Society in the Eighteenth Century* (New Haven, 1987).

Reid, Brian Holden, *The Origins of the American Civil War* (London, 1996).

Reynolds, Douglas R., *China 1898–1912* (Cambridge, Mass., 1993).

Richards, John F., *The Mughal Empire* (Cambridge, 1995).

Richards, John F., *The Unending Frontier: Environmental History in the Early Modern Centuries* (Berkeley, 2003).

Ricklefs, M., *A History of Modern Indonesia since 1300* (London, 1993).

Rizvi, S. A. A., *Shah Abd al-Aziz: Puritanism, Sectarian Polemics and Jihad* (Canberra, 1982).

Rizvi, S. A. A., *Shah Walli-allah and his Times* (Canberra, 1980).

Robinson, David, *The Holy War of Umar Tal: The Western Sudan in the Mid-Nineteenth Century* (Oxford, 1985).

Robinson, F. C. R., *Islam and Muslim History in South Asia* (New Delhi, 2001).

Robinson, Ronald and John Gallagher with Alice Denny, *Africa and the Victorians: The Official Mind of Imperialism* (London, 1981).

Roff, William R., *Islam and the Political Economy of Meaning: Studies in Muslim Discourse* (London, 1987).

Röhl, John G. C., *The Kaiser and his Court: Wilhelm II and the Government of Germany* (Cambridge, 1994).

Rolland, Romain, *Ramakrishna the Man God and the Universal Gospel of Vivekananda* (Calcutta, 1960).

Rostow, W. W., *The World Economy: History and Prospect* (Austin, Tex., 1978).

Rothschild, Emma, *Economic Sentiments: Adam Smith, Condorcet and the Enlightenment* (Cambridge, Mass., 2001).

Rowe, William T., *Hankow: Conflict and Community in a Chinese City 1796–1895* (Stanford, Calif., 1989).

Roy, Ram Mohun (ed. E. S. Bose), *The Selected English Works of Raja Ram Mohun Roy*, vol. 2 (Calcutta, 1887).

Roy, Tirthankar, *Traditional Industry in the Economy of Colonial India* (Cambridge, 1999).

Rule, John, *The Vital Century: England's Developing Economy 1714–1815* (Harlow, 1992).

Ruskin, John, *The Stones of Venice* (London, 1960).

Said, Edward, *Orientalism* (London, 1970).

Saidiq, M., *History of Urdu Literature* (London, 1964).

Saiz, M. C. G., *Las castas mexicanas: un genero pictorico americano* (Mexico City, 1989).

Salemink, Oscar, *The Ethnography of Vietnam's Central Highlanders: A Historical Contextualisation 1850–1930* (London, 2002).

Samson, Jane, *Imperial Benevolence: Making British Authority in the Pacific Islands* (Honolulu, 1998).

Schama, Simon, *Patriots and Liberators: Revolution in the Netherlands 1780–1813* (London, 1992).

Schölch, Alexander, *Egypt for the Egyptians* (Ithaca, NY, 1981).

Scott, James C., *Seeing like a State: How Certain Schemes to Improve the Human Condition have Failed* (New Haven, 1998).

Seal, Anil, *The Emergence of Indian Nationalism* (Cambridge, 1969).

Secord, James, *A Victorian Sensation* (Chicago, 2000).

Seddon, A., *Moroccan Peasants: A Century of Change in the Eastern Rif 1870–1970* (London, 1981).

Sevcenko, Ihor and Frank E. Sysyn (eds), *Eurcharisterion*, vol. 1 (Cambridge, Mass., 1978).

Sewell, William H., *Work and Revolution in France: The Language of Labour from the Old Regime to 1848* (Cambridge, 1980).

Shatzmiller, Maya, *The Berbers and the Islamic State* (Princeton, 2000).

Shaw, Stanford J., *A History of the Ottoman Empire and Modern Turkey*, vol. 2: *Reform, Revolution and Republic: The Rise of Modern Turkey 1808–1975* (Cambridge, 1975).

Shaw, Stanford J., *Between Old and New: The Ottoman Empire under Selim III 1789–1807* (Cambridge, Mass., 1971).

Sheehan, James J., *German History 1770–1866* (Oxford, 1989).

Showalter, Dennis, *The Wars of Frederick the Great* (London, 1996).

Shulze, Hagen, *The Course of German Nationalism: From Frederick the Great to Bismarck 1763–1867* (Cambridge, 1982).

Simon, Walter, *European Positivism in the Nineteenth Century: An Essay in Intellectual History* (Port Washington, NY, 1963).

Singha, Radhika, *A Despotism of Law: Crime and Justice in Early Colonial India* (Delhi, 2000).

Skaria, Ajay, *Hybrid Histories: Forests, Frontiers and Wildness in Western India* (Delhi, 1999).

Skowronek, Stephen, *Building a New American State: The Expansion of National Administrative Capacities 1877–1920* (Cambridge, 1982).

Smith, Anthony D., *Nationalism and Modernism* (London, 1998).

Smith, J. D., *The Epic of Pabuji: An Essay in Transcription and Translation* (Cambridge, 1991).

Smith, T. C., *The Agrarian Origins of Modern Japan* (Stanford, Calif., 1959).

Soleillet, C., *L'Avenir de la France en Afrique* (Paris, 1876).

Speck, W. A., *A Concise History of Britain 1707–1975* (Cambridge, 1999).

Spence, Jonathan, *The Search for Modern China* (New York, 1990).

Spencer, Herbert (ed. Duncan Macrae), *The Man versus the State* (1884, 1886, repr. London, 1969).

Sperber, Jonathan, *The European Revolutions 1848–1851* (Cambridge, 1994).

Stampp, Kenneth M., *The Peculiar Institution* (New York, 1956).

Stedman Jones, Gareth, Introduction to Karl Marx and Friedrich Engels, *The Communist Manifesto* (London, 2000).

Stedman Jones, Gareth, *Languages of Class* (Cambridge, 1983).

Stedman Jones, Gareth, *Outcast London* (Oxford, 1971).

Stein, Burton, *A History of India* (Oxford, 1998).

Stokes, Eric, *The English Utilitarians and India* (repr. Delhi, 1989).

Stokes, E. T., *The Peasant and the Raj* (Cambridge, 1979).

Stone, Lawrence (ed.), *The Imperial State at War: Britain from 1689–1815* (London, 1990).

Strachan, Hew, *The First World War*, vol. 1 (Oxford, 2001).

Sutherland, D., *France 1789–1815: Revolution and Counter-Revolution* (London, 1985).

Tambiah, Stanley J., *World Conqueror and World Renouncer* (Cambridge, 1972).

Tandan, Banmali, *The Architecture of Lucknow and its Dependencies 1722–1856*, 2 vols (Delhi, 2000).

Tanner, Duncan, Pat Thane, and Nicholas Tiratsoo (eds), *Labour's First Century* (Cambridge, 2000).

Tarlo, Emma, *Clothing Matters: What to Wear in Colonial India* (London, 1998).

Taylor, George R., *The Transportation Revolution 1815–1860* (London, 1951).

Taylor, Miles, *The Decline of British Radicalism 1847–1865* (Oxford, 1995).

Terasse, Henri, *Histoire du Maroc, des origines à l'établissement du protectorat français* (Casablanca, 1950).

Thomas, Hugh, *Cuba: Or the Pursuit of Freedom* (London, 1971).

Thompson, E. P., *The Making of the English Working Class* (London, 1993).

Thompson, E. P., *Whigs and Hunters: The Origin of the Black Acts* (London, 1975).

Thompson, John A., *Woodrow Wilson* (London, 2002).

Thompson, W. F. (ed.), *The Practical Philosophy of the Muhammadan People* (London, 1839).

Tilly, Charles, *Coercion, Capital and States AD 900–1992* (Cambridge, Mass., 1992).

Tinker, Hugh, *A New System of Slavery: The Export of Indian Labour Overseas 1830–1920* (London, 1974).

Tombs, Robert, *France 1814–1914* (London, 1996).

Tomlinson, B. R., *The Economy of Modern India 1860–1970* (Cambridge, 1993).

Tone, Theobald Wolfe (ed. R. Barry O'Brien), *The Autobiography of Theobald Wolfe Tone* (London, 1893).

Torpey, John, *The Invention of the Passport: Surveillance, Citizenship and the State* (Cambridge, 2000).

Totman, Conrad, *A History of Japan* (London, 2000).

Tretiakov, S., *A Chinese Testament: The Autobiography of Tan Shih-Hua as told to S. Tretiakov* (New York, 1934).

Trigger, Bruce G. (ed.), *The Cambridge History of the Native Peoples of the Americas*, vol. 1: *North America* (Cambridge, 1996).

Tripp, Charles, *A History of Iraq* (Cambridge, 2000).

Troll, Christian, *Sayyid Ahmad Khan: A Reinterpretation of Muslim Theology* (Delhi, 1978).

Tulard, J. (ed.), *Dictionnaire Napoléon* (Paris, 1987).

Tusi, Nasiruddin (tr. G. M. Wickens), *The Nasirean Ethics* (London, 1969).

van de Ven, Hans, *Military and Financial Reform in the Late Qing and Early Republic* (Taipei, 1999).

Vatikiotis, P. J., *The History of Modern Egypt: From Muhammad Ali to Mubarak* (London, 1991).

Vaughan, F., *The Political Philosophy of Giambattista Vico: An Introduction to La Scienza Nuova* (The Hague, 1972).

Vaughan, W. E. (ed.), *A New History of Ireland*, vol. 6, pt 2: *Ireland under the Union 1870–1921* (Oxford, 1986).

Vernadsky, G., et al. (eds), *A Source Book for Russian History from Early Times to 1917*, vol. 2: *Peter the Great to Nicholas II* (New Haven, 1972).

Vickery, Amanda, *The Gentleman's Daughter: Women's Lives in Georgian England* (London, 1998).

Vivekananda, *Chicago Addresses*, 16th impression (Calcutta, 1971).

Voll, Obert, *Islam: Continuity and Change in the Modern World* (Boulder, Colo., 1982).

Voth, Hans Joachim, *Time and Work in England 1750–1830* (Oxford, 2000).

Waley-Cohen, Joanna, *The Sextants of Beijing: Global Currents in Chinese History* (New York, 1999).

Wallerstein, Immanuel, *The Modern World System*, 1 (New York, 1974).

Walvin, James, *Black Ivory: Slavery in the British Empire* (Oxford, 2001).

Wardy, Robert, *Aristotle in China: Language, Categories and Translation* (Cambridge, 2000).

Watts, David, *The West Indies* (Cambridge, 1987).

Weber, Eugene, *Peasants into Frenchmen: The Modernisation of Rural France, 1870–1914* (Stanford, Calif., 1976).

Wesseling, H. L., *Divide and Rule: The Partition of Africa 1880–1914* (Westport, Conn., 1996).

Whitehouse, Harvey, *Arguments and Icons: Divergent Modes of Religiosity* (Oxford, 2000).

Wiener, Martin, *English Culture and the Decline of the Industrial Spirit* (Harmondsworth, 1981).

Wilks, Ivor, *Asante in the Nineteenth Century: The Structure and Evolution of a Political Order* (Cambridge, 1975).

Williams, Glyndwr and P. J. Marshall, *The Great Map of Mankind: British Perceptions of the World in the Age of Enlightenment* (London, 1982).

Wills, John E. II, *1688: A Global History* (London, 2001).

Wilson, Kathleen, *The Sense of the People: Politics, Culture and Imperialism in England, 1715–1785* (Cambridge, 1995).

Wilton, Andrew and Robert Upstone (eds), *The Age of Rossetti, Burne-Jones and Watts: Symbolism in Britain 1860–1910* (London, 1997).

Winichakul, Thongchai, *Siam Mapped: A History of the Geo-body of a Nation* (Honolulu, 1994).

Wong, J. Y., *Deadly Dreams: Opium and the Arrow War (1856–60) in China* (Cambridge, 1998).

Wong, J. Y., *The Making of a Heroic Image: Sun Yatsen in London 1896–7* (London, 1986).

Wong, R. Bin, *China Transformed: Historical Change and the Limits of European Experience* (Ithaca, NY, 1997).

Woodward, C. Vann, *The Origins of the New South* (Baton Rouge, La., 1951).

Woolf, Stuart, *A History of Italy 1700–1860* (London, 1979).

Woolf, Stuart, *Napoleon's Integration of Europe* (London, 1989).

Worden, Nigel, *The Making of Modern South Africa* (Oxford, 1994).

Worden, Nigel, *The Shaping of South African Society: Conquest, Segregation and Apartheid* (Oxford, 1994).

Wright, Stanley, *Hart and the Chinese Customs* (Belfast, 1950).

Wrigley, E. A., *People, Cities and Wealth: The Transition of Traditional Society* (Oxford, 1988).

Wu, Wang Gung, *The Chinese Overseas: From Earthbound China to the Quest for Autonomy* (Cambridge, Mass., 2000).

Wyatt, David K., *Thailand: A Short History* (New Haven, 1984).

Wyatt, David K., *The Politics of Reform in Thailand: Education in the Reign of Chulalongkorn* (New Haven, 1969).

Yang, Anand A., *Bazaar India: Markets, Society and the Colonial State in Bihar* (Berkeley, 1998).

Yashinaga, Toshinobu, *Ando Shoeki: Social and Ecological Philosopher in Eighteenth-Century Japan* (New York, 1992).

Yate, William, *An Account of New Zealand and of the Church Missionary Society's Mission in the Northern Island* (1835; repr. Shannon, 1970).

Zunz, Olivier, *Why the American Century?* (Chicago, 1998).

ARTICLES FROM JOURNALS, BOOK CHAPTERS, AND UNPUBLISHED PAPERS

Anderson, Perry, "Confronting defeat," *London Review of Books*, 24, 20 (17 Oct. 2002).

Bannerji, Himani, "Age of consent and hegemonic social reform," in Clare Midgely (ed.), *Gender and Imperialism* (Manchester, 1998), pp. 21–45.

Bayly, C. A., "The first age of global imperialism 1780–1830," in Peter Burroughs and A. J. Stockwell (eds), *Managing the Business of Empire: Essays in Honour of D. K. Fieldhouse* (London, 1998), pp. 28–43.

Bayly, C. A., "Orientalists, informants and critics in Benares, 1790–1860," in Jamal Malik (ed.), *Perceptions of Mutual Encounters in South Asian History, 1760–1860* (Wiesbaden, 2000), pp. 172–210.

Bayly, C. A., "South Asia and the great divergence," *Itinerario*, 24, 3/4 (2000), pp. 89–104.

Beasley, W. G., "Japan and the West in the mid-nineteenth century," offprint, *Proceedings of the British Academy* (London, 1969).

Bennison, Amira K., "Muslim universalism and Western globalisation," in A. G. Hopkins (ed.), *Globalization in World History* (London, 2002), pp. 74–97.

Breuilly, John, "Historians and the nation," in Peter Burke (ed.), *History and Historians in the Twentieth Century* (Oxford, 2002), pp. 55–87.

Carey, Peter, "Waiting for the Ratu Adil: the Javanese village community on the eve of the Java War," *Modern Asian Studies*, 20, 1 (1986), pp. 55–137.

Cole, J. R. I., "Printing in urban Islam," in L. T. Fawaz and C. A. Bayly, *Modernity and Culture from the Mediterranean to the Indian Ocean* (Columbia, SC, 2002), pp. 344–64.

de Vries, Jan, "The Industrial Revolution and the industrious revolution," *Journal of Economic History*, 54 (1994), pp. 240–70.

Doyle, William, "The Union in a European context," *Transactions of the Royal Historical Society*, 6 ser., 10 (2000), pp. 167–80.

el-din el-Shayyal, Gamal, "Some aspects of intellectual and social life in eighteenth-century Egypt," in P. M. Holt (ed.), *Political and Social Change in Modern Egypt* (London, 1968), pp. 117–32.

Fletcher, Joseph, "Turko-Mongolian tradition in the Ottoman Empire," in I. Sevcenko and Frank E. Sysyn (eds), *Eurcharisterion*, vol. 1 (Cambridge, Mass., 1978), pp. 240–2.

Gellner, Ernest, "Do nations have navels?," *Nations and Nationalism*, 10 (1996), pp. 366–70.

Godlewska, Anne, "Napoleon's geographers (1797–1815): imperialists and soldiers of modernity," in Anne Godlewska and Neil Smith, *Geography and Empire* (Oxford, 1994), pp. 31–53.

Harling, P. and P. Mandler, "From fiscal-military state to laissez-faire state, 1760–1850," *Journal of British Studies*, 32, 1 (1993), pp. 1–34.

Holsoe, S., "The Vai," in S. Miers and I. Kopytoff (eds), *Slavery in Africa* (Madison, Wis., 1977), pp. 287–304.

Hopkins, A. G., "Asante and the Victorians: transition and partition on the Gold Coast," in Roy E. Bridges (ed.), *Imperialism, Decolonisation and Africa: Studies Presented to John Hargreaves* (Basingstoke, 2000), pp. 25–65.

Innes, Joanna, "The domestic face of the military fiscal state in eighteenth-century Britain," in Lawrence Stone (ed.), *The Imperial State at War: Britain from 1689–1815* (London, 1990), pp. 96–127.

Joyce, Patrick, "The return of history: post-modernism and the politics of academic history in Britain," *Past and Present*, 158 (Feb. 1998), pp. 207–35.

Kaukiainen, Yrjo, "The improvement of communications in international freight markets c.1830–1870," in Hiram Morgan (ed.), *Information, Media and Power through the Ages* (Dublin, 2001), pp. 137–52.

Leask, Nigel, "Francis Wilford and the colonial construction of Hindu geography," in Amanda Gilroy (ed.), *Romantic Geographies: Discourses of Travel, 1775–1844* (Manchester, 2000), pp. 204–23.

Lewis, Colin, "Pulling teeth in eighteenth-century Paris," *Past and Present*, 166 (2000), pp. 100–45.

Makoto, Takeuchi, "Festivals and fights: the law and the people of Edo," in James L. McClain et al., *Edo and Paris: Urban Life and the State in the Early Modern Era* (Ithaca, NY, 1994), pp. 384–406.

Masao, Watanabe, "Science across the Pacific," in Ardath W. Burks (ed.), *The Modernisers: Overseas Students, Foreign Employees and Meiji Japan* (Boulder, Colo., 1985), pp. 369–92.

Morgan, Philip D., "Encounters between British and 'indigenous' peoples c.1500–c.1800," in Martin Daunton and Rick Halpern (eds), *Empire and Others: British Encounters with Indigenous Peoples 1600–1850* (London, 1999), pp. 42–78.

"Newspaper," in *Encyclopaedia Britannica*, 13th edn (London, 1911).

O'Brien, P. K., "The reconstruction, rehabilitation and reconfiguration of the British industrial revolution as a conjuncture in global history," *Itinerario*, 3/4 (2000), pp. 117–34.

Ozouf, Mona, "L'opinion publique," in Keith Baker (ed.), *The Political Culture of the Old Regime* (Oxford, 1987), pp. 419–34.

Parry, J. P., "The impact of Napoleon III on British politics 1851–1880," *Transactions of the Royal Historical Society*, 6 ser., 11 (2001), pp. 147–75.

Pomeranz, Kenneth , "Rethinking the late imperial Chinese economy: development, disaggregation and decline 1730–1930," *Itinerario*, 24, 3/4 (2000), pp. 29–75.

Ray, Rajat Kanta, "Asian capital in the age of European domination: the rise of the bazaar, 1800–1914," *Modern Asian Studies*, 29, 3 (1993), pp. 449–554.

Roberts, M., "Beyond Anderson: reconstructing and deconstructing Sinhala nationalist discourse," *Modern Asian Studies*, 30 (1996), pp. 690–8.

Robinson, Francis, "Technology and religious change: Islam and the impact of print," *Modern Asian Studies*, 27, 1 (1993), pp. 229–51.

Robinson, Ronald and John Gallagher, "The imperialism of free trade," *Economic History Review*, 2, ser. 6, 1 (1953), pp. 1–15.

Rothschild, Emma, "The East India Company and the American Revolution," unpublished paper, Centre for History and Economics, University of Cambridge, 2002.

Rothschild, Emma, "Globalisation and democracy in historical perspective," unpublished paper, Centre for History and Economics, University of Cambridge, 2000.

Rothschild, Emma, "*Smithianismus* and Enlightenment in nineteenth-century Europe," unpublished paper, Centre for History and Economics, University of Cambridge, 1998.

Singh, D. J., "Historical significance of Jhaggra Jatti te Katrani da," in F. Singh and A. C. Arora (eds), *Maharaja Ranjit Singh: Politics, Society and Economics* (Patiala, 1984), pp. 289–91.

Singha, Radhika, "Settle, mobilize, verify: identification practices in colonial India," *Studies in History* (Delhi), 16, 2, n.s. (2000), pp. 151–98.

"Spirit capture: the native Americans and the photographic image," *International Herald Tribune*, 25–6 Aug. 2001.

Stokes, Eric, "Late-nineteenth-century colonial expansion: the attack on the theory of economic imperialism: a case of mistaken identity?," *Historical Journal*, 12 (1969), pp. 285–302.

Subrahmanyam, Sanjay, "Du Tage au Gange au xvie siècle: une conjoncture millénariste à l'échelle eurasiatique," *Annales*, 1 (Jan.–Feb. 2001), pp. 51–84.

Taylor, Miles, "The 1848 revolutions in the British Empire," *Past and Present*, 166 (2000), pp. 146–81.

Waley-Cohen, Joanna, "Commemorating war in eighteenth-century China," *Modern Asian Studies*, 30, 4 (1996), pp. 869–99.

Ward, Helen, "Worth its weight in gold: women and value in northwest India," unpublished PhD dissertation, University of Cambridge, 1999.

Washbrook, D. A., "Economic depression and the making of 'traditional' society in Colonial India, 1820–1855," *Transactions of the Royal Historical Society*, 6, 3 (1993), pp. 237–63.

Wiebe, Robert, "Imagined communities: nationalist experiences," *Journal of the Historical Society*, 1, 1 (Spring 2000), pp. 33–63.

Wood, Gordon S., "The significance of the Early Republic," in Ralph D. Cray and Michael A. Morrison (eds), *New Perspectives on the Early Republic* (Urbana, Ill., 1994), pp. 1–22.

Wyse, Akintola J., "Britain's African junior partners: a re-examination of the role of the Krio in nineteenth-century West Africa," in Roy E. Bridges (ed.), *Imperialism, Decolonisation and Africa: Studies Presented to John Hargreaves* (Basingstoke, 2000), pp. 3–24.

INDEX

Abd al-Aziz, Shah, 127, 142, 338
Abd al-Wahhab, Muhammad ibn, 105–6,
    331–2
Abduh, Muhammad, 328, 402, 467, 477
Abdullah bin Abdul Kadir, Munshi, 296,
    387–8
Abu Lughod, Janet, 81
Abyssinia, 261, 397, 461
Africa, 38–9, 70–1, 188, 215–16, 222, 228–9,
    230, 261, 288, 335, 345–9, 407, 409–10
    southern, 41, 99, 133, 144, 188, 231–2, 233,
    253, 348, 437, 441–3, 463
Age of Consent Bill, 401–2
agriculture, 27–8, 38, 60, 132, 134–5, 156,
    172
    expansion of settled, 49–51, 167–8, 437,
    439–40, 456
    See also cash crops, slavery
Algeria, 113, 143, 145, 215, 261, 424
Altamirano, Ignacio, 296
American Civil War, 161–5, 444
American Revolution, 45, 86–7, 94, 95, 96,
    101, 108, 287, 336, 378
Amin, Qasim, 306
Anderson, Benedict, 68, 203–4, 211, 357
Anglicanism, 110, 338, 343
anthropology, 111, 223, 444, 447, 448
anticlericalism, 102, 157–8, 326–7
anti-Semitism, 108, 157, 190, 225–6, 241,
    281, 465
Appadurai, Arjun, 2, 44, 165
architecture, 196–7, 384–5
    religious, 333, 359–61, 368
Aristotle, 43, 79, 289, 403, 404, 409
art, history of, 367, 392
Arts and Crafts Movement, 197, 372, 383
arts, 333, 366–92, 485

Arya Samaj, 342, 351
Asante, 31, 61, 131, 255–6
atheism, 292, 327, 364
Atkinson, Alan, 116
Aubin, Jean, 47
Aurangzeb, 76, 91
Aurobindo Ghose, 466, 467
Australia, 51, 100, 112, 116, 119, 131, 160,
    163, 188, 273, 306, 378, 440
Austro-Hungarian Empire, 32, 33, 67–8, 132,
    140, 145, 176, 212, 412, 428
Awadh, 384

Baganda, 70
Bailyn, Bernard, 286
Baker, Keith, 102
Baker, Sir Herbert, 385
Bakunin, Mikhail, 310
Balkans, 179, 213, 363
Banks, Joseph, 110, 314
Bannerjea, Surendranath, 202
Basutoland, 71
Baudelaire, Charles, 388
Bayle, Pierre, 292
Bayly, Susan, 335–6
Beaumarchais, Pierre Augustin Caron de, 297
Beethoven, Ludwig van, 378–9
Beik, William, 30
Belgium, 175–6, 207–8, 228–9, 232, 418
Belley, Jean-Baptiste, 375
Benin, 370
Bernhardt, Sarah, 466
Bernier, François, 61
Birla, G. D., 457
Bismarck, Otto von, 161, 230, 232, 273, 303,
    356, 459
Blanc, Louis, 288

Blanning, T. C. W., 67, 202
Blanqui, Auguste, 309–10
Blériot, Louis, 456
Blyden, Edward W., 216
Boeke, Hermann, 410
Bolivar, Simon, 87, 126, 142, 376
books. *See* print culture
Bopp, Franz, 314
Bosnia, 363
Bougainville, Louis Antoine de, 45, 110
Boustany, Saladin, 387
Brading, David, 287
Brahmo Samaj, 308, 328
Braudel, Fernand, 2, 173–4, 411
Brazil, 119, 177, 130, 330, 403, 404, 405, 446
Breuilly, John, 203
Brewer, John, 250–1
Bright, John, 164
Britain, 35, 65, 93, 102, 105, 116, 139–40,
      159–60, 162, 250–1, 257, 425–6, 464
   "Englishness" in, 66, 418
   industrialization of, 171, 172–4, 175, 418
   See also colonialism
Brodzinski, Kazimierz, 362–3
Buddhism, 103, 328, 333, 334, 337, 339, 351,
      359, 402, 433
Burckhardt, Jacob, 367
bureaucracies, 32, 144–5, 248, 250, 258–61,
      264–5, 276–8, 280, 315
burkah, 15
Burke, Edmund, 107, 303
Burma, 90, 150, 222, 259, 275, 370, 433, 447
Byron, Lord, 377, 387

Cain, Peter, 171, 454
Cairo, 187, 385
Canada, 66, 99, 101, 115, 160, 163, 226,
      293–4, 297, 437, 439, 443
Cannadine, David, 426
Canova, Antonio, 376
Cardec, Alain, 364
Caribbean, 40, 55, 99, 159, 403–5, 408, 435
   See also slavery
Carpeaux, Jean-Baptiste, 379–80
cash crops, 50, 119, 129–31, 135, 138, 177–8,
      401–5, 411
caste, 46–7, 57, 119, 414–15
Cavour, Conte de, 303
Chadwick, Owen, 329
Chandra, Bipan, 329
Chartists, 159, 190, 287–8
Chatterjee, Bankim Chandra, 389
Chaudhuri, K.N., 82
China, 30–1, 32, 34, 55–6, 58, 69, 78, 90,
      103–4, 142–3, 179, 217–18, 259–60,
      268–9, 276, 282, 398, 341, 368–70,
      420–2, 463, 464

Boxer Rebellion, 217, 265, 369
Opium Wars, 137–8, 153, 267, 369
Taiping Rebellion, 143, 148–55, 421–2
Christianity, 82, 116, 287–8, 309, 310, 330–1,
      360–1
   expansion of, 88, 151, 154, 335–6, 343–50
   Orthodox, 332, 343, 362, 363
   Pietist, 68, 74, 102, 310, 343
Churchill, Winston, 211
cinema, 374, 391–2
cities. *See* urbanization
class differentiation, 21, 114–19, 187, 190–3,
      196–7, 198
Cleveland, Augustus, 438
clocks. *See* time-keeping
clothing, 12–17, 52, 238–9, 242
clubs and societies, 72–4
coal, 60, 175, 176, 192
Cobb, Richard, 15
Cohn, Bernard, 251
Colley, Linda, 2, 139–40, 207
colonialism, 88–9, 167–8, 182–3, 221–4,
      227–33, 397, 418, 423–4, 476
   British, 94–5, 99–100, 110, 111, 128–9,
      130, 136–8, 142, 153–4, 231–2, 434–5,
      437–8, 441–3
   Dutch, 90, 130–1, 233, 263–4, 418, 424,
      438, 462, 476
   French, 143, 150, 160, 161, 168, 215–16,
      230, 411, 438
   and electoral rights, 304–6
   and law, 337, 339–40
   and nationalism, 68–9, 113–14, 215–18,
      221–3, 455, 462–3, 477
   and religion, 237, 282, 337–8, 339–40,
      342–3, 348–50, 361
   and science, 317–20, 321, 322
   and the arts, 377–8, 383, 384–5, 387–8, 389,
      390
   and "the state," 111, 251–2, 253–4, 255–6,
      258, 262–3, 265, 267, 273, 279
Comaroff, Jean, 253
commerce, 40–1, 62, 115, 129, 130–1, 135
communalism, 329
communications, modern, 19–20, 132,
      211–12, 268, 315, 354, 456–7, 461–2
communitarianism, 108, 287–8, 289, 309
Comte, Auguste, 307, 308, 312, 473
Condorcet, marquis de, 95, 286, 291, 300
Confucianism, 78, 197, 334, 337, 341
consumerism, 44, 51–2, 56–7, 115, 116, 194,
      235, 369–70
Cook, James, 45, 110, 437
Coomaraswamy, Ananda Kentish, 368, 383
Copts, 305, 343, 348
Corn Laws, 136
Cornwallis, Lord, 111

cotton, 129–30, 135, 162, 405, 415
crime and punishment, 189–90, 262–4
Crimean War, 160, 177, 268
Crispi, Francesco, 232
Crossley, Pamela, 34
Cuba, 161, 404–5, 459–61, 462
Curie, Pierre and Marie, 322, 400, 466
Curzon, Lord, 228

dan Fodio, Usman, 347
Daniell, Thomas and William, 377
Darnton, Robert, 101, 102
Dars I-Nizamiya, 339
Darwin, Charles, 309, 313, 315–16, 363
David, Jacques-Louis, 375, 376
Davis, John A., 67
Dayananda, Swami, 342
de Tocqueville, Alexis, 127, 250, 303, 395
de Vries, Jan, 6, 40, 45, 51, 115, 171
Declaration of the Rights of Man, 87, 262
Degas, Edgar, 380
Delacroix, Eugène, 377, 378
Depretis, Agostino, 232
Descartes, René, 291
Dharmapala, Anagarika, 328, 466
Dickens, Charles, 388
Dikotter, Frank, 47
diseases and epidemics, 49, 88, 272, 321, 440
Dostoevsky, Fyodor, 387
Doyle, Arthur Conan, 454
Doyle, William, 33
Drayton, Richard, 111, 313
dress. See clothing
Dreyfus, Alfred, 226, 464
Drumont, Edouard, 226
Duara, Prasanjit, 468
Durkheim, Emile, 171, 308, 323

East India companies, 92, 296, 369
    Dutch, 62
    English, 45, 90, 94–5, 110, 142, 153–4, 259, 277, 301
ecological change, 50–1, 421, 433–4, 449–50, 481
education, 67–8, 272–3, 280, 349, 402
Edward VII, King, 397
Egypt, 129–30, 178–9, 206, 207, 215, 221, 233, 261, 274, 314, 376, 385, 461
Eisenstadt, S. N., 9, 10
emigration, 133–4, 272
    from Europe, 41, 119, 133–4, 155, 411, 439, 458
Engels, Friedrich, 170–1
Engermann, Stanley, 405–6
Estates General, 95
ethnicities. See minorities, race
Everest, George, 275

family structure, 188, 399–400
famine, 28, 135, 160, 256, 272, 402, 412
Fath Ali Shah, 376–7
Feraios, Rigas, 202
financial institutions, 21, 62, 185, 279–80
fingerprinting, 256
First World War, 4, 411, 455, 472, 479, 487
Fitzgerald, Edward, 386
Fogel, Robert, 405–6
folktales, 385–6
food and nutrition, 18–19, 28, 49, 51, 60, 177–8, 189
Ford, Henry, 175
forest-dwellers, 39, 40, 51, 222, 438
forests, 50, 51, 156, 279
Foucault, Michel, 251, 253
Fouché, Joseph, 145
France, 140, 141, 145, 150, 160, 176, 337, 411, 426, 464
    ancien régime, 30, 31, 32, 33, 65–6, 95
    Napoleonic, 97–9, 111, 139, 249, 256–7, 274
    See also colonialism, French Revolution
Franklin, Benjamin, 72–3, 74, 76, 471
Frederick the Great, 67, 92
freemasonry, 74, 78, 146, 195, 480
Fremiet, Emmanuel, 389–90
French Revolution, 5, 15, 68, 86, 93, 95–7, 101–2, 118, 126, 287, 326–7
Freud, Sigmund, 390, 485
Freyre, Gilberto, 409
Fulani, 345–7, 433
Furet, François, 102, 287
Furukawa Ichibe, 457

Gallagher, John, 137, 454, 472
Gandhi, Mohandas K., 18–19, 242, 283, 409, 467, 477
Garibaldi, Giuseppe, 4, 202, 208, 310
Gauguin, Paul, 368, 381, 485
Gellner, Ernest, 10, 203, 219, 473
Genovese, Eugene, 405, 406, 414
gentry classes, 187, 296–9, 418–26, 456
Géricault, Theodore, 377, 378
Germany, 30, 33, 66–7, 113, 117–18, 144, 175, 176, 206, 232, 252–3, 257, 273, 343, 425, 428, 456, 459
Ghulam Hussain Tabatabai, 387
Gibbon, Edward, 326
Girodet, Anne-Louis, 375, 376
Gladstone, W. E., 164, 210
globalization, "archaic," 41–5, 52, 234–6, 369
Goethe, Johann Wolfgang von, 65, 113, 314, 387
Gogol, Nikolai, 388
gold, 231, 235, 279
Goldstone, Jack, 470

Goya, Francisco, 366, 378
Greece, 137, 141, 213, 362, 377, 387
Gu Yanwu, 78
Guha, Ranajit, 111
Gunder Frank, André, 58, 410
gynecology, 401

Habermas, Jürgen, 71, 483–4
Habib, Irfan, 329
Haiti, 99
Hajj, 354–5
Hall, Catherine, 2
Hamilton, Lord Frederick, 364
Hardy, Thomas, 388
Harish Chandra, Bharatendu, 389
Harris, Jose, 251
Hastings, Adrian, 66, 202, 216
Haussmann, Georges Eugène, 384
Hawaii, 100, 112, 438
He Changling, 127
Hearst, William Randolph, 211, 462
Hegel, Georg Wilhelm Friedrich, 145, 250,
    303, 311, 473
Heisenberg, Werner, 390
Hinduism, 114, 241–2, 263, 308, 333, 336,
    339, 341–3, 351, 355, 359, 480
historical explanations, 5–11, 58–9, 88–9,
    227–8, 280–1, 284–5, 396–9, 430–1,
    454–5, 459, 468–73, 475, 484–5
    Annales school, 2, 411
    "civil society," 71–4, 82, 118, 483–4
    cultural nationalism, 202
    dependency theory, 410–11
    "gentlemanly capitalism," 171, 454
    industrial capitalism, 5, 7, 169, 329, 453,
        458–9
    "industrious revolution," 6, 45, 51–2, 55,
        56, 58, 59, 114–15, 171, 174, 474
    Marxist, 8, 10, 229, 250, 251, 329–30, 396,
        465
    modernization theory, 9–10, 203, 329–30
    nation-state, 5–6, 68–9, 203–4, 249–52,
        254–5
    "oriental despotism," 30, 61
    postmodernist, 8–9, 10, 329
    "Western exceptionalism," 40, 59, 71, 75,
        317–18, 469–70
Ho Chi Minh, 195, 205–6
Ho, Ping-ti, 421
Hobsbawm, Eric, 5, 7, 203, 280, 473
Hobson, J. A., 453–4
Hodgson, Marshall, 29
Hokusai, Katsushika, 382
Hong Xiuquan, 148, 153
Hopkins, Anthony G., 171, 454
Hosking, Geoffrey, 2
Hu Hanmin, 312

Hudson's Bay Company, 254
Hugo, Victor, 367
Hume, Allan Octavian, 304
Hume, David, 286, 291, 292
Hungary, 158, 159, 212, 412, 419
Hunt, Lynn, 102
Hurgronje, Snouck, 355

Ibn Khaldun, 39
Ibn Saud, 106
ideologies, civic republicanism, 43, 72, 285–8,
    304
    free trade, 136–8, 178, 238, 270–1, 300–2
    popular sovereignty, 101–2, 107, 147, 210,
        302–3
    "the people," 107, 167, 295
immigration controls, 237–8
Impressionism, 380–1
indentured labor, 133, 234–5, 408–9
India, colonial, 94, 111, 114, 130, 142, 155,
    182, 193, 216–17, 223, 239, 240, 241–2,
    319–20, 414–15
    Mughal, 33, 34, 36, 57, 58, 59, 89–90, 91,
        105
    Mutiny/Rebellion 1857, 151, 153–4, 424
Indian National Congress, 206, 217, 289, 299,
    304
indigenous peoples. See native peoples
Indonesia, 154
industrialization, 7, 49, 52, 93, 114, 157,
    168–9, 170–83, 188, 198, 270, 279,
    372–3, 418, 473, 482
Ingres, Jean-Auguste-Dominique, 98, 375–6
Internationale, 350
Iran, 89, 91, 151, 253, 260, 265, 376–7, 380
Ireland, 70, 99, 110, 113, 117, 135, 140, 141,
    160, 206–7, 224, 274–5, 297, 419, 426,
    462
Iroquois, 437
Ishmael Pasha, 376
Islam, 43, 47, 113, 289, 306, 336, 345–7,
    354–5, 359–60, 480
    reform movements in, 76–8, 87, 105–6,
        127, 142, 262–3, 265, 328, 338, 339,
        464
    See also Sufism, Wahhabism
Italy, 30, 111, 112, 132, 157–8, 176, 206, 208,
    232, 337, 370, 456, 415, 424
Ito Hirobumi, 428

Jackson, Andrew, 439
Jamal-al din al-Afghani, 477, 480
Japan, 56–7, 61–2, 80, 90, 104, 150, 232,
    269–70, 288–90, 318–19, 323, 334, 337,
    381–3, 402, 413, 414, 422–3, 428, 461
    industrialization of, 179–82, 457
Jaurès, Jean, 464

jazz, 374
Jefferson, Thomas, 109, 205, 326
Jerusalem, 43
Jesuits, 68, 78, 79, 146, 259, 341, 369, 435, 444–5
Jews, 74, 110, 157, 190, 220, 221, 224–6, 227, 264, 343
jihad, 113, 142, 289, 345–7, 355, 430
Johnson, William, 45, 437
Jones, William, 110, 314
Joyce, James, 389, 390
Judaism, 332, 340

Kames, Lord, 400
Kang Youwei, 305
Kant, Immanuel, 291
Kartik Prasad Khattri, 389
Kayali, Hasan, 215
Kedourie, Elie, 455
Kennedy, Paul, 89
Khilafat, 430, *460*
Khoi peoples, 144, 348, 437, 441, 442
kingship and monarchy, 30–5, 39, 42, 43, 75, 139–40, 220, 258, 288, 397, 426–30
Klimt, Gustav, 390, 485
Komlos, John, 28
Korea, 80, 461
Kossuth, Lajos, 159
Kraus, Karl, 194
Kruger, Paul, 463
Kuhn, Philip, 90, 103
Kurds, 436

Lafayette, marquis de, 95
Landes, David, 10, 75
Landseer, Edward, 390
languages, 17–18, 65, 66, 68, 358, 434, 435, 464
Lapps, 434, 435
Latin America, 50, 94, 126, 141–2, 147, 208, 287, 308, 339, 376, 404–5, 440
Latour, Bruno, 10
law, 21, 60–1, 81–2, 144–5, 234, 262–5
  religious, 336, 337, 339–40, 342
Lebanon, 213
Legge, Reverend James, 341
Lenin, Vladimir Ilyich, 231, 453, 458, 467, 472
Lermontov, Mikhail Yurievich, 387
Lewanika, 349
Lewis, Gwynne, 102
Li Hongzhang, 269, 275
liberalism, 88, 140, 290–306, 323–4, 464–7, 485
Liberia, 348, 407, 445
Lieven, Dominic, 2
Lincoln, Abraham, 163

Linnaeus, Carolus, 80, 313
List, Friedrich, 136, 301, 302
literature, 385–9
living standards, 57, 135, 172, 189, 406, 411–12
Locke, John, 286, 291, 302
London Corresponding Society, 102
London, 65, 185, 384
Longfellow, Henry Wadsworth, 388
Lourdes, *326*, 356
Lovejoy, P. E., 403
Lueger, Karl, 465
Lugard, Lord, 222, 397
Lutyens, Edwin, 392
luxury, 52, 56
Lyautey, Marshall, 397

Macaulay, T. B., 249
MacDonagh, Oliver, 251
Macfarlane, Alan, 10, 418
Macpherson, C. B., 286
Madagascar, 50
Mahabharata, 342, 386
malaria, 321
Malthus, Thomas, 272, 309
Manet, Edouard, 380, 384
Mann, Michael, 248
Manzoni, Alessandro, 367, 388
Maori, 14, 51, 304, 335, 349, 437–8, 441
mapping and surveying, 274–6
Marconi, Guglielmo, 456, *457*
Marie Antoinette, Queen, 101
marriage and sexual relations, 45, 57, 234, 235–6
Marshall, Alfred, 170
Marx, Karl, 10, 156, 166, 170–1, 309, 310–11, 312, 417, 473
Marxism, 11, 193, 290, 292, 308, 309, 310, 327, 465
Mayer, Arno, 396, 454
Mazower, Mark, 362
Mazzini, Giuseppe, 112, 140, 202, 327, 366–7
medical knowledge, 21, 44, 45–6, 314, 318–21, 401
Mendel, Franklin, 171
mercantilism, 136
Mexico, 3–4, 46, 147, 161, 178, 376, 465
Michelet, Jules, 388
Mieroslawski, Ludwig, 158
military technology, 62–4, 81, 91, 92, 165, 267–70, 274
Mill, John Stuart, 87, 297, 302, 304, 327
millenarianism, 11, 47, 103, 142–3, 148, 150, 153, 166, 253, 309, 421
minorities, 37–8, 39, 212–13, 219–27, 237, 238, 430

missionary endeavor, 100, 116, 118, 154, 315, 330–1, 332, 335–6, 341, 343–4, 345–51, 440, 441, 444–6
Mitchell, Timothy, 385
modernity, 9–12, 15, 158, 197, 399, 456
Monaco, 424–5
Montesquieu, baron de, 298
Moorcroft, William, 314
Morgan, Louis Henry, 444
mosques, 339, 359–60
Muhammad (Mehmet) Ali, 113, 129–30, 178, 215, 261
Murchison, Roderick, 315
Musa, Salama, 389
museums, 369, 370, 373
music, 109, 371, 372, 374, 378–9, 390, 391

Nabuco, Joaquin, 296
Nadir Shah, 91, 109
Nakae Chomin, 305
names, personal, 18
Naoroji, Dadhabhai, 289
Napoleon (Bonaparte), 43, 86, 93, 98, 99, 108–9, 139, 314, 327, 375–6, 395
Napoleon III (Louis Napoleon), 145, 160, 176, 210, 356, 377, 384, 427–8
nationalism, 68–9, 88, 141, 158, 199–228, 242–3, 301–2, 462–4
    and imperialism, 228–33
    and religion, 240–2, 282, 341–2, 362–4
    and the arts, 366–7, 379–80
    and "the state," 280–1
nation-states, emergence of, 64–5, 69, 70, 71, 108–9, 112–14, 163, 206–8, 234, 247–83, 474–5, 478–9
native peoples, 39–40, 50–1, 74, 111, 119, 127, 167–8, 227, 299–300, 348, 349–50, 378, 414, 432–50, 481–2
natural history, 110, 111, 314, 315
naval power, 62–4, 128, 129, 459
Ndebele, 216, 442
Needham, Joseph, 317, 318
Nepal, 438
Netherlands, 50, 51, 130–1, 304, 415, 418
    See also colonialism
New Caledonia, 168
New Zealand, 51, 100, 112, 160, 163, 273, 304, 306, 335, 437–8, 440, 441, 448–9
Newton, Isaac, 76
Nietzsche, Friedrich, 485
Nigeria, 222, 345–7, 355
Nightingale, Florence, 322
Nishi Amane, 308
Nobel Prize, 322, 367
nomadism, 39–40, 50, 299, 436, 438
novels, 373, 386–7, 388–9

O'Brien, Patrick, 171
O'Connell, Daniel, 117, 297
Ogyu Sorai, 288–9
Omar Khayyam, 386
Ooms, Herman, 414
opium, 44, 45, 235
Opium Wars, 137–8, 153, 267, 369
Ottoman Empire, 33, 34, 59, 76, 90, 137, 148, 151–2, 178–9, 213–15, 337–8, 398, 430, 464
    Tanzimat era, 105, 142, 147–8, 220–1, 260–1, 370, 376, 406–7
Ottoman Tariff Convention, 1838, 178
Ouvrard, Gabriel-Julien, 99
Ozouf, Mona, 101

Pacific Ocean region, 51, 71, 88, 100, 127, 258, 335, 349–50, 437–8, 440, 446
Padua, 356
Paine, Thomas, 87
Palmerston, Lord, 136, 137
pan-Africanism, 216, 466
pan-Islamism, 237, 464, 466, 480
Papal Infallibility, 338–9
Paris, 65–6, 185, 186, 194, 195, 361, 384
Paris Commune, 266, 267, 309, 322, 327, 384
Park, Mungo, 314
Parker, Geoffrey, 91
Parsons, Talcott, 250
Parthasarathi, Prasannan, 58, 174
passports, 239–40
Pasteur, Louis, 321–2
Pathé film company, 456
patriotism, 64–71, 101, 112–14, 141, 154, 158, 202, 207, 212–18, 280–1
peasantry, 27–29, 134–5, 156, 171–2, 398–9, 410–18, 479, 482
Peel, John, 288
Persia. See Iran
Peterloo Massacre, 143, *144*
photography, 165, 374
Picasso, Pablo, 368, 381, 485
pilgrimage, 43, *326*, 334, *340*, 351–7
Pipes, Richard, 61
Pitt, William (the Elder), 92
Pocock, John, 43, 286, 484
Poland, 113, 126, 141, 158, 267, 362–3, 480
policing and surveillance, 144, 145, 189–90, 239–40, 255, 256, 270
political parties, 210–11
Pomeranz, Kenneth, 2, 47, 58–9, 60, 179, 468
Pope Gregory XVI, 157–8
Pope Pius IX, 158, 343, 356
population growth, 49, 60, 93, 119, 129, 135, 155, 180, 181, 189, 270, 411–12
porcelain, 56, 368–70

Porter, Roy, 292
positivism, 307–8
Price, Richard, 455
primogeniture, 61, 419, 422
print culture, 19–20, 68, 78–9, 82, 100–1, 118, 119, 204, 205–6, 211–12, 319, 391–2
  religious, 333, 357–9
professions, specialization of, 20–1, 320–2, 483
property, 61–2, 111–12, 132, 145, 298–300, 303, 327, 424, 435, 440
Protestantism, 72–3, 102, 338, 343, 344

Quesnay, François, 136, 300
Quran, 358

race, 45, 46–7, 108–10, 119, 190, 196, 223, 226–7, 235–6, 237–9, 304–5, 323, 403, 409, 444, 447, 454, 466, 485
  See also caste
Ray, Rajat K., 133
rebellions, 103–4, 107, 126, 147, 148–53, 166–7, 481–2
  rural, 29, 56, 90, 141, 156, 419, 420
  slave, 99, 126, 403, 406
Red Cross, 240, *241*, 242
religion, 4, 20, 34–5, 42, 43, 87–8, 110, 154, 237, 325–65, 479–81
  disestablishment of, 326, 330, 336, 337, 338, 356
  and the arts, 367–72, 374, 390
  See also individual faiths
religious cults, 332, 356, 364, 479–80
Rendall, Jane, 306
Renoir, Auguste, 380
revolutions, 86–119
  Europe 1848, 147, 156–9, 311, 420, 424–5
  Russia 1905, 171–2, 192–3, 465
  Russia 1917, 266
  Young Turk, 213–15
Rhodes, Cecil, 230, 253
Rida, Muhammad Rashid, 306
rights, 86–7, 114, 158, 166, 237, 262, 264, 299, 306, 447, 456, 466
  electoral, 302–6
  See also property
Robertson, William, 110
Robespierre, Maximilien, 64–5
Robinson, Ronald, 137, 454, 472
Rodin, Auguste, 383
Roman Catholicism, 34–5, 73–4, 66, 101, 110, 327, 330, 337, 338–9, 343, 344, 355–6, 403, 444–5, 480
Romanticism, 377
Rome, 384–5
Roosevelt, Theodore, 277, 459–61, 465
Ross, Ronald, 321
Rousseau, Jean-Jacques, 287

Roy, Raja Ram Mohun, 114, 205, 237, 293–4
Ruskin, John, 283, 310, 329, 372
Russia, 33, 34, 39–40, 61, 64, 112–13, 141, 177, 192–3, 212, 416–17, 425

Sadik Rifat Pasha, 296
Sahlins, Marshall, 42
Said, Edward, 377
Saint Petersburg, 192–3, 197, 385
Saint-Simon, Henri de, 310, 327
samurai, 422–3
Santa Anna, Antonio López de, 147, 376
Sayyid Ahmad Khan, 306, 328
science, 79–80, 110, 312–24, 363, 457
  history of, 285
Scotland, 135, 272, 274, 321, 432, 436
Scott, James, 251, 252
Seal, Anil, 455
secularization, 325–7, 329, 330, 356
serfdom, 416–17
settler colonies, 41, 88, 112, 115, 116, 119, 132, 133, 227, 439–44
Seven Years War, 66–7, 86, 93
Shah Alam, 166
Shaka, 71
Shinto, 332, 334, 371
Sidi Mahomed, 70
Sierra Leone, 335, 348, 445
Sikhism, 78, 87, 105, 223, 332
silver, 91, 99, 126, 137, 413
Sinn Fein, 462
Skowronek, Stephen, 252
slavery, 19, 40–1, 50, 52–3, 58, 99, 127, 130, 132–3, 256, 344–5, 397–8, 402–10
  opposition to, 86, 117, 140, 164, 187, 481
Smiles, Samuel, 319, 474
Smith, A. D., 202, 219
Smith, Adam, 110, 135, 136, 170, 286, 291, 296, 300, 301
socialism, 308–12
Sokoto Khilafat, 345–7, 355, 436
South African War, 15, 211–12, 233, 231
Spain, 94, 141, 257
Spencer, Herbert, 312, 316–17
Spengler, Oswald, 485
Sperber, Jonathan, 205
spiritualism, 195, 364–5
sport, 19, 196
Stalin, Joseph, 417
Stead, W. T., 211, 212
Stedman Jones, Gareth, 287
Steensgaard, Niels, 64
Strachan, Hew, 4
Strauss, Richard, 390
strikes, 191–3
Subrahmanyam, Sanjay, 47
Sufism, 43, 292, 333, 345

Sun Yatsen, 217–18, 318, 341
Switzerland, 240

Taft, William Howard, 252
Tagore, Rabindranath, 367, 380, 454
Tahtawi, Rifaa al-, 318
Tasmania, 440
Taylor, Miles, 159
tea, 44, 45, *55*, 57, 95
Tehran, 187
Temorenga, 349
terra nullius, 299
Test Acts, 336–7
Tewodros, 261
textile production, 57, 58, 59, 134, 157, *173*,
     174, 176, 178, 181–3, 372
Thailand, 90, 259, 275
theosophy, 195, 365, 479–80
Thieu, Gilbert, 302
Thompson, E. P., 157, 251
Thompson, John A., 465
Tilak, Bal Ganghadhar, 193
Tilly, Charles, 126
time-keeping, 17, 51
Tinker, Hugh, 408
tobacco, 44, 45
Tolstoy, Leon, 283, 387, 467
Tone, Wolfe, 43
Tonga, 258
Torpey, John, 239
Toulouse-Lautrec, Henri de, 171, 373
Toussaint L'Ouverture, François-Dominique,
     99
trade, 19, 130–1, 135, 411, 455
   in exotics, 42, 44, 45–6, 52, 235, 369, 437,
      438
   maritime, 38
   See also cash crops, slavery
Trevelyan, G. M., 249
Trigonometrical Survey of India, 275
Twain, Mark, 388

Umar, Hajj, 261
United States of America, 115–16, 130, 161–5,
     174–5, 226, 250–1, 253, 257, 336, 344–5,
     405–6, 439, 440, 443–4, 456, 459–61,
     464–5, 470
universities, 81, 176, 276–7, 315, 316, 338, 458
urbanization, 170–2, 173, 183–9, 193, 194–8,
     204, 361, 384–5
Urdu, 387

van de Ven, Hans, 282, 398
van Gogh, Vincent, 380–1
Varma, Raja Ravi, 380
Velanganni, 356
Venice, 97, 126, 132, 194, 370

Vico, Giambattista, 80, 291–2
Victoria, Queen, *231*, 429
Vietnam, 32–3, 90, 113, 150, 207, 255, 259,
     334, 446–7
Viollet-le-Duc, Eugène, 361
Vivekananda, Swami, 241–2
Voltaire, 287, 326
von Ranke, Leopold, 303
Voth, Hans-Joachim, 51

Wagner, Richard, 171, 367, 379, 467
Wahhabism, 76, 87, 105–6, 354
Waitangi, Treaty of, 441
Waley-Cohen, Joanna, 2
Wali-Allah, Shah, 77, 471
Wallerstein, Immanuel, 410, 473
Wang Gung Wu, 2
Wardy, Robert, 289
warfare, 62–4, 81, 91–3, 96–7, 99, 125–6,
     143–4, 204–5, 242–3, 266–70
   Maori, 100, 438
Washbrook, David, 414, 415
Washington, George, 109, 166
Weber, Eugene, 411
Weber, Max, 10, 32, 72, 329, 362, 371, 372,
     478
welfare, 271–3
Wells, H. G., 454
whaling, 100, 440
Whistler, J. M., 368
Wiener, Martin, 171
William II, Kaiser, 252, 427, 428, 459, 484
Wills, John E., II, 470
Wilson, Kathleen, 67
Wilson, Woodrow, 465
Witte, Sergei, 427
women, 15, 39, 56, 74, 107, 118–19, 126, 194,
     303, 306, 334–5, 374–5, 400–2, 407,
     466
Wong, Roy Bin, 2, 58–9, 468
Woolf, Stuart, 108
World Parliament of Religions, 20, 240–1
Wrigley, E. A., 65

Xhosa, 144, 167, 222, 348, 377, 441

Yan Fu, 82
Yate, Reverend William, 349
Yoruba, 70, 288, 371, 424
"Young Bengal," 158, 328
Yuan Shikai, 398

Zimbabwe, 442
Zionism, 219, 224, 300
Zoffany, Johannes, 374
Zola, Émile, 194, 467
Zulus, 71, 167, 348, 437, 442